Handbook of
Pattern Recognition
and Image Processing

Volume 2

Handbook of Pattern Recognition and Image Processing: Computer Vision

Edited by

TZAY Y. YOUNG

Department of Electrical and Computer Engineering
University of Miami
Coral Gables, Florida

ACADEMIC PRESS
A Division of Harcourt Brace & Company
San Diego   New York   Boston
London   Sydney   Tokyo   Toronto

Academic Press, Inc.
525 B Street, Suite 1900, San Diego, California 92101-4495

United Kingdom Edition published by
Academic Press Limited
24–28 Oval Road, London NW1 7DX

Library of Congress Cataloging-in-Publication Data

Handbook of pattern recognition and image processing.

   Vol. 2 has title: Computer Vision.
   (Handbooks in science and technology)
   Includes bibliographies and index.
   1. Pattern recognition systems.   2. Image processing.
I. Young, Tzay Y., DATE.   II. Fu, K. S.
(King Sun), DATE.   III. Series.
   TK7882.P3H36 1986   006.4   85-13381
   ISBN 0-12-774560-2 (alk. paper : v. 1)
   ISBN 0-12-774561-0 (alk. paper : v. 2)

PRINTED IN THE UNITED STATES OF AMERICA
94 95 96 97 98 99   MM   9 8 7 6 5 4 3 2 1

Contents

Chapter 4 Recovery of Three-Dimensional Shape of Curved Objects from a Single Image

RAMAKANT NEVATIA, MOURAD ZERROUG, AND FATIH ULUPINAR

Chapter 5 Surface Reflection Mechanism

KATSUSHI IKEUCHI

Chapter 6 Extracting Shape-from-Shading

ALEX P. PENTLAND AND MARTIN BICHSEL

Chapter 7 Range Image Analysis
SARAVAJIT S. SINHA AND RAMESH JAIN

Chapter 8 Stereo Vision
LYNNE L. GREWE AND AVINASH C. KAK

Chapter 9 Machine Learning of Computer Vision Algorithms
STEVEN R. SCHWARTZ AND BENJAMIN W. WAH

Chapter 10 Image Sequence Analysis for Three-Dimensional Perception of Dynamic Scenes
GUNA S. SEETHARAMAN

Chapter 11 Nonrigid Motion Analysis
CHANDRA KAMBHAMETTU, DMITRY B. GOLDGOF, DEMETRI TERZOPOULOS, AND THOMAS S. HUANG

Chapter 12 Analysis and Synthesis of Human Movement

THOMAS W. CALVERT AND ARTHUR E. CHAPMAN

Chapter 13 Relational Matching

LINDA G. SHAPIRO

Chapter 14 Three-Dimensional Object Recognition
PATRICK J. FLYNN AND ANIL K. JAIN

Chapter 15 Fundamental Principles of Robot Vision
ERNEST L. HALL

Contributors

Numbers in parentheses indicate the pages on which the authors' contributions begin.

YIANNIS ALOIMONOS (1), Computer Vision Laboratory, Center for Automation Research, University of Maryland, College Park, Maryland 20742

MARTIN BICHSEL[1] (161), The Media Laboratory, Massachusetts Institute of Technology, Cambridge, Massachusetts 02139

KEVIN W. BOWYER (17), Department of Computer Sciences and Engineering, University of South Florida, Tampa, Florida 33620

THOMAS W. CALVERT (431), Schools of Computing Science, Kinesiology, and Engineering Science, Simon Fraser University, Burnaby, British Columbia, Canada V5A 1S6

ARTHUR E. CHAPMAN (431), Schools of Computing Science, Kinesiology, and Engineering Science, Simon Fraser University, Burnaby, British Columbia, Canada V5A 1S6

CHARLES R. DYER (17), Department of Computer Science, University of Wisconsin, Madison, Wisconsin 52706

PATRICK J. FLYNN (497), School of Electrical Engineering and Computer Science, Washington State University, Pullman, Washington 99164

DMITRY B. GOLDGOF (405), Department of Computer Science and Engineering, University of South Florida, Tampa, Florida 33620

LYNNE L. GREWE (239), Robot Vision Laboratory, School of Electrical Engineering, Purdue University, West Lafayette, Indiana 47907

ERNEST L. HALL (543), Center for Robotics Research, University of Cincinnati, Cincinnati, Ohio 45221

THOMAS S. HUANG (405), Department of Electrical and Computer Engineering, University of Illinois at Urbana-Champaign, Urbana , Illinois 61801

KATSUSHI IKEUCHI (131), School of Computer Science, Carnegie-Mellon University, Pittsburgh, Pennsylvania 15213

ANIL K. JAIN (497), Department of Computer Science, Michigan State University, East Lansing, Michigan 48824

RAMESH JAIN[2] (185). Artificial Intelligence Laboratory, Department of Electrical Engineering and Computer Science, The University of Michigan, Ann Arbor, Michigan 48109

[1]*Present address:* Institut für Informatik, UNI Irchel, 8057 Zürich, Switzerland.
[2]*Present address:* University of California, San Diego, La Jolla, California 92093.

AVINASH C. KAK (239), Robot Vision Laboratory, School of Electrical Engineering, Purdue University, West Lafayette, Indiana 47907

CHANDRA KAMBHAMETTU (405), Department of Computer Science and Engineering, University of South Florida, Tampa, Florida 33620

RAMAKANT NEVATIA (101), Institute for Robotics and Intelligent Systems, University of Southern California, Los Angeles, California 90089

ALEX P. PENTLAND (161), The Media Laboratory, Massachusetts Institute of Technology, Cambridge, Massachusetts 02139

AZRIEL ROSENFELD (1), Computer Vision Laboratory, Center for Automation Research, University of Maryland, College Park, Maryland 20742

STEVEN R. SCHWARTZ (319), Motorola, Inc., Arlington Heights, Illinois 60004

GUNA S. SEETHARAMAN (361), The Center for Advanced Computer Studies, University of Southwestern Louisiana, Lafayette, Louisiana 70504

LINDA G. SHAPIRO (475), Department of Computer Science and Engineering, University of Washington, Seattle, Washington 98195

WASIM J. SHOMAR[3] (53), Department of Electrical and Computer Engineering, University of Miami, Coral Gables, Florida 33124

SARVAJIT S. SINHA (185), Imageware, Ann Arbor, Michigan 48103

DEMETRI TERZOPOULOS (405), Department of Computer Science, University of Toronto, Toronto, Canada M5S 1A1

FATIH ULUPINAR (101), Department of Computer and Information Science, Bilkent University, Ankara, Turkey 06533

BENJAMIN W. WAH (319), Coordinated Science Laboratory, University of Illinois at Urbana-Champaign, Urbana, Illinois 61801

TZAY Y. YOUNG (53), Department of Electrical and Computer Engineering, University of Miami, Coral Gables, Florida 33124

MOURAD ZERROUG (101), Institute for Robotics and Intelligent Systems, University of Southern California, Los Angeles, California 90089

[3]*Present address:* IBM Corporation, Boca Raton, Florida 33432.

Preface

The first volume of the *Handbook of Pattern Recognition and Image Processing* was co-edited by the late Professor King-Sun Fu and myself. The volume, published in 1986, consisted of 27 chapters divided into four parts, Pattern Recognition, Image Processing and Understanding, Systems and Architecture, and Applications.

Computer vision research started in the early 1960s. The past decade has seen significant advances and the initiation of several journals on vision. One chapter on computer vision that summarized the progress up to the mid-1980s was included in Part II of the first volume. Volume 2 of the handbook is devoted solely to computer vision.

Computer vision can be divided into low-, intermediate-, and high-level visual tasks. Low-level vision refers to operations involved with individual pixels of an image. It is primarily concerned with detecting edges and segmenting the image into regions homogeneous in intensity or texture. Intermediate-level tasks include analysis of two-dimensional shapes, colors, texture, motion, shadows and occlusions, and the establishment of relationships between regions. In this way, regions in an image are described in terms of their properties and features, and a three-dimensional (3D) description can be inferred from a two-dimensional (2D) representation. The information to be extracted from an image depends on the particular application as well as on the prior knowledge about the objects and the 3D scene from which the image was obtained. High-level vision is concerned with the recognition of objects and the interpretation of the information contained in the image to understand the 3D scene.

Thus, the general goal of computer vision is to analyze an image or images of a given scene and to interpret the content of the scene. In some applications such as document processing, remote sensing, and analysis of certain biomedical images, the scenes can be treated as two-dimensional. In other situations, notably in robot vision, navigation, and 3D object recognition, the scene is three-dimensional. By observing a single image, humans obtain definite impressions about the 3D scene and the 3D shapes of the objects in the scene. To extract 3D visual information by a computer, however, is a difficult task. This volume is primarily concerned with methods for extracting 3D information and interpreting 3D scenes.

The 3D orientation of a surface can be inferred from shading (gray-level variation) in the image, which requires a thorough understanding of the surface reflection mechanism. Clues to 3D shape can also be derived from the 2D shapes and contours in an image and from texture variations. Alternatively, two or more cameras at different locations can be used to view the same scene. Stereo vision identifies the corresponding points in different images to recover the depth information in the scene. The performance of stereo vision algorithms can be improved by integrating machine learning techniques with vision. Depth information can also be obtained directly using a range sensor, and geometric information can be extracted by range image analysis. A commonly used range sensor is a laser scanner, which measures the return time of a laser beam reflected from object surfaces in the scene.

Representation of 3D object shape is a fundamental problem that permeates almost every aspect of 3D vision. Both object-centered and viewer-centered representations have been used. A major objective in 3D shape representations is to model the geometry of real objects. The models are then used to establish the correspondence between model features and image features. Object models are often expressed as relational graphs in which, for example, nodes represent object parts or surfaces labeled with various properties, and arcs connecting the nodes represent relationships among the parts. Similar graphs can be constructed from segmented images with nodes representing regions. Three-dimensional object recognition is then reduced to relational matching of the graph obtained from image data to subgraphs of object models stored in the model base. Other recognition techniques include search of the interpretation tree and recognition using invariant features. We note that 3D object recognition has applications in automation and manufacturing.

Analysis of 3D object motion from a time-ordered sequence of images has been a popular research in the past decade. One basic approach to extracting 3D motion information from rigid objects is based on establishing point correspondence, line correspondence, or region correspondence in the image sequence. Another approach computes the optical flow field, which is the apparent 2D velocity perceived directly from the image sequence. Actual 3D motion and geometrical structure of the objects can be computed from the established correspondences or the 2D optical flow field. In recent years, there has been a growing interest in nonrigid motion analysis, which has potential applications in areas such as robot vision and medical imaging. An interesting topic in articulated (piecewise rigid) motion is the analysis and synthesis (animation and simulation) of human movement. Most motion analysis techniques are expensive and time-consuming for real-world navigation tasks. It has been suggested that active vision, with the ability to actively control camera parameters such as orientation, focus, zoom, aperture, and vergence, can simplify many low- and intermediate-level vision problems and has the potential for real-time operations. In the near future, we expect advances in active vision and its application to navigation.

This volume consists of 15 chapters on various aspects of 3D computer vision. Several chapters in Volume 1 of the handbook are concerned with segmentation, 2D shapes, textures, and motion, and complement the chapters in this volume. The contents of Volume 2 will be useful to graduate students, scientists, and engineers interested in computer vision.

Chapter **1**

Principles of Computer Vision

YIANNIS ALOIMONOS and AZRIEL ROSENFELD

Computer Vision Laboratory
Center for Automation Research
University of Maryland
College Park, Maryland

1. VIEWPOINTS ABOUT VISION

Vision is the most powerful sense for many living organisms, including humans. We take it so much for granted, because it is ordinarily so effortless, that we often fail to seriously consider how it works. Students of visual perception include researchers in the fields of neuroanatomy and physiology, psychology, computational and robot vision, and engineering. But researchers in different fields ask different questions about vision. Some researchers ask empirical questions: How are existing biological visual systems actually designed? On the other hand, scientists and engineers try to answer theoretical and normative questions. The theoretical question in vision is, What is the range of possible mechanisms underlying perceptual capabilities in vision systems? The normative question is, How should a particular class of vision systems (or robots) be designed so that it

1

can efficiently perform a set of specific visual tasks? The three basic types of questions do not, in general, have the same answers.

A very large part of the human brain is devoted to visual perception (1). But what algorithms and data representations are used by the brain? Analogously, given a set of images acquired by a TV camera, what computer architectures, data structures, and algorithms should we use to create a machine that can "see" as we do (2–4)?

Many organisms possess visual capabilities, and their visual systems are not designed in the same way; moreover, they live in different environments and use vision for different purposes. But although a given visual capability—say, for obstacle avoidance—is not necessarily implemented in the same way in the fly, the rat, and the human, the principles underlying this ability may be the same. It is these principles that are the subject of research in computer vision. As our understanding of visual principles advances, we can build robots that perform various tasks through the use of vision.

2. THE PURPOSE OF VISION

What is vision for? Why do organisms have vision and why do we want to equip robots with it? We use vision (and other senses) to interact with our environments and survive—to navigate and avoid obstacles, to recognize and pick up objects, to identify food and danger, friends and enemies. In other words, we use vision to perform visual tasks; we engage in many kinds of behaviors that are guided by visual inputs.

How can we study the principles of visual perception? Should we study individual tasks? Since the nature of a task depends on the agent and the environment, what kind of agent should we assume in this study—an insect, a human, or a robot? Such questions demonstrate that one of the hardest problems we encounter in the study of visual perception is what questions to ask.

A set of specific questions was formulated in the work of the late David Marr (5), who suggested that we can study the principles of visual perception by considering the purpose of vision as describing scenes. In other words, we should regard the task of vision as being the construction of a detailed representation of the physical world, independent of the task under consideration. This viewpoint is prevalent; for example, we read in a recent survey article (6) that "The goal of an image understanding system is to transform two dimensional data into a description of the three-dimensional spatiotemporal world... [Such a system] must infer 3D surfaces, volumes, boundaries, shadows, occlusion, depth, color, motion, ..."

Regarding the central goal of vision as scene recovery makes sense. If we are able to create, using vision, an accurate representation of the three-dimensional world and its properties, then, using this information, we can perform any visual task. Because we will know where obstacles are, we can avoid them; because we will have an accurate representation of an object's properties, we will be able to match it against models in a database of possible objects and recognize it. The recovery methodology also allows us to study vision in isolation—something that is very desirable in the early stages of development of any new field.

The next section describes research on the problem of recovery, which has given rise to some interesting mathematical problems. It should be noted that treating recovery as a central vision problem raises a theoretical question: What properties of a scene can be recovered by means of vision? The study of the recovery problem tells us about the mathematical relationships between properties of the image and properties of the physical world. It does not necessarily tell us how to build a vision system for a specific purpose, because in order to perform a given visual task, we may not need to fully recover the scene; but it does shed some light on the problems of designing visual systems.

3. SCENE RECOVERY: HISTORICAL DEVELOPMENT

If we need to treat vision as a recovery problem, it is necessary to make the image-formation process explicit. Consider the simplified model of an observer illustrated in Fig. 1.1. The light going through a pinhole camera creates an image, that is, an array of light intensities. The problem of recovery is the "inverse optics" problem; optics maps the world onto the image, vision attempts to invert the process. It is important to note that recovery tasks and their applications (navigation, recognition, etc.) become easier if one has a specific model for the class of scenes in question. In this chapter, however, we will focus on techniques based on general scene models and on general-purpose tasks that visual systems might need to perform.

3.1. The Early Years (1955–1970)

The earliest work in the field dealt with the analysis of single images of static scenes. A great deal of effort was expended on images of "scenes"

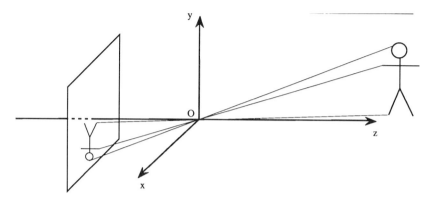

Figure 1.1. Geometry of vision. The optical image is formed by perspective projection through a point (a pinhole, or the nodal point of a lens)

that are (approximately) two-dimensional: documents, micrographs (where, because of the shallow depth of field, the image is an "optical section" of the specimen), and images of the earth's surface taken from high altitudes (in which terrain relief is negligible); the interpretation of such images is usually called "pattern recognition," not computer vision.

When work on robot vision began in the 1960s, it initially concentrated on the "blocks world"; that is, the scene was assumed to consist of a set of polyhedra. Because the image is a perspective projection of the scene, geometric analysis yields useful relationships between parameters of the block edges in the image and the three-dimensional structure of the blocks. Such relationships can be used to recover geometric properties, such as the concavity or convexity of an edge (7).

At the same time a lot of work was done on what was called "low-level processing," much of it devoted to the extraction of "important" intensity changes (edges) in an image. In a blocks-world image these should correspond to depth and slope discontinuities or to shadow boundaries. Edge detection was usually achieved by convolving images with local operators and thresholding the results. Finding homogeneous or smooth regions, which is essentially complementary to edge finding, was thought to have the potential of isolating image regions that were the images of surface patches with some physical significance. It was soon realized, however, that physically significant parts of a scene cannot be identified solely by analyzing the gray-level intensities in the image. By the early 1970s it had become clear that low-level vision could not generally derive useful scene descriptions from a single image, because even seemingly simple problems such as edge detection are in fact very complex.

At that time, which was a period of rapid progress in the development of artificial intelligence, it was suggested that "high-level" knowledge

about the scene could be used in conjunction with low-level visual processing to introduce additional constraints. To experiment with such ideas,
"complete" vision systems were constructed (6) that used information at
all levels, including both general knowledge about the imaging process as
well as domain-specific information. By and large, however, the performance of these systems was not impressive. Many researchers therefore
abandoned the system building approach and concentrated on the study of
specific visual abilities, possibly corresponding to identifiable modules in
the human visual system (8).

3.2. Modules and Uniqueness (1970–1985)

During the 1970s the field of computer vision became more mathematically sophisticated. David Marr proposed a paradigm in which a vision
system is conceptualized as a collection of individual autonomous components, or modules, each of which performs a different computational task.
The low-level modules operate directly on the image data in order to
recover useful 2D descriptions. The middle-level modules utilize these
descriptions to perform 3D recovery; and the high-level modules utilize
the results of recovery to reason about the world.

Low-level vision modules are devoted to extracting "simple" representations of the image intensity array that have some general physical significance. Tasks of particular interest at the low level are image restoration
(that is, estimation of the true intensities in a degraded image), edge
detection, segmentation into homogeneous regions, and texture representation.

Low-level modules operate on the image intensities and make no use of
higher-level knowledge about the scene. Some attempts were made to
introduce such knowledge into edge detection and segmentation processes
by treating them as image labeling processes and making use of local
consistency constraints on the labels (9, 10); but this approach did not
provide a sufficiently flexible means of representing and integrating global
knowledge.

Middle-level modules utilize the results of the low-level modules as well
as the image itself to recover the shapes, colors, spatial locations, and
motions of objects in the scene. These modules make use of various cues
in the image, such as shading, texture, contours, and motion. During this
period many mathematical techniques were developed for describing object geometry (11) and computing scene properties on the basis of various
types of information present in images (12–15).

It turns out, however, that nearly all of these low- or middle-level visual
tasks are ill-posed problems (16, 17); they are underconstrained and so do
not have unique solutions. For example, consider the problem of recover-

ing surface orientation from shading [the "shape from shading" problem (18)]. If we assume that reflectance is Lambertian (the object reflects light equally in all directions), the intensity I at a point (x, y) of the image is

$$I(x, y) = \rho \frac{1 + pp_s + qq_s}{\sqrt{1 + p^2 + q^2}\sqrt{1 + p_s^2 + q_s^2}},$$

where ρ is a constant (the albedo) that depends on the surface material, $(p_s, q_s, -1)$ is the direction of the light source, and $(p, q, -1)$ is the normal at the surface point whose image is (x, y). Thus measuring the intensity at any image point gives us one equation and two unknowns (p, q). Hence we cannot solve the shape from shading problem unless we impose additional constraints on the scene (19). The same is true for every recovery module.

    In general, suppose that we want to recover some quantity $\vec{\omega}$ that is a function of position in the image and that satisfies the equation $L(\vec{\omega}) = 0$. Since in many cases the equation $L(\vec{\omega}) = 0$ will not suffice for determination of $\vec{\omega}$, we need to make a further assumption about the scene. Let this assumption be of the form $S(\vec{\omega}) = 0$; this equation constitutes an additional constraint. Such constraints can be of various forms and can be related to various properties of the scene relevant to the quantities being computed. For example, if we need to compute surface shape, $S(\vec{\omega}) = 0$ can impose the condition that the surface is smooth, in other words, that shape variations are locally small, because most surfaces are piecewise smooth. In color processing, $S(\vec{\omega}) = 0$ can require that surface reflectance be describable using a small number of basis functions (20), based on the small number of retinal pigments. In the processing of general nonrigid motion, $S(\vec{\omega}) = 0$ can require that the deviation of the motion from rigidity be small. In segmenting an image into parts, $S(\vec{\omega}) = 0$ can require that the segmentation be as simple as possible with respect to some complexity measure (21).

    During the 1980s, Poggio and his colleagues (16) suggested that ill-posed visual recovery problems can be solved using the technique of regularization. [For simplicity and for consistency with the mathematical theory of regularization (22), we shall call the additional constraint $S(\vec{\omega}) = 0$ a "smoothness" condition even though it may not actually express the smoothness of the desired quantity $\vec{\omega}$. In general, $S(\vec{\omega}) = 0$ expresses the fact that some function of $\vec{\omega}$ should be small.] The solution is then obtained by minimizing a functional of the form $\int L^2(\vec{\omega}) + \lambda S^2(\vec{\omega})$. In other words, we find a solution that is as smooth as possible and at the same time satisfies the constraint $L(\vec{\omega}) = 0$. The coefficient λ determines the relative importance of smoothness in the solution. Figure 1.2 shows examples of surface recovery from shading and pattern cues, using various functionals.

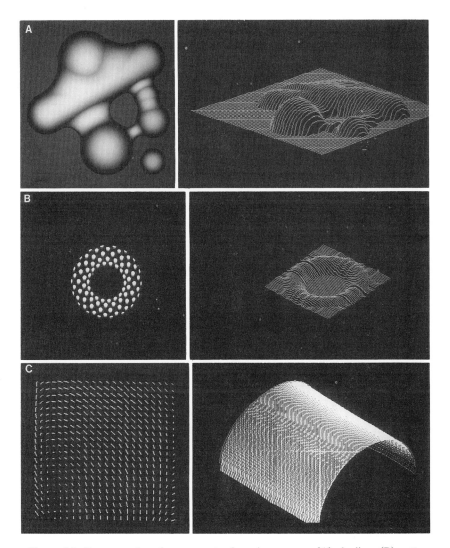

Figure 1.2. Recovery of surface geometry from image cues: (A) shading; (B) pattern; (C) motion. The left column shows the image (or image motion field); the right column shows the reconstructed surface.

In part (A) of Fig. 2.1, the intensity at every image point, assuming a Lambertian reflectance model, is

$$I(x, y) = p \frac{pp_s + qq_s + 1}{\sqrt{1 + p^2 + q^2}\sqrt{1 + p_s^2 + q_s^2}} \equiv R(p, q).$$

To obtain a unique solution, we minimize the functional

$$\iint\limits_{\text{image}} \left\{ (I - R)^2 + \lambda\left(p_x^2 + p_y^2 + q_x^2 + q_y^2 \right) \right\} dx\, dy;$$

this gives a surface that is as smooth as possible while satisfying the constraint $I = R$. The parameter λ weighs the relative importance of the two terms of the functional. In part (B), assuming that all the surface markings ("texels") have the same surface area, the area of an image texel S_I is related to the shape of the surface by

$$S_I = \frac{S_W}{d^2} \frac{1 - Ap - Bq}{\sqrt{1 + p^2 + q^2}} = R(p, q),$$

where S_W is the area of the surface texel, d is its distance from the viewer, and (A, B) is the centroid of the image texel. We obtain a unique solution by minimizing the same functional. In part (C), assuming that we know how every point of a rotating object moves on its (orthographic) image, the surface shape (p, q) is related to the local image motion by a quadratic expression of the form $f(p, q) = 0$. As before, we obtain a unique solution by minimizing the same functional.

The difficulty with regularization is that it tends to smooth over discontinuities (places where the constraint $S(\vec{\omega}) = 0$ is violated); but the visual world is rich in discontinuities. Another problem with regularization is that we need a systematic way of choosing a value for the coefficient λ. If λ is small, the solution involves less smoothing over discontinuities, but it then tends to be more sensitive to noise.

3.3. Some Current Research Areas (1985 – Present): Discontinuities and Active Vision

In the real world, the function $\vec{\omega}$ that we need to recover has discontinuities and discontinuous derivatives. Standard recovery techniques cannot deal fully with this situation.

One approach to dealing with discontinuities is to first segment the image (23) into homogeneous regions and then to regularize within each region. However, segmentation is not a solved problem. One of the reasons for attempting to recover the quantity $\vec{\omega}$ is to facilitate segmentation.

Another approach is to divide the image into boundary and nonboundary points. Assume there is a known probability that a random point is a boundary point and that at boundary points all values of S are equally likely. At nonboundary points, minimizing $\int[L^2 + \lambda S^2]$ is acceptable except that we do not excessively penalize large S (since large S means a probable boundary point). Thus we can minimize, for example, $\int[L^2 + \lambda g_T(S)]$ where $g_T(S) = \min(S^2, T^2)$. Here T is a threshold depending on the fraction of points that are discontinuities.

This problem has been studied in the case where $\vec{\omega}$ has discrete range (for instance, if $\vec{\omega}$ is a binary function) and the domain is a discrete lattice (24). This approach was later extended to the case where $\vec{\omega}$ is real-valued (25) and to a continuous domain (26). The minimization problem is solved using Monte Carlo techniques or deterministic approximations to them such as the mean-field approximation. In Blake and Zisserman (27) the problem was solved by a continuation method called "graduated nonconvexity." The solution is generally not unique. All these methods of finding the solution are either not guaranteed to converge to a global minimum or cannot be known to be reasonably efficient. The assumption that all $S^2 < T^2$ are equally good is also questionable.

Other approaches have been proposed in Nagel and Enkelmann (28) and Lee and Pavlidis (29). Some of these approaches first find the boundary points (at which λ can be set equal to 0); others make the amount of smoothing depend on the gradient magnitude (we smooth more where the gradient is small); still others allow some smoothing at boundary points, but only in the gradient direction ("oriented smoothness"). These theories can be augmented to incorporate the assumption that boundaries are smooth except at a few corner points, or other assumptions about boundary shape.

Another approach (30) is based on the observation that the errors and smoothness measures of nearby points are correlated and that we should therefore use terms involving the derivatives of L and S in the minimization problem. This makes it unnecessary to make a rigid binary distinction between boundary and nonboundary points, and to recover $\vec{\omega}$ while smoothing as little as possible over discontinuities.

Research will continue on the solution of ill-posed problems in which the quantity to be recovered is a function with discontinuous derivatives, and better algorithms will be developed. However, it should be pointed out that any recovery technique must be based on assumptions about scene and noise models. The dependence on a noise model leads to serious difficulties, because standard noise models are not adequate for describing images of real scenes. A scene often contains "clutter" that is difficult to model. Simple geometric and photometric models for a class of 3D scenes do not give rise to simple models for the 2D images of these scenes. For example, a quadratic Lambertian surface gives rise to a trigonometric shading function in the image. Statistically stationary surface markings in the scene do not necessarily yield stationary intensity fluctuations in the image; conversely, the stationarity of an image property is not

TABLE 1.1

How Observer Activity Simplifies Recovery Problems

Problem	Passive observer	Active observer
Shape from shading	Ill-posed problem; needs to be regularized—even then, unique solution is not guaranteed because of nonlinearity	Well-posed and stable; linear equation; unique solution
Shape from contour	Ill-posed problem; has not yet been regularized in the Tikhonov sense; solvable under restrictive assumptions	Well-posed problem; unique solution for either monocular or binocular observer
Shape from texture	Ill-posed problem; needs some assumption about the texture	Well-posed problem; no assumption required
Structure from motion	Well posed but unstable; nonlinear constraints	Well posed and stable; quadratic constraints, simple solution methods, stability

necessarily due to the stationarity of the corresponding scene property. In spite of these difficulties, the quest for noise-insensitive recovery algorithms continues, and can be expected to lead to a series of increasingly robust methods.

It was observed in the mid-1980s (31, 32) that many visual recovery problems become easier if the observer is active, that is, it can control its visual apparatus, for example, by making (known) "eye movements." It turns out that most of the low- and middle-level vision problems become much easier to solve (and often even become well posed) for an active observer. Examples of this phenomenon are shown in Table 1.1 (32). Observer activity is also a central theme in the design of "animate" or "purposive" vision systems, which will be discussed below.

After the 3D structure of the scene has been recovered from the images, the information can be used in a variety of ways. Objects of given types can be detected and located in the scene by finding parts of the scene that match stored object descriptions. (Of course, in many cases this can be done without first recovering 3D structure.) Knowledge of the structure of the scene allows a mobile robot (or a robot manipulator) to move around while avoiding obstacles. Object recognition and navigation are the two major areas of application of 3D computer vision. Many systems have been designed for recognizing given classes of objects from their geometric descriptions (33). Other systems have demonstrated successful control of robot movements using visual feedback; recent demonstrations involve autonomous outdoor vehicles that can be driven on roads under computer control (34–36).

3.4. Purposive Vision: A New Paradigm

In recent years it has become increasingly apparent that it is very difficult to create an accurate 3D description of the visible world from images. The recovery paradigm, which regards a vision system as a set of low- and middle-level modules that recover the structure of the scene, and that provide input to high-level modules that can then reason about the scene, has not led to the design of successful vision systems, that is, systems that robustly perform recognition or navigation tasks using vision.

General 3D scene recovery is a very complex problem. Many recovery problems are inherently unstable (37, 38). In order to correctly recover, we may need to formulate new classes of scene and noise models. General recovery would provide a powerful theoretical basis for solving recognition and navigation problems. However, we should not assume that practical results will flow out of successful theories rather than vice versa. In the past, it has at least as often been the case that successful theories have been constructed on the basis of engineering observations.

For many of the problems we need to solve using vision, complete and accurate recovery of the scene is not necessary. Brooks (39) has suggested that it is not necessary to achieve artificial intelligence before we can build successful robots. On the contrary, Brooks claims that we can achieve artificial intelligence (AI) by building robots, starting with simple ones and progressing to more complex ones. He has demonstrated how to build simple robots that have primitive behaviors.

Coming back to fundamentals, we should once again ask the basic question: What is vision for? Why does an organism (or a robot) need vision? Obviously, organisms use vision to accomplish various tasks, such as recognizing danger and food. Organisms have goals and purposes, and visual information makes it possible, or easier, to achieve these goals. It has been suggested (40) that perhaps vision can be more readily understood in the context of the vision-guided behaviors that the system (the organism or the robot) is engaged in.

This suggestion leads to the important realization that specific vision-guided behaviors may not require a very elaborate representation of the 3D world. If we are looking for an object that can be used for a certain purpose, we may only need to recognize some of its qualitative characteristics; we don't need to know its exact shape. Similarly, if we need to find a path out of a room, we don't need to know the exact shapes of all the pieces of furniture in the room. For many vision-guided behaviors, the visual processing needed is relatively simple; it does not require extensive numerical analysis, but involves only simple qualitative techniques that provide yes/no answers about the scene. For example, an active observer can robustly detect independently moving objects in its vicinity and can

estimate their trajectories, using simple analyses of the image motion field
(41). The results of this partial recovery can be used to control various
behaviors, such as dodging or catching an object.

This new paradigm of task-oriented, or *purposive*, vision, emphasizing
the study of specific vision-guided behaviors, will accelerate progress in the
field and will lead to systems having robust, reliable performance. At the
same time, the paradigm can be used to study the theory of visual
perception by developing and analyzing generic vision-based behaviors.
The paradigm still lacks theoretical foundations, however, including a
formal definition of a visual agent and the dependence of behavior on
agent characteristics (size, mobility, and so forth), a formal definition of
behavior (as a sequence of perceptual events and actions), a calculus of
behaviors or purposes that can generate new behaviors by combining
existing behaviors or by learning and provide the basis for controlling the
agent, and a corresponding repertoire of visual routines (42). The paradigm
treats vision as part of a larger system, with increasing emphasis on
high-level reasoning about the world, and will require interdisciplinary
approaches. The study of vision in organisms and computers continues to
be a rich source of interesting research problems.

4. CONCLUDING REMARKS

Those living organisms that have vision exhibit impressive abilities to
interact with their environments. This performance constitutes a challenge
to computer (and robot) vision; at the same time, it serves as an existence
proof that the goals of computer vision are attainable.

The theoretical foundations of computer vision are not yet fully developed; better models for noisy, cluttered, real-world scenes, and better
ways of solving ill-posed problems in the presence of discontinuities, are
needed. Meanwhile, tasks that require only partial descriptions of the
scene should be studied more closely, because such task tend to be better
posed and less computationally costly. Organisms seem to require only
partial scene descriptions (of various types) in order to perform visually
guided behaviors; similarly, the ability to construct appropriate partial
scene descriptions from images may be all that a computer or robot vision
system needs to function successfully in its environment.

Computer vision techniques have many practical applications in such
domains as document processing, industrial inspection, medical imaging,
remote sensing, reconnaissance, and robot guidance. There have been
successes in many of these domains, but many tasks are still beyond our
current capabilities. These potential applications provide major incentives
for continued research.

ACKNOWLEDGMENTS

This work was funded in part by DARPA (ARPA Order No. 6989, through Contract DACA76-89-C-0019 with the U.S. Army Engineer Topographic Laboratories), NSF (under a Presidential Young Investigator Award, Grant IRI-90-57934), Alliant Techsystems, Inc. and Texas Instruments, Inc. The authors thank Barbara Burnett and Janice Perrone for their expert help in preparing this paper.

REFERENCES

1. J. P. Frisby, "Seeing: Illusion, Brain and Mind." Oxford Univ. Press, Oxford, 1979.
2. D. H. Ballard and C. M. Brown, "Computer Vision." Prentice-Hall, Englewood Cliffs, NJ, 1982.
3. B. K. P. Horn, "Robot Vision." McGraw-Hill, New York, 1986.
4. A. Rosenfeld and A. C. Kak, "Digital Picture Processing," 2nd ed. Academic Press, New York, 1982.
5. D. Marr, "Vision: A Computational Investigation into the Human Representation and Processing of Visual Information." Freeman, San Francisco, 1982.
6. J. K. Tsotsos, Image understanding. In "Encyclopedia of Artificial Intelligence" (S. Shapiro, ed.), pp. 389–409. Wiley, New York, 1987.
7. M. Brady, Computational approaches to image understanding. *ACM Comput. Surv.* **14**, 3–71 (1982).
8. The existence of such modules is supported by the study of patients with visual disabilities resulting from brain lesions (8a) and by psychophysical experiments in which a particular source of information is isolated. Notable examples are Land's demonstrations on the computation of lightness (8b) and Julesz's demonstration of stereoscopic fusion without monocular cues (8c).
8a. M. J. Farah, "Visual Agnosia—Disorders of Object Recognition and what they Tell us about Normal Vision." MIT Press, Cambridge, MA, 1990.
8b. E. H. Land and J. J. McCann, Lightness and retinex theory. *J. Opt. Soc. Am.* **61**, 1–11 (1971).
8c. B. Julesz, "Foundations of Cyclopean Perception." Univ. of Chicago Press, Chicago, 1971.
9. L. S. Davis and A. Rosenfeld, Cooperative processes for low-level vision: A survey. *Artif. Intell.* **17**, 245–263 (1981).
10. O. D. Faugeras and M. Berthod, Scene labeling: An optimization approach. *IEEE Trans. Pattern Anal. Mach. Intell.* **PAMI-3**, 412–424 (1981).
11. J. J. Koenderink, "Solid Shape." MIT Press, Cambridge, MA, 1990.
12. S. Ullman, "The Interpretation of Visual Motion." MIT Press, Cambridge, MA, 1979.
13. T. S. Huang, ed., "Image Sequence Analysis." Springer, Berlin, 1981.
14. J. Aloimonos and C. M. Brown, Robust computation of intrinsic images from multiple cues. In "Advances in Computer Vision" (C. M. Brown, ed.), Vol. 1, pp. 115–163. Erlbaum, Hillsdale, NJ, 1987.
15. T. Poggio, E. B. Gamble, and J. J. Little, Parallel integration of vision modules. *Science* **242**, 436–440 (1988).

16. T. Poggio, V. Torre, and C. Koch, Computational vision and regularization theory. *Nature (London)* **317**, 314–319 (1985).
17. M. Bertero, T. A. Poggio, and V. Torre, Ill-posed problems in early vision. *Proc. IEEE* **76**, 869–889 (1988).
18. B. K. P. Horn and M. J. Brooks, eds., "Shape from Shading." MIT Press, Cambridge, MA, 1989.
19. R. T. Frankot and R. Chellappa, A method for enforcing integrability in shape from shading algorithms. *IEEE Trans. Pattern Anal. Mach. Intell.* **PAMI-10**, 439–451 (1988).
20. A. C. Hurlbert and T. A. Poggio, Synthesizing a color algorithm. *Science* **239**, 482–485 (1988).
21. Y. G. Leclerc, Constructing simple stable descriptions for image partitioning. *Int. J. Comput. Vision* **3**, 73–102 (1989).
22. A. N. Tikhonov and V. Y. Arsenin, "Solution of Ill-Posed Problems." Winston and Wiley, Washington, DC, 1977.
23. R. M. Haralick and L. G. Shapiro, Image segmentation techniques. *Comput. Vision, Graphics, Image Process.* **29**, 100–132 (1985).
24. S. Geman and D. Geman, Stochastic relaxation, Gibbs distribution, and the Bayesian restoration of images. *IEEE Trans. Pattern Anal. Mach. Intell.* **PAMI-6**, 721–741 (1984).
25. J. L. Marroquin, S. Mitter, and T. Poggio, Probabilistic solution of ill-posed problems in early vision. *J. Am. Stat. Assoc.* **82**, 76–89 (1987).
26. D. Mumford and M. Shah, Boundary detection by minimizing functionals. In "Image Understanding 1989" (S. Ullman and W. Richards, ed.), pp. 19–43. Ablex, Norwood, NJ.
27. A. Blake and A. Zisserman, "Visual Reconstruction." MIT Press, Cambridge, MA, 1987.
28. H. H. Nagel and W. Enkelmann, An investigation of smoothness constraints for the estimation of displacement vector fields from image sequences. *IEEE Trans. Pattern Anal. Mach. Intell.* **PAMI-8**, 565–593 (1986).
29. D. Lee and T. Pavlidis, One-dimensional regularization with discontinuities. *IEEE Trans. Pattern Anal. Mach. Intell.* **PAMI-10**, 822–829 (1988).
30. J. Aloimonos and D. Shulman, "Integration of Visual Modules: An Extension of the Marr Paradigm." Academic Press, Boston, 1989.
31. R. Bajcsy, Active perception vs. passive perception. In "Proceedings of the Third Workshop on Computer Vision: Representation and Control," pp. 55–59. IEEE Computer Society Press, Washington, DC, 1985.
32. J. Aloimonos, I. Weiss, and A. Bandopadhay, Active vision. *Int. J. Comput. Vision* **2**, 333–356 (1988).
33. T. O. Binford, Survey of model-based image analysis systems. *Int. J. Robotics Res.* **1**, 18–64 (1982).
34. A. M. Waxman, J. J. LeMoigne, L. S. Davis, B. Srinivasan, T. R. Kushner, E. Liang, and T. Siddalingaiah, A visual navigation system for autonomous land vehicles. *IEEE J. Robotics Autom.* **RA-3**, 249–265 (1987).
35. C. Thorpe, M. H. Hebert, T. Kanade, and S. A. Shafer, Vision and navigation for the Carnegie-Mellon Navlab. *IEEE Trans. Pattern Anal. Mach. Intell.* **PAMI-10**, 362–373 (1988).

36. E. D. Dickmanns and V. Graefe, [Application of] dynamic monocular machine vision. *Mach. Vision & Appl.* **1**, 241–261 (1988).

37. A. Verri and T. Poggio, Against quantitative optical flow. *Proc. Int. Conf. Comput. Vision, 1st,* pp. 171–180, (1987).

38. M. E. Spetsakis and J. Aloimonos, A unified theory of structure from motion. *Proc. Defense Advanced Research Projects Agency Image Understanding Workshop,* pp. 271–283 (1990).

39. R. A. Brooks, "Achieving Artificial Intelligence Through Building Robots," AI Memo 899. Massachusetts Institute of Technology, Artificial Intelligence Laboratory, Cambridge, MA, 1986.

40. D. H. Ballard, Animate vision. *Artif. Intell.* **48**, 57–86 (1991).

41. J. Aloimonos, Purposive and qualitative active vision. *Proc. Defense Advanced Research Projects Agency Image Understanding Workshop,* pp. 816–828 (1990).

42. S. Ullman, Visual routines. *Cognition* **18**, 97–159 (1984).

Chapter **2**

Three-Dimensional Shape Representation

KEVIN W. BOWYER

Department of Computer Science and Engineering
University of South Florida
Tampa, Florida

CHARLES R. DYER

Department of Computer Science
University of Wisconsin
Madison, Wisconsin

1. INTRODUCTION

Representing three-dimensional (3D) shapes is a fundamental problem in many areas of science and engineering. In computer-aided design and manufacturing, 3D models of the geometry of solid shapes are used to answer questions related to the design and manufacturability of objects. In computer graphics, models are used to generate dense surface descriptions

17

in order to render realistic images. In computer vision, models are used to infer 3D shape and scene structure from an image. In each area, specialized representations have been developed that have desirable properties for solving specific classes of tasks. Thus, while it is important in most cases to have a representation that is unambiguous, unique, accurate, stable, and compact (22, 27), the most critical issue is that the representation should make accessible key qualitative and quantitative structure so that efficient algorithms are possible for solving specific, basic operations.

In computer vision, a major use of 3D shape representations is to model the geometry of real objects, and then to use these models to interpret subsets of image features by finding correspondences between these image features and features of the model. Thus a good shape representation makes this matching process efficient, specifying what features are visible and invisible, and their spatial constraints. Lowe calls this relationship between an object model and an image the *viewpoint consistency constraint* (19).

This use of shape for interpreting image features occurs in many types of vision tasks. In 3D object recognition, the correspondence between an object model and a set of image features determines what object is present and its pose (4). Model-based tracking of 3D objects requires the dynamic tracking of features to compute the 3D motion of a given object (20, 23, 36). Terrain matching uses an elevation map to interpret optical or range terrain data (14). In navigation applications, models of selected terrain shape features (e.g., road markings and road signs) can be used to control vehicle motion for route planning and self-localization (24).

Because matching geometric models with image data is the primary operation of interest in computer vision, 3D shape representations that are appropriate for this field must be concerned with the following two issues: (1) modeling real, physical objects and classes of objects, and (2) the degree to which a geometric model facilitates matching features of the real shape represented by the model with image features.

The first issue is how to construct a set of models that adequately describe the physical properties of real objects. In this chapter we consider only the problem of describing the 3D geometry of opaque, solid objects. Incorporating other properties such as color and texture is also important, but will not be considered here. Because of the natural complexity of real objects, computer vision, as in computer graphics, must necessarily use models that are approximations to the geometry of real shapes. No representation can, in general, presume that all real shapes are described exactly using a given representation, no matter whether objects are specified by algebraic surfaces or polyhedra. In fact, most natural surfaces (e.g., bushes, bark, mountains) are not smooth at all, requiring a representation of a rough shape. It is important to know what are the essential elements of the model and what are irrelevant artifacts of the model. For example, if a polyhedron is used to model a sphere, the faces are the essential parts, approximating the surface of the sphere, and the vertices and edges are irrelevant. Similarly, if a piecewise-smooth surface representation is used, the intersection curves between surface patches are (usually) artifacts.

Experience in both computer vision and computer graphics indicates that the size and speed tradeoffs of using one approximation versus another are very dependent on the structure of the objects being represented. The speed and simplicity of linear representations can often compensate for size increases and approximation error, provided the appropriate feature information is retained (12, 21). For example, if surface curvature properties are important features, the representation must allow for reasonable approximations of this information. Other visible characteristics that may be of interest include projected locations of surface critical points (local maxima, minima, and saddlepoints), location of the occluding contour (surface depth discontinuities), curve tangent directions, and surface orientation discontinuity locations. The second major issue listed above emphasizes the fact that in vision, shape models are usually used to find correspondences between image features of the shape that is modeled (3). Depending on what shape features are selected as the basis for matching, the choice of how to represent those features in a shape model becomes a critical decision. In the case where the observed image features are the two-dimensional (2D) projection of scene features, we can differentiate between two classes of features. First, intrinsic features of the real object are viewpoint-independent features on the surface that are projected into the image and detectable by image operators of some kind. For example, corners, holes, and long, straight edges occur in many manufactured objects. A second class of features is generated by the image projection process where 3D opaque shape is projected into the 2D image plane. The geometry and topology of the occluding contour, silhouette, and T-junctions of a shape are viewpoint-dependent features that are not generated by any intrinsic feature of the real shape. The important point is that the features corresponding to detectable image features must be efficiently represented in (or computed from) a given model of the shape. Again, the processes that compute these features must distinguish between the relevant and irrelevant parts of the model in terms of the underlying shape that it approximates.

2. OBJECT-CENTERED REPRESENTATIONS

What does it mean to model the shape of an object? Most research in model-based vision has been based on geometric models that use an object-centered coordinate system to specify (approximately) the volume of three-dimensional Euclidean space that is filled by a solid shape. Object-centered approaches are compact because they do not represent any viewpoint-dependent properties. A separate projection mapping is used to generate the image appearance of an object represented in this manner. Representation of intrinsic local and global surface features of a shape is easily incorporated into this class of representations. Hence geometric matching operations that use viewpoint-independent shape features can be efficiently implemented. A major disadvantage is that features of appearance are not represented explicitly and may be difficult to calculate.

Object-centered representations can be divided into three main categories: boundary, volumetric, and sweep representations. The next section briefly reviews these standard approaches for representing rigid shapes. It should be noticed that all of these representations assume that a relatively smooth object is being modeled. There is a glaring lack of methods in computer vision representing rough surfaces and objects.

2.1. Exact Representations of Rigid Shape

2.1.1. Boundary Representations

Boundary representations describe a solid object in terms of its bounding surfaces. Except for simple objects, this means a piecewise collection of surface patch descriptions of the faces, plus a description of the connectivity of these patches, specifically, how they intersect at edges (curves) and vertices. Faces are usually constrained to be planar, quadric or superquadric surfaces.

Restricting the faces to polygonally bounded planar surfaces results in the class of *polyhedra*. Figure 2.1 shows three simple objects represented by polyhedra. Much of the work in both computer vision and computer

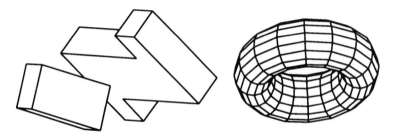

Figure 2.1. Three-dimensional objects represented by polyhedra.

graphics, including the seminal work by Roberts (28) and Sutherland (34), has used this approach because it enables the use of simple, efficient linear operations for manipulating them. When representing objects with curved surfaces, the errors in the representation can be made arbitrarily small by increasing the number of faces to obtain a better piecewise-linear approximation, but this increases the space requirements.

The object boundary is often represented as either lists of faces, edges, and vertices, or using Baumgart's *winged-edge* data structure that explicitly stores the interconnections between faces (2). The winged-edge representation maintains all the topological information in a record for each edge, describing the two vertices it connects, the two faces it separates, and containing forward and backward pointers to the next clockwise and counterclockwise edge of each face it separates. The vertex and face records contain pointers to an edge connected to them. Representations with interconnections between different surface patches are often referred to as *graph-based* or *topological representations*.

Polyhedral representations can require large amounts of space to adequately approximate objects with curved surfaces. Therefore other types of surfaces can be used to define the surface patches in a boundary representation. *Quadric surfaces* are second-degree equations implicitly defined by

$$\sum_{i+j+k \leq 2} a_{ijk} x^i y^j z^k = 0,$$

containing 10 coefficients. Quadric surfaces include cylinders, ellipsoids, paraboloids, and hyperboloids. *Superquadric surfaces* can also be used. The subclass superellipsoids will be discussed in the next section where they are used as volumetric primitives.

Parametric bicubic surfaces define points on a surface using bivariate cubic polynomials. Coons patches and Bézier surfaces are examples in this class. These surfaces have the advantage of allowing patches to be joined smoothly along an intersection curve, avoiding curvature discontinuity artifacts. In addition, point properties are easily computable; for example, the surface normal and whether a point is on the surface. Viewpoint-dependent properties are numerically quite complex, however, when using any piecewise-smooth surface representation. For example, the implicit equation of the occluding contour of a torus under orthographic projection is an 8th-degree polynomial containing over 170 terms (18).

2.1.2. *Volumetric Representations*

Volumetric representations of a solid object specify the subset of points in Euclidean space that are contained in the object. This is accomplished by specifying a set of simple, primitive 3D volumes, and a set of combining operators that join them into more complex volumes. Methods differ according to the types of primitives used, the types of combining operators, and whether the primitives are allowed to overlap one another. Because these representations emphasize the explicit encoding of all points in a solid object, computing surface properties is seldom very efficient. On the other hand, using volumetric primitives that describe semantically meaningful parts of a shape supports high-level operations such as articulations, structure deformations, and function-based analysis. In this section we briefly describe voxel arrays, octrees constructive solid geometry, and superquadric representations.

Voxel arrays are defined using a single primitive element, a unit-size cube, called a "voxel." An object is defined as the union of nonoverlapping cubes, where the positions of the cubes are restricted to points in a 3D square lattice, and the cubes are all oriented rectilinearly. This results in a description that is a partition of the space occupied by the object. Because of its regularity, it is simply implemented by a 3D array, where each array position specifies whether the correspondence voxel is contained in the shape. Figure 2.2 shows a torus represented by an array of voxels.

Octrees are a hierarchical extension of voxel arrays (30). The primitive elements are cubes with a side length of a power of 2. Objects are again defined by the union of nonoverlapping cubes. All cubes are oriented rectilinearly. The positions and sizes of the cubes used to partition the space covered by an object are defined recursively as follows. The entire

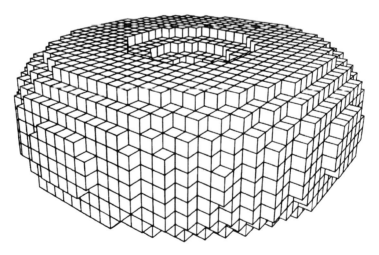

Figure 2.2. A torus represented by an array of voxels. From Christensen (10), courtesy of Association for Computing Machinery, Inc.

3D space in which an object is contained is assumed to be a cube with a power-of-2 side length. The root node of a tree is associated with this cube of space. If this cube is entirely contained in the object, the node is made a "black" leaf node. If this cube does not contain any points in the object, the node is made a "white" leaf. Otherwise, the cube is subdivided into octants and eight "children" nodes are created below the previous node to represent this decomposition of space. The process continues recursively until no more subdivisions are made. The result is an 8-ary tree, with each node corresponding to a cube of space.

The union of the cubes represented by the black leaf nodes represents the set of points contained in the object. The level of a black node implicitly determines its size, and the sequence of arcs traversed from the root determines its position. Because octrees contain voxels of variable size, they are generally more space efficient than voxel arrays. The number of nodes is usually proportional to the object's surface area. Consequently, the number of leaf nodes representing points on an object's surface will generally be proportional to the number of voxels on the surface in a voxel array.

Constructive solid geometry (CSG) uses a variety of types of primitive 3D volumetric solids such as spheres, cubes, and cylinders. More complicated objects are constructed by combining primitive solids using rigid transformations (rotation, translation, scaling) and regularized Boolean set operations (union, intersection, difference). An object is represented by an ordered, binary tree, where leaf nodes are primitives and nonleaf nodes correspond to transformation and combination operators. Because a torus is usually included as a primitive, only a single node is required to represent a torus-shaped object. To determine physical properties of an object requires a tree traversal in order to compute the shape of the object implicit in the tree. Hence, the efficiency of computing model features of the visible surfaces of an object, both intrinsic and viewpoint-sensitive properties, will depend on the number of primitives used to describe the object.

A variant of CSG representations uses *superquadric* volumetric primitives, increasing the range of types of component parts that can be specified (1, 25). One type of superquadric primitive is a generalization of an ellipsoid, called a *superellipsoid*, and is defined implicitly by

$$\left[\left(\frac{x}{a_1}\right)^{2/\epsilon_1} + \left(\frac{y}{a_2}\right)^{2/\epsilon_1}\right]^{\epsilon_1/\epsilon_2} + \left(\frac{z}{a_3}\right)^{2/\epsilon_2} - 1 = 0,$$

where ϵ_1 and ϵ_2 are shape parameters that control the squareness, roundness, or diamondness of the shape, and a_1, a_2, and a_3 determine the lengths in the three axis directions. Hence only five parameters are used to specify a shape (in a fixed position and orientation). By adding a few additional parameters, global deformations such as tapering, bending, and twisting can be included to build still more complex primitives. Because the primitives can be more complex than those used in conventional CSG representations, there will usually be fewer leaf nodes in the tree defining an object. Other types of primitives include cubes, pyramids and cones, plus variants that are truncated or have rounded corners.

2.1.3. Sweep Representations

While the previous section composed 3D solid primitives to define an object, in this section we consider methods that combine, using a sweeping transformation, 2D surfaces. *Generalized cylinders* (GC), also called *generalized cones*, are defined by a 3D space curve, called the "spine," and a 2D closed, planar "cross section" of the object perpendicular to the spine tangent (6). The cross-section function is parameterized by arc length along the spine, defining the "sweeping rule." The cross section is frequently specified by its boundary curve. For example, a torus is defined as a GC with a circular spine, a circular cross section, and a constant sweeping rule. Figure 2.3 shows a generalized cylinder representation of a telephone handset. GCs are intuitively appealing models for elongated shapes containing axial symmetry (9, 22). An object is represented as a union of overlapping elongated parts, each described by a GC. For nonelongated shapes or shapes that cannot be described in terms of a few elongated parts, GCs are not a natural representation.

In practice, restricted subclasses of GCs are usually studied and implemented. For example, *straight homogeneous generalized cylinders* are GCs that contain a straight spine, an arbitrary cross section, and a scaling sweeping rule (32). *Solids of revolution* are generated by rotating a planar curve around a straight axis. In the special case where the curve is a positive function of position along the axis, a GC is formed having a straight spine, a circular cross section, and an arbitrary sweeping rule.

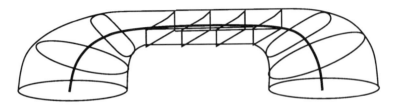

Figure 2.3. Generalized cylinder representation of a telephone handset showing selected cross sections and spine (dark curve).

Because of the relatively simple structure of GCs, both viewpoint-dependent and viewpoint-invariant properties can be derived and used.

2.2. More General Shape Representations

The shape representations described in the previous section all deal with representing rigid solid shape, and each has been used with at least some success for computer vision purposes. Recognition of rigid solid objects by matching shape-based features is a useful paradigm for many machine vision applications. However, it is clear that greater capabilities are required by a so-called general purpose and real-world vision system. Such a system must be able to deal with objects whose shape is not precisely defined or whose shape may vary. Such a system would also likely use different levels of detail in a representation, or even entirely different representations, for different tasks. This section will discuss shape representations that are meant to address the needs of more general-purpose and real-world computer vision systems.

2.2.1. Parameterized Shape Families

A first step toward greater generality in shape representation is to allow some specified range of variation in the parameters defining the shape. This can be done through relatively straightforward extensions to any of the geometric representations discussed in the previous section. All that is required is that some of the constants in the geometric representation be replaced by parameters that have associated ranges of allowed values. This usually requires only a minor modification in the format of the geometric representation. The resulting parameterized representation captures a continuous family of related shapes. An example of this type of parameterized shape family appears in Fig. 2.5 and can be contrasted with the simple boundary representation that appears in Fig. 2.4. This particular example of a parameterized shape family uses a boundary representation as its basis, but similar parameterizations can, of course, be defined using any form of geometric representation.

The *topology* of the parameterized representation and the nonparameterized representation, as defined by the connectivity of the faces that make up the shape, is identical. However, the *geometry* of the two representations, as defined by the coordinates of the vertices, is clearly different. In the nonparameterized representation, each vertex has fixed (x, y, z) coordinates. In the parameterized representation, three different groups of vertices have coordinates that depend on the value of one of the

Kevin W. Bowyer and Charles R. Dyer

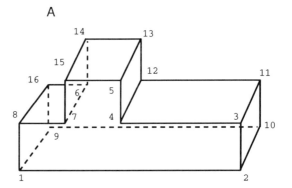

A

B

vertex	X	Y	Z
1	0	1	0
2	4	1	0
3	4	1	1
4	2	1	1
5	2	1	2
6	1	1	2
7	1	1	1
8	0	1	1
9	0	0	0
10	4	0	0
11	4	0	1
12	2	0	1
13	2	0	2
14	1	0	2
15	1	0	1
16	0	0	1

face	vertex list
right side	1,2,3,4,5,6,7,8
lower back	2,10,11,3
left side	9,16,15,14,13,12,11,10
lower front	9,1,8,16
upper front	15,7,6,14
upper back	12,4,5,13
top front	16,8,7,15
top mid	14,6,5,13
top back	12,4,3,11
bottom	9,1,2,10

Figure 2.4. Polyhedral boundary representation: (A) depiction of the shape represented; (B) the constitute vertex coordinates and the vertex lists for each face constitute a simple boundary representation. In this example, the vertex lists follow the convention of a counterclockwise listing as seen from outside the object.

parameters **H** or **L**. The y coordinate of the vertices that constitute the "lower back" face may vary over a range that effectively allows stretching of the back portion of the shape. The z coordinate of the vertices that constitute the "top front" and "top back" faces may vary over a range that effectively allows some lowering of the shape. The z coordinate of the vertices that comprise the "top mid-" face is specified as a constant offset from the value of the parameterized z coordinate.

Parameterized shape families have been used by computer vision researchers in several applications areas. In the analysis of images of piles of

A

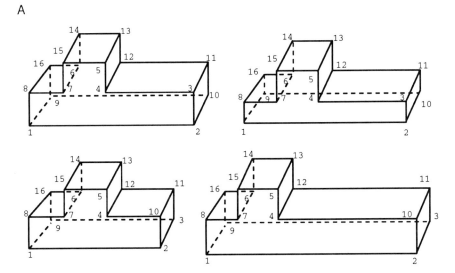

B

vertex	X	Y	Z
1	0	1	0
2	L	1	0
3	L	1	H
4	2	1	H
5	2	1	H+1
6	1	1	H+1
7	1	1	H
8	0	1	H
9	0	0	0
10	L	0	0
11	L	0	H
12	2	0	H
13	2	0	H+1
14	1	0	H+1
15	1	0	H
16	0	0	H
L = [3,6], H = [0.5,1]			

face	vertex list
right side	1,2,3,4,5,6,7,8
lower back	2,10,11,3
left side	9,16,15,14,13,12,11,10
lower front	9,1,8,16
upper front	15,7,6,14
upper back	12,4,5,13
top front	16,8,7,15
top mid	14,6,5,13
top back	12,4,3,11
bottom	9,1,2,10

Figure 2.5. Parameterized shape representation: (A) example shapes captured by the representation; (B) parameterized boundary representation.

postal packages, this type of representation makes it easy to define object types such as "parallelepiped" and "cylinder." In the analysis of images of outdoor scenes containing man-made objects, it is easy to define approximate shape representations for object types such as "house" and "truck."

2.2.2. Structural Representation of Shapes

In a structural representation, the shape is defined as a composition from some set of primitive parts. Each primitive part has its own shape representation. The overall shape representation includes the shape representation for each individual part as well as information for how the part shapes are put together to create the overall shape. Each individual part shape is typically defined in its own coordinate system, and so the information for composing the part shapes typically includes a transformation for each part to bring it into a common coordinate system for the overall shape (see Fig. 2.6). Taken by itself, a structural representation may be no more (or perhaps even less) complicated than a *constructive solid geometry* representation. However, the use of a structural representation may make it more convenient to specify a parameterized shape family, since it provides a logical grouping of portions of the overall object shape. Also, the use of a structural representation may make it easier to recognize objects in situations when only partial shape information is observed.

Structural models play an important role in Biederman's *recognition by components* (RBC) theory of human object recognition capabilities (5). The RBC theory suggests that there is some small number of fundamental, qualitatively defined part shapes called "geons" from which object representations are constructed. Biederman's original set of geons was defined by considering qualitative distinctions on the different elements in the definition of a generalized cylinder: straight vs. curved spine, polygonal versus curved cross section, and constant vs. monotonic vs. nonmonotonic sweeping rule. The types of the geons that compose a shape, along with qualitative distinctions of their sizes and qualitative distinctions of their relative positions, collectively define a generic representation for a category of objects. The RBC theory has inspired several computer vision research efforts aimed at implementing a system that operates along the general principles of the theory.

Once a structural representation is used, it becomes possible to parameterize not only the individual part shapes but also the structural composition of the overall shape. In this way, the number and location of some of the individual parts that make up the overall shape may be allowed to vary. This capability exists in the ACRONYM vision system (9). (The shape primitives used for the individual parts in ACRONYM are general-

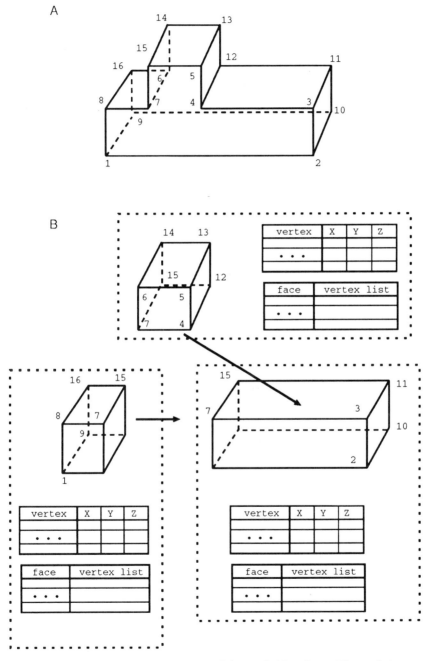

Figure 2.6. Structural shape representation: (A) overall object shape; (B) overall shape as a composition of three parts.

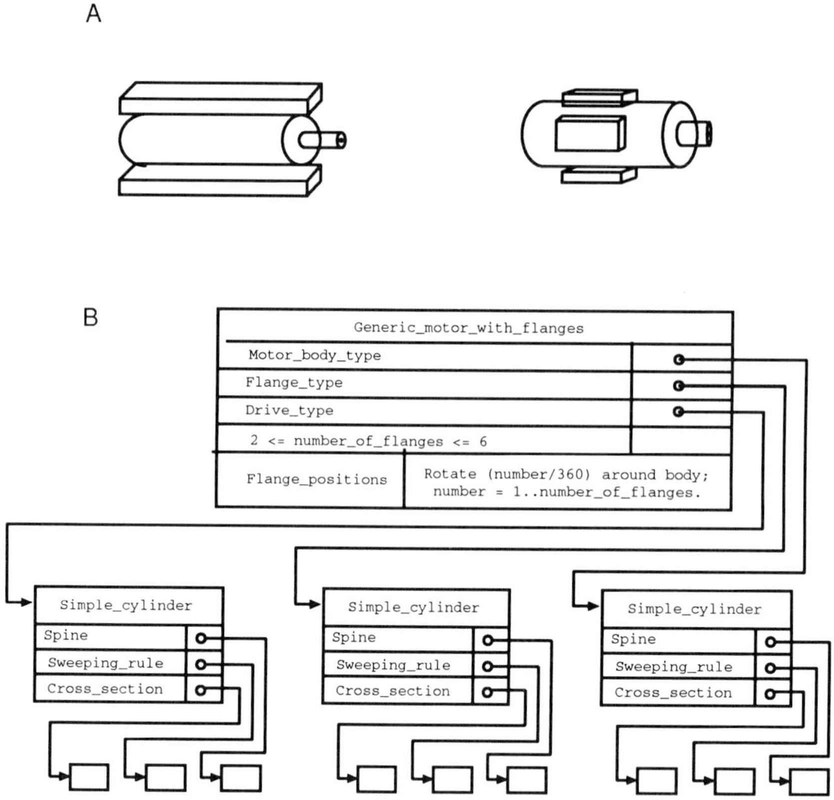

A

B

Figure 2.7. Parameterized structural representation: (A) shapes allowed by the representation; (B) representation of parameterized structure.

ized cylinders.) Example representations described in connection with ACRONYM include a family of aircraft shapes that allows a varying number of engines at different locations under the wings, and a family of small electric motor shapes that allows a varying number of flanges at different locations around the motor body. The representation for the family of small electric motor shapes is depicted in Fig. 2.7.

2.2.3. Articulated Shapes

We use the phrase *articulated shape* to indicate a particular type of nonrigid shape. With an articulated shape representation, the intention is to capture the range of shapes that can be realized by an object with movable parts. Each individual part of an articulated shape is rigid. However, the connections between parts are not fixed, but instead allow

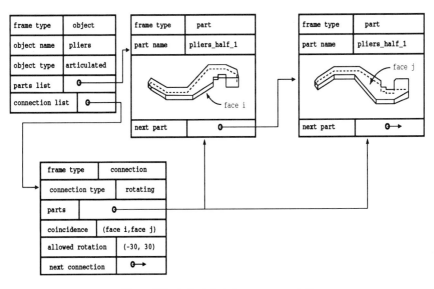

Figure 2.8. Articulated shape representation.

some parameterized range of relative movement between the parts. The information that must be specified is (1) the individual part shapes, (2) how the part shapes connect together, and (3) the type and the range of relative movement that is allowed at each joint (see Fig. 2.8).

In principle, it should be possible to specify the family of shapes for an object with moving parts by parameterizing a simple geometric model. However, in practice the task of properly specifying the family of allowed shapes is made much easier if it is approached as adding articulation information to a structural model. In fact, an articulated shape representation may be very similar in implementation to a parameterized structural representation. The differences are primarily in how the representation will be used. With the parameterized structural representation, the intention is generally to capture a range of shapes that corresponds to some generic family of objects. Thus the representation is parameterized on the geometry of individual parts or the structural plan of the shape. Then we imagine that any particular instance that belongs to the shape family modeled by the representation corresponds to some instance of the parameterization. With the articulated shape representation, the intention is generally to capture the range of shapes that an object may take on through the movement of its parts. In this case the representation would be parameterized on the geometry of the connections between the parts.

Articulated shape representations are appropriate for mechanical objects such as pliers and scissors, but would not be suitable for representing fundamentally non-rigid objects such as cloth and paper.

2.2.4. Deformable Shapes

A *deformable shape* is more fundamentally nonrigid than an articulated shape. For a deformable shape we imagine that there are no individual parts that can be specified as rigid. Although objects with deformable shape are ubiquitous in the real world, they have only recently begun to receive major attention in the computer vision research community. Examples of objects with deformable shape include the human face, cloth, paper, wire, plastic tubing, and so on. In the area of medical. imaging, organs such as the heart and the lungs have deformable shapes. Applications in medical imaging have, in particular, spurred some of the recent interest in deformable shape representation.

A broad categorization of different types of deformable shape representations is shown in Fig. 2.9. The range of representations for deformable shape is, if anything, even more varied than that for rigid shape. This is due at least in part to the fact that "deformable shape" encompasses such a broad range of phenomena. One approach to representing deformable shape is to parameterize a rigid shape representation. This approach is essentially the same as that already described for parameterized shape families; one or more of the constants in a rigid shape representation are replaced with parameters that may be constrained to take on values in some range. This type of approach has in fact been used by several researchers attempting to model the motion of the beating heart. (For an example of this, see Chapter 11 in this volume). Using the superquadric shape representation as the basic model, a superquadric shape is determined from 3D data of a heart volume at each of a sequence of time instants over one heartbeat period. The superquadric shape at each time instant will generally have different associated constants. It is then intended that the pattern of change in the constants in the superquadric equation can be used to characterize heart function. For additional detail on deformable superquadrics, although not on the heart modeling application, see Terzopoulos and Metaxes (35).

Other approaches to representing deformable shape may not assume any explicit parametric form for overall object shape. The shape may be

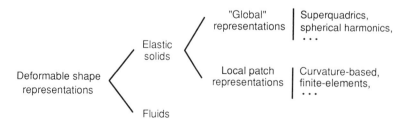

Figure 2.9. A broad categorization of deformable shape representations.

described only on a patch-by-patch basis rather than by some global parametric form. This approach is particularly reasonable when the object in question does not have a well-defined shape and the task is simply to track the deformations in the shape over time (15, 23).

A curvature-based classification of deformable shape was suggested by Goldgof *et al.* (13). Classes of shape deformation are described in terms of constraints on how the Gaussian curvature and the mean curvature at points on the shape are allowed to change. A measure of the curvature of a surface at a point may be found by considering the curve defined by the intersection of the surface with a plane that contains the point and is oriented according to the surface normal at the point. There is a family of such planes, and the Gaussian curvature K is the product of the maximal and minimal curvatures at a point. The mean curvature H is the average curvature at a point. (For further treatment of differential geometry and shape description, see, for example, Chapter 10 in this volume.)

Using this classification, a rigid shape is characterized as one for which the values of H and K are constant at every point. An *isometric* deformation of a shape is one in which K is constant at each point but H is allowed to vary. Isometric deformations preserve distances between points as measured along the surface, as well as angles between curves on the surface. An example of this type of deformation occurs when a flat sheet of paper is rolled into a cylinder. A *conformal* deformation is one that preserves the angles between curves on the surface but not the distances between points. In a conformal deformation, the shape may expand or contract by a different factor at each point, but the local effect is the same in all directions at a given point. A *homothetic* deformation is a subset of the conformal deformation, in which the degree of expansion or contraction is the same at every point on the surface. For example, a sphere undergoes a homothetic deformation when its size changes. However, a balloon that is being blown up is better described by a more general conformal deformation because the stretching is typically not equal at all points. The most general class of shape deformation, in which both angles between curves and distances between points on the shape are allowed to vary, is simply referred to as a *nonconformal* deformation.

For a more detailed description of some approaches to deformable shape description and its applications, see, for example, Chapter 11 of this volume.

2.2.5. Hierarchical (Multiresolution) Models

Precise shape representations may contain more detail than is needed for many purposes. Thus the notion of having a hierarchical representation that allows easy access to shape descriptions at different resolutions is

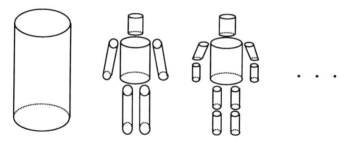

Figure 2.10. Hierarchical shape representation in the spirit of Marr (22).

attractive. However, it is not entirely clear how such a representation should be formulated. The alternatives that have been described in the literature are often very different in principle as well as in capabilities and none seems intuitively satisfying for use in a general-purpose vision system. We briefly outline two well-known approaches, each of which has some limitations.

Marr outlined an approach to hierarchical shape representation that initially seems quite appealing for computer vision (22). The primitive shape elements are simple generalized cylinders. At the coarsest level of detail, a single shape primitive is used. This gives just the approximate orientation of the shape. At each successive level of detail, additional parts are given explicit representation by having their own shape primitive introduced. The spirit of this type of hierarchical representation is given by the example in Fig. 2.10. The advantages claimed for this approach are that each unit of shape information is self-contained, that the units of shape information have uniform complexity, and that they occur in a natural context in which they are most meaningful. This type of hierarchical representation seems well suited to rough shape descriptions of natural objects, which often have a well-defined part decomposition and for which cylinders seem a useful approximate shape primitive. While it is generally clear what would constitute an increased level of detail relative to a current shape approximation for a given part, it is not so clear how to generate an overall shape approximation in which all parts are represented at a uniform level of detail. In general, it may be awkward to specify fine shape detail within this scheme. Also, it may be difficult in general to apply this scheme to many manufactured objects, where the decomposition into parts may not be so natural and it may not be possible to have a single type of shape primitive. Still, Marr's description of this approach has had substantial influence on thinking in this area.

Koenderink introduced an approach to hierarchical shape representation called *dynamic shape* (16). Koenderink's approach allows a principled method of determining a continuous family of different resolution shapes from an original shape instance. Consider that the original shape has some specified boundary, so that all points that lie inside the shape may be

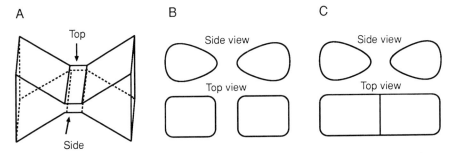

Figure 2.11. The effects of smoothing on a "bowtie"-shaped object (A); after "dynamic shape" smoothing (B); after "range" smoothing (C).

assigned the value 1 and all points that lie outside the shape may be assigned the value 0. Then imagine that a Gaussian smoothing kernel is applied at every point in space (both inside and outside the object). The result is a derived representation of space, in which each point has some associated value in the range between 0 and 1. The boundary of the object in this derived representation may then be declared to be at some level set, say, the set of points that have the value 0.5. If the same level set value is chosen for a sequence of derived representations obtained using Gaussian kernels with different σ, then a family of different resolution shapes is obtained.

One disadvantage of this approach is that the connectivity of the object may change in unexpected ways as the scale of the dynamic shape smoothing is changed. Also, the smoothing is geared toward the 3D shape in a way that is quite independent of the object's visual appearance. Consider the example shown in Fig. 2.11. For a given scale of dynamic shape smoothing, the central portion of the object shown in Fig. 2.11(A) will no longer exist and the object will be split into two pieces. While the appearance of the object in a side view may seem reasonable in this case, its appearance in a top view certainly is not [Fig 2.11(B)]. A more appropriate set of views to expect would be those in Fig. 2.11(C). In this case the small middle face is not distinguishable in the top view, but only because it has merged with the two sidefaces. This type of shape smoothing may be obtainable with a form of "range smoothing" that smooths the visible surfaces of the shape as seen from each viewpoint (11).

2.2.6. Function-Based Representation

A *function-based* representation of shape is defined in terms of the requirements for the shape to *function as* an instance of a particular object. One could think of function-based representation as an extreme form of parameterized description. However, the focus is really not on generalization from specific shapes, but instead is on using primitive chunks of knowledge about shape, physics, and causation to build minimally sufficient definitions of required function. The idea that function-based representations are an appropriate vehicle for "generic" models in computer vision is not new (7). However, implementation and experimentation with computer vision systems that use function-based representations for 3D object recognition has begun to occur only recently. We summarize one particular effort in this area in order to give a flavor of the general approach.

Stark (33) described a function-based object recognition system that uses a set of five "knowledge primitives" to construct a generic representation for the example object category chair. Each knowledge primitive takes some (specified portions of a) 3D shape as its input, along with specified parameter values, and returns an "evaluation measure" between 0 and 1 as its output. The five knowledge primitives used in this system are as follows:

1. `relative_orientation (normal_one, normal_two, range_parameters)`. This primitive can be used to determine whether the angle between the normals for two surfaces (normal_one and normal_two) falls within a desired range. Four range_parameters are specified: least, low_ideal, high_ideal, and greatest. These parameters are used to calculate the evaluation measure, according to where the relative orientation of the two surfaces falls within the specified range. A value between low_ideal and high_ideal results in a measure of 1. Values outside of this range but between least and greatest fall off linearly to 0. (Of course, low_ideal and high_ideal could be set to the same value for some cases, resulting in a "triangle-rule" for calculating the measure value.)

2. `dimensions (shape_element, dimension_type, range_parameters)`. This primitive is used to make decisions such as whether the width or depth of a surfaces lies within a specified range. The evaluation measure is again calculated using four range parameters in much the same manner as for relative orientation.

3. `proximity (shape_element_one, shape_element_two, range_parameters)`. This primitive is used to check qualitative relations between the shape_elements such as *above*, *below*, and *close to*. Again, the evaluation measure is calculated as described above.

4. `clearance (object_description, clearance_volume)`. This primitive can be used to check that there is a specified volume of unobstructed free space in a particular location relative to a particular element of shape. The evaluation measure is 1 if the volume specified is unobstructed and 0 if it is obstructed.

5. `stability (shape, orientation, applied_force)`. This primitive can be used to check that a given shape is stable when placed on a flat supporting plane in a given orientation and with a (possibly zero) force applied. It is assumed that the shape has homogeneous density, so that the center of mass may be calculated directly from the shape description. An evaluation measure of 1 is returned if the shape is stable in the specified orientation, and 0 is returned otherwise.

All of the system's representation of what is necessary for a 3D shape to function as a chair is constructed out of these primitives. (In fact, the particular set of "primitives" used is probably not so important. A different set of primitives might be defined that results in equivalent capabilities for the system.) The representation created with these primitives is structured as a "category tree" that specifies the "functional plan" for the object category. The system takes a polyhedral boundary representation as its input. The input shape can be in arbitrary orientation with respect to the actual orientation for the correct function of the object. The system analyzes the input shape to determine which of its known object categories, if any, the shape could belong to. Analysis of an input shape essentially follows a depth first traversal of the category definition tree. The system's performance was evaluated on a group of over 100 polyhedral shapes. A selection of the shapes recognized by the system as belonging to the (sub)category straight-back chair is shown in Fig. 2.12.

Function-based models clearly have the potential to come closer to capturing the intuitive human definition of an object category than do the other approaches that we have discussed. However, research into the use of function-based object representations is still in the early stages.

3. VIEWER-CENTERED REPRESENTATIONS

All of the representations discussed up to this point are oriented toward representing the 3D shape of an object. In this sense, they are *object-centered* representations. To the extent that computer vision is concerned with the task of recognizing objects by their appearance in 2D images, it may be that an object-centered representation is not the most appropriate. For this reason, computer vision researchers have also developed a large variety of *viewer-centered* representations. The goal of these representations is to summarize the set of possible appearances of a 3D object in a 2D image. One problem that arises immediately in pursuing this approach is that in general there is an infinity of possible viewpoints. Since the projection image of an object is generally different in some degree for

A

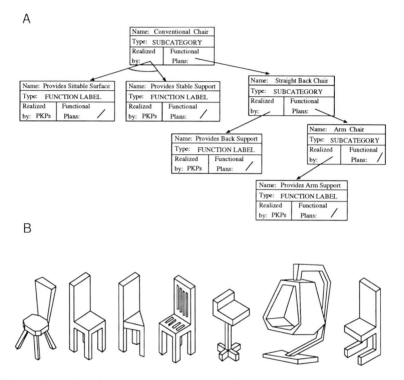

B

Figure 2.12. A function-based representation: (A) function-based representation as a frame system with procedural attributes; (B) a selection of 3D shapes recognized as providing "straight-back chair" function. Adapted from Stark and Bowyer (33).

every different viewpoint, there is also an infinity of possible 2D appearances. Thus it is necessary to develop some method of effectively sampling the viewpoint space and also to decide on some definition of similarity that can be used to group viewpoints from which the object appearance is essentially similar.

3.1. Models of Viewpoint Space

Two basic models of viewpoint space are commonly used. One is the *viewing sphere.* In this model, the space of possible viewpoints is the surface of a unit sphere. The sphere is considered to be centered around the object, which is located at the origin of the coordinate system. A viewpoint on the surface of the sphere defines a viewing direction vector from the origin toward the viewpoint. This direction vector can be used to create an orthographic projection view of the object.

A more general model of viewpoint space is to consider all points in 3D space. As was the case with the viewing sphere, the object can be considered to be located at the origin of the coordinate system. Specifying a direction vector for the line of sight and a focal length for the imaging process allows the creation of a perspective projection view of the object. The line of sight is assumed to be directed generally toward the object (toward the origin of the coordinate system). In object recognition tasks that include estimating the pose of the object, the exact line of sight is adjusted to produce the projected feature locations that best match the observed image features.

3.2. Symbolic Representation of a View

The most common symbolic representation for the object appearance in a 2D view is the *image structure graph*. To understand how the image structure graph of a view is defined, refer to Fig. 2.13. First, the intensity image of the object is abstracted to a *line drawing*. For polyhedral objects, the line drawing is entirely determined by the *lines* and the *junctions* formed where two or more lines meet. A *line* in the line drawing is a 2D projection in the image plane of a 3D *edge* on the object surface. An *edge* is a locus of points on the object surface where there is a discontinuity in the surface normal—for example, where two faces of a polyhedron meet. In addition to edges that project to lines in the line drawing, curved objects also have *contour generators* that project to *occluding contours*, or simply *contours*, in the line drawing. A *contour generator* (also called the *rim* or *limb*) is a locus of points on the object surface where the line of

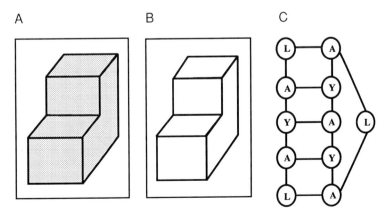

Figure 2.13. The image structure graph representation of an intensity image: (A) intensity image; (B) line drawing; (C) image structure graph.

sight is tangent to the surface. The lines or contours and junctions in a line drawing may be assigned symbolic labels that indicate their qualitative 3D interpretation. For example, for a polyhedral scene a line may be given the symbolic label convex to indicate that the internal angle between the two faces meeting at the correspondence edge on the object is less than 180°. Similarly, a junction may be given the label T to indicate that it represents the occlusion of one edge by one of the faces that meets at another edge. When curved objects are allowed, additional symbolic labels are required beyond those needed for polyhedral scenes. An image structure graph is created from the labeled line drawing by making a node in the graph for each junction in the line drawing and an arc in the graph for each line or contour between junctions. Thus the image structure graph specifies the type and configuration of the elements in the line drawing, but it is abstracted from the image-space and does not specify the lengths of lines or the size of the angles between lines. This form of image structure graph is a commonly used symbolic abstraction for the appearance of an object in a 2D image.

The symbolic representation of a view of an object by an image structure graph can be used to partition viewpoint space into regions of *general viewpoints* separated by boundaries of *accidental viewpoints*. Under either model of viewpoint space, a general viewpoint is one from which an infinitesimal movement can be made in any direction and the resulting image structure graph is isomorphic to the original. An accidental viewpoint is one for which there is some direction in which an infinitesimal movement will result in an image structure graph that is not isomorphic to the original. A *visual event* is said to occur on the passing from one region of general viewpoints through a boundary of accidental viewpoints into another region of general viewpoints.

3.3. Tessellations of the View Sphere

There are a variety of difficulties involved in developing an algorithm to compute the exact partition of viewpoint space into cells of general viewpoint. The most commonly applied approach is not to compute an exact partition at all, but rather to create an approximation based on a quasiuniform sampling of the viewing sphere. The approximation approach typically begins with an *icosahedron* centered around the origin of the coordinate system, so that the vertices of the icosahedron lie on the surface of a unit sphere. The icosahedron is the regular solid having the largest number of faces, with its faces forming 20 congruent equilateral triangles.

If we treat the center point on each face of the icosahedron as defining a viewing direction, the icosahedron provides a uniform sampling of 20 viewpoints on the sphere. Since 20 viewing directions are generally not sufficient to capture the visual complexity of an object, each face of the icosahedron is typically subdivided some number of times to provide a finer, quasiuniform sampling of the viewing sphere. The subdivision is done by connecting the midpoints of the three edges of the current triangular face to subdivide it into four triangles. The three new vertices are "pushed out" to the surface of the sphere, and the center of each of the new triangles defines a new viewing direction. In this way, a level 1 subdivision will provide a quasiuniform sampling of 80 viewing directions, a level 2 subdivision will provide 320, and so on. A projected view of the object is created for each sample point on the viewing sphere. Neighboring views of the same image structure are then merged and represented by one node in the aspect graph (17).

This approach has been employed by a large number of computer vision researchers and is now considered a standard technique in computer vision. A major advantage of this technique is that it is relatively easy to apply to an object of any shape. One disadvantage is that it is difficult to know a priori the appropriate resolution of the viewing sphere for an arbitrary object. If the resolution used is too coarse, some views of the object will not be included. If the resolution is too fine, unnecessary work will be done in creating the representation. Also, this approach requires the assumption of orthographic projection or a known viewer-to-object distance.

3.4. Aspect Graphs

The term *aspect graph* has come to be used to refer to a variety of related representations in which the partition of viewpoint space into cells of general viewpoint is used to generate a dual representation that takes the form of a graph. In the aspect graph representation there is (1) a node for each *general view* of the object as seen from some maximal, connected cell of *viewpoint space*; and (2) an arc for each possible transition, called a *visual event*, between two neighboring general views. Figure 2.14 shows an example of the aspect graph for a tetrahedron. A number of researchers have developed algorithms for computing the exact partition of viewpoint space for different classes of object shapes (8). It is not possible to describe all of the various approaches here, but we will briefly summarize one method in order to give a better feel for this type of object representation.

3.4.1. Aspect Graphs for Polyhedra

For polyhedra, there are just two fundamental types of accidental views: (1) edge–vertex alignments, and (2) edge–triplet alignments. An

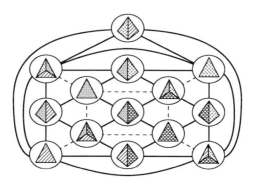

Figure 2.14. Aspect graph representation of a tetrahedron. For the tetrahedron object shape, the structure of the parcellation of viewpoint space is the same for either model of viewpoint space, and therefore is the structure of the aspect graph. The bold arcs indicate one convention for adjacency of cells of viewpoint space. The dotted arcs indicate additional connections that exist under an alternate convention.

edge–vertex alignment occurs when a vertex and some point on an edge of the object project of the same point in the image (see Fig. 2.15). In general, this event represents the beginning or ending of a T-junction in the image. (It includes, as a special case, the projection of an object face to a line segment in the image.) The viewpoints from which such an accidental alignment can be seen lie on a plane in the 3D model of viewpoint space, or on a great circle in the viewing sphere model.

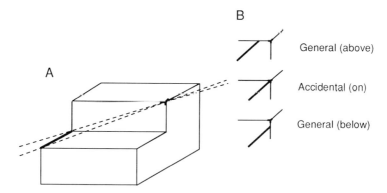

Figure 2.15. Visual event created by an edge–vertex interaction: (A) lines of sight defining plane of visual interaction; (B) views of edge and vertex. The bold edge and bold vertex interact to define a plane, as indicated by the dashed lines. In the region of the plane between the dashed lines, the vertex and edge project on top of each other in the image. The view just above or below the plane is represented by a different image structure graph than the view from on the plane. Thus the edge–vertex interaction defines a visual event separating regions of general viewpoint.

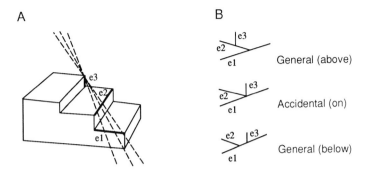

Figure 2.16. Visual event created by an edge–triplet interaction. (A) lines of sight defining quadric; (B) views of edges. The lines of sight passing through three skew edges define the rulings of a quadric surface in (A). The views of the three edges as seen from above, on, and below the surface are shown in (B).

An edge–triplet alignment occurs when points on three different edges of the object project to the same point in the image (see Fig. 2.16). In general, this event represents a change in the ordering of the visible T-junction relations between the three edges. The viewpoints from which such an accidental alignment can be seen lie on a quadratic surface in the 3D model of viewpoint space, or on a quadric curve on the surface of the viewing sphere.

In order to compute the exact aspect graph for polyhedra under either model of viewpoint space, one can first enumerate all of the possible edge–vertex alignments and edge–triplet alignments for the given object. For the viewing sphere model of viewpoint space, the result is a set of great circles and quadric curves on the surface of the sphere. For the 3D model of viewpoint space, the result is a set of planes and quadric surfaces in 3D. In either case, the next step is to determine how viewpoint space is partitioned by these accidental alignments into discrete cells of general viewpoint. This step is substantially more complicated for nonconvex polyhedra than it is for convex polyhedra.

In general, the viewpoint space is "overpartitioned" by these circles and curves found on the viewing sphere, or the planes and surfaces found in 3D. There are two reasons for this. One is that this partition of viewpoint space may have some neighboring cells that actually see the same image structure graph, but are separated by an apparent visual event that is actually occluded from view. Another reason is that since edges on the object have only finite length, a potential alignment is actually visible only over a subset of the circle or curve (or plane or surface) that it defines. Many of the potential accidental alignments can be discarded entirely, or the "active" subset reduced based on visibility tests. Thus some "extra" processing at an early stage of the algorithm can reduce the degree of overpartitioning of viewpoint space and reduce the need for processing in later stages. However, it is not possible to have an exact partition of viewpoint space at this stage for general polyhedra.

Once the partition of viewpoint space is determined, the aspect graph structure is created by traversing the partition. As the partition is traversed, final merging of overpartitioned cells is done and a node is created

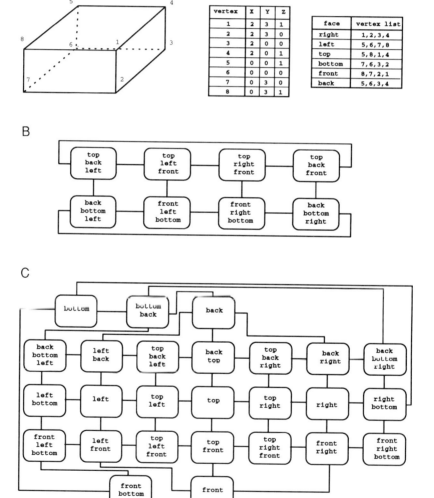

Figure 2.17. Aspect graph representation of a rectangular block; (A) using orthographic projection; (B) using viewing sphere as viewpoint space; and (C) using 3D space as viewpoint space.

in the aspect graph for each cell in the partition and an arc is created for each boundary between cells. Figure 2.17 shows a rectangular parallelepiped and the aspect graph created using each model of viewpoint space.

One disadvantage of the aspect graph is its large size. Under the viewing sphere model of viewpoint space, the maximum number of nodes in the aspect graph is $\Theta(n^2)$ for convex objects and $\Theta(n^6)$ for general polyhedra, where n is the number of faces. Under the 3D model of viewpoint space, the maximum sizes are $\Theta(n^3)$ and $\Theta(n^9)$ for the convex and general cases, respectively (26).

3.4.2. Aspect Graphs for More Complex Object Shapes

Computing the aspect graph of curved shapes follows the same basic steps as for polyhedra. First, the class of allowed shapes is defined. Then a method is developed for enumerating all the accidental alignments from any given instance of the class. From the set of accidental alignments, the partition of viewpoint space is determined. Finally, the aspect graph is created by traversing the partition of viewpoint space. The details of each step are substantially more complicated, however, for curved shapes than for polyhedra. One difficulty is that the models of curved objects are more complex than polyhedral models. Another is the existence of the viewpoint-dependent contour generators. Various algorithms have been developed that compute the aspect graph of different classes of curved shapes (8).

Researchers have also addressed the problem of computing the aspect graph of articulated shapes. Recall that an articulated shape is composed of rigid parts and a set of parameters that specify the possible articulations of the parts. The *configuration space* of a given articulated shape is defined simply as the cross-product space of each articulation parameter. The essential insight is to imagine a higher-dimensional space defined as (configuration space × viewpoint space). This higher-dimensional space can be partitioned into cells representing general views, separated by surfaces representing accidental views (29).

3.5. Aspect Space Representations

Rather than represent the set of topologically distinct views in a graph structure as defined by the aspect graph, we can instead describe an object in terms of its appearance in the image plane as a function of viewpoint. To do this, we first define multidimensional *aspect space* as the cross-product space of the image plane and viewpoint space. Assuming viewpoint space is defined using the viewing sphere, aspect space is 4D with 2 degrees of freedom in viewpoint space and 2 degrees of freedom in the image plane. Any object feature, such as a vertex, edge, or face, is parameterized as a hypersurface in aspect space, completely describing the appearance (with occluded parts removed) of that feature for all viewpoints.

For example, a one-dimensional (1D) space of viewpoints corresponding to a great circle of orthographic projection views around an object, can be represented by the unit circle $\mathbf{S}^1$. In this case aspect space is three-dimensional: $\mathscr{R}^2 \times \mathbf{S}^1$. Thus a point in aspect space corresponds to a point in the image from a particular viewpoint. Given a vertex in the world at coordinates (x_0, y_0, z_0), it traces a curve in this 3D aspect space. We can give an exact expression for this curve by deriving the image coordinates of the point as a function of the viewpoint. Letting (u, v) denote image coordinates and θ denote the viewpoint (as an angle from a fixed, but arbitrary, viewing direction), the curve describing this vertex in (u, v, θ) aspect space is given by

$$u = x_0 \cos \theta - z_0 \sin \theta$$

$$v = y_0$$

An edge can now be parameterized as a surface in aspect space bounded by the trace of the edge's two endpoints. In general, the dimensionality of the hypersurface for a feature depends on the dimensionality of the feature as well as the dimensionality of viewpoint case. If viewpoint space is defined using the viewing sphere, aspect space is four-dimensional (4D) (u, v, θ, ϕ), and the hypersurfaces for vertices, edges, and faces are 2D, 3D, and (4D), respectively (26).

A fundamental property of aspect space is that occlusion is equivalent to set subtraction in aspect space. To see this, consider two faces and their corresponding volumes in aspect space as shown in Fig. 2.18. A point in the intersection of the volumes for the two faces is a single image point generated by both faces. Since the faces are opaque, only one face can be visible at a time and therefore the point is removed from the volume for the face that is occluded. Thus the exact set of visible points of a face $\mathbf{F}$ from all viewpoints can be computed by subtracting from the volume for $\mathbf{F}$ all of the volumes for the faces in front of it [Fig. 2.18(B,C)]. The resulting volume for $\mathbf{F}$ is bounded by hypersurfaces corresponding to the visibility of the edges bounding the face. Although these hypersurfaces are not planar, they are algebraic ruled surfaces of degree at most three that can be computed exactly. Therefore the volume for a face can be represented and manipulated in much the same way as a polyhedron. For example, the intersection of two such volumes can be computed in closed form in a manner similar to polyhedral intersection.

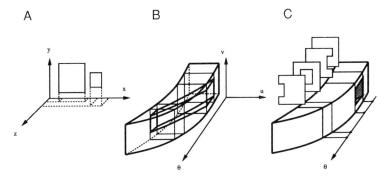

Figure 2.18. (A) Two square faces, the smaller one slightly in front of the larger one; (B) the volume of aspect space defining the visibility of the larger face, after subtracting the volume corresponding to the smaller face (shown as a wireframe); (C) the aspect space volume for the larger face, with cross sections shown at selected values of the viewpoint parameter θ.

The *asp* representation of a polyhedron is defined as the union of volumes in aspect space that describe the visibility of its constituent faces. Consequently, it is an exact, complete, viewer-centered description of the visibility of each vertex, edge, and face of a polyhedral object (26). Using the viewing sphere model of viewpoint space, the asp for a polyhedron is a 4D volume in a 4D aspect space that has several basic properties. First, the asp encodes the appearance of the polyhedron with hidden surfaces removed. Each face is represented such that occluded portions are removed. Second, a cross section of the asp for a face yields the appearance of that face with hidden parts removed. Third, the bounding hypersurfaces of an asp correspond to visual events that are not just intrinsic to the object (e.g., vertices), but also include the events caused by the image projection process, such as the apparent intersection of a pair of edges causing a T-junction in the image.

The asp is important not only because it is a complete, exact representation of appearance of a polyhedron as a function of viewpoint, but also because it can be used as an intermediate representation for constructing the aspect graph (26). Interestingly, the asp, which represents the appearance of an object from every viewpoint, has a worst-case size that is smaller than the aspect graph, which has a single vertex for each general viewpoint region [i.e., $\Theta(n^4)$ vs. $\Theta(n^6)$].

While the asp encodes the appearance of both intrinsic and viewpoint-dependent features of the model, this may include features that are not easily detectable in an image. Alternatively, the *rim-appearance representation* encodes a piecewise-linear approximation of the occluding contour only as a hypersurface in aspect space (31). This is a subset of the information contained in the image structure graph and represented in the asp. A polyhedral model is assumed to approximate a smooth 3D shape in

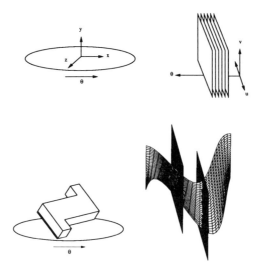

Figure 2.19. The appearance of a model edge (lower left, in bold) as the viewpoint parameter θ changes, forms a surface in 3D aspect space (grid in lower right; axes in upper right). The two black planes mark the values of θ where the edge joins or leaves the rim. The section of the rim surface between the two planes corresponds to the viewpoints where the edge is not on the rim because both faces for the edge are visible.

order to define which edges are on the rim (i.e., contour generator). The hypersurface in aspect space for a rim edge is that portion of the hypersurface for a given edge that is left after removing the sections for (1) the viewpoints where the edge is not on the rim, and (2) the viewpoints where the edge is not visible. Figure 2.19 shows the hypersurface in 3D aspect space for an edge and the vertical planar boundaries that indicate events when the edge joins or leaves the rim. These rim constraints significantly reduce the size of the representation and also eliminate edges that are part of the polyhedral model but do not correspond to observable features in the real object. Empirically, it has been shown that the number of visual events in the rim appearance representation is often 75% less than the number of events in the asp. This reduction in size is even more pronounced when compared with the aspect graph.

4. SUMMARY

A vision system must use some form of 3D object representation in order to carry out tasks such as recognition, navigation, and inspection. For many purposes, the representation used by a vision system is concerned primarily with object shape. Of course shape is not the only property of an object that is important. Color, texture, material substance, and many other properties enter into whether and how an autonomous system might interact with an object of a given shape. (One would not want to attempt to sit in a paper maché chair even though it might have the proper shape for a chair.) Still, shape tends to be of primary importance because the perceived shape will strongly influence how the system attempts to interact with the object in order to determine other properties. (Without having identified a part of the shape as a "seat," it would make no sense to attempt to use it as a chair at all.)

As evidenced by the variety of representations presented in this chapter, many different techniques exist for representing knowledge about 3D solid shape. These can be broadly divided into object-centered and viewer-centered representations. Some of the more popular types of object-centered representations, such as boundary and CSG, originated in other fields such as computer graphics and CAD/CAM (computer-aided design and manufacturing. Generalized cylinders are perhaps the best-known object-centered representation to have been developed primarily for use in computer vision. Viewer-centered representations based on quasiuniform sampling of the viewing sphere have been widely used in vision systems and can now be regarded as something of a "standard" technique. More exact methods of viewer-centered representation, such as aspect graphs, have been the subject of a great deal of research but have not yet been widely used in vision systems.

Representation of nonrigid shape is currently an active area of research. This is also true of representations meant to capture generic shape categories. Both of these topics promise to be active and important research areas for some time to come.

REFERENCES

1. A. Barr, Superquadrics and angle-preserving transformations. *IEEE Comput. Graphics and Appl.* **1**, 1–20 (1981).
2. B. G. Baumgart, A. Polyhedron representation for computer vision. *Proc. National Comput. Conf.* **75**, 589–596 (1975).
3. P. J. Besl, Geometric modeling and computer vision. *Proc. IEEE* **76**, 936–958 (1988).
4. P. J. Besl and R. C. Jain, Three-dimensional object recognition. *ACM Comput. Surv.* **17**, 75–145 (1985).
5. I. Biederman, Recognition-by-components: A theory of human image understanding. *Psychol. Rev.* **94**, 115–147 (1987).
6. T. O. Binford, Visual perception by computer. *IEEE Conf. Syst. Control* (1971).
7. T. O. Binford, Survey of model-based image analysis systems. *Int.J. Robotics Res.* **1**(1), 18–64 (1982).

8. K. W. Bowyer and C. R. Dyer, Aspect graphs: An introduction and survey of recent results. *Int. J. Imaging Syst. Technol.* **2**, 315–328 (1991).

9. R. A. Brooks, "Model-based Computer Vision." UMI Research Press, Ann Arbor, MI, 1984.

10. A. H. J. Christensen, Blocked puzzle. *Comput. Graphics* **14**(3) (Proc. SIGGRAPH '80 Conf.), title page (1980). (Figure used courtesy, Association for Computing Machinery, Inc.)

11. D. W. Eggert, K. W. Bowyer, C. R. Dyer, H. I. Christensen, and D. B. Goldgof, Applying the scale space concept to perspective projection aspect graphs. *In* "Theory and Applications of Image Analysis: Selected Papers from the 7th Scandinavian Conference on Image Analysis" (P. Johansen and S. Olsen, eds.). World Scientific Publ., Singapore, 1992, pp. 48–62.

12. O. Faugeras and M. Hebert, The representation, recognition, and locating of 3-D objects. *Int. J. Robot. Res.* **5**(3), 27–52 (1986).

13. D. B. Goldgof, H. Lee, and T. S. Huang, Motion analysis of nonrigid surfaces. *Proc. IEEE Conf. Comput. Vision Pattern Recognition, 1988*, pp. 375–380 (1988).

14. D. B. Goldgof, T. S. Huang, and H. Lee, Feature extraction and terrain matching. *Proc. IEEE Conf. Comput. Vision Pattern Recognition, 1988*, pp. 899–904 (1988).

15. R. Horowitz and A. P. Pentland, Recovery of non-rigid motion and structure. *Proc. IEEE Conf. Comput. Vision Pattern Recognition, 1991*, pp. 288–293 (1991).

16. J. J. Koenderink, "Solid Shape." MIT Press, Cambridge, MA, 1990.

17. M. R. Korn and C. R. Dyer, 3D multiview object representations for model-based object recognition. *Pattern Recognition* **20**, 91–103 (1987).

18. D. J. Kriegman and J. Ponce, On recognizing the positioning curved 3-D objects from image contours. *IEEE Trans. Pattern Anal. Mach. Intell.* **PAMI-12**, 1127–1137 (1990).

19. D. G. Lowe, The viewpoint consistency constraint. *Int. J. Comput. Vision* **1**, 57–72 (1987).

20. D. G. Lowe, Integrated treatment of matching and measurement errors for robust model-based motion tracking. *In* "Proceedings of the Third International Conference on Computer Vision," pp. 436–440. IEEE Computer Society Press, Washington, DC, 1990.

21. D. G. Lowe, Fitting parameterized three-dimensional models to images. *IEEE Trans. Pattern Anal. Mach. Intell.* **PAMI-13**, 441–450 (1991).

22. D. Marr, "Vision." Freeman, San Francisco, 1982.

23. D. Metaxas and D. Terzopoulos, Constrained deformable superquadrics and nonrigid motion tracking. *Proc. IEEE Conf. Comput. Vision Pattern Recognition, 1991*, pp. 337–343 (1991).

24. D. J. Orser and M. Roche, The extraction of topographic features in support of autonomous underwater vehicle navigation. *Proc. Int. Symp. Unmanned Untethered Submersible Technol.* **5th** (1987). Merrimack, NH. pp. 502–514, University of New Hampshire.

25. A. P. Pentland, Perceptual organization and the representation of natural form. *Artif. Intell.* **28**, 293–331 (1986).

26. H. Plantinga and C. R. Dyer, Visibility, occlusion and the aspect graph. *Int. J. Comput. Vision* **5**, 137–160 (1990).
27. A. Requicha, Representations for rigid solids: Theory, methods, and systems. *ACM Comput. Surv.* **12**, 437–464 (1980).
28. L. G. Roberts, Machine perception of three-dimensional solids. *In* "Optical and Electro-Optical Information Processing" (J. Tippett *et al.*, eds.), pp. 159–197. MIT Press, Cambridge, MA, 1965.
29. M. Y. Sallam, J. H. Stewman, and K. W. Bowyer, Computing the visual potential of an articulated assembly of parts." *In* "Proceedings of the Third International Conference on Computer Vision," pp. 636–643. IEEE Computer Society Press, Washington, DC, 1990.
30. H. Samet, "The Design and Analysis of Spatial Data Structures." Addison-Wesley, Reading, MA, 1990.
31. W. B. Seales and C. R. Dyer, Viewpoint from occluding contour. *Comput. Vision, Graphics, Image Process.: Image Understanding* **55**, 198–211 (1992).
32. S. A. Shafer and T. Kanade, "The Theory of Straight Homogeneous Generalized Cylinders," Tech. Rep. CMU-CS-83-105. Carnegie-Mellon University, Computer Science Department, Pittsburgh, 1983.
33. L. Stark and K. W. Bowyer, Achieving generalized object recognition through reasoning about association of function to structure. *IEEE Trans. Pattern Anal. Mach. Intell.* **PAMI-13**, 1097–1104 (1991).
34. I. E. Sutherland, Sketchpad: A man-machine graphical communication system. *Proc. AFIPS Spring Joint Comput. Conf.*, pp. 329–346 (1963).
35. D. Terzopoulos and D. Metaxas, Dynamic 3D models with local and global deformations: Deformable superquadrics. *IEEE Trans. Pattern Anal. Mach. Intell.* **PAMI-13**, 703–714 (1991).
36. G. Verghese, K. Gale, and C. R. Dyer, Real-time, parallel motion tracking of three dimensional objects from spatiotemporal sequences. *In* "Parallel Algorithms for Machine Intelligence and Vision" (V. Kumar, P. Gopalakrishnan, and L. Kanal, eds.), pp. 310–339. Springer-Verlag, New York, 1990.

Chapter **3**

Three-Dimensional Shape
Recovery from Line Drawings

WASIM J. SHOMAR and TZAY Y. YOUNG

Department of Electrical and
Computer Engineering
University of Miami
Coral Gables, Florida

1. INTRODUCTION

Valuable information about the three-dimensional (3D) structure and
orientation of objects is obtained from their edge lines in a two-dimen-

53

sional (2D) image, which are lines corresponding to the contour and
surface discontinuities. As a result, humans invented a graphical means
drawn on 2D planes for representing 3D shapes by specifying only the
edge lines of an object. This convention is used in our daily life and is
referred to as *line drawings*. A major advantage of line drawings is the fact
that they can be a quick graphical representation of an object, because the
line drawing is simply a collection of 2D lines on a paper. Also, such
representation seems to come naturally to humans because of the 3D clues
such lines offer. Line drawings are universal and are analogical in nature,
and thus do not require training, as opposed to languages that are typically
of symbolic nature. From a computer vision point of view, line drawings
have another advantage of being easily attained from gray-level images
through popular and relatively simple edge detection and segmentation
methods. The obvious disadvantage of line drawings is the fact that any
proper line drawing could have infinite possible corresponding 3D configurations. However, it seems that most of them are not evoked in human
perception, because of the implicit assumptions we make as a result of our
knowledge of the world around us, where coincidental alignments are not
expected to happen (the *general-viewpoint assumption*). As a result, "un-
usual" interpretations end up being excluded and humans seem to get
definite impressions about the 3D world through line drawings and have
no difficulties in understanding it.

A major difficulty in computer vision stems from the fact that we are
trying to conclude information in higher dimension than the dimension of
the provided data. More specifically, we try to conclude about the 3D
world (scene) from 2D images. However, a single image typically does not
contain enough information about its corresponding 3D world (scene),
which is due to the loss in dimensionality. Therefore, to solve this problem
one must consider one of two approaches. One approach may be to
analyze multiple (two or more) nonidentical images of the same 3D world
and try to extract 3D clues and information from each image and understand the relationships among such images and the corresponding 3D
world, in such a way that the collective information deduced from the 2D
images can describe uniquely the 3D scene. The second approach would
be to consider a single 2D image and impose enough assumptions and
constraints on the 3D scene in such a way that the problem of going from
an image to the world becomes invertible.

This chapter is concerned with the second approach to recover 3D
shape from a single line drawing. It turns out that the ability of interpreting line drawings can be realized by relatively simple computational and
mathematical methods and procedures when the objects in the scene are
restricted to planar-surfaced solids. Such objects that are bounded by a
finite number of planar surfaces are referred to as *polyhedrons*. Simple
computational methods on a single image proved to be sufficient for the

shape recovery of polyhedrons because the important shape information of such objects is contained in "skeletal structures" consisting of edges and vertices. Since line drawings are projections of skeletal structures, much information about polyhedrons are consequently obtained from line drawings. The polyhedral world assumption is a reasonable one for numerous applications. More specifically, many man-made objects and industrial objects are polyhedrons, or even trihedrons. Trihedrons are polyhedrons with exactly three surfaces meeting at each junction of the object. Furthermore, it can be argued that many nonpolyhedral objects could be reasonably approximated to polyhedrons.

Computational methods for shape recovery rely on mathematical constraints that the 3D objects impose on their corresponding line drawings. Many of these techniques assume world objects to have certain geometric regularities such as parallelisms and perpendicularities of edges, right corners, and symmetries. These regularities exhibit certain properties in the line drawing, and the attempt is to extract such regularities as 3D clues, for the purpose of shape recovery. Once such clues are extracted, they must be formulated in such a manner that one could arrive at the object's 3D structure and orientation.

We discuss in the following sections several methods for 3D shape recovery from line drawings, including rule-based expert systems for shape recovery.

2. CAMERA MODEL AND PROJECTIONS

2.1. Camera Model and Aspects of Image Formation

To be able to derive image constraints from 3D scenes, we must first have a clear understanding to the mapping relationship between the 3D scene and the image. This mapping is dictated by the image formation process of the camera system used to capture the image. For our image formation process, the coordinate system used will be Mackworth's (30): the x and y axes in the scene (world) are aligned parallel to the image coordinates x' and y', and the z axis points toward the viewer (i.e., a right-hand coordinate system). The eye (center of lens) is at the origin $(0, 0, 0)$ of the scene (world) coordinates and the image plane is at $z = f$, where f is the focal length of the lens (refer to Fig. 3.1). For clarity purposes, throughout the chapter, any parameter in the image is primed and all 3D scene parameters are not primed. Also, vector parameters are typically boldfaced.

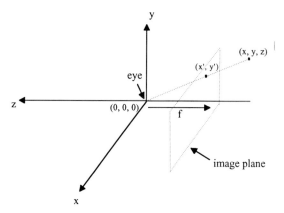

Figure 3.1. The camera model.

2.2. Orthographic versus Perspective Projections

Two popular projections exist in the study of computer vision. One is referred to as the *orthographic projection*, while the other is the *perspective* one.

In orthographic projection, the rays of light from the scene to the image are parallel to the z axis. Hence the scene point (x, y, z) is mapped onto the image point (x', y') such that

$$(x', y') = (x, y).   \qquad (1)$$

By examining the orthographic mapping in (1), it can be easily shown that parallel vectors in the scene map to parallel edges in the image.

In perspective projection, the rays of light converge to the center (focal point) of the lens, which happens to be at $(0, 0, 0)$ of our camera model. Under perspective projection, it can be easily seen from similar triangles that the scene point (x, y, z) is mapped onto the image point (x', y') such that

$$(x', y') = \left(f\frac{x}{z}, f\frac{y}{z} \right).   \qquad (2)$$

The image point is basically the point at which a line through the origin (eye) and the point (x, y, z) intersects the image plane. It is interesting to note that the orthographic projection is a special case of the perspective projection as $f \to \infty$. However, the two projections exhibit characteristics and impose mathematical constraints on the image that are quite different in nature from each other. Therefore, it is generally convenient to treat them independently. In most vision systems (including the human visual system), the images produced are perspective due to a finite focal length of the lens used. However, for many applications, the objects are so far from the camera relative to the focal length [i.e., $(z/f) \gg 1$] such that the rays of light could be estimated to be almost parallel, hence producing an almost orthographic projection.

The recovered scene parameters under perspective projection are always a scale factor from the true parameters because the problem is mathematically underconstrained. For example, it is impossible to tell the true size of an object just from its image; an object identical to another object in structure but twice in size would produce the same projection (image) if viewed from twice the distance. Since the scale factor is not recoverable, it is sometimes convenient to use the unit of measure in the image coordinate system to be the focal length of the camera lens. Also, choose the focal length to be a negative quantity, which results in a rotation around the origin to the image plane, to preserve the sense of "up," "down," "left," and "right" from the scene. Hence, if the focal plane is at $z = f$, then choose the image plane at $z = -1$ (focal length units).

2.3. Line Labeling

In 1971 Huffman (17) as well as Clowes (5) introduced the concept of line labeling, where information on the 3D structure of an object can be illustrated. Each line in a line drawing would be assigned one of three labels, that is, a line representing convex edges whose two sidefaces face toward a viewer (denoted by $+$); those representing convex edges, one of whose sidefaces is occluded (denoted by an arrow such that the visible surface is to the right of the arrow); and those representing concave edges (denoted by $-$). Huffman showed that for a trihedral world, certain combinations of line labels on a junction never occur and that the allowed labels on different junction types are very limited. Then he formed a list of all allowable combinations of junction labelings for each type of trihedral junctions (i.e., Y, W, T, and L) and proposed that an object can be consistently labeled if and only if all its junctions have allowable junction labels. The dictionary of allowable labelings for trihedral junctions are shown in Fig. 3.2.

It turns out that consistently junction-labeled objects constitute a very small subset of all possible line label combinations. Clowes proposed an equivalent method with different notation. Their labeling scheme is re-

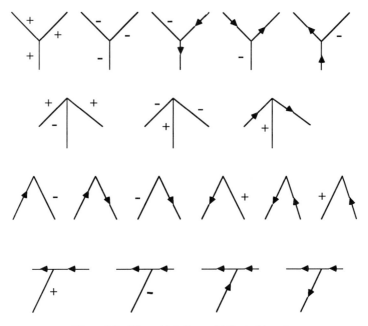

Figure 3.2. Allowed labelings of trihedral junctions.

ferred to as the Huffman–Clowes labeling scheme. It should be noted that the Huffman–Clowes labeling scheme provides a necessary but not sufficient condition for a line drawing to represent a polyhedral scene. A correct line drawing can always be consistently labeled, but a consistently labeled line drawing does not imply a correct polyhedral line drawing. A consistently labeled line drawing provides a mere candidate for a spatial interpretation of a line drawing. One must further examine the line drawing to verify whether the interpretation is correct. Figure 3.3 illustrates a labeled line drawing.

Numerous results have been developed based on the Huffman–Clowes labeling scheme. Their labeling scheme was extended to shadows and cracks, hidden line labeling, curved lines, and so on. There were also attempts to refine the scheme in a restricted object world consisting of right-angled objects (21, 34). Many methods were also developed to check the correctness of a labeled line drawing. Such methods include "reciprocal figures dualities" (17, 30), "spanning angles" constraints (18), "cyclic order property" of edges and vertices around faces (9, 42, 46), "sidedness reasoning" (6), and "maximal sets of relative place" (41). It is interesting to note that a consistency check of a line drawing can be implemented using a parallel-computation algorithm (29) or a neural network (37).

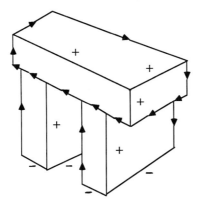

Figure 3.3. Possible consistent labeling of a line drawing.

3. SHAPE RECOVERY: ORTHOGRAPHIC PROJECTIONS

3.1. An Algebraic Approach to Shape Recovery

In this subsection, we explore the possibility of solving the "polyhedral shape recovery" problem using a purely algebraic approach, without resorting to making many assumptions about the world based on human knowledge and experience. This section is a partial summary of a system for machine interpretation of line drawings, implemented by Sugihara in the mid-1980s (47). This system operates on orthographic line drawings, and attempts to recover only polyhedral objects. One of the many interesting aspects about this system is the fact that it checks first if the line drawing is a proper one through labeling techniques. If the line drawing is "improper," it attempts to correct it first before going through the recovery process. Once the line drawing is considered a proper one, the system enters the computational stage, namely, the recovery–reconstruction stage. So, in a way this system considers the symbolic aspects of line drawings as well as their computational connotations. The computational stage of the system attempts to solve the problem from an algebraic degrees-of-freedom approach. The system does not rely on the forementioned geometric regularities of parallelism, perpendicularity, and symmetry, but the approach is from a point of view of solving matrix equations representing a system of simultaneous equations involving parameters of 3D vertex coordinates and surface orientations of the object. Even though the vertex and plane constraints narrow down the set of possible corresponding scenes, it is still an infinite one. However, this system attempts to include all these constraints in algebraic matrices. Then, once a system of matrices is obtained to characterize a line drawing, the degrees of freedom for the system of matrices are computed. The system then attempts to reduce the number of degrees of freedom by utilizing weighting functions and applying optimization functions. The algebraic analysis in the system is mathematically superstrict, and redundancy theorems as well as relaxation methods are used to resolve such superstrictness and reduce the program to a linear one.

The basic idea of this algebraic approach is the following. Given a properly labeled orthographic line drawing corresponding to a polyhedral scene, let $(x_\alpha, y_\alpha, z_\alpha)$ denote the position of the αth vertex of the object and $a_j x + b_j y + z + c_j = 0$ denote the surface on which the jth face lies. When the image is given, x_α and y_α are known constants whereas z_α, a_j, b_j, c_j are unknowns. Labels assigned to the image tell us which vertex should be on which face. If the αth vertex should be on the jth face, we get the equation

$$a_j x_\alpha + b_j y_\alpha + z_\alpha + c_j = 0, \tag{3}$$

which is linear in the unknowns z_α, a_j, b_j, c_j. The labeled image also contains information about relative distance; it tells us which part of the object should be nearer to the observer than other part. For example, if the βth vertex should be nearer than the kth face, we get

$$a_k x_\beta + b_k y_\beta + z_\beta + c_k > 0, \tag{4}$$

which is also linear in the unknowns z_β, a_k, b_k, c_k. Now, the most important point is how to extract from the image relevant equations and inequalities systematically.

One way to describe a 3D spatial structure $\mathbf{S}$, is by the quadruple $\mathbf{S} = (V, F, R, T)$, where the elements of V are the 3D vertices, $v_\alpha = (x_\alpha, y_\alpha, z_\alpha)$; F is a set of visible faces corresponding to 2D regions on the image plane; and R and T are used to represent relative depths among vertices and faces, and will be illustrated by examples later in this subsection.

Suppose that $\mathbf{S} = (V, F, R, T)$ is the spatial structure of a labeled line drawing $\mathbf{D}$. Let $|V| = n$ and $|F| = m$. For each vertex $v_\alpha = (x_\alpha, y_\alpha, z_\alpha)$ in V, x_α and y_α are given constants whereas z_α is an unknown variable. Hence, we have n unknowns $z_1, \ldots, z_n$. With each face f_j in F, we associate a planar surface given by Eq. (3), on which the face f_j should lie. Note that this equation cannot represent a surface that is parallel to the z axis. However, under the "general-viewpoint assumption," this case will not be considered. Thus we further obtain $3m$ unknowns $a_1, b_1, c_1, \ldots, a_m, b_m, c_m$.

An element (v_α, f_j) of R represents the fact that v_α lies on the planar surface f_j, and hence Eq. (3) is satisfied. Note that this equation is linear with respect to the unknowns. Gathering all such equations, one for each element of R, we get the system of linear equations

$$\mathbf{Aw} = \mathbf{0}, \tag{5}$$

where $\mathbf{w}^T = (z_1, \ldots, z_n, a_1, b_1, c_1, \ldots, a_m, b_m, c_m)$ and $\mathbf{A}$ is a constant matrix of size $|R| \times (3m + n)$.

Next we consider relative depth constraints represented by T. A triple of the form $(v_\alpha, v_\beta, FRONT)$ represents the fact that "vertex v_α is in front of vertex v_β." From the way $\mathbf{S}$ was constructed, we can see that if $(v_\alpha, v_\beta, FRONT)$ is an element of T, then the constraint represented by the triple can be paraphrased by

$$z_\alpha \geq z_\beta. \tag{6}$$

A triple of the form $(v_\alpha, f_j, PROPERLY - FRONT)$ indicates that the vertex v_α is properly in front of the planar surface on which the face f_j lies, and hence we get

$$a_j x_\alpha + b_j y_\alpha + z_\alpha + c_j > 0. \tag{7}$$

Similarly, a triple of the form $(v_\alpha, v_\beta, BEHIND)$ is equivalent to $(v_\beta, v_\alpha, FRONT)$, and also for the triple $(v_\alpha, f_i, PROPERLY - BEHIND)$, we get

$$a_j x_\alpha + b_j y_\alpha + z_\alpha + c_j < 0. \tag{8}$$

Any element of T belongs to one of the above four types. Gathering inequalities of the forms $(6), \ldots, (8)$, we can write

$$\mathbf{Bw} > \mathbf{0}, \tag{9}$$

where $\mathbf{B}$ is a constant matrix of size $|T| \times (3m + n)$, and the inequality symbol is an abbreviation of componentwise inequalities, some of which allow equalities. Now, for shape recovery, each and every solution to the system of matrix equations [Eqs. (5) and (9)] represents a unique solution of a spatial structure $\mathbf{S}$ to the line drawing $\mathbf{D}$. However, the problem here is that the system of Eq. (9) contains inequalities. The equations (5) and inequalities (9) form a polytope (i.e., a convex polyhedron) in the $(n + 3m)$-dimensional space.

Now, a line drawing does not specify a scene uniquely. Since the 3D structure is not unique for a given line drawing and infinitely many different objects can yield the same image, $\mathbf{S}$ is expected to have infinitely many solutions for a proper line drawing. Recall that the total number of unknowns is $n + 3m$; hence a solution to Eqs. (5) and (9) can be considered as a point in an $(n + 3m)$-dimensional Euclidean space. Each inequality in Eq. (9) represents an $(n + 3m)$-dimensional half space, and hence the set of all inequalities in Eq. (9) defines an intersection of the half spaces. The intersection usually forms an $(n + 3m)$-dimensional region, and (9) simply restricts the solutions to this region. Therefore, in what follows, we concentrate our attention on Eq. (5).

Each equation in Eq. (5) restricts the solutions to an $(n + 3m - 1)$-dimensional hyperplane in the $(n + 3m)$-dimensional space. Since (5) contains rank(A) independent equations, all the solutions to (5) form a region of dimension $n + 3m - \text{rank}(A)$. This means that there are $n + 3m - \text{rank}(A)$ degrees of freedom in the choice of a solution to Eq. (5); in other words, there exists a set of $n + 3m - \text{rank}(A)$ unknowns such that we can specify the values of these unknowns independently, and once we do we get a unique solution to Eq. (5).

It turns out that there is a lower bound on the degrees of freedom for a given image (47), as stated by the following theorem.

Theorem Let **D** be a labeled line drawing and **S** be a spatial structure associated with **D**. If **D**, together with **S**, represents a polyhedral scene and **S** has two or more faces, then there are at least 4 degrees of freedom in the choice of a polyhedral scene from **D** and **S**.

Sugihara (47) suggests an optimization method where different cues are considered that can lessen the degrees of freedom of the faces. Let d_k denote an observed value of the kth cue, and for any **w** satisfying Eqs. (5) and (9), let $d_k'(w)$ denote a theoretical value of the kth cue that should be observed if the exact scene is **w**. For example, if a face is covered with a grain texture of a known uniform density, one can adopt as d_k and $d_k'(w)$, respectively, the observed value and the theoretical one of the apparent grain density on the face. Another example of a cue is if the illumination condition and the surface reflectance are known, one can adopt d_k and $d_k(w)'$ as the observed value and the theoretical one of light intensity on the face. Let $g_k(w)$ be the difference between the two values:

$$g_k(\mathbf{w}) = d_k - d_k'(\mathbf{w}). \tag{10}$$

If there is no error in observation, the true scene **w** must satisfy $g_k(w) = 0$; this condition lessens the degrees of freedom of the face by 1. Since noises are inevitable in real-image data, we cannot expect $g_k(w) = 0$ exactly. However, if enough cues are available, we can seek a solution to the following optimization problem. Minimize

$$\phi(\mathbf{w}) = \sum_k s_k [g_k(\mathbf{w})]^2 \tag{11}$$

subject to Eqs. (5) and (9), where s_k denotes a positive weight of the kth cue, and the summation is to be taken over all available cues. In Sugihara's system, we can obtain different solutions if the weights are different in the relaxation and optimization functions to which the matrix system is optimized.

As we can see, the algebraic approach depends on various cues that are not always available in a line drawing to solve the shape-recovery problem. It was found that by imposing certain realistic heuristic constraints on the problem on the basis of our everyday experience, we can simplify the solution and relieve the superstrictness on the problem of shape recovery. Such heuristic assumptions are typically geometric regularities such as parallelism, perpendicularity, and symmetry. Therefore, the emphasis of the rest of this chapter will be on the detection of such regularities and their utilization for shape recovery.

3.2. The Gradient Space

The concept of gradient space is useful in describing surface orientations. Suppose a surface is defined as $-z = f(x, y)$; that is, any point on the surface can be described as $[x, y, -f(x, y)]$. Then define a domain (p, q) for the surface such that

$$(p, q) = \left(\frac{\partial f}{\partial x}, \frac{\partial f}{\partial y} \right) = \left(-\frac{\partial z}{\partial x}, -\frac{\partial z}{\partial y} \right). \tag{12}$$

The set of all points (p, q) is called the *gradient space*. The gradient space was first introduced by Mackworth (30) on the basis of Huffman's *dual space* (17). The gradient space has proved to be an extremely useful tool for describing 3D image constraints. From the definition of the gradient space described in Eq. (12), the surface normal **n** is

$$\mathbf{n} = (p, q, 1) \tag{13}$$

If the surface is a plane, then it can be described by the following general equation described in terms of the gradient space:

$$-z = px + qy + S. \tag{14}$$

Parallel planes have the same gradient. In other words, any point (p, q) in the gradient space represents an infinite set of parallel planes. From the gradient definition described in Eq. (12), the gradient of a plane represents how the planes are slanting relative to the view line (z axis). From the definition in Eq. (12), the direction $\tan^{-1}(q/p)$ is the direction of the steepest change of $-z$ (depth). The length of the vector is the rate of the change in depth along the direction of the steepest change. A plane's orientation is typically described by its gradient (p, q) as mentioned earlier. However, it is generally more intuitive for us to visualize 3D orientations by angular measurements. So, let us define the tilt angle τ and the slant angle σ, such that

$$\tau = \tan^{-1}\left(\frac{q}{p}\right),$$

$$\sigma = \tan^{-1}\left(\sqrt{p^2 + q^2}\right).$$

(15)

The definition of the gradient space suggests that the gradient can be established for differentiable surfaces only. However, the gradient space in reality can represent 3D orientation in general, and is not restricted to just orientation of differentiable surfaces. Let us define a direction vector of a line in space with arbitrary starting point as $(\Delta x, \Delta y, \Delta z)$, where Δx, Δy, and Δz represent the arithmetic difference between the two endpoints of the line in the x, y, and z directions, respectively. Define the gradient of the direction vector as follows:

$$\mathbf{G_v} = (p_v, q_v) = \left(\frac{\Delta x}{\Delta z}, \frac{\Delta y}{\Delta z}\right).$$

(16)

Observe that this definition of a vector gradient is very convenient since parallel vectors would have the same direction vector producing the same gradient, just as parallel planes have the same gradients. Therefore, a point in the gradient space describes an infinite family of parallel lines in space. Furthermore, note that, according to Eq. (13), the gradient of a vector normal to the surface is the same as the gradient of a surface.

3.3. Orthographic Constraints of Geometric Regularities

In this subsection, we will present algebraic constraints on images imposed by polyhedral scenes, utilizing the image formation model and our knowledge of the gradient space.

3.3.1. Relation of Image Line to Gradient Space

Under orthographic projection, from Eq. (1), the direction vector $l = (\Delta x, \Delta y, \Delta z)$ maps to $l' = (\Delta x, \Delta y)$ and from Eq. (16) the vector gradient is $G_v = (p_v, q_v) = [(\Delta x/\Delta z), (\Delta y/\Delta z)]$. Therefore, the line in gradient space from the origin to the point G_v is parallel to the edge in the image.

Suppose the vector $l = (\Delta x, \Delta y, \Delta z)$ is on a plane whose gradient is $G_0 = (p_0, q_0)$. From Eq. (13), the normal of the plane is $n_0 = (p_0, q_0, 1)$. Therefore,

$$l \cdot n_0 = 0, \tag{17}$$

which reduces to

$$G_0 \cdot l' = -\Delta z. \tag{18}$$

Therefore, we can recover the depth parameter Δz of a vector, provided we identify its orthographic projection and the orientation of the surface it falls on.

Now, suppose that the vector $l = (\Delta x, \Delta y, \Delta z)$ is the intersection of two planes of gradients $G_1 = (p_1, q_1)$ and $G_2 = (p_2, q_2)$. Under orthography, this vector corresponds to the edge $l' = (\Delta x, \Delta y)$. Then, from Eq. (18) one can write

$$-\Delta z = G_1 \cdot l' = G_2 \cdot l', \tag{19}$$

which reduces to

$$(G_1 - G_2) \cdot l' = 0. \tag{20}$$

Therefore, under orthography, the edge in the image is perpendicular to the line in the gradient space passing through G_1 and G_2. The relative position of G_1 and G_2 is related to the convexity or concavity of the edge between planar surfaces [Mackworth's relation involving connect edges (30)].

3.3.2. Two Image Lines on a Plane

Now, let us examine the information available from two vectors on a plane. Given two vectors $l_1 = (\Delta x_1, \Delta y_1, \Delta z_1)$ and $l_2 = (\Delta x_2, \Delta y_2, \Delta z_2)$ belonging to the same surface of gradient $G_0 = (p_0, q_0)$. Under orthography, their corresponding edges in the image are $l'_1 = (\Delta x_1, \Delta y_1)$ and $l'_2 = (\Delta x_2, \Delta y_2)$, respectively. Then from Eq. (18), we obtain

$$\begin{bmatrix} p_0 \\ q_0 \end{bmatrix} = - \begin{bmatrix} \Delta x_1 & \Delta y_1 \\ \Delta x_2 & \Delta y_2 \end{bmatrix}^{-1} \begin{bmatrix} \Delta z_1 \\ \Delta z_2 \end{bmatrix}. \tag{21}$$

Therefore, given the depth parameters (Δz values) for two vectors on a surface, the gradient of the surface can be found using the othographic image. Or conversely, knowing the gradient of a surface on which two lines fall on, we can recover the 3D scene lines from their corresponding image lines.

Now, suppose that the vectors l_1 and l_2 are perpendicular. The vector gradients are given by

$$\mathbf{G}_{v1} = (p_{v1}, q_{v1}) = \left(\frac{\Delta x_1}{\Delta z_1}, \frac{\Delta y_1}{\Delta z_1} \right),$$

$$\mathbf{G}_{v2} = (p_{v2}, q_{v2}) = \left(\frac{\Delta x_2}{\Delta z_2}, \frac{\Delta y_2}{\Delta z_2} \right). \tag{22}$$

Since l_1 and l_2 are perpendicular,

$$l_1 \cdot l_2 = 0, \tag{23}$$

which can be rewritten as

$$\mathbf{G}_{v1} \cdot \mathbf{G}_{v2} = -1. \tag{24}$$

Therefore, given one of the gradients, say, $\mathbf{G}_{v1}$, Eq. (24) is a line in the gradient space on which all possible solutions of the other gradient lie. This line is Huffman's dual line for an edge in the image whose gradient is $\mathbf{G}_{v1}$ (17). Further conclusions could be drawn from the relationship described in Eq. (24). For example, since two orthogonal planes have perpendicular surface normals, their gradients obey Eq. (24). Furthermore, if a plane contains a vector, then since the vector is perpendicular to the gradient of the plane, the vector and the gradient of the plane obey the relationship described in Eq. (24).

3.3.3. Parallel Lines and Gradient Space

Define *dual line* as the line in the gradient space passing through two gradient points $\mathbf{G}_1$ and $\mathbf{G}_2$, which are the gradients corresponding to two regions intersecting at line l. The dual line and l' are perpendicular [see Eq. (20)]. If the edge l is convex $(+)$, $\mathbf{G}_1$ and $\mathbf{G}_2$ are ordered in the same direction as are the corresponding regions shown in Figure 3.4. If the edge is concave $(-)$, then their order is reversed.

Consider two planes having parallel edges with direction $\mathbf{a} = (\cos \alpha, \sin \alpha)$. The 3D vectors corresponding to the two parallel lines are

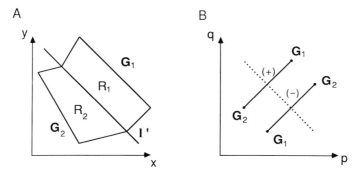

Figure 3.4. Gradient relationship to dual lines. From Kanade (19), ©1981 Elsevier.

identical:

$$(\cos \alpha, \sin \alpha, -\mathbf{G}_1 \cdot \mathbf{a}) = (\cos \alpha, \sin \alpha, -\mathbf{G}_2 \cdot \mathbf{a}). \qquad (25)$$

Note that the third components of these 3D vectors have no constant additive term ($S = 0$) since we are concerned with the incremental change in z corresponding to the translation from $(0, 0)$ to $(\cos \alpha, \sin \alpha)$.

3.3.4. Symmetry

A 2D region is symmetric if it has an axis for which the opposite sides of the axis are reflective. That is, for every point in the symmetric picture, there corresponds a point on the other side of the axis of the symmetry with equal perpendicular distance from it. In other words, the symmetric property is found along the transverse lines perpendicular to the symmetry axis.

Two-dimensional skewed symmetry is a more general case of 2D symmetry where the equal distance of the corresponding points are "angular" as opposed to perpendicular. In other words, the symmetry is found along lines not necessarily perpendicular to the axis, but at a skewed angle to it, as illustrated in Fig. 3.5. As noted earlier for 2D symmetry, the transverse lines are perpendicular to the axis of symmetry. Since angles between lines are not preserved under orthographic projection yet parallelism is, then the orthographic images of the transverse lines are parallel to each other, yet they are not perpendicular to the orthographic image of the axis of symmetry. This by definition is 2D skewed symmetry. So we conclude that a 2D symmetric surface projects orthographically to a 2D skewed symmetric patch in the image plane.

A   B

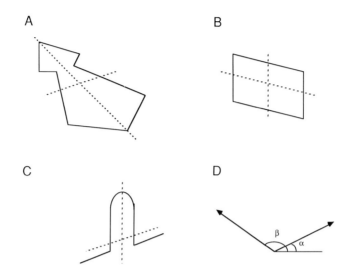

C   D

Figure 3.5. Two-dimensional skewed symmetry. From Kanade (19), ©1981 Elsevier.

Let α and β be the directional angles of the skewed symmetry and the skewed transverse axes, respectively. Let $\mathbf{G} = (p, q)$ be the gradient of the symmetric surface. The 3D vectors on the plane corresponding to the directions α and β are

$$\mathbf{A} = (\cos \alpha, \sin \alpha, -\mathbf{G} \cdot \mathbf{a}),$$

$$\mathbf{B} = (\cos \beta, \sin \beta, -\mathbf{G} \cdot \mathbf{b}),$$
(26)

where $\mathbf{a} = (\cos \alpha, \sin \alpha)$ and $\mathbf{b} = (\cos \beta, \sin \beta)$. If $\mathbf{A} \perp \mathbf{B}$, then we can write

$$\mathbf{A} \cdot \mathbf{B} = 0$$
(27)

Substituting Eq. (26) into Eq. (27), we obtain

$$\cos(\alpha - \beta) + (\mathbf{G} \cdot \mathbf{a})(\mathbf{G} \cdot \mathbf{b}) = 0.$$
(28)

Let us rotate $p - q$ by $\lambda = (\alpha + \beta)/2$ into $p_r - q_r$ and substitute into Eq. (28) to obtain

$$p_r^2 \cos^2\left(\frac{\alpha - \beta}{2}\right) - q_r^2 \sin^2\left(\frac{\alpha - \beta}{2}\right) = -\cos(\alpha - \beta),$$
(29)

where

$$p_r = p \cos \lambda + q \sin \lambda$$

$$q_r = -p \sin \lambda + q \cos \lambda$$

(30)

Equation (29) is the equation of a hyperbola. Hence, for skewed symmetry to be a projection of real symmetry, the gradient of the surface must fall on the hyperbola described in Eq. (29).

3.3.5. Literature Sources

The results on orthography discussed thus far are scattered in the literature. Most of the results can be found in works by Brady (4), Draper (6), Friedberg (8), Kanade (18–20), Shafer and Kanade (38), Stevens (45), and Weiss (48).

3.4. Geometrically Motivated Orthographic Metaheuristics

The previous subsection introduced us to different types of algebraic constraints that a scene imposes on a line drawing. These image constraints are always true, provided that the scene is known to have the corresponding regularities. However, in the problem of "shape recovery from line drawings," we are provided only with the image and the objective is to recover the scene. Unfortunately, because of the loss in dimensionality, the converses of the constraints developed in the previous section are not always true. Hence, to utilize such constraints for shape recovery, we must make certain assumptions about the scene. The main basic underlying assumption in solving this problem is the "general-viewpoint assumption," which states:

Regular properties and constraints observable in the image do not occur by accident, but are projections of some preferred corresponding 3D regularities and properties in the scene.

According to the "general-viewpoint assumption," if a relationship of certain image parameters is satisfied, and this relationship happens to be the same for the parameters of the projection of a certain 3D property, then it is highly unlikely that the relationship occurred coincidentally without the presence of a 3D regularity, and it must indeed correspond to the 3D scene property. There is vast amount of psychophysical evidence supporting the fact that humans indeed make such general-viewpoint assumption to interpret images. Since coincidental alignment is not considered, then we can utilize the image constraints established in the previous section in a converse manner to recover the 3D scenes from 2D images; more specifically, shape recovery from line drawings. The regularities discussed in this section and also discussed by Kanade (19) for 3D shape recovery are parallelism, perpendicularity (including right corners), and face symmetry.

1. *Parallelism*. As was evident by Eq. (1), parallelism is preserved under orthography. That is, parallel vectors in the 3D scene project to parallel edges in the image. Conversely, the parallelism heuristic states: "*If two lines are parallel in the image, they depict parallel lines in the scene.*" The heuristic fails only for those cases where two nonparallel lines are seen from a view direction such that if the two lines are properly translated so that they intersect at one point, then the plane defined by the two translated lines is perpendicular to the image plane.

2. *Perpendicularity*. "*If two adjacent planes P_1 and P_2 have respective gradients $\mathbf{G}_1$ and $\mathbf{G}_2$, then from Eq. (24), if*

$$\mathbf{G}_1 \cdot \mathbf{G}_2 = -1 \qquad\qquad (31)$$

the two planes are orthogonal, hence the lines in P_1 are perpendicular to the lines in P_2.

3. *Symmetry*. "*A skewed symmetry in the image depicts a real symmetry in the scene viewed from some (unknown) view direction.*"

The converse of this heuristic is always true as was discussed earlier. Stevens (15) presents a good body of psychological experiments suggesting that human observers can perceive surface orientations from figures with the property of skewed symmetry. Let us see an example of how symmetry can be used to determine orientations of planes. Take the line drawing of Fig. 3.6(A), which shows a cube with the angles and lengths. Figure 6(A) shows that there are three visible and adjacent planar faces P_1, P_2, and P_3. Let us say that the faces have gradients $\mathbf{G}_1$, $\mathbf{G}_2$, and $\mathbf{G}_3$. Since the faces are adjacent and nonparallel, their gradients should form a triangle in the gradient space. On the other hand, P_1, P_2, and P_3 have skewed symmetries. On the basis of the symmetry heuristic, if we assume these skewed symmetries to be projections of real symmetries, we can draw the hyperbola described in Eq. (29) for each surface as shown in Fig. 3.6(B).

The problem now is locating the triangle of Fig. 3.6(B) so that each vertex of the triangle falls on its corresponding hyperbola. It can be shown that the location shown in Fig. 3.6(A) is the only possible assignment of gradients for the given cube. For a complete proof and more complex examples, refer to Kanade (19).

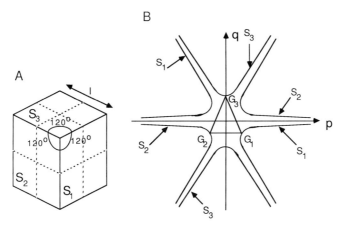

Figure 3.6. (A) Orthographic line drawing of a cube; (B) the use of hyperbolic constraint to determining the orientations of the surfaces of the cube. From Kanade (19), ©1981 Elsevier.

3.5. Orthographic Shape-Recovery Systems

The projections of 3D objects onto planes resulting in line drawings has been long studied by descriptive geometry and projective geometry. However, the converse problem of reconstructing 3D objects from line drawings drew attention only in the mid-1960s, with the advent and popularity of digital computers powerful enough to process digital images. One of the earliest attempts to the problem was a model-based system developed by Roberts in 1965 (36). The system had a dictionary of 3D objects, and attempted to match any object in a line drawing with one of the objects in its database (or dictionary). This system was very elementary and restrictive, where objects were assumed to be isolated in the images (i.e., no object occlusion). However, this system was important because it demonstrated that the solution to the line-drawing interpretation problem is feasible. As a result, many researchers followed Roberts' model-base approach, where some of the limitations of Roberts' system were further developed. Such limitations included occlusion and imperfect line drawings. Two such researchers were Falk (7) and Grape (10). Another popular approach to solving the problem was the interpretation of multiview drawings, pioneered by Shapira (40). Here, the problem was establishing point correspondence among the different views and then finding a consistent way of constructing the 3D objects based on the established point correspondences (31).

A popular "model-free" approach emerged in the late 1970s and early 1980s that extracted 3D structure from single-view drawings (9, 19, 24, 27).

It should be noted that the "model-free" interpretation of single-view line drawings was first studied in 1968 by Guzman (11), where he attempted to decompose an image into regions, with each region corresponding to a single 3D object. His method was too ad hoc in nature and his rules did not have enough logical foundation to them. Yet, his system showed that even with ad hoc rules, relatively complicated line drawings could be decomposed into objects. However, examples could be created to make his system fail (1). Mackworth (30) discussed geometric constraints using the gradient space, and his study dealt with accidental alignment as well as nontrihedral vertices. Draper (6) developed a recognition scheme based on which side of a plane a point lies. Lee and Fu (26) analyzed objects where parallelograms in the object image formed a basis for the analysis and were assumed to be rectangles in the object, which were distorted by the orientation of the object with respect to the camera. They also adopted the "least slant angle" preference rule. Kanade (19) used metaheuristics of parallelism of lines and skewed symmetry for shape recovery. His work and Sugihara's algebraic approach (47) were discussed in some detail in previous subsections.

4. SHAPE RECOVERY: PERSPECTIVE PROJECTION

4.1. Vanishing Points and Lines

Any line l in the scene containing a point (x, y, z) and having a direction vector $(\Delta x, \Delta y, \Delta z)$ can be described by

$$l = (x, y, z) + k(\Delta x, \Delta y, \Delta z), \tag{32}$$

where $k \in \mathscr{R}$. For a given k, the corresponding point $\mathbf{p}_k$ on the line is

$$\mathbf{p}_k = (x + k\,\Delta x, y + k\,\Delta y, z + k\,\Delta z). \tag{33}$$

The image point of $\mathbf{p}_k$ is $\mathbf{p}'_k$, which can be described according to Eqs. (2) and (33) as

$$\mathbf{p}'_k = \left(f\frac{x + k\,\Delta x}{z + k\,\Delta z}, f\frac{y + k\,\Delta y}{z + k\,\Delta z} \right). \tag{34}$$

As k grows large, $\mathbf{p}'_k$ converges to some point v'.

$$v' = \lim_{k \to \infty} \mathbf{p}'_k = \left(f\frac{\Delta x}{\Delta z}, f\frac{\Delta y}{\Delta z} \right), \tag{35}$$

where $\mathbf{v}'$ is the vanishing point of the line. The assumption in Eq. (35) is that $\Delta z \neq 0$; in other words, assume that the line l is not parallel to the image plane. A vector that is parallel to the image plane has no vanishing point in the image ($\mathbf{v}'$ is infinitely far away). The vanishing point $\mathbf{v}'$ depends solely on the direction vector of the line, namely, $(\Delta x, \Delta y, \Delta z)$. Hence parallel vectors have the same vanishing point; that is, each image point is a vanishing point for a family of parallel lines.

Straight lines in the scene map to straight lines in the image under perspective as well as orthographic projections. Therefore, the vanishing point $\mathbf{v}'$ of a vector l must lie along l', the image of the vector. Hence a set of parallel vectors map into image lines intersecting at (passing through) a single point in the image plane, namely, the vanishing point. We must also realize that the vanishing point is the projection of a point on the vector infinitely far away, and therefore it cannot be on the image line of the vector, but it typically lies on the extension of the image line.

Let us discuss vanishing lines. Consider a plane P with gradient $\mathbf{G} = (p, q)$. Let l be a vector on P having a vector gradient $\mathbf{G}_l = (p_l, q_l)$ and vanishing point $\mathbf{v}'_l = (v'_{xl}, v'_{yl})$. From Eq. (24), we know that

$$\mathbf{G} \cdot \mathbf{G}_l = -1. \tag{36}$$

It is easy to see from Eqs. (16) and (35) that $\mathbf{G}_l = \mathbf{v}'_i / f$, and with Eq. (36),

$$p v'_{xl} + q v'_{yl} = -f. \tag{37}$$

For a specific plane P with a given gradient $\mathbf{G}$, Eq. (37) defines a line in the image plane, called the *vanishing line* of the plane P. The vanishing line is the locus of vanishing points for all vectors on the surface. Since the vanishing line depends solely on $\mathbf{G}$, then parallel planes have the same vanishing line. Therefore, any line in the image is the vanishing line for a family of parallel planes.

4.2. Perspective Constraints of Geometric Regularities

4.2.1. Backprojection of Image Points

Let $\mathbf{p}$ be a point on a plane P with its perspective image point $\mathbf{p}' = (x', y')$. Under the perspective projection described by Eq. (2), we can write $\mathbf{p}$ in terms of the image coordinates as

$$\mathbf{p} = (ax', ay', af) \tag{38}$$

for some value of a real variable a ($a = z/f$), where $a \neq 0$. Since $\mathbf{p}$ is on

P, then substitute Eq. (38) into the plane equation [Eq. (14)] to obtain

$$p(ax') + q(ay') + (af) + S = 0. \tag{39}$$

Solving for a, we obtain

$$a = \frac{-S}{px' + qy' + f} = \frac{-S}{\mathbf{p}' \cdot \mathbf{G} + f}. \tag{40}$$

Substitute Eq. (40) back into Eq. (38) to obtain

$$\mathbf{p} = \frac{-S}{\mathbf{p}' \cdot \mathbf{G} + f}(x', y', f), \tag{41}$$

where $\mathbf{p}$ is the backprojection of image point $\mathbf{p}'$ onto plane P (22). Note that with $a = z/f$, if $a < 0$, then $\mathbf{p}$ is behind the viewer, and $\mathbf{p}'$ does not correspond to any point on the image of P. Also, note that in Eqs. (40) and (41) the assumption was made that $\mathbf{p}' \cdot \mathbf{G} + f \neq 0$. In other words, $\mathbf{p}'$ does not lie on the vanishing line of P.

4.2.2. 3D Vector Orientation

The orientation of a vector l in 3D has 2 degrees of freedom, so it can be described by two parameters. Let θ be the angle between the line and the z axis in the direction of the camera. Let ϕ be the angle of the orthographic projection of the line with respect to the x axis, as shown in Fig. 3.7. We assume without loss of generality that l passes through the lens center.

$$\tan \theta = \frac{\sqrt{v_x'^2 + v_y'^2}}{|f|}, \tag{42}$$

$$\tan \phi = \frac{v_y'}{v_x'}. $$

Thus the orientation of a line in 3D space can be determined by establishing the line's vanishing point, provided that the focal length of the camera is known. We can easily see from Fig. 7 that the direction cosine of l is

$$\mathbf{c}_1 = (\sin \theta \cos \phi, \sin \theta \sin \phi, \pm \cos \theta). \tag{43}$$

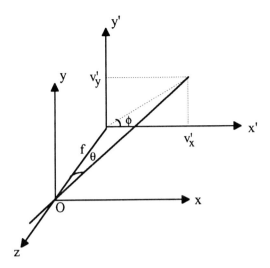

Figure 3.7. Orientation of a line in 3D space.

4.2.3. Perpendicularity

Consider two lines, l_1 and l_2, of orientations (θ_1, ϕ_1) and (θ_2, ϕ_2) with vanishing points $\mathbf{v}_1' = (v_{x1}', v_{y1}')$ and $\mathbf{v}_2' = (v_{x2}', v_{y2}')$, respectively. If the two lines are perpendicular, then their direction cosines given by Eq. (43) are perpendicular:

$$\mathbf{c}_{l_1} \cdot \mathbf{c}_{l_2} = 0, \tag{44}$$

which expands to

$$\sin\theta_1 \cos\phi_1 \sin\theta_2 \cos\phi_2 + \sin\theta_1 \sin\phi_1 \sin\theta_2 \sin\phi_2 + \cos\theta_1 \cos\theta_2 = 0. \tag{45}$$

Substituting Eq. (42) into Eq. (45) and simplifying, we obtain

$$\mathbf{v}_1' \cdot \mathbf{v}_2' = -f^2. \tag{46}$$

Manipulating Eq. (45) differently, we obtain

$$\cos(\phi_1 - \phi_2) = -\cot\theta_1 \cot\theta_2. \tag{47}$$

Since $0 \le \theta_1 < 90.0°$, and $0 \le \theta_2 < 90.0°$ are always true and using Eq. (42), it follows that

$$\cos(\phi_1 - \phi_2) = -\frac{f^2}{\sqrt{v'^2_{x1} + v'^2_{y1}} \sqrt{v'^2_{x2} + v'^2_{y2}}} < 0. \tag{48}$$

Therefore

$$90.0° < |\phi_2 - \phi_1| < 180.0°, \tag{49}$$

and if the difference angle is not in the second quadrant, then we know that the lines cannot be perpendicular.

4.2.4. Right Corners

In this subsection, we discuss trihedral vertices and the constraints they impose on a line drawing and mainly develop constraints on right corners. Utilizing Eq. (46) for a right corner, we can write

$$\mathbf{v}'_1 \cdot \mathbf{v}'_2 = \mathbf{v}'_1 \cdot \mathbf{v}'_3 = \mathbf{v}'_2 \cdot \mathbf{v}'_3 = -f^2, \tag{50}$$

where $\mathbf{v}'_i$ is the vanishing point of l_i of the right corner for $i = 1, 2, 3$.

Lines l'_1, l'_2, and l'_3 are image lines with vanishing points $\mathbf{v}'_1 = (v'_{x1}, v'_{y1})$, $\mathbf{v}'_2 = (v'_{x2}, v'_{y2})$, and $\mathbf{v}'_3 = (v'_{x3}, v'_{y3})$, respectively. The equations of these lines in the image plane are given by

$$y' = m_i x' + b_i \tag{51}$$

for $i = 1, 2, 3$, where m_i is the slope and b_i is the y-axis intercept of the line. Since the vanishing point of a line falls on the line, the three vanishing points must satisfy the relationship in Eq. (51). Hence

$$v'_{yi} = m_i v'_{xi} + b_i \tag{52}$$

for $i = 1, 2, 3$.

Assume that the three line segments are projections of a right corner. Then we may use Eqs. (50) and (52) to derive several constraints in terms of $\mathbf{v}'$, m, and b (44). For example, suppose that $\mathbf{v}'_1$ is known, and $\mathbf{v}'_2$ and $\mathbf{v}'_3$

are unknown. Using $\mathbf{v}_1' \cdot \mathbf{v}_2' = -f^2$ and the line equation for l_2', we obtain

$$v_{x2}' = -\frac{\left(f^2 + b_2 v_{y1}'\right)}{\left(v_{x1}' + m_2 v_{y1}'\right)},$$

$$v_{y2}' = \frac{\left(b_2 v_{x1}' - m_2 f^2\right)}{\left(v_{x1}' + m_2 v_{y1}'\right)}. \tag{53}$$

Similarly we can solve for v_{x3}' and v_{y3}'. A substitution of these two sets of equations into $\mathbf{v}_2' \cdot \mathbf{v}_3' = -f^2$ yields a constraint equation:

$$f^4(1 + m_2 m_3) + f^2 \left[v_{x1}'^2 + v_{x1}' v_{y1}'(m_2 + m_3) + m_2 m_3 v_{y1}'^2 \right.$$

$$\left. - v_{x1}'(m_2 b_3 + m_3 b_2) + b_{y1}'(b_2 + b_3) \right] + b_2 b_3 \left(v_{x1}'^2 + v_{y1}'^2 \right) = 0. \tag{54}$$

Now, assuming that $\mathbf{v}_1'$ and $\mathbf{v}_2'$ are known, but $\mathbf{v}_3'$ is unknown, we can derive, after algebraic manipulations, a constraint equation:

$$f^2 \left[v_{x2}' - v_{x1}' + m_3(v_{y2}' - v_{y1}') \right] - b_3(v_{x1}' v_{y2}' - v_{x2}' v_{y1}') = 0. \tag{55}$$

Additional constraints can be found in Shomar *et al.* (44).

Consider three image lines l_1', l_2', and l_3', forming a junction corresponding to a right corner in the scene. Line l_i' makes angle α_i' relative to the x' axis. Transform the right corner in the scene such that the vertex of the junction falls on the z axis (i.e., translate corresponding image junction to the origin of x'–y' coordinates). Denote the scene angles of the transformed right corner relative to the z axis by β_1, β_2, and β_3. Then, the angle constraint on the right corner can be shown to be (22)

$$\beta_1 = \tan^{-1} \sqrt{-\cos(\alpha_2' - \alpha_3')/\cos(\alpha_1' - \alpha_2')\cos(\alpha_3' - \alpha_1')},$$

$$\beta_2 = \tan^{-1} \sqrt{-\cos(\alpha_3' - \alpha_1')/\cos(\alpha_2' - \alpha_3')\cos(\alpha_1' - \alpha_2')}, \tag{56}$$

$$\beta_3 = \tan^{-1} \sqrt{-\cos(\alpha_1' - \alpha_2')/\cos(\alpha_3' - \alpha_1')\cos(\alpha_2' - \alpha_3')}.$$

4.2.5. Angle Constraints of Two General-Orientation Vectors

Consider two vectors l_1 and l_2 forming an angle α in the scene. If the orientations of l_1 and l_2 are (θ_1, ϕ_1) and (θ_2, ϕ_2), respectively. The dot product of the direction cosines c_1 and c_2 is

$$c_1 \cdot c_2 = \|c_1\| \|c_2\| \cos \alpha = \cos \alpha. \qquad (57)$$

Substituting Eq. (43), the equation for direction cosines, into Eq. (57) and simplifying, we can write

$$\cos \phi_1 \cos \phi_2 + \sin \phi_1 \sin \phi_2 + \cot \theta_1 \cot \theta_2 = \frac{\cos \alpha}{\sin \theta_1 \sin \theta_2}. \qquad (58)$$

Thus, if we obtain the vanishing points of l_1 and l_2 from the image, and use Eq. (42) to obtain (θ_1, ϕ_1) and (θ_2, ϕ_2), then, using Eq. (58), we can compute α (22). Note that under the special case where the two lines are perpendicular (i.e., $\alpha = 90°$), Eq. (58) reduces to Eq. (47). Now, substituting Eq. (42) into Eq. (58) and simplifying, we obtain

$$ak^2 + bk + c = 0,$$

$$a = 1 - \cos^2 \alpha,$$

$$b = 2(v'_{x1}v'_{x2} + v'_{y1}v'_{y2}) - \cos^2 \alpha \left(v'^2_{x1} + v'^2_{y1} + v'^2_{x2} + v'^2_{y2}\right),$$

$$c = (v'_{x1}v'_{x2} + v'_{y1}v'_{y2})^2 - \cos^2 \alpha \left(v'^2_{x1} + v'^2_{y1}\right)\left(v'^2_{x2} + v'^2_{y2}\right), \qquad (59)$$

where $k = f^2$. Note that $b^2 - 4ac > 0$.

The true angle (scene angle) between two segments l_1 and l_2 is α and the image angle (i.e., between l'_1 and l'_2) is α'. If the vanishing point of the normal of the plane on which l_1 and l_2 fall is given by $v'_n = (v'_{nx}, v'_{ny})$, and if the focal length is known to be f, then the following constraint is true (39):

$$\frac{1}{2}\left(v'^2_{nx} + v'^2_{ny} + \frac{v'^2_{nx} - v'_{ny}2}{\cos \alpha'}\right) + f^2 = f\frac{\tan \alpha'}{\tan \alpha}\sqrt{v'^2_{nx} + v'^2_{ny} + f^2}. \qquad (60)$$

Now if the two lines l'_1 and l'_2 form an L-junction, by translating the image vertex of the L-junction to the origin of x'–y' coordinates, we naturally transform l_1 and l_2 such that their common endpoint falls on the line of sight (the z axis). Let β_1 and β_2 denote the angles that the transformed l_1 and l_2 make with the z axis, respectively. Let α'_1 and α'_2 denote the angles the translated image lines make with the x' axis, and α be the angle between l_1 and l_2. Then, the following angle constraint must hold:

$$\sin \beta_1 \sin \beta_2 \cos(\alpha_1' - \alpha_2') + \cos \beta_1 \cos \beta_2 = \cos \alpha. \qquad (61)$$

4.2.6. Length Constraints

Consider an image line segment with endpoints $\mathbf{p}_0' = (x_0', y_0')$ and $\mathbf{p}_1' = (x_1', y_1')$, and let $\mathbf{p}_0$ and $\mathbf{p}_1$ be the corresponding endpoints in the scene. Assuming that the true 3D length of the vector is δ, consider the resulting constraint. Let $\mathbf{p}_1'' = (x_1'', y_1'')$ be the translated point $\mathbf{p}_1'$ such that $\mathbf{p}_0'$ is translated to the origin of x'–y' coordinates, resulting in $\mathbf{p}_0$ being translated to the line of slight (the z axis). Now, let α, $0 \le \alpha < (\pi/2)$ be the angle that a line passing through the origin of the scene coordinates and through $\mathbf{p}_1''$ makes with the z axis, and let β, $0 \le \beta < (\pi/2)$ be the angle that the transformed scene vector makes with the z axis. Then, it can be shown that the distance r of point $\mathbf{p}_0$ from the focal point is given by (22)

$$r = \frac{\delta \sin(\beta - \alpha)}{\sin \alpha},$$

$$(62)$$

$$\alpha = \tan^{-1} \frac{\sqrt{x_1''^2 + y_1''^2}}{|f|}.$$

4.3. Geometrically Motivated Perspective Metaheuristics

4.3.1. Parallelism

As discussed earlier, parallel lines in a scene project to lines converging at the vanishing point in perspective projections. Hence, parallelism of lines is depicted if their perspective projections converge to the same point. Recall that the vanishing point is far from the projection of the line segment in the image and does not fall on the actual line, but rather on the extension of the edge. Hence, lines that actually meet at a point to form a junction do not constitute projections of parallel lines. Furthermore, note that generally any two lines in the image would extend to meet at an image point (unless they happen to be parallel). Therefore, it is unwise to consider any two lines whose extensions intersect at a point to be projections of parallel lines in the scene. However, if three or more lines indeed extend to meet at one point, then under the general viewpoint assumption, they indeed depict parallelism. Hence, the heuristic for detecting parallelism in perspective line drawings is stated as follows:

If the extension of three or more lines in the perspective image intersect at the same image point, then these lines are projections of parallel lines in the scene and the image point at which they intersect is their vanishing point.

4.3.2. Perpendicularity and Right Corners

We have derived several constraints on perpendicularity and right corners that can be used as meta-heuristics under the general-viewpoint assumption. If two lines have two vanishing points v_1' and v_2', and if Eq. (46) is satisfied, then the two lines are perpendicular. To detect a right corner, if a Y (fork) or arrow junction has three lines with vanishing points satisfying Eq. (50), then the junction is indeed a projection of a right corner. Note that if only one of the lines in the junction had a known vanishing point, then we can first compute the vanishing points of the other two lines in the junction on the basis of the known vanishing point using Eq. (53). Then, check if Eq. (50) is satisfied, or equivalently check Eq. (54), and establish whether the junction corresponds to a right corner. If two of the vanishing points were already established, then check if Eq. (55) is satisfied.

4.3.3. Symmetry

Let us now discuss how symmetry can be useful for recovering perspective line drawings. Unfortunately, unlike orthography, there is no simple way of detecting real 2D symmetry of a surface from its perspective view. However, for each special case of a symmetric shape, a heuristic can be developed. Such special cases may include symmetric triangles, quadrilaterals, pentagons, and other shapes. For the sake of illustration, let us discuss one case of a quadrilateral face, and consider the quadrilateral in Fig. 3.8(B) as a perspective projection of a quadrilateral face. For a quadrilateral to be symmetric, at least two of its sides must be parallel and they must be perpendicular to a bisecting (i.e., passing through the midpoints of the lines) symmetry axis. We will rely on these facts to develop the heuristic. Assume that l_1' and l_3' have been established to be parallel with a known vanishing point $\mathbf{v}' = (v_x', v_y')$, and that the midpoint projections of the two parallel line segments have been computed [See Eqs. (71) and (72)]. Define l_5' to be the line connecting between the two midpoint projections, and assume it to correspond to the axis of symmetry

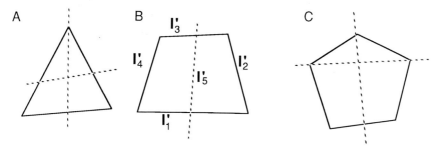

Figure 3.8. Perspective view of symmetric faces: (A) Triangular face; (B) quadrilateral face; (C) pentagonal face.

for the face. If the presumed axis of symmetry l'_5 has a 2D slope m_s and a y intercept b_s, and since the axis of symmetry is perpendicular to the two parallel lines in the quadrilateral face, then we can find the vanishing point $\mathbf{v}'_s$ of the axis of symmetry where Eq. (53) could be written as

$$v'_{xs} = -\frac{\left(f^2 + b_s v'_y\right)}{\left(v'_x + m_s v'_y\right)},$$

$$v'_{ys} = \frac{\left(b_s v'_x - m_s f^2\right)}{\left(v'_x + m_s v'_y\right)}. \tag{63}$$

Now that two lines on the planar face have known vanishing points, the gradient of the surface and the 3D coordinates of the vertices can be recovered completely (see the following subsections). Then check if the recovered surface is indeed symmetric. If that is indeed the case, then the assumption of symmetry was indeed valid, otherwise discard the assumption. For symmetry heuristics on triangles and pentagons refer to Shomar *et al.* (44).

We need a method to find the midpoint projection of a line segment with known orientation. Given a line segment l in 3D with endpoints $\mathbf{p_1} = (x_1, y_1, z_1)$ and $\mathbf{p_2} = (x_2, y_2, z_2)$ and orientation (θ, ϕ) [or equivalently, the vanishing point, $\mathbf{v}' = (v'_x, v'_y)$, is given]. Line l' is the perspective projection of l onto the image plane having endpoints $\mathbf{p}'_1 = (x'_1, y'_1)$ and $\mathbf{p}'_2 = (x'_2, y'_2)$, corresponding to $\mathbf{p_1}$ and $\mathbf{p_2}$, respectively. Line l may be described by the vector notation

$$\begin{bmatrix} x_2 \\ y_2 \\ z_2 \end{bmatrix} = \begin{bmatrix} x_1 \\ y_1 \\ z_1 \end{bmatrix} + t \begin{bmatrix} \sin\theta\cos\phi \\ \sin\theta\sin\phi \\ \cos\theta \end{bmatrix}, \tag{64}$$

where $t \in \mathcal{R}$.

Multiplying Eq. (64) by f/z_1 and substituting the perspective mapping described in Eq. (2) for the points $\mathbf{p_1}$ and $\mathbf{p_2}$, we obtain

$$\zeta \begin{bmatrix} x_2' \\ y_2' \\ f \end{bmatrix} = \begin{bmatrix} x_1' \\ y_1' \\ f \end{bmatrix} + \gamma f \begin{bmatrix} \sin\theta\cos\phi \\ \sin\theta\sin\phi \\ \cos\theta \end{bmatrix}, \tag{65}$$

where $\zeta = z_2/z_1$ and $\gamma = t/z_1$. Solving for γ from Eq. (65), we obtain

$$\gamma = \frac{x_2' - x_1'}{f\sin\theta\cos\phi - x_2'\cos\theta}. \tag{66}$$

Using the relationship between (θ, ϕ) and $\mathbf{v}'$ described in Eq. (42), Eq. (66) reduces to

$$\gamma = \frac{x_2' - x_1'}{(v_x' - x_2')\cos\theta}. \tag{67}$$

Substituting Eq. (67) into the last equation in Eq. (65), we obtain

$$\zeta = \frac{v_x' - x_1'}{v_x' - x_2'}. \tag{68}$$

If the midpoint of line l in the scene is $\mathbf{p_m} = (x_m, y_m, z_m)$ and the projection of $\mathbf{p_m}$ is $\mathbf{p_m'} = (x_m', y_m')$, then we can write

$$x_m' = f\frac{x_m}{z_m} = \frac{f(x_1 + x_2)/2}{(z_1 + z_2)/2} = \frac{fx_1}{z_1[1 + (z_2/z_1)]} + \frac{fx_2}{z_2[1 + (z_1/z_2)]}, \tag{69}$$

which reduces to

$$x_m' = \frac{x_1'}{1 + \zeta} + \frac{x_2'}{1 + (1/\zeta)}. \tag{70}$$

Substitute Eq. (68) into Eq. (70):

$$x_m' = \frac{v_x'(x_1' + x_2') - 2x_1'x_2'}{2v_x' - (x_1' + x_2')}. \tag{71}$$

The value of y'_m can be obtained by similar analysis:

$$y'_m = \frac{v'_y(y'_1 + y'_2) - 2y'_1 y'_2}{2v'_y - (y'_1 + y'_2)}. \tag{72}$$

4.3.4. 3D Orientation Recovery

Lines l_1 and l_2 are two vectors in the scene defining a plane P. If the orientations of l_1 and l_2 are (θ_1, ϕ_1) and (θ_2, ϕ_2), respectively; and P has a gradient $\mathbf{G} = (p, q)$, then the normal of P, call it $\mathbf{n}$, is given by Eq. (13) and the direction cosines of l_1 and l_2 are given by Eq. (43). Since $\mathbf{n} \perp \mathbf{c_i}$, for $i = 1, 2$, we can write

$$\mathbf{c_i} \cdot \mathbf{n} = 0. \tag{73}$$

Substitute Eqs. (13) and (43) into Eq. (73):

$$p \sin \theta_i \cos \phi_i + q \sin \theta_i \sin \phi_i \pm \cos \theta_i = 0. \tag{74}$$

Choose the negative sign in Eq. (74) without any loss of generality and solve the two linear equations of Eq. (74) for (p, q):

$$p = \frac{\cot \theta_1 \sin \phi_2 - \cot \theta_2 \sin \phi_1}{\sin(\phi_2 - \phi_1)},$$

$$q = \frac{\cot \theta_2 \cos \phi_1 - \cot \theta_1 \cos \phi_2}{\sin(\phi_2 - \phi_1)}. \tag{75}$$

Hence (p, q) of a planar surface could be computed by Eq. (75) if the orientation of two lines on that surface are known (35). Of course, if two lines with known vanishing points lie on a plane, we can again obtain the orientations of the lines, thus recovering gradient of the plane. Equivalently, if the vanishing line of a plane is known, then its orientation is determined.

Consider three planar faces of an object that are adjacent to one another. If the gradients of two adjacent surfaces were found, then the gradient of a third adjacent surface can be computed as follows. If P_1 and P_2 are the two adjacent faces with the known gradients and P_3 is the third adjacent face with the unknown gradient, and say that l'_1 is the edge common between the projections of P_1 and P_3 and l'_2 is the edge common between the projections of P_2 and P_3. Then use Eq. (37), the vanishing-line equation, and Eq. (52) to find the vanishing points of l'_1 and l'_2. The two computed vanishing points, substituted into Eq. (37), give us the gradient of P_3.

4.3.5. 3D Vertex Reconstruction

A plane P with a gradient $\mathbf{G} = (p, q)$ can be described by Eq. (14). Assume that $\mathbf{p_0} = (x_0, y_0, z_0)$ and $\mathbf{p_1} = (x_1, y_1, z_1)$ are two points on P such that

$$x_1 = x_0 + \Delta x,$$

$$y_1 = y_0 + \Delta y, \tag{76}$$

$$z_1 = z_0 + \Delta z.$$

Then, from Eq. (14) we can write

$$\Delta z = -p\,\Delta x - q\,\Delta y. \tag{77}$$

Assume that $\mathbf{p'_0} = (x'_0, y'_0)$ and $\mathbf{p'_1} = (x'_1, y'_1)$ are two points on the image plane corresponding to the projections of $\mathbf{p_0}$ and $\mathbf{p_1}$, respectively, such that

$$\Delta x' = x'_1 - x'_0,$$
$$\Delta y' = y'_1 - y'_0. \tag{78}$$

Substituting Eq. (2) into Eq. (78) and utilizing Eq. (76), we obtain

$$\Delta x' = f\frac{x_1}{z_1} - f\frac{x_0}{z_0} = f\left(\frac{x_0 + \Delta x}{z_0 + \Delta z} - \frac{x_0}{z_0}\right), \tag{79}$$

which reduces to

$$f\,\Delta x - (x'_0 + \Delta x')\,\Delta z = \Delta x'\,z_0. \tag{80}$$

Substitute Eq. (77) into Eq. (80) to obtain

$$(f + px'_1)\,\Delta x + qx'_1\,\Delta y = \Delta x'\,z_0. \tag{81}$$

By the same type of analysis on $\Delta y'$, we obtain

$$py'_1\,\Delta x + (qy'_1 + f)\,\Delta y = \Delta y'z_0. \tag{82}$$

Expressing Eqs. (81) and (82) in matrix notation, we obtain

$$\begin{bmatrix} \Delta x \\ \Delta y \end{bmatrix} = \begin{bmatrix} f + px'_1 & qx'_1 \\ py'_1 & f + qy'_1 \end{bmatrix}^{-1} \begin{bmatrix} \Delta x' \\ \Delta y' \end{bmatrix} z_0. \tag{83}$$

Substitute Eq. (83) into Eq. (76) to obtain

$$x_1 = \frac{(f + qy'_1)\,\Delta x' - qx'_1\,\Delta y'}{f^2 + f(px'_1 + qy'_1)} z_0 + x_0,$$

$$y_1 = \frac{(f + px'_1)\,\Delta y' - py'_1\,\Delta x'}{f^2 + f(px'_1 + qy'_1)} z_0 + y_0, \qquad (84)$$

$$z_1 = p(x_0 - x_1) + q(y_0 - y_1) + z_0.$$

Therefore, if we know the scene coordinates of a point on a plane for a corresponding image point, then we can obtain the scene coordinates of any other point on that plane from the image information, provided that the focal length is known.

Once the gradients of the planes are established, we are interested in recovering the 3D coordinates of the vertices. This can be accomplished by simply choosing arbitrarily a vertex and assigning it arbitrary 3D coordinates, and then using Eq. (84) to recover adjacent vertices on that plane. Propagate this process until all vertices are recovered. Recall that it is justified to assign an arbitrary vertex initial 3D coordinates due to the scale factor involved. Another way to recover the 3D coordinates is by using the backprojection equation of image points described by Eq. (41). Again, the value of S can be chosen arbitrarily due to the forementioned scale factor.

We've seen how parallelism, perpendicularity, and right corners can be detected in perspective images, and how such regularities can be used to recover the shape and orientation of objects in the scene. The perspective constraints discussed thus far can be found elsewhere in the literature (12, 14, 16, 30, 31, 34, 35, 41, 43–45, 49). There are also some other papers that have important results on perspective constraints that were not discussed here (2, 3, 13, 15, 21, 22, 39).

4.4. Perspective Shape-Recovery Systems

Most of the model-free approaches attempt to solve the shape recovery problem in two stages. The first stage involves the extraction of 3D geometric regularities from the line drawing. The second stage involves the utilization of such clues about the 3D objects for the shape-recovery process. The shape recovery involves 3D structure as well as orientation. Also, since orthographic and perspective projections exhibit different constraints on the line drawing from a computational point of view, the assumption on the type of projection of the line drawing must be made clear in the computational approach. Many researchers attempt to utilize the computational results and try to incorporate them into functional systems. An important approach is the rule-based expert systems approach. This is the approach of formulating the mathematical constraints developed in Section 3 and this section along with heuristic assumptions about the world in the form of rules. These rules would have the form IF ⟨conditions⟩ THEN ⟨actions⟩. Then have the computer allow all these rules to interact together to reach a conclusion or a finite number of conclusions about the 3D world. Two main works along such an approach to achieve a functional system are discussed in Section 5.

Many works on perspective shape recovery are based on parallel lines and vanishing points. Barnard (2) utilized perspective projection properties in determining the orientation of parallel lines and planes with a "Gaussian sphere formulation." Nelson and Young (35) utilized the vanishing point properties to detect parallelism of lines, then reconstructed 3D objects from their perspective views relying solely on the parallelism regularity and utilizing the primary face concept, where the shape and orientation of the faces in the model were adjusted iteratively so as to minimize the discrepancies between the object image and the image generated by the constructed model. Shakunaga and Kaneko (39) analyzed angle clues under perspective projection, but their formulations were complicated and limited. They provided a mathematical framework for shape-from-angle problems using a viewer-centered Gaussian sphere configuration. Mulgaonkar (32) used hypothesis based reasoning to reason about perspective line drawings using only the constraints supplied by the equations of perspective geometry, and showed that the problem is NP complete. He utilized the vanishing-point concept to develop constraints on focal length and projections of rectangles. He also developed constraints for the projections of circles.

Lin and Fu (28) used a model of an object to establish correspondence between points in the object image and points in the object model. Once this correspondence was established, the parameters of the camera system, including the orientation of the object with respect to the camera, were determined. Horaud (14), used model-based approach to interpret and derive properties of 3D physical world from viewing 2D perspective images. Image linear features and linear feature sets were backprojected onto the 3D space and geometric models were then used for selecting possible solutions. Horaud handled scenes from objects of simple geometric structure (rich in geometric regularities) as well as more complex scenes. The spatial position and orientation of each object was determined, and the method was successful for a large number of industrial objects, without requiring perfect low-level segmentation. In another paper, Horaud et al. (15) used point correspondence to find the position and orientation of a camera with respect to a scene object, using an analytical solution. An analytical solution for the perspective four-point problem was proposed, where the four points are replaced with a pencil of three lines, and the geometric constraints available with the perspective camera model were explored. Lamdan *et al.* (25), described model-based techniques for recognition of 3D objects from unknown viewpoints. Their method proved to be useful in the case of partially occluded objects and in recognition of flat industrial objects appearing in composite occluded scenes.

Haralick (12) reviewed the perspective transformation constraints, governing 2D images taken of a 3D world. He developed relationships using coordinates of points, direction cosines of lines on the image, to determine the perspective transformation parameters in closed form, as well as the 3D coordinates of the object. Haralick (13) also derived a number of perspective projection constraints, all in the reference frame of the camera, between 3D points, 3D lines, collection of 3D lines, the angles between lines lying in common planes, the planes in which lines may lie and the corresponding perspective projection of the 3D points, lines, and angles. He also pointed out that such constraints can serve as the geometric basis of a perspective projection expert system. Kanatani (22) studied the constraints on the 3D positions and orientations of line segments from a perspective view, assuming that their lengths and angles are known. He studied length constraint, where he observed two lines and assumed them to be perpendicular and was able to recover their true length uniquely. Kanatani also observed that the distinction between orthographic and perspective projections disappears for the interpretation of line or edge orientation in a *canonical position*, because in this case the 3D line orientation does not involve depth or the distance from the viewer at all.

5. RULE-BASED EXPERT SYSTEMS

5.1. System 1

This system (33) is a rule-based approach, which uses closed form equations for the inverse of the perspective transformation as modular inference engines. These inference engines use hypothesized spatial relationships between world (scene) entities to compute the unknown quantities such as distances between points, camera position, and focal length. The system is model-free, and takes a hypothesize-and-test approach to interpret the organization of the structure in the scene. The domain of the system is a world of solid objects made up of planar and cylindrical faces. The input to the system is an image consisting of edges and arcs corresponding to edges between surfaces in the scene (i.e., a "restricted" line drawing).

The system utilizes rules that govern the perspective projection process to provide tight constraints on ways in which 3D entities can be arranged in the world in order to give rise to the observed image. The system uses some of the equations of perspective geometry, organized as modular inference engines, to cooperatively process the image-level primitives and interpret the configurations in terms of a plausible arrangement of lines, points, arcs, and planes in 3D space. The system would operate on points, lines, and regions extracted by low-level feature extractors and group them into 3D structures without making any use of 3D models of a priori object-level description. The system can be thought of as two stages. The first stage is the one that incorporates the perspective constraints into the modular processes that cooperatively determine consistency of scene interpretations. The operation of these modular processes is proven to be stable and terminant, despite the fact that they operate in a distributed fashion on a shared data structure. The second stage of the system is the hypothesize-and-test paradigm for utilizing the perspective equations.

Inference engines are triggered based on their input requirements and compute values for some attributes. For example, if the hypothesis contains a relational tuple of the form (parallel $l_1 l_2$), the vanishing-point inference engine would be triggered since all parallel lines have the same vanishing point, and would compute a value for the vanishing-point attribute of l_1 and l_2. The processing involved in this case is to compute the intersection of the corresponding image lines l'_1 and l'_2. Subsequent inference engines whose computations use vanishing points may then be triggered. As we can see, inference engines are independent computational modules that compute values for attributes of an input set of relational tuples, on the basis of measurements from the image and possibly some previously computed attributes of some tuples in the input. A hypothesis is inconsistent if applications of these engines lead to distinctly different values for an attribute. To get a better understanding of how the inference engines are used, we provide the following three inference engines:

Inference engine 1. Given the hypothesis that two lines are parallel and whose images are not parallel in the image, determine the vanishing point of the lines as the intersection of their images.

Inference engine 2. Given the hypothesis that two lines are coplanar, and they do not have a common vanishing point, compute the vanishing line of their common plane.

Inference engine 3. Give a plane with a known vanishing line, compute the vanishing points of all lines hypothesized as lying in that plane.

Note that engines 1 and 3 both compute values for the same attribute—the vanishing point of the line. This is the basis for consistency checking. If a hypothesis consists of two tuples [(parallel $l_1 l_2$) (parallel $l_2 l_3$)] but does not contain the tuple parallel $l_1 l_3$, then it can be declared

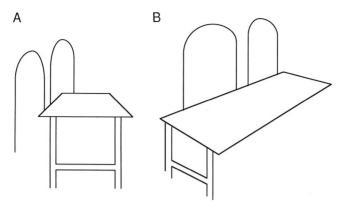

Figure 3.9. (A) A partial perspective image; (B) a perspective image of the system's outcome from another viewpoint. From Mulgaonkar *et al.* (33), ©1986 Academic Press.

inconsistent by virtue of being incomplete. Another example, if three lines l_1, l_2, and l_3 lie in a common plane with line l_2 perpendicular to both lines l_1 and l_3, then lines l_1 and l_3 must be parallel. Let us illustrate the performance of the system by an example. The system is supplied with a digitized line drawing of a perspective drawing of 3D solids taken from an unknown camera position with a camera of unknown focal length. The input can be augmented if necessary by supplying any of the unknowns such as position of some point in space or some of the camera parameters as a priori knowledge. The final output of the system is a listing of the best hypothesis along with the computed values for the numeric attributes such as coordinates of points, direction cosines of lines, and normals to planes. Figure 3.9(A) is the input digitized image. Figure 3.9(B) illustrates the result of the processing, shown as a perspective view of the structure hypothesized by the system taken from a different viewpoint.

It is noted that this approach of hypothesize and then verify is inefficient because of the large search space that the hypotheses create. The search space grows exponentially with respect to the number of lines in the image. For example, Mulgaonkar *et al.* (33) mention that four lines can participate in 12 relational tuples, resulting in a search space of $2^{12} = 4096$ possible sets of tuples. This inefficiency restricts this system from being able to use too many perspective constraints on such large search space, and limits the number of lines allowed in an image to very small (typically less than 15).

5.2. System 2

This expert system (44) formulates many of the perspective geometric constraints discussed earlier into heuristic rules and is structured in a way such that all these rules work cooperatively and interact together to deduce a conclusion on the 3D scene's orientation and structure from a single perspective line drawing. The system is model free. The expert system receives as input the perspective line-drawing image in the form of a line list. The approach here is to determine first the orientation of the line segments by geometric reasoning and then utilize the line orientations to recover *the gradient space* of all the faces in the scene. Then the expert system applies reconstruction rules to recover the 3D object coordinates, utilizing the gradient-space information of the faces. The graphics routines then transform object coordinates to camera coordinates and display the reconstructed objects and scene from different views.

The expert is divided into three primary modules: (1) low-level preprocessing of lines and junctions, (2) geometry rules, and (3) reconstruction rules for the generation of face orientation and three-dimensional object coordinates of the object's vertices. The first module of the expert is the preprocessing stage which traverses through the list of lines and detects higher level preliminary information about the object such as junctions. The list of lines may be actual edges of the object or even painted lines. Such information describe basic features about the perspective view of the object that are later utilized by the geometry rules of the expert system. The system assumes trihedral objects only, and therefore junctions are classified as arrow, Y-, L-, or T-junctions. All calculations in this preprocessing stage are carried out only in the 2D image plane. This preprocessing stage simplifies the software implementation of the rules in the expert system and accelerates the *conflict resolution* process in the *inference engine* of the rule-based expert system. The second module in the expert is the geometry rules. The expertise of the entire system is embedded in this module. The geometry rules contain low-level rules dealing with lines and higher level rules dealing with junctions, as well as the highest-level rules dealing with faces. These rules are responsible for detecting regularities in the object space that led to the given image instance recorded by the camera. The regularities consist of parallelism and perpendicularity of line segments, right corners, and parallelism of such corners. Also, symmetry rules are developed detecting symmetries of the object's faces. Furthermore, the system assumes no knowledge of the focal length of the camera that registered the image; hence geometry rules for estimating the camera's focal length were also developed and implemented. The rules of focal length estimation proved to be essential for many of the rules in the other groups. Many of the geometry rules also utilize the principle of *vanishing points*. The third module of the expert system contains the reconstruction rules. These rules utilize the established geometric regularities to represent the faces of the object in gradient space and determine the tilt and slant angles of the object's planar faces, which allow to interpret the 3D shape and orientation from the 2D image.

Since the problem of constructing a 3D model from a single perspective view is ill-posed and mathematically underconstrained, there is no guarantee that the resulting model is identical to the actual 3D object, and *certainty* (*confidence*) *factors* need to be associated with every rule, to provide the user with a measure of the system's reliability in its predictions. Associated to each of the rules are two different types of certainty factors, *evidences' certainty factors* as well as *rule's certainty factors*. These certainty factors provide a crude estimate of the probability of the rule making a correct observation or deduction. Since the certainty factors are probabilities, their values range from 0 to 1. *The evidence's certainty factor* is a measure of confidence based on the robustness and certainty factors of the parameters utilized in the rules. This certainty factor is a function of the elements' confidence of the subconditions of a rule and is computed by a formula. On the other hand, because of the certainty of the rules in general, each rule must also be assigned a subjective confidence factor, which is referred to as *the rule's certainty factor*. The rule's certainty factor simply indicates that in case the subconditions of a rule produce a certainty factor of 1, the rule itself should not; that is, the system can never be definite about a regularity prediction. *The total certainty factor* of a rule is the multiplicative product of its evidence's and rule's certainty factors. It is important to realize that each rule detects a specific regularity, and that different rules may arrive to the same conclusion, detecting the same specific regularity. Therefore, the system must have a built-in mechanism to incrementally change the certainty factor of the detected regularity as different rules arrive at the same conclusion. Obviously, the rules' total certainty factors must have direct impact on the certainty factor of the regularity it detected. This total certainty factor of a rule is incrementally assigned to the regularity the rule detects, by the simple equation

$$CF_n = CF_p + (1 - CF_p)CF_r, \tag{85}$$

where CF_n and CF_p are the new and previous certainty factors of the regularity, respectively; and CF_r is the total certainty factor of the rule that detected the regularity.

The geometry rules consist of five major groups and another group for recovering hidden lines. Each group is characterized by the geometrical regularity it detects. These regularities refer to the 3D object space and do not refer to the image plane. These regularities in turn provide us with information for reconstructing the object. The five major groups of rules detect parallelism of lines, perpendicularity of lines, right corners, parallelism of right corners, and the last major set of rules estimates the focal length of the camera lens. Note that right corners imply perpendicularity of lines, and parallel right corners imply perpendicularity as well as parallelism. Furthermore, the focal length is an essential parameter in all of the rule groups as will become evident after close examination of the geometry rules.

Some rules provide stronger evidences to the presence of a regularity than others, and therefore have higher rule's confidence factors. Also, some rules are implied in others, where the implied rule is guaranteed to be satisfied if its implying rule was satisfied. Such implied rules are not allowed to fire if the stronger rule have already fired, detecting the same regularity. A detailed architecture of the system is beyond the scope of this chapter (44).

The expert system consists of over 50 heuristic rules dealing with the detection of parallelism and perpendicularity of lines, right corners and parallelism of right corners, the focal length estimation, recovery of hidden lines and junctions, 3D reconstruction of vertices and surfaces, as well as symmetry rules. Let us illustrate what types of heuristic rules exist in the system by examining a small sample of these rules. For example, a rule for detecting parallelism was in fact stated as a heuristic in Section 4.3.1. Also, from Eqs. (46) or (50) and the fact that the extension of the perspective projection of parallel lines meeting in their vanishing point, the following two rules are stated:

Rule 1. Let μ'_1 be the intersecting point of two or more extended line segments and μ'_2 be the intersection point of another set of line segments. If the focal length of the camera lens is known, denoted by f, and if $\mu'_1 \cdot \mu'_2 = -f^2$, then μ'_1 and μ'_2 are vanishing points, and the two sets of parallel line segments are perpendicular.

Rule 2. Let μ'_1, μ'_2, and μ'_3 be the intersecting points of extended edges of two Y/arrow junctions. If $\mu'_1 \cdot \mu'_2 = \mu'_2 \cdot \mu'_3 = \mu'_3 \cdot \mu'_1 = -f^2$, then μ'_i are vanishing points for $i = 1, 2, 3$, and the two junctions are projections of parallel right corners.

The key idea and the underlying presumption behind rules 1 and 2 is the fact that it is highly unlikely for the dot product of two intersection points in the image plane to be accidentally equal to the negative of the square of the focal length, without having perpendicular sets of parallel lines in the original object. Note also that as the Hasian distance between lines increases, the discretization errors decrease. As a result, the evidences' certainty factors of rules 1 and 2 are proportional to the lengths of the line segments, the certainty of the focal length f, and the Hasian distances separating the parallel lines, and inversely proportional to the *equality error threshold*. The equality error threshold is simply the margin of error allowed because of the digitization truncations and approximations. So, for two quantities to be considered equal, the absolute difference between them must be less than a certain threshold level, which is determined based on the equipment specifications used in obtaining the experimental data. Rules 1 and 2 are relatively strong evidences, and hence are assigned a relatively high rule's certainty factor. Also note that rules 1 and 2 assume that the focal length of the camera lens has been established by other rules.

It is noted that right corners can be detected using rules based on constraints in Eqs. (54) and (55). In addition, a rule on parallelism of right corners that utilizes Eq. (55) states:

Rule 3. If two Y/arrow junctions share a common edge with slope m_3 and y intercept b_3, if the remaining two pairs of edges intersect by extension at μ'_1 and μ'_2 with $\mu'_1 \cdot \mu'_2 = -f^2$, and if Eq. (55) is satisfied, then the two junctions are projections of parallel right corners.

Since the focal length parameter is extensively used by many of the rules mentioned above, the focal length group is of utmost importance and essentiality. The focal length rules fall into three classes. The first class is dependent on parallelism (vanishing points) and perpendicularity of pairs of parallel lines. The second class would be dependent on single Y or arrow junction and the concepts of right corners. Finally, the third class is dependent on pairs of Y/arrow junctions and the concepts of parallel right corners. Many of the focal length rules are simply the inverse of rules of the other groups. Rule 1, for example, can be modified to estimate the focal length. This is illustrated by the following rule:

Rule 4. If two sets of parallel lines with vanishing points v'_1 and v'_2 are perpendicular, then $f = \sqrt{-v'_1 \cdot v'_2}$.

The evidences' certainty factor of rule 4 is directly proportional to the confidence of the parallelism of the two sets of lines as well as the confidence of the perpendicularity of the sets. The parallelism and perpendicularity of lines is assumed to have been established by other rules. Rule 4 is a very strong evidence for the focal length estimation and has a high rule's certainty factor.

For illustrative purposes, three more rules on focal length estimation are mentioned.

Rule 5. Given a broad Y or arrow junction. If v'_1, v'_2, and v'_3 are known and $v'_1 \cdot v'_2 = v'_2 \cdot v'_3 = v'_3 \cdot v'_1 < 0$, then $f = \sqrt{-v'_1 \cdot v'_2}$.

Rule 6. If the angle is α between the two sets of parallel lines with known vanishing points v'_1 and v'_2, then f can be estimated as $f = \sqrt{k}$, provided that a positive solution of k exists that satisfies Eq. (59).

Apply (55) on $\mu'_i = (u'_{xi}, u'_{yi})$ for $i = 1, 2$ and substituting $-\mu'_1 \cdot \mu'_2$ for f^2, then by simple algebraic manipulations, we could write the following:

$$-\mu'_1 \cdot \mu'_2 = \frac{b_3(u'_{x1}u'_{y2} - u'_{x2}u'_{y1})}{u'_{x2} - u'_{x1} + m_3(u'_{y2} - u'_{y1})} = c^2 \qquad (86)$$

Rule 7. If two Y/arrow junctions have a common edge with slope m_3 and y intercept b_3, if the remaining two pairs of edges intersect by extension at μ'_1 and μ'_2, and if Eq. (86) is satisfied for $\mu'_i = (u'_{xi}, u'_{yi})$ then μ'_i are vanishing points for $i = 1, 2$; and $f = |c|$.

One problem that arises in the shape recovery from line drawings which we have yet to stress is the hidden-line problem. Since most objects are opaque, the problem of occluded edges, vertices, and surfaces arises. That is the fact that in perspective view, many lines that belong to farther faces from the viewer are hidden by a closer opaque face. In the development of this expert system, scene labeling and symmetry assumptions were utilized for the recovery of occluded edges and vertices at three different levels: wireframe, face, as well as volumetric. Furthermore, some hidden-line recovery rules were applied on the image domain while others were applied on the parameters of the 3D scene domain that is already recovered from other rules. These rules will not be discussed in detail; however, for illustrative purposes we will mention a hidden-line recovery rule that does not require any knowledge of scene labeling or symmetry.

Rule 8. If the stems of two T junctions are separated by a negligible Hasian distance, then the stems are projections of two segments of the same line, and are replaced by a single line segment extending from the "extreme endpoints" of the two stems.

The system also includes symmetry rules for triangular, quadrilateral, and pentagonal faces. Also, the system utilizes the scene labeling information to distinguish multiple objects in the scene. At this point, the geometric regularities that have "high" certainty factors are established as true, and the ones with "low" certainty factors are discarded. Once the geometric regularities are established, the system uses these regularities to compute the gradients of the faces. For example, if a face contains line segments belonging to two different sets of parallel lines, then the orientations of these lines can be established from their vanishing points using Eq. (42); then Eq. (75) can be used to uniquely establish the gradient of that face. After determining the gradients of all the faces, then use Eq. (84) to recover the 3D scene coordinates, relative to some reference vertex, as discussed in Section 4.3.5.

Because of the computational complexity of some of the heuristic rules and with the vast number of rules and their interactions, efficiency considerations of the system was also an important issue. The system's performance was noticed to degrade significantly with the number of lines in the scene due to the vast combinations of computational complexities. Also, as the scene contained more lines, the amount of memory page swapping increased significantly and heavily slowed down the system. At this point, it was decided to modify the expert system, such that the system

A

B

C

D

E

F

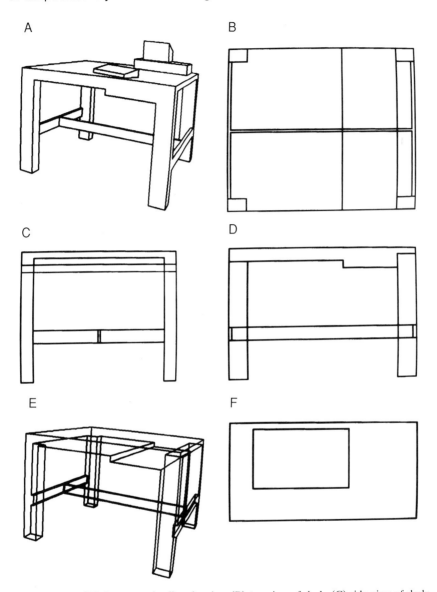

Figure 3.10. (A) A perspective line drawing; (B) top view of desk; (C) side view of desk; (D) front view of desk; (E) desk with recovered hidden lines; (F) top view of computer; (*Figure continues.*)

first counts the number of lines constituting the object. Then, if the object contains more than 30 lines, it would be partitioned into multiple sub-objects. If the subobjects also contain more than 30 lines, they are also partitioned. This process is carried out until all subobjects contain less than 30 lines. Then the system is sequentially applied on each partition independently. Then, when the regularities for all partitions are detected, the system groups the subobjects back together by utilizing the common edges among different parts of the total object and compares the regulari-

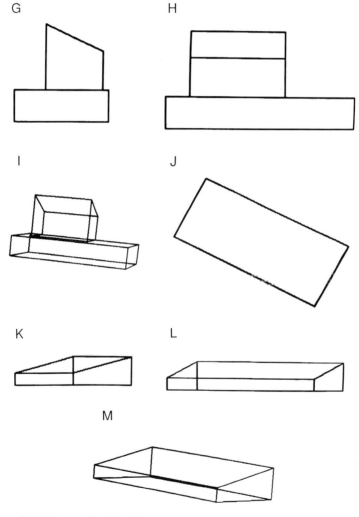

Figure 3.10 (*Continued*) (G) side view of computer; (H) front view of computer; (I) computer with recovered hidden lines; (J) top view of keyboard; (K) side view of keyboard; (L) front view of keyboard; (M) keyboard with recovered hidden lines.

ties for the entire object. Obviously, this method increased the performance of the system by a very large factor. However, the problem with such a strategy is that regularities that can be detected only across subobjects will not be detected. The justification to this strategy is the fact that if the object is so large, then the system should be able to find enough regularities in the subobjects to reconstruct the entire object.

The expert system was implemented in OPS5 (Official Production System 5), along with some Lisp and Pascal external routines for computations and graphics routines, on a VMS microVax system. Let us demonstrate the robustness of the system by illustrating an example. Consider the perspective line drawing in Fig. 3.10(A). The line drawing is an image of a simulated desk with a computer terminal and keyboard resting on it. This line drawing was input to the expert system in the form of a list of line segments described solely by the 2D image coordinates of their endpoints. Note that no other information was provided to the system, and the system had no a priori knowledge about the object. The system was able to successfully reconstruct and recover the 3D shape and orientation of the object, including the occluded parts, based on perspective rules and constraints similar to the ones discussed in this chapter. For clarity purposes, the outcome of the system for this example was partitioned into three different parts—the desk, the computer terminal, and the keyboard; each part was displayed and illustrated separately. To demonstrate the outcome of the system, the system has display capabilities to display the orthographic top, side, and front views of the object as well as the reconstructed perspective view of the object with the recovered hidden lines included. These views for the desk are illustrated in Figs. 3.10(B), (C), (D), and (E), respectively. Figures 3.10(F), (G), (H), and (I) demonstrate the reconstruction of the computer terminal; and Fig. 3.10(J), (K), (L) and (M) demonstrate the reconstruction of the keyboard. Note that in reality the system produced the outcome of the example as one entity, but the display was partitioned into logical entities simply for ease of interpretation for the observer. As one can see, the outcome of the system is in full agreement with human perception and expectations.

ACKNOWLEDGMENT

This work was supported in part by the National Science Foundation under grant IRI-8711405.

REFERENCES

1. D. H. Ballard and C. M. Brown, "Computer Vision" Prentice-Hall, Englewood Cliffs, NJ, 1982.
2. S. T. Barnard, Interpreting perspective images. *Artif. Intell.* **21**, 435–462 (1983).

3. P. Bellutta, G. Collini, A. Verri, and V. Torre, 3D visual information from vanishing points. *Proc. IEEE Workshop Interpretation 3D Scenes*, Austin, TX, *1989*, pp. 41–49 (1989).

4. M. Brady, Computational approaches to image understanding. *Comput. Surv.* **14**, 3–71 (1982).

5. M. B. Clowes, On seeing things. *Artif. Intell.* **2**, 79–116 (1971).

6. S. W. Draper, The use of gradient and dual space in line drawing interpretation. *Artif. Intell.* **17**, 461–508 (1981).

7. G. Falk, Interpretation of imperfect line data as a 3D scene. *Artif. Intell.* **3**, 101–144 (1972).

8. S. A. Friedberg, Finding axes of skewed symmetry. *Comput. Vision, Graphics, Image Process.* **34**, 138–155 (1986).

9. Y. Fukui, T. Ohira, and Y. Kishi, An Input Method for Solid Models by Drawing," Reprint. Industrial Products Research Institute, Ministry of International Trade and Industry of Japan, 1983.

10. G. R. Grape, "Model Based (Intermediate Level) Computer Vision," Stanford Artificial Intelligence Memo AIM-201 (STAN-CS-73-366) Stanford University, Stanford, CA, 1972.

11. A. Guzman, "Computer Recognition of 3D Objects in a Visual Scene," Tech. Rep. MAC-TR-59. Massachusetts Institute of Technology, Artificial Intelligence Laboratory, Cambridge, MA, 1968.

12. R. M. Haralick, Using perspective transformations in scene analysis. *Comput. Vision, Graphics, Image Process.* **13**, 191–221 (1980).

13. R. M. Haralick, Monocular vision using inverse perspective projection geometry: Analytic relations. *Proc. IEEE Conf. Comput. Vision Pattern Recognition*, San Diego, CA, *1989*, pp. 370–378 (1989).

14. R. Horaud, New methods for matching 3D objects with single perspective views. *IEEE Trans. Pattern Anal. Mach. Intell.* **PAMI-9** (3), 401–412 (1987).

15. R. Horaud, B. Conio, and O. Leboullex, An analytic solution for the perspective 4-point problem. *Proc. IEEE Conf. Comput. Vision Pattern Recognition*, San Diego, CA., *1989*, pp. 500–507 (1989).

16. B. K. P. Horn, Obtaining shape from shading information. In "The Psychology of Computer Vision" (P. H. Winston, ed.). McGraw-Hill, New York, 115–155, 1975.

17. D. A. Huggman, Impossible objects as nonsense sentences. In "Machine Intelligence" (B. Meltzer and D. Michie, (Eds.), Vol. 6, pp. 295–323. Edinburg Univ. Press, Edinburgh, 1971.

18. T. Kanade, A theory of origami world. *Artif. Intell.* **13**, 279–311 (1980).

19. T. Kanade, Recovery of the 3D shape of an object from a single view. *Artif. Intell.* **17**, 409–460 (1981).

20. T. Kanade, Geometrical aspects of interpreting images as a 3D scene. *Proc. IEEE* **71**, (7), 789–802 (1983).

21. K. Kanatani, The constraints on images of rectangular polyhedra. *IEEE Trans. Pattern Anal. Mach. Intell.* **PAMI-8** (4), 456–463 (1986).

22. K. Kanatani, Constraints on length and angle. *Comput. Vision, Graphics, Image Process.* **41**, 28–42 (1988).

23. J. R. Kender, Shape from texture: A computational paradigm. *Proc. DARPA Image Understanding Workshop*, *1979*, pp. 134–138 (1979).

24. G. Lafue, A theorem prover for recognizing 2D representations of 3D objects. In "Artificial Intelligence and Pattern Recognition in Computer Aided Design," (J. C. Latombe, ed.), pp. 391–401. North-Holland Publ., Amsterdam, 1978.

25. Y. Lamdan, J. T. Schwartz, and H. J. Wolfson, On recognition of 3D objects from 2D images. *Proc. IEEE Int. Conf. Robotics Autom.* Philadelphia, *1988,* pp. 1407–1413 (1988).

26. H. C. Lee and K. S. Fu, Generating object description for model retrieval. *IEEE Trans. Pattern Anal. Mach. Intell.* **PAMI-5,** 462–471 (1983).

27. M. Liardet, C. Holmes, and D. Rosenthal, Input to CAD systems—Two practical examples, "Artificial Intelligence and Pattern Recognition in Computer Aided Design," In J. C. Latombe, (ed.), pp. 403–427. North-Holland Publ., Amsterdam, 1978.

28. W. C. Lin and K. S. Fu, Estimation of three-dimensional object orientation for computer vision systems with feedback. *J. Robotic Syst.* **1**(1), 59–82 (1984).

29. H. Liu, T. Y. Young and A. Das, A multilevel parallel processing approach to scene labeling problems. *IEEE Trans. Pattern Anal. Mach. Intell.* **10**, 586–590 (1988).

30. A. K. Mackworth, Interpreting pictures of polyhedral scenes. *Artif. Intell.* **4**, 121–137 (1973).

31. G. Markowsky and M. A. Wesley, Fleshing out wire frames. *IBM J. Res. Dev.* **24**, 582–597 (1980).

32. P. G. Mulgaonkar, *Analyzing perspective line drawings using hypothesis based reasoning*. Ph.D. Thesis, Virginia Polytechnic Institute and State University, Blacksburg, 1984.

33. P. G. Mulgaonkar, L. G. Shapiro, and R. M. Haralick, Shape from perspective: A rule-based approach. *Comput. Vision, Graphics, Image Process.* **36**, 298–320 (1986).

34. H. Nakatani and T. Kitahashi, Inferring 3D shape from line drawings using vanishing points. *Proc. Int. Conf. Comput. Appl. 1st*, Peking, *1984*, pp. 683–688 (1984).

35. R. N. Nelson and T. Y. Young, Determining three-dimensional object shape and orientation from a single perspective view. *Opt. Eng.* **25**, 394–401 (1986).

36. L. Roberts, Machine perception of 3D solids. In "Optical and Electro-Optical Information Processing" (*J. Tippett* et al., pp. 159–197. MIT Press, Cambridge, MA, 1965.

37. G. J. Salem and T. Y. Young. A neural network approach to the labeling of line drawings. *IEEE Trans. Comput.* **12**, 1419–1424 (1992).

38. S. A. Shafer and T. Kanade, Gradient space under orthography and perspective. *Comput. Vision, Graphics, Image Process.* **24**, 182–199 (1983).

39. T. Shakunaga and H. Kaneko, Perspective angle transform and its application to 3D configuration recovery. *Proc. IEEE Conf. Comput. Vision Pattern Recognition*, Miami Beach, FL, *1986*, pp. 594–601 (1986).

40. R. Shapira, A technique for the reconstruction of a straight edge, wire frame object from two or more central projections. *Comput. Vision, Graphics, Image Process.* **3**, 318–326 (1974).

41. R. Shapira, The use of objects' faces in interpreting line drawings. *IEEE Trans. Pattern Anal. Mach. Intell.* **PAMI-6**, 789–794 (1984).

42. R. Shapira and H. Freeman, The cyclic order property of vertices as an aid in scene analysis. *Commun. ACM* **22**, 368–375 (1979).

43. W. J. Shomar, An expert system for recovering 3D shape and orientation from a single perspective view. Master's Thesis, University of Miami, Coral Gables, FL, Department of Electrical and Computer Engineering, 1988.

44. W. J. Shomar, G. Seetharaman, and T. Y. Young, An expert system for recovering 3D shape and orientation from a single view. *In* "Computer Vision and Image Processing" (L. Shapiro and A. Rosenfeld, eds.), pp. 459–515. Academic Press, San Diego, CA, 1992.

45. K. A. Stevens, The visual interpretation of surface contours. *Artif. Intell.* **17**, 47–73 (1981).

46. K. Sugihara, Picture language for skeletal polyhedra. *Comput. Vision, Graphics Image Process.* **8**, 382–405 (1978).

47. K. Sugihara, "Machine Interpretation of Line Drawings." MIT Press, Cambridge, MA and London, 1986.

48. I. Weiss, 3D shape representation by contour. *Comput. Vision, Graphics, Image Process.* **41**, 80–100 (1988).

49. T. Y. Young, G. Seetharaman, and W. J. Shomar, A rule based system for 3D shape recovery from a single perspective view. *SPIE Conf. App. Artif. Intell 6th*, Orlando, FL, *1988*, pp. 294–302 (1988).

Chapter **4**

Recovery of Three-Dimensional Shape of Curved Objects from a Single Image

RAMAKANT NEVATIA and MOURAD ZERROUG

Institute for Robotics and Intelligent Systems
University of Southern California
Los Angeles, California

FATIH ULUPINAR

Department of Computer and Information Science
Bilkent University
Ankara, Turkey

1. INTRODUCTION

A key task of a vision system is to recover a description of a scene from an image of that scene. Part of this description is the 3D shape of the different objects in the viewed scene. This is a difficult problem as the projection of the 3D world onto a 2D image is, in general, not invertible.

101

Use of multiple images does help as 3D measurements of at least several points in the scene can be obtained if these points can be matched and the relative geometry of the viewing positions of the different images is known. Such analysis, however, presents its own difficulties, and some of the approaches require elaborate calibration procedures. Single images are much more economical and easier to acquire and being able to use them would be 'highly useful for machine vision systems. Our faith in the possibility of 3D shape recovery from a single 2D image comes primarily from observations of the human visual system. For most tasks, humans can perform almost as well with one eye closed and no head (or object) motion.

Several cues, such as contour, shading and texture, can be used to recover shape from a single image. Object contours convey rich geometric information and are stable with respect to illumination changes. *Shading* refers to reflectance properties of an object's surface, which depend both on its shape and the illumination conditions. Thus, prior knowledge of photometric properties is needed to exploit shading. Use of texture requires presence (and assumption) of some uniform pattern on the surface. Experiments with humans indicate also that the contour is as good for recognition as a full-color image (2) and that in case of conflicts, contour cues generally dominate the shading cues (1). We will focus on methods to infer shape from contour, although it is possible to combine these methods with information from other cues (7).

Before engaging in a description of the different methods, we should clarify what is meant by shape recovery. Shape can be described in a number of ways. At the simplest level, the object surface is described by an array of 3D positions, or by a set of normal vectors to it. However, for many purposes, it is desirable to have more abstract, higher-level representations for the shape. By 3D shape recovery, we refer to the method(s) used for producing a description of an object in terms of the desired shape description scheme. This chapter does not deal with shape descriptions per se, but some of the techniques we describe do attempt to infer the higher level descriptions directly.

Note also that when we are given an image of a scene, the objects in it (and their contours) are not given to us in a segmented form. In fact, one of the reasons to recover 3D shape is to have more reliable object segmentation. Ability of a method to work with nonsegmented images (actually produce segmentations) is thus an important criterion by which to judge its suitability for specific tasks.

The methods that can be used thus may differ in the following ways: the types of cues used (contour, shading, texture), the nature of the input they assume (real images or segmented objects), the class of objects they handle, and the type of output they produce.

The discussion is organized as follows. In Section 2, we first describe the problems of inferring shape from contour. In Section 3, we describe methods for inferring shape given perfect contours. In Section 4, we describe methods that deal with real images. We summarize this chapter in Section 5.

2. ISSUES IN THREE-DIMENSIONAL SHAPE RECOVERY FROM CONTOUR

An inherent difficulty in recovering shape from contour is caused by the process of image formation, which consists of a projection of the 3D scene onto the 2D image. This is not an invertible transformation, and an infinite number of possible 3D shapes can produce the same 2D contours. Nonetheless, when presented with 2D line drawings, humans rarely experience this ambiguity and have no difficulty perceiving clear 3D shapes in most cases. Also, the perception of 3D shape is largely invariant to the viewpoint from which the image was acquired. This is not to say that the human visual system cannot be fooled, only that in our everyday experience, the 3D inference provided is rarely wrong. This leads us to believe that some additional assumptions can help provide constraints to resolve the ambiguities caused by projection, and that these assumptions hold in most real cases.

Understanding this problem from a computational standpoint, in order to develop methods of shape from contour, continues to be one of the most challenging problems in computer vision. Research on shape from contour has attempted to understand the constraints that the visible contours provide on the shapes they represent, and how to use those constraints, in a viewpoint-independent manner, in order to limit the set of possible solutions to just a few, possibly one. The constraints can come from purely geometric considerations or from some preference criteria that favor certain interpretations over others. Note that since the shape recovery problem from a single image is not completely solvable in a mathematical sense, our chief criterion for measuring success becomes that of comparing with human performance. Even in scenes where "ground" truth is known (i.e., where we know the 3D shape of the object), the correct answer could well be another shape that *could* have given rise to the same contours. Thus, throughout this chapter, we will appeal to the reader's own perception in judging whether a certain technique performs well.

One additional difficulty in relating image contour properties to 3D shape is that not all contours are projections of viewpoint-independent object edges, namely, surface intersections. For curved objects, having nonplanar surfaces, some of the viewed contours are inherently viewpoint-dependent. This is the case of *extremal contours* (also called "limbs") where the viewing direction is tangential to the surface. Although qualitative shape relationships exist between projections of extremal contours and 3D shape near those contours (10, 16), such extremal contours by themselves are not sufficient to recover the whole object shape.

Furthermore, image contours may result not only from geometric contours such as surface intersections or limb boundaries but also from surface markings (reflectance discontinuities), shadows (illumination discontinuities), and noise. We must distinguish between these kinds of boundaries to be able to correctly infer shape. The problem is compounded by the fact that the desired object boundaries are often fragmented as the result of noise and low contrast, and parts of them may be obscured by other objects in the scene. Completion of object boundaries, while separating the other boundaries, such as those from shadows and markings, is the problem of object segmentation; this is known, in psychology, as the *figure–ground* problem. While this chapter does not focus on *image* segmentation methods, *object* segmentation seldom can be separated from its shape recovery.

We first discuss methods that assume that the segmentation problem has been solved and that perfect contours are given and then describe some emerging approaches to deal with real images.

3. SHAPE FROM PERFECT CONTOURS

Even when a perfect contour is given, an infinite number of 3D shapes can project to this contour from some given viewpoint (see Fig. 4.1). We need some way of choosing a small set (usually a singleton) among these possibilities.

We classify the methods for inferring shape from contours into two broad categories. The first, which we will call *extremal* methods, attempt

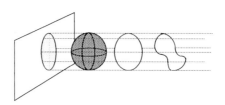

Figure 4.1. Ambiguities of shape from contour.

to recover the 3D shape by preferring the interpretation that optimizes a given measure from the observed contours, usually a regularity measure such as smoothness or compactness of shape. The second class of methods, which we will call *constraint-based* methods, use rules for generating constraints on the 3D surface orientations from 2D contours. The rigorous constraints, however, are seldom sufficient, and additional assumptions, such as regularity of the surface, need to be incorporated.

To make this chapter self-contained, we first provide a brief introduction to orthographic projection and gradient space representation, both of which are used in most methods we will discuss.

An orthographic projection of a 3D point $P = (x, y, z)^t$ on a plane $\mathscr{P}$ is the intersection point of the line orthogonal to $\mathscr{P}$ passing through P and the plane $\mathscr{P}$. Thus the direction of an orthographic projection is constant and parallel to the normal of the projection plane. For example, if the image plane $\mathscr{P}$ is parallel to the world x–y plane, then a point $P = (x, y, z)^t$ projects as point $p = (x, y)^t$. In most imaging situations, the more accurate projection model is that of *perspective* projection where the projection rays are not parallel but converge to a single point (the center of projection or the focal point). However, the orthographic projection is commonly used as the projected contours have simpler properties (e.g., parallel lines project into parallel lines) and it is a reasonable approximation when the viewed objects are far compared to the focal length of the imaging device. Although some of the methods we describe can be extended to perspective projection (27), we will limit ourselves to orthographic projection in this chapter.

The gradient space is used to represent surface normal vectors. A surface normal $N = (n_x, n_y, n_z)$ is represented in gradient space as $(p, q, 1)^t$, where $p = n_x/n_z$ and $q = n_y/n_z$ (assuming $n_z \neq 0$) (see Fig. 4.2); $n_z = 0$ only for orientations parallel to the image plane (orthogonal to the line of sight) which are not represented in gradient space. Only a two-dimensional space (also p–q space) is needed to represent surface normals. Each point $(p, q)^t$ in the gradient space corresponds to one 3D

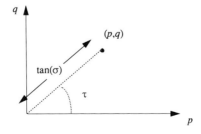

Figure 4.2. Gradient space representation of surface orientations.

vector (or its reverse orientation). Another slightly different representation of surface normals uses their 3D angles τ and σ called *tilt* and *slant*, respectively. For a gradient (p, q), the tilt is given by $\arctan(q/p)$ and the slant by $\arctan(\sqrt{p^2 + q^2})$.

3.1. Extremal Methods

Extremal methods select, among the potentially infinite set of solutions of the inverse projection problem, one solution that optimizes some chosen criterion. We discuss two such criteria: the compactness of shape and its smoothness.

3.1.1. Shape Compactness

Brady and Yuille (4) proposed a method for recovering the orientation of a planar surface that consists of finding the 3D orientation such that the recovered shape is the most *compact*. The compactness of a shape bounded by a closed curve is defined as

$$c = \frac{area}{(\,perimeter\,)^2}. \tag{1}$$

The selected interpretation is obtained through a search, over possible 3D orientations of the desired planar surface. This measure has an upper bound of $1/4\pi$, which holds for a circle, the most compact planar shape. Its lower bound is zero, which holds for a line segment. The search is over a 2D space of the slant and tilt of the desired orientation.

This method will interpret an ellipse as a slanted circle, usually in agreement with human perception (though humans sometimes just prefer to see the ellipse in the plane of the image). However, it can give counterintuitive results. For example, it interprets a rectangle as a slanted square. It is also restricted to planar shapes where the closed boundary is available.

3.1.2. Shape Smoothness

In this method, first proposed by Barrow and Tenenbaum (1), among all curves that could project into the given 2D curve, we choose the one that is the *smoothest*. The recovered curve is not necessarily planar, nor is the given 2D curve required to be closed. The smoothness measure used by

Barrow and Tennenbaum is the integral

$$\int (k'^2 + k^2 t^2)\, ds, \tag{2}$$

where k and t are, respectively, the curvature and torsion of the desired curve, k' is the derivative of k, and s is the arclength. The "best" interpretation under this criterion is the one that minimizes Eq. (2). The solution is found through an iterative optimization procedure. If planar shapes are assumed, the integral in Eq. (2) becomes simpler as the second term vanishes (zero torsion t), resulting in a faster search. Given the boundaries of an ellipse, for example, this method too recovers a slanted circle [for which Eq. (2) is identically zero]. This method recovers only a 3D curve. For points of that curve that lie on a limb boundary, the surface orientations are uniquely determined since, at each such point, the tangent plane is determined by the 3D curve tangent and the viewing direction. However, curve orientations at discontinuity boundaries only partially fix local surface orientations (to 1 degree of freedom). These boundary constraints are used in an interpolation process that recovers internal surface orientations.

A major drawback of the method is its sensitivity to noise in the boundary as it uses third-order derivatives. Thus, an ellipse with a small notch will no longer be interpreted as a slanted circle, as the corresponding errors will dominate Eq. (2).

Weiss (30) has proposed a modified smoothness measure using only the square of the curvature for planar shapes. For polygonal shapes the measure is based on squares of corner angles. The squared curvature method is less sensitive to noise than the method described above.

3.1.3. Discussion

The strong point of extremal methods is that they use well-defined computational tools that are simple and easy to implement. Their disadvantage, however, is that they ignore global information often captured by interactions between contours, such as symmetries. Our perception of a surface shape is affected not only by the contours that bound it but also by other surfaces. This is illustrated in Fig. 4.3.

To be able to provide a method with such ability requires explicit analysis of such global information. The discussion in the next section, includes some recovery methods that have this ability.

A   B

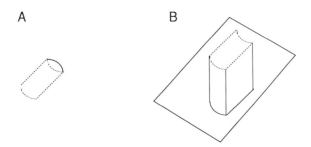

Figure 4.3. Shape perception depends on interaction of surfaces: (A) a cylindrical surface is perceived; (B) the same surface might be perceived as a planar side of a book.

3.2. Constraint-Based Methods

Unlike extremal methods that view shape recovery as a single uncon-strained optimization problem, constraint-based methods select a solution that satisfies certain constraints derived from observed properties of image contours. Those properties consist of regularity relationships between contours. The relationships are often captured by certain types of symme-tries that we introduce later. Such constraints often restrict the possible solutions to specific curves in the gradient space. Selection of "preferred" solutions requires usage of additional constraints based on other regularity criteria. Different proposed methods use different constraints and prefer-ence criteria.

Typically, these methods apply to only a certain class of shapes. In what follows, we will discuss four such methods. We begin with a method that applies to planar surfaces only but provides a foundation for extensions to more complex surfaces. The subsequent methods apply to surfaces of increasing complexity.

3.2.1. Recovering Planar Surfaces

This method exploits presence of skew symmetries, defined below, in an image [see Fig. 4.4(A)].

3.2.1.1. Definition

Definition 1. Two curves C_1 and C_2 are *skewed symmetric* if there exist a pointwise correspondence between points of C_1 and points of C_2 such that

- Segments joining corresponding points are mutually parallel.
- The locus of midpoints of those segments is a straight line, called *axis of skew symmetry*.

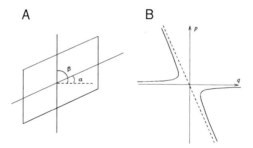

Figure 4.4. Example of skew symmetry: (A) symmetric figure; (B) its constraint hyperbola in gradient space.

The (constant) angle between correspondence segments and axis of symmetry need not be 90° in the image. An orthogonal symmetry in 3D can be easily shown to project to a skew symmetry; however, the inverse is not necessarily the case. Kanade (9) proposed a method that assumes that the inverse is also true (that the 2D skew symmetry is, in fact, a projection of an orthogonal 3D symmetry). This assumption can be used to obtain a constraint on the orientation of the plane in which the symmetric curves lie.

Let the curves lie on a plane given by (p, q) in the gradient space; let the unit vector, representing the direction of correspondence, form an angle α with the x axis of the image; and let β be the angle between the unit vector representing the direction of the axis of skew symmetry and the image x axis. Then, the 3D correspondence direction is given by the vector $a = (\cos \alpha, \sin \alpha, p \cos \alpha + q \sin \alpha)^t$, and the 3D axis direction by $b = (\cos \beta, \sin \beta, p \cos \beta + q \sin \beta)^t$.

The 3D symmetry is orthogonal if $a \cdot b = 0$, where "$\cdot$" denotes vector dot product. Rewriting the (p, q) coordinates of the planar surface orientation, after a rotation by $\lambda = (\alpha + \beta)/2$, we obtain the following *constraint equation*:

$$p'^2 \cos^2\left(\frac{\alpha - \beta}{2}\right) - q'^2 \sin^2\left(\frac{\alpha - \beta}{2}\right) + \cos(\alpha - \beta) = 0, \qquad (3)$$

where (p', q') is the gradient in the rotated system.

This is the equation of a hyperbola that constrains the orientation of the 3D plane [in gradient space; see Fig. 4.4(B)] but does not give a unique answer. For a single face, in absence of other evidence, one may choose the point nearest to the origin of the gradient space as the "preferred" interpretation (corresponding to the minimum slant orientation).

When observing several planes meeting at a single vertex, other constraints can be used. Suppose that three faces meet at a vertex and each one is skew symmetric. In this case, the orientation of each face is constrained to be on a hyperbola in gradient space. In addition, another constraint relates the relative orientations of those faces that intersect, as described below.

If two planes $\mathcal{P}_1$ and $\mathcal{P}_2$ intersect in a line L_{12}, then the line joining their corresponding orientations, (p_1, q_1) and (p_2, q_2) in the gradient space, must be perpendicular to the line L_{12} (in the image space). This constraint has been used in an earlier polyhedral scene analysis system (12). We will call this the *shared boundary constraint* (it can also be generalized to apply to curved surface intersections, as discussed later).

Returning to the example of three faces intersecting at a vertex, we can now add three shared boundary constraints between the three faces. These, in addition to the three skew symmetry constraints, give six equations for six unknowns. In general, a unique solution can be obtained.

3.2.2. Recovering Cylindrical Surfaces

Stevens (23) extended the orthogonal interpretation to curved surfaces and derived a method for recovery of cylindrical shapes. In this method, lines of minimum and maximum curvature are assumed to be given. Knowing that lines of curvature are orthogonal in 3D, we can use an approach similar to Kanade's to recover 3D orientations at the intersection of those lines. The method uses the slant–tilt representation of surface orientations. Observing that slant and tilt are bounded and that bounds depend on the 2D skew angle β between (projections of) lines of curvature, Stevens proposed to compute 3D orientation, first at minimum tilt error points then to propagate the results along lines of maximum curvature (for a cylindrical surface, surface orientations do not change along lines of minimum curvature). Initial computations are done at points near occlusion boundaries of the cylindrical surface, where $\beta = \pi$. The propagation is done using the relationship between tilts, τ_1 and τ_2, and the skew angles β_1 and β_2 at two neighboring points along each line of maximum curvature (see Fig. 4.5)

$$\tan \tau_1 \tan \beta_1 = \tan \tau_2 \tan \beta_2. \tag{4}$$

A generalization of this method to noncylindrical surfaces is given in Xu and Tsuji (31). This method too requires that the surface be cut along the lines of curvature. Further, the propagation method is only an approximation and can allow errors to build up.

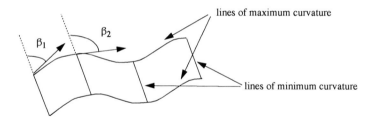

Figure 4.5. Cylindrical shape recovery.

3.2.3. Recovering Generalized Cylinders

Generalized cylinders are an attempt to find generic models for a variety of objects encountered in our normal environment. A generalized cylinder (GC) (3) is the surface obtained by sweeping a planar cross-section curve C, along an axis A while transforming it by a function f. Depending on the shape of the cross section, the shape of the axis and nature of the function f different attributes are used to denote the type of GC at hand (22). Here, we give some of the attributes related to the classes of GCs discussed in this chapter.

A GC is said to be *homogeneous* if the transformation f does not change the shape of the cross-section curve C, although it can change its size; f is said to be a *scaling function*. The GC is said to be *linear* if the transformation function f is a linear function of the position along the axis A. A special case of homogeneous GCs is *constant* where the cross-section size remains constant. The GC is said to be *planar* if the axis curve A is planar. It is said to be *straight* if the axis is a straight line. The GC is said to be *right* if the cross-section plane is always orthogonal to the axis.

Several such attributes can be used to specify and name certain classes of GCs. For example, a GC with a straight axis and a homogeneous cross section is named *straight homogeneous generalized cylinder* (SHGC). Examples of SHGCs include vases. If the scaling function is further constrained to be linear, it is named *linear straight homogeneous generalized cylinder* (LSHGC). Examples of LSHGCs include normal cylinders and cones. Another interesting case is that of *planar, right, constant generalized cylinder* (PRCGC). Examples of PRCGCs include tori and snakes. Figure 4.6 gives some examples of SHGCs, LSHGCs, and PRCGCs. It is believed that such GCs, and objects constructed from their composition, can model a significant fraction of objects found in our normal environment.

Several classes of GCs have been addressed in the research community. Solids of revolution (SORs), a special case of right SHGCs where the cross

A   B   C

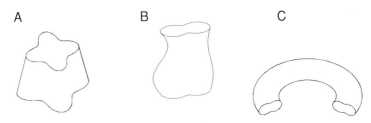

Figure 4.6. Sample generalized cylinders: (A) an LSHGC; (B) an SHGC; (C) a PRCGC.

section is circular, have been studied by Nalwa (15). The shape recovery of an SOR is greatly simplified, mainly because its (circular) cross section can be recovered from its elliptic image. LSHGCs have been addressed by Horaud and Brady (8), for example, who used a method that combines constraints on their orientation obtained from limb projections and their cross section. In another, more general, approach, Ulupinar and Nevatia (24–29) have addressed zero Gaussian curvature (ZGC) surfaces, SHGCs, PRCGCs, and surfaces made up of several ZGC patches. Nonstraight, nonconstant cross-section GCs are addressed in Zerroug and Nevatia (33). In this section, we discuss the method of Ulupinar and Nevatia (25) for recovering SHGCs as it is illustrative of others.

Their method is based on the observation that certain types of symmetries and surface adjacency relationships greatly influence our perception of surface shape. From this observation, which naturally captures surface interaction, they derived a number of properties and constraints that allow the formulation of constraint equations on surface orientations in gradient space.

We begin by giving a number of definitions introducing some of the related terminology, then state certain SHGC properties. For lack of space, the theorems we report are given without proof.

3.2.3.1. Definitions

Definition 2. Let the cross section of an SHGC be parameterized as $C(t) = [x(t), y(t)]$, its axis $A(s)$, and its scaling function $r(s)$; then curves of constant s are called *cross sections* (also *parallels*) and curves of constant t are called *meridians* (see Fig. 4.7).

Definition 3. Two curves $C_1(t)$ and $C_2(s)$ are said to be *parallel symmetric* if there exits a continuous and monotonic (pointwise correspondence) function f, such that $T_1(t) = T_2[f(t)]$, where T_i is the tangent vector of curve C_i.

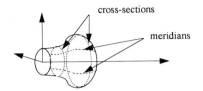

Figure 4.7. SHGC representation and terminology.

Figure 4.8 gives some examples. The correspondence is said to be *linear* if f is a linear function.

3.2.3.2. Properties of SHGCs

Property 1. Cross sections of an SHGC are mutually parallel symmetric with linear correspondences such that meridians join parallel symmetric points of the cross sections. This property holds both in 3D and in an orthographic projection.

Property 2. Tangents of the projections of the limb edges at the points they intersect the same cross section, when extended, intersect the image of the axis of the SHGC at the same point. This projective property has also been derived by Ponce *et al.* (17).

3.2.3.3. Constraints

Three types of constraint are used in Ulupinar and Nevatia's method: the *curved shared-boundary constraint*, the *inner surface constraint* and the *orthogonality constraint*. The first two are derived from pure differential geometric considerations, and the third corresponds to the assumption that certain observed 2D regularities originate from 3D orthogonality.

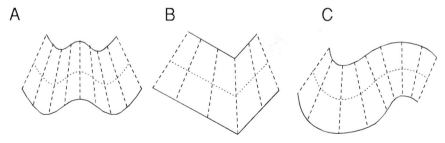

Figure 4.8. Examples of parallel symmetric curves. The dotted curves are axes of symmetry and the dashed lines are lines of symmetry.

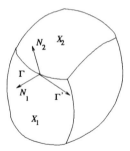

Figure 4.9. Curved shared-boundary constraint. Two curved surfaces meeting along a curve Γ.

Curved Shared-Boundary Constraint. The curved shared-boundary constraint (CSBC) is an extension of the shared boundary constraint for planar shapes described in Section 3.2.1. It relates the surface orientations of intersecting (curved) surfaces near their intersection curve. Letting $X_1(u_1, v_1)$ and $X_2(u_2, v_2)$ be the two intersecting surfaces as in Fig. 4.9, and $\Gamma(s) = X_1[u_1(s), v_1(s)] = X_2[u_2(s), v_2(s)]$ their intersecting curve, the CSBC can be formulated as follows:

$$N_1(s) \cdot \Gamma'(s) = 0 \quad \text{and} \quad N_2(s) \cdot \Gamma'(s) = 0, \tag{5}$$

where $N_i(s)$ is the normal to surface X_i along $\Gamma(s)$ and $\Gamma'(s)$ the tangent to the curve $\Gamma(s)$.

If one of the surfaces is planar with plane orientation given by the gradient (p_c, q_c), then $\Gamma(s)$ is also planar and can be written $\Gamma(s) = [x(s), y(s)]$ Letting $[p(s), q(s)]$ be the gradient, along $\Gamma(s)$, of the nonplanar surface, the CSBC can be rewritten as

$$x'(s)[p_c - p(s)] + y'(s)[q_c - q(s)] = 0. \tag{6}$$

Inner Surface Constraint. The inner surface constraint (ISC) relates orientations at neighboring points of a surface. Consider a curve $C(t)$ on a C^2 surface S. For each point P of C, associate a vector R belonging to T_p such that

$$\frac{dC}{dt} \cdot dN_R = 0, \tag{7}$$

where T_p is the tangent plane of S at P and dN_R the derivative of the normal N of S in the direction of R. The constraint is given by the following theorem

Theorem 1 Under orthographic projection, if an image curve C_I is the projection of the curve C on the surface S and $R_I = (r_x, r_y)$ is the projection of the vector R satisfying Eq. (7), then the change in gradient space of the orientation (p, q) of the surface S, along the curve C, is restricted by the image vector R_I as

$$d(p, q)_{C'} \cdot R_I = 0. \tag{8}$$

To apply this constraint, it is necessary to identify the C curves of interest for which the above directions R can be identified. The authors propose that parallel symmetric curves on a surface can be used for that purpose. This is the object of the following theorem.

Theorem 2 Let the family of curves $\{C_i\}$ be on a surface S such that the curves $\{C_i\}$ are mutually parallel symmetric in 3D. If the curves C_i are used as the above C curves, then the tangents of the curves obtained by joining the symmetric points of the family $\{C_i\}$ give the directions R of the ISC. Conversely, if the curves obtained by joining the parallel symmetric points of the curves $\{C_i\}$ are used as C curves then the tangents of the C_i curves give the directions R.

For an SHGC, the C_i curves are its cross sections and the R directions the tangents to its meridians (or vice-versa).

Orthogonality Constraint. The CSBC and the ISC are not sufficient to determine surface orientations uniquely. The authors propose to prefer interpretations, consistent with CSBC and ISC, such that the cross sections and meridians are "as much orthogonal" to each other as possible. (This is similar to imposing orthogonality in presence of a skew symmetry as in Section 3.2.1.) In fact, the cross sections and meridians may not be orthogonal to each other in 3D, except for surfaces of revolution. For this, the authors do not strictly enforce this constraint, but rather "maximize" it, thereby preferring the closest interpretation to an orthogonal ruling of the surface.

The formulation of the orthogonality constraint (OC) is as follows. Let α be the image angle between the tangent to the cross section, at some point P, and the image x axis, and β the angle of the tangent to the meridian at the same point. Let (p, q) be the gradient of the surface at that point; then the OC (orthogonality between the corresponding 3D tangents) gives the constraint

$$\cos(\alpha - \beta) + (p \cos \alpha + q \sin \alpha)(p \cos \beta + q \sin \beta) = 0. \tag{9}$$

(Use of this constraint is discussed in subsection 5).

3.2.3.4. *Cross Section and Axis Recovery*

Property 2 (above) gives the condition that corresponding points of limb projections should satisfy in order to both detect the image axis and hypothesize the presence of an SHGC. Ponce *et al.* (17) have used a "Hough-like" method that finds those correspondences in a perspective image of SHGCs. This method consists of finding, over the possible (discretized) orientations of the axis, linear patterns in the sets of points obtained by pairing all possible curve tangents. This method is rather computationally expensive. Ulupinar and Nevatia suggest a different method that uses the observed cross section of an SHGC. Their objective is not just to find limb correspondences but to recover image cross sections and meridians over the SHGC surface, as well. This allows application of the previous constraints to every cross section of the surface. The SHGC to recover is assumed to be cut along its cross-section plane. First, note that cross sections and limb projections are mutually tangential. (This follows from the nature of limb boundaries.) Let C_t be the visible cross section of the SHGC and C_l and C_r be the observed limbs, the steps are as follows (see Fig. 4.10):

For each point $P_l \in C_l$, do the following:

- Find the point $P_{cl} \in C_t$ such that $C_l'(P_l)$ is parallel to $C_t'(P_{cl})$, where C' is the tangent vector of the curve C.
- Translate the cross-section curve C_t such that the point $P_{cl} \in C_t$ coincides with the point P_l, obtaining the curve C_{tt}.
- Find the point $P_{cr} \in C_{tt}$ that minimizes the function $f(P_{cr}) = (d_1 + d_2)/d_1$, which is the amount of scaling required to be applied on the curve C_{tt} to bring the point P_{cr} to the point P_r. The quantities d_1 and d_2 are the lengths of the line segments from P_l to P_{cr} and from P_{cr} to P_r, respectively. It can be shown that local minima of the function

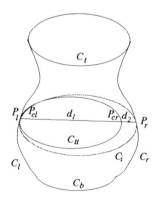

Figure 4.10. Cross-section recovery for an SHGC cut along its cross-section plane.

$f(\cdot)$ above give the correct point $P_{cr} \in C_{tt}$ such that the limb boundary condition: $C'_{tt}(P_{cr})$ parallel to $C'_r(P_r)$ is met.
• Scale the curve C_{tt} by $f(P_{cr})$ so that the point P_{cr} meets with the point P_r, obtaining the curve C_i.

The curve C_i obtained by this algorithm is precisely the image of the cross-section curve between points P_l and P_r of the SHGC. Once the correspondence of points P_l and P_r between limb boundaries C_l and C_r is obtained, the image of the axis of the SHGC can be recovered using property 2.

3.2.3.5. Shape Recovery

For each cross section so recovered, application of the CSBC on, say, n points provides n equations of the form given by Eq. (6). Application of the ISC provides $n - 1$ equations, which, combined with the CSBC equations, yields a system of $2n - 1$ equations on $2n + 2$ unknowns [the (p_i, q_i) at the n points of the cross section and the (p_c, q_c) of the cross-section plane].

Meridians of an SHGC are planar curves, thus the CSBC can also be applied to a given meridian in the same way it was applied to cross sections. Letting M be a meridian and (p_m, q_m) be its plane gradient, the surface normal gradient (p_j, q_j) at a point P_j on M is constrained by

$$(p_m - p_j, q_m - q_j) \cdot M'(p_j) = 0, \tag{10}$$

where $M'(P_j)$ is the meridian tangent at point P_j.

Therefore, over the whole SHGC surface (m cross sections and n points on each one of them), we obtain $2nm$ equations on $2nm + 4$ unknowns [surface normals at all points plus the cross-section gradient (p_c, q_c) and the chosen meridian gradient (p_m, q_m)]. This system of equations is clearly underconstrained, and an infinite number of solutions exist, subject to those constraints. At this point the OC is used to limit that number. As previously mentioned, the OC consists of preferring the interpretation that has the "most regular" grid of cross sections and meridians. The authors use the minimization of the sum of the cosines of the 3D angles between cross-sections and meridians over the whole surface. Its formulation is

$$\Xi = \sum_i \sum_j \cos(\theta_{ij}) = \frac{[C'_i(P_{ij})]_3 \cdot [M'_j(P_{ij})]_3}{|[C'_i(P_{ij})]_3| \, |[M'_i(P_{ij})]_3|}, \tag{11}$$

where $[C'_i(P_{ij})_3$ and $[M'_i(P_{ij})]_3$ are the 3D tangents of the cross section and meridian curves at point P_{ij}.

This minimization performed over (p_c, q_c) and (p_m, q_m). Assuming that the cross section is orthogonal to the axis, the latter gradients are related by

$$(p_m, q_m, 1)^t \cdot (p_c, q, 1)^t = 0. \tag{12}$$

Thus, with suitable rotation of the image coordinates, this yields $q_m = -1/q_c$ and the search for the minimum can be over q_c only: 1 degree of freedom. This degree of freedom is fixed by making the cross section compact and of medium slant. The method consists, first, of fitting an

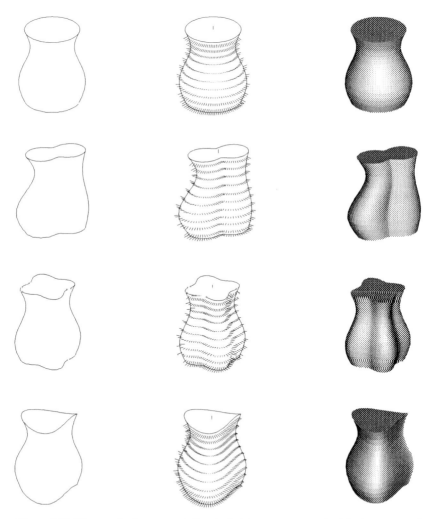

Figure 4.11. The needle images and the shaded images generated with the computed gradients at each point of the SHGCs shown. From Ulupinar (33).

ellipse to the cross section, then updating the corresponding 3D circle orientation with bias toward 45°.

Results of this method on some SHGC contours are given in Fig. 4.11. The figure shows input contours, computed surface gradients, and corresponding shaded images. The surface gradients are represented by needle diagrams showing normal vectors pointing outward from the surface. The shaded images have been computed using a point source light model and a Lambertian surface reflectance model, for which brightness is proportional to the cosine of the angle between the incident light rays and the surface normals. The results seem to be in good agreement with the human perception of the same contours.

In summary, constraint-based shape recovery follows a process whereby 3D shape is first constrained to specific (not any) solutions, possibly infinite in number. The process is completed by the usage of additional regularity assumptions corresponding to preferred interpretations. However, the methods we have described so far assume that perfect and segmented contours are given. In Section 4, we discuss some of the few methods that address scene segmentation.

4. METHODS OF SHAPE FROM IMPERFECT CONTOURS

In previous section, we assumed that perfect contours were available and that single objects were given before shape recovery methods were applied. In case the given contours are perfect (i.e., no breaks or markings), segmentation of an object can be viewed as a problem of labeling its edges as being occluding, limb, or similar (13). However, real images do not produce perfect contours. The detected contours are often fragmented and contours due to causes such as markings, shadows, and noise are present in addition to contours caused by object boundaries.

One approach to scene segmentation in real images is simply by recognition of objects in it. This is suitable when the number of models known to the system is rather small. Such techniques are discussed elsewhere in this book. Techniques specifically developed for GC models can be found in Brooks (5) and Richetin *et al.* (18).

Low-level analysis of contours, such as that given by corners and T-junctions, provides some useful information but is not sufficient to achieve object-level segmentation. Further, those local features are themselves difficult to detect and sensitive to image noise, and their detection may well depend on detection of higher level features such as surfaces. Thus, global properties of contours need to be used for segmentation.

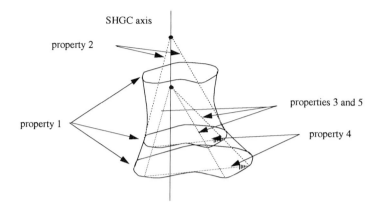

Figure 4.12. Properties of SHGCs.

In this section, we focus on segmentation and recovery of SHGCs without more specific knowledge of the objects. Properties of SHGCs that we have mentioned earlier as being useful for shape recovery can also be used for scene segmentation. We describe two methods, one developed by Sato and Binford at Stanford University and one by the first two authors of this chapter. It should be noted that these systems are rather recent attempts and the methods are less mature than the ones we have described earlier. Still, we hope that these are useful to the reader and that they convey a feel for the types of problems to be solved and the approaches that may be taken to them.

Some of the invariant properties of the contours of SHGCs were given earlier (in Section 3.2.3, properties 1 and 2). We state some additional ones below. All properties are illustrated in Fig. 4.12.

Property 3. Lines of correspondence between a pair of linearly parallel symmetric curves are either all parallel (for a unit scaling) or all intersect at the same point (which we will call *apex*).

Property 4. For a pair of parallel symmetric curves with a linear correspondence, line segments joining corresponding points are parallel and the ratios of their lengths is constant and equal to the scaling factor between the curves.

Property 5. Lines joining corresponding points of any pair of cross sections of a SHGC are either parallel to the axis or intersect on the axis at the same point. This property holds both in 3D and in a 2D orthographic projection.

Sato and Binford (20, 21) developed BUILDER I, a system for detection and recovery of SHGCs in a real contour image. The system is made up of four processing modules: the *end finder*, the *meridian finder*, the *cross-section finder*, and the *3D recoverer*. The principle of this system is to detect SHGCs in an edge image by detecting image contours that satisfy their projective-invariant properties.

The first module, end finder, consists of algorithms for finding the extremities ("ends") of an SHGC. Those extremities are the parallel symmetric parts of the extremal cross sections of the projection of an SHGC. Two algorithms are used for finding such ends. The first one detects unit-scaling symmetric curves. By property 3 above, the correspondence lines between such symmetric curves are all parallel, thus the detection method searches for their common direction. The second algorithm detects non-unit-scaling parallel symmetries. On the basis of property 3, which indicates that in this case lines of correspondence intersect at a common point ("origin of scaling" in the authors' terminology), their method uses a "Hough-like" transform, in the image space, to estimate this point. Normally, the two algorithms need to be applied for all pairs of curves in the image. The authors note that the methods are computationally expensive and suggest to manually select a reference curve (end) and search for symmetric ones.

The second module, the meridian finder, consists of detecting meridians connecting the previously detected ends. The method first finds junctions at the detected ends, then searches for pairs of curves joining pairs of junctions. For each such hypothesized pair of meridians, the lines of correspondence are assumed to be all parallel to a reference segment joining junctions at some end. Once those correspondences are determined, property 5 and property 2 are verified for the candidate meridians. A success is reported if those properties are satisfied, that is, if a line (projection of the axis) is found.

The third module, the cross-section finder, consists of finding closed cross sections at the detected ends and the fourth module consists of recovering the 3D shape of detected SHGCs. In this last module, the 3D recovery method assumes that the cross section is skew symmetric and that the axis pierces the cross section at its center. These two assumptions allow to fix a 3D orthogonal frame with the SHGC that is used for recovering the sweeping function.

This system uses strong constraints for the selection of image contours that are likely to project from SHGCs. Although the detection method of the meridian finder apply only to surfaces of revolution (SORs) and objects where the image contours are meridian projections, such as

LSHGCs, it automatically filters out markings and other non-SHGC contours. This system can be applied to scenes where there is no occlusion.

4.2. Zerroug – Nevatia Method

In an independent effort, Zerroug and Nevatia (32) have developed a method that also addresses the figure–ground problem for SHGCs. This method also uses the projective invariant properties discussed previously. The approach consists of exploiting the properties in a multilevel perceptual grouping process that addresses segmentation and description at three feature levels: the curve level, the parallel symmetry level, and the SHGC patch level. The fundamental difference between this method and the one of Sato and Binford is that it explicitly addresses problems of occlusion and discontinuities in image features such as broken contours and surfaces.

Figure 4.13 gives an example of a real image, this system handles, showing occlusion and other imperfections. At the heart of the method are hypothesize–verify processes that first detect local features, such as symmetry elements or surface patches, by local application of the invariant properties. The subsequent steps consist of generating grouping hypotheses between compatible features that are then verified for geometric and structural consistency. The final step consists of completing the discontinuous descriptions. The grouping, verification, and completion methods are derived from the projective properties of SHGCs. This process of local application of such invariant properties for feature detection and grouping allows occlusion and large gaps to be bridged.

The curve level consists of an edge-linking process followed by segmentation of contours at corners. Then, a conservative cocurvilinearity based grouping process is applied to bridge short breaks. In what follows, we will only describe the parallel symmetry level and the SHGC patch level.

4.2.1. Parallel-Symmetry-Level Grouping

In this level, the objective is to form parallel symmetry correspondences between contours. Such symmetries, by virtue of property 1, can be used to hypothesize cross sections of SHGCs. A multistep hypothesize–verify process is used for that purpose. The first step detects local parallel symmetry correspondences between all pairs of curves. The method uses an efficient quadratic B-spline-based method that finds correspondences analytically (19). Such correspondences, however, are not guaranteed to be

Figure 4.13. A real intensity image and its extracted edges.

linear and include both desired and undesired symmetries (involving markings, for example). The next steps, grouping, selection, and verification are used in order to group relevant symmetry elements and select those that are likely to correspond to cross sections of SHGCs. The grouping stage uses a local compatibility constraint, between pairs of symmetry elements, derived from property 4 above.

Verification uses consistency constraints, such as linearity of the correspondences, between global symmetries and component local ones. The final step of this process consists of completion of missing boundaries in consistent symmetries. The authors show how this can be done using the

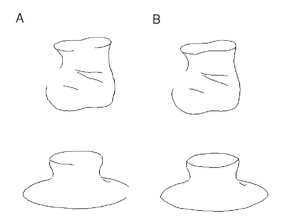

Figure 4.14. Examples of results obtained at the parallel symmetry level: (A) initial contours; (B) completed cross-sections. From Zerroug and Nevatia (37).

symmetries themselves. The idea is that missing sections of a curve can be inferred from visible sections of a symmetric curve. Symmetries involving curves that can be closed, by a cycle of continuous curves, are used to hypothesize presence of cross sections. Figure 4.14 shows some examples of the results of this process.

4.2.2. SHGC Patch-Level Grouping

At this level, hypothesized cross sections from the previous level are used for detection of SHGC surface patches. As mentioned previously, such surfaces may not be continuous because of occlusion or (large) gaps in bounding contours. The proposed approach is based on the definition of *local SHGC patches*, which is best explained by Fig. 4.15. These patches are continuous visible segments of an SHGC surface. Their detection is the first step of another hypothesize–verify process whose objective is to form global SHGC descriptions whenever possible.

Detection of local SHGC patches, for each hypothesized cross-section, consists of finding correspondences between *candidate limb patches*. The correspondence finding algorithm uses the method discussed in Section 3.2.3 for ruling the surface of an SHGC. Three types of local SHGC patches can be obtained: cylindrical patches, conical patches, and nonlinear patches, each giving a local estimate of the axis of a hypothetical SHGC it belongs to. From property 5 above, limbs of a cylindrical patch give only the direction of the projection of the axis. Also, intersection of (extension of) limbs of a conical patch gives a point (apex) of the projec-

A   B

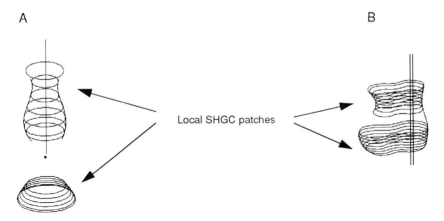

Figure 4.15. Examples of (geometrically compatible) local SHGC patches. From Zerroug and Nevatia (37).

tion of the axis and a nonlinear patch gives an estimate of the projection of the axis itself.

The next step of this level generates grouping hypotheses between such detected local SHGC patches. A combination of geometric and structural constraints are used for that purpose. Geometric compatibility constraints involve compatibility of axes of pairs of local SHGC patches. For example, two nonlinear patches are considered for grouping if their axes are (almost) collinear. Similarly, a conical patch and a nonlinear patch are compatible if the conical patch apex lies on the nonlinear patch axis, and a cylindrical patch and a nonlinear patch are compatible if the axis direction of the cylindrical patch is parallel to the axis of the nonlinear patch. Figure 4.15 shows examples of geometrically compatible local SHGC patches [example (A) shows the two local SHGC patches detected for the vase shown in Fig. 4.13).

Structural compatibility uses measures of proximity and continuity of limbs of local SHGC patches. It has been introduced in order to avoid grouping of patches that belong to different, although coaxial, SHGCs, such as is the case between separate components of some industrial parts (e.g., handle and the drive of a screwdriver).

Verification of hypothesized *global SHGC patches* (aggregates of compatible local SHGC patches) uses compatibility constraints between global axes descriptions and local ones. This is necessary as local compatibilities may not be transitive due to the usage of similarity measures.

The last stage of this level consists of completing SHGC surface descriptions using two consecutive methods: the *axis-based cross-section recovery* and the *limb reconstruction*. The axis-based cross-section recovery method

A   B

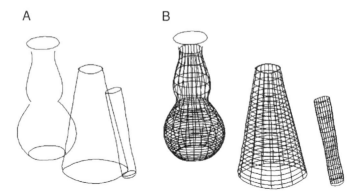

Figure 4.16. Results obtained at the SHGC patch level: (A) segmented and completed objects; (B) corresponding ruled surfaces. From Zerroug and Nevatia (37).

recovers cross sections for discontinuous portions of a detected SHGC. Although (at most) one side has a visible limb boundary, using property 5 and the detected axis, it is possible to recover cross sections (hence the surface) at such discontinuity regions. The limb reconstruction method consists of recovering the invisible limb boundary. Such recovery is necessary in that it indicates the extent of the surface and is also useful for recovering 3D shape. The method consists of finding the tangential envelope of the cross sections recovered by the axis-based cross-section recovery.

This level produces descriptions of detected SHGCs from a given image. Figure 4.16 shows detected SHGC descriptions from the edges of Fig. 4.13. Besides segmentation, the descriptions show the cross sections and meridians of each detected SHGC. At this stage only 2D information is available. To recover 3D shape, the authors use a method that combines these 2D descriptions and the viewer-centered descriptions, based on surface normals, obtained by applying the method of Ulupinar and Nevatia (25) discussed in Section 3.2.3. The method recovers a complete 3D

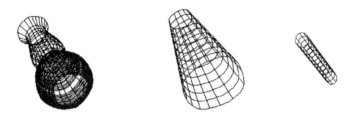

Figure 4.17. Recovered 3D SHGC primitives shown for different orientations. From Zerroug and Nevatia (37).

object centered description consisting of the 3D cross section, the 3D axis (and the point it pierces the cross section), and the scaling function, the necessary elements for a full description of an SHGC. Details of this method can be found in Zerroug and Nevatia (32). Figure 4.17 shows the resulting 3D volumetric descriptions, also using surface ruling in terms of cross sections and meridians. The figure shows the segmented objects of Fig. 4.16 for different 3D orientations.

5. CONCLUSION

We have described a few methods for recovering shape of curved objects from a single image. As observed earlier, this problem is inherently ambiguous, and no "correct" solution is possible without making some assumptions. The different techniques we have described make different assumptions about regularity in our world.

The most effective techniques rely on careful analysis of invariant properties of contours and the constraints they impose on the surface shape. These properties, however, are not sufficient to give a unique answer and some preference criteria must still be used. Moreover, the invariant properties apply only to certain generic classes of objects. We have focused on SHGCs, but some other classes have also been studied. It is our belief that the classes that have already been studied, in combination, are sufficient to describe many, although not all, shapes encountered in our normal environment.

We have also described some approaches to dealing with the complexities of analyzing real images rather than just synthetic contours. This is an extremely difficult problem, but some progress is being made. Our expectation is that in the next few years we will see more and more systems that are able to work by just acquiring a single image of the scene, which is perhaps the most convenient and economical way of sensing our environment.

REFERENCES

1. H. G. Barrow and J. M. Tenenbaum, Interpreting line drawings as three dimensional surfaces. *Artif. Intell.* **17**, 75–116 (1981).
2. I. Biederman, Recognition by components: A theory of human image understanding. *Psychol. Rev.* **94**(2), 115–147 (1987).
3. T. O. Binford, Visual perception of computer. Presented at *IEEE Conf. Syst. Controls*, Miami, *1971*.
4. M. Brady and A. Yuille, An extremum principle for shape from contour. *IEEE Trans. Pattern Anal. Mach. Intell.* **PAMI-6**, 288–301 (1984).

5. R. A. Brooks, Model-based three dimensional interpretation of two dimensional images. *IEEE Trans. Pattern Anal. Mach. Intell.* **PAMI-5**(2), 140–150 (1983).
6. J. F. Canny, A computational approach to edge detection. *IEEE Trans. Pattern Anal. Mach. Intell.* **PAMI-8**(6), 679–698 (1986).
7. A. Gross and T. Boult, Recovery of generalized cylinders from a single intensity view. *Proc. DARPA Image Understanding Workshop, Pennsylvania, 1990*, pp. 557–564 (1990).
8. R. Horaud and M. Brady, On the geometric interpretation of image contours. *Artif. Intell.* **37**, 333–353 (1988).
9. T. Kanade, Recovery of the three-dimensional shape of an object from a single view. *Artif. Intell.* **17**, 409–460 (1981).
10. J. J. Koenderink, "Solid Shape." MIT Press, Cambridge, MA, 1990.
11. D. G. Lowe, "Perceptual Organization and Visual Recognition." Kluwer Acad. Pub., Hingham, MA, 1985.
12. A. K. Mackworth, Interpreting pictures of polyhedral scenes. *Art. Intell.* **4**, 121–137 (1973).
13. J. Malik, Interpreting line drawings of curved objects. *Int. J. Comput. Vision* **1**(1), 73–103 (1987).
14. R. Mohan and R. Nevatia, Segmentation and description of scenes using perceptual organization. *Proc. IEEE Conf. Comput. Vision Pattern Recognition*, San Diego, CA, *1989*, pp. 333–341 (1989).
15. V. Nalwa, Line drawing interpretation: Bilateral symmetry. *Proc. DARPA Image Understanding Workshop*, Los Angles, *1987*, pp. 956–967 (1987).
16. V. Nalwa, Line-drawing interpretation: Straight lines and conic sections. *IEEE Trans. Pattern Anal. Mach. Intell.* **PAMI-10**(4), 514–529 (1988).
17. J. Ponce, D. Chelberg, and W. B. Mann, Invariant properties of straight homogeneous generalized cylinders and their contours. *IEEE Trans. Pattern Anal. Mach. Intell.* **PAMI-11**(9), 951–966, (1989).
18. M. Richetin, M. Dhome, J. T. Lapestre, and G. Rives, Inverse perspective transform using zero-curvature contours points: Applications to the localization of some generalized cylinders from a single view. *IEEE Trans. Pattern Anal. Mach. Intell.* **PAMI-13**(2), 185–192 (1991).
19. P. Saint-Marc and G. Medioni, B-spline contour representation and symmetry detection. *Eur. Conf. Comput. Vision, 1st*, Antibes, France, *1990*, pp. 604–606 (1990).
20. H. Sato and T. O. Binford, On finding the ends of SHGCs in an edge image. *Proc. DARPA Image Understanding Workshop*, San Diego, CA, 379–3868 *1992*.
21. H. Sato and T. O. Binford, BUILDER-I: A system for the extraction of SHGC objects in an edge image. *Proc. DARPA Image Understanding Workshop*, San Diego, CA, pp. 779–791 *1992*.
22. S. A. Shafer and T. Kanade, "The Theory of Straight Homogeneous Generalized Cylinders," Tech. Rep. CS-083-105. Carnegie-Mellon University, Pittsburgh, 1983.
23. K. A. Stevens, The visual interpretation of surface contours. *Artif. Intell.* **17**, 47–73, (1981).
24. F. Ulupinar and R. Nevatia, Inferring shape from contours for curved surfaces. *Proc. Int. Conf. Pattern Recognition*, Atlantic City, NJ, *1990*, pp. 147–154 (1990).

25. F. Ulupinar and R. Nevatia, Shape from contours: SHGCs. *Proc. IEEE Int. Conf. Comput. Vision*, Osaka, Japan, *1990*, pp. 582–586 (1990).
26. F. Ulupinar and R. Nevatia, Recovering shape from contour for constant cross section generalized cylinders. *Proc. IEEE Conf. Comput. Vision Pattern Recognition*, Maui, Hawaii, *1991*, pp. 674–676.
27. F. Ulupinar and R. Nevatia, Constraints for interpretation of line drawings under perspective projection. *Comput. Vision Graphics Image Process.* **53**(1), 88–96 (1991).
28. F. Ulupinar, Perception of 3-D shape from 2-D image of contours. Ph.D. Thesis IRIS-278. Institute for Robotics and Intelligent Systems, University of Southern California, Los Angles, 1991.
29. F. Ulupinar and R. Nevatia, Recovery of 3-D objects with multiple curved surfaces from 2-D contours. *Proc. IEEE Conf. Comput. Vision Pattern Recognition*, *1992*, pp. 730–733 (1992).
30. I. Weiss, 3-D shape representation by contours. *Comput. Vision Graphics and Image Process.* **41**, 80–100 (1988).
31. G. Xu and S. Tsuji, Inferring surfaces from boundaries. *Proc. IEEE Int. Conf. Comput. Vision*, London, *1987*, pp. 716–720 (1987).
32. M. Zerroug and R. Nevatia, Scene segmentation and volumetric descriptions of SHGCs from a single intensity image. *Proc. DARPA Image Understanding Workshop*. Washington DC, pp. 905–916 *1993*.
33. M. Zerroug and R. Nevatia, Quasi-invariant properties and 3D shape recovery of non-straight, non-constant generalized cylinders. *Proc. IEEE Conf. Comput. Vision Pattern Recognition*, New York, 1993, pp. 96–103 (1993).

Chapter **5**

Surface Reflection Mechanism

KATSUSHI IKEUCHI

School of Computer Science
Carnegie-Mellon University
Pittsburgh, Pennsylvania

1. OVERVIEW

Most machine vision problems involve the analysis of images that result from the reflection of light. The apparent brightness of a scene point depends on its ability to reflect incident light in the direction of the sensor; this is commonly referred to as the point's *reflectance properties*. Therefore, the prediction or interpretation of image brightness requires a sound understanding of the various mechanisms involved in the reflection process.

131

This chapter overviews how to model such reflection mechanisms and how to apply the resulting reflection models to computer vision research. Radiometric concepts and modeling techniques for surface profiles that are useful in analyzing surface reflection mechanisms are discussed in Section 2.

There are two approaches to the study of reflection: geometric optics and physical optics. Geometric optics assumes that light travels in a straight line. It calculates the geometric reflection distribution of incident light using a stochastic distribution of micro–surface patches. Physical optics treats light as electromagnetic waves and directly solves Maxwell's equations. Section 3 overviews the Torrance–Sparrow model, a representative geometric optics model, and the Beckmann–Spizzichino model, a representative physical optics model.

Although physics-based reflectance models, such as the Beckmann–Spizzichino and Torrance–Sparrow models, are derived rigorously, they are often cumbersome and impractical for computer vision applications. Section 4 introduces modified reflectance models that are customized for various applications. Each model is derived from physics-based reflectance models so as to emphasize the desired aspects of the models as well as to ignore their other unnecessary aspects.

2. BASIC CONCEPTS

2.1. Radiometric Definitions

In this section, we present definitions of radiometric terms that are useful in the study of surface reflection. Detailed derivations and descriptions of these terms are given by Nicodemus et al. (16) and Horn and Sjöberg (8).

As shown in Fig. 5.1, all directions are represented by the zenith angle θ and the azimuth angle ϕ with respect to the surface normal $\mathbf{n}$. The source is assumed to lie in the $(x$–$z)$ plane and is therefore uniquely determined by its zenith angle θ_i. Monochromatic flux $d\Phi_i$ is incident on the surface area dA_s from the direction θ_i. The irradiance E_i of the surface is defined as the incident flux density:

$$E_i = \frac{d\Phi_i}{dA_s}. \tag{1}$$

A fraction of the incident flux, $d^2\Phi_r$, is reflected in the direction (θ_r, ϕ_r) from the surface. The radiance L_r of the surface is defined as the flux

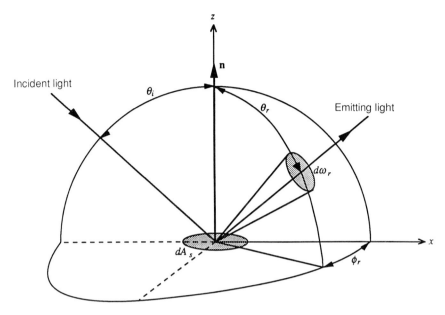

Figure 5.1. Local coordinate system.

emitted per unit foreshortened area per unit solid angle (Fig. 5.1). The surface radiance in the direction (θ_r, ϕ_r) is determined as

$$L_r = \frac{d^2\Phi_r}{dA_s \cos\theta_r \, d\omega_r}, \qquad (2)$$

where $d\omega_r$ is the spherical angle of a sensor measuring the surface radiance from the direction, (θ_r, ϕ_r).

Consider the illumination of a surface from a given direction θ_i; the *bi-directional reflectance distribution function* (BRDF) f_r of a surface is a measure of how bright the surface appears when viewed from another viewing direction, (θ_r, ϕ_r). The BRDF of the surface is defined as

$$F_r(\theta_i, \theta_r, \phi_r) = \frac{L_r(\theta_i, \theta_r, \phi_r)}{E_i(\theta_i)}. \qquad (3)$$

2.2. Surface Model

The manner in which light is reflected by a surface is dependent on, among other factors, the microscopic shape characteristics of the surface.

A smooth surface, for instance, may reflect incident light in a single direction, while a rough surface tends to scatter light into various directions, maybe more in some directions than in others. To be able to accurately predict the reflection of incident light, we must have prior knowledge of the microscopic surface irregularities; we need a model of the surface. All possible surface models may be divided into two broad categories: surfaces with exactly given profiles and surfaces with random irregularities. An exact profile may be determined by measuring the height at each point on the surface by means of a sensor such as the *stylus profilometer*. This method, however, is quite cumbersome and also inapplicable in many practical situations. Hence, it is often convenient to model a surface as a random process, where it is described by a statistical distribution of either its slope with respect to its mean slope or its height above a certain mean level.

2.2.1. Slope Distribution Model

A surface may be modeled as a collection of planar microfacets, as illustrated in Fig. 5.2 (25). A large set of microfacets constitute an infinitesimal surface patch that has a mean surface orientation **n**. Each microfacet, however, is represented by its own orientation, which may deviate from the mean surface orientation by an angle α. We will use the parameter α to represent the slope of independent facets. Surfaces can be modeled by giving a statistical distribution to the microfacet slope. If the surface is isotropic, the probability distribution of the microfacet slopes can be assumed to be rotationally symmetric with respect to the mean

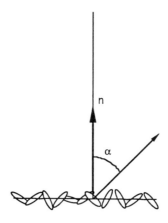

Figure 5.2. A surface may be modeled as a collection of planar microfacets.

surface normal **n**. Therefore, facet slopes may be described by a one-dimensional probability distribution function. For example, the surface may be modeled by assuming a normal distribution for the facet slope α with mean value $\langle \alpha \rangle = 0$ and standard deviation σ_α:

$$p_\alpha(\alpha) = \frac{1}{\sqrt{2\pi}\,\sigma_\alpha} e^{-(\alpha^2/2\sigma_\alpha^2)}. \tag{4}$$

It is seen that the surface model in this case is determined by a single parameter, namely, σ_α. Larger values for σ_α may be used to model rougher surfaces. The slope distribution model is popular in the analysis of surface reflection, as the scattering of light rays is found to be dependent on the local slope of the surface and not on the local height of the surface. For this reason, the slope model, although relatively ambiguous, is more directly applicable to the problem of surface reflection.

2.2.2. Height Distribution Model

The height coordinate h of the surface may be expressed as a random function of the coordinates x and y, as shown in Fig. 5.3. (3). The shape of the surface is then determined by the probability distribution of h. For instance, let h be normally distributed with mean value $\langle h \rangle = 0$, and standard deviation σ_h. Hence, the distribution of h is given by

$$p_h(h) = \frac{1}{\sqrt{2\pi}\,\sigma_h} e^{-(h^2/2\sigma_h^2)}. \tag{5}$$

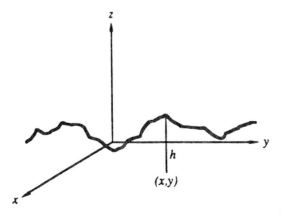

Figure 5.3. Surface height may be expressed as a random function of the spatial coordinates.

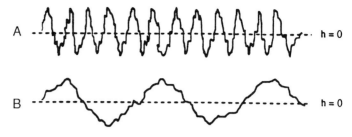

Figure 5.4. Random surfaces with (A) small and (B) large correlation distances. From (3) with permission.

The standard deviation σ_h is also the root mean square of h and represents the *roughness* of the surface. The surface is not uniquely described by the statistical distribution of h, as it does not tell us anything about the distances between the hills and valleys of the surface. In Fig. 5.4, both surfaces (A) and (B) have the same height distribution function, i.e., the same mean value and standard deviation. In appearance, however, the two surfaces do not strongly resemble each other. In order to strengthen the surface model, we use an autocorrelation coefficient $C(\tau)$ that determines the correlation (or lack of independence) between the random values assumed by the height h at two surface points (x_1, y_1) and (x_2, y_2) separated by a distance τ. We describe the autocorrelation coefficient by a fairly general function:

$$C(\tau) = e^{-(\tau^2/T^2)}, \tag{6}$$

where T is the *correlation distance*, for which $C(\tau)$ drops to the value e^{-1}. We see that the surfaces (A) and (B) shown in Fig. 5.4 have small and large correlation distances, respectively. By varying the parameters σ_h and T of our surfaces model we can generate surface that match in appearance with almost any rough surface met in the practice.

2.3. Surface Roughness

Human beings seem to have a rather loose definition of the term "roughness." A surface that appears to be rough from a short distance may appear smooth from far away. In some cases, by changing the direction of illumination, surface imperfections can be made less visible and a rough surface can be made to appear smooth. An observer who is unable to discern from its appearance how rough the surface is will be inclined to feel the surface and make a judgment on the basis of the resulting sensation.

In contrast to the human definition, surface reflection theories in optics offer a stronger definition of roughness; this definition must be one that relates surface irregularities to the wavelength of incident light and the angle of incidence. For incident light of a given wavelength, the roughness of a surface may be estimated by studying the manner in which the surface scatters light in different directions. If the surface irregularities are small compared to the wavelength of incident light, a large fraction of the incident light will be reflected *specularly* in a single direction. On the

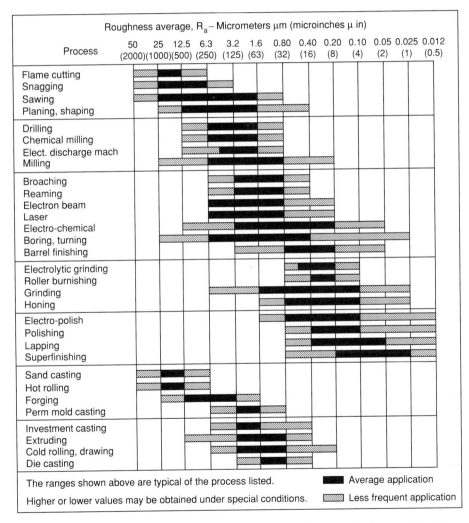

Figure 5.5. Surface roughness produced by common production methods. From (1) with permission.

other hand, if surface irregularities are large compared to the wavelength, the surface will scatter the incident light in various directions. Alternatively, the same surface can be made to appear smooth or rough by varying the wavelength of incident light; additionally, using this same wavelength, this surface can be made to appear smooth or rough by varying the angle of incidence.

In manufacturing engineering, surface roughness is defined from the statistical analysis of the output from the sensors such as stylus profilometers. The arithmetic average roughness R_a is defined as

$$R_a = \frac{1}{L} \int_0^L |y| \, dx, \tag{7}$$

where L is the sampling length and y is the ordinate of the profile's curve.

Surfaces finished by various manufacturing processes have the distributions of the arithmetic average roughness as shown in Fig. 5.5 (1).

3. PHYSICS-BASED REFLECTION MODEL

When light is incident on a boundary interface between two different media, one part of the incident light is immediately reflected on the boundary. This part of the reflection is referred to as the *surface reflection* component. The remainder part of the light penetrates the boundary. The part of the light hits internal pigments of the materials several times and eventually reemits from the inside of the object to the air. This part of the light is referred to as the *body reflection* components (see Fig. 5.6).

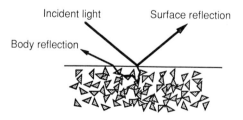

Figure 5.6. Body and surface reflection.

There are two different approaches to the study of surface reflection. *Geometric* optics uses the short wavelength of light to simplify many of the light-propagation problems. Geometric optics is generally able to explain the gross behavior of light when the wavelength is small compared to the pertinent physical dimensions of the system. *Physical* optics is directly based on electromagnetic wave theory and uses Maxwell's equations to study the propagation of light.

3.1.1. Geometric Optics Model

An outstanding feature of visible light is its short wavelength. Often, the wavelength of incident light is far shorter than the physical dimensions of the surface imperfections it encounters, and in such cases it is possible to solve the problem of reflection in an approximate way. The approximation that is valid for short wavelengths of light is known as *geometric optics*.

3.1.1.1. Phong Model

The Phong model (18) was developed in the computer graphics community, and is widely used there due to its simple form. The Phong model gives a good description of the reflection from dielectric materials if the angle of incidence and reflection are significantly less than $\pi/2$. The Phong model predicts reflection based on the angle of incidence and the angle between the reflection direction and the specular direction. The Phong model assumes that the maximum reflection occurs where the angle of reflection equals the angle of incidence. This direction, which satisfies $\theta_i = \theta_e$ and $\phi_e = 0$, is referred to as the *specular direction*. The Phong model is,

$$R = \cos^n \alpha. \qquad (8)$$

The component n determines how narrow the specular reflection is; n is related to the surface roughness. α is the angle between the specular direction and the viewer direction. Namely,

$$\cos \alpha = \sin \theta_i \sin \theta_e \cos \phi_e + \cos \theta_i \cos \theta_e. \qquad (9)$$

Although simple, the Phong model fails to predict an important characteristic of surface reflection: off-specular reflection. The maximum surface reflection does not occur at the specular direction. Instead, it occurs slightly at the outside direction with respect to the viewer. In order to predict this phenomenon, we need more precise reflection models such as the Torrance–Sparrow model.

3.1.1.2. Torrance–Sparrow Model

Torrance and Sparrow (25) model the surface as a collection of planar mirror-like micro-facets. The surface has a mean surface orientation **n**, and the slope α of each planar facet with respect to the mean orientation is described by a probability distribution. Each facet reflects incident light in the specular direction determined by its slope. Since the facet slopes are randomly distributed, light rays are scattered in various directions. Therefore, it is possible to assign a specific distribution function to the facet slopes and determine the radiance of the surface in any given direction.

Torrance and Sparrow assume the facet slopes to be normally distributed. Further, they have assumed the distribution to be rotationally symmetric about the mean surface normal **n**. Hence, facet slopes may be represented by a one-dimensional surface normal distribution:

$$p_\alpha(\alpha) = ce^{-(\alpha^2/2\sigma_\alpha^2)}, \tag{10}$$

where c is a constant, and the facet slope α has mean value $\langle \alpha \rangle = 0$ and standard deviation σ_α. As we have stated earlier, for this surface model, roughness is represented by the parameter σ_α.

Consider the geometry shown in Fig. 5.7. The surface area dA_s is located at the origin of the coordinate frame, and its surface normal points in the direction of the z coordinate. The surface is illuminated by a beam of light that lies in the $(x–z)$ plane and is incident on the surface at an angle θ_i. We are interested in determining the radiance of the surface in the direction (θ_r, ϕ_r). Only certain planar microfacets can specularly reflect the light flux incident at the angle θ_i into the infinitesimal solid angle $d\omega_r$. The microfacets having the capability of this specular reflection are those facets whose normal vectors lie in the solid angle $d\omega'$. Here, the local angle of incidence θ_i' and slope α of the reflecting facets are given from the angles θ_i, θ_r, and ϕ_r.

The number of facets, per unit area of the surface, that are oriented within the solid angle $d\omega'$, is equal to $(p_\alpha(\alpha)\,d\omega')$. Therefore, the number of facets in the surface area dA_s that are oriented within $d\omega'$ is equal to $[p_\alpha(\alpha)\,d\omega'\,dA_s]$. Let a_f be the area of each facet. Therefore, the area of points on dA_s that will reflect light from the direction θ_i into the solid angle $d\omega_r$ is equal to $(a_f p_\alpha(\alpha)\,d\omega'\,dA_s)$. All the reflecting facets are assumed to have the same local angle of incidence, θ_i'. The flux incident on the set of reflecting facets is determined by

$$d^2\Phi_i = L_i\,d\omega_i\left[a_f p_\alpha(\alpha)\,d\omega'\,dA_s\right]\cos\theta_i'. \tag{11}$$

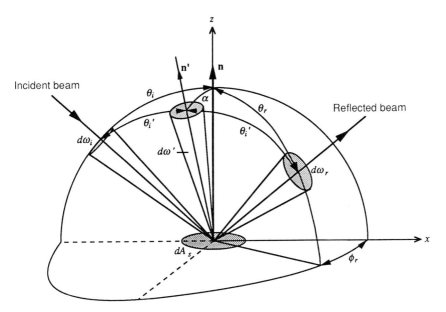

Figure 5.7. Coordinate system used to derive the Torrance–Sparrow model.

The fraction of incident light that is reflected by each planar facet is determined by the Fresnel reflectance coefficient. The Fresnel coefficients $F_\|(\theta_i', \eta')$ and $F_\perp(\theta_i', \eta')$ determine the electromagnetic field reflected in the specular direction by a planar surface. The Fresnel coefficient $F'(\theta_i', \eta')$ for the incident wave may be expressed as a linear combination of the Fresnel coefficients for parallel and perpendicular incident waves:

$$F'(\theta_i', \eta') = h |F_\|(\theta_i', \eta')|^2 + v |F_\perp(\theta_i', \eta')|^2, \tag{12}$$

where

$$h, v \geq 0 \quad \text{and} \quad h + v = 1. \tag{13}$$

Torrance and Sparrow have also considered the masking and shadowing of one microfacet by adjacent facets. Adjacent facets may obstruct flux incident on a given facet or they may obstruct the flux reflected by it. In order to compensate for these effects, the *geometric attenuation factor*[1] $G(\theta_i, \theta_r, \phi_r)$ is introduced. The obstruction of incident or reflected light will depend on the angle of incidence and the angles of reflection. Each facet is assumed to be one side of a V-groove cavity, and light rays are

---

[1] This factor plays the role of the shadowing function S mentioned in the previous section.

assumed to be reflected only once. The final expression $G(\theta_i, \theta_r, \phi_r)$ is

$$G(\theta_i, \theta_r, \phi_r) = \min\left(1, \frac{2\cos\alpha\cos\theta_r}{\cos\theta_i'}, \frac{2\cos\alpha\cos\theta_i}{\cos\theta_i'}\right). \tag{14}$$

Taking the Fresnel reflection coefficient and the geometric attenuation factor into consideration, the flux $d^2\Phi_r$ reflected into the solid angle $d\omega'$ may be determined from the flux $d^2\Phi_i$ incident on the reflecting facets as

$$d^2\Phi_r = F'(\theta_i', \eta')G(\theta_i, \theta_r, \phi_r)\, d^2\Phi_i. \tag{15}$$

The radiance L_r of the surface dA_s in the direction (θ_r, ϕ_r) is defined as

$$L_r = \frac{d^2\Phi_r}{d\omega_r\, dA_s\, \cos\theta_r}. \tag{16}$$

By using Eqs. (11) and (15), we may write Eq. (16) as

$$L_r = \frac{F'(\theta_i', \eta')G(\theta_i, \theta_r, \phi_r)L_i\, d\omega_i\big(a_f p_\alpha(\alpha)\, d\omega'\, dA_s\big)\cos\theta_i'}{d\omega_r\, dA_s\, \cos\theta_r}. \tag{17}$$

Earlier we stated that only facets with normals that lie within the solid angle $d\omega'$ are capable of reflecting light into the solid angle $d\omega_r$. Therefore, $d\omega'$ and $d\omega_r$ are related to one another:

$$d\omega' = \frac{d\omega_r}{4\cos\theta_i'}. \tag{18}$$

Hence, for a given $d\omega_r$, the shape and size of the corresponding $d\omega'$ is dependent on local angle of incidence θ_i' which is in turn dependent on the angle of incidence θ_i and the angles of reflectance (θ_r, ϕ_r).
Substituting Eqs. (10) and (18) in Eq. (17), we obtain

$$L_r = \kappa \frac{L_i\, d\omega_i}{\cos\theta_r} e^{-(\alpha^2/2\sigma_\alpha^2)}, \tag{19}$$

where

$$\kappa = \frac{c a_f F(\theta_i', \eta')G(\theta_i, \theta_r, \phi_r)}{4}. \tag{20}$$

Light is an electromagnetic phenomenon. Therefore, in a strict sense, optics should be studied as a branch of electrodynamics. The Beckmann–Spizzichino model (3) uses physical optics to describe the reflection of plane waves from smooth and rough surfaces. Owing to the electromagnetic character of light, this model is directly applicable to the reflection of light by surfaces.

3.1.2.1. Beckmann–Spizzichino Model

Consider a plane wave incident on a surface. The plane wave is represented by its electric field intensity. The incident field intensity at the surface point Y may be written as

$$\mathbf{P}_i = P_i \mathbf{e}_i e^{-i\mathbf{k}_i \cdot \mathbf{r}} e^{i\omega t}, \tag{21}$$

where $\mathbf{r}$ denotes the position of the surface point Y, P_i represents the electric field amplitude, $\mathbf{e}_1$ is the direction of the electric field, $\mathbf{k}_i$ is the wave propagation vector, and ω is the radian frequency of field oscillation (see Fig. 5.8).

We are interested in the instantaneous scattering of the incident plane wave by the surface. Hence, we can drop the second exponential term in Eq. (21) that represents the temporal variation of the incident field. We will not concern ourselves with the polarization of the scattered field, as we are interested only in the intensity. In future references, we will assume the polarization of the incident wave to be either parallel or perpendicular. The incident field will be denoted by the scalar P_i, where

$$P_i = \mathbf{e}_i \cdot \mathbf{P}_i. \tag{22}$$

A conducting surface will have an abundance of electrons that are very loosely bound to their atoms. When these electrons are subjected to the electromagnetic field carried by the incident wave, they experience forces. These forces result in a movement of the electrons, often referred to as *surface currents*. The surface currents give rise to new electromagnetic fields that interact with the incident field to determine the resultant field at the surface. Mathematically, the resultant field $(P)_s$ at a surface point Y must satisfy the *wave equation*

$$\Delta^2(P)_s + k^2(P)_s = 0, \tag{23}$$

where k is once again the propagation constant. Therefore, the field $(P)_s$ at the surface may be determined by solving the wave equation for the boundary conditions imposed by the surface profile.

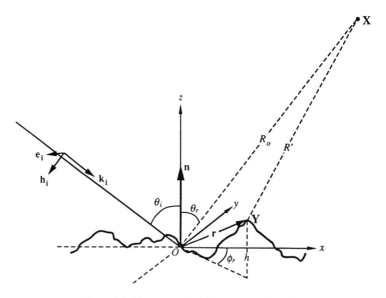

Figure 5.8. Plane wave incident on a rough surface.

The field scattered by the surface in any direction can be determined from the field at the surface. Let X be the point of observation and let the variable R' denote the distance between P and points on the surface S, as shown in Fig. 5.8. We would like to find the scattered field P_r at point X. To this end, let us consider a volume V that is bounded almost everywhere by the surface S but is extended such that point X lies just outside the volume. Therefore, it is reasonable to assume that the field $(P)_s$ is continuous and the wave equation [Eq. (23)] must be satisfied everywhere inside V. Further, a point inside the volume that is nearest to X will experience almost the same field as point X. Using these assumptions and Green's first and second theorems, we can determine the scattered field P_r at the point X from Eq. (23) as

$$P_r(X) = \frac{1}{4\pi} \int\int_A \left[(P)_s \frac{\partial \psi}{\partial n} - \psi \left(\frac{\partial P}{\partial n} \right)_s \right] dS, \tag{24}$$

where

$$\psi = \frac{e^{ikR'}}{R'}. \tag{25}$$

This is called the *Helmholtz integral* and provides us with the solution of the wave equation at any point inside (X is almost inside) of a region in terms of the values of the function [surface field $(E)_S$] and its normal derivative on the region boundary (the surface S). Although it is derived for a closed surface, it is also applicable for open surfaces such as the one in Fig. 5.8.

In order to evaluate the above integral, we must find $(P)_s$ and $(\partial P/\partial n)_s$, i.e., the field and its normal derivative on the surface S. Beckmann and Spizzichino use *Kirchhoff's assumption* to approximate the values of the field and its normal derivative at each point on the surface. The approximation is obtained by assuming that the surface does not have any sharp edges. Thus, the field at a point on the surface is equal to the field that would be present on a tangent plane at that point. Under this assumption, the field on S may be determined as

$$(P)_s = (1 + F)P_i \tag{26}$$

and by differentiating this equation, the normal derivative of the field is determined as

$$\left(\frac{\partial P}{\partial n}\right)_s = (1 - F)P_i\mathbf{k}_i \cdot \mathbf{n}', \tag{27}$$

where $\mathbf{n}'$ is the normal to the surface at the point under consideration and F is the *Fresnel reflection coefficient* for a smooth plane. Beckmann and Spizzichino assume that the surface medium is a perfect conductor, and that the incident wave is of perpendicular polarization: $F = F_\perp = -1$.

The normal height distribution model was described in the previous section. The surface height has the mean value $\langle h \rangle = 0$, standard deviation σ_h, and correlation distance T. The normal distribution $p_h(h)$ is given by Eq. (5), and the autocorrelation function $C(\tau)$ is given by Eq. (6). Beckmann and Spizzichino determine the statistics of P_r from the statistics of h and Eq. (24). Then, Beckmann and Spizzichino derive the mean field and mean power scattered by the surface into an arbitrary direction for any given angle of incidence, and derive the mean scattered power $\langle P_r P_r^* \rangle = \langle |P_r|^2 \rangle$.

For an incidence angle θ_i, the mean power scattered in the direction (θ_r, ϕ_r) by a rough surface, whose height h is normally distributed with mean value $\langle h \rangle = 0$, standard deviation σ_h, and correlation distance T, is given as

$$\langle P_r P_r^* \rangle = \frac{P_i^2 A^2 \cos^2 \theta_i}{\lambda^2 R_0^2} e^{-g}\left(\rho_0^2 + \frac{\pi T^2 D^2}{A} \sum_{m=1}^{m=\infty} \frac{g^m}{m!m} e^{-(v_{xy}^2 T^2/4m)}\right), \tag{28}$$

where

$$g = \left[2\pi \frac{\sigma_h}{\lambda} (\cos \theta_i + \cos \theta_r) \right]^2, \tag{29}$$

$$\rho_0 = \mathrm{sinc}(\nu_x A_x) \, \mathrm{sinc}(\nu_y A_y), \tag{30}$$

$$D = \frac{1 + \cos \theta_i \cos \theta_r - \sin \theta_i \sin \theta_r \cos \phi_r}{\cos \theta_i (\cos \theta_i + \cos \theta_r)}, \tag{31}$$

$$\nu_{xy} = \sqrt{\nu_x^2 + \nu_y^2}, \tag{32}$$

$$(\nu_x, \nu_y, \nu_z) = k(\sin \theta_i - \sin \theta_r \cos \phi_r)\mathbf{x},$$

$$+ k(\sin \theta_r \sin \phi_r)\mathbf{y},$$

$$- k(\cos \theta_i + \cos \theta_r)\mathbf{z}, \tag{33}$$

$$\mathbf{r} = x\mathbf{x} + y\mathbf{y} + h(x, y)\mathbf{z}, \tag{34}$$

where A_x and A_y denote a rectangular surface patch of A where the Helmholtz integral is evaluated.

3.1.2.2. Nayar–Ikeuchi–Kanade Modification

The physical optics reflection model predicts the mean field and mean power scattered by a rough surface. Radiance was defined as

$$L_r = \frac{d^2 \Phi_r}{d\omega_r \, dA_s \cos \theta_r}. \tag{35}$$

Using this relation, Nayar, Ikeuchi, and Kanade derive the image irradiance from the mean field (15).

Consider the image formation geometry shown in Fig. 5.9. For convenience, we will use the areas and solid angles shown in the figure to determine the surface radiance. The surface element dA_s is projected by the lens onto an area dA_{im} on the image plane. Since the solid angles subtended from the center X of the lens by both areas dA_s and dA_{im} are equal, we can relate the two areas as

$$dA_s = \frac{dA_{im} \cos \gamma}{\cos \theta_r} \left(\frac{z}{f} \right)^2. \tag{36}$$

As the viewing direction θ_r changes, we see that the surface area dA_s that

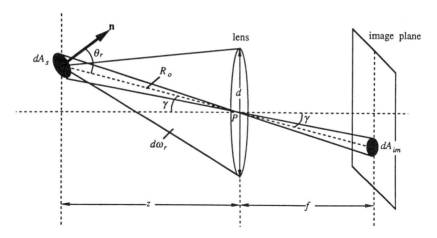

Figure 5.9. Image formation geometry.

is projected onto the same image element (pixel) area, changes as a function of θ_r. Since the image element area dA_{im} is constant for a given sensor, the surface area dA_s must be determined from dA_{im}. All light rays radiated from dA_s that are incident on the area dA_l of the lens, are projected onto the image area dA_{im}. Therefore, $d\omega_r$ in Eq. (35) corresponds to the solid angle subtended by the lens when viewed from the area dA_s, and is determined as

$$d\omega_r = \frac{dA_l \cos \gamma}{R_0^2}. \tag{37}$$

The flux $d^2\Phi_r$ in Eq. (35) is the energy of light received by the lens area dA_l, and can be determined as

$$d^2\Phi_r = S_a \, dA_l \cos \gamma = \frac{1}{2}\sqrt{\frac{\mu}{\epsilon}} \langle P_r P_r^* \rangle \, dA_l \cos \gamma. \tag{38}$$

By substituting Eqs. (36)–(38) in Eq. (35), we obtain

$$L_r = \frac{1}{2}\sqrt{\frac{\mu}{\epsilon}} \frac{R_0^2 f^2 \langle P_r P_r^* \rangle}{z^2 \, dA_{im} \cos \gamma}. \tag{39}$$

It is not possible to determine the exact value of the radiance from the statistics of the scattered field. The radiance L_r in Eq. (39) is actually the mean (expected) radiance, $\langle L_r \rangle$. The mean scattered power $\langle P_r P_r^* \rangle$ was determined as an integral over the entire area of the surface [Eq. (24)]. In

Fig. 5.9, we see that the image element dA_{im} receives light radiated only by the surface element dA_s and, therefore, the mean scattered power must be computed as an integral over the surface area $A = dA_s$. Since the image element area dA_{im} is constant for all viewing directions θ_r, the area of integration dA_s is determined by Eq. (36). Thus, for a given incidence angle θ_i, the radiance in the direction (θ_r, ϕ_r) of a rough surface, whose height h is normally distributed with mean value $\langle h \rangle = 0$, standard deviation σ_h, and correlation distance T, is given as

$$L_r = \sqrt{\frac{\mu}{\varepsilon}} \, \frac{P_i^2 \cos^2 \theta_i}{2\lambda^2} e^{-g}$$

$$\times \left[\left(\frac{z}{f} \right)^2 \frac{dA_{im} \cos \gamma}{\cos^2 \theta_r} \rho_0^2 + \frac{\pi T^2 D^2}{\cos \theta_r} \sum_{m=1}^{m=\infty} \frac{g^m}{m!m} e^{-(v_{xy}^2 T^2 /4m)} \right]. \quad (40)$$

It is important to note that the model under consideration only attempts to describe the reflection mechanism that is often referred to by the vision research community as "specular reflection." As seen from Eq. (28), the mean scattered power is the sum of two terms. The first term $e^{-g}\rho_0^2$ is the *specular spike* component of the specular reflection. It is seen from Eq. (30), that when the surface dimensions are small, ρ_0 becomes a very sharp function of θ_i and θ_r and is equal to zero for all scattering directions with the exception of a very narrow range around the specular direction. Since the mean slope of the surface is constant and is independent of the roughness of the surface, a privileged scattering in the specular direction is expected. The second term in Eq. (28) corresponds to the *specular lobe* or the diffusely scattered field that results from the roughness of the surface. The specular lobe component is distributed around the specular direction. For a perfectly smooth surface, $g = 0$ and the specular lobe vanishes while the specular spike is strong. As the roughness measure g increases, the spike component shrinks rapidly, and the lobe increases in magnitude.

The exponential series given by the summation in the lobe component may be approximated for smooth $(g \ll 1)$ and very rough $(g \gg 1)$ surfaces. The approximations result in simpler expressions for the scattered power for these two extreme surface conditions:

$$L_{r_{smooth}} = \sqrt{\frac{\mu}{\varepsilon}} \, \frac{E_0^2 \cos^2 \theta_i}{2\lambda^2} e^{-g} \left[\left(\frac{z}{f} \right)^2 \frac{dA_{im} \cos \gamma}{\cos^2 \theta_r} \rho_0^2 + \frac{\pi T^2 D^2 g}{\cos \theta_r} \right] \quad (g \ll 1),$$

$$(41)$$

$$L_{r_{rough}} = \sqrt{\frac{\mu}{\varepsilon}} \, \frac{E_0^2 \cos^2 \theta_i \, \pi T^2 D^2}{2\lambda^2 \cos \theta_r v_z^2 \sigma_h^2} \exp \left(\frac{-v_{xy}^2 T^2}{4 v_z^2 \sigma_h^2} \right) \quad (g \gg 1),$$

$$(42)$$

where g is the roughness measure in Beckmann–Spizzichino model. As given in Eq. (29), the factor g in Eq. (28) is proportional to the square of σ_h/λ. Therefore, g represents the roughness of the surface and the three cases $g \ll 1$, $g \approx 1$, and $g \gg 1$ correspond to *smooth surfaces,*[2] *moderately rough surfaces*, and *rough surfaces*, respectively.

3.2. Diffuse Reflection

3.2.1. Lambertian Model

Lambert (13) was the first to investigate the mechanisms underlying diffuse reflection. Surfaces that satisfy Lambert's law appear equally bright from all directions. In other words, the radiance of a Lambertian surface is independent of the viewing direction. As shown in Fig. 5.6, the light rays penetrate the surface and encounter microscopic inhomogeneities in the surface medium. The light rays are repeatedly reflected and refracted at boundaries between regions of differing refractive indices. Some of the scattered rays find their way to the surface with a variety of directions resulting in diffuse reflection. When diffuse reflection produced by either or both of the above mechanisms produce constant surface radiance in all directions, we have Lambertian reflection.

Surface radiance L_r of a Lambertian surface is proportional to the irradiance I_s (incident energy per unit area) of the surface. Consider an infinitesimal surface area dA_s illuminated by an infinitesimal source area dA_i. The flux incident on dA_s may be determined from the source radiance L_i as

$$d^2\Phi_i = L_i \, d\omega_s \, dA_i. \tag{43}$$

From the solid angles subtended by the surface and source areas, we obtain

$$dA_i = d\omega_i r^2, \tag{44}$$

$$d\omega_s = \frac{dA_s \cos \theta_i}{r^2}. \tag{45}$$

Substituting Eqs. (44) and (45) in Eq. (43), we obtain

$$d^2\Phi_i = L_i \, d\omega_i \, dA_s \cos \theta_i. \tag{46}$$

---

[2] We define a smooth surface as one that is either perfectly smooth or "slightly" rough.

The surface irradiance is determined from this equation as

$$E_i = \frac{d^2 \Phi_i}{dA_s}.\tag{47}$$

Since surface radiance is proportional to surface irradiance, and since it is meaningful only when it attains positive values, it can be expressed as

$$L_r = \kappa \max\left[0, (L_i \, d\omega_i \cos \theta_i)\right],\tag{48}$$

where κ determines the fraction of the incident energy that is diffusely reflected by the surface.

4. REFLECTION MODELS FOR COMPUTER VISION AND THEIR APPLICATIONS

The reflection models described in the previous sections are physics-based reflection models. However, some of them, in particular the Beckmann–Spizzichino models, are too complicated to use in computer vision research. Several approximate models have been proposed by the computer vision community.

4.1. Monochromatic Reflection Model

Nayar, Ikeuchi, and Kanade examined the Beckmann–Spizzichino model as well as the Torrance–Sparrow model and performed extensive computer simulations with these models (15). They found that the solutions for rough surfaces can be approximated by a Gaussian function, and that the solutions coincided with those obtained when the Torrance–Sparrow model—under a specific condition—was used. They also found that solutions for smooth surfaces can be roughly approximated by a delta function.

From these findings, they proposed the following three component model for computer vision research:

$$L(\theta_i, \theta_r, \phi_r) = C_b \cos \theta_i + \frac{C_{sl}}{\cos \theta_r} \exp\left(-\frac{\alpha^2}{2\sigma_\alpha^2}\right) + C_{ss}\delta(\theta_i - \theta_r)\delta(\phi_r).$$

$$\tag{49}$$

   The first component represents diffuse reflection due to body reflection components. The second component, referred to as the *specular lobe* component, corresponds to the Beckmann–Spizzichino solution for rough surfaces [Eq. (42)]. The third component, referred to as the *specular spike* component, corresponds to the smooth surfaces [Eq. (41)]. Figure 5.10(A) shows a schematic diagram of the model.

   In the previous schematic diagram, the lobe component had an asymmetric distribution with respect to the specular direction. Nayar, Ikeuchi, and Kanade showed that the lobe component becomes a symmetric distribution with respect to the specular direction as functions of the light source direction for a fixed sensor direction [see Fig. 10(B)].

   Using this new reflection model, for a surface that has both surface and body reflection components, Nayar, Ikeuchi, and Kanade developed a photometric sampling method to determine surface shape as well as the ratio between the specular spike and body reflection component under a moving light source. The object surface is illuminated using extended light sources and is viewed from a single direction. Surface illumination using extended sources makes it possible to ensure the detection of both body and specular spike reflections. Uniformly distributed source directions are used to obtain an image sequence of the object. This method uses the set of image brightness values at each surface point to compute orientation as well as to compute relative strength of the body and the surface reflection components. The simultaneous recovery of shape and reflectance parameters enables the method to adapt to variations in reflectance properties from one scene point to another.

   Tagare and deFigueiredo proposed a three-lobe reflection model (23), as shown in Fig. 5.11. Their normal and forescatter lobe correspond to Nayar-Ikeuchi-Kanade's body and surface reflection components: their model does not make any distinction between specular lobe and specular spike components. The backscatter lobe is the component that reflects the incident light back toward the incident direction. Tagare and deFigueiredo generalized the three-lobe model into a general *n* lobe reflection model.

   Tagare and deFigueiredo proved that if each lobe of the general *n*-lobe model is a monotonic decreasing function from each maximum direction, three lights can be sufficient for a unique inversion of the photometric stereo equation. They also obtained a constraint on the positions of light sources for obtaining this solution.

   By using the Nayar–Ikeuchi–Kanade reflection model, we can classify the several brightness analysis techniques in a uniform manner as shown in Fig. 5.12. Traditional shape from single image such as Horn (7), Ikeuchi and Horn (10), Pentland (17) as well as the shape-from-photometric stereo by Woodham (28), determine surface orientations using the body reflection component. Ikeuchi developed a photometric stereo method with three extended light sources to determine the surface orientations of

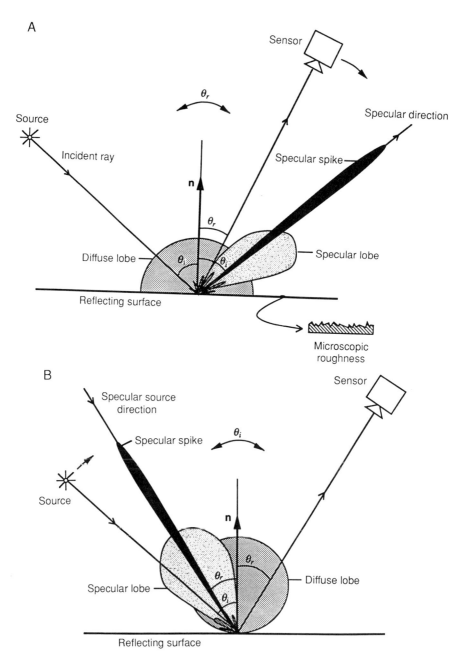

Figure 5.10. Polar plots of the three reflection components: (A) plot as functions of the sensor direction for a fixed source direction; (B) plot as functions of the light source direction for a fixed sensor direction.

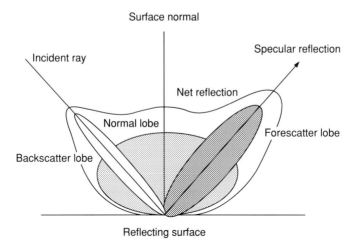

Figure 5.11. *N*-lobe model. From (23) with permission.

specular surfaces having dominant specular spike components, (specular photometric stereo) (9). Sanderson, Weiss, and Nayar also developed an inspection system, Shiny, for specular surfaces based on the specular spike reflection model (19). Healey and Binford developed a method to compute the local orientation, principal curvature and principal directions of a specular surface by examining on a specularity using the specular lobe model (6). Nayar, Ikeuchi, and Kanade proposed the photometric sampling method to determine the surface orientation as well as the reflectance parameters of surfaces with the body and specular spike reflection components (15). Sato, Nayar, and Ikeuchi implemented the 3D photometric sampling device (20). Ikeuchi and Sato proposed the Range brightness fusion method that determines surface reflectance parameters using a depth map and a brightness map. Their analysis was based on a model consisting both body and specular lobe components (11). Coleman and Jain develop a four-light photometric stereo method to determine orientations of surfaces on which both the body and specular lobe reflection components coexist (4). Solomon and Ikeuchi (22) further extended the four-light photometric stereo to determine not only surface orientation but also the reflectance parameters for the same kind of surfaces as Coleman and Jain. No methods have been developed to handle surfaces that have three reflection components simultaneously.

4.2. Dichromatic Reflection Model

So far the models described assume monochromatic incident light: black-and-white light. If an object body consists of inhomogeneous

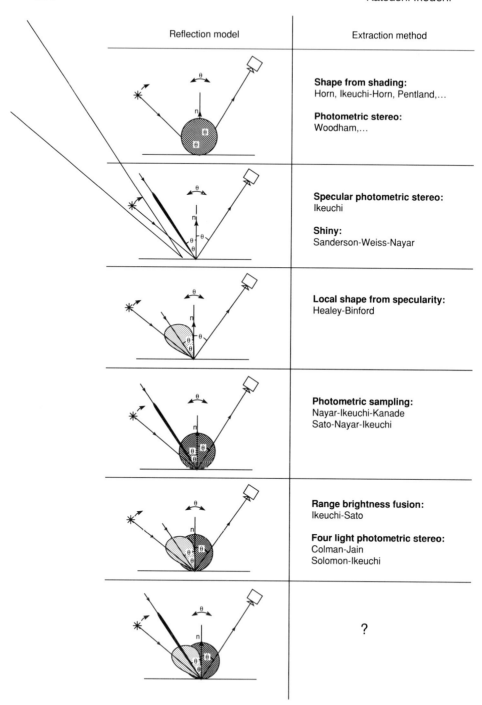

Figure 5.12. Classification of brightness analysis techniques.

dielectric materials, the emitted light has a different color from the incident light. When the light penetrates the surface, as a result of the absorption of a particular band unique to the materials of the body, the body reflection component has a different spectral power distribution (SPD) from the SPD of incident light. On the other hand, the surface reflection component, such as specular spike and specular lobe component, has the same SPD as the SPD of incident light. This is because the surface reflection component is immediately reflected by the boundary between the air and the body.

To capture this characteristic, Shafer (21) proposed dichromatic reflection model:

$$L(\lambda, \theta_i, \theta_r, \phi_r) = L_b(\lambda, \theta_i, \theta_r, \phi_r) + L_s(\lambda, \theta_i, \theta_r, \phi_r), \tag{50}$$

$$= m_b(\theta_i, \theta_r, \phi_r)c_b(\lambda) + m_s(\theta_i, \theta_r, \phi_r)c_s(\lambda), \tag{51}$$

where c_b and c_s denote SPD of the body and surface reflection component, and m_b and m_s denote the geometric coefficient of the body and surface reflection.

Tominaga and Wandell evaluated the dichromatic reflection model using a component analysis of the measured reflected light (24). They concluded that the dichromatic model is correct and that the SPD of the emitting light's specular component is the same as the SPD of the incident light. Lee, Breneman, and Schulte also evaluated the model and came to the same conclusion (14). Using the Reichman body-scattering model (5), Healey demonstrated the near independence of the spectral composition and geometrical scaling of light reflected from a surface. Healey combined the dichromatic reflection model for inhomogeneous dielectrics with a unichromatic reflection model for metals.

Shafer projected his dichromatic reflection model to the red–green–blue (RGB) color space and proved that the color vectors of a uniformly colored surface exist on a plane. Klinker, Shafer, and Kanade evaluated the theory using real data and developed an algorithm to separate a body color image from a color image (12) containing body and surface reflections.

In a color sensor such as the color camera, color filters are interposed between the incoming illumination and the camera. Each filter has a transmittance function, $\tau(\lambda)$, specifying the fraction of light transmitted at each wavelength; thus, the pixel value, p computed with a filter is specified by the integral

$$p = \int L(\lambda)\tau(\lambda)s(\lambda)\,d\lambda, \tag{52}$$

where $L(\lambda)$ denotes the SPD of incident light, and $s(\lambda)$ denotes the responsivity of the camera.

The color space is defined by the response of a color sensor. Typically, three filters (red, green, and blue) are used with transmittance τ_r, τ_g, and τ_b, resulting in a vector of three color values,

$$\mathbf{C}_L = \begin{bmatrix} r \\ g \\ b \end{bmatrix} = \begin{bmatrix} \int L(\lambda)\tau_r(\lambda)s(\lambda)\,d\lambda \\ \int L(\lambda)\tau_g(\lambda)s(\lambda)\,d\lambda \\ \int L(\lambda)\tau_b(\lambda)s(\lambda)\,d\lambda \end{bmatrix}. \tag{53}$$

This three-dimensional space is referred to as *RGB color space*.

This space is a linear transformation. Applying Eq. (53) to Eq. (51), we have

$$\mathbf{C}_L = \begin{bmatrix} r \\ g \\ b \end{bmatrix}$$

$$= \begin{bmatrix} \int m_b(\theta_i,\theta_r,\phi_r)L(\lambda)_b\tau_r(\lambda)s(\lambda) + m_s(\theta_i,\theta_r,\phi_r)L(\lambda)_s\tau_r(\lambda)s(\lambda)\,d\lambda \\ \int m_b(\theta_i,\theta_r,\phi_r)L(\lambda)_b\tau_g(\lambda)s(\lambda) + m_s(\theta_i,\theta_r,\phi_r)L(\lambda)_s\tau_g(\lambda)s(\lambda)\,d\lambda \\ \int m_b(\theta_i,\theta_r,\phi_r)L(\lambda)_b\tau_b(\lambda)s(\lambda) + m_s(\theta_i,\theta_r,\phi_r)L(\lambda)_s\tau_b(\lambda)s(\lambda)\,d\lambda \end{bmatrix}$$

$$= m_b(\theta_i,\theta_r,\phi_r)\begin{bmatrix} \int L(\lambda)_b\tau_r(\lambda)s(\lambda)\,d\lambda \\ \int L(\lambda)_b\tau_g(\lambda)s(\lambda)\,d\lambda \\ \int L(\lambda)_b\tau_b(\lambda)s(\lambda)\,d\lambda \end{bmatrix}$$

$$+ m_s(\theta_i,\theta_r,\phi_r)\begin{bmatrix} \int L(\lambda)_s\tau_r(\lambda)s(\lambda)\,d\lambda \\ \int L(\lambda)_s\tau_g(\lambda)s(\lambda)\,d\lambda \\ \int L(\lambda)_s\tau_b(\lambda)s(\lambda)\,d\lambda \end{bmatrix}$$

$$= m_b(\theta_i,\theta_r,\phi_r)\mathbf{C}_b + m_s(\theta_i,\theta_r,\phi_r)\mathbf{C}_s \tag{54}$$

where $\mathbf{C}_L$ is a vector of the emitted light in the color space, m_b and m_s are the magnitudes of the geometric component, and $\mathbf{C}_b$ and $\mathbf{C}_s$ are the vectors of the body and surface reflection components in the color space.

Consider the color vectors, $\mathbf{C}_L$, of a set of points for a uniformly colored surface. Because the geometry is different at each point, the geometric factors m_b and m_s vary from point to point. However, the color vector $\mathbf{C}_b, \mathbf{C}_s$ of the body and surface reflection components are simply the results of the triple integration of $c_b(\lambda)$ and $c_s(\lambda)$ and do not vary with geometry. Therefore, these color vectors are the same at all points on the same surface.

In other words, the pixel values are a linear combination of C_b and C_s with the coefficients determined by m_b abd m_s at each point. Namely, all the projected points of emitting light exist on a plane spanned by two vectors C_b and C_s in color space, as shown in Fig. 5.13(A). Klinker, Shafer, and Kanade developed an algorithm that used images in which both surface and body reflection components exist. From these images they extracted new images consisting solely of either the surface or the body reflection components. They also developed a new segmentation

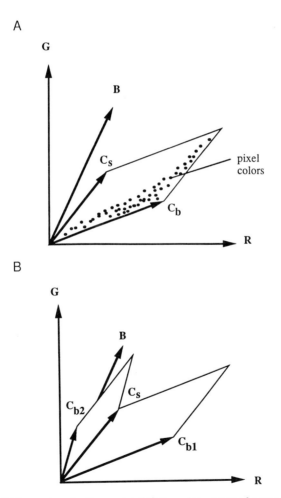

Figure 5.13. Dichromatic reflection model: (A) the color vectors of a set of points on the same uniformly colored surface exist on a plan spanned by the body color vector and the surface color vector; (B) the illuminant vector can be obtained as the intersection of two or more planes in the RGB space.

algorithm based on the model. Bajcsy, Lee, and Leonardis developed a similar technique using hue-saturation color space instead of the RGB color space (2).

Tominaga and Wandell showed how to use light reflected from pairs of surfaces to estimate the SPD of the illuminant. Each surface, i defines a plane in the RGB space defined by the body reflection vector, $\mathbf{C}_b^i$, and surface reflection vector $\mathbf{C}_s$. The surface reflection vector is common among the surfaces. Thus, the estimation problem of the illuminant spectrum can be reduced to finding the common spectral vector $\mathbf{C}_s$, which is defined as the intersection vector of two or more planes in the RGB space [see Fig. 5.13(B)]. Their method can obtain an illuminant SPD without using a reference white standard. Healey developed an algorithm to identify metals and dielectrics in color images, based on his unified reflection model.

Polarization is another dimension to be considered. Wolff proposed a polarization reflectance model (26, 27). This reflectance model accurately predicts the magnitudes of the polarization components of reflected light. By using the model, Wolff proposed a method for segmenting material surfaces according to varying levels of relative electrical conductivity; in particular, this model distinguishes dielectrics, which are nonconducting, from metals, which are highly conductive. Additionally, this method provides cues for distinguishing between three different intensity–edge types: those arising from intrinsic light–dark or color variations, those caused by specularities, and those caused by occluding contours in which the viewing direction has become nearly orthogonal to the surface normals. Analyzing the reflected polarization components enables the separation of diffuse and specular components of reflection.

5. CONCLUSIONS

This section overviewed reflection mechanisms that are useful for computer vision research. We have briefly discussed the Beckmann–Spizzichino and Torrance–Sparrow reflection models. Subsequently, we have shown how to apply these models to computer vision research.

REFERENCES

1. American National Standards Institute, *Surface Texture, ANSI / AMSE B46.1-1978*. ANSI, New York, 1978.
2. R. Bajcsy, S. W. Lee, and A. Leonardis, Color image segmentation with detection of highlights and local illumination induced by interreflections. *Proc. Int. Conf. Pattern Recognition*, pp. 785–790 (1990).

3. P. Beckmann and A. Spizzichino. "The Scattering of Electromagnetic Waves from Rough Surfaces." Pergamon, London, 1963.
4. E. N. Coleman and R. Jain, Obtaining 3-dimensional shape of textured and specular surface using four-source photometry. *Computer Graphics Image Process.*, **18**(4), 309–328 (1982).
5. G. Healey, Using color for geometry-insensitive segmentation. *J. Opt. Soc. Am. A* **6**(6); 920–937 (1989).
6. G. Healey and T. O. Binford, Local shape from specularity. *Comput. Vision, Graphics, Image Process.*, **42**; 62–86 (1988).
7. B. K. P. Horn, Obtaining shape from shading. *In* "The Psychology of Computer Vision" P. H. Winston, ed., pp. 115–155. McGraw-Hill, New York, 1975.
8. B. K. P. Horn and R. W. Sjőberg, "Calculating the Reflectance Map," Tech. Rep. AI Memo 498. Massachusetts Institute of Technology, Artificial Intelligence Laboratory, Cambridge, MA, 1978.
9. K. Ikeuchi, Determining surface orientation of specular surfaces by using the photometric stereo method. *IEEE Trans. Pattern Anal. Mach. Intell.*, **PAMI-3**(6); 661–669 (1981).
10. K. Ikeuchi and B. K. P. Horn, Numerical shape from shading and occluding boundaries. *In* "Computer Vision" (M. J. Brady, ed), pp. 141–184. North Holland Publ., Amsterdam, 1981.
11. K. Ikeuchi and K. Sato, Determining reflectance properties of an object using range and brightness images. *IEEE Trans. Pattern Anal. Mach. Intell.* **PAMI-13**(11); 1139–1153 (1991).
12. G. J. Klinker, S. A. Shafer, and T. Kanade, The measurement of highlights in color image. *Int. J. Comp. Vision* **2**(1) (1988).
13. J. H. Lambert, "Photometria sive de mensura de gratibus luminis colorum et umbrae." Eberhard Klett, Augsburg, 1960.
14. H. C. Lee, E. J. Breneman, and C. P. Schulte, Modeling light reflection for computer color vision. *IEEE Trans. Pattern Anal. Mach. Intell.* **PAMI-12**(4); 402–409 (1990).
15. S. K. Nayar, K. Ikeuchi, and T. Kanade, Surface reflection: Physical and geometrical perspectives. *IEEE Trans. Pattern Anal. Mach. Intell.* **PAMI-13**(7); 661–634 (1991).
16. F. E. Nicodemus, J. C. Richmond, and J. J. Hsia, "Geometrical Considerations and Nomenclature for Reflectance," NBS Monogr., Vol. 160. Department of Commerce, National Bureau of Standards, Washington, DC, 1977.
17. A. P. Pentland, Local shading analysis. *IEEE Trans. Pattern Anal. Mach. Intell.* **PAMI-6**(2); 170–187 (1984).
18. B. T. Phong, Illumination for computer generated pictures. *Commun. ACM* **18**(6); 311–317 (1975).
19. A. C. Sanderson, L. E. Weiss, and S. K. Nayar, Structured highlight inspection of specular surfaces. *IEEE Trans. Pattern Anal. Mach. Intell.* **PAMI-10**(1); 44–55 (1988).
20. H. Sato, S. Nayar, and K. Ikeuchi, Extracting shape and reflectance of glossy surfaces by using 3d photometric sampling method. *International Association for Pattern Recognition Workshop Mach. Vision Appl.*, *1990*, pp. 82–88 (1990).

21. S. Shafer, Using color to separate reflection components. *Color Res. Appl.* **10**(4); 210–218 (1985).

22. F. Solomon and K. Ikeuchi, Inspecting specular lobe objects using four light sources. *Proc. IEEE Int. Conf. Robotics Autom., 1992.* pp. 1707–1712. Nice, France (1992).

23. H. D. Tagare and R. J. P. deFigueiredo, A theory of photometric stereo for an class of diffuse non-lambertian surfaces. *IEEE Trans. Pattern Anal. Mach. Intell.* **PAMI-13**(2); 133–152 (1991).

24. S. Tominaga and B. Wandell, Standard surface reflectance model and illuminant estimation. *J. Opt. Soc. Am. A* **6**(4); 576–584 (1989).

25. K. E. Torrance and E. M. Sparrow, Theory for off-specular reflection from roughened surfaces. *J. Opt. Soc. Am.* **57**; 1105–1114 (1967).

26. L. Wolff, Polarization-based material classification from specular reflection. *IEEE Trans. Pattern Anal. Mach. Intell.* **PAMI-12**(11); 1059–1071 (1990).

27. L. Wolff and T. Boult, Constraining object features using a polarization reflectance model. *IEEE Trans. Pattern Anal. Mach. Intell.* **PAMI-13**(7); 635–657 (1991).

28. R. J. Woodham, "Reflectance Map Techniques for Analyzing Surface Defects in Metal Castings," Tech. Rep. AI-TR-457. Massachusetts Institute of Technology, Artificial Intelligence Laboratory, Cambridge, MA, 1978.

Chapter **6**

Extracting Shape-from-Shading

ALEX P. PENTLAND and MARTIN BICHSEL*

The Media Laboratory
Massachusetts Institute of Technology
Cambridge, Massachusetts

Shading appears to me to be of supreme importance in perspective, because, without it opaque and solid bodies will be ill-defined . . . .

Leonardo Da Vinci, Notebooks

1. INTRODUCTION

As we look around us, most of the time we see a mosaic of relatively smooth, homogeneous surfaces. This makes it natural to model images as being composed of homogeneous (but possibly textured) patches.

Present address: Institut für Informatik, UNI Irchel, Winterthurerstr. 190, 8057 Zürich, Switzerland.

161

**HANDBOOK OF PATTERN RECOGNITION
AND IMAGE PROCESSING: COMPUTER VISION**

However, the prevalence of homogeneous patches creates a problem when trying to recover 3D structure from a image. This is because most of the most familiar vision techniques—stereo, structure-from-motion, depth-from-focus—function best at edges, and only weakly or not at all in the interior of a homogeneous region. Consequently, we can only recover a skeleton of the surrounding scene's geometry using these standard vision techniques.

Such considerations provide strong motivation for developing algorithms that can extract shape from the variations in intensity that exist within a single homogeneous patch. It is not surprising, therefore, that this problem was one of the first addressed by the field of computer vision.

Perhaps the first modern work was Horn's 1970 doctoral thesis (5), which defined the shape-from-shading problem as follows:

> Given an intensity image of a continuous surface with constant, known reflectance and illumination, recover the shape of that surface.

This problem can be shown to be underdetermined, so typically it is also assumed that the depth and orientation of a few points, such as the brightest points or the edge points, are also known.

The overall idea is that images are composed of homogeneous patches, and that stereo, motion, or focus can provide depth information at the patch edges. Shading can then be used to "fill in" the surface between these edges. This general framework for thinking about recovering shape-from-shading has remained the dominant one to date.

Perhaps the major defect in this approach is that the assumed image model is too cartoon-like: smooth variations in surface color, nearby illuminants, and reflection from nearby surfaces are all ignored. Still, however, many images are at least reasonably well modeled as a mosaic of homogeneous patches, so that often this is a useful approach to the problem of recovering 3D structure from the image.

There have been two general classes of algorithm developed: local algorithms, which attempt to estimate shape from local variations in image intensity, and global algorithms, which attempt to propagate information across a shaded surface starting from points with known surface orientation.

Local algorithms, originally suggested by Pentland (14) as being more similar to human visual processing, attempt to extract qualitative estimates of surface shape from the shading information within a small image neighborhood. These local methods of estimating surface orientation have been shown generally capable of producing good qualitative estimates of shape (4, 14, 16), and are perhaps the best computational model of human visual processing. Except for certain imaging conditions, however, they do not recover metrically accurate estimates of surface shape.

Global algorithms, primarily due to Horn and his students (5–9) offer the hope of extracting metrically accurate models of surfaces from their images. Following some initial research using the characteristic strips method, all of these algorithms have made use of strong continuity assumptions in order to extract estimates of surface orientation. The resulting *regularization algorithm* uses this smoothness constraint to relate adjoining points, enabling spatially isolated information about absolute surface orientation (which must be derived using some other technique) to be iteratively propagated across the surface. Typically thousands of iterations are required to obtain convergence. Moreover, the use of a strong smoothness constraint implies that the algorithms will not produce exact solutions except under certain limited situations (17).

In 1991 Oliensis and Dupuis showed that another approach to global shape-from-shading was feasible (10–12). They proved that, given initial values at the singular points of an image (i.e., the points of maximum brightness), use of a conservative minimization process to successively approximate the solution surface would lead to a stable solution—*without* the need of any strong smoothness or shape assumptions. Unfortunately, their algorithm and its derivation are rather complex.

There are, however, some simple truths underlying their work: first, that the shape-from-shading problem typically has a unique, well-posed solution, and second, that a stable solution method will require successively approximating the surface in a conservative manner. In fact, in the second half of this chapter we will show that the simple characteristic-strips method, originally used by Horn in his 1970 doctoral thesis (5), can be made to produce a stable, accurate, and efficient solution simply by modifying the integration step to successively approximate the solution surface in a conservative fashion (2, 3).

2. BACKGROUND AND NOTATION

By assuming that surface patches are homogeneous and uniformly lit by distant light sources, then the brightness $E(x, y)$ seen at the image plane often depends only on the orientation of the surface. This dependence of brightness on surface orientation can be represented as a function $R(\vec{n}) = R(n_1, n_2, n_3)$ defined on the Gaussian sphere, i.e., by representing the brightness as a function of the unit surface normal $\vec{n} = (n_1, n_2, n_3)$.

In the past, authors have often chosen to represent the reflectance properties of a surface in terms of the partial derivatives of the surface height,

$$p = \frac{\partial z(x, y)}{\partial x}, \qquad q = \frac{\partial z(x, y)}{\partial y}, \qquad (1)$$

rather than as a function of the surface normal. The function $R(p, q)$ is known as the *reflectance map*. The representation of reflectance $R(\vec{n})$ on the Gaussian sphere and the reflectance map are related to each other by

$$\vec{n}^T = \left(\frac{-p}{\sqrt{p^2 + q^2 + 1}}, \frac{-q}{\sqrt{p^2 + q^2 + 1}}, \frac{1}{\sqrt{p^2 + q^2 + 1}} \right). \qquad (2)$$

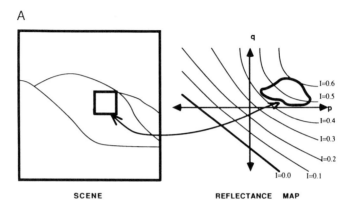

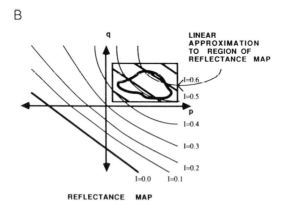

Figure 6.1. (A) Each continuous patch in the image maps to a continuous patch in the reflectance map space; (B) for small patches, the isointensity lines may be well approximated by a linear function, so that the shape-from-shading problem can be solved using linear techniques.

Given the simplification to homogeneous, uniformly lit patches, we can formulate the shape-from-shading problem as finding a solution to the *brightness equation*:

$$R(\vec{n}(x, y)) = E(x, y). \qquad (3)$$

A continuous surface $z(x, y)$ with normal $\vec{n}(x, y)$ is a solution as long as it is consistent with the brightness equation.

The mathematical difficulty in finding such a solution surface is that for any brightness $E(x, y)$ there are typically an infinite number of normals $\vec{n}(x, y) = (n_1, n_2, n_3)$ that satisfy Eq. (3). These normals form a contour of constant brightness on the Gaussian sphere, and only by considering surrounding points can we determine which normal is the correct one. The only exception to this is the brightest possible image value, which can be generated by only one normal (typically one that points in the mean illumination direction). An additional complication is that we cannot observe the brightness $E(x, y)$ directly, but only $I(x, y)$, a measurement of image-plane intensity that is (hopefully!) a well-behaved function of brightness.

This situation is illustrated in Fig. 6.1(A). A continuous patch of surface maps to a continuous patch in (p, q), the surface orientation space. Similarly, each point in the image corresponds to some point in the reflectance map; the problem is that each measured image intensity can lie anywhere along the corresponding isointensity line.

3. LOCAL SHAPE-FROM-SHADING

As illustrated in Fig. 6.1(B), for suffciently small image patches the isointensity lines in the corresponding portion of the reflectance map are nearly parallel lines. Thus over a small region we can always approximate the reflectance map by a linear function of the partial derivatives (p, q).

This approximation can be determined by taking a first-order Taylor series expansion of $R(p, q)$ about the central point (p_0, q_0), to obtain

$$
\begin{aligned}
E(x, y) &\approx R(p_0, q_0) \\
&+ (p - p_0) \left. \frac{\partial R(p, q)}{\partial p} \right|_{p=p_0, q=q_0} \\
&+ (q - q_0) \left. \frac{\partial R(p, q)}{\partial q} \right|_{p=p_0, q=q_0} \\
&= k_1 + k_2 p + k_3 q.
\end{aligned}
\qquad (4)
$$

In the case of the Lambertian reflectance function, $k_1 = \cos \sigma$, $k_2 = \cos \tau \sin \sigma$, $k_3 = \sin \tau \sin \sigma$, where τ and σ are the tilt and slant angles of the illuminant. This linear approximation of the reflectance function becomes accurate over a larger area as the illuminant becomes more oblique, and over a smaller area as the illuminant moves closer to the viewer's direction.

Equation (4) may be transformed into the Fourier domain in order to obtain a convenient and efficient solution. Letting $F_z(f, \theta)$ be the complex Fourier spectrum of $z(x, y)$ (where f is radial frequency and θ is orientation) then because p and q are the partial derivatives of $z(x, y)$ their Fourier transforms $F_p(f, \theta)$ and $F_q(f, \theta)$ are simply

$$F_p(f, \theta) = 2\pi \cos \theta f e^{i\pi/2} F_z(f, \theta), \tag{5}$$

$$F_q(f, \theta) = 2\pi \sin \theta f e^{i\pi/2} F_z(f, \theta). \tag{6}$$

Equation (4) can now be rewritten in the Fourier domain as

$$F_E(f, \theta) = H(f, \theta) F_z(f, \theta), \tag{7}$$

where $F_E(f, \theta)$ is the Fourier spectrum of the brightness image and $H(f, \theta)$ is a linear transfer function that relates the Fourier transform of the brightness to that of the surface.

Thus given a linear reflectance function approximation, the surface shape can be estimated in closed form by use of the inverse transfer function, $H^{-1}(f, \theta)$:

$$F_z(f, \theta) = H^{-1}(f, \theta) F_I(f, \theta)$$

$$= \left(2\pi f e^{i\pi/2} [k_2 \cos \theta + k_3 \sin \theta]\right)^{-1} F_E(f, \theta). \tag{8}$$

Note that in this linear formulation, the Fourier components of the surface that are exactly perpendicular to the illuminant (i.e., when $\cos \theta / \sin \theta = -k_3/k_2$) cannot be seen in the image data, and must either be obtained from other information sources or simply set to some default value. When such boundary conditions are not available (as is often the case), the assumption of general viewing position may be invoked to argue that these unseen Fourier components should be assumed to be zero, because if they were large, then small variations in viewing geometry would produce large changes in the estimated surface shape.

The recovery process can be improved by use of Wiener filtering to remove noise and nonlinear components of the image-intensity pattern (1). If the contaminating noise $N(f, \theta)$ is modeled as being a fixed fraction of the spectral power along each image orientation, and the surface $S(f, \theta)$ is modeled as a fractal Brownian function (15) whose power spectrum is proportional to f^{-4} (or, equivalently, as a second-order Markov random field or as a "thin-plate model") then the optimal RMSE (root-mean-square error) estimate of surface shape is

$$F_z(f, \theta) = H^{-1}(f, \theta) \|H(f, \theta)\|^2 \left[\|H(f, \theta)\|^2 + \frac{\|N(f, \theta)\|}{\|S(f, \theta)\|} \right]^{-1} F_E(f, \theta)$$

$$= (2\pi f e^{i\pi/2} \{\text{sign}[\cos(\tau - \theta)] d + (k_2 \cos\theta + k_3 \sin\theta)\})^{-1} F_E(f, \theta),$$

$$(9)$$

where τ is the angle of illumination in the image plane and $0.5 < d < 0.75$. In actual practice Eq. (9) has been found to perform much better than Eq. (8). For more detail, see Pentland (16).

3.1. A Biological Mechanism

The ability to recover surface shape by use of Eq. (9) suggests a parallel filtering mechanism for recovering shape-from-shading. Such a mechanism may be relevant to biological vision, as it is widely accepted that early stages of the human visual system can be regarded as being composed of filters tuned to orientation, spatial frequency and phase. Figure 6.2 illustrates a mechanism based on filters with similar characteristics. The transformation $\vec{T}$ is a decomposition of the image using filters that form an orthonormal basis set and are localized in both space and spatial frequency.

In order to recover surface shape from this filter set, the transformations indicated in Eq. (9) must be performed, as indicated in Fig. 6.2. These transformations are (1) phase-shift the filter responses by $\pi/2$, accomplished by switching the outputs of the sine and cosine phase filters; (2) scale the filter amplitude by $1/f$, where f is the filter's central spatial frequency; (3) normalize average filter responses within each orientation to remove the illumination's directional bias; and (4) reconstruct an elevation surface from the scaled amplitudes of the filter set. The final step, reconstruction, can be accomplished by passing the signal through a second, identical set of filters. This produces the estimated surface shape within the windowed area of the image (the "receptive field" of the filters). For more detail, see Pentland (16).

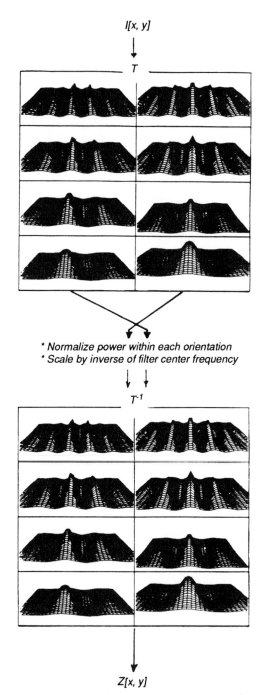

Figure 6.2. A shape-from-shading mechanism. A transformation $\vec{T}$ produces localized measurements of sine and cosine phase frequency content, and then the inverse transformation is applied, switching sine and cosine phase amplitudes and scaling the filter amplitude in proportion to the central frequency. The output of this process is the recovered surface shape.

3.2. Surface Recovery Results

   The first example is one that has a very nearly linear reflectance function, so that it satisfies the assumptions of the theory almost exactly and thus we can expect accurate surface recovery. Figure 6.3(A) shows an image of a plaster cast of a nickel. The surface shape was estimated using Eq. (9); the illuminant direction was estimated from the Fourier transform of the image, as described in Appendix A.

   The recovered shape is illustrated in Fig. 6.3(B). This image is generated by using standard computer graphics techniques to first render a shaded, perspective view of the recovered surface shape, and then to project straight lines onto the surface. These straight lines are seen as bending surface contours in the resulting image. The resulting image gives most viewers an accurate impression of the actual surface shape.

   By comparing Fig. 6.3(B) to a real nickel, the reader can determine that the surface recovery is in fact quite accurate. The main defect is that the areas surrounding the head are not sufficiently flat.

   Figures 6.3(C) and (D) show a second example of recovering surface shape, this time using an image of the very shiny metal surface of a new nickel. In this case we can expect surface recovery to be somewhat less accurate, as the surface is quite specular. Figure 6.3(D) shows the surface recovered from Fig. 6.3(C). As expected the surface recovery is somewhat less accurate than when a diffusely reflecting plaster nickel was used; however, the differences between the two examples are surprisingly small.

   A third example of surface recovery is shown in Fig. 6.4. Figure 6.4(A) is a complex image widely used in image compression research. Figure 6.4(B) shows a shaded perspective view of the recovered surface in the neighborhood of the face. The eyes, cheek, chin, lips, nose, and nostrils can all be clearly seen in the recovered surface, and are generally correct. The wavy, dark area in the lower right is a small portion of the woman's hair.

4. GLOBAL SHAPE-FROM-SHADING

   We have seen how the shape-from-shading problem may be solved by a very simple linear mechanism within a sufficiently small region of the image. We would now like to link adjoining patches together, to obtain a global solution to the brightness equation.

   If we know the normal of a surface patch in an image, then we can "grow" a solution by integrating that information along the direction of steepest descent on the reflectance map. This technique is known as the

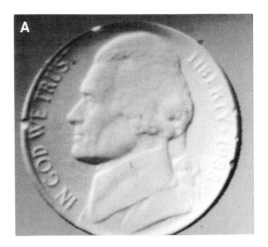

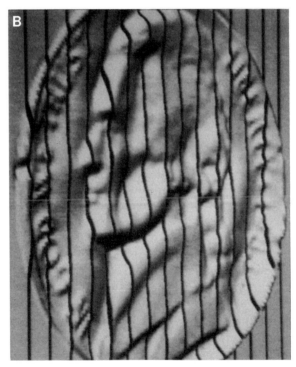

Figure 6.3. (A) Image of a plaster cast of a nickel; (B) a shaded perspective view of the surface extracted from the plaster cast image. (*Figure continues.*)

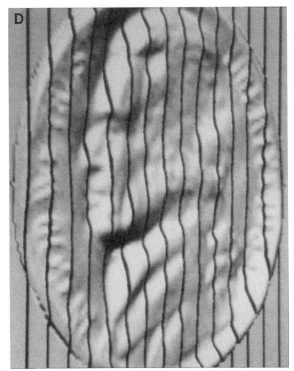

Figure 6.3 (*Continued*). (C) image of a shiny new nickel; (D) a shaded perspective view of the surface extracted from the shiny nickel image.

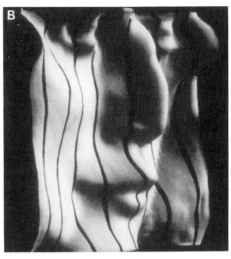

Figure 6.4. (A) An image widely used in image compression research; (B) a shaded perspective view of the recovered surface.

method of characteristic strips, and was perhaps the first method tried for solving the shape-from-shading problem (5). This approach, however, is unstable; characteristic strips originating from a single smooth surface patch will tend to separate, leading to a fractured, chaotic solution surface. This lead researchers to investigate regularization methods, which smooth the surface in order to produce a continuous, stable solution.

Singular points play a key role in this integration process, because each singular point introduces a threefold ambiguity (locally convex, concave, or saddle-shaped) to the solution. This ambiguity can be removed by employing a conservative "minimum downhill" rule while performing the integration step. This rule is of the following form:

- Pass surface information only to points that are more distant from the light source (i.e., to points "downhill" from the singular point). This guarantees causality (directionality) while propagating information across the surface.
- Among different possible paths at a point, choose the path that leads the least away from the light source (a "minimum downhill" integration rule).

Bichsel has shown that use of this integration rule converts the characteristic strips method into a simple, stable, and efficient algorithm (2). Appendix B provides Bichsel's C code program, which implements this algorithm.

4.1. Integration to Determine Surface Height

In order to update the height at (x, y) let us scan over the neighboring points on an infinitesimal circle around (x, y) trying to propagate height information from the points on this circle toward (x, y). A planar surface patch obeys the surface equation

$$xn_1 + yn_2 + (z - z_0) n_3 = 0 \Leftrightarrow z = z_0 - \frac{xn_1 + yn_2}{n_3}, \qquad (10)$$

where z_0 is an arbitrary vertical offset of the patch. Taking a small step (dx, dy) and expressing it in polar coordinates $(dx = \cos(\phi) \, ds, \; dy = \sin(\phi) \, ds)$ allows us to express the slope $\sigma(\phi, \vec{n}) := (dz/ds(\phi, \vec{n}))$ in the direction $(\cos(\phi), \sin(\phi))$ as a function of the surface normal:

$$\sigma(\phi, \vec{n}) = -\frac{\cos(\phi)n_1 + \sin(\phi)n_2}{n_3}. \qquad (11)$$

For each direction $(\cos(\phi), \sin(\phi))$ let us choose the slope $\sigma(\phi)$ corresponding to the steepest descent in the direction $(-\cos(\phi), -\sin(\phi))$ toward (x, y) or, equivalently, the direction of steepest ascent in the direction $(\cos(\phi), \sin(\phi))$. This choice will guarantee that the final surface fulfills the brightness equation. The steepest ascent in the direction $(\cos(\phi), \sin(\phi))$ is given by

$$0 = \frac{d}{d\alpha}(\cos(\phi) \, p(\alpha) + \sin(\phi) \, q(\alpha)) \qquad (12)$$

where α is an arbitrary parameter along the curve of constant brightness in the brightness map for which the brightness equation is fulfilled.

For each direction $(\cos(\phi), \sin(\phi))$ there are usually two solutions $(p(\phi), q(\phi))$ corresponding to opposite points on the Gaussian sphere that fulfill Eq. (12). Causality of the algorithm can be guaranteed by always choosing the solution that leads away from the light source when moving from a point on the circle toward (x, y):

$$(\cos(\phi), \sin(\phi), \sigma(\phi)) \cdot \vec{l} \geq 0 \qquad (13)$$

where "$\cdot$" denotes the scalar product and $\vec{l}$ is the illumination direction. This downhill rule will guarantee that solutions can propagate from a neighboring point (x_0, y_0) to (x, y) only if this neighboring point is closer to the light source, that is, if $(x, y, z(x, y)) \cdot \vec{l} \leq (x_0, y_0, z(x_0, y_0)) \cdot \vec{l}$, so that loops and infinite spirals are avoided.[1]

Requiring that the surface be continuous in the direction ϕ and propagating the solution from a point $(x + ds \cos(\phi), y + ds \sin(\phi))$ toward (x, y) usually leads to a different estimated height $\hat{z}$ for each ϕ:

$$\hat{z}^{t+1}(x, y, \phi) = z^t(x + ds \cos(\phi), y + ds \sin(\phi)) - ds\, \sigma(\phi) \quad (14)$$

where superscript t denotes the time step in the propagation across the image. Among the possible directions ϕ let us choose the estimate $\hat{z}$ which brings $z(x, y)$ closest to the light source, retaining the previous value if it was closest:

$$z^{t+1}(x, y) = \max\{\sup_\phi[\hat{z}^{t+1}(x, y, \phi)], z^t(x, y)\} \quad (15)$$

Note that instead of computing the distance to the light source, only the local surface height needs to be computed and maximized for selecting the optimum ϕ, as x and y remain fixed at each image location. Consequently, as long as the angle between the illumination direction and the optical axis is less than 90°, then the distance to the light source is a monotonically increasing function of the surface height only.

This minimum distance rule will guarantee the convergence of the algorithm. When viewed from the light source direction, Eqs. (13) and (15) can be summarized as a *minimum downhill rule*.

This method of integration can be proven to converge to a unique, correct surface. For additional details, see Bichsel and Pentland (3).

4.2. Implementation on a Discrete Grid

On a discrete grid we have to replace the maximization over all angles by a maximization over a finite number of angles. In the present algorithm this maximization is carried out over the eight angles $\phi_k = k\pi/4$, $k \in \{0 \cdots 7\}$. For a move in a diagonal direction the surface height is linearly interpolated at a distance $\sqrt{\frac{1}{2}}$, whereas for a horizontal or vertical move the height of the nearest neighbor is selected. For each direction and each image location the slope $(dz/ds)_k(x, y, \phi)$ leading farthest away from the light source can be precomputed and thus needs to be calculated only once.

---

[1]If there is more than one solution to these constraints it is possible to add more constraints to remove the ambiguity, so that we end up with a unique slope $\sigma(\phi)$ for each direction $(\cos(\phi), \sin(\phi))$. If no solution is compatible with Eq. (13), on the other hand, a step leading most away from the light source would be the corresponding choice.

What kind of solutions do we expect for Eq. (12)? The curves of constant brightness in the reflectance map can be either closed contours or curved lines that go to infinity at both ends, because they form closed contours on the Gaussian sphere. If such a contour happens to cross the horizontal great circle, then the corresponding curve in the reflectance map will go to infinity in the direction of the normal on the Gaussian sphere. As the light source becomes tilted, there will be more and more curves in the reflectance map that have their ends at infinity, and these curves will tend to become straight lines.

Looking for a steepest descent solution for low brightness values $E(x, y)$, we will find a $\sigma = \infty$ for most step directions. The directions for which a solution exists will form a narrow angle with respect to the illumination direction. Thus the maximum criterion in Eq. (15) will pick out neighboring points in this sector so that, for low brightness values, the surface height is determined approximately by integration in the direction opposite to the direction of light. This provides us with a nice link to linear shape from the shading methods described above.

For low brightness values an infinite slope may be found in all the discrete directions, so that no solution can be constructed. If one of the discrete directions aligns with the projected illumination direction, on the other hand, then the existence of a solution is not further restricted by the discrete approximation.

Therefore we first rotate the original image in order to align one of the discrete directions with the illumination direction. Best results are obtained for alignment with a diagonal. After the processing, the resulting depth map is rotated back, ending up with the original orientation.

4.3. An Example: Lambertian Reflectance

The Lambertian reflectance law, for an illumination direction $\vec{l}$, with additional uniform ambient light, leading to an overall increase in brightness I_a, takes the form

$$\tilde{R}(\vec{n}) = \frac{R(\vec{n}) - I_a}{I_0 - I_a} = \frac{i_1 p + i_2 q + i_3}{\sqrt{1 + p^2 + q^2}}, \tag{16}$$

$$\tilde{R}^2(1 + p^2 + q^2) = (-i_1 p - i_2 q + i_3)^2, \tag{17}$$

where I_0 is the maximum possible brightness, that is, the brightness at a singular point. (p_s, q_s) describes the surface orientation at a singular point. Let us choose a step direction $(\cos(\phi), \sin(\phi))$ and rotate our coordinate system in the image plane such that the x axis is aligned with this direction. In this rotated coordinate system the reflectance law takes the same form, except that the illumination vector (i_1, i_2, i_3) has to be replaced with $(\cos(\phi)i_1 - \sin(\phi)i_2, \cos(\phi)i_2 + \sin(\phi)i_1, i_3)$. Then we have again

$$\tilde{R}(p, q) = \frac{-i_1 p - i_2 q + i_3}{\sqrt{1 + p^2 + q^2}}. \tag{18}$$

The constraint of parallel slope means that the derivative with respect to q has to vanish:

$$0 = \frac{d}{dq} \tilde{R}(p, q) = \frac{-i_2}{\sqrt{1 + p^2 + q^2}} - q \frac{-i_1 p - i_2 q + i_3}{\left(1 + p^2 + q^2\right)^{3/2}}, \tag{19}$$

$$= \tilde{R} \frac{i_2}{i_1 p + i_2 q - i_3} - \frac{\tilde{R}^3 q}{\left(i_1 p + i_2 q - i_3\right)^2}, \tag{20}$$

$$0 = i_2(i_1 p + i_2 q - i_3) - \tilde{R}^2 q = q\left(i_2^2 - \tilde{R}^2\right) + p i_2 i_1 - i_2 i_3, \tag{21}$$

$$q = \frac{p i_2 i_1 - i_2 i_3}{\tilde{R}^2 - i_2^2}. \tag{22}$$

Combining this with Eq. (17), the brightness equation, and solving a quadratic equation results in

$$p = \frac{-i_1 i_3 \pm \sqrt{\left(1 - \tilde{R}^2\right)\left(\tilde{R}^2 - i_2^2\right)}}{\tilde{R}^2 - i_2^2 - i_1^2}. \tag{23}$$

The $\pm$ in Eq. (23) has to be replaced by a "$-$". If the numerator of Eq. (23) is positive, then the "$-$" corresponds to the solution leading away from the light source whereas in the case of a negative numerator the "$-$" corresponds to a surface normal with positive z component. In the latter case a solution is valid only if $i_1 \le 0$; that is, the displacement vector is pointing away from the light source.

4.4. Surface Recovery Results

   Two experiments are shown here, one using synthetic images in order to illustrate noise sensitivity, and the other using a real object. In these experiments a simple Lambertian reflectance law was assumed and only one iteration was used to determine the step vector $d\vec{s}$, as described in Section 4.3. The computer code for these experiments is included in Appendix B.

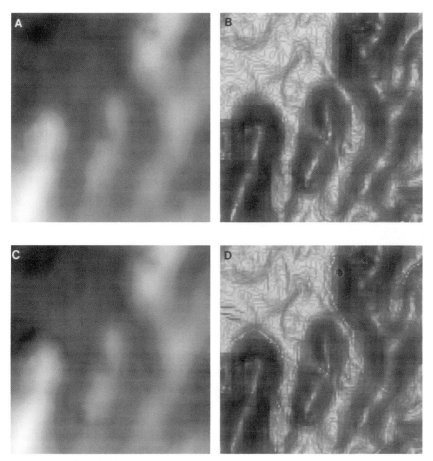

Figure 6.5. (A) Original depth map; (B) shaded version of the original depth map, illumination vector; $(0, 0, 1)$; (C) recovered depth map, assumed illumination direction $(0, 0, 1)$; (D) shaded version of recovered depth map, illumination vector; $(0, 0, 1)$. RMS depth error is 3.3% of dynamic range.

4.4.1. Using A Synthetic Image

Figure 6.5(A) shows an experiment in which a range map of a mountainous area was synthetically shaded with a Lambertian reflectance law, to produce the image shown in Fig. 6.5(B). Eleven singular points were then specified, and the surface recovered using the program in Appendix B. Figure 6.5(C) shows the recovered range surface after eight iterations, which has an RMS depth error of 8.4 depth units, i.e., 3.3% of the total depth range. Figure 6.5(D) shows a synthetically shaded image produced from the recovered depth map.

In order to get an estimate of the sensitivity of the algorithm to image noise, white Gaussian noise was added to the image in Fig. 6.5(B). Table 6.1 shows the resulting RMS error in the recovered depth map for various amounts of noise.

In an additional experiment the RMS depth error was measured for an erroneous estimate of the light-source direction. The angle between the true light source and the estimated light source was chosen to be 10° in a first test and 20° in a second test. The tests were again carried out using the synthetic image in Fig. 6.5(B). The results were that for a 10° error in the light-source direction the recovered depth map showed an RMS error of 14.8 depth units, while for a 20° light-source error an RMS error of

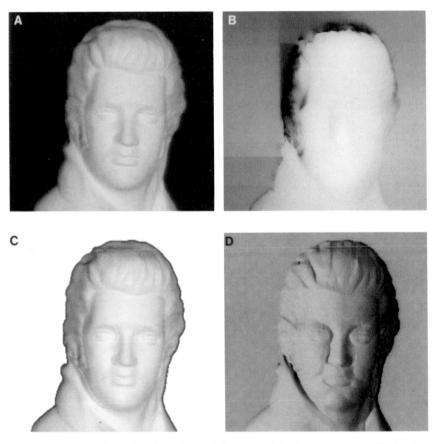

Figure 6.6. (A) Original brightness image; (B) recovered depth map, assumed illumination direction $(0, 0, 1)$; (C) shaded version of recovered depth map, original illumination vector; $(0, 0, 1)$; (D) shaded version of recovered depth map, illumination vector, $(1, 0, 1)$. Self-illumination from the cheeks and the lip to the nose seems to be the main cause of error.

TABLE 6.1

Sensitivity Analysis

	σ_n				
	0	10	20	30	40
$E_{RMS}(\sigma_n)^a$	8.4	8.5	9.8	13.4	16.9
$E_{RMS}(\sigma_n)/E_{RMS}(0)$	1.00	1.01	1.16	1.60	2.01

[a]Root-mean-square depth error E_{RMS} (depth units) as a function of image noise standard deviation σ_n [gray levels].

24.6 depth units was observed. Almost half of this error was due to an overall, average tilt to the recovered surface, corresponding directly to the magnitude of erroneous light-source tilt.

4.4.2. Using A Real Image

Figure 6.6(A) shows a stone bust of Elvis illuminated from the front. In Fig. 6.6 only one singular point, on the nose tip, was specified. Figure 6.6(B) shows the depth map recovered after eight iterations. Figures 6.6(C) and (D) show the recovered depth map illuminated from two different directions. As can be seen, an accurate depth map was recovered. The most pronounced deviations from the true surface are around the edge of the nose, and seem to be due mainly to self-illumination of the surface.

5. SUMMARY

The problem of extracting surface shape from homogeneous, uniformly lit regions has been described, and two solutions presented. The first solution uses linear filters and point nonlinearities to obtain local estimates of shape, and provides a plausible theory of biological functioning. The second links boundary conditions and local shading information together to obtain a global solution to the shape-from-shading problem.

Experiments confirm that both algorithms are capable of good performance. The local analysis algorithm provides surprisingly robust estimates of surface shape, while the global algorithm efficiently produces accurate estimates of the 3D surface shape. The computer code for the global algorithm is included in Appendix B.

APPENDIX A: ILLUMINANT DIRECTION

Pentland (13) introduced a method of estimating illuminant direction from the distribution of image derivatives as a function of image direction. The method works by assuming a statistically uniform distribution of surface orientations, and then performing a maximum-likelihood analysis to estimate the cosine variation in image gradient magnitude induced by the directionality of the illuminant. In summary, the result is that

$$(x_L^*, y_L^*) = (\beta^T\beta)^{-1}\beta^T(dI_1, dI_2, \ldots, dI_n), \tag{24}$$

where (x_L^*, y_L^*) are the unnormalized x and y components of the illuminant direction, β is a $2 \times n$ matrix of directions (dx_i, dy_i), and dI_i is the mean magnitude of $dI(x, y)/dx_i + dI(x, y)/dy_i$.

Given (x_L^*, y_L^*), one may then find the complete illuminant direction, which is simply

$$x_L = x_L^*/k \qquad y_L = y_L^*/k \qquad z_L = \sqrt{1 - x_L^2 - y_L^2}, \tag{25}$$

where

$$k = \sqrt{E(dI^2) - E(dI)^2} \tag{26}$$

and $E(dI)$ is the expected value of $dI/dx_i + dI/dy_i$ over all directions i.

This method has proven to be quite robust, however the assumption of uniformly distributed surface orientations is disagreeably strong. This method can be substantially improved by observing that in Eq. (8) the illuminant produces a similar effect in *each frequency band*. Thus, using the much weaker assumption that the power in a particular spatial frequency band is uniformly distributed over orientation,[2] the same formula can be used to estimate the illuminant direction, by substituting the magnitude of the Fourier components for magnitude of the first derivatives. In particular, Eq. (24) becomes

$$(x_L^*, y_L^*) = (\beta^T\beta)^{-1}\beta^T(m_1, m_2, \ldots, m_n), \tag{27}$$

where the m_i are the magnitude of the Fourier components within the selected frequency band in direction (dx, dy).

[2]Or, more precisely, is not distributed in a way that is correlated with the illuminant's effects.

APPENDIX B: COMPUTER CODE

```
/*
Basic code for global shape from shading
        Author: Martin Bichsel,  15-Mar-1992
*/


void DirectionalSlope(float ***dz, float **Pic,long nCol,long nRow, float *vI)
{ /* dz[0..nRow-1][0..nCol-1][0..7]: Change of surface height step in direction
     i*45 degrees, i in[0..7], assuming a Lambertian reflectance law  (output)*/
  /* Pic[0..nRow-1][0..nCol-1]: Rotated normalized brightnesses */
  /* vI[0..2] Normalized illumination vector pointing towards light source */

  long i,j,iDir;
  float sq05=sqrt(0.5),e3,i1[8],i2[8],sina,Det,temp,nom,eps=1.0e-6;

  for (iDir = 0; iDir < 8; iDir++) {
     i1[iDir] = -cos(iDir*0.785398)*vI[0]-sin(iDir*0.785398)*vI[1];
     i2[iDir] =  sin(iDir*0.785398)*vI[0]-cos(iDir*0.785398)*vI[1];}
  for (j=0; j< nRow; j++) {
     for (i=0; i< nCol; i++) {
        for (iDir = 0; iDir < 8; iDir++) {
           temp = Pic[j][i]*Pic[j][i]-i2[iDir]*i2[iDir];
           Det  = (1.0-Pic[j][i]*Pic[j][i])*temp;
           dz[j][i][iDir] = -10e10; /* default */
           if (Det>= 0.0) {
              nom = temp-i1[iDir]*i1[iDir]+1.0e-10;
              if ((nom > 0.0) || (i1[iDir]<eps)) {
                 dz[j][i][iDir] = (-i1[iDir]*vI[2] - sqrt(Det)) / nom;}}
           if (iDir % 2 == 1) dz[j][i][iDir] *= sq05; /* diagonal move */}}}
} /* end of DirectionalSlope */


float  GetHeight(float **Height,long iIter,float ***dz,long nCol,long nRow)
{ /* Height[-1..nRow][-1..nCol]: Local surface height in image
     coordinates. The initial Height has to be a large negative value
     except for a list of singular points where a fixed Height is given */
  /* iIter: Iteration counter */
  /* dz[0..nRow-1][0..nCol-1][0..7]: Change of suface height
     for a unit step in direction i*45 degrees, i in[0..7] */
  /* Note: At each iteration only 4 multiplications (factor 0.5) per pixel */

  long  i,j,i2,j2,iStep,*di,*dj;
  long  diS[8][2] = {{1},{1,0},{0},{0,-1},{-1},{-1, 0},{ 0},{ 0,1}};
```

```
long  djS[8][2] = {{0},{0,1},{1},{1, 0},{ 0},{ 0,-1},{-1},{-1,0}};
float z, h, DisplTot=0.0, eps=1.0e-5;

for (j2=0; j2< nRow; j2++) {
  if ((iIter % 4 == 0) || (iIter % 4 == 1)) j = j2;
  else j = nRow-1-j2; /* change vertical direction of pass */
  for (i2=0; i2< nCol; i2++) {
    if (iIter % 2 == 1)  i = i2;
    else i = nCol-1-i2; /* change horizontal direction of pass */
    for (iStep = 0; iStep < 8; iStep+= 2) {
        dj = &djS[iStep][0]; di = &diS[iStep][0]; /* hv-neighbour */
        z = Height[j + dj[0]][i + di[0]] + dz[j][i][iStep];
        if (z > Height[j][i] + eps) {
           DisplTot    += z - Height[j][i];
           Height[j][i] = z;}
        dj = &djS[iStep+1][0]; di = &diS[iStep+1][0]; /* diagonal neighbours */
        z   = 0.5*(Height[j+dj[0]][i+di[0]] + Height[j+dj[1]][i+di[1]])
              + dz[j][i][iStep+1]; /* interpolate z in diagonal direction */
        if (z > Height[j][i] + eps) {
           DisplTot    += z - Height[j][i];
           Height[j][i] = z;}}}}
  return(DisplTot); /* Return total displacement */
} /* end of GetHeight */
```

ACKNOWLEDGMENTS

We would like to thank Mr. J. Oliensis and Profs. E. Adelson and B. K. P. Horn for their many helpful comments. I would also like to thank Prof. E. Adelson for use of the nickel images.

REFERENCES

1. E. Adelson, Personal communication (1990).
2. M. Bichsel, (1991) "A Simple Algorithm for Shape from Shading," Tech. Rep. No. 172. MIT Media Laboratory, Vision and Modeling Group, Cambridge, MA, 1991.
3. M. Bichsel, and A. Pentland, A simple algorithm for shape from shading. *Proc. IEEE Conf. Comput. Vision Pattern Recognition*, Champaign-Urbana, IL, *1992*, pp. 459–465 (1992).
4. F. P. Ferrie, and M. D. Levine, Where and why local shading works. *IEEE Trans. Pattern Anal. Mach. Recognition* **PAMR-17**, (1) (1989).
5. B. K. P. Horn, Shape from shading, a method for obtaining the shape of a smooth opaque object from one view. Ph.D. Thesis, Massachusetts Institute of Technology, Department of Electrical Engineering, Cambridge, MA, 1970.
6. B. K. P. Horn, Understanding image intensities. *Arti. Intell.* **8**(2), 210–231 (1977).
7. B. K. P. Horn, and M. J. Brooks, The variational approach to shape from shading. In "Shape from Shading," (B. K. P. Horn and M. J. Brooks, eds.) MIT Press 1989.
8. B. K. P. Horn, Height and gradient from shading. *Int. J. Comput. Vision* **5**(1), 37–76 (1990).
9. K. Ikeuchi and B. K. P. Horn, Numerical shape from shading and occluding boundaries. *Arti. Intell.* **17**, 141–185 (1981).
10. J. Oliensis, and P. Dupuis, Direct method for reconstructing shape from shading. *SPIE Geometric Methods Comput. Vision*, San Diego, CA, *1991*, p. 1570 (1991).
11. J. Oliensis, Shape from shading as a partially well-constrained problem. *Comput. Vision, Graphics, Image Process.: Image Understanding*, **54**(2), 163–183(1991).
12. J. Oliensis, Uniqueness in shape from shading. *Int. J. Comput. Vision*, **6**(2), 75–104 (1991).
13. A. P. Pentland, Finding the illuminant direction. *J. Opt. Soc. Am.* **72**(4), 448–455 (1982).
14. A. P. Pentland, Local analysis of the image. *IEEE Trans. Pattern Anal. Mach. Recognition*, **PAMR-6**(2) 170–187 (1984).
15. A. P. Pentland, Fractal-based description of natural scenes. *IEEE Trans. Pattern Anal. Mach. Recognition*, **PAMR-6**(6), 661–674 (1984).
16. A. P. Pentland, Linear shape from shading. *Int. J. Comput. Vision* **4**(2), 153–162 (1990).
17. G. B. Smith, Shape from shading: An assessment. SRI AI Cent. Tech. Note 287. SRI International, Menlo Park, CA, 1985.

Chapter **7**

Range Image Analysis

SARVAJIT S. SINHA

Imageware
Ann Arbor, Michigan

RAMESH JAIN*

Artificial Intelligence Laboratory
The University of Michigan
Ann Arbor, Michigan

Present Address: Department of Electrical and Computer Engineering. University of California, San Diego, La Jolla, California 92093.

HANDBOOK OF PATTERN RECOGNITION
AND IMAGE PROCESSING: COMPUTER VISION

1. INTRODUCTION

Computer vision research attempts to recreate the mechanisms of the biological vision system on a general-purpose computer. This link to biological systems has biased research in the field toward working with intensity images and attempting to extract information from (usually) 8-bit gray-scale intensity images. A primary goal of vision as a sensory mechanism is to recognize objects in a scene by extracting their shapes. There is no explicit shape information contained in an intensity image, yet humans are able to extract depth, and therefore, three-dimensional shape information with relative ease. In fact, humans *impose* a three-dimensional surface structure even on two-dimensional images. Computer vision researchers have therefore recognized the importance of representing and extracting three-dimensional surface structure from images.

Extracting geometric information from intensity images has proved to be a very difficult task. Computer vision has, until recently, concentrated on developing algorithms to extract three-dimensional information from this passive source, reflecting light. The complexity of these algorithms and the development of sensors capable of providing geometric information directly have lead to the creation of algorithms that will analyze and extract information from *geometric signals* [see Besl in Jain and Jain (12)]. A geometric signal is defined as a collection of three-dimensional points x_i, y_i, z_i in a known coordinate system. Explicit three-dimensional information makes the extraction of geometric information easier, since there is a direct correspondence between the geometric signal and the geometric model to be acquired.

There has been rapid development in the hardware of range sensors, making them faster, more accurate, and much more reliable. A common range sensor, a laser scanner, provides three-dimensional information by measuring the return time of a laser beam reflected off an object in the scene. It produces a three-dimensional coordinate for each measurement, and with a scanning mechanism it can create a matrix or image of range measurements. The terms *range image*, *depth map*, and *geometric signal* are used interchangeably in this chapter.

The process of extracting geometric information from a range image consists of first deciding *what* features are to be created (i.e., the shape representation or data structure), and second deciding on *how* to extract these features (i.e., the algorithm). Before an object can be percieved, its model must be available. The *model* can be of various types, on the basis of intensity, texture, or shape. This chapter will be concerned only with shape or geometric models. The question of deciding which features of a surface need to be represented leads us to one of the central questions in computer vision, that of the representation of solid shape. This has been an open question for many years (14). An object can be represented by a combination of volume primitives or of bounding surface primitives. It may also be studied as a volumetric model, or analyzed in terms of its surface elements or the boundaries of those elements.

Most signal and image processing techniques are not suitable for extracting *geometric* information from a range signal. In order to deal with this deficiency, a large number of new algorithms have been developed with roots in functional analysis, approximation, and differential geometry. These algorithms remove the errors in noisy, voluminous sensor output, segment the data set into its constituent parts, and extract a concise, meaningful geometric representation of the objects in the scene. This representation is compatible with the original model of the object so that they can be compared and the part can be recognized.

This chapter is divided into three sections: Section 2 discusses the firmware involved in obtaining range images: Section 3, the geometric representations to be extracted from range data: and Section 4, the algorithms used to extract these representations from the range data.

2. FIRMWARE

Range image sensor firmware is the combination of hardware and software used to compute the distance of points on an object in the scene from the sensor. Some sensors are hardware devices that provide explicit range data using active illumination. Other "sensors" are software algorithms that passively measure ambient scene reflections and subsequent derive range. While very little computation is required for range estimation with active sensors, passive sensors require involved algorithms to compute range. For the purpose of this chapter, both types of "sensors" will be discussed together as range sensors.

Range image sensor technology has expanded and improved tremendously in the last 10 years. Sensors are now more accurate, faster in scanning an image, and easier to use. With these improvements, they can now be applied to a number of areas where they were previously considered esoteric. Engineering design, inspection, and verification are some of the manufacturing applications. Laser sensors create a dense depth map of an surface, which can then be used for inspection of manufacturing flaws. Range image processing systems are also used in medical imaging. Computer-aided tomography (CAT) and nuclear magnetic resonance (NMR) imaging, although not "range" sensing techniques in the true sense, provide volumetric images from which the geometry of internal organs can be derived as an assistance to medical personnel for diagnosis and surgical planning. Algorithms for range image processing are also used in creating spatial databases for geographic information systems. Photogrammetry, a passive technique of ranging, is utilized to create elevation maps from satellite or aerial imagery. Yet another application of range image processing algorithms is to find defects on chips from depth maps produced by as scanning electron microscope (SEM) or scanning tunneling microscope (STM). As one can see, range image processing algorithms can be utilized in a variety of applications—from the microscopically small to the macroscopically large.

Range sensors can be divided into many categories based on different criteria active versus passive, scan mechanism, or physical principle. This section focuses particularly on the categorization of active and passive range sensors. The features of active and passive sensors are described below. For an extensive review of range sensor technology, readers are referred to Besl (3) or Jarvis (13).

2.1. Active Sensors

An active sensor is generally defined as one that provides and controls its own illumination. It radiates energy onto the surfaces to be measured and computes range from the reflected energy, either by measuring the time of flight of the illuminant or by triangulating a projected pattern. A variety of physical phenomenon are used as the radiant source. The sensors discussed below use the time of flight of a laser beam, triangulation of a white light pattern, Moire interference of white light patterns, and sonar or radar beams. The term *active sensors* must not be confused with *active sensing* used in high-level vision, which refers to goal-directed or purposive sensing strategies.

2.1.1. Laser

Laser sensors use a focused beam of light and employ either the time of flight (TOF) or phase difference to find the range. The TOF lasers measure the time interval between the emission of a subnanosecond laser pulse and the reception of the echo or reflected beam. The relationship between the time and range is simple:

$$r = \frac{c\tau}{2},\tag{1}$$

where r is the range, c is the speed of light, and τ is the time interval between emission and reception of the wave.

Phase-difference laser sensors use a continuous-wave amplitude-modulated laser beam, and measure the phase difference between the emitted wave and the sensed wave. The relationship between the phase difference $\Delta\phi$ and the range r is given by

$$r = \frac{c}{4\pi f_{am}}\Delta\phi, \qquad (2)$$

where f_{am} is the modulating frequency. Since the phase difference can be measured only up to λ_{am}, the range resolution of such a system is restricted to the ambiguity interval $\lambda_{am}/2$. A laser sensor consists of a laser source mounted on a mechanical assembly that allows the beam to be tracked in the θ and ϕ direction of a virtual spherical coordinate system situated at the sensor (see Fig. 7.1). The coordinates obtained must be converted from this spherical coordinate system to cartesian coordinates to derive range data. Range measurements are usually averaged to remove the effect of noise. Noise results from either thermodynamic quantum effects or the jitter in the electromechanical assembly of the laser.

In using a laser sensor, three important aspects must be considered. The first is the power of the sensor. High-power lasers cause a stronger reflected signal and, therefore, better range data. However, such lasers are costlier and more harmful for an unprotected eye, which prevents their use in a human environment. The second aspect is the viewing volume.

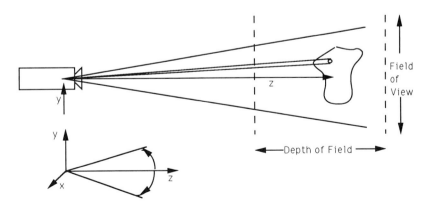

Figure 7.1. Typical laser sensor setup.

TABLE 7.1

A Comparison of Range Image Sensor [a]

	Criterion			
Sensor	Range	Accuracy	Data density	Figure of merit
Passive				
Stereo	†	1 in 250	Sparse	15,750
Focus	1 mm–10 m	1 in 50	Sparse	
Active				
Laser	0.1 mm–100 m	100 μm	Dense	100,000
Structured light	1 μm–100 m	1 in 200	Dense to sparse	100,000
S n M	1 pm	1 pm	Dense	$2000/\sqrt{t}$
CMM	10 cm–10 m	10 μm	Sparse	10,400
Moire	1 μm–10 m	50 μm	Dense	121,43

[a]These are only typical values; actual implementation numbers vary greatly. Shape-from-motion is not shown since no real system is available. The symbol † indicates that the result depends on the particular implementation. (From Besl (3).)

The viewing volume of a sensor is determined by the area of projection and the depth of field. The area of projection is controlled by the field of view of the scanning mirrors. The third aspect is the range resolution. Typically, a range sensor produces 8–12 bits of information and a resolution of 25–500 μm. The range accuracy for laser sensors is given in Table 7.1.

The problem with laser sensors (and active sensors in general) is that they depend on the reflection from the object's surface. The reflected energy is determined by the incident angle of the beam and the reflective properties of objects' material. Inaccurate readings result when the object surface is tangent to the beam direction and the incident angle is 0°. The measurements are also inaccurate for specular surfaces, as shiny surfaces scatter the light. Objects with transparent material such as glass obviously cannot be ranged with optical lasers.

2.1.2. Structured Light

Structured light systems are active triangulation-based sensors. A spot, sheet, or grid pattern of light is projected onto the object, and this pattern is detected by a camera. The range to the object can be computed by straightforward trigonometry given a priori knowledge of the positions of the illuminant projector and detector. A simple setup is shown in Fig. 7.2. With a camera of focal length f located at the origin, a projector is set up so that it emits the structural pattern at an angle θ to the baseline. The

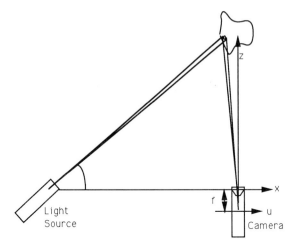

Figure 7.2. Typical structured light geometry.

distance between the projector and the camera is the baseline b. A point (X, Y, Z) in the world is projected onto the camera at pixel (u, v), so that

$$u = \frac{Xf}{Z}$$

$$v = \frac{Yf}{Z}.$$

(3)

The world coordinates of the points in the structured light pattern are given by

$$X = \frac{bu}{f \cot \theta - u}$$

$$Y = \frac{bv}{f \cot \theta - u}$$

$$Z = \frac{bf}{f \cot \theta - u} C$$

(4)

The quantities f, b, θ are known from the setup of the equipment and the pixel locations u, v are found by simple peak detection across scan lines of the image. The advantage of the structured light sensors is that they are fairly cheap. However, they are not very accurate, since the resolution of the system is limited by the resolution of the pixel measurement u, v. Another disadvantage of the structured light sensors is the missing parts problem. The light source and camera are not coaxial, and some areas of the projected pattern may be occluded by other surfaces of the part itself. By increasing the baseline b, better resolution can be achieved from the sensor. Unfortunately, the problem from occlusion is also increased at the same time. A possible solution to this problem is to set up multiple cameras, and integrate the information from each of these sources.

2.1.3. Moire Interferometry

Moire sensors are light source–detector pairs in which a grating is placed in front of both the projector and camera. A typical setup is shown in Fig. 7.3. An interference pattern is created when light is processed through the two gratings that have regularly spaced patterns. If p_0 is the period of the fringes on the object surface, and θ_l, θ_v the angles of the light source and the viewer, then the relative change in range is given approximately by

$$\Delta z \approx \frac{p_0}{\tan(\theta_l) + \tan(\theta_v)} \tag{5}$$

A projection Moire sensor is used to measure the relative depth of a smooth surface.

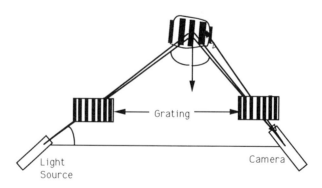

Figure 7.3. Moire sensor setup.

2.1.4. Tactile Sensing

One of the most accurate ways of measuring the three-dimensional coordinates of a point is to actually touch it using a probe. Two very dissimilar tactile probes exist: the scanning probe microscopes (S × M) and the coordinate measuring machines (CMM).

2.1.4.1. S × M

Scanning probe microscopy, which includes techniques such as STM and SEM microscopy (hence the "×" in the title), is a useful tool for the measurement of surface structure at the atomic level. It allows the analysis of surface structure down to 0.1 nm and has great potential for applications in material science and semiconductor manufacturing. It is employed as a ranging device in order to find flaws on semiconductor wafers. There is also great scope for its applications in molecular biology.

The S × M operates on the basis of quantum-mechanical phenomena. A very small probe or stylus is brought into close contact with the surface to be measured. At such close proximity, quantum-mechanical interactions occur between the probe and the surface. Range can be computed by measuring this phenomenon. Image analysis techniques can be used to extract information from the dense range images produced when the probe is scanned over the surface. A drawback to S × M sensors is that the measurements are dependent on the size of the probe used, as Fig. 7.4 illustrates.

In STMs, the interaction phenomenon is a tunnelling current that flows between the probe and the surface when they are brought close together. The tunneling current varies inversely with the distance between the probe and the surface

$$i_t = \frac{e^2 \kappa_0 V A_{\mathrm{eff}} e^{-2\kappa_0 Z}}{4\pi h Z},$$ (6)

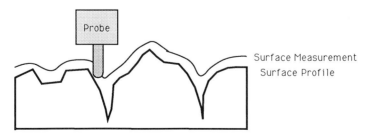

Figure 7.4. The effect of probe size on the range measurements.

where e is the electron charge, V is the voltage bias between the probe and the surface, A_{eff} is the effective area through which the tunneling current flows, and Z is the distance between the probe and the surface or "range"; κ_0 is given by

$$\kappa_0 = \sqrt{\frac{2m_e\phi}{h^2}}\,,\qquad(7)$$

where m_e is the electron mass and ϕ is the work function of the sample. The tunneling current is fed back to the positioning mechanism to keep the probe a constant distance from the surface.

2.1.4.2. CMM

A coordinate measuring machine is an accurate robotic arm with a tactile probe or laser sensor attached to its wrist. The arm is an ultra-high-tolerance mechanical linkage providing precise measurements even in large volumes. CMMs are in wide use in industry for measurement and verification of manufactured parts. The great advantage of the CMM is its accuracy. A typical CMM has an accuracy of the order to 10 μm. One disadvantage is that the device is either manually moved to points on the surface or programmed to follow a particular path. In either case the process is laborious and time-consuming. Another disadvantage of CMM is the cost of the high precision machinery involved.

2.1.5. Sonar

Sonar sensors are range sensors that use ultrasonic waves as their active "illumination." They emit modulated ultrasonic waves and bounce them off the object to be measured. The range to the object can be computed from the phase difference of the returned wave with the emitted wave. Sonar sensors are employed as range sensors in robot navigation for close-range obstacle avoidance. They cannot, however, be considered as true "geometric" sensors since their output is very noisy.

2.2. Passive Sensors

Passive sensors, as their name implies, merely absorb ambient radiation and derive range by first extracting an intermediate representation. Most passive sensing techniques fall under the title of shape-from-X (SfX) methods, where X may be stereo, motion, focus, or similar. Only a few techniques are described below, as other techniques are discussed throughout this volume. While much energy has gone into the development of passive ranging systems, such systems remain for the most part in the realm of academicians. There are few commercially available passive ranging systems, notable examples being autofocus cameras.

2.2.1. Stereo

Shape-from-stereo is an old and well-studied problem in computer vision. The principles behind stereo vision are similar to those of triangulation. Range is derived from the disparity between the images formed on cameras which are viewing the same scene but are placed apart. Figure 7.5 shows the idealized setup for binocular stereo system where the cameras are placed parallel to each other. The camera geometry is usually set up so that one can match features across an epipolar line (i.e., the same line in the left and right images). This makes the search for corresponding features a linear search across a scan line of the image pair. Since the cameras are placed apart with a baseline separation, the image formed on the retinas or cameras are slightly different in their u values, but a feature can be found on the same scan line v in either image. The *disparity d* between the two images is defined as the distance between projections (u_l, v) and (u_r, v) of the same scene point on the two cameras. The disparity, along with a knowledge of the baseline, can be used to compute the range to the object in the scene with the simple relationships

$$d(u_l, u_r) = \frac{bf}{Z},$$

$$X = \frac{b(u_l + u_r)}{2d},$$

$$Y = \frac{bv}{d},$$

$$Z = \frac{bf}{d},$$

(8)

where (u_l, v) and (u_r, v) is the perspective projection of the point (X, Y, Z) onto a camera pair of focal length f separated by a baseline b.

Disparity can be calculated by performing local-area correlation between regions in the left and right images or by matching distinct features in the images. The area correlation method produces a dense disparity map, but is less accurate than feature matching. On the other hand, matching features in the left and right images results in a sparse depth map, which must be interpolated get complete information. The problem

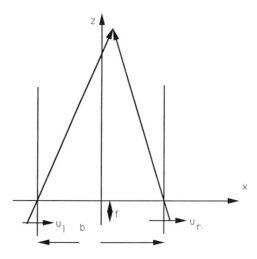

Figure 7.5. Parallel stereo setup.

with passive stereo ranging is, therefore, twofold: (1) establishing correspondence between features in the left and right images is difficult
because of the occlusion of features when viewed from different positions;
and (2) depth can be computed only at the discrete points where correspondence has been established, and in order to produce a dense depth
map, the depth (or disparity) values found must be interpolated. Thus,
overall range accuracy depends on both the feature correspondence and
interpolation. Reviews of several shape-from-stereo algorithms can be
found in Barnard and Fischler (1). This volume contains a chapter on
stereo ranging.

2.2.2. Motion

Shape-from-motion has been a large area of research and includes two
basic subtopics: structure from instantaneous optical flow and structure
from sequences of images. Optical flow is the instantaneous velocity field
produced on the retina of a system by the ego-motion of the observer.
Researchers have attempted to extract optical flow from a sequence of
images using regularization, and then extract structure parameters from
optical flow. The vector geometry of structure-from-optical-flow is elegant
but involved. The weakness of the approaches lies assumption that the
optical flow field is known. Robust estimation of optical flow has eluded
researchers for many years.

The basic equations involving range Z and optical flow $(\dot{u}, \dot{v})$ are

$$\dot{u} = \frac{V_X - xV_z}{Z} - \omega_X xy + \omega_Y(1 + x^2) - \omega_Z y$$

$$\dot{v} = \frac{V_Y - yV_z}{Z} - \omega_X(1 + y^2) + \omega_Y xy - \omega_Z x,$$

(9)

where a point (X, Y, Z) moving in space with velocity (V_X, V_Y, V_Z) is imaged onto x, y with an optical flow of $(\dot{u}, \dot{v})$.

Researchers have also attempted to extract structure form a temporal sequence of images. This problem is similar to recovering shape-from-stereo. Time adjacent pairs of images from a sequence form (temporal) stereo pairs. Knowledge of the speed of the camera system is equivalent to knowledge of the baseline of a stereo system. In the simplest case of shape-from-motion system, the axis of the camera is aligned to the direction of motion. The (temporal) disparity between features in consecutive frames of an image sequence is found by correspondence techniques. The range can be obtained by straightforward trignometry.

2.2.3. Focus

Shape-from-focus is the recovery of range information from an image according to whether the objects of interest are in or out of focus. Objects lying inside the finite depth of field of a convex lens are in focus on the imaging plane. The basic thin-lens law is a simple relationship between objects in focus and their range. The law states that a thin lens of focal length f will focus a point source located at a range Z onto a focal plane located at a distance z, or

$$\frac{1}{Z} + \frac{1}{z} = \frac{1}{f},$$

(10)

as illustrated in Fig.7.6. By varying z and having a method to find the image in focus, the appropriate z can be read off and the range Z can be computed. Given that a real lens will suffer from blurring due to diffraction, Eq. (10) must be modified to correct this:

$$Z_\pm = \frac{zf}{z - f \pm \sigma f/D},$$

(11)

where D is the lens diameter. The range signified by $Z_+ - Z_-$ is the depth of field, the region in which all points are in focus.

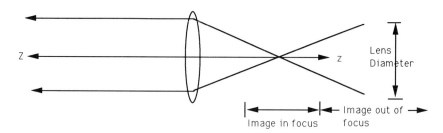

Figure 7.6. Depth-by-focus setup.

A number of researchers have presented measures of image focus. A measure suggested by Jarvis (13) is the maxima of the expression

$$\text{Sum modulo difference} = \sum_{i=2}^{N} |x_i - x_{i-1}|, \tag{12}$$

which is a maxima when the image is in focus.

3. GEOMETRIC REPRESENTATIONS

A geometric model is the starting point in recognizing and manipulating objects in a scene. Solid objects can be described by either the volume enclosed, or by the bounding surfaces. Hence, modeling schemes are either volumetric or surface-based.

Computer-aided design (CAD) literature provides a wealth of geometric modeling primitives. The common object descriptors in CAD are as follow:

- Wireframe
- Spatial occupancy, including voxel and octree representations
- Sweep, which includes what is known in computer vision as the general-ized cylinder (GC) model
- Constructive solid geometry (CSG)
- Boundary representation (BRep)

Since CAD is a large area by itself, only a brief description of the representations is given here. The readers are referred to Faux and Pratt (8) and Requicha (15) for further information.

Complex objects can be represented by combinations of two-and three-dimensional primitives. Primitive surfaces can be looked at as half-spaces, defining an "inside" and an "outside." There half-spaces generally have an implicit low-order planar or quadric polynomial form. The halfspaces collectively define a primitive solid such as a cube, sphere, cone, cylinder, and torus. These solid primitives can, in turn, be combined together with the use of the Boolean operators: union, intersection, and difference. A representation is called *constructive solid geometry* (CSG) when the object is described in terms of the primitive solid. On the other hand, when the description is based on bounding half-spaces, it is called *boundary representation* (BRep) Figure 7.7 shows two different representations of an object produced by these schemes. It is the classical portrayal of the CSG–BRep distinction. Most human-engineered objects can be represented by Boolean operations on a few primitive solids. Some objects, though, have a complex shape that cannot be represented as a combination of fixed primitives. For such objects, a boundary representation is utilized with free-form parametrized surfaces as the primitives. Comercially available solid modeling systems use the CSG approach, while surface modelers use a BRep model for representing solid objects. The discussion in this section is concerned mostly with surface models, since it is the exterior bounding surfaces that are visible to a typical range sensor.

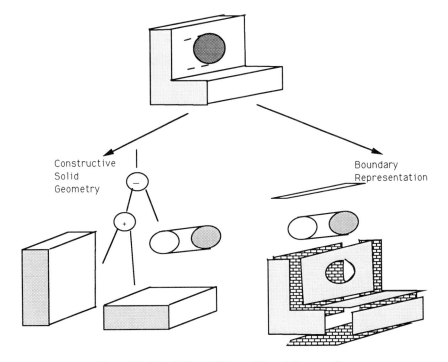

Figure 7.7. The CSG and BRep solid modeling paradigms.

Surface representations can be categorized as implicit or explicit according to the form of the mathematical functions employed. Bivariate polynomials fall under the first category, while parametric free-form surfaces into the other.

1. **Implicit.** A surface can be written as an implicit function of the three space variables X, Y, Z. The surface f is written as

$$f(X, Y, Z) = 0. \tag{13}$$

Planar surfaces can be written as

$$f(X, Y, Z) = a_0 + a_1 X + a_2 Y + a_3 Z, \tag{14}$$

where the vector (a_1, a_2, a_3) is the normal to the plane and a_0 is the normalized distance to the origin. Quadric surfaces can be written as

$$f(X, Y, Z) = a_0 + a_1 X + a_2 Y + a_3 Z + a_4 X^2 + a_5 Y^2$$

$$+ a_6 Z^2 + a_6 Z^2 + a_7 XY + a_8 YZ + a_9 XZ. \tag{15}$$

Spheres, cones, cylinders, ellipsoids, and hyperboloids can be represented by this function for different values of the coefficients $a_0 \cdots a_9$. While such a representation is useful for low-order polynomials, implicit surfaces get cumbersome to manipulate when the order of the polynomial increases and their usefulness decreases.

2. **Explicit.** A surface can also be written as an explicit function of some parameter set (s, t) for each of its coordinates (X, Y, Z):

$$f(X, Y, Z) = f[\mathbf{X}(s, t), \mathbf{Y}(s, t), \mathbf{Z}(s, t)]. \tag{16}$$

Such a parametrized representation leads to different types of surfaces depending on the functions $\mathbf{X}(s, t), \mathbf{Y}(s, t), \mathbf{Z}(s, t)$. Some of these are

a. Coons patches—a description based on surface boundary-curves and blending functions.

b. Tensor product surfaces of the form

$$f(s, t) = B(s)[Q]B^T(t), \tag{17}$$

where B is a set of basic B-splines functions, and $[Q]$ the control points. The basis functions may be either Bézier curves or B-splines. Nonuniform (in knot spacing) rational (tensor-product) B-spline surfaces (NURBs) are the most popular surface representation in CAD systems.

A simplified form of the parametrized surface is the graph surface. In this case $X(s, t) = s$ and $Y(s, t) = t$. Range data from one viewpoint can be represented as a single-valued function $Z = Z(X, Y) = f(s, t)$ by assigning $s = X, T = Y$. This is very useful in range image processing, as we shall see later.

The discussion so far has concentrated on surface primitives from CAD. Some computer vision researchers have used CAD primitives to define the shape extracted from range data; however, the requirements of primitives from a shape-extraction viewpoint are different from those from a modeling viewpoint. Extraction of geometric information requires that the models satisfy three constraints. First, the primitives must be constructive, that is, they must form the building blocks for describing complex objects. Geometric signal processing requires a combination of free-form and implicit BRep schemes. Second, the representation must be invariant to viewpoint, and to rotations and translations of the object. CAD models depend on the position of the object in space. Third, computer vision requires the model to be a unique representation to facilitate recognition. While CAD provides the models we would *like* to use, it is not clear whether these models are canonical. For example, a CSG tree is an inherently ambiguous description of a solid, since the same object can be represented by different CSG trees. A BRep model of a cylinder presents a similar problem in that it can be expressed in different ways—as a simple quadric or as a complex nonuniform rational B-spline.

As the requirements of CAD and computer vision are different, a CAD model always cannot be used for shape extraction. For this reason, computer vision research has gone back to the roots of the geometric basis of three-dimensional representations. It has attempted to create canonical models of objects and find robust estimators for these models. Computer vision research studies an object in three dimensions by computing and comparing features of one, two, or three dimensions. One-dimensional space curve descriptions can tell us a great deal about the object. Curves that lie on a surface such as bounding curves (or *jump boundaries* in range data), lines of curvature, asymptotes, and surface intersection curves (or *surface creases*) characterize that surface (6). Two-dimensional surface models are critical, since their robust extraction describes the shape of an object's boundary. Most research has been based on differential geometry principally because this area of mathematics gives a number of different techniques for a unique and stable representation of bounding surfaces and curves thereon. For example, one of the major concerns for computer vision researchers is that the model used for representing an object must be invarient to rotations and translations. This is provided by a representation characterizing a surface based on the mean and Gaussian curvatures. Instead of the bounding surface approach, some researchers have also advocated a direct three-dimensional volumetric models fitting strategy to studying objects. An object is represented as a union of primitive solids, as is the case for CSG. The most common volumetric primitive is the generalized cylinder, a subset of which is the superquadrics [see Bajscy *et al.* in Jain and Jain (12)].

Certain objects representations are unique to the computer vision community. For example, some researchers have created the extended Gaussian image (EGI) to model objects. An EGI is a plot of the normals of the surfaces and reveals the changes of an object's surface. The EGI is viewpoint invariant, satisfying one of the requirements discussed above. For more information on other representations, the reader is referred to Brady *et al.* (6) and Chapter 2 in this volume.

3.1. Surface Characterization

Surface characterization involves the computation of spatial properties of a two-dimensional manifold. The concepts of differential geometry are employed for such computation. The equations necessary to obtain an intrinsic, viewpoint-independent characterization of a surface are pro-vided. For the following section, it is assumed that a given surface can be described parametrically as $Z = f[X(s, t), Y(s, t), Z(s, t)]$, that it is at least twice differentiable, and that the function and its derivatives are continuous.

Differential geometry states that the mean and Gaussian curvatures of a surface are viewpoint invariant properties and provide a representation that does not depend on the rotations and translations of an object. In order to derive the equations for the curvatures, the concepts of first and second fundamental forms of a surface must be introduced. The first fundamental form measures the movement $|dx|^2$ on the surface at a point (s, t) for a given infinitesimal movement on the parameter space s, t. The second form measures the correlation between the changes in the normal vector $d\vec{n}$ and the surface position $d\vec{x}$ with respect to infintesimal changes in the parameter space s, t. Computation of these two quantities at every point on a surface provides a complete description of the local shape of the surface.

The *first fundamental form* of a surface is given by

$$I = d\vec{z} \cdot d\vec{z} = d\vec{s}^T [\mathbf{g}] \, d\vec{s} \qquad (18)$$

where the $[\mathbf{g}]$ matrix elements are defined as

$$g_{11} = E = \vec{z}_s \cdot \vec{z}_s,$$

$$g_{22} = G = \vec{z}_t \cdot \vec{z}_t, \qquad (19)$$

$$g_{12} = g_{21} = F = \vec{z}_s \cdot \vec{z}_t,$$

and the subscripts denote partial differentials

$$\vec{z}_s(s,t) = \frac{\partial \vec{z}}{\partial s}, \qquad \vec{z}_t(s,t) = \frac{\partial \vec{z}}{\partial t}. \tag{20}$$

The *second fundamental form* of a surface is given by

$$\mathrm{II} = d\vec{z} \cdot d\vec{n} = d\vec{s}^T [\mathbf{b}] d\vec{s}, \tag{21}$$

where the $[\mathbf{b}]$ matrix elements are defined as

$$b_{11} = L = \vec{z}_{ss} \cdot \vec{n},$$

$$b_{22} = N = \vec{z}_{tt} \cdot \vec{n}, \tag{22}$$

$$b_{12} = b_{21} = M = \vec{z}_{st} \cdot \vec{n},$$

and the double subscripts denote second partial differentials

$$\vec{z}_{ss}(s,t) = \frac{\partial^2 \vec{z}}{\partial s^2},$$

$$\vec{z}_{tt}(s,t) = \frac{\partial^2 \vec{z}}{\partial t^2}, \tag{23}$$

$$\vec{z}_{st}(s,t) = \vec{z}_{ts}(s,t) = \frac{\partial^2 \vec{z}}{\partial s \partial t}.$$

Considering a point on the surface as a vector $\vec{z}(s,t) = [s\, t\, f(s,t)]^T$, the partial drivatives required for the curvature calculations can be easily determined as shown below:

$$\vec{z}_s = [1\ \ 0\ \ f_s]^T,$$

$$\vec{z}_t = [0\ \ 1\ \ f_t]^T,$$

$$\vec{z}_{ss} = [0\ \ 0\ \ f_{ss}]^T,$$

$$\vec{z}_{st} = [0\ \ 0\ \ f_{st}]^T, \tag{24}$$

$$\vec{z}_{tt} = [0\ \ 0\ \ f_{tt}]^T,$$

$$\vec{n} = \frac{1}{\sqrt{1 + f_s^2 + f_t^2}} [-f_s\ -f_t\ 1]^T.$$

Therefore, the fundamental form matrix coefficents can be expressed as

$$E = 1 + f_s^2, \qquad G = 1 + f_t^2, \qquad F = f_s f_t,$$

$$L = \frac{f_{ss}}{\sqrt{1 + f_s^2 + f_t^2}}, \quad M = \frac{f_{st}}{\sqrt{1 + f_s^2 + f_t^2}}, \quad N = \frac{f_{tt}}{\sqrt{1 + f_s^2 + f_t^2}}. \tag{25}$$

The Gaussian curvature is then given quite simply as

$$K = \frac{LN - M^2}{g} \tag{26}$$

and the mean curvature as

$$H = \frac{LG + NE - 2FM}{2g}, \tag{27}$$

where $g = EG - F^2$. The first fundamental form I can be written as $E \dot{s}^2 + 2F \dot{s}\dot{t} + G \dot{t}^2$ by expanding Eq. (18), and expansion of Eq. (21) leads to $\mathrm{II} = L \dot{s}^2 + 2M \dot{s}\dot{t} + N \dot{t}^2$.

The *normal curvature* of a surface is the ratio II/I. It is the curvature of the intersection curve between a surface and a cutting plane normal to it. The directions of maximum and minimum normal curvature are the

B

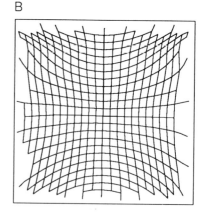

A

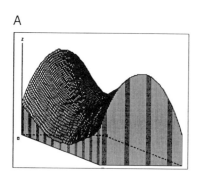

Figure 7.8. (A) A saddle-shaped region of range data as a perspective plot; (B) lines of principal curvature on the saddle.

principal directions and are always mutually perpendicular to each other. The curvature in either principal direction is called the *principal curvature*, κ_1, κ_2. The Gaussian curvature can be expressed as the product of the principle curvatures, $K = \kappa_1 \cdot \kappa_2$, and the mean curvature by half the sum of the two, $H = 1/2(\kappa_1 + \kappa_2)$. If both principal curvatures are of the same sign (i.e., positive Gaussian curvature), the surface is *elliptic* or *convex* in the region. If they are of opposite signs (i.e., negative Gaussian curvature), the surface is *hyperbolic* or *saddle-shaped*. If either of the two are zero, the surface is said to be *parabolic*. Figure 7.8(A) shows a saddle-shaped region in a orthogonal projection, and Fig. 7.8 (B) shows the surface as an image

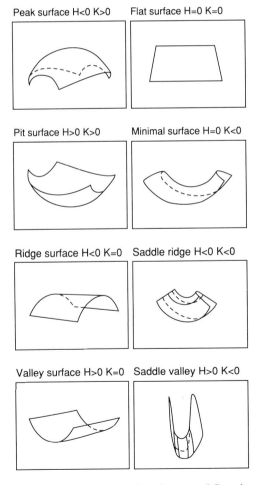

Figure 7.9. Surface types based on sign of mean and Gaussian curvature.

TABLE 7.2

Surface Types Based on Sign of Mean and Gaussian Curvature

	$K > 0$	$K = 0$	$K < 0$
$H < 0$	Peak	Ridge	Saddle ridge
$H = 0$	None	Flat	Minimal surface
$H > 0$	Pit	Valley	Saddle valley

with the lines of principal curvature overlaid. It should be pointed out that although the lines of principle curvature form a locally orthogonal mesh on the surface, they will not appear orthogonal on the image. Table 7.2 and Fig. 7.9 provide a characterization of surface types based on the sign of the mean and Gaussian curvatures.

As we move along a smooth curve on the surface, the surface characterization also changes. Such changes are continuous since the surface is smooth and the curvatures continuous. Figure 7.10 shows the allowable transitions between surface types.

A change in the surface characterization creates local umbilics, which are singularities in the principal direction field. They are located where the principal curvatures are equal. An umbilic point must be traversed when moving along the surface from a peak to a pit where the surface becomes locally planar.

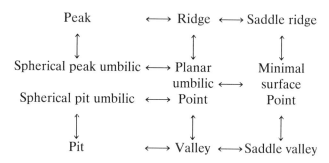

Figure 7.10. Allowable transitions in surface types.

3.2. Curve Networks

A network of curves on a surface defines a parametrization for that surface. The parametric surface model has been found the most convenient form for representing a surface BRep among CAD researchers. This section describes a method that creates a network of curves from range data, and thereby produce a parametric representation of the surface.

In order to create a parametric surface model, the data must first be parametrized along some axes u, v. The parametrization can be achieved by creating a network of curves on the surface, and using the curves as the parameter lines of a surface representation. A curve network leads to a viewpoint-independent, intrinsic, CAD-compatible surface model. A curve network parametrized surface serves as a data-reduction scheme, and also enables ripple control on the surface model by eliminating tensor product effects.

Principal patches, perhaps the most useful of curve network geometric descriptions, can be created from lines of principle curvature. Brady *et al.* (6) were the first computer vision researchers to attempt to computer the lines of principle curvature from range images, and to publicize the significance of such patches. Other researchers have studied the projections of curves on surfaces and proposed that the given curves are often interpreted as lines of curvature of that surface.

Geometric descriptions based on lines of curvature will be increasingly important in the future. There are definite advantages of using such a parameterization. For instance, if the lines of curvature are used as u, v parameter curves, the first and second fundamental forms are diagonal and the Weingarten mapping is a diagonal matrix that contains the principal curvatures.

In theory, principal patches can be constructed locally. Nonetheless, automatically extending the network to arbitrary regions of unknown data is difficult because of the presence of isolated singular points (i.e., *umbilics*). Umbilic points cause significant problems in creating complete and consistent u, v parametric domains.

The principal patch representation is based on the fact that the lines of minimum and maximum curvature (i,e., the principal curvatures) on a generic smooth ($\mathscr{C}^2$) surface are orthogonal at almost every point. Mathematical literature provides a theorem (18) that says that the principal patches can be created locally on a mesh of these lines. However, it is a difficult task to create such a representation over the whole surface when working with real range data. Range data, as we know, suffers from noise, and this leads to inaccurate computation of the curve.

A robust algorithm for creating principal patches from range data requires the following computations. A point on a surface is parametrically defined as $[s(r), t(r)]$, where r is the arc length. A direction on the surface is given by $(\dot{s}, \dot{t})$, when the derivatives are defined. The expression for the normal curvature of a surface at a point (s, t) on the surface is given by

$$\kappa = -\frac{L\dot{s}^2 + 2M\dot{s}\dot{t} + N\dot{t}^2}{E\dot{s}^2 + 2F\dot{s}\dot{t} + G\dot{t}^2}. \tag{28}$$

Principal directions are defined as those directions in which the curvature is either maximum or minimum. This occurs when

$$\frac{\partial \kappa}{\partial \dot{s}} = 0 \quad \text{and} \quad \frac{\partial \kappa}{\partial \dot{t}} = 0. \tag{29}$$

After some trivial algebraic manipulations, these conditions can be written as

$$(L - \kappa E)\dot{s} + (M - \kappa F)\dot{t} = 0,$$
$$(M - \kappa F)\dot{s} + (N - \kappa G)\dot{t} = 0. \tag{30}$$

They can also be rewritten as

$$[\mathbf{g}]^{-1}[\mathbf{b}]\,\dot{\mathbf{s}} = \kappa\,\dot{\mathbf{s}}, \quad \text{where} \quad \dot{\mathbf{s}} = \begin{pmatrix} \dot{s} \\ \dot{t} \end{pmatrix}. \tag{31}$$

For these equations to possess a consistent solution, κ must be an eigenvalue of the system of equations, and satisfy the characteristic equation

$$\kappa^2 - 2H\kappa + K = 0, \tag{32}$$

which, when solved, leads to the principal curvatures

$$\kappa_{max} = H + \sqrt{H^2 - K},$$
$$\kappa_{min} = H - \sqrt{H^2 - K}. \tag{33}$$

Finding the eigenvectors in equation 30 leads to the pair of coupled ordinary differential equations

$$\begin{bmatrix} \dot{s} \\ \dot{t} \end{bmatrix} = \begin{bmatrix} \frac{1}{2}(EN - GL) + g\sqrt{(H^2 - K)} \\ FL - EM \end{bmatrix}, \text{minimum}$$

$$\begin{bmatrix} \dot{s} \\ \dot{t} \end{bmatrix} = \begin{bmatrix} GM - FN \\ \frac{1}{2}(EN - GL) + g\sqrt{(H^2 - K)} \end{bmatrix}, \text{maximum} \tag{34}$$

for the minimum and maximum curvature directions. Given the coupled nonlinear first-order ordinary differential equations for the principal directions, a numerical procedure can be used to integrate them. Figure 7.8 (B) illustrates the lines of principle curvature on a saddle surface, resulting from the application of a Runge–Kutta integrator to the preceding equations.

3.2.1. Umbilics

The presence of umbilic points on surfaces presents problems in creating a mesh of principal curvature lines because they do not allow the creation of a simple quadrilateral mesh. Umbilic points occur on elliptic surfaces where the magnitude of the principle curvatures are equal. They are not found in regions with negative Gaussian curvature such as the saddle surface [Fig. 7.8 (A)] since $K = \kappa_1 \cdot \kappa_2$. Spheres and planes are pathological cases because they are umbilic everywhere. Isolated umbilic points can be characterized as either generic or degenerate according to whether the location and behavior of the umbilic are affected by small changes in the parameters of the surface. Generic umbilic points do not change their behavior and location appreciably over small changes in surface parameters. They have been characterized into exactly three types according to the patterns of the curvature lines around the umbilic: LeMon, Star, and MonStar. The flow of principal curvature lines around the three types of generic umbilics can be seen in Fig. 7.11. The pattern in Fig. 7.11 (A) represents the plot of the surface $z = \partial^2 G / \partial x \, \partial y$, where $G = \exp[-(x^2 + y^2)]$. The symbolic math package Mathematica was used to compute the magnitude of the principal curvatures. In Fig. 7.11 the difference between the principal curvatures $\kappa_1 - \kappa_2$ is represented. It displays four umbilic points at the peak and pits of the function.

A degenerate umbilic point changes location if the parameters of the underlying surface are changed. A degenerate umbilic occurs on an ellipsoidal parabola

$$z = \frac{x^2}{a} + \frac{y^2}{b} \tag{35}$$

at the point $(0, 0, 0)$. If $a = b \neq 0$, the lines of curvature meet at one degenerate umbilic point. Even the slightest variation in the parameters a

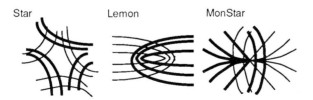

Figure 7.11. Principal curvature lines near isolated umbilics.

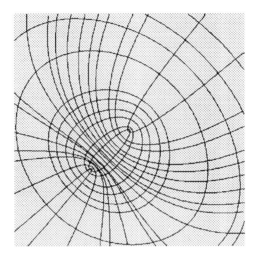

Figure 7.12. Two lemon umbilic points on an ellipsoidal surface.

or *b* causes the umbilic to split into two points of the type shown in
Fig 7.12.

The stable detection and characterization of the umbilic points is an
area of ongoing research. One technique to find locations of umbilic points
is to first compute the principal direction fields and then infer the location
from the index of the fields. This involves the computation of a local
isotropic bicubic approximation of the surface at the umbilic and evaluation of the discriminant based on the coefficients of this bicubic. The sign
of the discriminant distinguishes the type of the umbilic. Another technique is to apply divergence and curl operators to find discontinuities in
the principal direction field.

4. EXTRACTING GEOMETRIC INFORMATION

The extraction of geometric information from range is the conversion of
a set of points into higher order geometric forms. This process involves
two tasks. The first task, the identification of the appropriate geometric
primitives, is application-specific and -dependent. The previous section
dealt with the representation of objects in general. The actual selection of
primitive(s), however, is left up to the applications engineer. The second
task is the extraction of geometric information from the range data. This

involves the segmentation of point data and the estimation of corresponding geometric forms. Techniques utilized for such procedures will be described in this section.

The processes of segmentation and shape representation are interrelated, as has been pointed out by Bajcsy *et al.* [in Jain and Jain (12)]. If segmentation is performed first, then shape extraction is simplified; on the other hand, if scene were known to consist of just a few shape primitives, then segmentation would involve the search for only these primitives. The two problems must, therefore, be studied together.

An overview of the extraction procedure is illustrated in Fig. 7.13. It shows two major components of this procedure, segmentation and approximation. A range image can be segmented into regions of similar geometric properties by either edge-based or region-based techniques. The segmented regions are merely lists of points, and are converted into their corresponding geometric form with the application of approximation and estimation techniques. The extracted shape primitives are then assembled into a canonical description of the complete object.

An example of range image processing is shown in Figs. 7.14 and 7.15 (courtesy of Francis Quek, A. I. Laboratory, The University of Michigan). Figure 7.14(A) shows a rendered perspective view of the three-dimen-

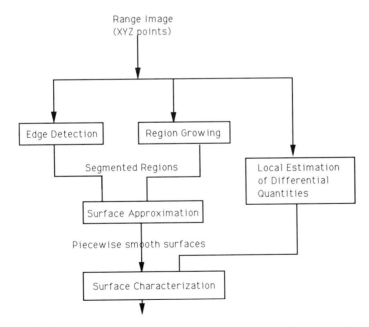

Figure 7.13. Flow of control through a system to extract geometric information from range data.

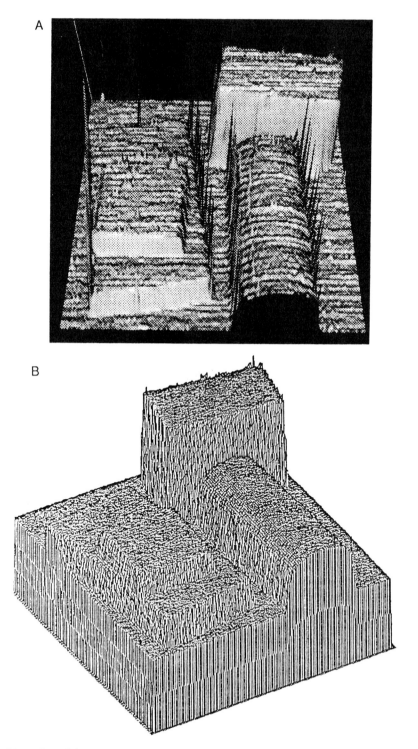

Figure 7.14. (A) Rendered perspective view of the three-dimensional image of blocks and a cylinder; (B) image after filtering through a LMS procedure to eliminate these outliers.

A

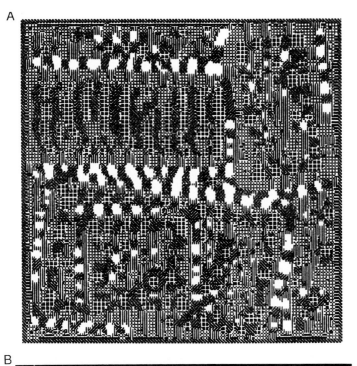

B

Figure 7.15. (A) The curvature sign map of the image obtained using a 7×7 kernel operator; (B) the rendered perspective view of the three-dimensional surfaces found in the image.

sional image of blocks and a cylinder lying on a table. It reveals erroneous data points at the range discontinuities. Figure 7.14(B) presents the image after it has been filtered by a least-median-of-squares procedure. This eliminates the anomalous bad data and does not smooth the discontinuities. Figure 7.15(A) shows the curvature sign map of the image obtained using a 7×7 kernel operator, showing the effect of noise in computing the differential quantities directly from the data. Figure 7.15(B) shows the rendered perspective view of the segmented and approximated three-dimensional surfaces found in the image.

Prior to a detailed discussion of segmentation (Section 4.2) and approximation (Section 4.3), certain issues must be considered.

4.1. Issues in Extraction of Geometric Information

Extraction or geometric information is a complicated problem with many variables. The data may be scattered or dense: it may be clean or very noisy. The scene may consist of a single smooth surface, or it may be cluttered with different objects. Surfaces in the scene may be representable by combination of primitives, or they may be free-form. The user may want real-time response, or the processes may operate in batch mode. These issues must be taken into account when selecting an appropriate surface approximant function and a computational algorithm. They are discussed in depth below.

4.1.1. Spatial Distribution of Data

The different sensors described in Section 2 provide data with differing distributions. For example, structured light systems and CMMs provide *sparse* but uniformly distributed data. The usual assumption made here is that the surface is smoothly varying between measurements. Shape-from-X also provides very sparse data, but the data sets are completely unstructured. These sensors usually depend on changes in surface albedo or illumination. Laser scanning sensors, on the other hand, provide volumes of *dense* data that may not be gridded. Laser sensors can also provide dense *gridded* data in the form of an image once the spherical parametrization is eliminated. This distribution of the data will affect the choice of surface approximation algorithm.

4.1.2. Noise and Outliers

There are three distinct types of problems that arise in the measurement of range data: (1) outliers, which are data points not obeying a

Gaussian distribution and which are caused by sensor errors; (2) data dropouts, which are caused by specular reflection or large slopes near the edges of objects; and (3) Gaussian noise, which is caused by internal electronics and software. The data must be smoothed and low-pass-filtered to remove the effect of these errors. The amount of noise determines the degree of smoothing to be performed on the data. However, smoothing tends to blur discontinuities in the range data leading to a loss of geometric information. This necessitates adaptive smoothing techniques as in Sinha and Schunck (17). Confidence in the data and knowledge about the amount of noise also determines whether interpolation or approximation techniques are used for fitting a surface through the data.

4.1.3. Order of Differentiability

There are three conflicting requirements on the reconstructed surface: (1) it should be allowed to tear at step edges to satisfy the assumption that the surface is piecewise-continuous; (2) it should be $\mathscr{C}^0$, or position-continuous, at orientation discontinuities or crease edges; and (**3**) it should be at least $\mathscr{C}^2$, curvature-continuous, within smooth regions so that the intrinsic properties of the object, which are dependent on the second differential, may be extracted.

4.1.4. Global-versus Local-Extent Functions

A surface approximant with a global extent will be affected by distant data points, which is inappropriate. It also does not allow local control of the surface. For example, polynomial and thin-plate spline fitting techniques are global by nature, and cannot be used over the whole data set. In contrast, B-splines and other compact-basis surfaces such as the ν-splines affect only a local area of the surface. Local basis functions are preferred, since (1) there is no correlation between faraway points, and (2) they allow discontinuities to appear between surface patches.

4.1.5. Segmentation

The segmentation problem is central to range image analysis. One approach is to segment the data, and then fit surfaces to the segmented regions. Region-based and edge-based techniques are examples of this approach. The computation of the criteria for segmentation involves the differential properties of the surface, which cannot be computed reliably from raw data. Better values are obtained once a surface has been fit and the derivatives obtained from the coefficients of this surface. This leads to a chicken-and-egg problem. That is, the surface cannot be extracted until the data is segmented, but the data cannot be segmented until surface derivatives are known, and accurate derivative values cannot be obtained unless the surface is fit!

Another approach is to fit one global "visual surface" over the whole data. This technique is especially suited to sparse data such as that from the passive range sensors, where criterion for segmentation become difficult to compute. This visual surface approach creates a surface approximant to the data, from which differential quantities are computed. Adaptive surface fitting allows the computation of reliable differential quantities even though the data are not segmented. Segmentation can be easily performed on this surface.

4.1.6. Viewpoint-Independent Reconstruction

One problem with most functional minimization in surface fitting is that it is dependent on the viewpoint. The norm chosen for minimization must not depend on the viewing direction, as it would result in different representations of the objects. Simple least-squares norms, which are extensively used for surface fitting, are not recommended for they do not have the viewpoint-invariance property.

4.1.7. Computational Effort

The computational effort involved in finding the surface approximant is a crucial criterion in the selection of an algorithm, since range image analysis usually deals with large amounts of data. There are two important points to note regarding computational efficiency: (1) local-basis methods usually result in sparse coefficient matrices to be solved, offering computational advantages over global methods whose coefficient matrices are dense; and, (B) the computational effort increases rapidly as the order of the basis function increases. A comparison of the computational efficiency of various surface fitting methods is presented in Table 7.4.

Related to the computational effort is the question of convergence of the algorithm. It is important to remember that there is a tradeoff between the rate of convergence and the amount of computation. In choosing an algorithm for surface approximation, the following questions must be answered:

1. Does the method converge to a unique solution and can this be proven?
2. If so, what is the rate of convergence?

4.2. Segmentation

There are two distinct approaches to the segmentation of range data: region-based and edge-based. The first approach, region-based, presupposes that a patch (or region) on the object with similar spatial properties describes a surface feature. The patch can be extracted by first fitting a surface function to the data and then computing the desired properties such as curvature from this function. The second, and edge-based approach, has its roots in edge detection, which is a classical area of computer vision. In this approach, edges are extracted from the range image and boundaries of surface patches are identified. The area within patch boundaries is assumed to be a smooth surface, which can easily be approximated.

A region-based approach to surface description has been developed by Besl and Jain (5). Their basic assumption is that of spatial coherence; in other words, the scene consists of piecewise-smooth surface patches separated by jump discontinuities. Patches can be represented by low-order polynomials. Besl and Jain segment an image by "growing" regions of polynomial fits of variable order until some cutoff criteria is satisfied.

Their algorithm proceeds as follows:

1. Compute differential properties of data.
2. Select regions of similar mean and Gaussian curvature.
3. Shrink these regions to obtain seed region list.
4. For each seed region,
   a. $i = 1$, $S_i^j = NULL$.
   b. If $(i > 4)$, remove those seed regions from list that are covered by S_i^j, and go on to next seed region.
   c. Fit a polynomial function S_i^j to seed region j.
   d. If goodness-of-fit criterion is not exceeded, add neighboring points to region. Go to step (3).
   e. If goodness-of-fit criterion is exceeded, $i = i + 1$. Go to step (3).
   f. If goodness-of-fit criterion has not changed over two iterations, go to step (3).
5. Output S_i^j as segmented, fitted regions.

An edge-based surface description has been advocated by Fan *et al.* (7). Their basic philosophy is to fit a surface *after* finding the discontinuities and patch boundaries. Surface boundaries must be inferred from higher-order differential properties of a surface. Therefore, the first task, as in the region-based schemes, is to find the curvature related quantities from the surface. While jump boundaries can easily be computed by standard edge detectors, crease boundaries are much more difficult to locate since they are discontinuities in the surface normals. A jump boundary can be detected by finding zero crossings of the curvature in a direction normal to the bounding curve. Crease boundaries can be detected by finding local extrema of the curvature. On the basis of these facts, Fan presented the following algorithm.

1. Compute surface curvature quantities.
2. Extract and localize significant properties of these curvature properties.
3. Use a multiscale Gaussian edge detection and linking scheme to find edge labels.
4. Interpret sets of curvature features in terms of physical boundaries of the surface, and define the regions.
5. Reconstruct surface inside each region. Since the segmentation at the end of this procedure guarantees that the enclosed surfaces are simple, a biquadratic polynomial is fit to the internal points.

Region- and edge-based approaches have been combined by Vemuri and Aggarwal (21). They characterize an object in terms of its jump boundaries and surface primitives. Their algorithm consists of the following steps:

1. The range data is divided into $L \times L$ windows ($L = 7$), which overlap by 2 pixels.
2. Each window of data is tested to see if it contains a jump boundary by looking for significant range discontinuity between the pixels in the neighborhood.
3. If a discontinuity is detected, the region is rejected.
4. If no discontinuity is detected, a tensor product *spline-under-tension* is fitted to the data.
5. Surface characteristics are computed from this analytical surface element. The labels used are elliptic, hyperbolic, parabolic, umbilic, and planar.
6. A region growing algorithm is utilized to create a region adjacency graph. A graph node corresponds to a region and contains information about it, and graph edges link regions that abut each other.

The algorithms by Besl and Jain (5) and Fan *et al.* (7) are complementary in their use of range information, and provide good examples of range image processing. All three methods show the general framework of range image processing algorithms represented in Fig. 7.13.

4.3. Surface Approximation

Surface approximation is the process of fitting a surface primitive to range data with techniques from approximation theory and statistics. It is

required for both shape extraction and the estimation of surface properties during segmentation. Existing surface fitting algorithms include a
variety of different approximation schemes: simple bivariate polynomial
approximation for planes and low-order polynomials; nonlinear approximation for the standard set of quadrics such as spheres, cylinders, cones,
and superquadrics; and spline approximation for free-form surfaces.

Surface approximation is cast as a minimization problem. Approximation schemes minimize the error between the data and a bivariate model.
The statisical error measure in this procedure is the basis for the following
discussion of surface approximation. Least-squares regression is the simplest and most common norm used in the solution. The beauty of the
least-squares method lies not only in its mathematical simplicity but also in
its computational efficiency. However, it is inadequate in many circumstances. This leads to the use of other norms and methods. For instance,
when the data are sparse, the minimization problem is ill-posed, but can
be solved through regularization. When the data are extremely noisy,
robust statistical methods are warranted. Sections 4.3.1 through 4.3.4
describe these methods in detail.

4.3.1. Least-Squares Norm

Traditional least-squares or L_2 regression assumes the data model to be

$$z = f^*(x,y) + \varepsilon \qquad (36)$$

where f^* is a linear model and is the expected value of $f(x, y)$ given the
data z, and ε is a normal (Gaussian) noise. The noise has zero mean and
variance σ^2, that is, $\varepsilon \sim N(0,\sigma^2)$. The ε are independent, identically
distributed random variables.

Least-squares approximation is a *best approximation* for a L_2 norm $\|\cdot\|$,
derived from an inner product $\langle,\dots,\rangle$ of the discrete form

$$\langle g, h \rangle = \sum_{i=0}^{N_p} g(i)h(i). \qquad (37)$$

If the approximating function belongs to a finite linear space $\mathcal{L}$, a best
approximation to the data z implies finding $f^* \in \mathcal{L}$ such that

$$\|g - f^*\|_2 = \min_{f \in \mathcal{L}} \|z - f\|_2$$

The function f^* is a best approximation from $\mathcal{L}$ to z with respect to

$\| \cdot \|_2$, if and only if, the function f^* is in $\mathscr{L}$:

$$\forall f \in \mathscr{L}, \langle f, z - f^* \rangle = 0.$$

If $\{\phi_i\}$, $i = 1, \ldots, n$ is a basis for $\mathscr{L}$, then

$$\text{for } i = 1, \ldots, N_p \qquad \langle \phi_i, z - f^* \rangle = 0 \tag{38}$$

that is, the error is perpendicular to the basis functions. Here f^* has a unique representation $f^* = \sum_{j=1}^n a_i \phi_i$ in terms of the basis functions; hense the linear system

$$\text{for } i = 1, \ldots, N_p \qquad \left\langle \phi_i, z_i - \sum_{j=1}^n a_j \phi_j \right\rangle = 0 \tag{39}$$

has a unique solution a_i, where N_p is the number of data points. These equations can be rewritten as the *normal equations*

$$\text{for } i = 1, \ldots, N_p \qquad \sum_{j=1}^n \langle \phi_i, \phi_j \rangle a_j = \langle \phi_i, z_i \rangle. \tag{40}$$

Polynomials and B-splines are possible candidate as basis functions for approximation and are discussed below.

4.3.1.1. Polynomial Fitting

Polynomial surface reconstruction is usually applied in sequence over small regions of the range image. A set of points are selected in the local neighborhood of the place where the fit needs to be performed. Each data point in the set may be weighted with a constant according to the affect of that point. The solution of the normal equations is equivalent to minimizing the sum of the difference between the data values and polynomial model estimate $f(x, y)$. The normal equations of

$$\min \left\{ \sum_{k=1}^N w_k [z_k - f(x_k, y_k)]^2 \right\}, \tag{41}$$

can be written compactly in matrix form as

$$\mathbf{XWA} = \mathbf{Z}, \tag{42}$$

and has the solution

$$\mathbf{A} = (\mathbf{X}^T \mathbf{W} \mathbf{X})^{-1} \mathbf{X}^T \mathbf{W} \mathbf{Z}, \tag{43}$$

where N is the number of points in the neighborhood, w_k is the weight associated with each point, and the parameter vector $\mathbf{A} = (a_0, \ldots, a_n)$ consists of the coefficients of the bivariate polynomial. The coefficients can be computed using well-known numerical techiniques.

When fitting implicit quadrics, the minimization becomes nonlinear, and methods such as the Levenberg–Marquandt solver must be used for gradient descent.

Many researchers have used polynomial least-squares fit to *directly* extract the differential quantities from the data. For instance, Haralick and Watson (10) employ the *local-facet model*, which relies on discrete orthogonal polynomials to find local fits and compute differential quanties from the coefficients. This method is computationally efficient since the use of orthogonal polynomials implies that the solution is seperable and does not require inversion of a matrix. However, there are two disadvantages: (1) it is applicable only to gridded depth maps, and (2) the local nature of the computation implies that the quantities computed are not continuous.

4.3.1.2. Spline Fitting (Local or Global)

Tensor product spline surface(s) can be fit to range data as an intermediate step in the computation of curvature quantities. This approach has been taken to fit local patches in a subwindow of the data to determine the differential quantities needed. It has also been used to perform a global fit of the surface over the whole data set. While Vemuri and Aggarwal employ a spline under tension, other splines can also be used. One of the more common approaches to fitting uses cubic B-splines as the basis function.

One-dimensional B-splines may be expressed as the recursion between basis functions of varying degrees over a knot vector $\{t_i\}$,

$$b_{ki}(x) = \frac{(x - t_{i-k})b_{k-1,i-1}(x) + (t_i - x)b_{k-1,i}(x)}{t_i - t_{i-k}}, \qquad (44)$$

$$b_{1i}(x) = \begin{cases} \dfrac{1}{t_i - t_{i-1}} & \text{when} \quad t_{i-1} \leq x < t_i, \\ 0 & \text{otherwise.} \end{cases} \qquad (45)$$

It is well known that a cubic spline curve can be represented as a linear combination of B-splines $b_{k\,i}(x), i = 1, \ldots, g$ of order $k = 4$. This forms a set of basis functions that are identically zero outside of a $(k + 1)$-knot local support interval. The cubic $_{4i}(x)$ is the minimal basis function needed to ensure continuous curvature quantities.

The two-dimensional basis function is given as a linear combination of the tensor products of one-dimensional B-splines,

$$f(x, y) = \sum_{i=1}^{g+k} \sum_{j=1}^{h+k} c_{ij} b_{ki}(x) b_{kj}(y). \tag{46}$$

$b_{k\,i}(x)$ and $b_{kj}(y)$ are one-dimensional B-splines of degree $k - 1$, $b_{k\,j}(y)$ is described in the same manner as $b_{k\,i}(x)$ above, and g and h are the number of knots in x and y. The coefficients of the B-spline are determined by substituting the expression for $f(x, y)$ in Eq. (46) into the normal Eq. (38), and solving the resulting system of equations. In matrix notation, Eq. (46) can be represented as

$$\mathbf{F} = \mathbf{B_X C B_Y^T} \tag{47}$$

The coefficients can be obtained by solving the normal equations

$$\mathbf{C} = \left(\mathbf{B_x^T B_x}\right)^{-1} \mathbf{B_x^T Z B_y} \left(\mathbf{B_Y^T B_Y}\right)^{-1}. \tag{48}$$

An advantage of the tensor product B-spline basis functions over other spline basis is that the normal equations revert to a solution of two $N \times N$ matrices instead of an $N^2 \times N^2$ matrix for an data set of size $N \times N$. deBoor (22) asserts that the piecewise cubic elements of the B-spline have fewer degrees of freedom, enough to approximate the underlying data, but not enough to follow the noise. Another advantage is that cubic B-spline basis functions provide a computationally convenient representation. They have local support and result in a well-conditioned, banded positive-definite system.

There is an inherent problem with global B-spline approximation, however. Qualitative analysis of the surface obtained by this method shows a large amount of "ringing" at the boundaries of regions. One way of viewing the effect of the noise suppression property of regression is to study the geometry associated with the ringing (i.e., Gibbs phenomenon) caused by the fit. Surface fitting is a low-pass filtering procedure that does not achieve an exact cutoff in the frequency domain resulting in Gibbs phenomenon. This phenomenon manifests itself at ripples on the surface, which leads to inflection points that are an artifact of the fit, not the underlying data.

4.3.2. Regularization-Based Norms

Sparse depth maps arise from visual processes such as binocular stereo correspondence. The recovery of the *visual surface* from such data by approximation is a problem central to computer vision. When the available range data is sparse, surface reconstruction becomes an ill-posed problem since there are more unknowns than equations. Regularization techniques can be utilized for solving such a problem. The minimization problem is "regularized" by augmenting the least-squares norm with additional constraints, possibly on the smoothness of the solution. Recently, these reconstruction methods been applied to other types of range data. A review of the theory of surface approximation is available in Schumaker (16), and a bibliography of the latest technology in Franke and Schumaker (9).

The *regularized* approximation problem is to find $f^* \in \mathcal{F}$, such that f^* minimizes $\mathcal{I}(f)$ with respect to all $f \in F$, where

$$\mathcal{I}(f) = \sum_{i=1}^{N_p} |z_i - f(x_i, y_i)|^2 + \nu^2 \mathcal{S}(f)^2. \tag{49}$$

The first term $\mathcal{E}(f) = \sum_{i=1}^{N_p} |z_i - f(x_i, y_i)|^2$ is the error in the fit of the surface to the data. The second term, the stabilizing functional $\mathcal{S}(f)$, is a measure of the "consistency" or smoothness of the surface and is related to the variation in the normal to the surface (i.e., the curvature). The general form of the stabilizers is derived for the case in which the smoothest function is chosen from the Sobolev space W_p^2. It is given by

$$\mathcal{S}_1(f) = \left\{ \int_a^b \sum_{i=0}^{p} w_i(x) \left(\frac{d^i f}{dx^i} \right)^2 dx \right\}^{1/2}, \tag{50}$$

where $w_0(x), \ldots, w_{p-1}(x)$ are nonnegative functions and $w_p(x)$ is a positive function. A suitable choice of stabilizer is the quadratic variation:

$$\mathcal{S}_2(f) = \left\{ \int\int_\Omega \left(f_{xx}^2 + 2f_{xy}^2 + f_{yy}^2 \right) \right\}^{1/2}. \tag{51}$$

The quadratic variation is preferred to a Laplacian stabilizer since it has a smaller null space, that of the set of linear functions, as opposed to the set of all harmonic functions that satisfy the Laplacian.

The use of regularization is an elegant solution to the problem. However, its major weakness is that the stabilizing term imposes the same smoothness criteria over the whole image. This is not a good strategy for range image processing. A single measure of smoothness fails to incorporate discontinuities in depth and orientation because the approximating surface cannot be equally smooth everywhere over a depth map that usually consists of surfaces separated by discontinuities. Therefore, it is inappropriate to have global squared second-order derivative operators, such as the quadratic variation, in the stabilizing term.

4.3.2.1. Solution of Regularization Based Approaches

The functional $\mathcal{F}(f)$ presented in Eq. (49) must be minimized to obtain f. It can be minimized by variational calculus, thin-plate splines or finite-element methods.

Variational Calculus. The calculus of variations takes the partial derivative of the variation of the functional $\mathcal{F}$ and sets it equal to zero to obtain the Euler equations. In general, minimizing a functional

$$\int\int \mathcal{F}(x, y, f, f_x, f_y, f_{xx}, f_{xy}, f_{yy}, \ldots)\, dx\, dy \tag{52}$$

with a solution f leads to the Euler equations

$$\mathcal{F}_f - \frac{\partial}{\partial x}\mathcal{F}_{fx} + \frac{\partial}{\partial x^2}\mathcal{F}_{fxx} - \cdots - \frac{\partial}{\partial y^2}\mathcal{F}_{fy} + \frac{\partial}{\partial y^2}\mathcal{F}_{fyy} - \cdots = 0. \tag{53}$$

The minimization problem is, therefore, reduced to solving a set of differential equations by finite difference or conjugate gradient methods.

Finite-Element Approach. The finite-element approach represents the minimial function f^* as a linear combination of elements. The finite elements may be bivariate elements as used by Terzopoulos (20), or B-splines as used by Sinha (17). In the bivariate element approach, the basis functions, or finite elements, are given by either bilinear quadrilateral or triangular element. The nodal shape functions are given by

$$N_i(\xi, \eta) = \tfrac{1}{4}(1 + \xi\xi_i)(1 + \eta\eta_i), \tag{54}$$

where (ξ_i, η_i) are the reference coordinates of the node i. This basis function is substituted into the integrals of Eq. (49) and solved using standard numerical techniques. B-Splines may also be used for the basis function. The same approach is followed in this case—the minimal function is represented as a combination of the B-spline bases; it is substituted into Eq. (49); each term is evaluated to produce a diagonal system of equations; and the linear system is solved for the coefficients of the B-spline.

Thin-Plate Splines. Thin plate splines are couched in the theory of *reproducing kernel splines.* The minimizing function $f(x, y)$ can be expressed as a linear combination of basis functions, and is given by

$$f(x, y) = \sum_{i=0}^{N_p} a_i K[(x, y);(x_i, y_i)] + \sum_{i=1}^{d} b_i P_i(x, y). \qquad (55)$$

Here, $K[x, y);(x_i, y_i)]$ is the reproducing kernel for the space $\mathscr{F}$ of admissible functions, $f \in \mathscr{F}$, $d = 3$, and p_i is a basis for the null space $N = \text{span}\{1, x, y\}$ of $\mathscr{F}(16)$. The reproducing kernel is of the form

$$K[(x, y);(x_i, y_i)] = r_i^2(x, y)\ln[r_i(x, y)],$$

When the smoothness norm of Eq. (49) is the quadratic variation, and where the basis functions are $r_i(x, y) = [(x - x_i)^2 + (y - y_i)^2]^{1/2}$. The coefficients a_i, b_i can be determined by the solution of a $(N_p + d)$ by $(N_p + d)$ dense linear system, with $N(f) = \{z_1, z_2, \ldots z_{N_p}\} = \{f(x_1, y_1), \ldots, f(x_{N_p}, y_{N_p})\}$

There are three drawbacks to the thin-plate spline method. First, it is difficult to obtain the reproducing kernel for new classes of smoothness norms, for example, for the adaptive norm discussed below. Second, the method has a limitation in that it is satisfied by globally $\mathscr{C}^2$ continuous splines, while the data usually consist of *piecewise*-smooth surfaces. Third, the solution is computationally expensive as the coefficient matrix is dense. In contrast, B-splines are not as costly since they have local basis and result in a banded system of equations.

4.3.3. *Adaptive-Regularization-Based Approaches*

An adaptive smoothing or regularization approach has been introduced to alleviate the global smoothness constraint that has plagued surface approximation. In this approach, the regularization stabilizers are adaptively adjusted according to the smoothness of the underlying surface. Adaptive (or controlled-continuity) stabilizers were first proposed in computer vision by Terzopoulos (19). They are represented as a weighted sum of the energies associated with a membrane and a thin plate over the surface. This is given by

$$\mathscr{S}_3(f) = \left\{ \begin{aligned} \iint_\Omega &\rho(x, y)\{\tau(x, y)(f_{xx}^2 + 2f_{xy}^2 + f_{yy}^2) \\ &+ [1 - \tau(x, y)](f_x^2 + f_y^2)\} \, dx \, du, \end{aligned} \right\}^{1/2} \qquad (56)$$

where $\rho(x, y)$ and $\tau(x, y)$ are real-valued weighting functions whose range is in [0,1]. If $\rho(x, y) = \tau(x, y) = 1$, the stabilizer reduces to the quadratic variation. If $\rho(x, y) = 1$ and $\tau(x, y) = 0$, the stabilizer is equivalent to a membrane. If $\rho(x,y) = 0$, the surface can be discontinuous (i.e; it may tear). However, solving for the optimal value of ρ and τ is a difficult problem, as this is equivalent to segmenting the data. If all three unknowns f, ρ, τ are solved simultaneously, the problem becomes nonlinear and the solution may not be unique. Terzopoulos (in Algorithm VP2) (20) estimates the weighting functions during surface approximation iterations, while Sinha and Schunck (17) suggest a two-stage process that seperates the computation of ρ and τ from the computation of f.

In the solution of the adaptive regularization problem, the use of local-basis finite elements is advantageous. Even though the basis functions for thin-plate splines are global, it should be theoretically possible to construct solutions that are restricted to continuous regions, given the continuity control functions. This is, however, difficult in practice, as it is equivalent to segmenting the image. Local bases, such as B-splines, are much better suited to computing continuity control functions containing jump transitions, since discontinuities may readily emerge between adjacent elements.

4.3.4. *Robust Estimators*

Most of the reconstruction methods described above suffer from two problems; the methods (1) break down in the presence of outliers, and (2) smooth over discontinuities or edges of patches. These problems can be overcome by the use of robust estimators. The term *robustness* refers to the fact that these estimators are not affected by the presence of outliers in the data. Outliers and discontinuities can be looked at as a single type of error, as illustrated in Fig. 7.16 The symbol ⊞ at the center of the neighborhood denotes the location at which reconstruction is performed, and the symbol ⊕ denotes the location of the data. At least half the points in the neighborhood around the ⊞ are expected to lie on the same underlying surface as that point. Thus, an optimal technique for surface reconstruction should allow for at most half the points to be outliers to the distribution. This behavior, of allowing a large amount of outliers, is exhibited by robust algorithms, and accounts for their discontinuity preserving behavior. Robustness is, therefore, an advantage when fitting across discontinuities in both depth and orientation. The distribution on one side of the discontinuity is not affected by the population on the other, which are outliers to the other population.

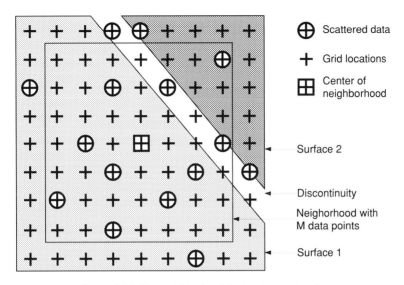

Figure 7.16. The neighborhood for local reconstruction.

Robust algorithms are characterized by their statistical efficiency and breakdown point. *Efficiency* measures the degree to which optimal estimates can be obtained with a particular algorithm. The *breakdown point* of an algorithm refers to the smallest percentage of points incorrect to an arbitrary degree at which the estimation procedure can produce an arbitrarily wrong estimate. Least-squares, a nonrobust algorithm, is optimally efficient for normal noise in large sample sets, but can be very inefficient if the noise does not obey the Gaussian distribution. For a mixed model of noise such as

$$(1 - \epsilon)N(\mu, \sigma^2) + \epsilon N(\mu_1, \sigma_1^2), \tag{57}$$

the estimation of location in one dimension by the least-squares method is more efficient than the median for normal noise ($\epsilon = 0$). However, a mix of even $\epsilon = 10\%$ of noise from another distribution can make the median more efficient. The least-squares method also has the disadvantage in that even a single outlier will affect the reconstruction, as illustrated in Fig. 7.17 Therefore, its breakdown point is 0%.

While a simple combination of a median filter and least-squares fitting can be used for processing gridded data, other nonlinear methods must be developed for sparse data. Two robust estimation techniques—"M-estimators" and "least median of squares"–are commonly used in vision. They are described below.

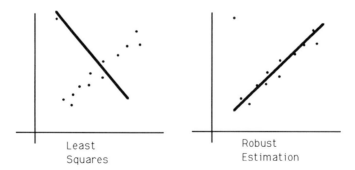

Figure 7.17. Even one outlier can wreak havoc on least-squares estimates. Robust methods are immune to outliers.

4.3.4.1. M-Estimators

M-Estimators (11) are a generalization of the maximum-likelihood estimators. They are based on the idea of replacing the square of the residual with a symmetric function ρ of the residuals. The cost function to be minimized is given by

$$\min_{\hat{a}} \sum_{i=1}^{N_p} \rho(r_i). \tag{58}$$

The function ρ makes the effects of points in the tail of the Gaussian distribution constant after a certain point, or actually sets them to zero in the case of redescending ρ functions. This cost function leads to normal equations of the form

$$\sum_{i=1}^{N_p} \mathbf{A}_{ij}\psi(r_i) = 1, j = 1, 2, \ldots, p, \tag{59}$$

where ψ is the derivative of the function ρ. Huber (11) suggest using

$$\rho(x) = \begin{cases} \frac{1}{2}x^2 & \text{for} \quad |x| \le c, \\ c|x| - \frac{1}{2}c^2 & \text{for} \quad |x| > c, \end{cases} \tag{60}$$

and

$$\psi(x) = \begin{cases} x & \text{for} \quad |x| \le c, \\ c\,\mathrm{sign}(x)c^2 & \text{for} \quad |x| > c. \end{cases} \tag{61}$$

Figure 7.18 shows the shape of the ρ function

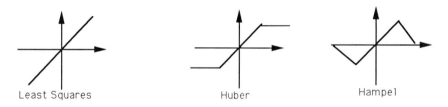

Figure 7.18. ρ function of M-estimators.

The use of robust operators for surface reconstruction in computer vision was first introduced by Besl *et al.* (2) They used an iterative M-estimator to smooth data even across discontinuities, without losing the location of the edges. Interested readers are referred to Huber (11) for more details on M-estimators.

4.3.4.2. Least Median of Squares (LMS)

The least median of squares method of estimation is similar to the least squares method described above, except that the sum of the squares of the residual is replaced by the median of the squared residuals. It is also related to the median filter used in image processing to remove impulse noise from images, and is nearly optimal in suppressing noise with a large amount of outliers. The use of LMS for surface reconstruction is based on the fact that the median of a finite set of independent and identically distributed random variables is a useful statistical estimate of the mean when the underlying distribution has a very large tail. The LMS algorithm has been used in various vision tasks such as fitting lines to edge data and smoothing salt-and-pepper noise. The LMS method is described as

$$\min_{\hat{a}} \left\{ \operatorname*{median}_{0 \leq i < N} \left[(z_i - f^*(x_i, y_i))^2 \right] \right\}, \tag{62}$$

where the f^* is an estimate of the actual value of the function at x_i, y_i; $\hat{a}$ is an estimated parameter vector; and N is the number of points in a local neighborhood. The LMS procedure has a breakdown point of 50%.

The algorithm used to find the LMS fit consists of the following steps:

1. First, chose M closest neighbors of the grid point.
2. From this set, repeatedly draw random samples of N points.
3. With each of these subsamples, associate an index L.
4. Determine the regression surface approximation of these points, and denote the corresponding coefficient vector $\mathbf{a}_L$.
5. For this estimate of the grid value, find the LMS objective function with respect to all the M points $\operatorname*{median}_{0 \leq i < N} [(z_i - f^*(x_i, y_i))^2]$.
6. Finally, retain the trial, L, for which this value is minimal, and output the parameter vector $\mathbf{a}_L$

TABLE 7.3

Number of Subsamples Required to Assure P (good) = .95 for |a| = 6

ε	.05	.1	.2	.3	.4	.5
m	3	4	10	24	63	191

It should be noted that this procedure is very compute-intensive because $C_{N_p}^M$ subsamples have to be selected. In actual practice, only a certain number of samplings are performed such that the probability of one of the samples being "good" tends to 1. A sample is "good" if it consists of p true data points and a fraction ε of noisy points. The expression for this probability is

$$P(good) = 1 - \left[1 - (1 - \varepsilon)^p\right]^m. \tag{63}$$

Table 7.3 shows values of m, the number of random subsamples for various amounts of noise ε in the data. These values are true for a parameter vector $\mathbf{a}, |\mathbf{a}| = 6$, and are the number of subsamples required to assure a probability of 0.95 that a good sample is selected. The efficiency of the least sum of median estimator is $2/\pi = 0.637$.

Table 7.4 compares properties of various techniques for surface fitting based on different criteria. The symbol "†" (dagger) indicates that the result depends on the particular implementation. For instance, polynomial fitting does not generally handle outliers. However, when the normally quadratic least-squares norm is changed to an appropriate ψ-function as is done by Boal *et al.* (2), the method does reject outliers.

TABLE 7.4

Comparison of Surface Reconstruction Techniques[a]

Representation technique	Scattered data	Local basis	Efficiency	Preserve discontinuities	Handle outliers
Bivariate polynomials	Y	†	$O(N)$		
Tensor-product B-splines		Y	$O(N \log N)$		
Thin-plate splines	Y		$O(k^2)$		
Regularized approximation	Y		$O(N^2)$		
Controlled continuity splines	Y	Y	$O(N \log N)$	Y	
Adaptive regularization	Y	Y	$O(N \log N)$	Y	†
Robust estimation	Y		†	Y	Y

[a]The symbol k is the number of data points, and N is the number of grid locations. They symbol † indicates that the result depends on the particular implementation.

5. APPLICATIONS

Applications of range imaging systems are numerous, encompassing a wide variety of fields such as product design, manufacturing, medical imaging, geographic information systems, and vehicle navigation. The core processes involved in these disparate areas are modeling, inspection, or guidance and control.

5.1. Modeling

The creation of a geometric CAD model from a physical part is referred to as reverse engineering. Reverse engineering has applicability in the design and redesign of parts in the automotive, aerospace, shipping, and ancillary industries. This technique is often utilized in design studios, where designers first work in a physical medium such as clay or foam

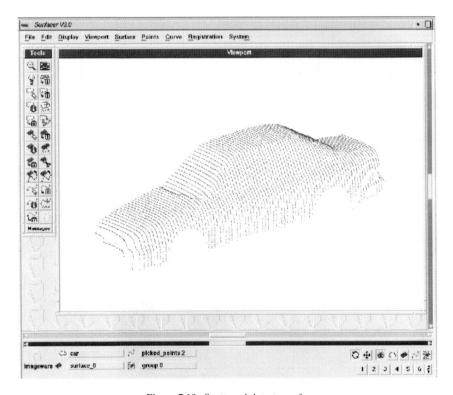

Figure 7.19. Scattered data to surfaces.

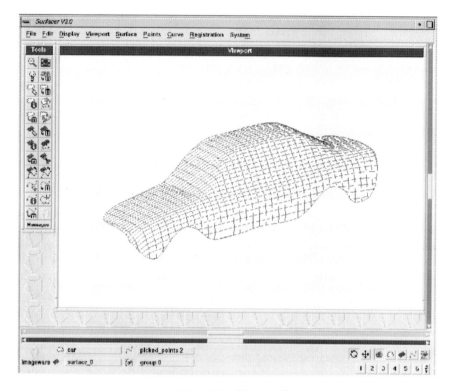

Figure 7.19. (*Continued*)

before creating a CAD model of a part. Figure 7.19 shows three-dimensional data obtained from the clay model and the surfaces fit to it. Reverse engineering can also be used to update an exiating CAD model when a part is modified based on functional constraints. Design applications require the range sensor and processing algorithms to be extremely precise. Yet another application of reverse engineering is the manufacture of one-of-a-kind artificial limbs and bones. In this usage, the fit between the body and the prosthesis must be exact, but the accuracy required of the ranging system is not as great as that in design applications.

Surface fitting algorithms play a central role in reverse engineering, as illustrated in Fig 7.20. They convert three-dimensional measurements to surface models, which can then be directly imported into a CAD system. The CAD model is output in IGES[1] format and can be shipped to

---

[1]Initial Graphics Exchange Standard, an obtuse CAD community standard for exchange of geometric information.

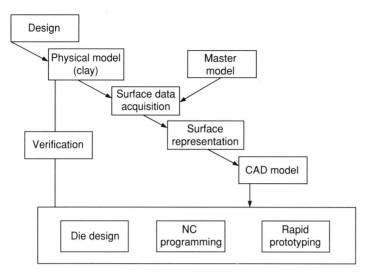

Figure 7.20. The role of range image processing in reverse engineering.

finite-element systems for analysis, to stereo-lithography systems for rapid prototyping, and to numerically controlled machines for manufacturing.

5.2. Inspection

Inspection of production parts is a critical component of the manufacturing process. The term is utilized in a variety of contexts. For instance, it is used in dimensional inspection to determine whether critical dimensions are within the tolerance limits (metrology) and whether the assembly locations for parts are precisely situated. The critical dimensions of a part (e.g; hole diameters, concentricity of circles, lengths, width, thicknesses, angles between surface) can be measured directly from surfaces fit to data. In terms of overall accuracy required of the sensing and fitting processes, metrology is the most demanding process.

The inspection of surface flaws and component defects is an obvious application for range image processing. Scanning followed by surface fitting offers a fast and complete inspection procedure for finding surface quality flaws such as waviness and dents. Quantitative and qualitative measures of the surface can be estimated from the average roughness R_a and the curvature properties. Measurement accuracy and inspection time can be traded off by varying the spatial density of the scan and smoothing parameters of the fitting procedure. This use of range image sensors replaces laborious optical methods for surface inspection.

5.3. Guidance and Control

Range image processing algorithms can be used for guidance and control in applications that require continuous geometric information. Range data serve as feedback information for servoing robot arms and mobile vehicles. For example, range data are utilized for guidance in the CMU Navlab (12) vehicle. The Navlab has an Environmental Research Institute of Michigan range sensor and general-purpose computers on board, which create an elevation map as a data structure for terrain representation. This 2 1/2 D terrain map is used for path-planning and avoiding obstacles. Many smaller mobile robots employ sonar senors to provide real-time feedback of range information to prevent collisions.

A somewhat futuristic application of range image processing is the real-time monitoring of machining processes during the manufacture of expensive and precise parts such as turbine blades. Since the machining process warps the stock itself, a structured light system can be employed to monitor the progress of the part being cut. The current shape of the stock can be compared to the initial CAD model, and the cutter path can be changed if the stock geometry varies from the model. This application requires the registration and comparison of range data with a CAD model.

6. CONCLUSION

The extraction of three-dimensional information from a scene is an important cognitive task that must be re-created on a computer. This process has been broken down into three steps in this chapter, not necessarily in this order: generating the models of the objects ot be sensed, measuring three-dimensional information, and extracting the corresponding models from the range data. A prerequisite to shape extraction is shape modeling. Computer vision has produced many geometric primitives to represent objects and has also borrowed representations from CAD. Some of these descriptors, such as polynomials and splines, have been presented. Shape extraction is facilitated with the advent of range image sensors that provide shape explicitly in the form of range images. A number of sensors have been described in this chapter. These range sensors produce data that must be processed to extract the shape of objects in a scene. The processing operates on raw three-dimensional point data and segments range data into different objects extracts corresponding geometric primitives. This chapter has focused particularly on these two processes, as they are central to range image processing.

There are a number of interesting ideas in range image processing that have not as yet been fully explored. These include the integration of information from multiple sources and the relationship of the shape extracted to the model of the object (for registration and recognition).

- **Multiview integration and multisensor fusion**. Multiview integration becomes an important problem in reverse-engineering the model of a *whole* object, as information from different viewpoints must be coalesced into a single representation. Unfortunately, very few deal with multiple views or with assimilating information from different data sets from either multiple views or multiple sensors. There are two schools of thought on how to integrate information from multiple views—to convert all the data into a single coordinate frame and then run the range image analysis algorithms, or to extract the surfaces from each view and merge these higher level primitives. Multiview integration is presented in Vemuri and Aggarwal (21).
- **Shape representation and object recognition**. There are a number of computer vision specific shape representation schemes, which seem to be waiting in the wings for faster processing units. Examples are the view-centered models obtained from aspect graphs or from tessellations of the viewing sphere. These topics are dealt with in depth in Chapter 2 in this volume. Object recognition is another area requiring greater processing speed. Even though the low-level range image processing described in this chapter creates a concise description of a scene, it is still necessary to search through a database of objects and match descriptors. Chapter 14 in this volume provides more details on the problem.
- **Registration**. Many applications, including object recognition, require the registration of measured range data with an internal geometric model. Registration entails the comparison of lower-dimensional point data with higher-dimensional surface primitives, and requires the formulation of a "distance" norm between these two entities. A possible solution is to bring the two entities to the same dimension either by fitting a surface to the range data, or by sampling the surface model at sufficient points to get point data. Then a distance norm can be defined between the one- or two-dimensional entities.

The material for this chapter has been collected from various sources. The bibliography in this chapter will provide a starting point for further research. Readers are also referred to the proceedings of the NSF

Range Image Processing Workshop (12) as a source of information. An early reference to range image work in Computer Vision is Jarvis' paper (13). For a comprehensive study of range image sensor hardware, readers may consult Besl (3). Some other notable papers in the range image processing literature are Besl and Jain (4), Brady (6), Fan *et al.* (7), and Vemuri and Aggarwal (21).

REFERENCES

1. S. T. Barnard and M. A. Fischler, Computational stereo. *Comput. Surv.* **14**(4); 553–572 (1982).
2. P. J. Besl, J. B. Birch, and L. T. Watson, Robust window operators. Proc. 2nd Int'l. Conf. Comput. Vision, Dec. 5–8, 1988. *IEEE-CS*, pp. 591–600.
3. P. J. Besl, Active, optical range imaging sensors. *Mach. Vision & Appl.* 1, 127–152 (1988).
4. P. J. Besl and R. C. Jain, Three-dimensional object recognition. *Comput. Surv.* **17**(1); (1985).
5. P. J. Besl and R. C. Jain, Segmentation through variable-order surface fitting. *IEEE Trans. Pattern Anal. Mach. Intell.* **PAMI-10**(2); 167–192 (1988).
6. M. Brady, J. Ponce, A. Yuille, and H. Asada, Describing surfaces. *Comput. Vision, Graphics, Image Process.* **32**(1); 1–28 (1985).
7. T. J. Fan, G. Medioni, and R. Nevatia, Segmented descriptions of 3-d surfaces. *IEEE J. Robotics Autom.* **3**(6); 527–538 (1987).
8. I. D. Faux and M. J. Pratt, *"Computational Geometry for Design and Manufacture."* Ellis Horwood, Chichester, UK, 1979.
9. R. Franke and L. L. Schumaker, Bibliography of multivariate approximation. *In "Topics in Multivariate Approximation"* (C. K. Chui, L. L. Schumaker, and F. I. Uteras, eds.), pp. 275–335 (1987).
10. R. M. Haralick and L. Watson, A facet model for image data. *Comput. Graphics and Image Process.* **15**; 113–129 (1981).
11. P. J. Huber, *" Robust Statistics"* Wiley, New York, 1981.
12. R. C. Jain and A. K. Jain, eds., *"Analysis and Interpretation of Range Images."* Springer-Verlag, Boston, 1990.
13. R. A. Jarvis, A perspective on range finding techniques for computer vision. *IEEE Trans. Pattern Anal. Mach. Intell.* **PAMI 5**(2); 122–139 (1983).
14. J. J. Koenderink and A. J. van Doorn, The internal representation of solid shape with respect to vision. *Biol. Cybernet.* **32**; 211–216 (1979).
15. A. A. G. Requicha, Representations for solid objects: Theory, methods and systems. *Comput. Surv.* **12**(4); 437–464 (1980).
16. L. L. Schumaker, Fitting surfaces to scattered data. *In "Approximation Theory II"* (G. G. Lorentz, C. K. Chui, and L. L. Schumaker, eds.), pp. 203–268. Academic Press, London and Orlando, Fl., 1979.
17. S. S. Sinha and B. G. Schunck, a two stage algorithm for discontinuity-preserving surface reconstruction. *IEEE Trans. Pattern Anal. Mach. Intell.* **PAMI 14**(1); 36–55 (1992).
18. M. Spivak, *"A Comprehensive Introduction to Differential Geometry,"* 2nd ed. vols. I–V. Publish or Perish Press, 1979.

19. D. Terzopoulos, Regularization of inverse visual problems involving disconti-
    nuities. *IEEE Trans. Pattern Anal. Mach. Intell.* **PAMI 8**(4); 413–424 (1986).
20. D. Terzopoulos, The computation of visible surface representations. *IEEE
    Trans. Pattern Anal. Mach. Intell.* **PAMI 10**, 417–438 (1988).
21. B. C. Vemuri and J. K. Aggarwal, Representation and recognition of objects
    from dense range maps. *IEEE Trans. Circuits Syst.* **CAS-34**; 1351–1363
    (1987).
22. C. deBoor, *A Practical Guide to Splines*. Springer-Verlag, New York (1978).

Chapter **8**

Stereo Vision

LYNNE L. GREWE and AVINASH C. KAK
Robot Vision Laboratory
School of Electrical Engineering
Purdue University
West Lafayette, Indiana

HANDBOOK OF PATTERN RECOGNITION
AND IMAGE PROCESSING: COMPUTER VISION

1. INTRODUCTION

One way in which humans perceive depth is through a process called *binocular stereopsis* or *stereo vision*. Stereo vision uses the images viewed by each eye to recover the depth information in the scene. A point in the scene is projected into different locations in each eye, and this difference is called the *disparity*. Using geometric relationships between the eyes and the computed disparity value, the depth of the scene point can be calculated. Stereo vision, as used in computer vision systems, is similar.

While there are other techniques known for recovering depth, stereo vision has the advantage of being a passive technique meaning that an active sensor is not required. Historically, stereo vision has been used in many areas including cartography, industrial object recognition, and mobile robot navigation.

The stereo vision process can be summarized by the following steps: (1) detection of features in each image, (2) matching of features between the images under certain geometric and other constraints, and (3) calculation of depth using the disparity values and the geometric parameters of the imaging configuration. While each of these steps is important in the stereo vision process, the matching of features is generally thought to be the most difficult step and can easily become the most time-consuming.

In the sections to come, we hope to inform the reader of the vast work that has been accomplished in the area of stereo vision. We begin in Section 2 by discussing the geometry of a camera and how a scene point is projected into a camera. In Section 3, we describe the imaging configuration used in a stereo vision system and how the difference in the projected locations of a scene point yields a measurement called *disparity*. Also, we discuss how the depth of a point can be calculated from its disparity measurement. Section 4 contains the main contribution of this chapter. Here we describe the different stereo vision systems that have been developed paying particular attention to the issues of feature detection and matching. To help the reader interpret the differences in many of the existing stereo vision algorithms, we have classified them into the following three categories: low-level-feature-based, high-level-feature-based, and object-level-feature-based. In Section 5, we discuss resolution issues and the factors that influence the selection of the various parameters that characterize a stereo vision system. The topic of Section 6 is trinocular stereo vision, where instead of two cameras, three are used in an attempt to improve the results obtained by a binocular system. The effects of scene illumination are discussed in Section 7. Finally, in the last section, Section 8, the topic of error analysis in stereo vision is discussed.

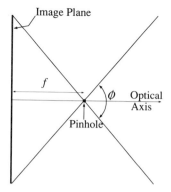

Figure 8.1. Illustration of the dependence of the view angle ϕ on the focal length f.

2. OPTICAL CONSIDERATIONS

Before discussing stereo vision itself, we first describe how the imaging process works in a camera. The process involved in capturing a scene point in the image is referred to as *perspective projection* and is mathematically described by what is called a *perspective transform*. In this section, we explain perspective projection and we also discuss a method of camera calibration that yields the parameters involved in this projection.

2.1. About the Camera Lens

A camera unit consists of two major components: the sensor plane and the lens. A typical sensor plane is 5.0×3.75 cm in size. The lens used is characterized by its focal length or a range of focal lengths if it is a zoom lens. As shown in Fig. 8.1, for a given sensor (image) plane size, the focal length f will determine the view angle ϕ. This angle determines the region of the scene in the field of view.

Another characteristic of a camera is its depth of field. The depth of field is defined as the range over which objects are in focus, meaning that their details will be sharply captured in the image plane. The depth of field is usually shallower in extent in the foreground and deeper in the background. The depth of field depends on the distance o from the lens center to the point at which the camera is focused and the size of the aperture as follows:

$$\text{Depth of field} = \frac{2HN(m + 1)}{m^2},$$

where

H = permissible diameter of the circle of confusion
N = f-stop (aperture) number of the lens = f/A, where A is the diameter of the aperture
m = magnification = i/o, where i is the distance between the lens plane and the image plane

A typical value for H is $f/1000$. Note that o, i and f are related by the following equation:

$$\frac{1}{o} + \frac{1}{i} = \frac{1}{f}.$$

2.2. Perspective Projection

We model the imaging process through the use of the pinhole model of a camera, shown in Fig. 8.2. This model treats the camera lens as a pinhole at a distance of f, the focal length, along the optical axis from the center of the image plane. The line that is drawn through the image plane's center (u_o, v_o) and is perpendicular to the image plane is referred

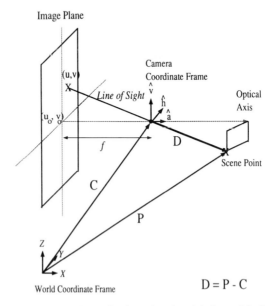

Figure 8.2. Perspective projection using the pinhole model of a camera.

to as the *optical axis*. The camera's 3D location is denoted by the vector C, which represents the world coordinates of the camera's focal point. The camera's orientation is described by the three vectors of the camera coordinate frame denoted by $\hat{h}$, $\hat{v}$, and $\hat{a}$. The image plane has two axes denoted by u and v that are parallel to the $\hat{h}$ and $\hat{v}$ vectors of the camera coordinate frame, respectively. Notice that the $\hat{a}$ vector is coincident with the optical axis.

In terms of $\hat{h}$, $\hat{v}$, and $\hat{a}$, any point on the image plane, (u, v), can be described in world coordinates as follows:

$$C - f\hat{a} + u\hat{h} + v\hat{v}.$$

We derive the perspective transformation equations for a given scene point P and its corresponding image point (u, v) by comparing the appropriate similar triangles in Fig. 8.2. The following is obtained:

$$\frac{u}{f} = \frac{D \cdot \hat{h}}{D \cdot \hat{a}}, \qquad \frac{v}{f} = \frac{D \cdot \hat{v}}{D \cdot \hat{a}},$$

where $D = P - C$ is the vector from the focal point to the scene point. An image is represented in a discrete domain in terms of pixels. Thus we now rewrite the above equation in terms of pixel coordinates, (i, j), instead of the continuously valued points (u, v). We know that the following is true where δu is the horizontal sampling interval and δv is the vertical sampling interval:

$$u = (i - i_o)\delta u, \qquad v = (j - j_o)\delta v.$$

Note that i_o, j_o is the center position of the image in pixel coordinates. We can rewrite the perspective transformation equations as follows:

$$\frac{(i - i_o)\delta u}{f} = \frac{D \cdot \hat{h}}{D \cdot \hat{a}}, \qquad \frac{(j - j_o)\delta v}{f} = \frac{D \cdot \hat{h}}{D \cdot \hat{a}},$$

therefore

$$\frac{i}{f} = \frac{D \cdot H}{D \cdot \hat{a}}, \qquad \frac{j}{f} = \frac{D \cdot V}{D \cdot \hat{a}}, \tag{1}$$

where

$$H = \frac{f}{\delta u} \hat{h} + i_o \hat{a}, \qquad V = \frac{f}{\delta v} \hat{v} + j_o \hat{a}.$$

We can rewrite Eq. (1) in matrix form as follows:

$$\begin{bmatrix} i' \\ j' \\ w \end{bmatrix} = \begin{bmatrix} H_x & H_y & H_z & 0 \\ V_x & V_y & V_z & 0 \\ a_x & a_y & a_z & 0 \end{bmatrix} \begin{bmatrix} D_x \\ D_y \\ D_z \\ 1 \end{bmatrix} \qquad \text{and} \quad i = \frac{i'}{w}, \quad j = \frac{j'}{w}. \quad (2)$$

Given $D = P - C$, Eq. (2) becomes

$$\begin{bmatrix} i' \\ j' \\ w \end{bmatrix} = \begin{bmatrix} H_x & H_y & H_z & -C'_x \\ V_x & V_y & V_z & -C'_y \\ a_x & a_y & a_z & -C'_z \end{bmatrix} \begin{bmatrix} P_x \\ P_y \\ P_z \\ 1 \end{bmatrix} = T \begin{bmatrix} P_x \\ P_y \\ P_z \\ 1 \end{bmatrix}, \quad (3)$$

where

$$C' = RC \qquad \text{and} \qquad R = \begin{bmatrix} H_x & H_y & H_z \\ V_x & V_y & V_z \\ a_x & a_y & a_z \end{bmatrix}$$

The pinhole model is accurate for fixed-focal-length cameras with high-quality lenses. However, this model breaks down when a thick or poor-quality lens is used. There are other methods of modeling a camera and, if appropriate, they should be used (25).

2.3. Camera Calibration

As we will see later, the parameters of a camera, C, $\hat{h}$, $\hat{v}$, $\hat{a}$, f, δu, δv, i_o, and j_o can be calculated if the matrix T of Eq. (3) is known. In this section, we will discuss a camera calibration procedure that calculates the matrix T. The matrix T, commonly referred to as the *camera calibration matrix* or *perspective transformation matrix*, transforms a point in world coordinates (x_m, y_m, z_m) to the corresponding point (i_m, j_m) in the image plane:

$$
\begin{bmatrix} i'_m \\ j'_m \\ w_m \end{bmatrix} = \begin{bmatrix} T_{11} & T_{12} & T_{13} & T_{14} \\ T_{21} & T_{22} & T_{23} & T_{24} \\ T_{31} & T_{32} & T_{33} & T_{34} \end{bmatrix} \begin{bmatrix} x_m \\ y_m \\ z_m \\ 1 \end{bmatrix}, \quad \text{where} \quad i_m = \frac{i'_m}{w_m}, \quad j_m = \frac{j'_m}{w_m}.
$$

$$(4)$$

Therefore, we have 12 unknowns (T_{ij}'s), which can be calculated if the camera is shown at least six scene points whose 3D world coordinates are known and whose corresponding image coordinates can be found. Each of these correspondences will generate two constraints on T as described in Eq. (1). Thus, a total of 12 equations will be generated. The form of these equations can be expressed as follows:

$$
i_m = \frac{T_{11}x_m + T_{12}y_m + T_{13}z_m + T_{14}}{T_{31}x_m + T_{32}y_m + T_{33}z_m + T_{34}},
$$

$$(5)$$

$$
j_m = \frac{T_{21}x_m + T_{22}y_m + T_{23}z_m + T_{24}}{T_{31}x_m + T_{32}y_m + T_{33}z_m + T_{34}}.
$$

$$(6)$$

To create a solution from this set of equations we arbitrarily set T_{34} equal to one (this can be thought of as merely a scaling factor). Therefore, Eqs. (5) and (6) can be rewritten as follows:

$$
T_{11}x_m + T_{12}y_m + T_{13}z_m + T_{14} + T_{31}(-i_m x_m)
$$

$$
+ T_{32}(-i_m y_m) + T_{33}(-i_m z_m) = i_m,
$$

$$(7)$$

$$
T_{21}x_m + T_{22}y_m + T_{23}z_m + T_{24} + T_{31}(-j_m x_m)
$$

$$
+ T_{32}(-j_m y_m) + T_{33}(-j_m z_m) = j_m.
$$

$$(8)$$

Thus, given N correspondences we can write the constraints produced from Eqs. (7) and (8) in matrix form:

$$
\begin{bmatrix}
x_1 & y_1 & z_1 & 1 & 0 & 0 & 0 & 0 & -i_1 x_1 & -i_1 y_1 & -i_1 z_1 \\
0 & 0 & 0 & 0 & x_1 & y_1 & z_1 & 1 & -j_1 x_1 & -j_1 y_1 & -i_1 z_1 \\
\vdots & \vdots & \vdots & \vdots & \vdots & \vdots & \vdots & \vdots & \vdots & \vdots & \vdots \\
x_N & y_N & z_N & 1 & 0 & 0 & 0 & 0 & -i_N x_N & -i_N y_N & -i_N z_N \\
0 & 0 & 0 & 0 & x_N & y_N & z_N & 1 & -j_N x_N & -j_N y_N & -j_N z_N
\end{bmatrix}
$$

$$
\times
\begin{bmatrix}
T_{11} \\
T_{12} \\
T_{13} \\
T_{14} \\
T_{21} \\
T_{22} \\
T_{23} \\
T_{24} \\
T_{31} \\
T_{32} \\
T_{33}
\end{bmatrix}
=
\begin{bmatrix}
i_1 \\
j_1 \\
i_2 \\
j_2 \\
\vdots \\
i_N \\
j_N
\end{bmatrix}.
\tag{9}
$$

or, equivalently, by the shorter form

$$ \mathbf{AU} = \mathbf{B}, $$

where **A** is the $2N \times 11$ matrix shown at the left above, **U** the vector of unknowns and **B** the vector of known pixel coordinates. If N is greater than 6, we have an overdetermined system of equations, and thus an optimal solution can be determined. A common optimization goal with such equations is to find a solution that minimizes the squared error. The squared error involved is defined as $E = [AU - B]^T[AU - B]$. Minimization of this error is equivalent to solving the *normal equations*, $A^TAU = A^TB$. The resulting solution is

$$ U = (A^TA)^{-1}A^TB. $$

This solution exists if A^TA is invertible, which is the case when A has linearly independent columns. Consequently, this stipulates that the world points (x_i, y_i, z_i) do not lie on a single plane.

Other techniques for solving for U, including using the QR decomposi-
tions of A and the pseudoinverse method with subsequent nonlinear
optimization, are discussed in Lopez-Abadia and Kak (25).

2.3.1. Calculation of Camera Parameters from T

Using the matrix T, the camera parameters can be calculated. The
relationships between the elements of T and the parameters can be shown
to be

$$T_{11} = \frac{(f/\delta u)h_x + i_o a_x}{-C \cdot \hat{a}}, \tag{10a}$$

$$T_{12} = \frac{(f/\delta u)h_y + i_o a_y}{-C \cdot \hat{a}}, \tag{10b}$$

$$T_{13} = \frac{(f/\delta u)h_z + i_o a_z}{-C \cdot \hat{a}}, \tag{10c}$$

$$T_{14} = -\frac{(f/\delta u)C \cdot \hat{h} + i_o C \cdot \hat{a}}{-C \cdot \hat{a}}, \tag{10d}$$

$$T_{21} = \frac{(f/\delta v)v_x + j_o a_x}{-C \cdot \hat{a}}, \tag{10e}$$

$$T_{22} = \frac{(f/\delta v)v_y + j_o a_y}{-C \cdot \hat{a}}, \tag{10f}$$

$$T_{23} = \frac{(f/\delta v)v_z + j_o a_z}{-C \cdot \hat{a}}, \tag{10g}$$

$$T_{24} = -\frac{(f/\delta u)C \cdot \hat{v} + j_o C \cdot \hat{a}}{-C \cdot \hat{a}}, \tag{10h}$$

$$T_{31} = \frac{a_x}{-C \cdot \hat{a}}, \tag{10i}$$

$$T_{32} = \frac{a_y}{-C \cdot \hat{a}}, \tag{10j}$$

$$T_{33} = \frac{a_z}{-C \cdot \hat{a}}, \tag{10k}$$

$$T_{34} = 1. \tag{10l}$$

These equations have all been scaled by T_{34} to account for the assumption
that $T_{34} = 1$ (Eq. 10l). A procedure to recover the parameters from Eqs.

(10a–l) was developed by Ganapathy (10). This method actually solves for C, $\hat{h}$, $\hat{v}$, $\hat{a}$, i_o, j_o, $f/\delta u$, and $f/\delta v$. If the sampling intervals (δu and δv) are known then f can be recovered. These sampling intervals are typically given by the camera's manufacturer. In the following derivations, T_i, denotes $[T_{i1} T_{i2} T_{i3}]$. Now, using Eqs. (10a–c) the following is obtained:

$$T_1 \cdot T_1 = \left(\frac{f/\delta u}{-C \cdot \hat{a}} \right)^2 + \left(\frac{i_o}{-C \cdot \hat{a}} \right)^2. \tag{11}$$

Using the fact that $\hat{h}$, $\hat{v}$ and $\hat{a}$ are mutually orthogonal we can similarly obtain

$$T_2 \cdot T_2 = \left(\frac{f/\delta v}{-C \cdot \hat{a}} \right)^2 + \left(\frac{j_o}{-C \cdot \hat{a}} \right)^2, \tag{12}$$

$$T_3 \cdot T_3 = \left(\frac{1}{-C \cdot \hat{a}} \right)^2, \tag{13}$$

$$T_1 \cdot T_3 = \left(\frac{i_o}{(-C \cdot \hat{a})^2} \right), \tag{14}$$

$$T_2 \cdot T_3 = \left(\frac{j_o}{(-C \cdot \hat{a})^2} \right). \tag{15}$$

From Eq. (13) we can compute $C \cdot \hat{a}$, and using this and Eqs. (14) and (15), we can compute i_o and j_o. In addition, using Eqs. (10i–k), the values for a_x, a_y, a_z, and $\hat{a}$ can be determined.

Now, Eqs. (11) and (12) are used to find the magnitudes of $f/\delta u$ and $f/\delta v$. We will now show how the signs of $-C \cdot \hat{a}$, $f/\delta u$ and $f/\delta v$ can be determined. We can set $-C \cdot \hat{a}$ and $f/\delta u$ to have positive signs, and then determine the appropriate sign of $f/\delta v$. Notice that the signs of $f/\delta u$ and $f/\delta v$ depend on the polarity of the axes of the camera coordinate frame; that is, the directions in which the row and column numbers of the pixels (i, j) increase. Given that we have assumed a positive sign for both $-C \cdot \hat{a}$ and $f/\delta u$, we will assume for a moment that $f/\delta v$ is positive. Given that we know $-C \cdot \hat{a}$, $f/\delta u$, i_o, j_o, a_x, a_y, a_z, and $\hat{a}$, we can determine h_x, h_y, and h_z from Eqs. (10a), (10b), and (10c), respectively. Similarly, v_x, v_y, and v_z can be determined from Eqs. (10e), (10f), and (10g), respectively. Also, $\hat{v}$ can be obtained by using the relationship $\hat{v} = \hat{a} \times \hat{h}$. If the two vectors $\hat{v}$ obtained by the different methods are the same then the choice of a positive sign for $f/\delta v$ was correct otherwise the sign must be reversed.

The components of the vector C can be recovered with the use of Eqs. (10d) and (10h). As mentioned above, the value of f can be calculated if δu or δv is known.

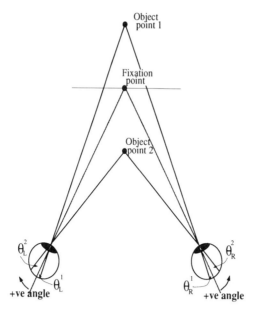

Figure 8.3. Object point 1 posses divergent disparity $d = -\theta_L^1 + -\theta_R^1$ since it lies behind the fixation point whereas object point 2 has convergent disparity, $d = \theta_L^2 + \theta_R^2$.

3. OVERVIEW OF THE STEREO VISION PROCESS

Binocular stereo vision or stereopsis is the process of matching features in one image with the corresponding features in the other image and then using these matches to derive the depth information in the scene being viewed. Figure 8.3 depicts the human stereo vision system. At any one moment a person's perception is centered on one point in space, called the *fixation point*. More specifically, the fixation point is the intersection of the two optical axes for the two eyes. Projection of a scene point into each eye's retina takes place as described in Section 2. As shown in Fig. 8.3, an object point will be projected into each eye's retina in a different position with respect to the directions of positive and negative movement from the center point. This leads to the definition of disparity, which is the difference between these positions. From the disparity the depth of the object point can be calculated by effectively inverting the projection process for each eye. When an object point is nearer than the fixation point, the disparity is called *convergent* or *crossed* and will be of a sign opposite to the disparity value produced by an object point behind the fixation point; the latter disparity is referred to as the *divergent* or *uncrossed disparity*. The term *crossed* refers to the fact that the optical axes of the two eyes or cameras will have to cross or converge further to fixate on the object point.

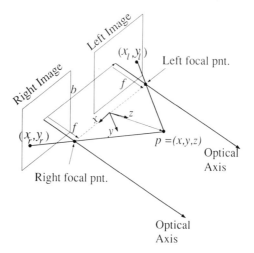

Figure 8.4. The canonical stereo camera configuration where the point p is projected to (x_l, y_l) in the left image plane and (x_r, y_r) in the right-image plane.

In Fig. 8.4, we show a point being projected into the image planes of a pair of stereo cameras. In this configuration, the optical axes are parallel and are also perpendicular to the line (baseline b) connecting the center of the image planes. In addition, the baseline is coincident with the horizontal (x axis) axis of each image plane, meaning that the two camera images are row registered; i.e., the nth row of the left image is collinear with the nth row of the right image. We will henceforth refer to this configuration as the canonical configuration. While other configurations can also be used, we will initially assume this one for convenience in our discussion of depth calculation. In any camera configuration, the disparity of a projected scene point is defined as the difference between the projected locations in the two image planes.

It is fairly trivial to compute depth from a disparity measurement given that a few parameters of the stereo camera setup are known. In our canonical camera configuration, shown in Fig. 8.4, notice that the origin of the world coordinate frame is located on the baseline half-way between the image centers. From the geometry of the projections, it follows trivially

$$\frac{x_l}{f} = \frac{x + b/2}{z}, \qquad \frac{x_r}{f} = \frac{x - b/2}{z}, \qquad \frac{y_l}{f} = \frac{y_r}{f} = \frac{y}{z}, \qquad (16)$$

where b is the length of the baseline connecting the two image centers and f is the focal length of each camera. These equations lead to the following expressions for the recovery of the coordinates of the scene point:

$$
x = \frac{b(x_l + x_r)/2}{(x_l - x_r)}, \qquad y = \frac{b(y_l + y_r)/2}{(x_l - x_r)}, \qquad z = \frac{bf}{(x_l - x_r)} \quad (17)
$$

where the disparity is equal to $(x_l - x_r)$. Because we are using the canonical camera configuration, a scene point will project into each image so that the only difference in location is along the x axis. It is interesting to note that depth (the z component) is inversely proportional to the disparity and is proportional to both b, the baseline length, and f, the focal length. In Section 5, we will discuss these relationships and how they affect the design of an appropriate stereo camera configuration.

The geometry of the camera configuration influences not only how the depth is calculated but also the efficiency of search for establishing correspondences between the image features from the two cameras. Many systems use what is called the *epipolar constraint*, which states that given an object point p and its projection in the left image p_l, then the corresponding right image point p_r must be located on the corresponding epipolar line. As shown in Fig. 8.5, the epipolar line is formed by the intersection of the epipolar plane with the right image plane. The epipolar plane is defined as the plane that passes through the points p_l, C_l, and C_r. C_l, and C_r are the focal points of the left and right images, respectively. This constraint is a direct result of the geometry of perspective projection.

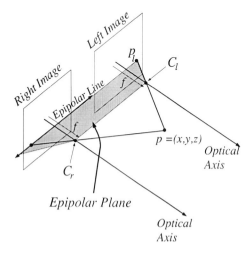

Figure 8.5. Illustration of epipolar plane and line. The corresponding right-image point can lie anywhere along the epipolar line.

It is interesting to note that the epipolar lines for a canonical camera configuration fall on horizontal scan lines of the images.

While a canonical camera configuration is nice for describing how depth values are calculated, its use may not be feasible for a particular set of system requirements. For example, the depth of field required in a scene at a certain depth z can result in the necessary use of a noncanonical camera configuration. An example of a noncanonical, or convergent, system is shown in Fig. 8.6. Generally, in a convergent system the cameras are set up so that the cameras are symmetrically oriented with respect to the y axis in Fig. 8.6. Here, for any scene point, the epipolar line will not fall on a horizontal scan line of the image. Therefore, the search space becomes complicated. In such cases, it is best to reproject the camera images, or the feature points extracted therefrom, into planes that would correspond to a canonical configuration, as illustrated in Fig. 8.7. This reprojection process, referred to as rectification in the literature, described below for each image, uses the position of the focal points of the cameras in 3D space (C), and the perspective transformation matrices T. Both the matrices and the focal point positions are results of the camera calibration procedure of Section 2. The goal is to reproject each image plane so that it is coplanar with the other one and also is parallel to the line that connects the two camera centers (focal points) in order to obtain epipolar lines that are parallel to the horizontal axis of each image. In addition, the focal points of the cameras should not move. The derivation of this method can be found in Ayache and Hansen (1). We will denote the transformation matrices of the two cameras as T_1 and T_2 and similarly the focal points as C_1 and C_2.

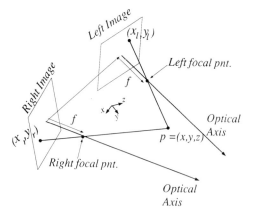

Figure 8.6. A stereo camera configuration with nonparallel optical axes.

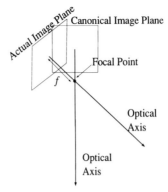

Figure 8.7. Illustration of the actual camera's rotation from a canonical camera.

For each point $p = (u, v)$ in image i, $p' = (u', v')$ is computed as follows:

$$\begin{bmatrix} a \\ b \\ w \end{bmatrix} - R_i \begin{bmatrix} u \\ v \\ 1 \end{bmatrix} \quad \text{and} \quad u' = \frac{a}{w}, \quad v' = \frac{b}{w},$$

where the following are 3×3 matrices

$$R_1 = \begin{bmatrix} [(C_1 \times C_2) \times C_1]^t \\ (C_1 \times C_2)^t \\ [(C_1 - C_2) \times (C_1 \times C_2)]^t \end{bmatrix} \cdot \begin{bmatrix} t_2 \times t_3 \\ t_3 \times t_1 \\ t_1 \times t_2 \end{bmatrix}^t ,$$

where t_i denotes the ith row of the matrix T_1

$$R_2 = \begin{bmatrix} [(C_1 \times C_2) \times C_2]^t \\ (C_1 \times C_2)^t \\ [(C_1 - C_2) \times (C_1 \times C_2)]^t \end{bmatrix} \cdot \begin{bmatrix} t_2 \times t_3 \\ t_3 \times t_1 \\ t_1 \times t_2 \end{bmatrix}^t ,$$

where t_i denotes the ith row of the matrix T_2

As a result of this procedure on each image, the newly created images have epipolar lines that lie on the horizontal scan lines of each image. In addition, the reprojected images are row registered, meaning that the nth row of one image corresponds to the nth row of the other image.

In the next section, we will discuss in detail various types of stereo vision algorithms.

4. PARADIGMS FOR STEREOPSIS

Historically, research in stereo vision can be described by two paradigms, which we will refer to as *low-level-feature-based stereo vision* and *high-level-feature-based stereo vision*. Initially, it was believed that recognition of high-level features such as straight-line edges in each of the two images must first be accomplished and then binocular matching of these features would take place. This belief is the foundation of what we call *high-level-feature-based stereo*. Then in 1960, Julez (18) performed a series of random-dot stereogram experiments that revolutionized the field and led to a new paradigm for modeling stereo vision, which we refer to as *low-level-feature-based stereo*. These psychophysical experiments indicated that humans in fact did not have to produce monocular cues before binocular fusion could take place. Subsequently, Marr and Poggio (26) advanced a computational theory, later implemented by Grimson (11, 12), that explained the observations made by Julez.

Various researchers and different psychophysical experiments have separately supported each of the paradigms, and as such each paradigm can be thought of as explaining different aspects of vision. The low-level-feature-based paradigm leads to a bottom–up procedure where the system starts with low-level features. On the other hand, the high-level paradigm results in a top down or expectation-driven process because high-level features are extracted and this implies the expectation that these high-level features exist in the two images of the scene. Most recently, investigators have been implementing hybrid systems that use both high- and low-level features (23, 44). This we believe is currently the most robust method of achieving good stereo vision performance. Following is a detailed discussion of each paradigm in which the issues of feature extraction and methods of establishing correspondences are emphasized.

4.1. Low-Level-Feature-Based Stereo Vision

"Low" and "high" are subjective descriptors in the English language, and thus there are no set criteria for a feature to be classified as a low- or high-level feature. Tradition dictates that image features that are semantically significant, such as long straight lines or curved lines possessing particular attributes, be called "high-level" and the other semantically nonsignificant, such as zero-crossings of the derivatives of the image gray levels, be called "low-level." In this section, we will deal with stereo vision using low-level features. We will start out with a discussion of what is certainly the most famous algorithm founded on the low-level paradigm, the Marr–Poggio–Grimson (MPG) algorithm.

4.1.1. The MPG Algorithm

4.1.1.1. Feature Extraction

The Marr–Poggio theory (26) proposes extracting point features by filtering the images with a set of 12 orientation-specific filters where each is represented by the difference of two Gaussian functions and then extracting zero-crossing points. Marr and Hildreth (27) showed that intensity changes occurring at a particular resolution may be detected by locating such zero-crossing points. In Grimson's implementation (11, 12) called the MPG algorithm, a single circularly symmetric Laplacian-of-a-Gaussian (LOG) filter is used. The use of a single filter is not only more computationally efficient, but, as discussed in Mayhew and Frisby (30), there is psychophysical evidence that humans may utilize a single circularly symmetric filter.

The LOG operator is often referred to as a primal sketch operator where a primal sketch can be defined as the representation of an image that makes explicit the information about gray-level variations. As will be illustrated below, the LOG is a smoothed second derivative of the image signal. The LOG operator assumes the following form:

$$\nabla^2 G(x, y) = \left(\frac{x^2 + y^2}{\sigma^2} - 2 \right) \exp\left(\frac{-(x^2 + y^2)}{2\sigma^2} \right), \tag{18}$$

where ∇^2 is the Laplacian $\nabla^2 = (\delta^2/\delta x^2) + (\delta^2/\delta y^2)$ and $G(x, y)$ is the Gaussian function, which acts to low-pass-filter the image:

$$G(x, y) = \sigma^2 \exp\left(\frac{-(x^2 + y^2)}{2\sigma^2} \right). \tag{19}$$

Figure 8.8(A) shows the Gaussian function and Fig. 8.8(B), the LOG function. The "width" of the LOG function is the diameter of the circle formed by the ring of zeros of the function; this width is related to σ as follows: $w_{2D} = \sqrt{2}\,\sigma$.

Before continuing, let's observe how a zero-crossing of the second derivative of a signal can indicate a point of gray-level variation. For ease of illustration suppose we have the 1D (one-dimensional) gray-level signal of Fig. 8.9(A). Shown in Figs. 8.9(B) and (C) are the results of taking the

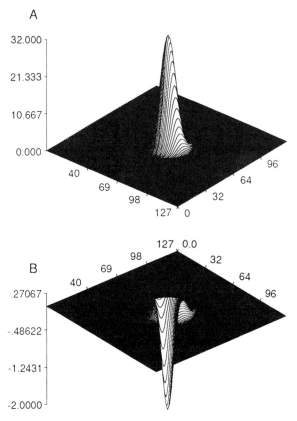

Figure 8.8. (A) 2D Gaussian function at $w_{2D} = 8$; (B) corresponding Laplacian-of-a-Gaussian function (viewed from below the x–y plane).

first and second derivatives. [Actually, the results shown in Figs. 8.9(B) and (C) are obtained by applying discrete approximation to the derivative operators to the discrete signal in Fig. 8.9(A)]. Observe that the zero-crossing of Fig. 8.9(C) is located at the center of the gray-level variation of Fig. 8.9(A). A left-to-right transition from a positive to a negative value at the zero-crossing is referred to as a *positive zero-crossing* and indicates that the corresponding gray-level variation is from low to high. Likewise a negative zero crossing, which is a negative-to-positive transition in values at the zero-crossing, indicates a gray-level variation from high to low.

The LOG function takes the second derivative after low-pass filtering with the Gaussian function, which is characterized by the width w_{2D}. Changing the width of the LOG function in effect captures gray-level variations at different scales or resolutions. Figure 8.10 shows a gray-scale

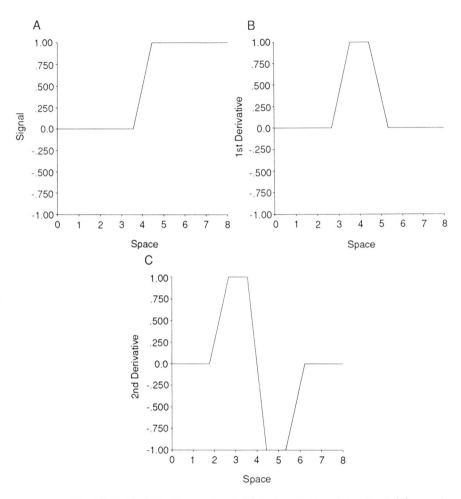

Figure 8.9. (A) Original 1D discrete signal; (B) first derivative of the signal; (C) second derivative of the signal.

image and the results of LOG filtering at different widths. As w_{2D} becomes smaller, finer gray-level variations are retained. The LOG operator is defined in the continuous domain and, theoretically speaking, it extends over the entire xy plane. The domain of the operator must evidently be truncated for computer implementation. It is usual to use only that piece of the LOG operator that is defined over the $2w_{2D} \times 2w_{2D}$ patch, centered at the origin, of the xy plane. This portion of the LOG function, appropriately sampled, will be referred to as the *LOG kernel*.

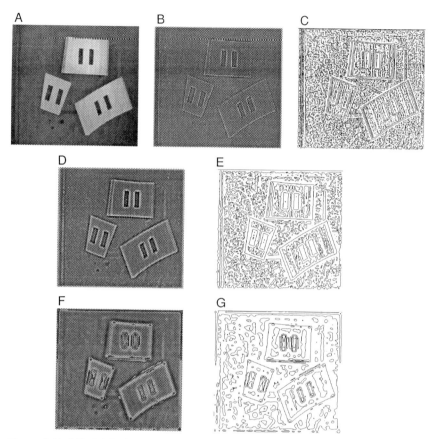

Figure 8.10. (A) Original gray-scale image; (B) image convolved with LOG filter at $w_{2D} = 4$; (C) extracted zero-crossings for $w_{2D} = 4$; (D) image convolved with LOG filter at $w_{2D} = 8$; (E) extracted zero-crossings for $w_{2D} = 8$; (F) images convolved with LOG filter at $w_{2D} = 16$; (G) extracted zero-crossings for $w_{2D} = 16$. Note that all zero-crossing images are displayed by gray-scale values that reflect the strength of the zero-crossing, i.e., indicate the difference in the gray values across the zero-crossing point.

After convolution with the LOG kernel, a simple algorithm such as the following one from Tanaka and Kak (44) may be used to extract the zero-crossings from the LOG filtered data.

```
1)  Label all of the positive pixels in the LOG filtered
    image with +1's
2)  Label all of the negative pixels in the LOG filtered
    image with 0's
3)  The zero-crossing contours are extracted by following
    the boundaries of the positive regions, where the
```

```
boundaries are defined as the 4-connectedness neighbor
of negative regions.
```

```
During the contour extraction process, label each zero-
crossing as either `p' or `n', depending upon whether or
not its immediate-left neighbor is lesser or greater than
its immediate-right neighbor. If one of the neighbors in
this left-right comparison is a boundary pixel than the
zero-crossing is classified as `o' which stands for
`other'. Notice that `p' denotes a positive zero-crossing
and `n' a negative zero-crossing.
```

If subpixel accuracy is desired, the exact location of a zero-crossing can be estimated by interpolating between the positive and negative values on either side of the zero-crossing found above. Subpixel calculation is feasible only in cases where the zero-crossings are fairly isolated.

As discussed by Grimson (13) there is support that the human visual system uses data from five different-sized LOG filters where each application of a LOG filter is commonly referred to as "passing the image through a channel of width w_{2D}." Figure 8.11 illustrates the flow of control in the MPG algorithm and shows the use of five channels with differing widths. The larger-width (coarser) channels capture the larger gray-level variations in the image, whereas the smaller width (finer) channels capture fine variations. The use of multiple channels will be explained in the next subsection on matching.

Besides the classification of a zero-crossing as either positive or negative, a zero-crossing point also has the additional attribute of orientation. It is theoretically known that the output of a LOG filtered image will have zero-crossing points that form continuous contours. Thus, the orientation of a zero-crossing can be defined as the orientation of the locally connected contour of zero-crossings passing through the point in question. Examination of the zero-crossings that are neighbors of the point in question can yield an estimate of the orientation using bit patterns as discussed in Tanaka and Kak (44). Also, the ratio of local Sobel operators applied to the original gray-scale image can be used to find the orientation as described in Kak (20).

4.1.1.2. Matching

Before discussing the multichannel matching algorithm of the MPG process, we will examine how matching is done for one channel independently. As discussed before, the right-image correspondent of a left-image zero-crossing point must lie on the epipolar line of the left image zero-crossing point in question. If we assume a canonical camera configuration, the epipolar line will lie on a horizontal scan line (row) of the right image. Now, assuming that we know an estimate of the average disparity, d_{av}, in

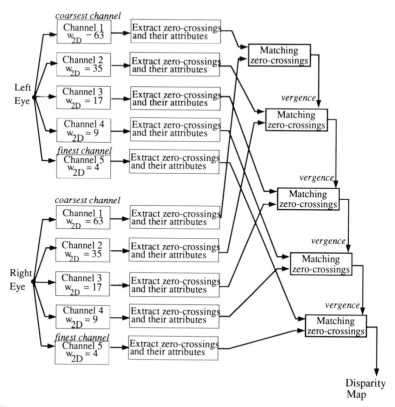

Figure 8.11. Block diagram of Marr–Poggio–Grimson algorithm. In each channel box the image is convolved with a Laplacian-of-a-Gaussian operator of width w_{2D}.

the image then the following steps are performed to find matches for a left-image zero-crossing point, $p = (x_l, y_l)$:

1) Search on the y_l scan line of the right image in a 1D window $\pm w_{2D}$ centered at the point $(x_l + d_{av}, y_l)$ for the possible candidate zero-crossing matches.

2) If a zero-crossing on the window is of the same sign type and is of approximately the same orientation as the left image zero-crossing in question then this zero-crossing produces a match.

See Fig. 8.12 for step 1 above.

It should be clear to the reader at this point that the choice of w_{2D} determines the range of disparities that can be calculated in the scene as

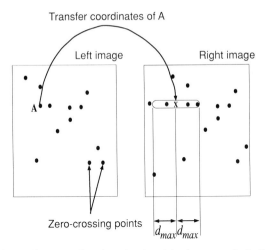

Figure 8.12. A search must take place in the right image to find all of the potential matching points for a left image point. The search space is shown in the figure to span the left-image point's position in the right image by $d_{\max}$ in both directions.

given by the following equation:

$$d_{\min} = d_{av} - w_{2D} \leq \text{disparity} \leq d_{av} + w_{2D} = d_{\max}. \qquad (20)$$

Given a camera configuration, if the maximum disparity range in the scene is known, then the w_{2D} that should be used can be calculated. If d_{av} is not known, then w_{2D} must be set to equal the maximum absolute disparity expected in the scene. Note that d_{av} could be an average over all of the image or, if available, a function of the location in the image. An important feature of using the $\pm w_{2D}$ search window is that the number of possible candidates is considerably reduced from the case of searching the entire scan line. The reader should not be misled into thinking that this choice of window size is arbitrary. Marr and Poggio (26) have shown that there is a 95% probability that there will be only one right-image zero-crossing in a window of size $\pm w_{2D}/2$. However, the choice of $\pm w_{2D}/2$ is too restrictive for practical use since, especially for large window sizes, adjacent gray-level variations can cause a shift in the location of a zero-crossing. Figures 8.13(A) and (B) show a pair of stereo images taken from Tanaka and Kak (44), and Fig. 8.14 shows the graphs that illustrate the shifts in the locations of zero-crossings along the *PQ* scan line for each image in the stereo pair as a function of applying LOG operators with different widths. Observe that there is more variation in the position of the left-image zero-crossing, which is due to the presence of a shadow illumi-

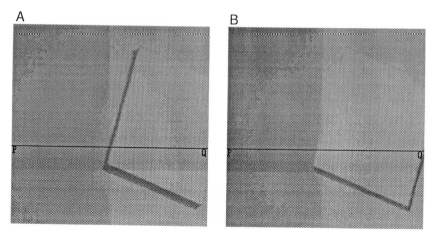

Figure 8.13. Stereo pair of images of a block on a flat background. A PQ scan line is shown across each image: (A) left image; (B) right image.

nation pattern in the left image that does not exist in the right image. This difference in illumination patterns between the images is due to the fact that each camera is at a different viewing position. The size of the search window is usually increased to $\pm w_{2D}$ in order to cope with the difficulties caused by the shifts in the locations of zero-crossings. The disadvantage of expanding the search window is that the probability of finding only a single zero-crossing in this window decreases to 50%, and thus the number of left-image zero-crossings with more than one possible match in the right-image increases.

When the scene objects are opaque, there can be only one right image correspondent for each left-image zero-crossing. The MPG algorithm assumes this uniqueness constraint. If the reader is interested in techniques that work with transparent objects she is referred to Prazdny (38).

The processing of multiple channels in a coarse to fine sequence using what is called *vergence control* allows for a more accurate determination of the disparity values in the scene. In such multichannel systems, more low-pass filtering is performed in the coarser channels than in the finer channels. As a result, small variations in intensity disappear in the coarser channels so that very accurate disparity calculations are not possible. In addition, a coarse channel will produce a sparse disparity map. In a finer channel, the positions of the zero-crossings will be more accurate since not as much smearing of the intensity variations occurs, and thus a more accurate disparity calculation can be achieved. However, a correct value of d_{av} for the point in question in Eq. (20) is more critical for finer channels because the search window is much smaller than the one used by a coarser channel. This leads to the concept of vergence control, which is an

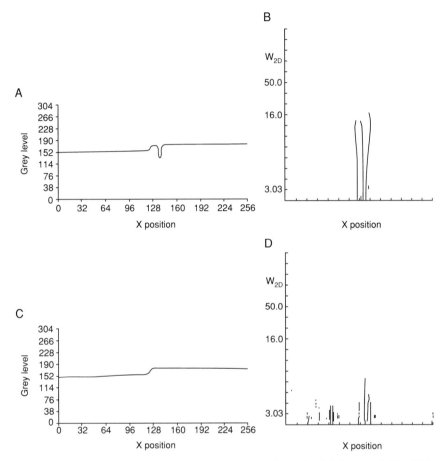

Figure 8.14. (A) Gray-level variations across line *PQ* in the left image of Fig. 8.13; (B) locations of left-image zero-crossings along *PQ* for different w_{2D}; (C) gray-level variations across line *PQ* in the right image of Fig. 8.13; (D) locations of right-image zero-crossings along *PQ* for different w_{2D}.

implementation of the idea that the disparities calculated from the coarser channels can be used to locally bring regions of the right image into range for appropriate matching to take place with the left image at the next finer channel. More specifically, the disparities from the coarser channels will be used to calculate the average disparity in a neighborhood of the left-image point in question, and then this is used to shift the search window [via d_{av} value of Eq. (20)] to the appropriate position in the right image for matching to occur.

In Grimson's implementation, for the $w_{2D} = 9$ channel a neighborhood of size 25×25 is examined, and if less than 70% of the points in this region have matches, the region is considered to be out of the range for fusion in this channel. For each region that does not pass this test, a vergence shift must take place to bring the right-image region into the range of fusion for this channel. In another implementation, vergence is used everywhere the coarse channel produces disparity values without first applying a threshold to the number of matches. The disparity calculated for each matched pair of zero-crossings is stored in a buffer commonly called a *disparity map*, or the $2\frac{1}{2}$D sketch. If there exists more than one match at a zero-crossing point, the average of the corresponding dispari- ties is stored. Notice that there is no theoretically correct size for the region that must be examined to determine whether its points are within the range of fusion for the current channel. However, this size should be a function of the density of the zero-crossings in the images, which is dependent on the scene being viewed. For example, in Kak (20) a neighborhood of 10×10 and a threshold of 50% yielded superior results. It is worth noting that vergence control is akin to humans observing a scene in an unfocused manner, forming a crude idea of the locations of the objects in the scene, and then fixating on each object of interest.

Instead of averaging the disparities when multiple matches occur for a particular left-image zero-crossing, a unique match may still be established by what Marr and Poggio (26) have termed as the "pulling effect." The pulling effect consists of enforcing some form of a continuity constraint over the disparities in a region surrounding the left-image zero-crossing in question. The validity of desiring that the disparities be continuous in value in a local region comes from the assumption that the scene consists of object points that vary continuously. There is no theoretically correct choice for the size of the neighborhood to be used for the disambiguation of multiple matches. However, in Kak (20) a 10×10 neighborhood for 256×256 images was used successfully. After disambiguation has taken place, the disparity map is updated.

We will now discuss some important ancillary issues that would be relevant to a modern-day implementation of the MPG algorithm. The first one of these deals with the concept of vertical disparity. Psychophysical experiments have demonstrated that when a pair of stereo images is not row-registered, human subjects are still able to make the correct matches when there is only a small amount of vertical difference (disparity) be- tween the corresponding points. A similar capability may be given to a computer implementation, which has the additional desired effect of correcting for small vertical displacements of the images that can result from less than perfect row registration. This can be accomplished by using two-dimensional search windows spanning a few rows above and below the apparent epipolar line.

Another issue is that of figural continuity that can be used to further constrain the matching between the zero-crossings. Figural continuity is

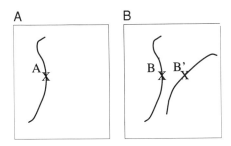

Figure 8.15. The match pair (A, B) will pass the figural continuity constraint but the match pair (A, B') will fail the figural continuity constraint: (A) left image; (B) right image.

derived from the notion that surfaces vary smoothly in a scene and thus disparity values should be continuous (30). Its computer implementation is based on the realization that the contours on a scene surface will project into each image as continuous contours with approximately the same shape. Although the exact nature of the implementation varies from system to system, the common denominator consists of comparing the shapes, say, by comparing chain codes, of the zero-crossing contours. The idea is illustrated in Fig. 8.15. In order for the zero-crossing A in the left image to be considered matchable to the zero-crossing B in the right image, the figural continuity constraint demands that the shape of the zero-crossing contour passing through A be similar to the shape of the zero-crossing contour passing through B. A local shape comparison would reject a match between the point A and the point B' also shown in Fig. 8.15. Mayhew and Frisby (30) have advanced psychophysical evidence to support the conjecture that the stereopsis in the human visual system also uses a figural continuity constraint.

It is interesting to note that the region-based disparity continuity constraint and the figural continuity constraint play a complementary role in the fusion process. For those regions of object surfaces that are away from the boundaries, it makes intuitive sense to use a region-based disparity constraint for disambiguation. However, such a constraint will serve no purpose in the vicinity of depth discontinuities. Since figural continuity constraint is applied only along contours, it is less sensitive to the problems caused by depth discontinuities. The reader's attention is also drawn to a recent contribution by Fleck (9) who has taken scene topology into account and presented a generalization of the figural continuity constraint.

In addition to the region-based disparity and figural continuity constraints, it is also possible to apply what has been called a *disparity gradient constraint* (37). Pollard *et al.* have shown that there is an upper bound to the maximum difference in the disparities of two potential matches as a function of their separation in the image space. Therefore, potential matches that violate this upper bound can be discarded. The reader is referred to Baunegg (5) for a recent implementation of the MPG algorithm that includes an implementation of the disparity gradient constraint.

4.1.2. Low-Level Features besides Zero-Crossings

At this point, the reader is probably wondering whether low-level features besides the zero-crossings of the LOG output can be used for stereopsis. Mayhew and Frisby (30) claim that, in addition to the zero-crossings, points located at the peaks of the LOG-filtered images are also necessary low-level features. They show psychophysical evidence that humans use these peaks in binocular fusion to perceive the depth in some scenes. If only LOG zero-crossings are used in such scenes, incorrect depth perception results. Shown in Fig. 8.16(A) are the images of a stereo pair. The brightness function along one row of the images is shown in Fig. 8.16(B). The output of the LOG operator for a single channel MPG implementation is shown in Fig. 8.16(C) for each image. Figure 8.16(D) shows the brightness values along one row in each of the images in part (C). Figures 8.16(E) and (F) show the zero crossings and the peaks detected along a single row of the images in (C). When a human subject is shown the stereo pair of Fig. 8.16(A), the perceived depth profile is approximately as shown in Fig. 8.17(A). The depth profile constructed from just the LOG zero-crossings is presented in Fig. 8.17(B), while the profile constructed by using just the peaks of the LOG output are shown in Fig. 8.17(C). Finally, Fig. 8.17(D) shows the depth profile constructed by using both the LOG zero-crossings and peaks. The similarity of this computed depth profile to the perceived depth profile of Fig. 8.17(A) lends credence to the claim of Mayhew and Frisby.

Besides the LOG operator, it is also possible to use other operators to extract points of high gray-level variance. For example, the Movarec interest operator has been used and also the Sobel, Roberts, and Prewitt, along with other first-derivative operators, have been used for edge point detection [see Rosenfeld and Kak (40) for a general discussion of edge detection]. Marr and Poggio (28) and Medioni and Nevatia (31) suggest the use of oriented masks to extract edge points. However, it is the opinion of the authors that the extraction of zero-crossings from a LOG-filtered image is in general a good choice because the circular symmetry of the LOG filter is supported by psychophysical evidence (30) and because convolution with a single LOG filter is computationally more efficient than using multiple-oriented filters.

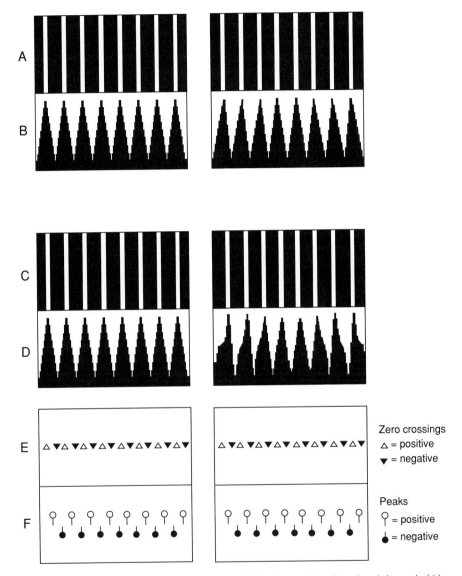

Figure 8.16. (A) Left and right stereo images; (B) brightness function of each image in (A) along a single row; (C) resulting images after convolution of filter with images in (A); (D) brightness function of each image in (C) along a single row; (E) extracted zero-crossings from each image in (C) along a single row; (F) extracted peaks from each image in (C) along a single row. From Mayhew and Frisby (30), with permission from the authors and Elsevier Science Publishers BV.

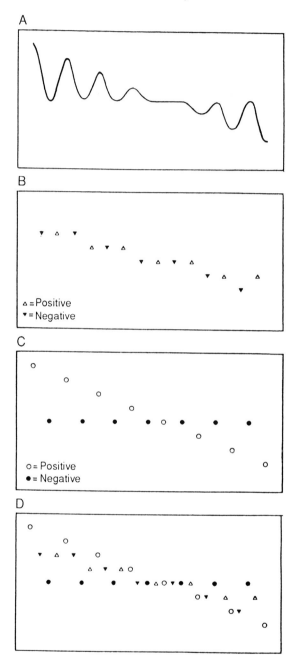

268 Lynne L. Grewe and Avinash C. Kak

Figure 8.17. Depth profiles: (A) perceived depth profile (along a single row); (B) depth profile constructed from zero-crossings alone; (C) depth profile constructed from peaks alone; (D) depth profile constructed from zero-crossings and peaks. From Mayhew and Frisby (30), with permission from the authors and Elsevier Science Publishers BV.

4.1.3. Other Matching Techniques for Low-Level Features

Other methods have been advanced for solving the correspondence problem in stereo vision. In what follows, we will briefly review some of the more prominent of the alternatives to the MPG algorithm.

4.1.3.1. Relaxation-Based Matching

Probablistic relaxation is a process whereby the probability of a candidate match is iteratively updated depending on the probabilities of other neighboring matches. Thus, the disambiguation process in not performed in one step but in an iterative fashion. As discussed in Marr and Poggio (29) and Julesz and Chang (19), there is psychophysical evidence that a cooperative process between local matches occurs, which is used to arrive at a globally consistent set of matches. In addition, it has been shown that the closer the disparity values are of two matches in a neighborhood, the stronger will be their cooperation. The evidence of such cooperative processes validates the use of relaxation techniques for the disambiguation of multiple matches.

Most relaxation schemes for disambiguation will iterate a fixed number of times or until the desired matching results are obtained. An example of a desired result is that for each set of multiple matches, there exists one match that has a probability measure greater than the other probability measures by some fixed threshold. One of the nice features of a relaxation based method is that the update procedure is a function only of the probability values in a discrete neighborhood and thus can be implemented in a parallel fashion. In this way, the computation involved in each iteration can be greatly reduced.

The use of probabilistic relaxation in stereo was first advanced by Barnard and Thompson (4). They use a region-based disparity continuity constraint in updating the probabilities of the matches. For such schemes, the situation where a region encompasses a physical discontinuity will cause the same difficulty as it did for the original MPG algorithm. In a more recent contribution, Kim and Aggarwal (21) have proposed a modification of the Barnard and Thompson algorithm in which both the initial probabilities of the matches and the update procedures use the disparity information along the local zero-crossings contour. We will next discuss this algorithm.

Kim and Aggarwal's stereo vision algorithm (21) begins with the detection of the zero-crossings of the LOG-filtered stereo images. Next, initial matches are set up in the same manner as in the MPG algorithm for a single channel, and each candidate match is assigned a weight value. Suppose we are considering the ith zero-crossing in the left image, which has n candidate matches in the right image. Let $w_i(d_j)$ denote the weight assigned to the match of the ith left-image zero-crossing (x_i, y_i) and its

jth candidate (x_j, y_j) in the right image where d_j is the corresponding disparity. This weight is a function of how similar the left and right zero-crossings are in terms of the local orientations of their zero-crossing contours (w^1) and an intensity gradient measure (w^2) as follows:

$$w_i(d_j) = a * w^1(d_j) + b * w^2(d_j), \tag{21}$$

where a and b are constants and

$$w^1(d_j) = \frac{1}{1 + |DP_{ij}|},$$

$$w^2(d_j) = \frac{1}{1 + |G_l(x_i, y_i) - G_r(x_j, y_j)|},$$

$$G_l(x_i, y_i) = \frac{\text{intensity}(x_i + 1, y_i) - \text{intensity}(x_i - 1, y_i)}{2},$$

$$G_r(x_j, y_j) = \frac{\text{intensity}(x_j + 1, y_j) - \text{intensity}(x_j - 1, y_j)}{2}.$$

where DP_{ij} is a measure of the difference in orientation of the zero-crossing contours that fall in the 3×3 neighborhoods of the zero-crossings of the left image (x_i, y_i) and the right image (x_j, y_j), respectively. This can be easily measured by looking at the zero-crossing patterns in each 3×3 neighborhood. Figure 8.18 shows some examples of possible zero-crossing patterns that can occur. Assume that $D_1(x, y)$ and $D_2(x, y)$ represent the position of the first and second zero-crossings found in a counterclockwise traversal starting in the east direction of a 3×3 neighborhood centered at the zero-crossing (x, y) where the position assignments are shown in Fig. 8.18(I). For example, in Fig. 8.18(A) D_1 is 3 and D_2 is 7. The difference in local orientations is measured as follows:

$$DP_{ij} = DIFF_1 + DIFF_2,$$

where

$$DIFF_1 = |D_1(x_i, y_i) - D_1(x_j, y_j)|$$

$$DIFF_2 = |D_2(x_i, y_i) - D_2(x_j, y_j)|$$

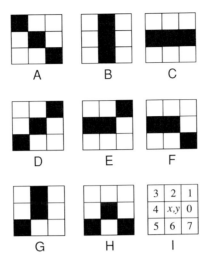

Figure 8.18. Parts (A)-(H) are examples of 3×3 zero-crossing patterns than can occur. Part (I) illustrates the position assignment given to the neighboring zero-crossing points.

and

$$\text{If } (DIFF_k > 4) \text{ then } DP_{ij} = |8 - DIFF_k|.$$

So far, we have assumed that each neighborhood will have two zero-crossings in it but, if that is not the case then the value of $DIFF$ will be set to 20, which is a number large enough to ensure that the resulting weight w^1 will be small, thus indicating that the matched zero-crossings do not have similar surrounding zero-crossing patterns (i.e., orientations).

Next, initial probability values are assigned to each candidate match as a function of the weight values that we calculated above as follows:

$$P_i^0(d_j) = \frac{w_i(d_j)}{w_i(no\ match) + \sum_{k=1}^n w_i(d_k)}, \qquad d_j = no\ match, d_1, \ldots, d_n,$$

(23)

where $w_i(no\ match)$ is equal to $1 - \max[w_i(d_j)]$. Thus, the initial probability of the jth candidate match of the ith zero-crossing in the left image is the weight of this match normalized by the sum of the weights of all the other candidate matches where there are n such candidates.

The iterative step of the relaxation-based matching procedure updates the probability of each match with supporting matches that pass a regional

disparity continuity constraint and a disparity gradient constraint. The
following equations describe the update procedure at the $(k + 1)$th iteration:

$$P_i^{k+1}(d_j) = \frac{\tilde{P}_i^{k+1}(d_j)}{\tilde{P}_i^{k+1}(no\ match) + \sum_{r=1}^{n} \tilde{P}_i^{k+1}(d_r)},$$

$$d_j = no\ match, d_1, \ldots, d_n, \tag{24}$$

where

$$\tilde{P}_i^{k+1}(d_j) = P_i^k(d_j) + c\,F\big(P_i^k(d_j)\big)P_S^k - d\,P_i^k(d_j)I(P_{FS})$$
$$\tilde{P}_i^{k+1}(no\ match) = P_i^k(no\ match) \tag{25}$$

and

$$P_F^k = \max\big[P_f^k(d_j - 1), P_f^k(d_j), P_f^k(d_j + 1)\big]$$

$$P_S^k = \max\big[P_s^k(d_j - 1), P_s^k(d_j), P_s^k(d_j + 1)\big]$$

$$F\big[P_i^k(d_j)\big] = \begin{cases} \big[P_i^k(d_j)\big]^2 & \text{if} \quad 0.0 < P_i^k(d_j) \leq 0.5 \\ \big[P_i^k(d_j)\big]\big(1 - P_i^k(d_j)\big) & \text{if} \quad 0.5 < P_i^k(d_j) < 1.0 \end{cases}$$

$$I(P_{FS}) = \begin{cases} 0 & \text{if} \quad P_F^k + P_S^k \neq 0 \\ 1 & \text{if} \quad P_F^k + P_S^k = 0 \end{cases}$$

Note that the subscripts f and s indicate the two zero-crossings found in
the 3×3 neighborhood of the left image zero-crossing in question where
f denotes the first zero-crossing found in the counterclockwise scan of the
neighborhood and s denotes the second zero-crossing found. Therefore,
$P_s^k(d_j)$ is the probability at the kth iteration that the second zero-crossing
in the neighborhood has a match of disparity d_j. If there does not exist a
first or second zero-crossing, then probabilities involving them are set to
zero. The third term in Eq. (25) implements a disparity gradient constraint. The value $I(P_{FS})$ is set to 1, which activates a decrease in support,
if both of the two neighboring zero-crossing produce a disparity gradient
with respect to the zero-crossing match in question that is larger than 1.
Because the two neighboring zero-crossings must lie on the same local
contour, this is much like the limit of one in the disparity gradient limit
constraint presented in Pollard et al. (37). The second term of Eq. (25)
increases the support of a match if a neighboring zero-crossing has a

nonzero probability for disparities similar in value to the disparity of the match in question. This is what the authors refer to as a "regional" disparity constraint even though only a single neighboring zero-crossing point is considered.

4.1.3.2. Dynamic-Programming-Based Matching

Dynamic programming is a problem solving technique that is commonly applied to problems for which a recursive algorithm would tend to solve many of the same subproblems over and over again. The basic idea is that small subproblems are solved and their results are stored. Then larger subproblems and eventually the problem itself are solved by looking up the results of the smaller subproblems. Edge-point matching can be solved using dynamic programming when the problem is viewed as finding an optimal path through the set of all nodes where a node represents a possible match of a left-image edge point and a right-image edge point. Below we discuss an algorithm that is typical of the stereo algorithms that utilize dynamic programming.

Ohta and Kanade (35) present an algorithm that uses dynamic programming in a two-stage fashion for solving the stereo correspondence problem. The first stage finds the optimal set of matches along each epipolar scan line pair. Each such intra–scan line search is interpreted as the problem of finding a matching path on a two-dimensional (2D) search plane whose axes are the left and right scan lines being searched. Figure 8.19 illustrates the search space where a vertical line represents an edge-point position on the left-image scan line and a horizontal line represents the edge-point position on the right-image scan line. For convenience the 0th vertical and horizontal lines denote the leftmost pixel of each scan line; the Nth vertical line of the search space represents the right most pixel of the left image scan line and the Mth horizontal line represents the right most pixel of the right image scan line. An intersection point of a vertical and a horizontal line is referred to as a *node* and can be thought of as representing a potential match between the two corresponding edge points. Now, the goal is to find an optimal path between the nodes $(0, 0)$ and (N, M) in Fig. 8.19, where every node on this path represents an accepted match between two edge points.

Finding the optimal path from any node (p_l, p_r) to the starting node $(0, 0)$ is considered to be a subproblem in their dynamic-programming-based algorithm. However, to use dynamic programming there must exist an ordering from smaller to larger subproblems: for the intra–scan line search problem this is accomplished by the following constraint: When considering the match of two edge points (p_l, p_r), the edge points that are to the left of p_l on the left-image scan line and the edge points to the left of p_r on the right-image scan line should have already been processed. This constraint is referred to as the *left-to-right ordering of matches*. This constraint is valid if the objects and their edge points in the scene retain a left-to-right ordering in the two stereo images and this will be true for most scenes.

When we say that we want the optimal path, we mean that the cost of this path is smaller than all of the other possible paths where the cost of a path is defined to be the sum of the costs of its primitive paths. A primitive path is defined as a link directly connecting two nodes. A link such as link c in Fig. 19 represents a continuous interval of pixels along each scan line. A measure of the cost of such a link is defined as how much the two intervals (one on the left-image scan line and one of the right-image scan line) are similar in terms of their gray-level values. Because the intervals may be of different lengths, the cost is defined in terms of the average gray-level variance of each interval with respect to the average of their mean gray-level values as follows:

Suppose $a_1, \ldots, a_k \in$ left-image interval and

$$b_1, \ldots, b_t \in \text{right-image interval},$$

$$m = \frac{1}{2} \left(\frac{1}{k} \sum_{i=1}^{k} a_i + \frac{1}{t} \sum_{j=1}^{t} b_i \right) = \text{average of means},$$

$$\sigma^2 = \frac{1}{2} \left(\frac{1}{k} \sum_{i=1}^{k} a_i - m^2 + \frac{1}{t} \sum_{j=1}^{t} b_i - m^2 \right) = \text{average of variances } wrt\, m,$$

$$\text{Cost of link} = \sigma^2 \sqrt{k^2 + t^2}. \tag{26}$$

This cost measure will be smaller for smaller values of the variance σ^2 that will occur for intervals of similar gray-scale content.

A cost measure of the optimal path from node (N, M) to node $(0, 0)$ is determined iteratively by adding the cost of each added primitive path to the already known optimal partial path. To clarify the ordering of nodes and how this iterative processing occurs, we define the distance of a node (i, j) as being equal to $i + j$. At the first iteration, the optimal path to the node $(0, 0)$ from each node that is at a distance of 1 is determined and these paths will be primitive by definition. At the second iteration the optimal path to the node $(0, 0)$ from each node at a distance of 2 is determined using the partial optimal paths calculated at the previous iteration. This iterative process continues until the (N, M) node is reached. The italicized number next to each node in Fig. 8.19 is the distance from the node to the node $(0, 0)$.

Although an optimal path of matches for each scan line pair can be found using the above dynamic programming procedure, the formation of

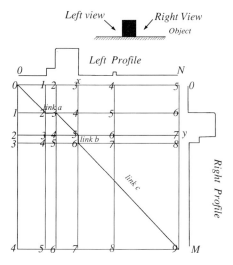

Figure 8.19. This illustrates the 2D search plane used in intra–scan line search. Along the top is a gray-scale profile of a row in the left stereo image, and along the right side is the gray-scale profile of the corresponding row in the right image. The vertical lines indicate positions of edge points in the left profile, and similarly, the horizontal lines indicate the positions of edge points in the right profile. Intersections of these lines denote possible edge point matches. Italicized numbers at intersection points denote their visitation order in the intra–scan line search procedure.

these matches does not take into account the figural constraints that must consider edge points across scan lines. To get around this shortcoming, Ohta and Kanade propose a dynamic programming approach that integrates intra–scan line search with inter–scan line constraints. Inter–scan line search is interpreted as searching in a 3D space that is constructed from stacking the 2D intra–scan line search spaces in order of the scan line numbers. The goal now is to find an optimal surface of matches (nodes) that minimizes the intra–scan line costs and at the same time satisfies inter–scan line consistency. A similar left-to-right ordering of edge contours of the two images is assumed and the reader is referred to Ohta and Kanade (35) for details.

The assumption of left-to-right ordering of edge points or contours in an image is not valid for scenes where neighboring long thin vertical objects exist at varying depths. In this case, the projections of these objects may actually reverse position in a left–right sense between the two camera images. For example, hold up your two index fingers in front of you at very different depths but very close in terms of a projected distance along a horizontal line (see Fig. 8.20). Now, alternate looking through your left eye and your right eye and you will observe that the fingers project in a

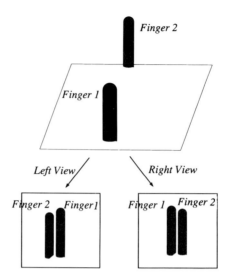

Figure 8.20. Scene where the reversal of the left-to-right ordering of the objects occurs between the two stereo images.

different left–right order for each eye. This is one limitation of the dynamic programming approach that the previous two matching paradigms do not suffer from.

The advantage of using a dynamic programming approach is that an optimal set of matches are obtained. The disadvantages are the large execution time typically needed for dynamic programming algorithms and the large amount of storage needed for the results of subproblems. In Ohta and Kanade (36), an attempt is made to reduce the processing time algorithm by implementing portions of the algorithm in hardware. A reader interested in another stereo vision system that uses dynamic programming is referred to Lloyd (24).

4.2. High-Level-Feature-Based Stereo Vision

As the reader should have surmised by now, one of the difficulties with the use of low-level features for stereo, such as the zero-crossings produced by an LOG operator, is the problem of disambiguation, meaning the difficulty associated with deciding which candidate match to accept if there is more than one contender. This difficulty with disambiguation is ameliorated when higher-level features are used. In the rest of this section, we will review four contributions, by Medioni and Nevatia (31),

Tanaka and Kak (44), Boyer and Kak (6), and Horaud and Skordas (16), for matching straight line segments in two images. Another contribution we will discuss after these is by Nasrabadi and Liu (34) on the matching of curved segments. There is an interesting tradeoff between the use of relational constraints in the matching process and the computational efficiency of the algorithms presented in Tanaka and Kak (44) and Medioni and Nevatia (31), on one hand, and those presented in Boyer and Kak (6), Horaud and Skordas (16), and Nasrabadi and Liu (34) on the other. In comparison to Tanaka and Kak (44) and Medioni and Nevatia (31), the algorithms of Boyer and Kak (6), Horaud and Skordas (16), and Nasrabadi and Liu (34) have a stronger relational flavor, but at the expense of decreased computational efficiency. Algorithms that utilize relationships between features come under the rubrik of *structural stereopsis*, and those that do not, we will simply refer to as *edge-based stereopsis*.

4.2.1. Edge-Based Stereopsis

Medioni and Nevatia (31) propose an iterative method for solving the correspondence problem using straight line segments as features. These features are composed of zero-crossing points and each feature is described by its endpoints, orientation, and the average gray-level variation across the line. Initially, all right-image lines that fall in the search space for a given left image line and have similar attribute values with respect to the attribute values of the left-image line are considered to be candidates for matching (and vice versa). The search space is bounded in one direction by the epipolar lines of the left-image line's endpoints and in the perpendicular direction by a span w, which is a function of the maximum expected disparity in the scene. Every match, (l_i, r_j), where l_i is a left-image line and r_j is a right-image line, is assigned a value, $v(l_i, r_j)$, that measures how well the disparity of the other line matches in neighborhoods of both l_i and r_j agree with the average disparity d_{ij}, computed along the matched lines (l_i, r_j). This evaluation function implements a region-based disparity continuity constraint and is set up so that a small value indicates a better match. The following algorithm describes the iterative scheme presented in Medioni and Nevatia (31) that removes matches from the initial match set using the measure v.

```
M={set of initially constructed matches}
∀l_i Q(l_i)=initially constructed matches for l_i
∀r_i Q(r_i)=initially constructed matches for r_i
t=0
```

Until (Termination_Condition)

```
{

    Calculate vᵗ(1ᵢ, rⱼ) for all (1ᵢ, rⱼ) ∈ M using only sur-
    rounding matching segments in Q.
```

$\forall\ 1_i$ { Eliminate any $r_j \in Q(1_i)$ that does not form a "preferred" match }

$\forall\ r_i$ { Eliminate any $1_j \in Q(r_i)$ that does not form a "preferred" match }

```
    t++


}
```

where a match $(1_i, r_j)$ is "preferred" if

$\forall\ r_k$ where $(1_i, r_k) \in M$ and r_k and r_j overlap then
$v^t(1_i, r_j) < v^t(1_i, r_k)$

AND

$\forall\ 1_h$ where $(1_h, r_j) \in M$ and 1_h and 1_i overlap then
$v^t(1_i, r_j) < v^t(1_h, r_j)$

A simple termination condition requiring the number of iterations t to be equal to three is used and the matches with the smallest v values are accepted. An advantage of this method is that more than one preferred match is allowed for a particular line segment. For example, line segment l_i of the left image is allowed the following two matches (l_i, r_j) and (l_i, r_s) if r_j and r_s do not overlap. This capability handles the situation where a line segment in one image corresponds to more than one line segment in the other image. A drawback of this system is that the number of iterations needed to totally disambiguate the match set is unknown and stopping at a prechosen number will not guarantee that the results yield the best match set. Another problem that can arise is a result of the assumption that a region-based disparity constraint is desirable for line features. Depending on the size of the neighborhood and the type of objects in the scene this assumption can lead to incorrect results. For example, consider the situation where neighboring lines are produced from the physical edges of two nearby objects that are at very different depths. These lines should produce very different disparities, and they will incorrectly inhibit each other as valid matches using a regional disparity constraint. It is our opinion that the use of relational constraints such as collinearity and adjacency are more appropriate than region-based disparity constraints for use in segment feature matching systems.

Tanaka and Kak (44) present a hierarchical stereo algorithm in which one step of this hierarchy involves straight line feature matching. Like the previous algorithm, this algorithm also allows an edge in one image to correspond to multiple edges in the second image. Since the algorithm does not take into account any relational constraints during the matching of the line segments, it is computationally efficient. (Note that, unlike the Nevatia–Medioni algorithm, not taking into account relational constraints while matching straight line segments does not degrade the performance of stereo fusion since the edge matching takes place in a larger hierarchical framework.) An outline of the algorithm follows (it is assumed that the canonical camera configuration is used and the images are row-registered):

Feature Extraction

1) For each image extract straight line segments using modified Freeman criteria so that each segment is S pixels long. Represent a line longer than S pixels by overlapping segments such that their starting pixels are spaced s pixels apart. Segments that are nearly parallel to epipolar lines are removed from the image.

Generate Initial Candidate Matches
2) Consider every right image line segment, R, to be a candidate match for a left image line segment, L, if:

   $Start\_row(R) = Start\_row(L) \pm t$
   $Start\_col(R) = Start\_col(L) \pm d_{max}$

The value of t is 1. (t accounts for the possible misregistration of the epipolar lines and perspective effects that can result from the fact that the two cameras may not have truly parallel axes.) The value of d_{max} is the maximum expected disparity.

Disambiguation of Multiple Candidates
3) Evaluate each candidate match (L, R) by comparing the similarity of their orientations using chain code descriptions of the line segments. Let $L(i)$ and $R(i)$ be the i-th element of the chain codes along L and R. L is similar to R if

   $\forall i$
   $if(L(i) == R(i)) \{similarity{+}{+}\}$
   $if(L(i) == R(i-1) OR (L(i) == R(i+1)))$
        $\{similarity = similarity + w\}$

The second test is needed in the case where the chain codes of diagonal lines are being compared.

Consider the two following chain codes:
1 2 1 2 1 2 1 2 1 2... and 2 1 2 1 2 1 2 1 2 1... which represent
lines at approximately 45°. These two segments would
be considered to have similar orientations by a human observer. The second test ensures that the algorithm will also judge them as similar.

4) If *similarity* is larger than a threshold then accept
the match (L, R) and delete L from left image. If no
match for L, delete L from left image.

5) Go to step 2 until no more edges exist in the left
image.

Disparity Calculation
6) For every match (L, R) found, compute the disparity
values along the segments as follows: $D(i) = L_{col}(i) - R_{col}(i)$ where col indicates the column value of the
current chain code position.

In the work reported by Tanaka and Kak (44), the length parameter S
was set to 41 and s to 4 pixels; these choices were dictated by empirical
considerations. Also, the threshold in step 4 was empirically chosen to be
50 pixels. It is assumed in this algorithm that dominant edges, meaning
edges that are long and straight, are few and will in most cases result in
unique matches. The scene lines constructed by fusing long edges then
serve as anchors for testing hypotheses regarding the presence or absence
of planar surfaces in the scene.

For scenes in which the objects have edges far apart in comparison to
d_{max}, this algorithm will yield good results and do so in linear time with
respect to the number of edges in either image. As we will see in the next
two examples, it is possible to construct straight line and contour matching
algorithms that are capable of matching straight line edges even when they
do not obey the d_{max} separation constraint, but by entailing exponential
computational burden.

4.2.2. Structural Stereopsis

While the previous two approaches enforce constraints on the continuity
of disparity along line segments, the approaches described in this section
use the relationships between the line segments to improve the robustness
of stereopsis. In this way, the structure present in the images is explicitly
used; hence the name *structural stereopsis*.

Boyer and Kak (6) present a system that seeks to find a mapping
between the set of straight line edge segments in the left image to the set

of straight line edge segments in the right image that best preserves the relational constraints between the matched line segments. Each line segment is described by attributes such as its length in pixels, and mean orientation of the edge segment. The relationships used between two segments are as follows: the orientation and the length of the line that connects the centroids of the two segments in question, and the length of the line that connects the closest pair of endpoints of the two segments in question.

In the Boyer–Kak approach, a mapping from the segments in the left image to those in the right image is constructed by minimizing a cost function that has two components; the first component measures the dissimilarity of the attributes of the matched segments, and the second measures the inconsistency of the relations between the matched segments. The cost function is formulated using information-theoretic considerations, which means specifying probabilities for the image-to-image distortion of the attributes of the segments and their relations. *Nilmapping*, which consists of assigning nils to the segments of the left image, (necessitated by the fact that in the presence of occlusions there may not exist a right-image correspondent for a left-image segment), plays an important role in the discovery of a best-mapping function. The mapping function itself is constructed by employing a backtracking search; the structure of the search space is such that each level of the search tree corresponds to one left-image segment and the different nodes at a level represent the different possible right-image candidate segments. A principal shortcoming of the Boyer–Kak approach is that the system is incapable of dealing with the fragmentation of segments. What that means is that if a left-image segment shows up as two or more disconnected segments in the right image, this system would be incapable of discovering that fact. Another problem, which we will not describe here in any detail for reasons of space limitation, is caused by large depths of field in a scene. Both these shortcomings of the Boyer–Kak method have been rectified in a recent contribution by Kosaka and Kak (22).

In Horaud and Skordas (16), structural stereopsis is implemented with a graph-theoretical approach where straight line edge segments are used as features. In graph-theoretic approaches, the set of line segments and their relations in each image are represented by a graph data structure, in particular the relational attributed variety. In general, a relational attributed graph (RAG) is constructed for each image where a node of the graph represents a segment and the arcs indicate relationships between segments of the connected nodes. Each node in the graph has a set of attributes that describe the structure of the edge segment assigned to the node. The problem of establishing correspondences between the line segments in the two images then becomes an exercise in finding the largest

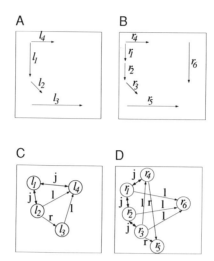

Figure 8.21. Example relational attributed graphs (RAGs) are constructed for a set of stereo images: (A) straight line segments found in the left image; (B) straight line segments found in the right image; (C) RAG of left image; (D) RAG of the right image. Note in (C) and (D) the meanings of the labels on the links are as follows: j = junction, l = left-of, r = right-of, c = collinear. Also note that for every link with label l (or r) there is another link in the other direction with the label r (or l) that is not drawn.

double-subgraph isomorphism.[1] Note that "double" subgraph isomorphisms are required rather than subgraph isomorphisms because a segment in one image may correspond to more than one segment in the other image as a result of occlusion, illumination differences, and so on that can occur between the images and effect the extraction of segments. Another reason for stating the problem as a double-subgraph isomorphism problem is that a relation between a particular pair of segments in one image may be different from the relation for the corresponding pair of segments in the other image. For example, left-to-right ordering is a common relationship used, and, as illustrated by Fig. 8.20, a reversal of this ordering can occur for thin vertical objects that are spatially close in the image domain but separated by a large depth.

Horaud and Skordas (16) use adjacency, collinearity, and intersection for the relations. *Adjacency* is indicated by whether a line segment is directly adjacent to another segment in a left or right sense. For a given line segment, these left and right adjacencies are detected by scanning in a direction perpendicular to the orientation of the segment and recording

[1] As stated in Ballard and Brown (3), the problem of solving "double" subgraph isomorphisms consists of finding all isomorphisms between the subgraphs of a graph and the subgraphs of the other graphs.

hits with other line segments. *Collinearity* is simply a measure that indicates that two line features lie on the same line in the image plane. Finally, an intersection point (junction) occurs when two line segments intersect. Figures 8.21(A) and (B) show, for the purpose of illustration, a schematic of line segments that could be the output of an edge detector applied to the two images of a stereo pair. The arrowheads on the line segments indicate the orientation of the underlying edges with respect to the black-to-white transitions. Figures 8.21(C) and (D) are the corresponding relational attributed graphs. As explained in the legend, the labels correspond to the different relations.

Horaud and Skordas (16) solve the problem of finding the largest double-subgraph isomorphism by using what they call a *correspondence graph* (GC). A CG has a node for every feasible match between the lines of the left and right images. Arcs are connected between two nodes in the CG if they are compatible, meaning that all the relations concerning the lines in question in the RAGs match or at least do not dispute each other. For example, say we have two nodes of the CG called $n_1 = (l_1, r_2)$ and $n_2 = (l_2, r_3)$ then the two nodes are compatible if the relations (arcs in RAG) between l_1 and l_2 exist between r_2 and r_3 or at least do not conflict and vice versa. Using the CG derived from a stereo pair of images, the solution to the correspondence problem is to find the "best" maximal clique.[2]

As Horaud and Skordas discuss, there may be more than one largest maximal clique, and in practice even if there is a unique largest maximal clique, it may not result in the best stereo matching. Thus, as presented below, a benefit value is calculated for each node and the benefit of a clique is the sum of the benefits of its nodes. Consequently, the "best" maximal clique is defined as the maximal clique with the largest benefit. The following steps outline the process of matching line features in their system:

1) Create nodes of CG
            for every 1, a line of the left image, find all of
            the possible lines of right image, r, that can
            match given the epipolar line, position and orien-
            tation constraints. The search space for finding
            candidate lines in right image is bounded by the
            epipolar lines of the endpoints of line 1. The po-
            sition constraint delimits the span along the
            epipolar line that a valid candidate right line
            must be in and this is a function of the field of

---

[2]A "clique" is a completely connected subgraph; each node is connected to all the other nodes of the subgraph. A maximal clique is a clique that cannot be extended to include any other nodes of the graph.

views of the cameras (no expected disparity information is used). The orientation constraint requires that two matching lines be within 30° of
each other in orientation.

2) For each node=$(l,r) \in$ CG calculate its benefit:

$$Benefit(node)=1/4 \left(\frac{min(C_l,C_r)}{max(C_l,C_r)} + \frac{min(L_l,L_r)}{max(L_l,L_r)} \right.$$

$$\left. + \frac{min(\Theta_l,\Theta_r)}{max(\Theta_l,\Theta_r)} + \frac{min(N_l,N_r)}{max(N_l,N_r)} \right)$$

where C_i=contrast across line i.
        L_i=length of line i.
        Θ_i=orientation of line i.
        N_i=# of relations line i has with other lines of
        same image.

3) Remove nodes with $Benefit(node)<$ Threshold
    Note that Threshold is empirically chosen.

4) Place arcs between nodes in CG that are compatible.

5) Find maximal cliques in CG.

6) Take maximal clique with max $Benefit(clique)$
    where $Benefit(\textbf{clique})= \sum_{nodes \, \in \, clique} Benefit(node)$

An advantage of this system is that it allows one edge in an image to
match to two or more edges in the other image. The major drawback of
this algorithm is that finding all of the maximal cliques (step 5) in the CG
is an NP-hard problem, and as such this step will be of exponential time
complexity in terms of the number of nodes in the CG. For one example
of an office scene it took 26 minutes to run the line correspondence
algorithm on a 11/780 VAX. The authors attempt to reduce the actual
time spent in finding the maximal cliques by removing nodes in the CG
that have a low benefit value (step 3). There are also other heuristic
methods that possess smaller time complexities, however at the risk of not
finding all of the maximal cliques and therefore possibly not finding the
best stereo match.

Nasrabadi and Liu (34) present an approach, similar to the one proposed by Horaud and Skordas (16), in which curve segments consisting of
zero-crossing points are used as features. Like the Horaud–Skordas algorithm, this algorithm forms a correspondence graph and finds its maximal
cliques. Each curve segment is described by its centroid location, length,

and Hough transform. The Hough transform is used here to describe the shape of a curve segment. After a RAG is formed for each image a CG is constructed, but only the distance between the curve segments' centroids is considered to determine whether two nodes of a CG are compatible. Unlike the previous system, this system simply chooses the largest maximal clique. Nasrabadi and Liu have implemented a coarse-to-fine processing strategy using curve segments derived from zero-crossing contours generated by LOG operators at different scales. As was the case in the MPG algorithm, the use of LOG operators also allows the authors to implement vergence control.

Nasrabadi and Liu argue that using curve segments is better than straight line segments since the extraction of straight lines via a piecewise segmentation process can introduce problems with edge localization. They extract semantically significant curve segments through a curve tracing routine that traces only zero-crossings that are above a chosen gradient threshold. Tracing is iteratively started at a maximum gradient zero-crossing point and the current curve is ended when the next zero-crossing in the trace is at an orientation[3] 10° different from the orientation of the previously visited zero-crossing or if it has a gradient magnitude that is below a certain threshold. The lengths of the extracted zero-crossings will be a function of the gradient and orientation thresholds chosen. The larger curve segments generally correspond to the physical edges of the objects in the scene or significant (nonrandom) texture patterns on the objects and therefore small curve segments are ignored.

In the algorithm reported in Nasrabadi and Liu (34), the disparities along the matching curve segments are calculated after the largest maximal clique is found. The system attempts to resolve the ambiguity that arises when part of a matching curve is occluded or when some of the pixels on a curve are along the epipolar line by assigning the disparity of these pixels to be equal to the disparity at the curve segment's centroid.

4.3. Incorporation of Object-Level Information in Stereo Vision

There are two distinctive ways in which object-level information is used in stereo vision systems. The first is in the use of very high level features in matching such as vertices, junctions, and surfaces. The advantage of using ultra-high-level features is that the probability of mismatches occurring is very low because of the sparseness of these features in the scene. A second use of object-level information is in the area of surface reconstruction where knowledge of the surface characteristics can be used to correct

---

[3]"Orientation" here refers to the direction of the maximum gray-level variation at the zero-crossing point in question.

mismatches. Surface reconstruction techniques are usually applied to dense disparity maps that are produced from the matching of lower-level features. Below we describe a few systems that illustrate each of the ways in which object-level information is used.

4.3.1. Object-Derived High-Level Features

In the preceding sections, the goal of the stereo system has been to recover the depth information of any type of scene. However, in this section we relax this goal and now only wish to recover the depth information of a particular type of scene, namely, one populated with particular objects. In this sense these stereo vision systems will be domain-dependent and will most probably not function well with a scene from a different type of domain. We will describe two systems that differ in the breadth of their domains. The first system is more specific in that it is only for scenes of a particular set of objects. The importance of discussing such a system is that it is very fast and tuned to the eventual recognition of the objects in question, which is often the goal of many industrial projects. The reader is also referred to Mohan and Nevatia (33), which briefly discusses a stereo system that matches ribbons where a ribbon is a surface-like feature that is extracted by the system using perceptual organization techniques. The system of Mohan and Nevatia (33) differs from the two systems presented in this section mainly in that it uses perceptual organization techniques for feature extraction.

Currently, we are working on a stereo vision system for the recognition and pose estimation of a set of industrial objects. There are four unique types of objects, three of which are shown in Fig. 8.22(A). Because our goal is very specific, we are able to adopt an object/domain-dependent approach where we use object-derived high-level features for stereo matching. The system takes on a hierarchical flavor in the sense that first objects are monocularly recognized, then these objects are matched, then the corners of each pair of matched objects are matched, and these are used to create a sparse disparity map. "Corners" are defined as the physical vertices of the objects. Matching the objects takes place first because there are only a few objects in the scene and the chance of mismatching is very low. Subsequently, the matching of corners can take place using constraints from the previous object-level matching. More specifically, corners of a particular left-image object must match with corners of the matching right-image object. This method works well for the type of scenes we are dealing with and is much faster than a low-level-feature-based stereo vision algorithm. Figure 8.23 illustrates the processing steps of this system.

Objects are monocularly detected through the use of their boundary edges. These edges are detected via Sobel edge detection and thinning

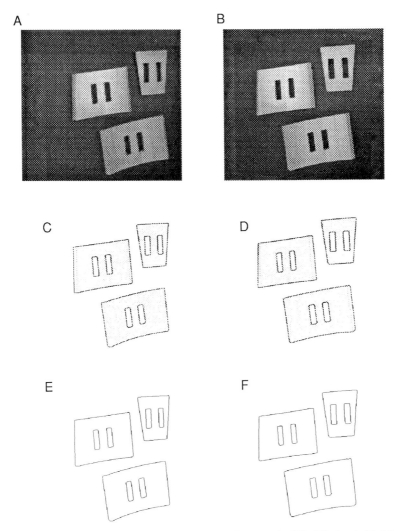

Figure 8.22. (A), (B) Original gray-scale stereo image pair; (C), (D) thresholded images convolved with Sobel operator; (E), (F) results after thinning edges (*Figure continues.*)

and a skeleton tracing procedure. First, the stereo pair of images are thresholded in order to remove the background noise. The results of convolving the thresholded images with a Sobel operator are shown in Figs. 8.22(C) and (D), and the output after thinning is shown in Figs. 8.22(E) and (F). The resulting images are passed to a skeleton tracing procedure that removes skeletons that do not correspond to object boundary edges. During skeleton tracing, the corners and their connecting linear boundary edges are found where corners are defined to be points of high curvature. Objects can be monocularly recognized from the information

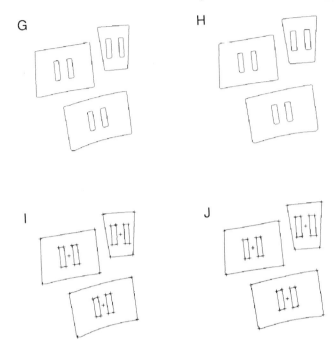

Figure 8.22. (*Continued*) (G), (H) results after skeleton tracing; (I), (J) corners found in the images are marked by cross symbol, and the object centers are also marked.

gleaned during this processing step. At this point, each detected object has three skeletons associated with it. The largest skeleton corresponds to the object's outside boundary edges, and the two smaller skeletons are the bounding edges of the two grasping holes inside of the object. Figures 8.22(I) and (J) show the corners that are detected for our example.

Because the detected objects are large with respect to the image size, both left-to-right and top-to-bottom ordering of the objects can be used to make object matches between the images. Actually, the objects can be matched with respect to their centers, where a "center" is defined as the centroid point of the pixels in the object's outside bounding edges. First, all of the object center points must be reprojected so that the points lie in image planes of the canonical camera configuration (see Section 3 for discussion on reprojection). Now, a search window can be set up in the right image surrounding each object center point in the left image with a $\pm d_{max}$ span along the horizontal direction and a $\pm t$ span in the vertical direction. As before, d_{max} is the maximum expected disparity, and a small value of t such as 1 accounts for errors in the reprojection process. In our scenes, there is only one candidate right-image object center in this window. If this candidate is of the same object type, then the two objects are considered to be matched.

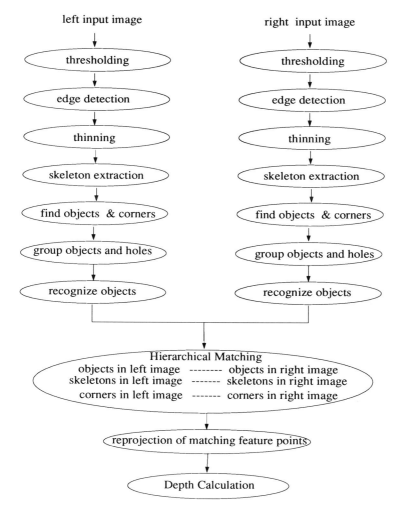

Figure 8.23. Block diagram illustrating the processing steps in the high-level-feature-based stereo vision algorithm for the eventual recognition of a set of industrial parts.

Each object has at most three skeletons associated with it, and each of these skeletons can have at most four corners. Before corner matching can occur, matching of the set of skeletons of each previously found pair of matched objects must take place. It is very obvious that the two largest skeletons that are the outside bounding edges of the matched objects must match. Therefore, only the two inside skeletons of each object remain to be matched, and this is easily accomplished with the use of a vector comparison test that maintains the left-to-right and top-to-bottom ordering that exists for these skeletons. Vectors are created from the center of each inside skeleton to the center of its object. Then a skeleton of the left-image object will match to the skeleton of the corresponding right-image object whose vector is most similar in orientation. Because of the very large difference in the orientation of these vectors, this scheme efficiently captures the left-to-right and top-to-bottom ordering of the inside skeletons. A similar matching scheme for the corners of each pair of matched skeletons takes place, but this time the vectors are with respect to the centers of the skeletons that contain them.

Lim and Binford (23) present a system that is in some ways similar to the previous one in that it uses a hierarchy of scene features. While it is true that the set of objects for which this system is geared is larger, we believe that the system will perform best for polygonal objects that do not occlude one another in the scene. The high-level features used are bodies, surfaces, curves, junctions, and edgels. A "body" is a set of connected surfaces in the scene and a surface is described by a set of boundary curves that are connected at junction points. These curves are listed in order of a directional traversal of the surface's boundary. "Surfaces" can be either open or closed. A closed surface is a surface whose boundary curves form a closed loop. An open surface does not form such a loop and can occur as a result of an occluding surface or breaks in the curves due to noisy data or illumination patterns. "Curves" are either straight line or conic edge segments and junctions are points where curves intersect. Finally "edgels" are loosely defined here as short linear edge segments.

Monocular detection of the features in each image begins with the detection of edgels, where an edgel is characterized by its direction and position. Next, edgels are grouped into ordered sets that correspond to extended edges and curves are fit to these sets where a curve can be either a straight line or a conic section. Junctions are detected in the image as points where more than two curves intersect; curves are broken up at junctions. Now a curve tracing procedure takes place to find the surfaces. Unlike the previous system, this tracing routine is not fine-tuned to any particular set of objects, and thus surfaces can be found that are actually a composite of more than one surface or only part of a surface in the scene. Finally, bodies are detected as groups of surfaces that share edges, and as such, a body may consist of more than one object in the scene.

Matching occurs in a top–down fashion in the following order: bodies, surfaces, curves, junctions. The higher-levels of matching produce constraints for the lower levels that greatly reduce the number of match candidates. The matching process begins by matching bodies according to how similar they are in terms of the number of surfaces they contain, the order of these surfaces, and the relative positions of the bodies in each image. For each pair of matched bodies, their surfaces are matched on the basis of characteristics such as the number of junctions and the relative positions of the surfaces in the body. Finally, for each surface match, their curves and junctions are matched according to ordering constraints. Disparity and depth values are computed at the matched curves and junctions.

The authors mention that a subsequent step of surface interpolation could take place on the sparse disparity map. However, this can happen only if each surface can be recognized from its boundary curves along with its pose, as was accomplished by the system described previously.

4.3.2. Surface Reconstruction Techniques in Stereo Vision

Surface reconstruction can be a process that is totally independent from the matching process in stereo vision and takes place after an unambiguous disparity or depth map has been produced. More recently, surface reconstruction has been incorporated into the feature matching stage of stereo vision systems and used to disambiguate multiple matches. This integration of surface reconstruction obviously assumes that some types of surfaces exist in the scene and as such utilizes object-level information. In this section, we describe two systems that use surface reconstruction to perform disambigution of multiple matches. The main difference between the two systems lies in the fact that in the first, surface reconstruction takes place only in selected local regions, whereas in the second, surface reconstruction is attempted everywhere.

Surface reconstruction, also called *surface fitting* and *surface interpolation*, is the process of finding the surface that most of the 3D points in question will lie on or close to. In stereo vision systems, these 3D points are either the points of the disparity map or its corresponding depth map. It is important to note that fitting a particular type of surface to a set of depth points is equivalent to fitting the same type of surface to the corresponding set of disparity points. Commonly, planar or quadratic surfaces, in mathematical terms called the *first-* and *second-order surfaces*, are fit to the data. Higher-order surfaces are not used because accurate fitting requires a larger density of data points, which seldom is available.

Tanaka and Kak (44) present a hierarchical stereo vision algorithm that, unlike the systems described in Section 4.3.1, produces a dense disparity map. The following is a list of the processing steps of this system in order of their execution: (1) straight line matching, (2) application of geometric constraints, (3) curve segment matching, and (4) zero-crossing point matching. The denser disparity map is a result of the second processing step, which we will discuss below, and the last step, where an MPG-type algorithm is invoked for pixels in the disparity map that are not assigned values from the previous three steps. We will now discuss the step of the algorithm that deals with the application of geometric constraints. The algorithm assumes that the surfaces in the scene are all planar and the orientation of each planar surface is one of a known set of orientations.

Evidently, this assumption severely limits any practical usefulness of the algorithm, but the algorithm is of historical interest since it is one of the first stereo algorithms that imposes top–down constraints on the stereo fusion process. Here is a description of the algorithm:

```
For each θ ∈ {Finite Set of Assumed Orientations}
    1) Grow/Fit a 16 pixel wide region to a plane of ori-
    entation θ that contains the pair of matched straight
    lines in question.

    2) The goodness of the fit is evaluated by matching
    the zero-crossings in this 16 pixel region from the
    finest channel. The disparity values corresponding to
    the planar strip produced in step 1 are used to center
    the search windows used in matching. The number of
    zero-crossing matches is recorded.
```

```
The planar strip (θ) that leads to the largest number of
zero-crossing matches is regarded as the best fit and the
corresponding disparity values are stored in the final dis-
parity map of the scene.
```

Hoff and Ahuja (15) describe a system that integrates low-level-feature-based matching with surface reconstruction at every point in the image. An MPG-type algorithm is used to produce zero-crossing matches at three different resolutions and a coarse-to-fine matching strategy is used. All of the multiple zero-crossing matches produced are kept, and surface fitting is used for disambiguation where the points that lie on or closest to the surface are kept. Both planar and quadratic surfaces are locally fit to the data. In addition, a final global surface fitting operation takes place after occluding and ridge edges in the scene have been detected.

First, a sparse grid is created at a spacing of w_{2D}, which is the size of the LOG operator used to find the zero-crossing points. A planar surface is fit to a circular patch centered at each grid point with a radius in the range of w_{2D} to $2w_{2D}$. The two best fit planes are kept. A fit is accepted only if the number of unmatchable points in the region is less than an empirically determined threshold and if the sum of the squared errors is less than another empirically determined threshold. The squared error at a point is the square of the distance from the point to the surface. Points whose distances to the plane being fit are greater than what is commonly called an "outlier distance" are considered unmatchable and are not included in the sum of the squared errors.

One way in which a planar surface can be fit to a set of data points is through the use of a least-squares method where all of the combinations of points are tried for each surface fitting. The data set that has a planar patch fit with the minimum squared error and passes the threshold tests mentioned above is considered as the best-fitting plane. The total number of these combinations is exponential in the number of ambiguous points. However, the system in Hoff and Ahuja (15) avoids this exponential complexity by using a Hough transform of the data points as the surface fitting procedure. A surface can be described by a set of parameters, as in $z = ax + by + c$ for a planar surface. The 3D planar parameter space, also called the *Hough space*, spanned by the parameters a, b, and c, is discretized and a Hough transform is computed for all of the data points. The maximum point in the Hough accumulator space yields the parameters of the best-fitting plane. The amount of time it takes to find the best planar fit using the Hough transform method is a function of the size of the 3D Hough space, specifically, the coarseness of the discretization of the parameters used. While using this Hough technique will decrease the time spent in finding the best-fitting plane, it is also true that it is at the cost of finding the best-fitting plane from only a discrete set of planes.

Next, for each grid point, a quadratic patch is fit to the points of the planar patches at this grid point and the planar patches of neighboring grid points. Therefore, the quadratic patches are fit to a larger local region of the scene; this is acceptable since the previous fittings of planar patches would have removed many of the ambiguous matches. This time a least-squares method is used, but only the two most compatible sets of the planes covering this larger region are used as input to the quadratic patch fitting procedure. Two neighboring planar patches are compatible if the differences in depth and orientation between them are less than empirically chosen thresholds. Only the two most compatible sets of planes in the region are used, and consequently the exponential time complexity that can occur for surface fitting is avoided. The quadratic patch with the minimum squared error that also is less than an empirically determined threshold is taken as the best-fitting quadratic patch. If the quadratic patch with the minimum squared error does not pass the threshold test, then no patch is fit to the corresponding grid point.

After quadratic fitting, all of the ambiguous matches are resolved. Before a final global surface interpolation can take place, the occluding and ridge contours in the scene must be detected. This is performed by fitting bipartite circular planar patches to each grid point. Bipartite circular planar patches are formed by dividing a circular patch into two halves by cutting along a diameter at a particular orientation. If the two planes differ in depth or orientation by more than some threshold, then an occluding or ridge edge may exist along the split circular patch's diameter. The final surface interpolation follows the calculation of a weighted average of the surrounding quadratic surface points at each grid point where the weights reflect the distance from the surrounding surface point to the center grid point in question. This interpolation step does not cross edges when averaging in the surrounding surface points.

The main disadvantage of using surface reconstruction techniques at every point in the scene is the computational expense. For example, for the finest LOG channel for a 512×512 pixel image, it took this system approximately 3 hours to perform planar patch fitting on a Sun 3/160 workstation. The authors suggest special dedicated hardware to implement the Hough transform as a way of significantly improving this time and parallel processing techniques where each processor can be assigned the task of a single planar patch fitting. In addition, this system also runs the risk of spending too much time performing surface fitting in areas where no surfaces exist or where background surfaces exist which may be unimportant to the subsequent recognition tasks. As suggested by the Tanaka–Kak system (44), it may be desirable to perform surface fitting only over local areas that are most likely to contain semantically significant object surfaces such as the areas surrounding straight line features.

5. DEPTH RESOLUTION AND DESIGN OF STEREO CAMERA CONFIGURATION

The process of designing a stereo camera configuration is a function of many considerations such as the desired depth resolution, the typical scene depths, and the portion of the scene you wish to capture. The parameters of a stereo camera configuration are the baseline length b, the focal length of the cameras f, the angle of the optical axes, and the image sampling intervals in the images. We assume that the cameras have the same focal length and sampling intervals simply because there is no reason for these parameters to differ, and if they did, it would complicate feature extraction and matching. In the following paragraphs, we will attempt to elucidate the interdependencies of the system parameters with the task-dependent considerations.

In Section 3, we briefly mentioned two types of configurations: the canonical and convergent camera configurations shown in Figs. 8.4 and 8.6, respectively. In the canonical configuration, the optical axes are parallel, whereas in the convergent configuration they are not parallel. Before feature matching can occur for the convergent case, a reprojection process must take place as described in Section 3. This reprojection process utilizes estimates of the cameras' positions and orientations and because these are only estimates, errors can be introduced. Therefore, whenever possible the canonical configuration should be used. Unfortunately, for given b and f values chosen to achieve a desired depth resolution, the cameras may be spaced too far apart to view enough of the same portion of the scene for the particular task in question. In this case, a convergent camera system must be utilized.

A design criterion, which often is the most important, is the desired depth resolution. The depth at a point is defined as the z component of the (x, y, z) value recovered from the corresponding stereo point match as described by Eq. (17). The depth resolution, which we will denote as Δz, is defined as the smallest detectable change in depth and is a function of the smallest detectable change in disparity. The smallest displacement of a point in an image is one pixel unless subpixel detection of points is performed. Therefore, the smallest change in disparity, which we denote as Δd, is equal to δu, the spacing between pixels, or in the case of subpixel calculations, an appropriate fraction of δu. Using Eq. (17), we can solve for Δd as follows, where d = disparity:

$$d = \frac{bf}{z}, \qquad d + \Delta d = \frac{bf}{z + \Delta z},$$

$$\Delta d = \frac{bf}{z + \Delta z} - \frac{bf}{z},$$

$$\Delta d(z + \Delta z)z = bfz - bf(z + \Delta z),$$

$$\Delta z = \frac{-\Delta d z^2}{bf + \Delta d z}. \tag{27}$$

Observe that the depth resolution is inversely proportional to b and f and directly proportional to the square of the distance to the scene. This last relationship leads to the fact that for a given b and f the depth values computed for objects that are closer are more accurate than for objects that are farther away. Another way to think about this is that closer object points will project farther away from the optical axis of each camera and thus produce a larger disparity (see Fig. 8.3). Therefore, it is not possible to calculate the depth of distant object points whose disparities are less than the smallest detectable disparity. Supposedly, this phenomenon is also responsible for the observation that, through the mechanism of binocular fusion, humans cannot perceive depth beyond approximately 60 m. Fortunately, in a camera-based system, we can set the b and f parameters so that appropriate disparity resolution is achieved for the perception of any depth; of course, some values of b and f may not be practically feasible. Given that the maximum depth value z_{max} is known, the following equation describes the bounds on Δz:

$$\frac{-z_{max}^2 \Delta u}{bf + z_{max} \Delta u} \leq \Delta z \leq \frac{z_{max}^2 \Delta u}{bf - z_{max} \Delta u} \tag{28}$$

If either the baseline length b or the focal length f is increased, then the two images will view less of the same portion of the scene. When relatively large objects populate the scene and there is a task-specific requirement that the objects be all viewable from both cameras, then bounds must be placed on how large b and f are allowed to be. The values of these two parameters are also limited by the extent of occlusion acceptable to the system.

In addition to depth resolution, there is also a similar notion of resolution in the x and y directions. However, the constraints placed on the parameters of the stereo configuration are usually not as strict as those created by the desired depth resolution. This is especially true when the x,y span of the objects is smaller than the depth of the objects.

Dhond and Aggarwal (8) derive a similar expression for Δz for the convergent camera configuration where the second camera's optical axis is rotated by a pan angle ϕ with respect to the optical axis of the first camera. This expression is as follows:

$$\frac{\Delta z}{\Delta d} = \cos^2(\phi - \beta)[A + B],$$

where

$$\beta = \tan^{-1}\left[\frac{b - (zu_1/f)}{z}\right], \qquad A = \frac{z^2}{bf}, \qquad \text{and}$$

$$B = \frac{b}{f}\left[1 - \frac{zu_1}{bf}\right]^2$$

Note that in this equation u_1 indicates the horizontal coordinate of the point in image 1 for a particular match pair. Therefore, Δz for the convergent camera setup is a function of the coordinates of the pixels used in a matched pair, besides, of course, being a function of z, b, f, and ϕ. In other words, for a given set of z, b, f, and ϕ values, Δz will vary according to the position of the edge point in image 1 that is being matched.

6. TRINOCULAR STEREO VISION

Trinocular stereo vision is a relatively new technique for depth recovery. It is similar in many ways to binocular stereo vision except for the fact that now three cameras are used. The addition of the third camera helps to reduce the ill effects of occlusion and adds additional epipolar constraints that can be used to produce more robust disparity calculations. More specifically, a third image may capture regions in the scene visible in image 1 but occluded in image 2, or vice versa. Also, the additional epipolar constraints, discussed below, can be used to reject erroneous matches that might otherwise be accepted by a binocular stereo algorithm.

Figure 8.24 illustrates a trinocular camera configuration. Notice that the scene point P is projected into each of the three image planes at p_1, p_2, and p_3, respectively. Now, given the point p_1, an epipolar line can be

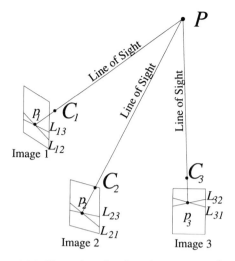

Figure 8.24. Illustration of a trinocular camera configuration.

drawn in each of the other image planes; these lines are denoted by L_{21} and L_{31} for the second and third images, respectively. Given an initial match between p_1 and p_2, the epipolar constraints dictate that the corresponding point in the third image should be located at the intersection of the epipolar lines, L_{31} and L_{32}. This extra set of epipolar constraints can be used to find the point p_3 in the third image. If such a point is found in the third image and the local properties of this point are similar to those observed at p_1 and p_2, then (p_1, p_2, p_3) can be accepted as a triplet of candidate matching points.

An initially matched pair p_1, p_2 is selected in a manner similar to how matched pairs are formed for regular binocular stereo, that is, by using local properties to establish similarity between the two points. If two points p_1 and p_2 are strongly similar, one can go ahead and accept them for disparity calculations. But, if for point p_1 there exist multiple candidates in the second image, searching in the third image for the corresponding point p_3 with similar properties can be used as a method of disambiguation. In this way, trinocular matching can reduce the number of mismatches that may result from a binocular stereo algorithm.

Given a triplet of matches, (p_1, p_2, p_3), the depth of the corresponding scene point is ideally recovered by finding the 3D intersection point of the three lines of sight (see Fig. 8.24). A line of sight for the point p_i is the 3D line that goes through the point p_i on the image plane and the focal point C_i. Because we are dealing with discrete images, the three lines may not intersect at a single point. Therefore, the corresponding scene point is taken to be the 3D point that minimizes the sum of the squared distances to the three lines of sight. Since we are using more than the two lines of sights available to a binocular stereo vision system, it can be said that the calculation of a 3D point in the scene will be on average more accurate.

In the next subsection, we present two trinocular vision algorithms, one that utilizes edgels (edge points) and the other, which uses straight lines as features. In the following subsection, we discuss the rectification of the three trinocular images that result in the epipolar lines being parallel to the axes of the image coordinate frames. In the last subsection, we will discuss the added computational complexity of trinocular vision with respect to binocular stereo vision and also discuss the quantitative improvement in depth recovery.

6.1. Example Trinocular Stereo Vision Systems

In this section, we present two algorithms that are indicative of the work that has been accomplished in trinocular stereo vision. We present two algorithms, one that uses low level features and the other, high-level features.

Ito and Ishi (17) describe a trinocular stereo vision system that uses edgels (edge points) as features for matching. In this system, the edge image extracted from one of the images is treated as a "base" image. The goal is to recover the depth of all of the points in the "base" image. Unlike the more recent trinocular vision systems, image rectification is not performed, and thus the epipolar lines will generally not fall along the scan lines of the images, as shown in Fig. 8.24. The next step in their procedure is to determine all of the epipolar lines corresponding to the edgels in the base image. Now, the matching procedure outlined below is invoked where image 1 is the base image. In the following procedure, a two-sided correlation coefficient of a candidate match between two points p_a and p_b is defined as a function of the correlation of the gray-scale information in the neighborhoods surrounding each point. A large correlation coefficient indicates that the matched points have neighborhoods with similar gray-scale content. Similarly, a one-sided correlation coefficient is defined as a function of the correlation of the gray-scale information only on one side of the neighborhoods that surround the candidate matching points. The reader is referred to Ito and Ishi (17) for further implementation details.

1) For each $p_1 \in$ image 1 find all of the candidate matches, $p_2{}^i$, in image 2 that have 2-sided correlation coefficients above a certain threshold.

For each $(p_1, p_2{}^i) \in \{$Matches to $p_1\}$

{

    Find the corresponding point, $p_3{}^i$, in image 3 using epipolar constraints. Compute the 2-sided correlation coefficient of the points p_1 and $p_3{}^i$

}

Retain the triplet match $(p_1, p_2{}^i, p_3{}^i)$ which has the largest correlation coefficient

2) For all unmatched $p_1 \in$ Image 1 find all of the candidate matches, $p_3{}^i$, in image 3 that have 2-sided correlation coefficients above a certain threshold.

For each $(p_1, p_3{}^i) \in \{$Matches to $p_1\}$

{

    Find the corresponding point, $p_2{}^i$, in image 2 using epipolar constraints. Compute the 2-sided correlation coefficient of the points p_1 and $p_2{}^i$

}

Retain the triplet match $(p_1, p_3{}^i, p_2{}^i)$ which has the largest correlation coefficient

3) Do the same as step 1 except use 1-sided correlation coefficients where necessary.

4) Do the same as step 2 except use 1-sided correlation coefficients where necessary.

5) For any points in image 1 that are unmatched, use a binocular stereopsis algorithm with the other images to produce matches. The search region along an epipolar line is bounded using the information of the surrounding disparity values calculated from matches previously found in steps 1–4.

It is interesting to note that through the actions of steps 3–5 the ill effects of occlusion may be reduced. Consider the situation in Fig. 8.25, where in image 1 the point p_1, because of occlusion, can be compared only in terms of one side of its neighborhood with one side of the neighborhoods of the corresponding points p_2 and p_3 of images 2 and 3, respec-

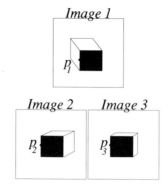

Figure 8.25. In this scene, the neighborhood of point p_1 can only be compared on one side of the neighborhoods of the points p_2 and p_3.

tively. Steps 3 and 4, perform a one-sided correlational test that will result in this triplet of points forming a match. Observe in Fig. 8.26, that the point p_1 has a corresponding point in image 3 but none in image 2. This is a result of occlusion and is handled by step 5 of the algorithm.

In (2, 14), a trinocular stereo vision algorithm is described that matches straight line segments. This algorithm uses different combinations of the images to set up the candidate matches. This helps to reduce the occurrence of missed matches that can result from the fact that one segment in an image may correspond to more than one segment in another image as a result of occlusion and other factors (14). Below is an outline of the algorithm called, `Trinocular`.

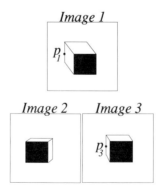

Figure 8.26. In this scene, the point p_1 has a corresponding point in image 3 but not in image 2 because of occlusion.

Trinocular

```
{

   Matcher(1,2,3)

   Matcher(2,1,3)

   Matcher(3,2,1)

}
```

where

```
Matcher(i,j,k)
```

```
{

   For each unmatched segment S_i ∈ image i

      {

            calculate |α_i| where |α_i| is the angle formed by S_i and
            the corresponding epipolar line in image j

      if |α_i| > 45°

            Generate_Hypotheses (i,j,k,S_i)

      else

            Generate_Hypotheses (i,k,j,S_i)

   }

}
```

```
Generate_Hypotheses (i,j,k,S_i)
```

```
{

   perform a search in image j for candidate matches with
   S_i.
   if a match is found then check validity by looking for a
   corresponding segment S_k in image k.

}
```

Generate_Hypotheses (i, j, k, S_i) is the procedure that finds the candidate matches for the segment S_i in image i. Basically, this procedure operates by first calculating the midpoint, a_i, of the straight line segment, S_i (see Fig. 8.27). Then any segment S_j that intersects with the epipolar line of the point a_i in image j (denoted as L_{ji}) and also has similar geometric characteristics such as orientation and length with respect to S_i

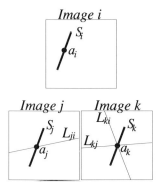

Figure 8.27. Illustration of epipolar line constraints used in the matching of segment S_i.

is considered to be a candidate match. For each candidate match (S_i, S_j), the epipolar lines L_{ki} and L_{kj}, associated with points a_i and a_j, respectively, are used to find point a_k in image 3. This point should lie on the corresponding segment in the third image. A neighborhood of 3×3 pixels is searched and if a segment, which we will call S_k, is found in this region that also has similar characteristics with respect to S_i and S_j, then the triplet (S_i, S_j, S_k) is kept as a candidate match.

As discussed in Hansen *et al.* (14), before the procedure `Trinocular` is invoked, the three images are rectified so that the epipolar lines become parallel to the axes of the image coordinate frames. This allows for fast epipolar line search. We will discuss this procedure in more detail in the next subsection.

Subsequent to the `Trinocular` procedure, the 3D line segments are reconstructed from the triple segment matches. Because each pairwise reconstruction of the 3D line from a triplet segment match will differ, the 3D line that minimizes the least-squared error is chosen. Actually, a Kalman filter approach that computes a recursive weighted least-squares solution is used. Finally, a comparison involving neighboring 3D segments is invoked to remove erroneous matches.

6.2. Trinocular Image Rectification

An example camera configuration for a trinocular vision system is shown in Fig. 8.24. Rectification of the three images is important because it allows for fast epipolar search. It is best to reproject the camera images, or the feature points extracted therefrom, into planes that would correspond

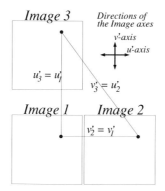

Figure 8.28. Resulting images from a trinocular system after image rectification has been performed.

to a trinocular canonical configuration (see Fig. 8.28). As a result of this reprojection, the images will be coplanar and lie in the plane containing the focal points of the three cameras. This reprojection process uses the position of the focal points of the cameras in 3D space (C), and the perspective transformation matrices T. As a result, the horizontal scan lines of images 1 and 2 will be row-registered; that is, the nth row of image 1 will be coincident with the nth row of image 2. In addition, the columns of images 1 and 3 will be registered after reprojection. Therefore, the following relations on the newly rectified images will be true where u'_i is the coordinate of a pixel along the horizontal axis of the ith image and v'_i is the coordinate of the same pixel along the vertical axis of the ith image:

$$v'_2 = v'_1, \qquad u'_3 = u'_1, \qquad v'_3 = u'_2.$$

Consequently, the epipolar line of point (u'_1, v'_1) in image 2 is the line $v'_2 = v'_1$ and in image 3 is the line $u'_3 = u'_1$. In the following reprojection process, we will denote the transformation matrix of camera i as T_i and the focal point of camera i as C_i.

For each point $p = (u, v)$ in image i, the reprojected point $p' = (u', v')$ is computed as follows:

$$\begin{bmatrix} a \\ b \\ w \end{bmatrix} = R_i \begin{bmatrix} u \\ v \\ 1 \end{bmatrix} \qquad \text{and} \qquad u' = \frac{a}{w}, \quad v' = \frac{b}{w},$$

where

$$R_i = \begin{bmatrix} (C_{i-1} \times C_i)^t \\ (C_i \times C_{i+1})^t \\ (C_1 \times C_2 + C_2 \times C_3 + C_3 \times C_1)^t \end{bmatrix} \cdot \begin{bmatrix} t_2 \times t_3 \\ t_3 \times t_1 \\ t_1 \times t_2 \end{bmatrix}^t$$

where t_j denotes the jth row of the matrix T_i. Note that in this procedure $i + 1 = 1$ if $i = 3$ and $i - 1 = 3$ if $i = 1$. The reader is referred to Ayache and Hansen (1) for details.

6.3. Comparison of Trinocular and Binocular Stereopsis

A quantitative analysis of the reduction in the number of stereo matching errors for a trinocular system over a binocular system is performed in (8). Both real digital elevation map (DEM) data and computer-generated random-dot stereograms are used. The trinocular systems use an extra image of each test scene besides the two images used by the binocular system. A subset of the data points for which ground truth is known is processed by each stereo algorithm. The percentage of mismatched points is argued by Dhond and Aggarwal (8) to be an estimate of the probability of a mismatch occuring for a scene point with no a priori knowledge of its true depth. The computational complexity of a generic trinocular stereo algorithm and a generic binocular stereo algorithm are evaluated.

The error involved in a match for which the actual 3D point is known is calculated as follows:

$$\varepsilon = |d_{calc} - d_{truth}|.$$

The value d_{calc} is the disparity calculated by the stereo algorithm, and d_{truth} is the corresponding disparity of the actual 3D point that is found by using the perspective projections of the known 3D point into images 1 and 2 and measuring the resultant displacement. It is important to note that in this study the disparity of a triplet match (p_1, p_2, p_3), produced from the trinocular algorithm, is defined to be the disparity between points p_1 and p_2. If the error ε is greater than a chosen threshold τ, the match is considered to be erroneous.

Different values of the threshold τ were used, and for values exceeding 5 pixels, the trinocular stereo algorithm cut in half the number of matching errors produced by the binocular stereo algorithm. This was true for both the DEM data and the random-dot stereograms. Even for smaller disparity thresholds, the trinocular stereo algorithm always produced a smaller number of matching errors. It should be emphasized that the depth in a trinocular stereo system is usually calculated using all three points in the match triplet, and as such the error in the depth values may be less on average than if only two of the points are used as was performed in this study.

Dhond and Aggarwal (8) also evaluate the computational complexity of a generic trinocular stereo algorithm and of a generic binocular stereo algorithm in terms on the number of multiplications (M), additions (A), and comparisons (C) for each matched point in image 1. The following numbers were obtained:

Binocular   76M, 130A, 110C

Trinocular 96M, 162A, 115C

Thus, in the worst case the increase in computational cost of the trinocular algorithm over the binocular algorithm is approximately one-fourth.

In conclusion, if an increase in computational complexity of one-fourth is acceptable, an decrease of up to 50% in the number of matching errors can be obtained by using a trinocular stereo vision system. It should be stressed that these performance measures were calculated using the particular trinocular and binocular stereo algorithms in Dhond and Aggarwal (8) and that for other algorithms these values may change.

7. ILLUMINATION EFFECTS

In this section, we will briefly discuss the effects of scene illumination on the stereo vision process. In addition, we will discuss the use of a special lighting technique referred to as *unstructured lighting*.

The locations of the scene light sources will effect the edge information that is extracted from a view of the scene. For example, consider Figs. 8.29(A–D), where the light sources used are placed at four different angles. Each image in Fig. 8.29 shows only the strongest zero-crossings detected in the image. Notice that a different set of zero-crossing contours appear in each image. In some cases, contours exist in one image, but not in another image. In other cases, the shapes of the corresponding contours have altered between images. From the fact that different edge images will result from the movement of the light sources, we can deduce that for different views, different edge patterns in the commonly viewed scene regions may result.

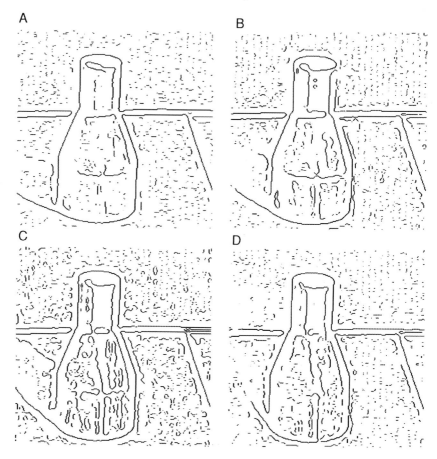

Figure 8.29. Zero-crossings extracted from the same scene with the illumination sources at different angles: (A) illumination 1; (B) illumination 2; (C) illumination 3; (D) illumination 4.

Most of the features used in stereo vision algorithms are constructed from the edgels detected in the images of the scene. To produce dense depth maps, it would be ideal to have features everywhere in the image. Unfortunately, in areas of approximately uniform gray level, few edge points will be detected. For example, consider Fig. 8.30(A), which shows a gray-level image of a scene and notice that there is little gray-level variation in the surfaces in the image. In Fig. 8.30(B), the corresponding zero-crossing image is shown, and as we expect, there are very few zero-crossings detected inside of the fairly uniform gray-level regions of the scene.

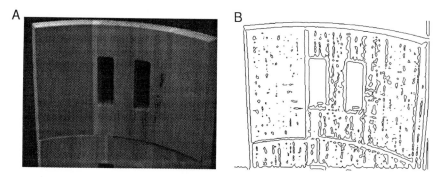

Figure 8.30. (A) Gray-scale image of objects against a black background; (B) zero-crossings extracted from the LOG-filtered image with $w_{2D} = 8$.

One lighting technique, called *unstructured* or *textured lighting*, can be used to induce edge features in regions that would appear to have constant gray levels under normal room lighting. Unstructured lighting of a scene is accomplished by illuminating the scene with a randomly textured pattern of light. Such a textured pattern of light can be produced by illuminating the scene with a slide projector where the slide is an image of a random-dot gray-scale pattern. Figure 8.31(A) shows the scene in Fig. 8.30(A) but with unstructured lighting, and Fig. 8.31(B) illustrates the resulting increase in the number of zero-crossings detected. Figure 8.32 shows the results of stereopsis on both the normal and unstructured illumination of a scene. As in the previous example, superior results are obtained for the unstructured lighting case.

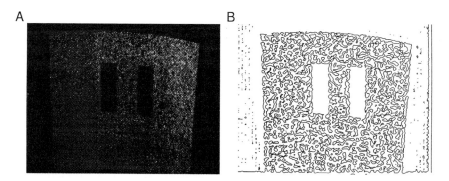

Figure 8.31. (A) Objects of Fig. 8.30(A) illuminated with unstructured light; (B) zero-crossings extracted from the LOG-filtered image with $w_{2D} = 8$.

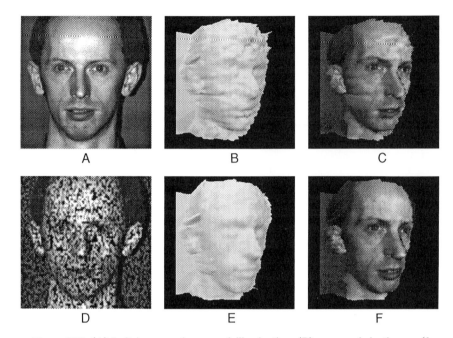

Figure 8.32. (A) Left image under normal illumination; (B) recovered depth map (for normal illumination case) rendered with Gouraud shading; (C) recovered depth map (for normal illumination case) rendered with texture mapping; (D) left image under unstructured illumination; (E) recovered depth map (for unstructured illumination case) rendered with Gouraud shading; (F) recovered depth map (for unstructured illumination case) rendered with texture mapping. Images were supplied by P. Siebert and C. Urquhart at the Turing Institute Ltd. in Glasgow, UK (under the DTI project IED3/1/2109). See Siebert and Urquhart (41) for a previous contribution from the authors on the use of unstructured lighting.

8. CORRECTION AND ANALYSIS OF ERRORS

The errors that can occur in a stereo vision system can be classified into three types. The first, which we will call *quantization error*, is a consequence of the fact that images are 2D discrete signals and thus a scene point is projected to a pixel in the image. Thus, a scene point's location can be displaced by as much as $\pm \frac{1}{2}$ pixel. The second type of error, which we will refer to as *camera distortion error*, occurs as a result of camera sensor and lens distortions. This type of error is difficult to model because they are systematic and not random. More specifically, it is a function of the particular camera or lens that is being used. The last type of error we refer to as *matching error*, which results from incorrect matching of stereo features. In this section, we will discuss each type of error and its effects. In addition, we discuss methods for correcting these errors.

8.1. Quantization Errors

Quantization error is defined as the change in the calculated depth value at a point as a function of the corresponding change in the disparity value on account of the quantization or digitization of the images. Equation (27) describes this relation, where Δd is the change in disparity and Δz is the quantization error. While Eq. (27) is useful, the quantization error can also be modeled stochastically. In the next few paragraphs, we present the stochastic model as derived in Rodrigues and Aggarwal (39).

We can consider Δz to be a function of the random variables Δd and z in Eq. (27). We assume a canonical camera configuration as shown in Fig. 8.4. Thus $\Delta d = \Delta x_l - \Delta x_r$, where Δx_l is the quantization error of the x_l position and Δx_r is the quantization error of the x_r position. We assume that Δx_l and Δx_r are independent of each other and of z. This assumption is true if the disparity $(x_l - x_r)$ is not too small (39). In addition, Δx_l and Δx_r are assumed to be uniformly distributed between $-\delta u/2$ and $\delta u/2$, which corresponds to a displacement of up to $\pm \frac{1}{2}$ pixel. The probability density functions (pdf) of Δx_l and Δx_r are

$$f_{\Delta x_l}(\Delta x_l) = \frac{1}{\delta u}, \quad \text{for} \quad -\frac{\delta u}{2} \leq \Delta x_l \leq \frac{\delta u}{2};$$

$$f_{\Delta x_r}(\Delta x_r) = \frac{1}{\delta u}, \quad \text{for} \quad -\frac{\delta u}{2} \leq \Delta x_r \leq \frac{\delta u}{2} \tag{29}$$

Using the fact that the pdf of the sum of two independent variables is the convolution of their pdfs we can derive the following:

$$f_{\Delta d}(\Delta d) = f_{\Delta x_l}(\Delta x_l) * f_{\Delta x_r}(\Delta x_r)$$

$$= \begin{cases} \dfrac{\delta u + \Delta d}{(\delta u)^2} & -\delta u \leq \Delta d \leq 0 \\[3mm] \dfrac{\delta u - \Delta d}{(\delta u)^2} & 0 \leq \Delta d \leq \delta u \end{cases} \tag{30}$$

Next, using Eq. (27) and (30) we can show that the following is true:

$$f_{\Delta z}(\Delta z \mid z) = f_{\Delta d}(\Delta d)\left|\frac{d(\Delta d)}{d(\Delta z)}\right|$$

$$= \frac{bf}{(z + \Delta z)^2}\begin{cases} \dfrac{\delta u + \Delta d}{(\delta u)^2} & -\delta u \le \Delta d \le 0 \\[2ex] \dfrac{\delta u - \Delta d}{(\delta u)^2} & 0 \le \Delta d \le \delta u \end{cases}.$$

Our goal is to find the pdf of Δz, which we do using the above conditional probability as follows:

$$f_{\Delta z}(\Delta z) = \int_{-\infty}^{\infty} f_{\Delta z}(\Delta z \mid z) f_z(z)\, dz$$

$$= \begin{cases} \dfrac{bf}{\delta u^2}\displaystyle\int_{-\infty}^{\infty} \dfrac{z^2\, \delta u + z\, \delta u\, \Delta z + bf\, \Delta z}{z(z + \Delta z)^3} g^-(z) f_z(z)\, dz & -\delta u \le \Delta d \le 0 \\[3ex] \dfrac{bf}{\delta u^2}\displaystyle\int_{-\infty}^{\infty} \dfrac{z^2\, \delta u + z\, \delta u\, \Delta z - bf\, \Delta z}{z(z + \Delta z)^3} g^+(z) f_z(z)\, dz & 0 \le \Delta d \le \delta u \end{cases}$$

$$(31)$$

where

$$g^+(z) = \begin{cases} 1 & \text{if} \quad -\delta u \le \Delta d \le 0 \\[1ex] & \text{equivalently} \quad z \ge \dfrac{-\delta u\, \Delta z + \sqrt{\delta u^2\, \Delta z^2 + 4bf\, \delta u\, \Delta z}}{2\delta u} \\[2ex] 0 & \text{otherwise} \end{cases},$$

$$g^-(z) = \begin{cases} 1 & \text{if} \quad 0 \le \Delta d \le \delta u \\[1ex] & \text{equivalently} \quad z \ge \dfrac{-\delta u\, \Delta z + \sqrt{\delta u^2\, \Delta z^2 - 4bf\, \delta u\, \Delta z}}{2\delta u} \\[2ex] 0 & \text{otherwise} \end{cases}.$$

Notice that $f_z(z)$ is the pdf of the random variable z and this is domain-dependent. Assuming that the distribution of depth values in the scene is uniformly distributed between z_{min} and z_{max}, the following is true:

$$f_z(z) = \frac{1}{z_{max} - z_{min}}, \qquad z_{min} \le z \le z_{max}.$$

After plugging this into Eq. (31) and integrating, we obtain

For $0 < \Delta z \le z_{max}^2 \dfrac{\delta u}{bf - z_{max} \delta u}$,

$$f_{\Delta z}(\Delta z) = \frac{bf}{2 \delta u^2 \Delta z^2 (z_{max} - z_{min})}$$

$$\times \left[\frac{4bfz - 2\delta u \Delta z^2}{z + \Delta z} - \frac{bfz^2}{(z + \Delta z)^2} + 2bf \ln\left(1 + \frac{\Delta z}{z}\right) \right]\Bigg|_{z_0}^{z_2} ; \tag{32}$$

For $-z_{max}^2 \dfrac{\delta u}{bf + z_{max} \delta u} \le \Delta z < 0$,

$$f_{\Delta z}(\Delta z) = \frac{bf}{2 \delta u^2 \Delta z^2 (z_{max} - z_{min})}$$

$$\times \left[\frac{bfz^2}{(z + \Delta z)^2} - \frac{4bfz - 2\delta u \Delta z^2}{z + \Delta z} - 2bf \ln\left(1 + \frac{\Delta z}{z}\right) \right]\Bigg|_{z_1}^{z_2} ; \tag{33}$$

For $\Delta z = 0$,

$$f_{\Delta z}(0) = \frac{bf}{z_{min} z_{max} \delta u}, \tag{34}$$

where

$$z_2 = z_{max} \quad \text{and} \quad z_0 = \max\{z_{min}, z^+\} \quad \text{and} \quad z_1 = \max\{z_{min}, z^-\}$$

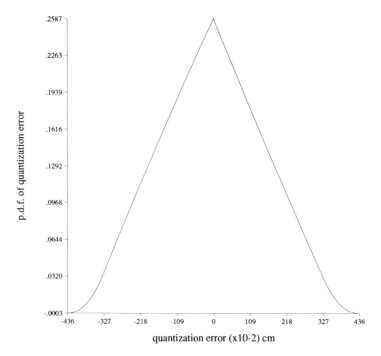

Figure 8.33. Plot of the probability density function of the quantization error.

and

$$z^{+} = \frac{-\delta uz + \sqrt{\delta u^2 \Delta z^2 + 4bf\,\delta u\,\Delta z}}{2\delta u}$$

$$z^{-} = \frac{-\delta uz + \sqrt{\delta u^2 \Delta z^2 - 4bf\,\delta u\,\Delta z}}{2\delta u}$$

Figure 8.33 is a plot of the pdf, $f_{\Delta z}$, where the following parameters were used: $b = 53.8$ cm, $f = 16$ mm, $z_{\min} = 187.49$ cm, $z_{\max} = 158.79$ cm, $\delta u = 0.00153$ cm.

In addition to the pdf of the quantization error, the expected value of the magnitude of the quantization error was derived in Rodrigues and Aggarwal (39). The following is an approximation to this expected value under the assumption that the depth is uniformly distributed between $z_{\min}$ and $z_{\max}$:

$$E[\,|\Delta z|\,] = \frac{\delta u}{9bf}\left(z_{\min}^2 + z_{\min}z_{\max} + z_{\max}^2\right) \qquad (35)$$

For the stereo parameters used to create Fig. 33, the expected value is 1.297 cm.

There are three ways to reduce quantization error. The first is to perform subpixel detection of features. Unfortunately, subpixel detection of features, as mentioned before, is appropriate only when the features are relatively well separated. Second, as discussed in Section 5, the camera configuration parameters can be altered, and if possible the cameras could be moved closer to the objects in the scene. Finally, a practical solution would be to use a high-resolution camera where the pixel size δu is smaller. In any case, there will always be some quantization error existent in the system.

8.2. Camera Distortion Errors

We have defined this type of error to be a consequence of the distortions present in the lens and camera sensors. This type of error will vary from camera to camera and lens to lens. A practical solution to reducing camera distortion errors is to buy a fine-quality lens and camera. One place in which the effect of camera distortion errors can be reduced is in the reprojection process of the stereo images that is performed for a convergent camera configuration (see Section 3). The reprojection process uses information derived in camera calibration. Typically most systems use the pinhole model of the camera for calibration. However, other models can be used, such as the one described in (45), which incorporates radial lens distortion and therefore produces more accurate calibration results. In practice, camera distortion errors in general do not contribute as much to the total error as do the quantization and matching errors.

8.3. Matching Errors

Unlike quantization errors, the errors that result from mismatching have not been adequately modeled since they can result from a number of very different factors that are difficult to identify. Examples of these factors are missing features in one image, and the local invalidity of the particular matching constraints used such as a regional disparity continuity constraint. Therefore, instead of pursuing the difficult task of modeling the statistics of these errors, researchers have attempted to develop algorithms to detect matching errors. Often the goodness of a stereo matching algorithm is evaluated by counting the number of incorrect matches formed for different scenes.

In some sense, one can think of the algorithms used for disambiguation of matches as algorithms that detect and correct matching errors. However, in this section we will concentrate on methods that detect and correct matching errors after a unique disparity map has been produced.

One method of detecting and correcting matching errors uses domain-dependent knowledge in the guise of surface reconstruction. As discussed in Section 4.3.2, if surface boundaries can be found (for either local surface patches or entire surface regions) and the type of the underlying surface can be recognized, surface reconstruction can take place in these bounded regions. Points that are outliers with respect to the best-fit surface are replaced by the corresponding disparity values of the fit surface. An outlier is a point whose distance to the fitted surface is too large, ostensibly a result of mismatching. In the same manner, holes in the disparity map can be filled in. This procedure will work only if surfaces exist in the scene and they can be detected, meaning that the physical discontinuities of the scene should be detectable. In addition, the type(s) of the surfaces must be predefined, and as such this method will work in only some domains. The reader is referred to Cochran *et al.* (7) and Sinha *et al.* (42, 43) for details on some surface reconstruction techniques that have been used on stereo data.

Another method is described in Mohan *et al.* (32) using the figural continuity constraint to correct mismatches along contours. This algorithm will work on the output of any low-level-feature-based stereo algorithm. It is important to note that even if figural continuity is used as a constraint in a low-level-feature-based algorithm, it will only be used locally and thus a long contour can have some of its points mismatched. Mohan *et al.* (32) classify matching errors along contours into two types. Type 1 errors correspond to matching errors on a contour where the majority of matches on this contour are correct. Type 2 errors on a contour indicate the situation where the majority of the matches on the contour are incorrect. On the basis of figural continuity alone, only type 1 errors can be detected and corrected. Unfortunately, this algorithm runs the risk of trying to correct type 2 errors and thus producing contours with an even larger majority of erroneous matches.

In Mohan *et al.* (32), only linear segments are used. The fact that the disparity along a pair of matched linear segments varies linearly in proportion to the length of the segment is used as a constraint. First, the linear segments in each image are detected. For each linear segment, a 2D plot of all of its matched points is constructed. The disparity of each matched point on the segment is plotted as a function of its distance to the end of the segment. Next, for each such plot a straight line is fit to the plot since it is known that in the absence of matching errors the plotted points should form a straight line. This fitting is accomplished via a modified Hough transform, and the reader is referred to Mohan *et al.* (32) for details. This best-fit line is then used to calculate with subpixel accuracy the disparity at each point along the line, and these are the values retained in the final disparity map.

One advantage of this method is that it has a linear time complexity, $O(N)$, where N is the number of line segments in the two images. A disadvantage of this algorithm is that erroneous matches along straight lines only will be corrected. In addition, the number of type 2 errors along a contour may increase if originally a sufficiently large number of type 2 errors form a straight line in the 2D disparity-length plot.

ACKNOWLEDGMENT

Work in section 4.3.1 was supported by Hitachi Construction Machinery Corporation, Limited and in collaboration with Zhaohui Li.

REFERENCES

1. N. Ayache and C. Hansen, Rectification of images for binocular and trinocular stereovision. *Proc. Int. Conf. Pattern Recognition, 9th*, Rome, Italy, *1988*, pp. 11–16 (1988).
2. N. Ayache and F. Lustman, Fast and reliable passive trinocular stereovision. *Proc. Int. Conf. Comput. Vision, 1st*, London, *1987*, pp. 422–427 (1987).
3. D. Ballard and C. Brown, "Computer Vision." Prentice-Hall, Englewood Cliffs, NJ, 1982.
4. S. Barnard and W. Thompson, Disparity analysis of images. *IEEE Trans. Pattern Anal. Mach. Intell.* **PAMI-2**(4), 333–340 (1980).
5. D. Baunegg, Stereo feature matching in disparity space. *Proce IEEE Int. Conf. Robotics Autom.*, Cincinnati, OH, *1990*, pp. 796–803 (1990).
6. K. Boyer and A. Kak, Structural stereopsis for 3-D vision. *IEEE Trans. Pattern Anal. Mach. Intell.* **10**(2), 144–166 (1988).
7. S. Cochran, G. Medioni, and R. Nevatia, Correcting matches and inferring surface patches inpassive stereo. *Proc. IEEE Comput. Soc. Workshop Comput. Vision*, Miami Beach, FL, *1987*, pp. 333–335 (1987).
8. U. Dhond and J. Aggarwal, A cost-benefit analysis of a third camera for stereo correspondence. *Int. J. Comput. Vision* **6**(1), 39–58 (1991).
9. M. Fleck, A topological stereo matcher. *Int. J. Comput. Vision* **6**, 197–226 (1991).
10. S. Ganapathy, Decomposition of transformation matrices for robot vision. *Proc. IEEE Int. Conf. Robot. Autom.*, *1984*, pp. 130–139 (1984).
11. W. E. L. Grimson, A computer implementation of a theory of human stereo vision. *Philos. Trans. R. Soc. London, Ser. B* **292**, 217–253 (1981).
12. W. E. L. Grimson, Computational experiments with a feature based stereo algorithm. *IEEE Trans. Pattern Anal. Mach. Intell.* **PAMI-7**(1), 17–34 (1985).
13. W. E. L. Grimson, "From Images to Surfaces: A Study of the Human Early Visual System." MIT Press, Cambridge, MA, 1981.
14. C. Hansen, N. Ayache, and F. Lustman, Towards real-time trinocular stereo. *Proc. Int. Conf. Comput. Vision, 2nd*, Tampa, FL, *1988*, pp. 129–133 (1988).

15. W. Hoff and N. Ahuja, Surfaces from stereo: Integrating feature matching, disparity estimation, and contour detection. *IEEE Trans. Pattern Anal. Mach. Intel.* **PAMI-11**(2), 121–136 (1989).

16. R. Horaud and T. Skordas, Stereo correspondence through feature grouping and maximal cliques. *IEEE Trans. Pattern Anal. Mach. Intell.* **PAMI-11**(11), 1168–1180 (1989).

17. M. Ito and A. Ishi, Three-view stereo analysis. *IEEE Trans. Pattern Anal. Mach. Intell.* **PAMI-8**(4), 524–532 (1986).

18. B. Julesz, Binocular depth perception of computer-generated patterns. *Bell Syst. Tech. J.* **39**, 1125–1162 (1960).

19. B. Julesz and J. Chang, Interaction between pools of binocular disparity detectors tuned to different disparities. *Biol. Cybernet.* **22**, 107–119 (1976).

20. A. C. Kak, Depth perception for robots. *In* "Handbook of Industrial Robotics" (S. Y. Nof, ed.) Chapter 16. Wiley, New York, 1985.

21. Y. C. Kim and J. K. Aggarwal, Positioning three-dimensional objects using stereo images. *IEEE J. Robotics Autom.* **RA-3**(4), 361–373 (1987).

22. A. Kosaka and A. Kak, A useful generalization of the theory of structural stereopsis for 3D robot vision. Submitted.

23. H. Lim and T. Binford, Stereo vision correspondence: A hierarchical approach. *Proc. DARPA Image Understanding Workshop*, Los Angeles, *1987*, pp. 234–240 (1987).

24. S. Lloyd, Stereo matching using intra- and inter-row dynamic programming. *Pattern Recognition Lett.* **4**, 273–277 (1986).

25. C. Lopez-Abadia and A. Kak, "Vision-Guided Mobile Robot Navigation," Tech. Rep. TR-EE 89-34. Purdue University, West Lafayette, IN, 1989.

26. D. Marr and T. Poggio, A computational theory of human stereo vision. *Proc. R. Soc. London, Ser. B* **204**, 301–328 (1979).

27. D. Marr and E. Hildreth, Theory of edge detection. *Proc. R. Soc. London, Ser. B* **207**, 187–217 (1980).

28. D. Marr and T. Poggio, A theory of human stereopsis. *Proc. R. Soc. London, Ser. B* **204**, 301–328 (1979).

29. D. Marr and T. Poggio, Cooperative computation of stereo disparity. *Science* **194**, 283–287 (1976).

30. J. E. W. Mayhew and J. P. Frisby, Psychophysical and computational studies towards a theory of human stereopsis. *Artif. Intell.* **17**, 349–385 (1981).

31. G. Medioni and R. Nevatia, Segment-based stereo matching. *Comput. Vision, Graphics Image Process.*, **31**, 2–18 (1985).

32. R. Mohan, G. Medioni, and R. Nevatia, Stereo error detection, correction, and evaluation. *IEEE Trans. Pattern Anal. Mach. Intell.* **11**(2), 113–120 (1989).

33. R. Mohan and R. Nevatia, Perceptual organization for scene segmentation and description. *IEEE Trans. Pattern Anal. Mach. Intell.* **14**(6), 616–633 (1992).

34. N. Nasrabadi and Y. Liu, Stereo vision correspondence using a multichannel graph matching technique. *Image Vision Comput.* **7**(4), 237–245 (1989).

35. Y. Ohta and T. Kanade, Stereo by intra- and inter-scanline search using dynamic programming. *IEEE Trans. Pattern Anal. Mach. Intell.* **7**(2), 139–154 (1985).

36. Y. Ohta and T. Kanade, A high speed stereo matching system based on dynamic programming. *Proc. Int. Conf. Comput. Vision, 1st*, London, *1987*, pp. 335–342 (1987).

37. S. B. Pollard, J. E. W. Mayhew, and J. P. Frisby, PMF: A stereo correspondence algorithm using a disparity gradient limit. *Perception* **14**, 449–470 (1981).

38. K. Prazdny, Detection of binocular disparities. *Biol. Cybernet.* **52**, 93–99 (1985).

39. J. Rodrigues and J. Aggarwal, Stochastic analysis of stereo quantization error. *IEEE Trans. Pattern Anal. Mach. Intell.* **12**(5), 467–470 (1990).

40. A. Rosenfeld and A. C. Kak, "Digital Picture Processing." Academic Press, New York, 1982.

41. J. Siebert and C. Urquhart, Active stereo: Texture enhanced reconstruction. *Electron. Lett.* **26**(26), 427–429 (1990).

42. S. Sinha, S. Moezzi, and B. Schunck, Robust stereo vision. *Proc. SPIE — Opt. Illum., Image Sens. Mach. Vision V* **1835**, 259–266 (1990).

43. S. Sinha, S. Moezzi, and B. Schunck, A two-stage algorithm for discontinuity-preserving surface reconstruction. *IEEE Trans. Pattern Anal. Mach. Intell.* **14**(6), 36–55 (1992).

44. S. Tanaka and A. C. Kak, A rule-based approach to binocular stereopsis. *In* "Analysis and Interpretation of Range Images" (R. C. Jain and A. K. Jain, eds.), Chapter 2. Springer-Verlag, Berlin, 1990.

45. R. Y. Tsai, A versatile camera calibration technique for high accuracy 3D machine vision metrology using off-the-shelf TV cameras and lenses, *IEEE J. Robotics Autom.*, **RA-3**(4), 323–344 (1987).

Chapter **9**

Machine Learning of Computer Vision Algorithms

STEVEN R. SCHWARTZ

Motorola Inc.
Arlington Heights, Illinois

BENJAMIN W. WAH

Center for Reliable and High-Performance Computing
Coordinated Science Laboratory
University of Illinois, Urbana-Champaign
Urbana, Illinois

**HANDBOOK OF PATTERN RECOGNITION
AND IMAGE PROCESSING: COMPUTER VISION**

1. INTRODUCTION

Both human vision and human learning are far from fully understood, yet machine imitation of these abilities has proved very useful. Research up to now has made much progress in tracing the desired result backward to the algorithms that implement it. For example, we know how or what we want the machine to perform, but lacking a complete understanding of the biological processes, we proceed to find an algorithmic solution. In both the fields of machine learning and computer vision this has been the case. This chapter presents an approach to integrating machine learning techniques to improve the performance of computer vision algorithms. The topics considered here are the techniques for machine learning, examples of how they can be applied, and a specific case study detailing the application of the methods. Topics not considered here include reasoning about detected objects and planning interaction with the environment.

Before discussing the integration of learning and vision it is best to start with a brief description of the sought-after result: namely, what vision tasks do we now expect the machine to perform. This will lead to the difficulties that must be overcome and how machine learning can play a role in surmounting them. The full utility of human vision is far beyond our current reach with computational techniques, yet our present demands are often less ambitious than full human vision and are within our grasp. Three general and important goals are effective performance of (1) two-dimensional object recognition, (2) three-dimensional object recognition, and (3) integration with robotics.

These goals are general, but applications toward achieving limited forms of these goals are of key interest here. Two-dimensional object recognition has found much application in manufacturing as an assembly automation technique. Other uses lie in spotting equipment and hostile movement for defense purposes from aerial surveillance imagery. Three-dimensional object recognition is also of use in manufacturing and is vital to systems that interact in the real world. Effective 3D vision is one of the key requirements for automatic navigation in mobile robots. The last goal, integrating vision with robotics, is primarily an application of the first two but also underlines a motive for computer vision in the first place: vision in environments where it is more practical to send a machine. An example of the tasks in demand is in parsing scenes viewed by an exploratory mobile robot. Such robots are often outside the reach of remote operation by humans, thus necessitating a degree of autonomy.

2. THE NEED FOR MACHINE LEARNING IN VISION

The goals outlined above are achievable in a limited sense, but to go beyond them it is necessary to overcome a variety of problems. The first problem is that simple cognitive tasks are difficult for machines because the algorithm designer must specify every step in the task. This is exemplified in that gaining Gestalt information from a scene is often very difficult. Often we ourselves don't know the correct way of combining components to make the whole. Also, much of the difficulty in computer vision lies in getting the machine to ignore unimportant details. Another problem is that the design of practical vision systems is still very much an art. What is needed is to take advantage of the machine to develop and refine the algorithm itself.

In real-world applications we need to be pragmatic. To incorporate machine learning we must first approach a reasonable portion of the vision task. A logical partitioning of the algorithm construction effort relys on human expertise for the design of the general algorithmic framework, while relying on computer exploration within this framework to search for the appropriate complete algorithm. This necessitates using machine learning techniques to achieve effective results, and can work well with many vision algorithms because of the large number of heuristic components. With this approach, given the parametric form of the algorithm, it becomes the responsibility of the machine to find suitable "values." Here the term *parameter* is used loosely to refer to any adjustable component and can be numeric as well as symbolic; the value in the latter case is the particular expression used for the component.

These parameters in the algorithm may have varied roles. Some examples include detection thresholds, set sizes, and the configuration of image preprocessing stages. Frequently, the parameter values that are used in the final algorithm are set heuristically. There is often little or no theory behind the values that are used, and a significant amount of hand-tuning is used to find acceptable values. (Developers of real-world systems can attest to this.) Since parameter tuning is a tedious process, machine automation allows more extensive testing than humans may find personally tolerable. As recognized in a panel discussion chaired by Sklansky in 1988 (14), one of the bottlenecks to effective vision applications is the amount of effort necessary for tuning the algorithm. Tuning is necessary not only for the initial implementation in the laboratory but also for the installation of the system in the field. Additional factors that necessitate modification include varying image domains, different lighting conditions, drifting camera parameters, and the implementation of the algorithm on different computer systems. In the latter case, the performance bottleneck can change, thus shifting the time critical area of the algorithm elsewhere.

As an example, different sets of parameters may be needed for a system designed for both day- and night-vision applications. Additionally, parameters may need adjusting after the vision system is ported to another computer; for example, one that might lack special image processing hardware. These adjustments can be costly because the novice user is typically unqualified to make them. Worse yet, even an expert can be inadequate because many systems require the extensive knowledge of the original code to make appropriate adjustments. A benefit of machine assistance is the ability to train for different domains and automatically switch context as necessary. By putting the responsibility for tuning in the machine, the need for human intervention can be greatly reduced. This results in a cost savings of both time and effort.

3. THE ROLE OF MACHINE LEARNING

Computer vision encompasses everything from low-level image preprocessing to high-level construction and interpretation of visual information. Machine learning can be applied at any stage in this cognitive process. The procedures for integrating learning techniques with existing vision algorithms is best done incrementally. The initial step is to recognize areas in the vision task where the strengths of machine learning can be exploited. Massive bookkeeping and computation can prove very fruitful when guided by relatively simple learning techniques. Before addressing these points further, however, it is necessary to outline what machine learning is and what can be expected.

Most people assume they know what learning is for humans, but anthropomorphizing the term for machines does not clarify what is meant by machine learning. A useful working definition is supplied by Simon (13): "[Machine] Learning denotes changes in the system that are adaptive in the sense that they enable the system to do the same task or tasks drawn from the same population more efficiently and more effectively the next time."

With this interpretation the purpose of using machine learning techniques is to improve computer vision performance by *automating algorithm improvement*. Machine learning can address problems in both low- and high-level computer vision. In low-level vision the machine can learn what should be seen, that is to say, what should be detected from the image for use in the higher levels of the vision algorithm. Parameters can have a strong influence on what the machine "sees." In high level vision, the machine can help learning by "seeing." This includes generalizing from examples. Each of the problems mentioned above can be addressed through learning techniques.

Learning can be performed over the target domain by allowing the vision algorithm to adapt and improve its performance. Feedback from the measured algorithm performance can also be used by the learning mechanisms at the initial image processing stage. This can have the effect of training the system to eliminate any unnecessary detail. This is a very powerful technique that is evident in biological systems (5, pp. 12–15). Gestalt knowledge of a scene can be obtained by a vision system that is able to generalize. An example of this is generalization by training the system to associate various sets of image primitives with the same label. For instance, differentiating rivers from roads in reconnaissance images can be done by learning techniques that select the discriminating features rather than through hand analysis by experts. Finally, because machine learning systems must be able to judge algorithm fitness, it forces the use of an objective algorithm-quality measure. Of course, quality measures will vary for individual vision tasks, but consistent use of objective metrics can give needed insight into system performance.

4. MACHINE LEARNING TECHNIQUES

This section presents an overview of available learning techniques. These techniques are described relative to the domain of computer vision, and with the goal of improving the performance of the algorithm. First, common components in learning systems are explored, then in each subsection that follows the technique is presented along with example application domains. It is hoped that from this information the designer will be able to select the most appropriate learning mechanism for the intended application. This information is presented in a general form to stress how the methods are applicable to a variety of domains. To clarify the information, a specific case of applying the techniques and strategies is presented in the second half of this chapter (Section 5).

Before presenting the individual learning mechanisms, it is useful to discuss some characteristics common to all the learning methods that will be discussed. One common attribute is the use of stored knowledge. "Knowledge" is simply the term used for the collection of tools or building blocks that the learning system has available to it. Indeed, the strength of a learning system stems from its ability to manipulate knowledge into useful forms. Therefore, both the mechanism to manipulate knowledge and the structure of the knowledge itself can have an impact on system performance. For example, in a particular system, the knowledge might take the form of a rule-base used to represent the archetype of an object's 3D framework. Initial knowledge could be "hard-coded" into the system, and new knowledge could be acquired through manipulation or extrapolation of existing rules. Another example of knowledge would be the structure of preprocessing stages used to extract edges in the scene for use in a recognition task. The knowledge base would be the set of stage organizations that have been explored or are currently under consideration. The rules for manipulating the stages are also part of the system knowledge. It is important to note, however, that the goal of learning is not simply to acquire new knowledge but to work with existing knowledge to develop a better algorithm.

An effective system may also choose to forget, or to "prune" knowledge. In the example given above, this would include removing stage combinations that have proved less effective. In this case it may also be necessary to construct a class of knowledge that was purged to avoid generating it in the future.

The method of classifying and storing knowledge is closely related to another common attribute of the learning mechanisms: a learning bias (11). This determines what can and cannot be learned and, therefore, should be adjusted carefully. Bias is exhibited in both the knowledge representation scheme and the knowledge manipulation tools. In terms of computer vision, this will limit the form of algorithms that can be discovered and that need to be avoided.

Nevertheless, bias is a necessary restriction. Without bias, the learning system can have an infinitely wider domain of potential solutions to discover. Such a system, however, would have little focus, and as a result, little hope of discovering anything promising. Balancing the tradeoffs of bias can be performed dynamically and to some degree automatically. By properly scheduling the operations in a learning system, the system can gradually increase its bias throughout the learning process. Figure 9.1 shows this graphically over the concept space. As time progresses, the bias

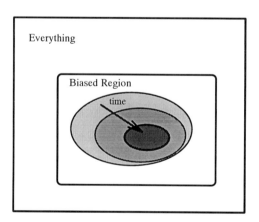

Figure 9.1. Bias (size of concept space) increasing over time.

should become stronger and stronger, limiting the search space to smaller regions. The tradeoff is that with a smaller space, the relative performance can be better. This form of scheduling helps determine what areas should be given preference. In practical applications, it is important to balance bias with scheduling in order to narrow the search, since only a finite amount of time is available.

Machine learning can be divided into several different strategies. Common divisions include (9):

- Rote learning
- Learning by instruction
- Deductive learning
- Learning by analogy
- Inductive learning

Rote learning and learning by instruction are the most primitive. *Rote learning* simply refers to knowledge being directly implanted. *Learning by instruction* differs from rote learning only in that the machine is responsible for compiling the knowledge into a readily usable format. These methods are inappropriate as a primary mechanism because none of the burden of discovery is taken on by the machine. *Deductive learning* is the process of using a set of axiomatic knowledge and truth-maintaining transformation rules to construct more useful forms of knowledge. This method is also of little utility in computer vision because the foundation of many practical algorithms is heuristic in nature. *Learning by analogy* is the process of mapping knowledge from one domain to another. This method is useful primarily when the learning domains are very similar. Because the knowledge must already be in a machine-usable form, it is often coupled with another learning technique used in the original domain. An example of learning by analogy would be transforming the algorithmic knowledge learned for a simulated vision domain to that of the real world. The domain change could also be less drastic, perhaps consisting of the extension of day-vision to a night-vision system. This transformation could be performed under user supplied rules formed independently of the knowledge in the source domain.

4.1. Inductive Learning

Learning by induction is by far the most powerful of the learning strategies for the domain of computer vision algorithms. This strategy encompasses many subcategories, some of which can be combined: learning by example, learning by exploration, data-driven learning, and model-driven learning.

The first category, learning by example, is both simple and powerful. In this case, training samples are presented from an external entity, and it is the responsibility of the system to structure the knowledge constituting the presented class. For example, a high-level vision system may be trying to recognize flat parts on an assembly line based on their 2D outline. Part of the recognition algorithm is the model used by the machine to perform identification. A system to tackle this problem could be composed of an edge detector and an outline constructor. Sample images of the object to recognize, along with its correct identity, would be presented to the system. In each training instance, the system would construct a model for the object. As more examples are presented, the object model used by the machine would adjust to accommodate variances. In this case the machine is learning the knowledge that will be used by the system to perform the recognition task.

Training samples presented in this way can be either positive or negative. In the case mentioned above, positive samples were used. The object to be recognized—say, a bracket for a car—is presented in image form, and the system is told to associate the label "bracket" with the model that it built. The training sample, however, could also have been a negative one. This would mean presenting something that the system should not recognize as being a bracket. The model modification algorithm would then make sure that the stored outline for a bracket did not fit the outline extracted for the negative example. Training with both positive and negative examples can be important for a system that must differentiate multiple objects. This kind of training ensures that key *differentiating* traits are emphasized in the models rather than just *identifying* traits.

The presentation of training samples to the learning system can have an impact on the type of algorithm that is learned and also how much training is necessary to achieve adequate results. Because formation of the acquired or learned portions of the algorithm is performed incrementally, the initial training samples can play a more significant role than latter ones. Additionally, it is important that the training domain represent the intended target domain and not simply a single case of each type of the scenes that will be encountered. This point is best illustrated by an example.

Suppose a vision system is constructed to recognize navigable terrain for a mobile robot. There are several factors that must be considered in training the system. If the system operates on solar power, it may be necessary to explore primarily during sunlight. Therefore, the training domain would emphasize brightly-lit daytime scenes with perhaps a small number of dawn and dusk images. The algorithm learned for one domain may not be best suited for all. If the risk of making a mistake is higher during the period of lower light, however, it may be best to over-represent training images during these periods as a counter measure.

Ideally the system would perform its learning by actually working in the domain for which it was intended. This is called learning by exploration. However, in this situation it becomes more difficult to verify the performance of the algorithm, so the result is that the system receives less effective guidance in modifying existing and creating new forms of the algorithm.

Learning by exploration can still be effective if an oracle is available to provide feedback to the system. One method of implementing the concept of an oracle is to make the entire training database available to the vision system, but have the system responsible for selecting the training cases. This can be especially beneficial if training is expensive in terms of image acquisition costs or available time. Typically training time greatly exceeds the time to apply the algorithm that has been learned. If the training database is available, the system can apply the current algorithm to training cases only in the cases where the algorithm produces undesirable results. An example of this would be in an artificial neural network designed for character recognition (8). The inputs would be the grid of pixels containing the character. In this case it would save time to train only over the cases where the existing network weights led to incorrect classification. Nevertheless, a predetermined database does not have to be created for the disposal of the system. A human could act as the oracle, or another vision system could be used as the oracle. (This would be useful if the oracle system has either impractical cost or size to be used in the target system.) This approach still allows the system to explore on its own and train based on its own scene selections.

Another division in the structure of an inductive learning algorithm is data-driven learning versus model-driven learning. The data-driven approach starts from a specific form and generalizes (relaxes the model) as more examples are presented. The model-driven approach starts with a generalization (a user-supplied model) and refines (specializes the model) as more examples are presented. In the example of learning the archetype for the car-bracket recognition problem, either the data-driven or the model-driven approach could be used. In the data-driven approach the system may start initially without a model. The first training instance would supply the initial concept of the archetype. Additional training instances would broaden the model to encompass the new instance as well. This could be accomplished by increasing matching tolerances in the model. Depending on the format of the model, the tolerances might be for lengths of edge segments or angles of connection of the segments.

The same target problem could be model-driven. In this case the system would be primed with a very broad description of the part and would have wide tolerances. Then the model could be refined by training with either positive or negative training cases. With negative training cases the model tolerances would be reduced if an accidental classification of the negative example occurred. For positive training cases a stepwise procedure could be used to reduce the tolerances to more aptly fit the training case.

In summary, inductive learning can be applied under a variety of conditions. It is primarily effective when training data is available either as positive or negative examples. The training data can be a prepared set, or can be selected by the machine under its own guidance. (In either case, however, the correct answer needs to be available for the purposes of feedback to the learning system.) An indication of algorithm learning performance can always be obtained by reserving some instances of the training set for testing purposes.

One drawback of learning systems is that it may be forced to make a tradeoff with its bias. If the system is strongly biased, it will have a narrower set of solutions that can be learned. This can lead to a higher learning rate by bypassing ranges of knowledge, but if an effective concept lies in the excluded range then it will never be discovered.

5. CASE STUDY

This section presents a case study to demonstrate how the methods presented in the last section can be applied. The design of the system is developed step by step, and the rationale for the necessary tradeoffs is presented as appropriate. Finally, results are presented to show what type of gain a system can experience with the addition of learning techniques.

The target system is a general stereo vision system. It is designed to be used as an integral stage in a 3D object recognition system or an image understanding system. It is general in the sense that it performs standard feature matching to achieve correspondences used to gauge depth. The following section briefly describes the stereo matching system. This is necessary to understand the rationale for the tradeoffs to be made in the system with the addition of a learning component.

5.1. System Background

In our study, we use a correspondence-based stereopsis algorithm whose local correspondences are constrained by a number of parameters such as epipolar constraints and orientation. Our algorithm belongs to Marr and Poggio's paradigm that uses monocular feature extraction, local stereopsis, and global stereopsis (6). Other models of stereopsis (16, 18) are not considered in this study.

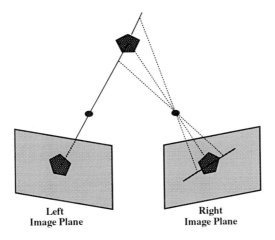

Figure 9.2. Stereo camera setup.

The standard two-camera (binocular) stereo vision setup is shown in Fig. 9.2. Here the two cameras are pictured facing into the page. The object being imaged is the pentagon. One image alone (left) narrows the position in 3D space to a line passing through the focus of the camera and the position of the object in the image. The matching position of the object in the second image (right) conveys where along that line the object lies. The general procedure for discrete binocular stereo vision can be summarized in five steps:

1. Obtain two images from different viewpoints.
2. Extract the tokens, or scene features, from each image to use for matching. (This information is known as the *primal sketch*.) (5, pp. 188–193).
3. Determine the correspondence between tokens found in each image. (This results in the disparity map.)
4. Translate disparity values into depth values. (This results in the depth map.)
5. Interpolate over the depth map as necessary for the desired resolution of depth information.

The first step can be accomplished using two cameras separated by a small distance, say, 25 cm. A typical image might be 512 × 512 pixels with 8 bits for recording pixel intensity, i.e., 256 gray levels.

In the second step, the matchable features are extracted from the intensity information. Edge detection preprocessing is used to extract these higher-level tokens. Tokens, such as edges, tend to emphasize areas of interest for object identification, and these are points at which depth information can be useful.

The third step, known as the *correspondence problem*, has traditionally been the most difficult. If the matching criteria are too loose, then depth information is lost because of ambiguous potential matches. However, if the matching criteria are too restrictive, then depth information is lost because no match can be found. There is no known analytic function to optimize for the selection of the matching criteria. The problem is best approached by heuristic methods generated by either human experts or machines.

The fourth step in the stereo matching procedure is to transform disparities into depths. This is straightforward when given the geometry of the camera setup. Horn (3) gives a concise outline of this procedure.

The fifth and final step of interpolating depth values can be solved with a variety of interpolation methods as well as with knowledge-driven interpolation schemes. For the sake of simplicity, the nearest-neighbor method is used here.

The procedure in steps 2 and 3 is repeated iteratively to refine the depth measurements made by the system. The idea is to start by extracting few, but prominent, tokens using a large search region. This provides a good initial depth estimate. Further stages extract more tokens but can use previous depth information to reduce the size of the search region. Each stage of this algorithm is called a *channel*, and each channel has a granularity defined by the "coarseness" of the tokens extracted at that stage. One attractive aspect of this approach is that it is thought to be similar to the process used in biological visual systems (2). A pictorial view of the algorithm is shown in Fig. 9.3.

The matching of corresponding features in the images occurs on a medium level. The tokens that are matched consist of edge pixels or *edgels*. The edgel extraction is done using an enhanced version of the Canny edge detector (1) that employs hysteresis for greater edge continuity and retains midprocessing information to be used for matching.

5.2. System Analysis

After choosing the vision algorithm to be used, the designer needs to analyze the algorithm and determines the goals of the learning system. At this point, the exact learning mechanisms are of secondary importance as compared to the goals of learning, which drives the strategy-selection process. (Strategy selection is presented in Section 5.3.)

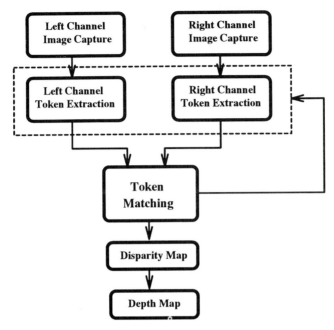

Figure 9.3. Stereo algorithm flowchart.

5.2.1. Specification of the Target Domain

This first step is to select the target domain based on the application requirements. Since the system will be learning on its own, it is necessary to provide it with training cases. The main effort of this step is, therefore, to decide the types of images that are representative of the domain. In our study, we have chosen day scenes of an outdoor environment. A sample stereo pair is presented in Fig. 9.4. The image training domain consists of 30 image pairs. Each stereo pair is a 128×128 gray-scale image with 256 gray levels.

To allow for automated experimentation, it is also necessary to supply the system with correct results for guidance. Here we want to ensure the accuracy of token matching; hence, we enhance the image database by adding the correct matches for sample components within the image. We manually selected and matched 10 sample test points from each image and recorded the correct disparity in the database.

At this point, it is also necessary to divide the training set in order to reserve some of the samples for testing the final vision algorithm to be learned. Another reason for reserving samples is to help detect common problems among learning systems: sometimes systems become very proficient at processing over their training set, yet they become so optimized that their performance actually drops on other test cases. Having a

A   B

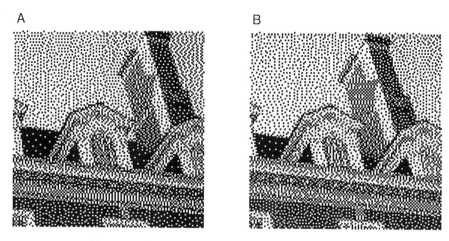

Figure 9.4. Sample stereo pair: (A) right image; (B) left image.

fraction of the training set reserved for testing can identify when this problem occurs.

5.2.2. Component Selection

The next step in the analysis phase is to isolate the components, or parameters, that are appropriate for machine learning. Using the general algorithm as outlined above, the methods suited for machine tuning lie in steps 2 and 3. These areas have the greatest impact on system performance and also the greatest flexibility. From these steps, the designer may first enumerate what exactly is open to machine adjustment. Table 9.1 lists the adjustable components that may be selected in this general token-based stereo matching algorithm. (Note that the unit of "pixel" as used in the table is a distance measure equal to the width of one pixel.) The list of parameters considered in Table 9.1 assumes a vision algorithm similar to Marr and Poggio's (6).

There are two problems facing the selection of the appropriate parameters. First, as is evident from Table 9.1, the parameters are continuous and can sometimes be unbounded. This means that the potential parameter space is infinite and, without a strong bias in the learning system, it becomes impossible to explore many of the possible combinations. The second problem is that there is little information available to guide the search for the appropriate parameters. Our approach is to use parameters determined intuitively by designers as a good starting point, and apply a machine-coordinated search for better values.

TABLE 9.1

Stereo Algorithm Parameter List

Parameter	Function and Purpose	Range	Units
Number of channels	Aids matching density by refining the search region and obtaining increasingly dense depth estimates	≥ 1	
Blurring kernel size	Width (σ) of the Gaussian filter used to select the strength of detected edges; along with the edge detection thresholds, this controls the density of edges detected in a particular channel	0.1–5.0	pixels
High threshold	Upper limit of gradient strength for hysteresis of edge thresholding	1–255	$\dfrac{\partial \text{ intensity}}{\partial \text{ pixel}}$
Low threshold	Lower limit on gradient strength allowed for edge classification	0–255	$\dfrac{\partial \text{ intensity}}{\partial \text{ pixel}}$
Initial search window	Size of region to initially consider for a match	1–200	pixels
Similarity thresholds	Used to determine if tokens are a match (similar)		
Gradient	Difference in gradient magnitude	1–50	$\Delta \dfrac{\partial \text{ intensity}}{\partial \text{ pixel}}$
Orientation	Difference in edgel orientation	$\lvert \cdot \rvert \leq 30$	degrees
Vertical position	Difference in vertical position	± 1–3	pixels

The first step is to narrow the possible component space to the most important factors. The choice for the initial subset is made regarding the effect and function that the parameters had on performance. Of the parameters listed, the number of channels, the blurring factor for each channel, and the edge detection gradient thresholds have been selected as the domain for the machine to search through. The other parameters were assigned values selected by experimentation and were held constant throughout the experiments. This set provides an acceptable balance between the size of the search space and the importance of the parameters; it is best to start with a small learning domain and increase the range searched incrementally. For a typical candidate, the number of channels varied from one to five, and the σ of the blurring kernel varied from 0.1 to 5.0.

The final form for a candidate parameter can be viewed as a set of triplets. Each triplet gives the parameters for a particular channel. For example, the expression

$$\{(\sigma_1, lt_1, ht_1), (\sigma_2, lt_2, ht_2)\}$$

would represent the parameters comprising a two-channel candidate.

5.2.3. Expressing the Learning Objective

For the learning system to operate autonomously, it must be able to gauge its performance. The designer must specify the performance metric precisely so that it can be expressed in a machine-usable form. This metric is known as the *objective function*, whose inputs can be thought of as the algorithm components to be learned. In general terms, the goal of the system is to maximize the objective function over the learnable component space given the training database as input. To formulate the objective function, the designer must assess the goals of the vision system and represent them concisely for the learning system to use. Note that one possible way that the objective can be expressed is an equation with both symbolic and numerical components. Other possible forms include constraint equations that define where desirable parameter sets would lie.

In most applications, the designer is faced with overall performance requirements that must be met. It is from this that the quality of an algorithm is measured. For example, requirements could consist of a time limit or a minimum accuracy. In this respect, however, the objective is ill-defined. In other words, the precise performance tradeoff of accuracy or speed is not known and can be left to the system to decide. With respect to the stereo-matching problem, there are three factors used to judge its general performance:

1. *Speed*—the rate at which a unit area of the depth map is calculated
2. *Density*—the fraction of the image for which depth information is determined
3. *Accuracy*—the average error in depth measurements

The relative importance of each factor, of course, depends on the parent application employing the stereo system. The bias of application-specific modifications to the algorithm can be set by the user by formulating a particular equation of these three measurements. Without specifying minimum allowable values in the performance criterion, a simple performance equation might be

$$\text{Performance} = \text{speed} \times \text{density} \times \text{accuracy}. \qquad (1)$$

This example objective function is specified as a mathematical function of three parameters, but because the actual objective is ill-defined, we should use a more flexible objective that can adapt to various application requirements. One possibility is to parametrize Eq. (1) as a family of functions and set bounds on allowable time, acceptable density, and acceptable accuracy of depth information. For example, the accuracy component can be expressed parametrically and could take a functional form itself. Similarly, other application-specific measures may be substituted as components in the objective function. An example might be the end goal of the vision system, such as the 3D model to be matched. This would allow the stereo vision system to be tuned with respect to its specific impact on the vision task at hand. An example of a formulation used in our case study is given in Eq. (4) later in this chapter. This function consists of a time penalty, an accuracy weight, and a density weight to measure performance.

In the rest of this chapter, we assume that it is the task of the learning system to hypothesize a set of more specific alternative objectives by performing tests. These objectives will be implicitly arrived at by natural tradeoffs made by the system. In turn, the particular objective function defined indirectly determines the types of candidates that the system finds. The objective function would be a function of only the stereo vision algorithm parameters and would return a measure of quality. It is expressed as a function of intermediate values gathered by performing tests on the candidate component set. Of course, it is the user's responsibility to review the machine-generated results and determine the most appropriate *explicit* tradeoff needed.

The objective defined in Eq. (1) involves tradeoffs among the cost of running the vision algorithm and the quality of the matched tokens returned by the algorithm. We assume that a fixed amount of time is allowed for completing the algorithm. Exceeding (and even approaching) this limit penalizes the fitness of a candidate. This is consistent with many real-world situations in which the vision system plays a role in a chain of cognitive acts and reacts to inputs in real time. Performing faster than this deadline would not be considered particularly useful. *Cost* is then defined as a penalty in exceeding the specified time limit, where the penalty function is defined in terms of t, the time for the test

$$p(t) = \frac{1 + e^{-qt_0}}{1 + e^{q(t-t_0)}}.$$

(2)

The parameter q allows tailoring the penalty function with respect to the time limit t_0. The graph of the penalty function for $q = 0.05$ and $t_0 = 120$ seconds is shown in Fig. 9.5.

Other than the speed of the stereo vision algorithm, it is also important to maximize the density as well as the accuracy. *Density* is measured in

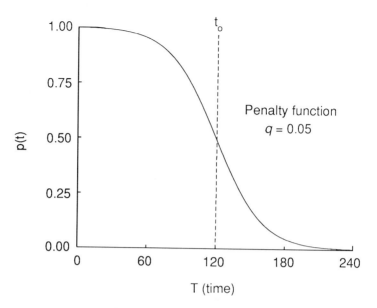

Figure 9.5. Time penalty function.

terms of the fraction of the image for which corresponding edgels were found. *Accuracy* is measured by probing the resulting disparity map and comparing the values with known disparities. For the test images in our database, 10 points were measured per image. The accuracy used by the objective function is the normalized average disparity error with 0 error mapping to 1, and an error of e_{max} pixels or more mapping to 0. (The value of e_{max} used for our system was varied to simulate the effect of different application requirements. See Section 4.)

The final form of the objective function [Eq. (4)] is then a product of density (in matches per square pixel), normalized accuracy, and the time penalty function. It is computed as the average quality of the candidate as measured over each test image in the database. The quality measure over one image i with parameter set P is $q(i, P)$. This is a function of three intermediate test results that are each functions of the image and the algorithm parameters. The three components are $d(i, P)$, density of disparity measurements; $a(i, P)$, average accuracy of disparity measurements; and $t(i, P)$, time to process the image

$$q(i, P) = d(i, P) \times a(i, P) \times p[t(i, P)]. \qquad (3)$$

The objective function, $O(P)$, now takes the form shown in Eq. (4), where P is the set of candidate parameters and B is the set of the N

images in the database

$$O(P, B) = q_{av} = \frac{1}{N} \sum_{i \in B} q(i, P).$$ (4)

The objective function stated here is really one in a large family of possible objectives. By varying components such as t_0, q, and e_{max}, the user can make the system search for particular parameter sets for different applications (cf. Tables 9.4 and 9.5). This kind of information is of interest because it shows how the system focuses on different classes of candidates under different system requirements.

5.3. Machine Learning Enhancements

After analyzing the vision problem from an algorithmic perspective, we need to select the appropriate learning mechanisms. These mechanisms include the structure of system knowledge and the methods for manipulating knowledge. Together these components will form the bias of the system and determine what can and cannot be learned.

5.3.1. Knowledge Selection

To specify the format for system knowledge, it is helpful to analyze how a human would behave in the machine's place. A person would track candidate performance and would develop an understanding of what makes one candidate better than another. A person would also keep track of the deadline for finding the solution. This would have an influence on how many experiments would be performed as time passed. In the beginning of the process, it might be best to try a variety of different strategies to gain a feeling for the relationship that particular parameters have on system performance. As time runs out, it would be best to focus on fine-tuning the parameters.

With this view, the system will need to store and manipulate three types of knowledge: (1) past candidate performance, (2) candidate performance relationships, and (3) system constraints and goals.

Past candidate performance can be stored in a performance database indexed by candidate identifiers. These identifiers are simply tags unique to the algorithm components. The values of past performance are the intermediate performance measurements obtained by applying the algorithm to sample images. There will be a performance entry in this database for every test image to which the candidate has been applied.

The relationship between candidates is important because it can be used to guide the creation of new candidates. Each relationship is stored as a "delta" vector in the candidate components with an associated value for the measured change in performance. This type of knowledge must be carefully maintained for two reasons. First, it can grow exponentially with the number of candidates. Therefore, it is best to limit remembered relationships to neighbors that are close within the component space. The second reason for maintaining the knowledge is that ineffective relationships can cause an unnecessary waste of time and storage space. The system must be able to track relationships and learn when a potentially promising one has created only false leads. The specific details of relationship knowledge and how they are to be used are discussed in more detail in Section 5.3.2.

The final piece of knowledge that the system must maintain is the set of constraints and the goals of the system. Any practical learning system will be faced with resource constraints, and, therefore, must tailor its actions to best reach the assigned goals in view of the constraints. The goals are represented in either the objective function or in the cost and quality constraints, and can take the form of a mathematical function or a symbolic expression. The knowledge of the time constraints are stored explicitly in the form of a deadline, but the knowledge that guides how to coordinate achievement of the goals under the deadline is stored implicitly in the candidate-generation mechanism. This mechanism is described next.

5.3.2. Candidate Creation

Initially, some sample parameter sets (or candidates) are specified by the user. As testing progresses, however, the system needs to be able to create new candidates. Since each candidate the system creates represents a potential increase or decrease of algorithm performance, it is important to create new candidates that are guided by structures of promising candidates (those with good sample performance values). If they were created haphazardly, we could almost be guaranteed to spend our computational resources on many poorly performing ones.

The generation of new candidates is handled by using rules to represent knowledge in candidate generation. Because of the limited amount of time available for testing, the candidate generator should refer to the performance of previous candidates when generating new ones. Two methods are used here: pseudorandom and greedy. In the pseudorandom approach, a new candidate is generated by a perturbation from one of the existing candidates. The candidate used as a basis for this perturbation must lie in the top third of the existing candidates. In the greedy approach, the generator tries to follow the "direction" of the greatest improvement in performance, based on the performance of candidates already generated. This direction is expressed as a vector of the delta values between the parameters of the two candidates.

The knowledge for candidate creation is stored in the form of rules. This rule-based implementation is flexible enough to allow the addition of further domain knowledge as it becomes available. New operators and rules can easily be added to give incremental improvement. The rule base consists of a set of assertions called *working memory* and a set of rules for operating on it. A rule consists of two parts: a list of conditions and a list of actions. When all conditions within a rule are met, the rule is said to fire, and all the associated actions are carried out. In general, a rule-based system allows asynchronous execution of rules by relying on a conflict-resolution strategy to select one rule to fire at a time. In this case, however, the rule base executes the rules sequentially. A condition can be either a pattern or a function. A pattern is considered met by finding a unification between the pattern and an assertion within the working memory, whereas a function is considered met when it returns a nonempty value. Variable assignments and wildcards can be used in both patterns and functions. There are three basic types of actions: (1) delete an existing assertion from working memory, (2) add a new assertion to working memory, and (3) execute a function.

Actions can use values of variables assigned in the conditional parts of rules. This approach allows a flexible system for analyzing existing candidates and for generating new ones.

The creation of a candidate follows a regular procedure. During this process, only well-tested candidates are considered worthy of reference. (Relatively untested candidates are avoided because their "goodness" may not yet be particularly reliable or stable.) A candidate is considered well tested if the confidence of its performance is above a given level for its sample mean to lie within a certain range of its population mean.

The first step in candidate creation is to select a reference candidate from which to create the new one. This candidate is randomly selected from the top third of the well-tested candidates in the pool. Next, the candidate's neighbors are checked to see if they have better performance. If so, then the reference candidate is updated to be the best neighbor. This candidate will now serve as the basis for the new candidate. Following this, the neighbors of the reference candidate are again polled for their performance values. The "direction" of the greatest change in performance is then recorded. This direction is represented as a numerical vector (called a *transform*) that specifies the change in the parameters between the two candidates. If no existing candidates lie in the path of this transform, then the transform is applied to the reference candidate to generate the new one. However, if this transform leads into a region of the parameter space already occupied by a candidate, then a random transformation is created to move into unexplored space. The random transform is created by first recording the transforms from the reference candidate to the neighbors. One of the channels of the transform is then selected for modification. An individual replacement channel transformation is then randomly created. If it is found to be similar to any of the existing transforms for that channel, then the channel transform is recreated, but with a greater magnitude. This process continues until the new transform leads to an unexplored region of the parameter space.

This method of candidate generation combines two important concepts. The first is that existing good transformations are followed. This gives an effect similar to hill-climbing in the parameter space. The second benefit of this method is that randomness is employed as a hedge against stagnation in a local maximum on the objective-function "surface." This randomness is exploited in two ways. First, it is used as the reference candidate and is set by randomly selecting from the top third of all candidates, rather than just using the top, or *incumbent*, candidate. Second, as the local regions of the parameter space become more well searched, the transforms try to break away from the current region by issuing larger perturbations.

Table 9.2 lists the candidate-generation rules more explicitly. In the table, C_{ref} is the chosen reference candidate, C_{max} is the best neighbor of the reference candidate, and C_{inc} is the incumbent (or best) candidate.

TABLE 9.2

Rules Used for Candidate Generation

Rule no.	Description
1	Randomly select C_{ref} from the top third of the well-tested candidates
2	If there is a candidate in the same neighborhood as C_{ref} that is better than C_{ref} and has a greater quality disparity from C_{ref} than all others in the neighborhood, then use that candidate instead of C_{ref}
3	If no candidate in the neighborhood of C_{ref} has a performance in the top $\frac{2}{3}$ of all well-tested candidates, then use C_{inc} instead of C_{ref}
4	Find a candidate C_{max} with the greatest disparity from C_{ref} among all candidates in the neighborhood; record T_{max} as the transformation that creates this disparity and Δ as the change in quality
5	Use the transform that caused the highest increase in performance in the neighborhood of C_{ref} as the basis transform for generating a new candidate
6	If there are no existing candidates in the direction of the basis transformation, then use the basis transformation to generate the new candidate
7	Otherwise, generate progressively greater transforms until one is found that leads to an unexplored region of the parameter space; then apply this transform to C_{ref} to generate the new candidate

Unfortunately, the domain of stereo vision parameter tuning is knowl-edge-lean; that is, the knowledge that leads to the generation of better candidates is either very difficult to acquire or too expensive to be useful. Therefore, it is more important to have an efficient procedure for testing the generated candidates than to develop methods for capturing new knowledge for candidate generation. Generating parameter sets and test-ing them in a controlled manner is commonly used by knowledgeable experts who hand-tune the parameters themselves. This tedious task is best handled by automated machine learning; the difficulty, of course, is to transfer some of the expertise from the designer to the system so that the added speed and patience are put to proper use.

Each unique set of parameter values is considered a separate entity, or candidate, that could possibly lead to an improvement. The creation mechanism decides how many new candidates to create, how to create them, and how to schedule the available testing time. On the basis of a statistical model, the system trades between the quality and the cost of the vision algorithm learned, and incorporates methods such as gradient ascent to overcome the knowledge-lean aspect of the learning problem.

Even with the measure of the algorithm quality clearly defined, it is still not straightforward to automate the process of finding better parameter values. To fully evaluate the performance of a parameter set, it is neces-sary to test it over the entire training domain database. Clearly, a gradient-ascent-type method is impractical here. For such a method to work, it would be necessary to perform full evaluation frequently. The primary tradeoff is between the number of candidates to be evaluated and the amount of evaluation performed on each.

The generate-and-test framework used here is geared toward searching an ill-defined space under a given time constraint (see Fig. 9.6). Before examining its structure, it is necessary to define some terms. The set of all candidates currently under consideration for testing is called the *candidate pool*, and the set of images used for testing the candidates is called the *test database*.

The three main parts that constitute the core of the framework are the *candidate generator*, the *candidate evaluator*, and the *resource scheduler*. The candidate generator creates new candidates for consideration; the candidate evaluator tests the candidates on the test images and records their performance; and the resource scheduler determines which candi-date to test next.

If there is much domain knowledge available, then the candidate gener-ator can be very sophisticated. In this case, the candidate evaluator plays a subordinate role. However, in knowledge-lean domains, the candidate generator is relatively primitive. Therefore, the burden of selecting good

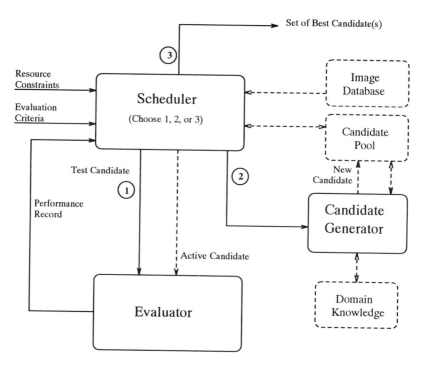

Figure 9.6. Generate-and-test framework.

heuristics shifts to the resource scheduler and the candidate evaluator. Such is the case in the stereo vision domain. Consequently, the focus is placed on the resource scheduler and the candidate evaluator. (It is worth noting, however, that the strategies presented here are general enough to be applicable to knowledge-rich domains as well.)

To avoid spending a large amount of time on poor candidates, the evaluation process is divided into small subtests called *quanta*. This allows the system to perform additional tests on candidates *only* if they demonstrate some merit during prior quanta. During one quantum of time, tests are performed on the selected candidate using test images from a data-base supplied by the user. There are two possibilities for the test images used here. They can be either relatively small images (64 × 64) that give only a mild indication of fitness of the candidate, or they, can be fairly large images (512 × 512) that give a good indication of candidate fitness. The advantage of the latter approach is that the candidate is tested under more realistic conditions; however, its drawback is that the duration of one quantum must be large enough to accommodate the test. This can then have an adverse effect on the system's performance. In the stereo vision domain, parameter-set performance scales relatively well from small to large test images. Therefore, candidates are tested using small images, with the goal being to find the candidate with the greatest average performance. Of course, the optimal objective is to find a candidate that performs the best in all cases. This, however, is impractical or impossible to verify unless all candidates are evaluated over the exact same (and possibly infinite) set of test images representing the application domain. This would imply that all candidates (including the worst) must be evaluated to an equal degree.

At the end of each quantum the scheduler selects one of the following actions to perform:

1. Select the next candidate to test from the candidate pool.
2. Generate a new candidate to be placed in the candidate pool (and possibly remove an existing one from the pool).
3. If the deadline has been reached, select a set of the best candidates and terminate testing.

The decision between choices 1 and 2 is based on the current performance of the candidates in the pool and the amount of evaluation that has been performed on each. One simple method for determining when to generate new candidates for the pool is to generate new ones whenever existing ones have been evaluated to have a performance value known to within a statistical confidence level.

If the decision is made to pursue choice 1 or 3, then the candidate(s) is (are) selected on the basis of an *evaluation criterion*. This consists of two parts: the *goodness function* and the *guidance strategy*.

The goodness function is an estimator of the value of the objective function [Eq. (4)]. It is used to select from the pool the candidate that most likely performs the best. It is needed because candidates may not be fully evaluated to within a statistical confidence when testing is terminated.

The guidance strategy is used (if testing is continued) to select the candidate to be evaluated during the next quantum. The goal of the guidance strategy is to choose a candidate that maximizes the probability that the candidates with the highest objective values also have the highest goodness values. It is not always best to select the most promising candidate to test because a candidate may show less promise when limited tests have been performed but might appear better with more tests. Moreover, with limited resources, it might be necessary to explore more candidates early in the generate-and-test process and focus on a limited set of promising ones as time runs out. This tradeoff is addressed by using a statistical model for sequential selection.

If the decision is made to pursue choice 2, then a new candidate must be generated. The candidate generator used here is driven by a fixed set of

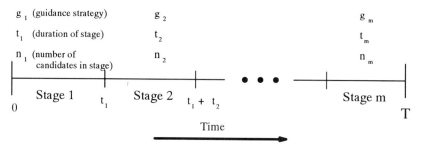

Figure 9.7. The multistage testing procedure.

rules. An outline of the actual code comprising this framework can be found in Schwartz (12).

Guidance strategies must be developed to take into account limited resources such as testing time, and that can deal with situations in which there are so many candidates that it would be impossible to test them all even once. Because of these conditions, the guidance strategies must trade between the number of candidates that can be tested and the accuracy of the sample mean for selecting the best candidate in the end. If more candidates are tested, then the accuracy of the estimated performance would decrease, and the final selection of the best candidate would likely be in error. If a candidate is tested more thoroughly, then fewer total candidates can be tested and, therefore, a greater chance of missing a good one entirely.

To overcome these problems, it is necessary to formulate a general guidance strategy $G(T)$. This is accomplished as a series of stages in which each stage is represented by $G_i(g_i, t_i, n_i)$, where i ranges from 1 to m, the number of stages. Each stage is then characterized by the triplet g_i, t_i, n_i. The particular guidance strategy to be used for stage i is g_i; the duration of the stage is t_i; and the number of candidates to be considered for testing during that stage is n_i (see Fig. 9.7). In this methodology, the early stages correspond to coarse initial testing used to weed out unworthy candidates, and the latter stages correspond to more careful evaluation of the better candidates. Of course, only the candidates that have the top n_{i+1} sample-mean performance values at the end of stage i are carried over into stage $i + 1$ for further testing. Finally, only the top candidate is selected at the end of the last stage. This entire procedure is a way of incrementally increasing the bias of the learning system by allowing many candidates to be tested in the early stages, and by obtaining accurate sample-mean values for the better candidates by more thorough tests in later stages. For a full discussion of a variety of guidance strategies the reader is referred to Ieumwananonthachai *et al.* (4).

This section presents some of the actual results of implementing the system described in the previous sections. The results were generated from actual runs of different durations and with different objective-function formulations. (In addition, simulated runs are presented to provide a more complete picture.) Before performing the experiments in the actual runs, the candidate pool was seeded with six candidates that were tuned by hand (see Table 9.3). All experiments started with these candidates to show the different types of candidates that can be discovered as the available time and the objective function are modified. From these initial candidates, the rules shown in Table 9.2 were applied to generate new candidates as necessary. At the end of each run, all candidates were then fully evaluated over all images in the database. Here the database consisted of 30 images. Testing of the candidates was performed on a Sparc IPC workstation using the general binocular stereo algorithm implemented in C language. Typical execution times were roughly 20 seconds per channel on the 128×128 gray-scale images. Of course, this time varied widely depending on the number of tokens found in each channel. This full evaluation allows judging the performance of the system by giving insight into the quality/time tradeoff. The quality loss is the difference between the best found under the guided system and the best found by

TABLE 9.3

Hand-Tuned Seed Candidates

Candidate number	Channel width	Low threshold	High threshold
1	1.3	2.0	5.0
2	0.6	2.0	5.0
3	0.9	2.0	5.0
	0.6	2.0	5.0
4	1.8	2.0	5.0
	1.5	2.0	5.0
5	2.4	2.0	5.0
	1.7	2.0	5.0
	1.0	2.0	5.0
6	3.0	2.0	5.0
	1.0	2.0	5.0
	0.4	2.0	5.0
7	1.8	2.0	5.0
	1.3	2.0	5.0
	0.8	2.0	5.0
	0.6	2.0	5.0

TABLE 9.4

Performance from Actual Tests with Varying Objectives

Objective parameters	Total duration (in no. of tests)	
	200	400
$t_0 = 60$	2.4–2.0–5.0/1.7–2.0–5.0/ 1.3–0.5–2.2(22)	2.4–2.0–6.6/1.5–1.7–5.0/1.0–2.0–5.0(18)
$e_{max} = 5$	0.0369	0.0416
$t_0 = 60$	1.3–0.5–4.3/1.5–2.0–4.8(29)	2.4–2.5–5.0/1.7–2.0–5.0/1.0–1.6–5.0(140)
$e_{max} = 2.5$	0.0143	0.0251
$t_0 = 45$	1.6–1.4–2.5/0.7–4.0–8.3(30)	3.0–2.0–5.0/1.4–2.1–2.1/1.1–1.7–2.2(109)
$e_{max} = 5$	0.0284	0.0430
$t_0 = 30$	2.4–2.0–5.0/1.4–2.0–6.2/ 1.0–2.0–5.0(48)	1.8–0.6–5.0/1.7–4.0–4.9/1.3–2.0–5.0/ 0.9–0.7–5.6(134)
$e_{max} = 2.5$	0.0199	0.0200

exhaustive tests. The time gain is the amount of time saved by using a guidance strategy rather than blind exhaustive tests. The full evaluation corresponds to finding the values of the objective function for the given candidates.

During actual tests, the testing strategy that was used was a two-stage round-robin–minimum-risk strategy (4, 12). The division of time between the two stages was equal.

Results from a combination of actual and simulated runs are combined to present a full picture, because it is very time-consuming to perform extensive tests on candidates whose individual test times can range from 1 to 2 minutes. (Simulated runs were performed by using preevaluated candidates rather than generating them on the fly.) For 200 candidates tested on 30 images, the total testing time can last up to 7 days. For this reason, it can be beneficial to perform additional simulations using results recorded from actual tests, if the simulations are close to observed actual results. Since a simulation can take less than an hour to complete, it clearly results in a great time savings. The problem with simulation, however, is that candidate generation is not modeled. Therefore, the candidates that were generated by the one recorded run will be the only ones used during the simulation. Nevertheless, empirical evidence has shown that simulation performance is very close to that of actual tests. Some justification for this conclusion can be found by comparing the results shown in Table 9.4 for real tests (those with candidate generation) and the results shown in Table 9.5 (the simulations).

For the actual (nonsimulated) tests of the system, three objective functions were tested for three different durations. The parameters of the objective functions that were used as well as the test durations are

TABLE 9.5

Performance from Simulated Tests with Varying Objectives

Time limit (t_0 in seconds)	Error Cutoff (e_{max})			
	2.5	5	7.5	10
5	2.4-2.0-5.0/1.7-2.0-5.0/ 1.0-2.0-5.0 0.0163	1.5-2.3-2.7(24) 0.0225	3.0-2.0-5.0/1.4-2.1-2.1/ 1.11-1.7-2.2(109) 0.0319	1.5-2.3-2.7(24) 0.0342
10	2.3-2.0-5.0/2.3-1.0-4.3/ 1.0-2.0-3.7(156) 0.0146	3.1-1.2-5.8/1.1-4.6-4.6/ 0.8-1.1-3.7(122) 0.0225	2.8-2.0-5.0/1.9-3.5-4.4/ 1.2-2.5-6.1(48) 0.0312	1.5-2.3-2.7(24) 0.0350
20	2.2-0.7-3.6/1.5-2.4-3.1/ 1.0-2.2-5.0(34) 0.0167	2.7-2.7-7.2/1.7-2.0-5.0/ 1.0-2.0-3.7(85) 0.0264	3.0-2.0-5.0/1.4-2.1-2.1/ 1.1-1.7-2.2(109) 0.0384	3.0-2.0-5.0/1.4-2.1-2.1/ 1.1-1.7-2.2(109) 0.0408
30	2.2-0.7-3.6/1.5-2.4-3.1/ 1.0-1.5-4.1(58) 0.0173	2.8-2.0-5.0/1.9-3.5-4.4/ 1.2-2.5-6.1(48) 0.0319	3.0-2.0-5.0/1.4-2.1-2.1/ 1.1-1.7-2.2(109) 0.0431	2.4-1.0-6.4/1.7-2.0-5.0/ 1.0-2.0-3.7(104) 0.0390
60	2.4-2.0-5.0/2.1-2.0-5.4/ 1.0-0.5-5.2(69) 0.0266	2.4-1.0-6.4/1.7-2.0-5.0/ 1.0-2.0-3.7(104) 0.0392	2.4-1.3-6.3/1.7-2.0-5.0/ 1.0-2.0-3.7(45) 0.0460	2.8-2.0-5.0/1.3-3.5-4.6/ 0.6-2.5-6.1(39) 0.0456

presented in Table 9.4. Each entry of this table lists the identity of the best parameter set that was found, as well as its performance, that is, the value of the objective function after 30 tests. The parameter set for each channel is encoded in the form (channel width–low-threshold–high-threshold) with channels separated by a "/". The number in parentheses at the end of the candidate name indicates that this was the nth candidate to be generated.

Simulated results for the case of a fixed duration and different objectives are shown in Table 9.5. Here two of the parameters constituting the objective function are shown on different axes (horizontal and vertical) of the table. Each entry in the table shows the identity of the best candidate as well as its performance value. The duration for each learning experiment was 400 tests.

As can be seen from Table 9.5, the objective function plays a major role in determining the sought-after solution. The difference in the results for varying t_0 and e_{max} demonstrates the two purposes of the objective function: the ability to express the goals of the designer, and the guidance of the search in an automated fashion. It is also beneficial to see the effect of extending the available testing time. As would be expected, spending more time should produce better solutions.

The best candidates found by the various objectives shown above are difficult to appreciate when the results are listed in a strictly numerical format. Presented here are some graphical results in the form of input images and matched results for the best performing seed candidate and the candidate found after 200 tests. These were generated with $t_0 = 30$, and $e_{max} = 5$. Each set of images consists of the stereo pair, the left and right edge maps found on the original channels, and those found on the discovered channels. The 3D relief of the matched edges and the disparity map are also presented for both parameter sets. The disparity map is generated by interpolating the entire image area by nearest-neighbor disparity values. It is meant to give only an indication of depth throughout the scene, since this type of interpolation does *not* preserve object outlines and appearances. The left and right images are displayed with the right image on the left so that it is possible for the viewer to merge them by crossing the eyes if desired. One thing that is not appreciable from the pictures, however, is the speed-up in execution. In all cases, the machine-tuned parameters performed faster and resulted in a 15–30% improvement as measured by the objective function. In the cases shown here, the best original parameter set was candidate number 5 from Table 9.3. The best parameter set found after a simulation with 600 time units with the above stated objective was used for the results shown below. This candidate was 2.2–2.0–7.0/1.6–3.8–3.8/1.3–3.0–3.6(41).

This first example, shown in Fig. 9.8, is of a sample building scene. Figures 9.9–9.14 show the old and new edge maps extracted for each channel. This image was processed in 115.26 seconds with the original

A   B

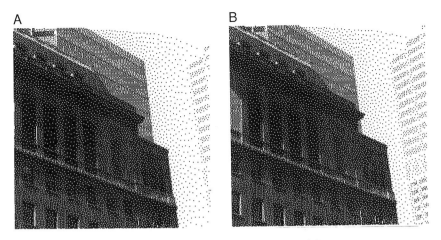

Figure 9.8. Building stereo pair: (A) right image; (B) left image.

parameters, and 78.83 seconds with the discovered (new) ones. The accuracy, however, dropped from 2.83 pixels to 3.12, but as the objective function emphasized speed, the new parameter set had a performance of 0.021 as opposed to the original 0.017. Figures 9.15(A) and (B) compare the 3D outline for the original and the new parameters, respectively. Figure 9.16 displays the same scene except in the form of an interpolated depth map with intensity representing depth.

Figure 9.17 shows a sample street scene. This image was processed in 130.71 seconds with the original parameters, and 100.10 seconds with the

A   B

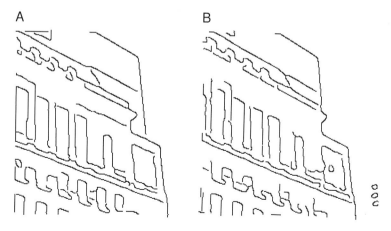

Figure 9.9. Original channel 1: (A) right; (B) left.

A   B

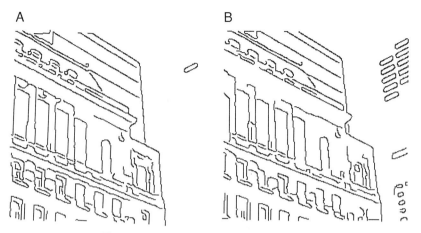

Figure 9.10. Original channel 2: (A) right; (B) left.

discovered (new) ones. In this case, the accuracy dropped from 1.4 pixels to 2.4. Nevertheless, the great increase in speed allowed the objective function to increase from 0.024 to 0.034, a 42% improvement. Figures 9.18–9.23 show the old and new edge maps extracted for each channel. Figures 9.24(A) and (B) compare the 3D outline for the original and the new parameters, respectively. Figure 9.25 displays the same scene except in the form of an interpolated depth map with intensity representing depth.

A   B

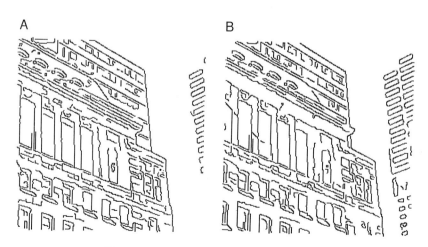

Figure 9.11. Original channel 3: (A) right; (B) left.

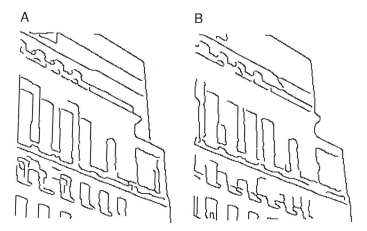

Figure 9.12. New channel 1: (A) right; (B) left.

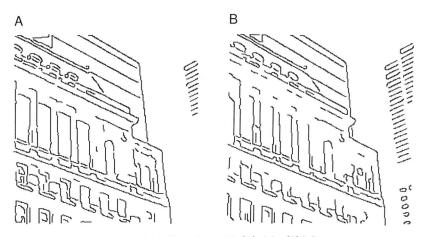

Figure 9.13. New channel 2: (A) right; (B) left.

A   B

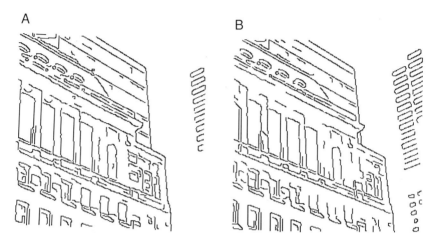

Figure 9.14. New channel 3: (A) right; (B) left.

A   B

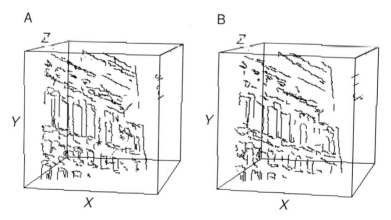

Figure 9.15. Scatter plot of points, 3D comparison: (A) original; (B) new.

A B

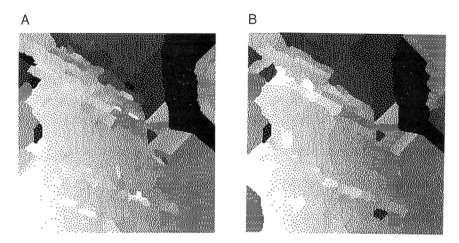

Figure 9.16. Three-dimensional interpolation comparison: (A) original; (B) new.

A B

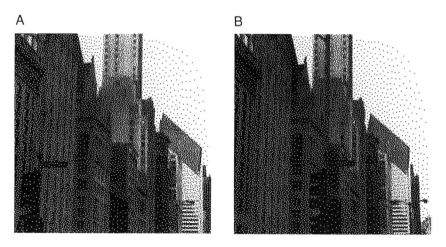

Figure 9.17. Building stereo pair: (A) right image; (B) left image.

A   B

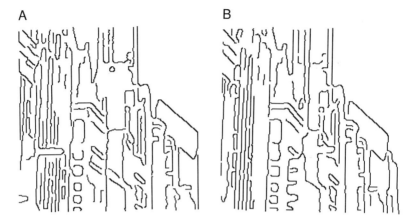

Figure 9.18. Original channel 1: (A) right; (B) left.

A   B

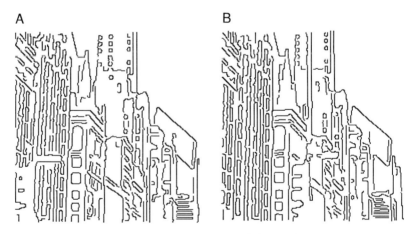

Figure 9.19. Original channel 2: (A) right; (B) left.

A   B

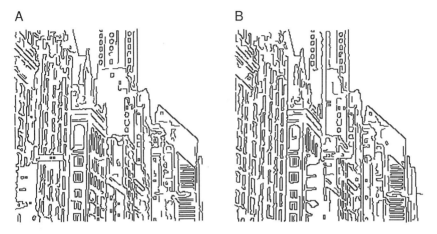

Figure 9.20. Original channel 3: (A) right; (B) left.

A   B

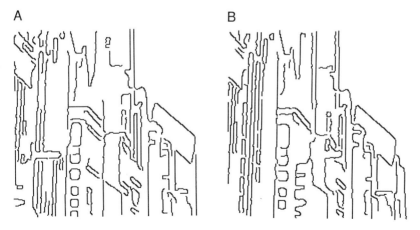

Figure 9.21. New channel 1: (A) right; (B) left.

A   B

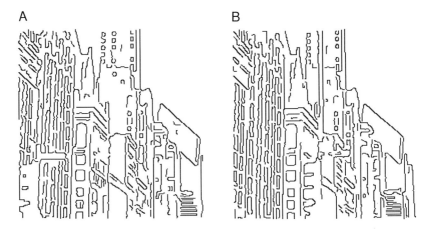

Figure 9.22. New channel 2: (A) right; (B) left.

A   B

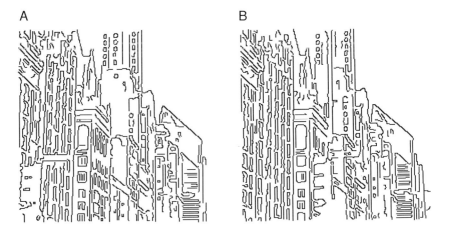

Figure 9.23. New channel 3: (A) right; (B) left.

A   B

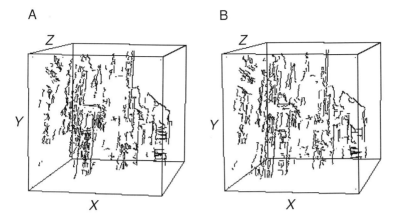

Figure 9.24. Scatter plot of points, 3D comparison: (A) original; (B) new.

A   B

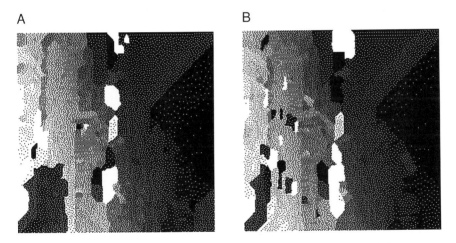

Figure 9.25. Three-dimensional interpolation comparison: (A) original; (B) new.

6. CONCLUSION AND FUTURE WORK

As can be seen from the case study, the addition of a learning component to an existing vision system can have a significant impact on performance. The approach to take is one of pragmatism with an eye toward
incremental improvement. The key decisions that the designer must make

in this task are:

1. Analyze the current structure of the vision algorithm.
2. Select the areas where a learning component will perform best.
3. Express the learning objective and constraints formally.
4. Choose the learning mechanisms that will act on the algorithm.

For the first step, the designer should "dissect" the system and view it as a set of logical modules. To accomplish the second step, it is best to focus on tasks that are tedious or areas that have little theory to guide decisions. The third step can be straightforward, but any oversight in specifying the objective will certainly cause the machine to find an algorithm that satisfies the objective in a trivial way. Here it is best to express everything of importance in the objective that must be optimized and constraints that must be satisfied. If there is a tradeoff that the machine should not be allowed to make on its own, then penalty components might be included in the objective or constraints to guide it. The last step is the most difficult. For many systems, an inductive learning approach will serve best. Also, it can be helpful at this stage to review how a human expert might address the problem. This can help significantly in designing ways to perturb the vision algorithm. In any case there will be a variety of options available, and it is best to focus on what is feasible before attempting a task more complex than redesigning the vision algorithm itself.

One limitation of our case study is that we did not consider objectives other than that defined in Eq. (3). We have found that anomalies in cost and quality of the algorithm learned may happen when learning is carried out under a single objective function defined as a mathematical function of subobjectives (15). An alternative way to learn is to define constraints (or requirements) on the cost and quality of the algorithm to be learned, and direct the learning system to find good feasible algorithms satisfying the constraints. We plan to carry out this approach in our future study.

Another restriction of our case study is that we did not consider domain knowledge already known about the performance of the vision algorithm with respect to changes in these parameter values. In the future, we plan to incorporate existing error analysis methods on various aspects of binocular stereo vision (7, 10, 17) in our objective function.

Finally, our stereo vision algorithm is based on a paradigm that recovers dense-range maps via interpolation of sparse feature maps. There exist other stereo vision algorithms in the literature. We plan to study in the future the applicability of our learning system for these other algorithms.

ACKNOWLEDGMENT

Research was supported by National Aeronautics and Space Administration Contract NCC 2-481 and National Science Foundation Grant MIP 92-18715.

REFERENCES

1. J. Canny, A computational approach to edge detection. *IEEE Trans. Pattern Anal. Mach. Intell.* **PAMI-8**, 679–698 (1986).
2. W. E. L. Grimson, "From Images to Surfaces: A Computational Study of the Human Early Visual System." MIT Press, Cambridge, MA, 1981.
3. B. K. P. Horn, "Robot Vision." MIT Press, Cambridge, MA, 1986.
4. A. Ieumwananonthachai, A. Aizawa, S. R. Schwartz, B. W. Wah, and J. C. Yan, Intelligent process mapping through systematic improvement of heuristics. *J. Parallel Distributed Comput.* **15**, 118–142 (1992).
5. D. Marr, "Vision." Freeman, New York, 1982.
6. D. Marr and T. Poggio, "A Theory of Human Stereo Vision," AI Memo 451. Artificial Intelligence Laboratory, Massachusetts Institute of Technology, Cambridge, MA, 1977.
7. D. Marr and T. Poggio, A computational theory of human stereo vision. *Proc. R. Soc. London, Ser.*, **204**, 301–328 (1979).
8. J. L. McClelland, D. D. Rumelhart, and G. Hinton, The appeal of parallel distributed processing, *In* "Parallel Distributed Processing: Explorations in the Microstructure of Cognition" (D. E. Rumelhart, J. L. McClelland, and the PDP Research Group, eds.), No. 1. MIT Press, Cambridge, MA, 1986, pp. 3–44.
9. R. S. Michalski, Understanding the nature of learning: Issues and research directions. *In* "Machine Learning: An Artificial Intelligence Approach" (R. S. Michalski, J. G. Carbonell, and T. M. Mitchell, eds.), No. 2. Morgan Kaufmann, Los Altos, CA, 1986, pp. 3–25.
10. H. K. Nishihara, Practical real-time imaging stereo matcher. *Opt. Eng.* **23**, 536–545 (1984).
11. L. Rendell, R. Seshu, and D. Tcheng, More robust concept learning using dynamically-variable bias. "Machine Learning." Boston, 198, pp. 66–78..
12. S. R. Schwartz, "Resource Constrained Parameter Tuning Applied to Stereo Vision." M.Sc. Thesis, University of Illinois, Department of Electrical and Computer Engineering, Urbana, IL, 1991.
13. H. A. Simon, Why should machines learn? *In* "Machine Learning: An Artificial Intelligence Approach" (R. S. Michalski, J. G. Carbonell, and T. M. Mitchell, eds.), pp. 25–37. Morgan Kaufmann, Los Altos, CA, 1983.
14. J. Sklansky, Bottlenecks to effective application of machine vision. *In* "Machine Vision: Algorithms, Architectures, and Systems" (H. Freeman, ed.), pp. 187–192. Academic Press, San Diego, CA, 1988.
15. B. W. Wah, Population-based learning: A new method for learning from examples under resource constraints. *Trans. Knowl. Data Eng.* **4**, pp. 454–474 (1992).
16. J. Weng, A theory of image matching. *Proc. Int. Conf. Comput. Vision, 3rd,* Osaka, Japan, 1990, pp. 200–209, IEEE.
17. R. P. Wildes, Direct recovery of three-dimensional scene geometry from binocular stereo disparity. *IEEE Trans. Pattern Anal. Mach. Intell.* **PAMI-13**, 761–774 (1991).
18. A. Witkin, D. Terzopoulis, and M. Kass, Signal matching through scale space. *Proc. Natl. Conf. Artif. Intell., 5th,* Philadelphia, 1986, pp. 714–719.

Chapter **10**

Image Sequence Analysis for Three-Dimensional Perception of Dynamic Scenes

GUNA S. SEETHARAMAN

The Center for Advanced Computer Studies
University of Southwestern Louisiana
Lafayette, Louisiana

1. PROBLEM STATEMENT AND BASIC MODELS

1.1. Introduction and Motivation

Consider a simple intelligent robotic system (IRS), whose operation involves picking the parts as they arrive at a station and assembling them. The primary task of its sensory subsystem is to identify and locate precisely

361

each object present in its workspace. This pragmatic requirement is similar to Marr's (1) view of vision: What is there? Where is it located? In practice, IRSs employ videocameras to monitor the environment, and use several vision algorithms to effectively perceive the 3D nature of their workspace.

Several limitations become inevitable in sensing and perceiving the exact 3D nature of a dynamic scene through its video images. First, the images recorded by practical videocameras suffer a noninvertible loss of depth information due to the inherent projection of the 3D world onto a 2D image. Second, practical applications are full of opaque objects, and thus self-occlusion of objects is inherent as each object tends to hide part of itself. Furthermore, a large opaque object closer to the camera could completely occlude smaller objects behind it, and thus defeat the purpose of the vision subsystem.

These problems are effectively handled by (1) monitoring the scene through more than one camera from distinctly different vantage points, or (2) suitably exploiting the dynamic events occurring in the scene by analyzing the sequence of images recorded from a single vantage point, and (3) the combination of 1 and 2. In all cases, the goal is to *extract* the 3D orientation and motion *information* of the objects from a set of images as a whole, which is *not available from any single image*. The objective of image sequence analysis is to answer the following: What is there? Where is it located? How and in what orientation is it positioned in space? If any of these are changing in time, then What is the dynamics? The canonical models of the underlying computation for cases 1 and 2 above are very similar. The techniques described in this chapter, for the most part, deal with case 2, called *monocular image sequence analysis*. All these algorithms can be easily mapped to case 1 as well.

The 3D state of nature of the dynamic scene, being monitored, changes when (1) one or more objects in the scene experience a 3D displacement over time, or (2) the videocamera undergoes a 3D motion, or (3) both 1 and 2 takes place, and (4) the lighting conditions change in time. With very few exceptions, an occurrence of such dynamic events in the 3D world almost always introduce an apparent change between the images recorded before and after that event. This idea is captured as follows:

$$S(\mathbf{X}; t-1) \xrightarrow{\text{dynamic events}} S(\mathbf{X}; t) \xrightarrow{\text{dynamic events}} S(\mathbf{X}; t+1)$$

$$\cdots \quad \downarrow \phi \qquad\qquad\qquad \downarrow \phi \qquad\qquad\qquad \downarrow \phi \quad \cdots$$

$$f(\mathbf{x}; t-1) \xrightarrow{\text{induced change}} f(\mathbf{x}; t) \xrightarrow{\text{induced change}} f(\mathbf{x}; t+1)$$

where S defines the scene, f defines the image function, ϕ represents the imaging process. The purpose, then, is to study and represent the nature of these 3D event-triggered 2D dynamic features of the image sequences.

Several factors influence the overall complexity of the computer perception of a dynamic scene. To effectively implement the methods described in this chapter, it becomes necessary to decide as to (1) how to represent the input data, and the desired output; (2) if the 3D world is not structured, then whether the chosen representation can accommodate unforeseen objects; (3) what is the suitable representation for representing the dynamics of each object, hence the scene; and (4) what is the role of partially occluded objects, and fully occluded objects in arriving at the final result.

1.2. Representation of Input Images and Output Three-Dimensional Scene Description

The input to a monocular image sequence analysis system is a set of images

$$f(\mathbf{x}; t); \quad t = 0, \pm 1, \pm 2, \ldots, \pm N; \quad \text{and} \quad \mathbf{x} = (x, y)^{\mathrm{T}} \in \mathbb{R}^2.$$

The objective is to extract the 3D motion and surface orientation parameters of each object in the scene from its image sequence.

The flow of information through the vision system may be hierarchically modeled into three levels. The lowest level in the hierarchy is called the *sensor level*, where the information is essentially available in the form of one or more video images as

$$\mathcal{I}_s \equiv \{f(x, y; t) | f(x, y; t) \quad \text{is an image recorded at an instant } t\}.$$

The sensor level data $\mathcal{I}_s$ must then be transformed into a set of piecewise surfaces called *intrinsic surfaces* whose 3D position and orientation are to be derived from $\mathcal{I}_s$. Knowledge derived about the scene, at this *intermediate level* of 3D perception, is easily represented as

$$\mathcal{I}_i \equiv \left\{ \left(X, Y, Z, \frac{\partial Z}{\partial X}, \frac{\partial Z}{\partial Y} \right) \middle| (X, Y, Z) \in \text{surface of some object in the scene} \right\}$$

It is known from the basic principles of differential geometry that a solid object is completely described by all the points located on its surface, and the surface normal at every point. In fact, at each pixel (x, y), $\mathcal{I}_i$, derived directly from the input images $\mathcal{I}_s$, represents the orientation of local surface normal. The transformation of sensor-level data $\mathcal{I}_s$ into intermediate form $\mathcal{I}_i$ is called the *recovery of intrinsic surfaces* (RIS). The loss of depth information is inherent in projective imaging systems. As a consequence, the information to be recovered from a single image is of the form

$$\mathcal{I}_i \equiv \left\{ x, y, p(x, y), q(x, y), \lambda(x, y) | \lambda(\mathbf{x}^T, f_C) \in \text{the object surface} \right\},$$

where, f_C is the focal length of the camera, both (p, q) represent the local-surface orientation parameters commonly described in a two-dimensional space known as *gradient space*. The parameter λ describes the absolute distance Z of each point measured in terms of focal length.

A significant portion of Marr's book (1) on vision emphasizes the importance and the role of intrinsic surfaces in the overall perception of images. A set of high-level processes are believed to act on $\mathcal{I}_i$ and $\mathcal{I}_s$ in arriving at the final abstraction, $\mathcal{I}_h$, of the scene. The objective of these processes is to group the intrinsic surfaces to several candidate objects, and then choose a meaningful interpretation that best satisfies the observed data $\mathcal{I}_s$ and any a priori knowledge and beliefs that may be available. At this point, several objects in the scene have been recognized, and the 3D position and the pose (orientation) of each object extracted with varying degrees of certainty.

The purpose and operation of motion analysis systems is broadly classified into understanding of the 3D state of nature of (1) a structured scene consisting of a known class of objects and (2) that of an unstructured environment where the presence of alien (unknown) objects is inevitable. The representation is very critical to be able to accommodate alien objects.

1.3. The Motion Parameters

A column vector $\mathbf{X}_P^C$ would be used to describe the position of a certain point P expressed in a specific coordinate system C. The superscript C would be dropped whenever the underlying coordinate system is apparent. It is well known that an arbitrary motion of a point P in 3D space can be decomposed into a canonic form

$$\mathbf{X}_P(t + 1) = \mathbf{R}(t)\mathbf{X}_P(t) + \mathbf{T}(t) \tag{1}$$

where $\mathbf{R}$ describes the net rotation and $\mathbf{T}$ describes the net translation. The index t describes the time dependence of the motion parameters. Let $f(\mathbf{x}; t)$ be the image of a scene $S(\mathbf{X}; t)$ at a given time t. Then we have

$$
\begin{array}{ccc}
S(\mathbf{X}; t) & \xrightarrow{\mathbf{R}_{(t)}, \mathbf{T}_{(t)}} & S(\mathbf{X}; t + 1) \\
\downarrow{\phi} & & \downarrow{\phi} \\
f(\mathbf{x}; t) & & f(\mathbf{x}; t + 1)
\end{array}
\tag{2}
$$

where f is a nonnegative scalar function representing the spatial organization of intensity patterns. Also, ϕ represents the imaging transformation, which takes into account the variations in illumination, specular effects, and the geometric and projective nature of the imaging process. The problem at hand is to recover $\mathbf{R}_t$ and $\mathbf{T}_t$ from $f(\mathbf{x}; t)$ and $f(\mathbf{x}; t + i)$, $i = \pm 1, \pm 2 \cdots \pm N$. The exact number of frames N may vary for different techniques.

Various cases arise when (1) only one object is moving in space, (2) two or more objects are moving independently with respect to the camera, and (3) the effective rotation axis of an object's motion is parallel to the optical axis of the camera. Other factors include (1) the angle between the translation component of the composite 3D motion and the effective rotation axis of each moving object, and (2) the expected range of motion parameters and the disparity between successive images in the image sequence.

There are several ways to describe an arbitrary rotation matrix $\mathbf{R}$. However, its intrinsic dimensionality is always 3. The degree of freedom of $\mathbf{T}$ is also 3. Thus the motion parameters can be uniquely described with 6 degrees of freedom. Let $\mathbf{n}$ be the effective rotation axis and θ be the effective rotation angle, of the matrix $\mathbf{R}$. Then, $\mathbf{R}$ is uniquely described by

$$\mathbf{R} = (1 - \cos \theta) \begin{bmatrix} n_x^2 & n_x n_y & n_x n_z \\ n_y n_x & n_y^2 & n_y n_z \\ n_z n_x & n_z n_y & n_z^2 \end{bmatrix}$$

$$+ (\cos \theta)\mathbf{I}_3 + (\sin \theta) \begin{bmatrix} 0 & -n_z & n_y \\ n_z & 0 & -n_x \\ -n_y & n_x & 0 \end{bmatrix}. \tag{3}$$

In particular, this representation of $\mathbf{R}$ is more suitable for representing the 3D motion of the camera in time.

When two or more objects are moving independently in the scene, it becomes necessary to associate a 3D rotation matrix and a translation vector for each object and represent them in terms of *object centered* coordinate systems. Let K be the frame of reference attached (permanently) to object k. The position of an arbitrary point P located on the object K at time t may expressed in the form

$$\mathbf{X}_P^C = \mathbf{R}_K^C(t)\mathbf{X}_P^K + \mathbf{T}_K^C(t), \tag{4}$$

where $\mathbf{T}_K$ and $\mathbf{R}_K$ describe the position and orientation of the coordinate system K with respect to the (absolute) camera coordinate system C. The position of the point P after a composite motion can then be expressed as

$$\mathbf{X}_{t+1}^{C} = \mathbf{R}_{m}^{C}(t)\mathbf{X}^{C}(t) + \mathbf{T}_{m}^{C}(t), \tag{5a}$$

$$\mathbf{X}_{t+1}^{K} = \mathbf{R}_{m}^{K}(t)\mathbf{X}^{K}(t) + \mathbf{T}_{m}^{K}(t), \tag{5b}$$

where $\mathbf{R}_{m}^{K}(t)$ and $\mathbf{T}_{m}^{K}(t)$ represent the instantaneous motion of the object with respect to the coordinate system K. The motion parameters, $\mathbf{R}_{m}^{C}$, $\mathbf{R}_{m}^{K}$, $\mathbf{T}_{m}^{C}$, and $\mathbf{T}_{m}^{K}$ are mutually related in the form

$$\mathbf{X}_{t+1}^{K} = \left[\mathbf{R}_{K}(t+1)\right]^{-1}\left[\mathbf{R}_{m}^{C}(t)\right]\left[\mathbf{R}_{K}(t)\right]\mathbf{X}^{K}(t),$$

$$+ \left[\mathbf{R}_{K}(t+1)\right]^{-1}\left(\left[\mathbf{R}_{m}^{C}(t)\right]\mathbf{T}_{K}(t) + \mathbf{T}_{m}^{C}(t)\right), \tag{5c}$$

$$- \left[\mathbf{R}_{K}(t+1)\right]^{-1}\mathbf{T}_{K}(t+1).$$

In particular, $\mathbf{R}_{m}^{C}(t) = \mathbf{R}_{m}^{K}$, if $\mathbf{R}_{K}^{C}(t+1) = \mathbf{R}_{K}^{C}(t) = \mathbf{I}_{3}$.

The rotation of the object K can then be decomposed to the form

$$\mathbf{R}_{m}^{K}(t) \equiv R_{z|k}(\phi)R_{y|k}(\theta)R_{z|k}(\psi), \tag{6a}$$

where

$$\psi = \arctan\left(\frac{r_{23}}{r_{13}}\right), \qquad\qquad -90° < \psi < 90°,$$

$$\theta = \arcsin\left(\frac{r_{13}}{\cos\phi}\right), \qquad\qquad -90° < \theta < 90°, \tag{6b}$$

$$\psi = \arcsin(r_{21}\cos\psi - r_{11}\sin\phi), \qquad -90° < \theta < 90°,$$

as shown in Seetharaman (2). Eulerian decomposition facilitates a unique interpretation of the spin of each object.

1.4. Perspective Projection Model of the Cameras

In general, videocameras project a certain object point $\mathbf{X}$ located on opaque objects onto an image point $\mathbf{x} = (x, y, z = f)^{\mathrm{T}}$ in the image plane. The image plane is uniquely determined by the focal length f_C of the camera, and satisfies the equality $Z = f_C$. The projection model of the image sensor is either *orthographic* or *perspective* depending on the lens

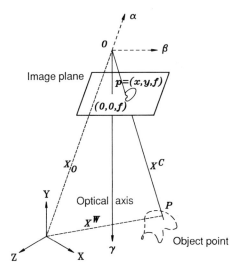

Figure 10.1. A simple perspective imaging system with its origin located at $\mathbf{O}_C$.

characteristics and the relative dimensions of the image sensor and the lens. Loss of depth information is inevitable in both the types of projections. The intrinsic geometric model of an intensity camera is illustrated in Figs. 10.1 and 10.2.

The irreversible loss of depth information introduced by the underlying perspective projection is expressed as

$$
\begin{bmatrix} x \\ y \\ f \end{bmatrix} = [\mathbf{P}] \begin{bmatrix} X \\ Y \\ Z \end{bmatrix}, \quad \text{where} \quad \mathbf{P} = \begin{bmatrix} \dfrac{1}{\lambda} & 0 & 0 \\ 0 & \dfrac{1}{\lambda} & 0 \\ 0 & 0 & \dfrac{1}{\lambda} \end{bmatrix}, \quad \lambda = \dfrac{Z}{f_C}, \text{ and } \lambda > 1.
$$

$$(7)$$

That is, both $\mathbf{X}$ and $a\mathbf{X}$, $\forall_a$, $a \neq 0$, result in the same image point $\mathbf{x}$. Equation (7) is noninvertible in that given $\mathbf{X}$ one can determine $\mathbf{x}$ but not the opposite. However, given a point $\mathbf{x}$ on the intensity image, $\mathbf{X}$ is constrained to a line (of points) passing through the focal point $\mathbf{O}$, $\mathbf{O}^C = (0, 0, 0)$ and the image point $\mathbf{x}^C$. Symbol $\mathbf{O}_C^W$ would be used to describe the position of the origin $\mathbf{O}_C$ measured with respect to the world coordinate system.

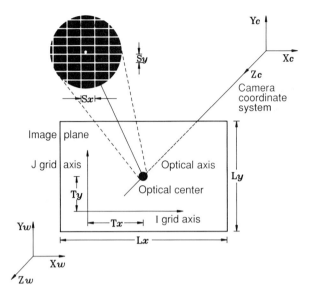

Figure 10.2. The intrinsic parameters of a perspective camera and the discrete sampling process.

Given the absolute position $\mathbf{X}^W$ of a point X measured with respect to the world coordinate system, both $\mathbf{X}^C$ and $\mathbf{X}^W$ are related as follows:

$$
\begin{bmatrix} X \\ Y \\ Z \\ 1 \end{bmatrix}^W = \begin{bmatrix} \mathbf{T}_C^W \end{bmatrix} \begin{bmatrix} X \\ Y \\ Z \\ 1 \end{bmatrix}^C ,
$$

$$
\text{where} \quad \mathbf{T}_C^W = \begin{bmatrix} \boldsymbol{\alpha}_C^W & \vdots & \boldsymbol{\beta}_C^W & \vdots & \boldsymbol{\gamma}_C^W & \vdots & \mathbf{O}_C^W \\ \cdots & \vdots & \cdots & \vdots & \cdots & \vdots & \cdots \\ 0 & & 0 & & 0 & \vdots & 1 \end{bmatrix} \quad (8)
$$

and

$\boldsymbol{\alpha}_C^W, \boldsymbol{\beta}_C^W, \boldsymbol{\gamma}_C^W$ = direction cosines of the X, Y, and Z axes of the camera
$\mathbf{O}_C^W$ = vector position of the origin of the camera coordinate system.

The matrix $\mathbf{T}_C$, uniquely characterized by six parameters called *extrinsic camera parameters*, is always invertible. These parameters are easily calculated when the position and orientation of the camera is known with respect to the absolute coordinate system. They can also be extracted using calibration techniques. From Eqs. (7) and (8) it follows that

$$
\begin{bmatrix} X \\ Y \\ Z \\ 1 \end{bmatrix}^W = [\mathbf{T}_C] \begin{bmatrix} \lambda x \\ \lambda y \\ \lambda f_C \\ 1 \end{bmatrix}^C \equiv [\mathbf{T}_C] \begin{bmatrix} \lambda \mathbf{x}^C \\ \hline 1 \end{bmatrix}. \tag{9}
$$

Clearly, given $\mathbf{x}^C$, additional information is required to uniquely locate $\mathbf{X}^W$ along that line.

In practice, the images are obtained from a videocamera through a *digitization* process. The purpose of the *digitizer* is to discretely *sample* the continuous image, and *quantize* each sample to facilitate intensity-based image processing. The sampled, and quantized, image is generally described over a 2D grid whose origin need not necessarily coincide with $(0, 0, f_C)^C$ where the optical axis intersects with the image plane. The location of an image point $\mathbf{x}_{CG}$ is thus expressed in terms of its position grid coordinate system CG.

The parameters that relate $\mathbf{x}_C$ and $\mathbf{x}_{CG}$ are called the intrinsic parameter of the video imaging system. The intrinsic parameters include: the sampling intervals s_x, s_y in x, y directions, respectively, of the rectangular grid; and the position (τ_x, τ_y) of the true image center, $(0, 0, f)^C$ measured in the grid (pixel) coordinate system. These parameters are illustrated in Fig. 10.2. Their relationship is expressed as

$$
\begin{bmatrix} x_C \\ y_C \\ 1 \end{bmatrix} = \begin{bmatrix} s_x & 0 & -s_x \tau_x \\ 0 & s_y & -s_y \tau_y \\ 0 & 0 & 1 \end{bmatrix} \begin{bmatrix} x_G \\ y_G \\ 1 \end{bmatrix}. \tag{10}
$$

A commonly repeated mistake is to assume that the uniform sampling intervals are equal, $s_x = s_y$. This is not the case for many practical image acquisition systems. While this may not seriously affect early vision tasks (e.g., edge detection) an erroneous assumption here would contribute to misleading interpretation of 3D motion from 2D images at later stages. In particular, it poses very serious problems in computing and interpreting optical flow. It is very critical that the camera be calibrated, and that $\mathbf{x}^C$ be expressed accurately in terms of the observed quantities, $\mathbf{x}^{CG}$.

1.5. Orthographic Projection Model of the Cameras

In certain circumstances, it is desirable to model the camera by an orthographic projection. Practical cameras are inherently perspective. A truly orthographic camera would require the film (video sensor) to have

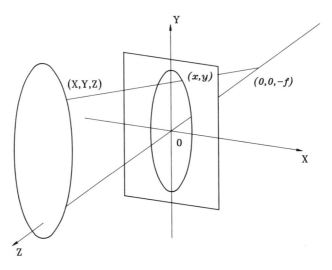

Figure 10.3. A simple orthographic imaging system.

the same dimensions as the objects, and thus would not be useful in practical applications. However, favorable conditions occur when focal length of the camera is much larger than the diagonal of the video sensor and/or the lens's diameter. The nonlinearity due to perspective imaging is uniformly distributed, since the lens covers only a very narrow beam of light, consisting essentially of almost parallel lines. The projection is illustrated in Fig. 10.3.

The basic equations are similar to that of the perspective imaging model. However, the difference can be emphasized if the object points are described with respect to an object-centered coordinate system. Let $\mathbf{X}^C = (X, Y, Z)^O + (0, 0, Z_0)^C$, where, Z_0^C is the distance of the object from the camera. Then, it is easy to show that:

$$ x = \frac{fX^O}{f + Z_0 + Z^O} = \frac{fX^O}{(f + Z_0)}\left(1 + \frac{Z^O}{Z_0 + f}\right)^{-1}, $$

$$ \tag{11} $$

$$ y = \frac{fY^O}{f + Z_0 + Z^O} = \frac{fY^O}{(f + Z_0)}\left(1 + \frac{Z^O}{Z_0 + f}\right)^{-1}. $$

In particular, when both f and Z_0 assume very large values, the resulting projection is of the form

$$
x = \lim_{Z_0 \to \infty, f \to \infty} X^O \left(1 + \frac{Z_0}{f}\right)^{-1} \left(1 + \frac{Z^O}{Z_0 + f}\right)^{-1} \approx X^O \left(1 + \frac{Z_0}{f}\right)^{-1},
$$

$$
y = \lim_{Z_0 \to \infty, f \to \infty} Y^O \left(1 + \frac{Z_0}{f}\right)^{-1} \left(1 + \frac{Z^O}{Z_0 + f}\right)^{-1} \approx Y^O \left(1 + \frac{Z_0}{f}\right)^{-1}.
$$

$$(12)$$

Both X and Y components of the position vector $\mathbf{X}^O$ are scaled by the same amount, and the scale is independent of the exact Z position, $Z^C = Z_0 + Z^O$, of the object points. In essence, this is a scaled orthographic projection, and it preserves various second-order geometric properties. In fact, it is of affine nature, expressed as

$$
\begin{bmatrix} x \\ y \end{bmatrix} = \left(1 + \frac{Z_0}{f}\right)^{-1} \begin{bmatrix} 1 & 0 & 0 \\ 0 & 1 & 0 \end{bmatrix} \begin{bmatrix} X^O \\ Y^O \\ Z^O + Z_0 \end{bmatrix}, \tag{13}
$$

(*Note:* It was assumed that the origin of object centered coordinate system was located on the optical axis. The method may not work for larger values of $Y^O = Y^C$ and $X^O = X^C$.)

2. KNOWN COMPUTATIONAL MODELS FOR THREE-DIMENSIONAL MOTION ANALYSIS

The recovery of 3D information from 2D images is similar to solving any other *ill-posed inversion* problems (3). The general approach to solving such problems requires a set of consistency tests (functions) based on a priori knowledge of the solution space. The problem is *regularized* by imposing a set of appropriate constraints in order to narrow the class of feasible solutions. Thus, the approach is restricted to structured scenes with a known class of objects. These are not suitable for IRSs who must navigate through 3D scenes with unexpected object configurations (possibly still structured) that may occur as a result of dynamic (failures) events in the environment.

Existing models of human perception of images indicate that, because of the nature of application, and the specific 3D features of the objects involved, images are perceived as a collection of (1) prominent points, (2) a collection of lines, (3) a collection of piecewise surfaces, (4) any combination of the above, or (5) none of the above. In practice, these instances form the rationale behind (1) the point correspondence method, (2) the line correspondence method, (3) the region correspondence method, (4) various combinations of the above, and (5) the optical-flow-based methods, respectively, used for the 3D motion analysis of a given image sequence.

Current state of knowledge (4) in 3D perception of dynamics scenes may be broadly categorized into (1) dynamic scene analysis of monocular image sequences [motion-based techniques for objects with planar (2, 5) and quadratic surfaces (6)], including photogrammetric techniques (7), and (2) fusion of images derived from multiple views (8), and multiple sensors [stereo analysis of intensity and range images (9)].

Recovery of depth information based on multiple view offers certain additional advantages. It is possible to resolve the inherent ambiguities otherwise inevitable in the 3D perception from a single view because of self-occlusion and multiple occlusion of opaque objects.

2.1. Correspondence-Based Methods

In principle, depth information can be recovered from two images, say, f_1 and f_2, without severely restricting the objects in the scene. However, for every point ξ_1 in image f_1 it is required to find exactly one point ξ_2 in image f_2, such that they both represent the image of the same 3D object point, and hence the same intrinsic surface. The depth of the 3D point and orientation of its local normal are easily recovered if the relative orientation and displacement between the two cameras are known. It is possible to calibrate a stereo imaging system for $\mathbf{R}$ and $\mathbf{T}$ using objects that are rich in vanishing points, while also calibrating the intrinsic parameters of these cameras (10).

In the absence of such information, the problem becomes a 3D motion and structure recovery problem. It has been independently established (2, 6), that three consecutive images are required to uniquely recover $\mathbf{R}, \mathbf{T}$ and the orientation of the intrinsic surfaces. However, it is not possible to locate the objects uniquely in 3D space since an object twice bigger kept twice farther away would also give rise to the same image sequence; hence the depth ambiguity.

In practical applications it is extremely difficult to identify and establish registration between images. One approach is to extract a set of (token) points in each image where its intensity function exhibits certain distinct features, and match such tokens across the images. Basic limitations are inevitable: (1) in selecting the spatial tokens, in general *geometric features* in smooth images; (2) in establishing the isomorphic correspondence, which is inherently NP-complete; and (3) limitation due to the finite sampling rate, in the form of geometric uncertainties (11). Physically meaningful objects do exist for which these methods don't work.

2.1.1. Point Correspondence Method

When the rigid body undergoes motion, the image of almost every point on its surface undergoes a 2D displacement in the image plane. The technique essentially involves identifying these points in each image and comparing their positions in consecutive images. The required number of points and the number of consecutive images are determined by the type of surface to be recovered. A detailed survey is available in Huang (12). However, the equations will be reproduced to suit the context. Let $\mathbf{x}_t$ and $\mathbf{x}_{t+1}$ be two corresponding points, related such that

$$\mathbf{X}_{t+1} = \mathbf{R}_m(t)\mathbf{X}_t + \mathbf{T}_m(t)$$

$$= \lambda_{t+1}\mathbf{x}_{t+1}, \tag{14}$$

$$\lambda_t\mathbf{x}_t = \mathbf{X}_t.$$

Then, it can be shown that

$$\begin{bmatrix} x_{t+1}, & y_{t+1}, & f \end{bmatrix}^C \begin{bmatrix} e_{1x} & e_{2x} & e_{3x} \\ e_{1y} & e_{2y} & e_{3y} \\ e_{1z} & e_{2z} & e_{3z} \end{bmatrix} \begin{bmatrix} x_t \\ y_t \\ f \end{bmatrix}^C = 0, \tag{15}$$

with

$$[E] = \begin{bmatrix} \vdots & \vdots & \vdots \\ \mathbf{r}_1 \times \mathbf{t} & \vdots & \mathbf{r}_2 \times \mathbf{t} & \vdots & \mathbf{r}_3 \times \mathbf{t} \\ \vdots & \vdots & \vdots \end{bmatrix}, \tag{16}$$

and $\mathbf{T} = $ to $|\mathbf{T}|\mathbf{t}$ where $\mathbf{r}_1, \mathbf{r}_2, \mathbf{r}_3$ are the columns of the rotation matrix $\mathbf{R}$. The physical interpretation of Eq. (15) is as follows. Given a point $\mathbf{x}_t$ in the image at time t, its true corresponding point is constrained to a line uniquely determined by a set of eight numbers called *essential parameters*. Different values of $\mathbf{x}_t$ would generate distinctly different lines, called *epipolar lines*, which all converge at a point e, called the *epicenter*, which is the image of the translation vector $\mathbf{e}_{t+1} \equiv \mathbf{t}$. Thus the direction cosines of $\mathbf{t}$ is easily obtained when two or more pairs of corresponding-points are available. It is also shown that, given the point correspondences of eight points in general positions, the motion parameters computed from essential parameters are unique. In fact, seven points in two views are sufficient to extract unique solutions under certain cases.

The computational difficulties and uncertainties are associated with the process of establishing a set of corresponding point pairs. This method requires very high spatial resolution in sampling the image. The effect of finite resolution used in sampling on the uniqueness of the motion parameters is explained in Lee (13) and Weng *et al.* (14). In particular, a numerical example is used to illustrate (13) the conditions where the robustness of this approach breaks down. The location and separation of these points influence the computational error in the overall system (14, 15), and some kind of averaging over a large number of points is necessary.

For reliable results it is necessary that (1) the focal length of the lens be shorter than its cross section (i.e., a wide-angle lens must be used), and (2) the translation must be large to allow stable estimation of **t**.

2.1.2. Line Correspondence Methods

The basis of the tokens or features used for correspondence is often decided by the availability and the reliability of measurements. Even when it is not possible to establish a large number of point correspondences, it may be possible to measure and extract higher-level features such as lines, edges, and piecewise contours. Since these higher-level features are determined by a collection of pixels, the uncertainties in measuring the geometric location of these features is effectively reduced. Furthermore, establishing line correspondence is somewhat easier than point correspondence.

The 3D motion parameters can be recovered by solving a set of nonlinear equations (16) from a minimum of 13 corresponding lines over three consecutive frames. In a recent paper, a closed-form solution is reported (17) that also gives a unique solution. Let $\mathbf{x}_1$ and $\mathbf{x}_2$ be the images of two points $\mathbf{X}_1$ and $\mathbf{X}_2$, respectively. Let L_{12} the line passing through $\mathbf{X}_1$ and $\mathbf{X}_2$. The equation of the line is described by

$$L_{12}(t0): \mathbf{X} = \mathbf{X}_1 + k\mathbf{l},$$

$$\mathbf{l} = \frac{\mathbf{X}_2 - \mathbf{X}_1}{|\mathbf{X}_2 - \mathbf{X}_1|}, \tag{17}$$

where the column vector **l** is called the *direction cosine*. The parametric equation of the line changes as these points undergo a rigid motion in space in time. Let the motion parameters $\mathbf{R}, \mathbf{T}, \mathbf{S}, \mathbf{U}$ describe three consecutive instances of a rigid object:

$$X_1(t_1) = RX_1(t_0) + T, \tag{18}$$

$$X_1(t_2) = SX_1(t_0) + U. \tag{19}$$

Then the line L_{12} can be expressed in the form

$$L_{12}(t_1): \quad X = RX_1(t_0) + T + k\,R\mathbf{l}, \tag{20}$$

$$L_{12}(t_2): \quad X = SX_1(t_0) + U + k\,S\mathbf{l}. \tag{21}$$

At any given time, the points, $\mathbf{o}, \mathbf{x}_1, \mathbf{x}_2, \mathbf{X}_1, \mathbf{X}_2$ all lie in a plane, whose normal $\mathbf{n}_0$ is readily computed from $\mathbf{x}_1$ and $\mathbf{x}_2$. The parametric form of the normal at each instant is given by

$$t_0: \quad \mathbf{n}_0 = \mathbf{X}_1 \times \mathbf{l} \tag{22}$$

$$t_1: \quad \mathbf{n}_1 = R(\mathbf{n}_0 + R^{-1}T \times \mathbf{l}) \tag{23}$$

$$t_2: \quad \mathbf{n}_2 = S(\mathbf{n}_0 + R^{-1}U \times \mathbf{l}) \tag{24}$$

Using the vector identity, $\mathbf{a} \times (\mathbf{b} \times \mathbf{c}) = (\mathbf{a} \cdot \mathbf{c})\mathbf{b} - (\mathbf{a} \cdot \mathbf{b})\mathbf{c}$, Eq. (23) is reduced to give

$$\mathbf{n}_0 \times R^{-1}\mathbf{n}_1 = -(\mathbf{n}_0 \cdot R^{-1}T)\mathbf{l}, \tag{25}$$

which is further simplified to

$$\mathbf{n}_0 \times R^{-1}\mathbf{n}_1 = -(\mathbf{n}_1 \cdot T)\mathbf{l}. \tag{26a}$$

Similarly

$$\mathbf{n}_0 \times S^{-1}\mathbf{n}_2 = -(\mathbf{n}_2 \cdot U)\mathbf{l}. \tag{26b}$$

Letting $R = [\mathbf{r}_1, \mathbf{r}_2, \mathbf{r}_3]$ and $S = [\mathbf{s}_1, \mathbf{s}_2, \mathbf{s}_3]$, further reductions lead to

$$[\mathbf{n}_0]_\times \begin{bmatrix} \mathbf{n}_1^T(\mathbf{r}_1 U^T - T\mathbf{s}_1^T)\mathbf{n}_2 \\ \mathbf{n}_1^T(\mathbf{r}_2 U^T - T\mathbf{s}_2^T)\mathbf{n}_2 \\ \mathbf{n}_1^T(\mathbf{r}_3 U^T - T\mathbf{s}_3^T)\mathbf{n}_2 \end{bmatrix} \triangleq [\mathbf{n}_0]_\times \begin{bmatrix} \mathbf{n}_1^T E\mathbf{n}_2 \\ \mathbf{n}_1^T F\mathbf{n}_2 \\ \mathbf{n}_1^T G\mathbf{n}_2 \end{bmatrix} = \mathbf{o}, \tag{27}$$

where (E, F, G) are defined as the intermediate parameters. Given one *line correspondence* over three consecutive images, $\mathbf{n}_0$, $\mathbf{n}_1$, and $\mathbf{n}_2$ are easily observed, by quantitatively extracting their values. If we have at least 13 lines from 3 images, the intermediate parameters can be computed, from which, in turn, the motion parameters can be computed. The problem essentially involves solving up to 26 independent scalar equations. For a detailed analysis, the reader is referred to Weng *et al.* (17). The accuracy still depends on the reliability of the segmentation procedures responsible for extracting these lines.

2.1.3. Region Correspondence Methods

There are several reasons to expect that motion analysis, based on *region correspondence*, could be more accurate and robust than the foregoing methods. Establishing point correspondence in the images, in general, is a difficult task and is more susceptible to noise. On the other hand, identifying a region correspondence is relatively easier and is more accurate. The inherent integration involved in forming the regions from a collection of pixels makes it less sensitive to noise and other causes of inaccuracy.

The region correspondence method exploits the fact that the dynamic changes in the observed shape of the visible faces of rigid objects gives rise to a meaningful interpretation of the underlying motion. Both the motion and orientation of each face of the objects can be recovered using this approach.

To best illustrate the concepts, let the parametric form of a visible planar surface (patch) of the object be

$$Z = -pX - qY - s. \tag{28}$$

This piecewise plane would be referred to as a rigid planar patch (RPP). The parameters (p, q) are defined in a space called the *gradient space*. The physical significance of p and q is that they represent respectively the slant and tilt angles at which the plane under consideration is being viewed. Each point in the gradient space represents a unique family of parallel planes. The variable s describes the distance at which the plane of interest cuts the Z axis.

For simplicity, consider an orthographic imaging system, $\mathbf{x} = (X, Y)^T$, and assume that the composite motion consists of rotation only. Young and Wang (18) introduced the basic relationship between the 2D shape changes of the segmented face and the 3D *object-centered* rotation that induces the change. It is shown that

$$\mathbf{x}_{t+1} = \begin{bmatrix} r_{11} - pr_{13} & r_{12} - qr_{13} \\ r_{21} - pr_{23} & r_{22} - qr_{23} \end{bmatrix} \mathbf{x}_t + \begin{bmatrix} -sr_{13} \\ -sr_{23} \end{bmatrix} \tag{29}$$

$$= \mathbf{A}\mathbf{x}_t + \mathbf{c},$$

where the r_{ij} values are the elements of the rotation matrix, and $\mathbf{A}$ and $\mathbf{c}$ define an affine transformation in the image space. Both $\mathbf{A}$ and $\mathbf{c}$ are referred to as the *shape change parameters*.

Given two images, drawn from an image sequence, it is possible to extract both $\mathbf{A}$ and $\mathbf{c}$ from which $\mathbf{R}$ can be recovered if p, q, and s are known, by solving the six individual linear equations contained in Eq. (29). It is particularly convenient to decompose $\mathbf{R}$ into a sequence of Eulerian rotations as described in Eq. (6). The preceding example is only a simple case, which captures the essential idea of region correspondence approach. A detailed study of this method is available in Seetharaman (2). The performance of the region correspondence method depends on the accuracy of the segmentation process, and requires at least one visible planar face for each object being monitored. This method is explained in detail in Section 3.

2.2. Optical Flow Approach

When an object moves in the dynamic scene, it induces an apparent motion within the 2D images over time. The principal idea behind optical flow is that the temporal variations in brightness patterns give rise to the apparent 2D motion, perceived directly from the image sequence. This visually apparent motion is quantitatively described by a 2D optical flow field (19) from which the actual 3D motion and surface structure of the objects can be computed (5).

First, the velocity at each pixel is computed by some local operators, and thus a velocity field is formed as

$$\mathbf{u}(x, y; t) = \begin{bmatrix} 1 & 0 & 0 \\ 0 & 1 & 0 \end{bmatrix} [\boldsymbol{\omega} \times \mathbf{X} + \mathbf{T}]. \tag{30}$$

However, the velocity can be resolved only in the direction of the gradient of intensity function

$$
\frac{\partial}{\partial t} f(x, y; t) = -\mathbf{u}^T(x, y; t) \cdot \begin{bmatrix} \dfrac{\partial}{\partial x} \\[2mm] \dfrac{\partial}{\partial y} \end{bmatrix} f(x, y; t),
$$

(31)

$$
\mathbf{u}_p(x, y; t) = -\frac{|\nabla_t f(\mathbf{x}; t)|}{|\nabla \mathbf{x} f(\mathbf{x}; t)|} \hat{\mathbf{u}}_p(x, y),
$$

where $\hat{\mathbf{u}}_p(x, y)$ is the direction cosine of the local intensity gradient. The truly induced 2D motion field has to be computed (20) from this partial velocity field, by imposing various smoothness conditions on the resulting, globally consistent 2D velocity field. Many techniques have been proposed to interpret these velocity fields. Adiv (5) employed a more general model, and presented methods for computing the 3D motion parameters from the optical flow.

Motion analysis based on optical flow techniques consists of two phases: First, an optical flow field, specifically, the velocity or displacement field describing the instantaneous velocity at each pixel, is computed over the image plane. The second stage involves the interpretations of these fields. The basic principle is that a rigid motion in the 3D space induces a connected set of flow vectors in the velocity field such that the vectors within a set are consistent in some sense (5). First, the given flow field is partitioned into several segments, each one satisfying the above criterion. Then these segments are grouped such that each group represents a single 3D motion. For example, consider a multifaced 3D object in motion; then for each of its visible faces we have one affine metric governed by the 3D motion and the orientation parameters. Hence many segments in the flow field corresponding to its visible faces represent the same 3D motion forming a consistent group of segments. Many such groups indicate the presence of several independently moving objects in the scene. Consider the imaging geometry given in Fig. 10.4.

Let the instantaneous motion (relative to the camera) of an object be decomposed into a rotation $\mathbf{\Omega}$, followed by translation $\mathbf{T}$. It is important to note that $\mathbf{\Omega}$ is a small rotation-angle model of the nonorthonormal rotation matrix that represents the rotation of the camera's coordinate frame as shown in Fig. 10.4 (21). Then

$$
\mathbf{X}_{t+1} = \mathbf{X}_t + (\mathbf{\Omega} \times \mathbf{X}_t) + \mathbf{T}
$$

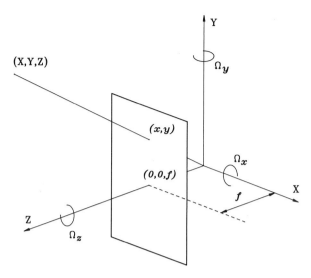

Figure 10.4. A perspective imaging system illustrating the angular velocities of its camera frame. Reproduced from Seetharaman and Young (21) with permission from World Scientific Press.

$$= \begin{bmatrix} 1 & -\omega_Z & \omega_Y \\ \omega_Z & 1 & -\omega_X \\ -\omega_Y & \omega_X & 1 \end{bmatrix} \begin{bmatrix} X_t \\ Y_t \\ Z_t \end{bmatrix} + \begin{bmatrix} T_X \\ T_Y \\ T_Z \end{bmatrix}. \tag{32}$$

Also,

$$x_t = \frac{X_t}{Z_t}, \quad y_t = \frac{Y_t}{Z_t}, \quad x_{t+1} = \frac{X_{t+1}}{Z_{t+1}}, \quad y_{t+1} = \frac{Y_{t+1}}{Z_{t+1}}. \tag{33}$$

Let $(\alpha, \beta)^T = \mathbf{x}_{t+1} - \mathbf{x}_t$; it can then be shown that

$$\alpha = \frac{(T_X - xT_Z)}{Z} - xy\omega_X + (1 + x^2)\omega_Y - y\omega_Z$$

$$\beta = \frac{(T_Y - yT_Z)}{Z} - (1 + y^2)\omega_X + xy\omega_Y + x\omega_Z \tag{34}$$

when $|T_Z/Z| \ll 1$ and the field of view of the camera is small. When a roughly planar patch in motion is considered, Eq. (33) takes the form of a Ψ transformation that describes the 2D motion in the image plane by eight parameters $b_1, b_2, \ldots, b_8$, as follows. First, let the planar surface be defined by the equation

$$k_X X + k_Y Y + k_Z Z = 1, \tag{35}$$

or

$$\frac{1}{Z} = k_X x + k_Y y + k_Z.$$ (36)

Then

$$\alpha = b_1 + b_2 x + b_3 y + b_7 x^2 + b_8 xy,$$

$$\beta = b_4 + b_5 x + b_6 y + b_7 xy + b_8 y^2,$$ (37)

where

$$b_1 = w_Y + k_Z T_X, \qquad b_4 = -w_X + k_Z T_Y,$$

$$b_2 = k_X T_X - k_Z T_Z, \qquad b_5 = -w_Z + k_X T_Y,$$

$$b_3 = -w_Z + k_Y T_X, \qquad b_6 = k_Y T_Y - k_Z T_Z,$$ (38)

$$b_7 = -w_Y - k_X T_Z, \qquad b_8 = -w_X - k_Y T_Z.$$

A multipass segmentation algorithm using the Hough transform technique is developed to combine the flow vectors that are consistent with an affine transformation. Then, the components that are compatible with the same optimal Ψ transform are merged into segments, using a multipass multiresolution search combined with least-squared error verification. Those segments that satisfy the same 3D motion are grouped to represent a rigid object. Many groups of segments, each group representing a 3D rigid object, are derived from the scene to determine the structure of the scene. The ambiguities due to noisy flow fields are noted to be inherent, and their effects on the final interpretations are significant.

In a recent paper (22) it is discussed that the interpretation of 3D motion from 2D velocity field is clearly nonunique. In particular, two examples are given to indicate that two entirely different 3D motion and structure combinations give rise to identical optical velocity fields.

2.3. Motion Analysis from Regional Features

Kanatani (23, 24) highlights the problems that are generally associated with the point correspondence methods and suggests two methods for tracking planar faces in motion. The first method is concerned with orthographic projection and considers rotation and 2D translation only. The method is robust, is reasonably accurate, and involves many approximations; also it is applicable for small rotations only. We are particularly interested in his second method, since it is exact. Generally speaking, the following formulation is an example of Amari's feature spaces that accept transformations in the feature domain.

The analysis considers the rigid motion of a planar patch in an orthographically projected image sequence. It is assumed that the given planar face is available in the form of a closed contour in the image plane. Also, it is required that the values of p, q, and r be explicitly known for the first frame. A feature I_k of the contour is defined as line integral along the closed contour C such that

$$I_k = \oint_C F_k(x, y)\, ds, \tag{39}$$

where $ds = \sqrt{dx^2 + dy^2}$ measured along the contour C. Then, by using Stoke's theorem it is established that its time derivative is of the form

$$\frac{d}{dt} I = C_1 T_X + C_2 T_Y + C_3 T_Z + C_4 \omega_X + C_5 \omega_Y + C_6 \omega_Z, \tag{40}$$

where $C_1, C_2, \ldots, C_6$ are expressed in terms of in p, q, r, dF/dx, dF/dy, dx/ds, and dy/ds. In particular they are linear in p, q, and r. For the exact expressions, the reader is referred to Kanatani (24). It is then required to choose six linearly independent functions $F_1(x, y)$, $F_2(x, y)$, $\ldots, F_6(x, y)$ and compute the six feature functions, $I_1, I_2, \ldots, I_6$ over two frames. Also, for each feature function $F_k(x, y)$ the six C_{kj} values are computed as in Kanatani (24). Then a set of six linear equations in six unknowns are formed as given Eq. (41), and can be readily solved by standard methods:

$$[C_{kj}](T_X, T_Y, T_Z, \omega_X, \omega_Y, \omega_Z)^T = (I_1, I_2, \ldots, I_6)^T \tag{41}$$

Once the motion parameters are available from Eq. (41), the values of p, q, r can be computed for the second frame to facilitate tracking over the subsequent frames.

From the fact that C_1, C_2, C_3 are linear in p, q, r, Kanatani suggested a method by which the initial orientation can be extracted from multiple views of the initial static scene. The planar face is assumed to be stationary, and the camera is moved by a known distance in X, Y, and Z directions and three new images are recorded. Again a set of three linear equations in p, q, and r are formed and solved. However, this method requires at least three views, and may be viewed as a region-based stereoscopy. As will be shown later, the dynamic nature of the scene can be utilized to extract the initial orientation by different methods.

It is also emphasized that the choice of the feature functions is crucial since a wrong choice may lead to degeneracy in Eq. (41). For example, x, y, x^2, xy, y^2, and x^2y^2 have been chosen as the feature functions in Kanatani (24).

2.4. Combined Optical Flow – Correspondence Approach

From our studies of biological systems (1, 25), it is clear that optical flow plays an important role in perceiving a slowly varying dynamic scene. The computation of optical flow is geared mainly from pixel levels, and the resulting abstraction is unidirectional. However, recent models in cognitive sciences support a particular control structure that is bidirectional. We, the humans, are able to interpret the 3D structures and the depth information from 2D images. Spatial structures of the scenes readily lend themselves to our visual perception process (26, 27).

It is more effective and practical to combine the optical-flow- and correspondence-based methods. Any uncertainties faced in one of the methods, is generally a plus in the other. Consequently, strong evidence available for correspondence-based partial perception can be utilized to activate a more rigorous and biased computation of the optical flow field, if necessary. Alternatively, a set of consistent signatures in two flow fields may be used to group corresponding regions. Evidence accumulation (28) and evidence-based object recognition (29, 30) use such control structures. Although some authors have combined these techniques, more work is necessary in this aspect.

Mitiche and Aggarwal (31) applied the principle of conservation of distance to optical flow field. In particular, their approach blends both point correspondence and optical flow. Then, given a set of four-point correspondence, or given the true 2D optical flow at four points in the image plane, it is possible to compute $\mathbf{T}$ and $\mathbf{\Omega}$. This method is applicable for perspectively projected images.

Zhao (32) and Young (33) describe a set of objective functions to estimate a globally consistent 2D velocity field. It is assumed that the smoothly varying image sequence of a rigid planar patch has already been segmented, and that the boundary points are available. Let $\mathbf{u} = \mathbf{x}_{t+1} - \mathbf{x}$ be the velocity vector. A quadratic objective function is then defined of the form

$$\hat{\mathbf{u}} = \mathbf{G}\xi_t. \tag{42}$$

The meaning of $\mathbf{G}$ and ξ will become apparent after reading Section 3 in this chapter. Let $\mathbf{x}_i$ be a point on the boundary of the image segment corresponding to a planar region. Also, let γ be the component of $\mathbf{u}$ along the local normal $\mathbf{n}$ (to the boundary) at that point i. A globally consistent 2D velocity field would minimize the total error defined below:

$$\epsilon^2 = \sum_{i=1}^{|B|} \left[\left(\mathbf{u}_i^T \mathbf{n}_i - \gamma_i \right)^2 + \eta (\mathbf{u}_i - \hat{\mathbf{u}}_i)^T (\mathbf{u}_i - \hat{\mathbf{u}}_i) \right]. \tag{43}$$

The minimization procedure is an iterative relaxation algorithm, written compactly as

$$\mathbf{u}_i(k+1) = \hat{\mathbf{u}}_i(k) - \frac{1}{\eta+1} \mathbf{n}_i \left[\mathbf{n}_i^T \hat{\mathbf{u}}_i(k) - \gamma_i \right]. \tag{44}$$

The quadratic objective function $\hat{\mathbf{u}}$ has to be computed iteratively from previous iteration, when $\mathbf{G}$ is not available. Let

$$\begin{aligned} \mathbf{w}^T &= \left[\mathbf{u}_1^T, \mathbf{u}_2^T, \ldots, \mathbf{u}_N^T \right] \\ \hat{\mathbf{w}}^T &= \left[\hat{\mathbf{u}}_1^T, \hat{\mathbf{u}}_2^T, \ldots, \hat{\mathbf{u}}_N^T \right]. \end{aligned} \tag{45}$$

Then

$$\hat{\mathbf{w}}(k) = \mathbf{Q}(\mathbf{Q}^T\mathbf{Q})^{-1}\mathbf{Q}^T\mathbf{w}(k), \tag{46}$$

where $\mathbf{Q}$ is a $2N \times 12$ matrix, where N is the number of points on the boundary of the specific region being tracked. The odd numbered rows, $1, 3, 5, \ldots, (2i+1), \ldots, (2N-1)$, are of the form

$$\left[1, x_i, y_i, x_i^2, x_i, y_i, y_i^2, 0, 0, 0, 0, 0, 0 \right].$$

The even-numbered rows, say, $2i$th row, consists of the same numbers, except that the six zeros are moved to the front of the row vector. The initial value is computed from basic optical flow equation. The experimental results show a good agreement with motion parameters estimated using region-based methods and the objective-function-based flow field interpretations.

Waxman's (34) approach to combine the region correspondence and optical flow methods assumes that a region correspondence has already been established. Thus, a pair of corresponding contours is made available, facilitating the identification of a large number of noisy point correspondences implying a sparse set of noisy optical flow vectors. Since the regions have already been assumed to be planar, the flow field must satisfy some properties. These properties are used to develop a globally consistent 2D optical flow field. The optical flow field and the shape change parameters are used together to extract the 3D motion parameters.

3. REGION-BASED APPROACH TO THREE-DIMENSIONAL MOTION ANALYSIS

As stated earlier, the purpose of this chapter is to represent new results that would complement Chapter 14 (12) of the first volume of this book series. The emphasis is on region-based techniques. The flow of computation in region-based techniques is given in the flowchart in Fig. 10.5.

The analysis considers both orthographic and perspective imaging environments. The relationship between an arbitrary 3D motion of a finite-sized rigid planar face and the resulting change in its observed shape are

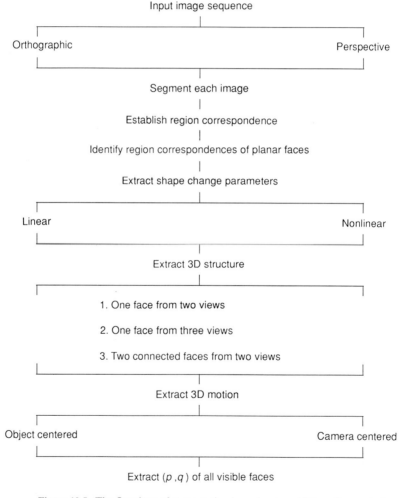

Figure 10.5. The flowchart of computation in region-based 3D motion analysis.

explained. The resulting 2D shape change is linear for orthographic images, and quadratic and nonlinear for perspective images.

Given the observed shape of a rigid planar face and the shape change parameters, in principle, it is possible to predict its shape in other images within the image sequence. For example, given $f(\mathbf{x}; t)$ and $(\mathbf{A}, \mathbf{c})$, it is possible to predict $f(\mathbf{x}; t + 1)$. In order to predict the shape of a patch at time $t + 1$ from its shape at time t, it is required that for every image pixel in the target image, its position in the image be computed at time t. This is possible in the case of orthographic images:

$$\hat{f}(\mathbf{x}; t + 1) \leftarrow f\left[\mathbf{A}^{-1}(\mathbf{x} - \mathbf{c}); t\right]. \tag{47}$$

However, it is not the case for perspective images because of the nonlinear nature of underlying dynamic shape changes. A method called *time-reversal technique* is used to predict the shape of the patch at time t based on its image at $t + 1$ as

$$\hat{f}(\mathbf{x}; t) \leftarrow f\left[\mathbf{\Phi}(\mathbf{x}); t + 1\right]. \tag{48}$$

The objective is to estimate, iteratively, the values of $\hat{\mathbf{A}}, \hat{\mathbf{c}}$ that minimize the mean-squared error between $f(\mathbf{x}; t + 1)$ and $\hat{f}(\mathbf{x}; t + 1)$. It is not clear if both $(\mathbf{A}, \mathbf{c})$ extracted from the images are unique. However, the 3D interpretation of the dynamic scene based on three consecutive frames is uniquely resolvable.

The next step is to interpret the 3D state of nature of the dynamic scene from these shape change parameters extracted from several images. Three similar cases are considered in both orthographic and perspective imaging environments.

3.1. Motion Analysis from Orthographic Images

Given a pair of corresponding regions, several algorithms (2) may be used to compute the shape change parameters, $\mathbf{A}$ and $\mathbf{c}$. Once the shape change parameters have been computed, the 3D motion parameters are recovered using Eq. (29). The computation requires a knowledge of the initial 3D orientation of the RPP (rigid planar pitch) being tracked. It is shown that the initial orientation of the RPP can also be recovered. Selected cases will be considered in this subsection for which both the 3D orientation and motion parameters can be recovered from orthographic image sequences.

It is assumed that at least two segments, among others, have been identified as the images of two distinct RPPs in the scene, in two consecutive image frames, specifically, in $f(x, y; t)$ as well as $f(x, y; t + 1)$. One of these faces is called the *primary face* and the others, *secondary faces*. The secondary faces may be chosen to have the desirable properties such as symmetry, skewed symmetry, and region of maximum connectivity. The purpose of the *primary face* is to provide an *object-centered* coordinate system whose origin is located at the center of the *primary face* with its axes being parallel to the corresponding axes of the camera coordinate system. A *one-point correspondence* can be used when it is not possible to establish a primary region.

Then, the 3D translation of the object with reference to the stationary observer is simply the translation of the origin of the moving frame measured with reference to the observer coordinate system. The rotation of the rigid body is readily described by Eulerian angles, with reference to the moving frame. Because of the inherent nature of orthographic imaging, neither the Z component of the 3D translation nor the distance between the camera and the object can be recovered from the given images alone.

The orthogonality of the rotation matrix **R** is used to explore the mutual constraints between the linear shape change parameters. Their interdependence is compactly represented by a pair of circles in a parametrically scaled gradient space. When the constraint is transformed into the gradient space, it results in a nonlinear curve $\phi(p, q) = 0$, called the *solution curve*, which is essentially a specific form of gradient ambiguities, similar to that of the hyperbolic curves derived by Kanade (35) based on *skewed symmetries*. In forming this *solution curve*, no explicit assumption is made about the shape of the planar face. Thus, by suitably choosing one or more constraints in the gradient space, in conjunction with the *solution curve*, one can solve for p, q, and s first, followed by the recovery of the 3D motion parameters.

Different spatial configurations for which the initial orientation itself can be recovered are presented in the subsequent sections.

3.1.1. Gradient Ambiguities: A Mutual Constraint in (A, c)

Six equations in p, q and s parameters, a_{ij} and c_k values and r_{ij} (unknown) values could be developed from Eq. (29). Since **R** is an orthogonal matrix, it follows that

$$\sum_{k=1}^{3} r_{ik} r_{jk} = \begin{cases} 1 & \text{if } i = j, \\ 0 & \text{otherwise.} \end{cases} \tag{49}$$

Then, Eq. (29) can further be reduced to show that

$$\left(\frac{p}{s} - \frac{a_{11}}{c_1}\right)^2 + \left(\frac{q}{s} - \frac{a_{12}}{c_1}\right)^2 = \frac{1}{c_1^2} - \frac{1}{s^2},$$

$$\left(\frac{p}{s} - \frac{a_{21}}{c_2}\right)^2 + \left(\frac{q}{s} - \frac{a_{22}}{c_2}\right)^2 = \frac{1}{c_2^2} - \frac{1}{s^2}, \tag{50}$$

and

$$\left(\frac{p}{s} - \frac{a_{11}}{c_1}\right)\left(\frac{p}{s} - \frac{a_{21}}{c_2}\right) + \left(\frac{q}{s} - \frac{a_{12}}{c_1}\right)\left(\frac{q}{s} - \frac{a_{22}}{c_2}\right) = -\frac{1}{s^2}. \quad (51)$$

A simple geometric interpretation of the equations in Eq. (50) is possible. Consider a plane, spanned by the scaled gradient space by a factor $1/s$. Then, Eq. (50) represents a pair of intersecting circles, which, in a limiting case, are tangential to each other, when $s \to \sqrt{c_1^2 + c_2^2}$. It can be shown that the third equation is linearly dependent, since it defines the line of intersection of the above circles. Also, it can be shown that

$$\left(\frac{a_{11}}{c_1} - \frac{a_{21}}{c_2}\right)^2 + \left(\frac{a_{12}}{c_1} - \frac{a_{22}}{c_2}\right)^2 = \frac{1}{c_1^2} + \frac{1}{c_2^2}, \quad (52)$$

and

$$0 \le \frac{1}{s^2} \le \frac{1}{c_1^2 + c_2^2}. \quad (53)$$

For a given value of $1/s$ within the permissible range, the value of p/s and q/s can be readily computed; hence (p, q). In addition, it can be

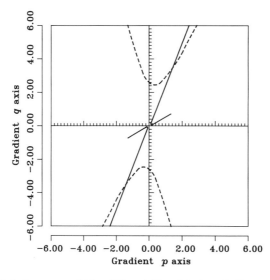

Figure 10.6. Solution curve of Eq. (50) and Kanade's hyperbolic constraints in (p, q) space. Reproduced form Seetharaman and Young (21) with permission from World Scientific Press.

proved (2) that the permissible range of s corresponds to the points located on the common chord of the two largest circles in the parameter space. Every point on this chord represents a unique solution (p, q, s). The loci of such reconstructed values of (p, q) is given in Fig. 10.6.

The solution curve is nonlinear, and a closed-form expression would be extremely useful. It has interesting applications as that of Kanade's (35) results based on skewed symmetry. Also, it is important to note that the gradient ambiguities are constrained from the dynamic shape change parameters only. No assumptions are made on the shape of the object. In the following sections, we present a few methods that take advantage of the *solution curve* in the gradient space or the *constrained line segment* in the parameter space, to extract the 3D orientation parameters of the given plane(s).

3.1.2. Two-Region Correspondence from Three Images

In this section we will be concerned with the extraction of (p, q, s) from three time sequential images of a rigid body in motion. It is assumed that the images have been segmented beforehand and that at least two-region correspondence have been identified. The *primary face* is used mainly for the choice of the origin of the moving frame. A *one-point correspondence* can be used as well. Let $f(\mathbf{x}; t)$, $f(\mathbf{x}; t_1)$, and $f(\mathbf{x}; t_2)$ be three images in a sequence. Let $(\mathbf{A}, \mathbf{c})$ and $(\mathbf{B}, \mathbf{d})$ describe the shape disparity between $\langle f_0, f_1 \rangle$ and $\langle f_0, f_2 \rangle$, respectively. The underlying 3D motion can be described by $(\mathbf{R}, \mathbf{T})$ and $(\mathbf{S}, \mathbf{U})$, respectively. Then in the parametrically scaled gradient space $[(p/s), (q/s)]$, the following four equations will hold:

$$\left(\frac{p}{s} - \frac{a_{11}}{c_1}\right)^2 + \left(\frac{q}{s} - \frac{a_{12}}{c_1}\right)^2 = \frac{1}{c_1^2} - \frac{1}{s^2},$$

$$\left(\frac{p}{s} - \frac{a_{21}}{c_2}\right)^2 + \left(\frac{q}{2} - \frac{a_{22}}{c_2}\right)^2 = \frac{1}{c_2^2} - \frac{1}{s^2},$$

$$\left(\frac{p}{s} - \frac{b_{11}}{d_1}\right)^2 + \left(\frac{q}{s} - \frac{b_{12}}{d_1}\right)^2 = \frac{1}{d_1^2} - \frac{1}{s^2}, \tag{54}$$

$$\left(\frac{p}{s} - \frac{b_{21}}{d_2}\right)^2 + \left(\frac{q}{s} - \frac{b_{22}}{d_2}\right)^2 = \frac{1}{d_2^2} - \frac{1}{s^2}.$$

The first two equations determine a pair of intersecting circles, whose common chord represents a locus of solution points. The latter two equations give rise to a common chord of two intersecting circles. The point of intersection of these two common chords (within the scaled gradient space) can be obtained directly by solving

$$\frac{p}{s}\left(\frac{a_{11}}{c_1} - \frac{a_{21}}{c_2}\right) + \frac{q}{s}\left(\frac{a_{12}}{c_1} - \frac{a_{22}}{c_2}\right) = \frac{a_{11}^2 + a_{12}^2 - 1}{c_1^2} - \frac{a_{11}a_{21} + a_{12}a_{22}}{c_1 c_2},$$

$$\frac{p}{s}\left(\frac{b_{11}}{d_1} - \frac{b_{21}}{d_2}\right) + \frac{q}{s}\left(\frac{b_{12}}{d_1} - \frac{b_{22}}{d_2}\right) = \frac{b_{11}^2 + b_{12}^2 - 1}{d_1^2} - \frac{b_{11}b_{21} + b_{12}b_{22}}{d_1 d_2}.$$

$$(55)$$

The computation of (p, q, s) is then carried out simply by substituting the intersection point (α, β), in the $[(p/s),(q/s)]$ plane, into any of the above four equations. Although there is only one point of intersection in the $[(p/s),(q/s)]$ plane, two solutions are expected: both positive and negative values of s.

The existence of the solution breaks down in the following three cases: when (1) **S** and **R** both represent only a rotation about the Z axis—that is, none of them have a nonzero rotation about the X or Y axes; (2) some combinations of $\mathbf{R}_1$, $\mathbf{T}_1$, **S**, and **U** may cause these lines to be parallel in the $[(p/s),(q/s)]$ space (a trivial example of such degenerate case occurs when $\mathbf{S} = \mathbf{R}$; and (3) also, a known degenerate case is

$$\Delta_{31}\tilde{\Delta}_{32} - \Delta_{32}\tilde{\Delta}_{31} = 0, \tag{56}$$

where Δ_{ij} represents the minor$_{ij}$ of the matrix **R**. Note that case (2) is a direct consequence of case (3) stated above.

3.1.3. Three-Region Correspondence over Two Images

Assume that the segmented images represent at least three planar faces present in the object. Since the rotation and translation will be resolved with reference to the centroid of the primary face, the remaining two faces should have the same rigid motion parameters governing their shape deformations. It is assumed that these two faces are adjacent, and that they are not parallel in the 3D space. The *primary face* is used mainly for the choice of the origin of the moving frame. A *one-point correspondence* can be used as well.

Let (p_1, q_1, s_1) and (p_2, q_2, s_2) represent two distinct and nonparallel planar faces under observation. Let $(\mathbf{A}, \mathbf{c})$ and $(\mathbf{B}, \mathbf{d})$ describe the shape change parameters of these two planes. Both **R** and **T** remain the same for both the planes. Then, from Eq. (29), we note that the following equations hold:

$$\frac{s_1}{s_2} = \frac{c_1}{d_1} = \frac{c_2}{d_2}. \tag{57}$$

From Eq. (50) it readily follows that

$$\left(\frac{p_1}{s_1} - \frac{a_{11}}{c_1}\right)^2 + \left(\frac{q_1}{s_1} - \frac{a_{12}}{c_1}\right)^2 = \frac{1}{c_1^2} - \frac{1}{s_1^2},$$

$$\left(\frac{p_1}{s_1} - \frac{a_{21}}{c_2}\right)^2 + \left(\frac{q_1}{s_1} - \frac{a_{22}}{c_2}\right)^2 = \frac{1}{c_2^2} - \frac{1}{s_1^2},$$

$$\left(\frac{p_2}{s_2} - \frac{b_{11}}{d_1}\right)^2 + \left(\frac{q_2}{s_2} - \frac{b_{12}}{d_1}\right)^2 = \frac{1}{d_1^2} - \frac{1}{s_2^2},$$

$$\left(\frac{p_2}{s_2} - \frac{b_{21}}{d_2}\right)^2 + \left(\frac{q_2}{s_2} - \frac{b_{22}}{d_2}\right)^2 = \frac{1}{d_2^2} - \frac{1}{s_2^2}. \tag{58}$$

Notice that these equations are written in terms of $[(p_1/s_1),(q_1/s_1)]$ and $[(p_2/s_2),(q_2/s_2)]$ as

$$\frac{p_1}{s_1}\left(\frac{a_{11}}{c_1} - \frac{a_{21}}{c_2}\right) + \frac{q_1}{s_1}\left(\frac{a_{12}}{c_1} - \frac{a_{22}}{c_2}\right) = \frac{a_{11}^2 + a_{12}^2 - 1}{c_1^2} - \frac{a_{11}a_{21} + a_{12}a_{22}}{c_1 c_2}, \tag{59a}$$

$$\frac{p_2}{s_2}\left(\frac{b_{11}}{d_1} - \frac{b_{21}}{d_2}\right) + \frac{q_2}{s_2}\left(\frac{b_{12}}{d_1} - \frac{b_{22}}{d_2}\right) = \frac{b_{11}^2 + b_{12}^2 - 1}{d_1^2} - \frac{b_{11}b_{21} + b_{12}b_{22}}{d_1 d_2}. \tag{59b}$$

In contrast to the previous example, the point of intersection of these lines does not necessarily signify the solution. However, such an instance simply indicates a possibility that $(p_1/q_1) = (p_2/q_2)$.

Let L_1 be the solution line segment in the parameter space satisfying Eq. (59a) for valid ranges of s_1. Also, let L_2 be the line segment in the parameter space satisfying Eq. (59b) for valid ranges of s_2. For an arbitrary s_1 one can compute the corresponding s_2 from Eq. (57). Then the points $(\alpha_1, \beta_1) \in L_1$ and $(\alpha_2, \beta_2) \in L_2$ within the parameter space can be readily calculated.

A careful inspection of the problem reveals that we need one more constraint to recover the initial orientations of the two planes. It is shown by Kanade (35) that the image of the line of interface between two arbitrary planes in space satisfies the following relationship. Let two planes defined by (p_1, q_1, s_1) and (p_2, q_2, s_2) intersect in the 3D space at a line whose image in the image plane subtends and angle γ; then it is required that

$$(p_1 - p_2, q_1 - q_2)(\cos \gamma, \sin \gamma)^T = 0. \tag{60}$$

Then, a one-dimensional search algorithm, parameterized by s_1, can be devised to extract the initial orientation of both of the planar faces as follows:

Step 1. Identify the image of the line of interface L_3 between the two secondary faces within the image plane and measure its slope. Let this slope be γ.

Step 2. Chose an arbitrary value of s_1, in the valid range, and compute the corresponding s_{2_i}.

Step 3. Compute the corresponding orientation parameters (p, q) in the gradient plane, as explained in the foregoing sections, and label them as $\mathbf{p}_{i1}$ and $\mathbf{p}_{i2}$, respectively.

Step 4. Check if the vector joining $\mathbf{p}_{i1}$ and $\mathbf{p}_{i2}$ is perpendicular to the line L_3. If so, we have arrived at the solution; exit to step 6, or else continue.

Step 5. If the entire range of s_1 has been exhausted, then exit with failure message, or else choose another value of s_1, and go to step 3.

Step 6. Label the solution values as $\mathbf{p}_{i1}, s_1$ and $\mathbf{p}_{i2}, s_2$ and exit with success message.

An iterative scheme seems to be possible, however, and is left for future research.

3.1.4. Two-Region Corresponding in Two Images

In practice, most of the vision systems employed for industrial applications deal with objects of certain geometrical regularities (symmetries). In such cases, as stated earlier, the skewed symmetry observed in the image enables us to compute the gradient ambiguities, as developed by Kanade.

The two axes of skewed symmetry observed in the image are assumed to represent two perpendicular lines in the 3D space. Let the two axes of skewed symmetry subtend the angles β_1 and β_2, respectively, with the x axis. Then Kanade (35) arrives at a hyperbolic equation relating p and q in the (p, q) plane, from the basic equation

$$\cos(\beta_1 - \beta_2) + (p \cos \beta_1 + q \sin \beta_1)(p \cos \beta_2 + q \sin \beta_2) = 0. \quad (61)$$

Basically, Eq. (61) constrains an infinite number of (p, q) pairs that can result in the same image, similar to our *solution curve*. With β_1 and β_2 measured from the image, the 3D orientation of the given planar face (p, q, s) can be computed by solving Eqs. (61) and (50).

3.2. Motion Analysis from Perspective Images

This method is applicable for tracking rigid objects consisting of at least one visible planar face. First, it is shown that as the rigid body undergoes motion, the associated shape changes of its image are described by a nonlinear (quadratic) transformation. The analysis assumes a *viewer coordinate* system with its origin located within the focus of the camera.

Given a region correspondence in two perspective images, the iterative algorithm developed by Seetharaman and Young (36) can be applied for estimating the nonlinear shape change parameters. Certain heuristics to improve the initial estimates and the convergence of the iterative algorithm are also explained (2).

When the initial orientation of the RPP is available, the motion parameters are computed directly from the shape change parameters by solving a set of linear equations. Also, when the 3D structure is not known, a nonlinear technique is used to estimate the initial orientation, followed by the computation of rotation parameters. The translations terms, however, can be extracted up to an unknown scale factor. The method involves solving a sixth-order nonlinear equation and deals with an instance of one-region correspondence over two images. Also, this method provides an elegant graphical interpretation of the results.

The basic equations governing the recovery of 3D structures are emphasized and various possibilities are discussed. Given a one-region correspondence over three consecutive images, the orientation parameters can be extracted uniquely, followed by the recovery of the 3D motion parameters. Also, given two-region correspondence in two images, one arrives at a set of 10 nonlinear equations in nine unknowns. In addition, we develop an additional equation in the gradient space, similar to the orthographic environment. As a result, we have 11 equations in nine unknowns, which can be solved using a standard numerical method. A partial analysis of these methods is presented, and the preliminary results indicate that the solutions do exist. The problems such as uniqueness have not been considered for these techniques, and further investigation is necessary.

3.2.1. Quadratic Shape-Change Analysis

The perspective imaging system shown in Fig. 10.4 is considered for the analysis. Let $\mathbf{x}$ be the image of a 3D point $\mathbf{X}$ such that

$$x = F\frac{X}{Z}, \qquad y = F\frac{Y}{Z} \tag{62}$$

An arbitrary motion of a rigid body in space can be represented by a rotation followed by translation as follows:

$$\mathbf{X}_{t+1} = \mathbf{R}\mathbf{X}_t + (\mu_x, \mu_y, \mu_z)^T \tag{63}$$

In particular, we adopt the small rotation model of $\mathbf{R}$ that represents the instantaneous angular velocity. It is known that the angular velocity matrix is skewed symmetric as shown below.

$$\mathbf{R} = \begin{bmatrix} 1 & r_{12} & r_{13} \\ r_{21} & 1 & r_{23} \\ r_{31} & r_{32} & 1 \end{bmatrix} \qquad r_{ij} = -r_{ji}, \qquad j \neq i \tag{64}$$

In order to emphasize the significance of the linear and quadratic terms in describing the shape changes, we defer the suppression of focal length F from the equations. Let the planar face in the rigid body be described by

$$Z = -pX - qY - s. \tag{65}$$

Under certain conditions, where

$$\left| \frac{\mu_z}{Z_t} \right| \ll 1 \qquad \text{and} \qquad \left| \frac{r_{31}x_t + r_{32}y_t}{f} \right| \ll 1,$$

the nonlinear shape change is expressed in the form

$$\mathbf{x}_{t+1} = \mathbf{x}_t + \mathbf{G}\xi_t, \tag{66}$$

where ξ is an augmented vector defined such that $\xi^T = (1, x, y, x^2, xy, y^2)$ and $\mathbf{G}$ is a 2×6 matrix whose coefficients are given below:

$$g_{10} = F\left(r_{13} - \frac{\mu_x}{s}\right), \qquad g_{20} = F\left(r_{23} - \frac{\mu_y}{s}\right),$$

$$g_{11} = \left(\frac{\mu_z - p\mu_x}{s}\right), \qquad g_{21} = \left(r_{21} - \frac{p\mu_y}{s}\right),$$

$$g_{12} = \left(r_{12} - \frac{q\mu_x}{s}\right), \qquad g_{22} = \left(\frac{\mu_z - q\mu_y}{s}\right),$$

$$g_{13} = \frac{1}{F}\left(r_{13} + \frac{p\mu_z}{s}\right), \qquad g_{23} = 0, \tag{67}$$

$$g_{14} = \frac{1}{F}\left(r_{23} + \frac{q\mu_z}{s}\right), \qquad g_{24} = \frac{1}{F}\left(r_{13} + \frac{p\mu_z}{s}\right),$$

$$g_{15} = 0, \qquad g_{25} = \frac{1}{F}\left(r_{23} + \frac{q\mu_z}{s}\right).$$

There are only eight distinct parameters that describes the nonlinear shape changes of the image of an RPP in motion. The nonlinear shape change matrix is similar to the Ψ transformation developed by Adiv (5).

The estimation shape change parameters follow the time-reversal technique, as described earlier. The method examines the shape changes of the visible face backward from the $(t + 1)$th image to the tth image in a tractable form. Given a particular value of $\mathbf{G}$, say, $\hat{\mathbf{G}}$, the shape of the visible face at time t is expressed in a functional form as follows:

$$\hat{s}(\mathbf{x}; t) \leftarrow s(\mathbf{x} + \hat{\mathbf{G}}\xi; t + 1). \tag{68}$$

Then, the objective is to find the $\hat{\mathbf{G}}$ such that the mean-squared error

$$\epsilon^2(\hat{\mathbf{G}}) = \sum_{\mathbf{x}} \|\hat{s}(\mathbf{x}; t) - s(\mathbf{x}; t)\|^2 \tag{69}$$

is minimized. Then, the iterative algorithm

$$\hat{\mathbf{G}}_{k+1} = \hat{\mathbf{G}}_k - \rho_k \frac{\partial}{\partial \hat{\mathbf{G}}} \epsilon^2(\hat{\mathbf{G}}) \tag{70}$$

seeks the value of $\hat{\mathbf{G}}$ for which ϵ^2 is minimum, where

$$\frac{\partial}{\partial \hat{\mathbf{G}}} \epsilon^2(\hat{\Gamma}) = 2 \sum_{\mathbf{x}} [\hat{s}(\mathbf{x}; t) - s(\mathbf{x}; t)][\nabla \hat{s}(\mathbf{x}; t)] \xi^T. \tag{71}$$

Generally speaking, it is possible that the algorithm converges into a local minimum instead of the true minimum. The nature and the existence of multiple extrema in the objective function are not clearly known. The experimental results indicate that the iterative method is sensitive to the initial estimates (i.e., $\hat{\mathbf{G}}_0$) and that oscillations are inevitable if ρ_k is not chosen carefully.

In order to improve the convergence performance, it is desired to have a good estimate of the initial value $\hat{\mathbf{G}}_0$ for the iterative procedure. It is effective (2) to find the best linear terms first, which are then followed by a suitable estimation of the quadratic terms, g_{13} and g_{14}. Another approach is to exploit certain mutual constraints on the elements of the $\mathbf{G}$ matrix. In particular, if the initial orientation of the RPP [i.e., (p, q)] is known, then the quadratic terms estimated using the linear terms of the partially estimated $\mathbf{G}$ matrix. That is, in tracking, we can always compute an estimate of (p, q) from the values of (p_{t_2}, q_{t_2}) as well as the extracted $\mathbf{R}$. Also, it is assumed that the linear terms have been computed to a reasonable degree of accuracy. Once the quadratic terms are estimated, then the iterative estimation algorithm is activated with the suitably initialized $\hat{\mathbf{G}}$ matrix.

In situations where (p, q) is not known, a large set of candidate points will be considered in the vicinity of the most likely orientations. For example, if $(\hat{p}, \hat{q})$ denotes the expected orientation of the planar face, then search for all (p, q) such that $(p - \hat{p}^2) + (q - \hat{q}^2) \le \delta^2$, where the radius of search δ has been chosen experimentally. Once again the method requires at least a rough estimate of (p, q).

3.2.2. Extraction of Three-Dimensional Motion Parameters

Consider a region correspondence over two image frames, whose orientations in the 3D space is known, that is, where p, q, and s are known. The first step is to extract $\hat{\mathbf{G}}$. The next step is to extract the 3D motion parameters. By suitably rearranging the equations in Eq. (67), eight linear equations are obtained in six unknowns, namely, (T_X, T_Y, T_Z) and

r_{12}, r_{13}, r_{23}, as follows:

$$
\begin{bmatrix}
0 & 1 & 0 & -\dfrac{1}{s} & 0 & 0 \\[2mm]
0 & 0 & 0 & -\dfrac{p}{s} & 0 & \dfrac{1}{s} \\[2mm]
1 & 0 & 0 & -\dfrac{q}{s} & 0 & 0 \\[2mm]
0 & 1 & 0 & 0 & 0 & \dfrac{p}{s} \\[2mm]
0 & 0 & 1 & 0 & 0 & \dfrac{q}{s} \\[2mm]
0 & 0 & 1 & 0 & \dfrac{1}{s} & 0 \\[2mm]
-1 & 0 & 0 & 0 & -\dfrac{p}{s} & 0 \\[2mm]
0 & 0 & 0 & 0 & -\dfrac{q}{s} & \dfrac{1}{s}
\end{bmatrix}
\begin{bmatrix}
r_{12} \\ r_{13} \\ r_{23} \\ \mu_x \\ \mu_y \\ \mu_z
\end{bmatrix}
=
\begin{bmatrix}
\dfrac{g_{10}}{F} \\[2mm]
g_{11} \\[2mm]
g_{12} \\[2mm]
Fg_{13} \\[2mm]
Fg_{14} \\[2mm]
\dfrac{g_{20}}{F} \\[2mm]
g_{21} \\[2mm]
g_{22}
\end{bmatrix}
\tag{72}
$$

The basic equations describing the nonlinear shape changes as given in Eq. (67). When one is concerned with tracking, it is assumed that p, q, and s are known at time t, and that the $\hat{G}$ matrix has been evaluated as explained in the previous sections. Thus, Eq. (72) represents a set of eight linear equations in $r_{12}, r_{13}, r_{23}, \mu_1, \mu_2$, and μ_3. Then, one can solve these overdetermined equations by a standard linear least-square techniques and extract the motion parameters. A standard, least-squared approach for solving overdetermined linear equations is adopted to solve Eq. (72).

3.2.3. Extraction of Three-Dimensional Orientation Parameters

In this section we are concerned with certain methods of extracting the 3D orientation and the depth information of a rigid, planar-faced object from its perspective image sequence. Unlike the *gradient ambiguity* experienced with the orthographic images explained earlier, an easy interpretation of the underlying relationships is not available at present. The methods to be described follow a set of nonlinear equations developed from Eq. (67).

If p, q, and s at time t are not known, we notice that Eq. (73) represents eight nonlinear equations in nine unknowns. Through simple manipulations, one can eliminate the r_{ij} terms and arrive at the following set of five equations in six unknowns given below:

$$p\mu_3 + \mu_1 - h_1 s = 0,$$

$$p\mu_1 - \mu_3 + g_{11} s = 0, \qquad\qquad h_1 = \left(Fg_{13} - \frac{g_{10}}{F}\right),$$

$$p\mu_2 + q\mu_1 - h_2 s = 0, \qquad \text{where} \qquad h_2 = -(g_{12} + g_{21}), \quad (73)$$

$$q\mu_2 - \mu_3 + g_{22} s = 0, \qquad\qquad h_3 = \left(Fg_{25} - \frac{g_{20}}{F}\right).$$

$$q\mu_3 + \mu_2 - h_3 s = 0,$$

These equations play an important role in extracting the 3D structure of a dynamic scene of rigid objects. With properly chosen conditions, a system of nonlinear equations can be formulated and solved, as will be described in the following text.

By substituting $v_i = \mu_i/s$, and reducing Eq. (73) by a series of eliminations, it is shown that

$$p = \frac{(q^2 + 1)(h_1 q - h_2)}{(h_3 q^2 + 2g_{22} q_2 - h_3)},$$

$$\qquad\qquad\qquad\qquad\qquad\qquad\qquad\qquad (74)$$

$$q = \frac{(p^2 + 1)(h_3 p - h_2)}{(h_1 p^2 + 2g_{11} p - h_1)}.$$

Further reductions of Eqs. (74) is possible by substituting for q in the first expression from the second expression. Such a reduction results in an eighth-degree polynomial equation in p whose roots can be found by standard numerical methods. A closer look at Eq. (74) reveals two solutions $[p = (h_2/h_3), q = 0]$ and $[p = 0, q = (h_2/h_1)]$, which are meaningless. After eliminating these two roots by a factorization process, however, we are still left with a sixth-degree polynomial equation in p to be solved numerically.

To facilitate our understanding of the underlying solutions of Eq. (73), a graphical solution is desired. By substituting $\alpha = \tan^{-1} p$ and $\beta = \tan^{-1} q$, we can rewrite Eq. (74) such that

$$\alpha = \tan^{-1}\left[\frac{(\tan^2 \beta + 1)(h_1 \tan \beta - h_2)}{h_3 \tan^2 \beta + 2g_{22} \tan \beta - h_3}\right],$$

$$\beta = \tan^{-1}\left[\frac{(\tan^2 \alpha + 1)(h_3 \tan \alpha - h_3)}{h_1 \tan^2 \alpha + 2g_{11} \tan \alpha - h_1}\right], \qquad \text{where} \qquad -\frac{\pi}{2} \le \alpha, \beta \le \frac{\pi}{2}$$

$$\qquad\qquad\qquad\qquad\qquad\qquad\qquad\qquad\qquad\qquad (75)$$

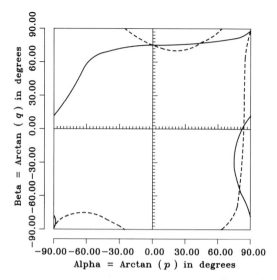

Figure 10.7. The gradient ambiguity [Eq. (74)] shown in $(\tan^{-1} p, \tan^{-1} q)$ space. Reproduced from Seetharaman and Young (21) with permission from World Scientific Press.

It is to be noted that the graphical solution plotted in (α, β) plane is essentially a different form of gradient ambiguities in which two loci of permissible orientations intersect at the expected solution points. The experimental results indicate that the performance still leaves much to be desired. In Fig. 10.7 we present a graphical solution to Eq. (75) using an experimental result illustrated in Seetharaman (2).

It is expected from the fundamental works of Tsai and Huang (15) that there are only one (repeated) or two distinct roots of the sixth-order polynomial in p. We note that in arriving at Eq. (73) from Eq. (67), only a set of linear substitutions were made at each step; hence there exists only one set of q, ν_1, ν_2, ν_3, and r_{ij} values corresponding to each one of the six roots of the polynomial equation in p.

There are alternate ways to determine the initial orientations. A recent work (37) indicates that for 3D objects that are rich in parallel lines, the surface orientations can be determined from a single perspective view. If there is only one set of parallel lines, however, a linear constraint equation in p and q can be developed through the vanishing point of the images of the parallel lines. Then the linear constraint in conjunction with Eq. (74) can resolve the uniqueness considerations.

3.2.4. One-Region Correspondence in Three Frames

Another possibility of extracting the 3D orientation is to observe two or more visible faces (planar faces) in two or more images and analyze their quadratic shape change parameters. Consider a situation where we are given the image of a visible planar face in three consecutive images. For convenience, we represent the three images as f_2, f_0, and f_1. Let $\mathbf{G}^{(1)}$: $f_0 \rightarrow f_1$ and $\mathbf{G}^{(2)}$: $f_2 \leftarrow f_0$; describe the shape changes of the visible face in time. Also, let the 3D translation components of the underlying forward and inverse motion be described by $\mu_i^{(1)}$ and $\mu_i^{(2)}$, respectively. Then one can easily formulate a set of nonlinear equations in p, q, s, $\mu_i^{(1)}$, and $\mu_i^{(2)}$, values using Eq. (87). Further reductions show that

$$\left[h_3^{(2)}p - h_2^{(2)} \right]\left[h_1^{(1)}p^2 + 2g_{11}^{(1)}p - h_1^{(1)} \right]$$

$$- \left[h_3^{(1)}p - h_2^{(1)} \right]\left[h_1^{(2)}p^2 + 2g_{11}^{(2)}p - h_1^{(2)} \right] = 0 \qquad (76)$$

and

$$\left[h_1^{(2)}q - h_2^{(2)} \right]\left[h_3^{(1)}q^2 + 2g_{22}^{(1)}q - h_3^{(1)} \right]$$

$$- \left[h_1^{(1)}q - h_2^{(1)} \right]\left[h_3^{(2)}q^2 + 2g_{22}^{(2)}q - h_3^{(2)} \right] = 0. \qquad (77)$$

These two equations can be solved for p and q independently. Another approach is to obtain the graphic solution, for each motion problem independently, and choosing the solution common to both subproblems.

3.2.5. Two Adjacent Regions in Two Frames

Consider the instance where we are provided with two region correspondences in two images. It is assumed that the faces belong to the same rigid object; therefore, their individual shape changes are governed by the motion parameters of a single rigid motion. Let $\mathbf{G}^{(1)}$ and $\mathbf{G}^{(2)}$ be the two sets of shape change parameters of the two visible faces under inspection, and let (p_1, q_1, s_1) and (p_2, q_2, s_2) be the orientation parameters. Then, using Eq. (73), one can arrive at a set of nonlinear equations in $p_1, q_1, s_1, p_2, q_2, s_2, \mu_1, \mu_2, \mu_3$.

In addition to these equations, three more independent constraints on $\mu_1, \mu_2, \mu_3, s_1, s_2$ can be developed. Furthermore, if these two faces are assumed to be adjacent in 3D space, that is, if they intersect in space within the field of view, one can develop a quadratic constraint in p and q.

Let α be the slope of the line of interface between the two regions being tracked. Also, let (x_0, y_0) be one endpoint of that line. Then the following equation can be derived as an additional constraints on

p_1, q_1, p_2, q_2:

$$(q_1 - q_2)\tan \alpha + (p_1 - p_2) - (x_0 \tan \alpha - y_0)(p_1 q_2 - q_1 p_2) = 0.$$

$$(78)$$

Thus a system of overdetermined nonlinear equations in nine variables can be formulated and solved using any of the standard techniques.

4. CONCLUSION

Motion analysis has been an area of intensive research over the past decade. Substantial advancements have taken place since 1983, after Tsai and Huang's fundamental works (6) on point-correspondence-based methods. Their method offers closed-form solutions and insight into the inherent conditions with regard to tractability. However, in real applications the point correspondence method is faced with many practical problems.

The optical flow method offers an attractive solution because of its largely localized computational structure. Its simplicity is also evidenced by our understanding of vision systems in biological creatures. From a computational standpoint, it involves too many approximations, and unique interpretation of 3D motion from 2D velocity field is not a reliable process (22). However, it should be noted in the context here that humans do make use of other information in successfully grouping and perceiving the motion fields. An improvement in the overall control structure is necessary.

The region correspondence method and the line correspondence methods are somewhat less sensitive to noise, and are also realistic if our goal is to solve real-world problems. Nonetheless, a combination of optical-flow- and correspondence-based methods is more promising, and should be examined in detail. A comprehensive computational following such an approach would also facilitate multiview image sequence analysis, in which the correspondence-based techniques would be applicable across different views (recorded simultaneously), and optical-flow-based computation individually within each monocular image sequence. Research on this hybrid approach is currently in progress at The Center for Advanced Computer Studies.

ACKNOWLEDGMENTS

The author would like to acknowledge Prof. J. Gerbrands and Prof. B. Sankur, Delft University of Technology, for their comments on the initial draft of this chapter. Credits are also due to Phil Barnes and Anup Nayak for preparing the figures and experimental setups to evaluate different methods at the Computer Vision and Pattern Recognition Laboratory, University of Southwestern Louisiana.

This work was supported in part by a grant from the NSF, NSF-IRI-9210926 and a grant from the Louisiana Educational Quality Support Funds, LEQSF FY91-RAD-42.

REFERENCES

1. D. Marr, "Vision." Freeman, New York, 1982.
2. G. Seetharaman, "Estimation of 3-D motion and orientation of rigid objects from an image sequence: A region correspondence approach." Ph.D. Thesis, University of Miami, Coral Gables, FL, 1988.
3. T. Poggio, V. Torre, and C. Koch, Computational vision and regularization theory. *Nature (London)* **317**(2), 314–319 (1985).
4. W. B. Thompson, ed., *IEEE Transactions on Pattern Analysis and Machine Intelligence:* Special Issue on Visual Motion, Vol. 11. IEEE Computer Society, IEEE Press, 1989.
5. G. Adiv, Determining 3-D motion and surface structure from optical flow generated by several objects. *IEEE Trans. Pattern Anal. Mach. Intell.* **PAMI-7**(6), 384–401, (1985).
6. R. Y. Tsai and T. S. Huang, Uniqueness and estimation of three dimensional motion parameters of rigid objects with curved surfaces. *IEEE Trans. Pattern Anal. Mach. Intell.* **PAMI-6**, 545–554 (1984).
7. B. K. P. Horn, "Robot Vision." MIT Press, Cambridge, MA, 1987.
8. P. G. Mulgaonkar, Multiview image acquisition for postal parcels. *Adv. Imaging* No. 2, p. 44 (1991).
9. R. O. Duda, D. Nitzan, and P. Barrett, Use of range and reflectance data to find planar surfaces. *IEEE Trans. Pattern Anal. Mach. Intell.* **PAMI-1**, 259–271 (1979).
10. G. Seetharaman, "Calibration of Intrinsic Parameters of Videocameras and Stereo Systems Using Vanishing Points," Tech. Rep. TR 93-1-12. University of Southwestern Louisiana, Center for Advanced Computer Studies, Lafayette, 1993.
11. M. A. Snyder, The precision of 3-d parameters in correspondence based techniques. *IEEE Trans. Pattern Anal. Mach. Intell.* **PAMI-11**(5), 523–528 (1989).
12. T. S. Huang, Determining three dimensional motion and structure from two perspective images. In "Handbook of Pattern Recognition and Image Processing" (T. Y. Young, and K. S. Fu, eds.), pp. 334–354, Academic Press, San Diego, CA, 1989.
13. C. H. Lee, Time varying images: The effect of finite resolution on uniqueness. *Comput. Vision, Graphics, Image Process.*: **54**(3), 325–332 (1992).
14. J. Weng, T. S. Huang, and N. Ahuja, Motion and structure from two perspective views: Algorithm, error analysis and error estimation. *IEEE Trans. Pattern Anal. Mach. Intell.* **PAMI-11**(5), 451–476 (1989).
15. R. Y. Tsai and T. S. Huang, Estimating 3-dimensional motion parameters of a rigid planar patch. *iii*. Finite point correspondences and three views

problem. *IEEE Trans. Acoust., Speech, Signal Process.* **ASSP-32**(2), 213–220 (1984).

16. Y. Liu and T. S. Huang, A linear algorithm for determining motion and structure from. *Comput. Vision, Graphics, Image Process.* **44**(1), 35–57 (1988).

17. J. Weng, T. S. Huang, and N. Ahuja, Motion and structure from line correspondences: Closed-form solution, uniqueness and optimization. *IEEE Trans. Pattern Anal. Mach. Intell.* **PAMI-14**(3), 318–336 (1992).

18. T. Y. Young and Y. L. Wang, "Analysis of Linear Nonlinear Shape Changes," Tech. Rep. UM-ECE-82-1. University of Miami, Coral Gables, FL, 1982.

19. B. K. P. Horn and B. G. Schunck, Determining optical flow. *Artif. Intell.* **17**(8), 1855–1873 (1981).

20. E. C. Hildreth, Computations underlying the measurement of visual motion. *Artif. Intell.* **23**, 304–354 (1984).

21. G. S. Seetharaman and T. Y. Young, A region correspondence approach to the recovery of 3-D motion and structure in dynamic scenes. *In "Series in Automation"* (S.-S. Chen, ed.), Vol. 2, pp. 75–124. World Scientific Pulbl., NJ, 1989.

22. G. Adiv, Inherent ambiguities in recovering 3-d motion and structure from noisy flow field. *IEEE Trans. Pattern Anal. Mach. Intell.* **PAMI-11**(5), 477 (1989).

23. K. Kanatani, Tracing planar surface motion from a projection without knowing the correspondence. *Comput. Vision, Graphics, and Image Process.* **29**(1), 1–12 (1985).

24. K. Kanatani, Detecting motion of a planar surface by line and surface integrals. *Comput. Vision, Graphics, Image Process.* **29**(1), 13–26 (1985).

25. M. Egelhaaf, A. Borst, and R. Werner, Computational structure of biological motion-detection systems as revealed by local detector analysis in the fly's nervous system. *J. Opt. Soc. Am.* **6**(7), 1086–1087 (1989).

26. J. J. Gibson, "The Ecological Approach to Visual Perception." Houghton Mifflin, Boston, 1979.

27. J. J. Gibson, "The Senses Considered as Perceptual Systems." Houghton Mifflin, Boston, 1966.

28. K. M. Andress and A. C. Kak, Evidence accumulation and flow of control in a spatial reasoning system. *AI Mag.* **9** (Summer), 75–93 (1988).

29. A. K. Jain and R. Hoffman, Evidence-based recognition of 3-D objects. *IEEE Trans. Pattern Anal. Mach. Intell.* **PAMI-10**(6), 783–802 (1988).

30. G. Seetharaman, "Sira: Segment, Inspect and Refine Algorithms for Model Based Vision," Tech. Rep. CACS-TR-92-1-3. University of Southwestern Louisiana, Center for Advanced Computer Studies, Layfette, 1992.

31. A. Mitiche and J. K. Aggarwal, Analysis of time varying imagery. *In* "Handbook of Pattern Recognition and Image Processing" (T. Y. Young and K. S. Fu, eds.), pp. 311–332. Academic Press, Orlando, FL, 1986.

32. W. Z. Zhao, F.-H. Qin, and T. Y. Young, Dynamic estimation of optical flow field using linear and nonlinear objective functions. *Vision Image Comput.* **7**(4), 259–267 (1989).

33. T. Y. Young, G. Seetharaman, and W. Zhao, Analysis and extraction of three dimensional motion analysis information from an image sequence. *Adv. Artif. Intell. Res.* **1**, 290–223 (1989).

34. A. M. Waxman and K. Wohn, Contour evolution, neighborhood deformation
     and global flow: Planar flow in motion. *Int. J. Robotics Res.* **4**(3), 95–108
     (1985).
35. T. Kanade, Recovery of the 3d shape of an object from a single view. *Artif.*
     Intell. **17**, 409–460 (1981).
36. G. S. Seetharaman and T. Y. Young, A region-based approach to 3d motion
     analysis. *Adv. Comput. Vision Image Process.* **3**, 63–99 (1988).
37. W. J. Shomar, G. S. Seetharaman, and T. Y. Young, An expert system for
     recovering 3d shape and orientation from a single perspective view. *In*
     "Computer Vision, and Image Processing." (L. Shapiro and A. Rosenfeld,
     eds.), pp. 459–515, Academic Press, San Diego, CA, 1992.

Chapter **11**

Nonrigid Motion Analysis

CHANDRA KAMBHAMETTU and DMITRY B. GOLDGOF

Department of Computer Science and Engineering
University of South Florida
Tampa, Florida

DEMETRI TERZOPOULOS

Department of Computer Science
University of Toronto
Toronto, Canada

THOMAS S. HUANG

Department of Electrical and Computer Engineering
University of Illinois, Urbana-Champaign
Urbana, Illinois

405

1. INTRODUCTION

Motion analysis has been an important research area in computer vision for the last two decades. The motion analysis problem was defined traditionally as the problem of finding the motion of an object based on 2D or 3D images of it acquired at two or more time instances. The so-called structure from motion problem has an additional goal, which is to obtain the geometric structure as well as the motion parameters from a sequence of projections. A large body of work has been done in this area because of its importance in dynamic scene understanding (1, 2), essentially under the assumption that all the objects involved have constant shapes throughout the time sequence. The rigidity assumption fails in numerous motion analysis situations, as many real-world objects are nonrigid. For example, trees sway, a piece of paper bends, cloth wrinkles, and the living human body is in continuous nonrigid motion.

In recent years, a growing trend toward research in nonrigid motion analysis has become apparent. A significant impetus for this work derives from potential applications in areas such as medical imaging and model-based image compression. Numerous applications exist in the biomedical area, such as study of heart and lung motion, blood flow, and analysis of tumor growth. One of the goals in cardiac imaging, for instance, is to analyze nonrigid motion and estimate the deformation characteristics of the heart. In this application, computed tomography (CT) or magnetic resonance imaging (MRI) scanners collect 3D density data of the heart at a series of time instants during the cardiac cycle. An analysis of the range of motion parameters can help screen patients and decide on the extent of cardiac injury. Another example is model-based image compression in high-speed teleconferencing. Once the motion parameters or point correspondences of a facial movement can be estimated, they can be encoded and transmitted. This reduces the information bandwidth significantly when compared to the traditional statistical approaches. There are many more applications of nonrigid motion analysis. They include the study of lip motion for lip reading, human face recognition for security, material deformations for visual inspection of structures (such as dams, bridges, and crystal growth inspection), and the tracking of cloud formations for weather prediction. Machine vision for robotics applications will also need to handle nonrigid shapes: articulated and bendable parts are found in industrial settings. Nonrigid objects are also clearly unavoidable for a robot operating in natural environments. Additionally, virtual-reality applications require methods for the construction and simulation of both rigid and nonrigid object models.

The nonrigid motion analysis problem is difficult because *nonrigid motion* implies varying shape and possibly varying topological structure. A nonrigid object cannot be represented by a fixed set of parameters unless certain restrictions are placed on the object's behavior. Thus, we cannot have a general algorithm for determining motion parameters as we can have for rigid motion. Consequently, we need a classification for nonrigid motion that can guide the choice of applicable approaches. Nonrigid objects can be separated into different types such as articulated objects, elastic objects, and fluids. Different methods for motion analysis may be suitable for each type. Narrowing the scope of nonrigid analysis problem to a particular type allows one to define specific "nonrigidity assumptions" that may be incorporated as computational constraints within nonrigid motion analysis algorithms.

The last 5–10 years have seen significant progress in the analysis of nonrigid motion. In this chapter, we classify the different approaches in nonrigid motion analysis and indicate the assumptions and conditions that they utilize. Our goal in surveying the state of the art in nonrigid motion research is not to attempt an exhaustive review of the literature, but to provide some guidance in deciding the approaches most suitable to particular applications.

It is important to realize that the questions of motion analysis and shape modeling become inseparable when we consider nonrigid motion. Our review therefore includes some of the relevant work on shape modeling. The modeling perspective suggests one possible classification of nonrigid shape and motion research. Nonrigid shape models may be categorized into two main groups: local models and global models. Local modeling schemes concentrate on local shape representations, which include differential geometric methods and physics-based finite-element techniques. Global modeling schemes include various parameterized models (which are often suitable for both rigid and nonrigid objects) such as spherical harmonics, global polynomial models, and hyperquadrics. The local/global classification is not the only one possible, and, in fact, recent research has yielded shape models with both global and local characteristics.

A coarse classification of nonrigid motion was first proposed by Huang (3). He suggested three broad groups of objects: articulated, elastic, and fluid objects. We will follow this broad classification and supplement it with the curvature-based classification of elastic nonrigid motion suggested by Goldgof *et al.* (4). This will yield what we believe to be a natural classification ranging from near-rigid objects to highly nonrigid objects. Our survey concentrates on the analysis of 3D objects at the expense of work related to 2D curve deformations and fluid motion.

Section 2 presents an overview of our nonrigid motion classification. Sections 3 and 4 survey the literature associated with each motion class.

Figure 11.1. Classification of nonrigid motion analysis algorithms.

Section 5 discusses local and global shape models for nonrigid objects. Section 6 concludes the chapter with a summary.

2. CLASSIFICATION OF NONRIGID MOTION

This section proposes a classification of nonrigid motion. Figure 11.1 is a chart depicting the classification of nonrigid motion analysis algorithms, together with some of the references. A much larger set of references is cited in the text throughout this chapter and listed in the reference section. The motion of objects can generally be classified according to the degree of nonrigidity. We will consider primarily the relative motion of 3D objects, especially of their surfaces; this is the major distinction between rigid and nonrigid motion. In contrast to nonrigid motion, rigid motion preserves the 3D distances between any two points in an object. The object does not stretch or bend; hence both mean curvature and Gaussian curvature on the surface of the object remain invariant.

3. RESTRICTED CLASSES OF NONRIGID MOTION

3.1. Articulated Motion

Articulated motion is piecewise rigid motion. It involves motion of rigid parts connected by nonrigid joints. Examples are animal skeletons and robot manipulators. Clearly, the rigidity constraint is more relaxed in this case. An *articulated* object is a very restricted type of nonrigid object composed of rigid parts with connections between them that may allow defined ranges of movement. Arms, legs, scissors, and pliers are some simple examples of articulated objects. The relevance of articulated motion in robot movement is one of the reasons for its importance in motion analysis.

An object can be categorized as articulated by observing its behavior over some time period and comparing the image sequences with all the valid shapes that can be generated by an articulated model in the database. Another reliable approach is to consider all the image sequences of an object and integrate them depending on the articulation degrees of freedom at each point. Extensive research has been done in the modeling, recognition, and analysis of articulated motion. Webb and Aggarwal (5) considered the *fixed-axis assumption*, assuming that all movements consist of translations and rotations about an axis that is fixed in direction for short periods of time. Hoffman and Flinchbaugh (6) and Bennett and Hoffman (7) discuss the movement of linked rigid rods in one plane, and points in motion rotating about a fixed axis. O'Rourke and Badler (8), Asada *et al.* (9) also consider restricted motion of articulated objects. Goldgof *et al.* (4) use surface curvature to segment an articulated object into its rigid parts. The computation of aspect graphs for 3D articulated object recognition is proposed by Sallam and Bowyer (10). The representation of articulated objects for purposes of machine vision is considered by Bruno *et al.* (11). Additionally, authors suggest *function-based* models that allow the generic recognition of all objects that are the members of the modeled category. For more details, see Chapter 2 of this book.

On the whole, there has been significant development in the research of articulated motion than in other kinds of nonrigid motion analysis. This is because once we break up the articulated body into its rigid parts, we can apply rigid motion analysis. We will now proceed to different approaches in nonrigid motion analysis, in increasing degrees of nonrigidity.

3.2. Quasirigid Motion

Quasirigid motion restricts the degree of deformation. A general nonrigid motion is quasirigid when viewed in a sufficiently short time interval, say, between image frames when the sampling rate is sufficiently high.

Initial work in nonrigid motion was premised on the fact that a real-world object cannot change shape instantaneously as a result of inertia. When a translating, rotating, and deforming object is imaged at high temporal sampling rates, the nonrigid motion which occurs between image frames will be small.

Ullman (12) proposed an incremental rigidity scheme, based on the human perception of nonrigid transformations, to recover the shape of an object from its motion. The scheme has an internal model of the viewed object, which it modifies at each instant by the minimal nonrigid change, which suffices to account for the observed transformation; in other words, at each instant the estimated 3D structure of the viewed object is updated over that of the previous model. It integrates information from an extended viewing period to improve the approximation of the current 3D structure. However, the success of the scheme depends on the reliability of its initial model of the 3D structure, as well as the availability of point correspondences between 2D frames, which itself is a hard task in nonrigid motion. On similar lines, Shulman and Aloimonos (13) used a regularization approach to find the smoothest motion consistent with image data and the known object structure. The assumption was that the parameters characterizing the motion are approximately constant in any sufficiently small region of the image.

The problem of point correspondences in nonrigid motion is addressed by Jain and Sethi (14). They presented a method of establishing correspondences of nonrigid objects in a sequence of image frames using a motion smoothness constraint. Using path coherence, they formulate an optimization problem that assumes that the object cannot change its shape instantaneously. Their approach involves hypothesizing the 2D trajectories of points (i.e., projections of 3D trajectories) to be smooth over an extended space–time region. Thus, they choose maximally smooth trajectories from the set of all possible trajectories. This automatically solves the correspondence problem. However, this approach is computationally intensive (complexity depends on the number of frames) and relies on the smoothness of the 2D motions. A similar approach for measuring the point trajectories on deformable objects from image sequences is addressed by Duncan *et al.* (15). They model the boundary of the object as a deformable contour and then track the local segments of the contour through the temporal sequence. Small motion is assumed between tokens from frame to frame to hypothesize the candidate match points. The motion estimation is done by matching the local segments between pairs of contours by minimizing the deformation between the segments using a measure of bending energy. They have used this approach for tracking left-ventricle (LV) endocardial motion.

3.3. Isometric Motion

Isometric motion is defined as nonrigid motion that preserves lengths along the surface as well as angles between curves on the surface. It can be described as a motion which preserves Gaussian but not mean curvature. A well-known example is a bending deformation: a piece of paper or a metal plate bending from a planar configuration into a cylindrical shape (Fig. 11.2). Isometric motion severely limits the nonrigidity, since for many curved objects, such as spheres, no isometry is possible.

There have been several approaches to estimating isometric motion from 2D image sequences. It is important to note that all of them assume known point correspondences between images.

Koenderink considered the shape from motion assuming bending deformation in Koenderink (16). Koenderink and Doorn (17) proposed a method for solving shape from motion under bending deformations, using polyhedral approximations of a smooth surface. Polyhedral approximation results in a piecewise rigid surface, unless there is sufficient spatial resolution. The authors concentrate on obtaining partial solutions of 3D

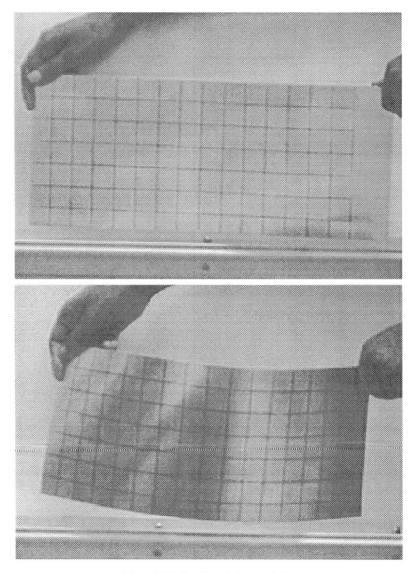

Figure 11.2. Bending of the metal plate.

shape and motion up to a relief transformation using the projected positions of points and their temporal derivatives.

By contrast, Jasinschi and Yuille (18) triangulate the surface approximation. They use Regge calculus to approximate a general surface by a net of triangles, and allow bending at the common edges of these triangles to accommodate nonrigid flexing motion. Again, a jointed triangulation may be suitable only for articulated motion unless the spatial resolution is sufficiently high. The authors have modified Ullman's incremental rigidity scheme to estimate depth information at the vertices of triangles, assuming correspondences between vertices of triangles. They initially consider the object to be a flat structure and update the model between time frames by assuming a minimal nonrigidity (*quasirigidity*) occurring between time frames. The minimal change is enforced by a cost function, thus yielding a series of estimated depth values that converge towards the correct result.

Chen and Penna (19, 20) apply differential geometry to nonrigid motion analysis. They relax the rigidity constraint but consider mostly isometric motion. Their approach is to approximate the transformation using Taylor expansion. They first consider a general elastic motion, and present three approaches for motion recovery: (1) an infinitesimal approach, (2) a global approach, and (3) a hybrid of the former two approaches. The infinitesimal approach is based on the local surface geometry of the object. The authors first recover the image transformation between two images using point correspondences and the least-squares approach. The Jacobian of the image transformation is coupled with the Jacobian of the orthographic or planar perspective projection to recover the Jacobian (i.e., linear approximation) of the generalized motion. A closed-form solution is possible only in the case of isometric motion in this approach. The global approach is concerned with determining the generalized motion completely from point correspondences. They illustrate this approach by using projective geometry under affine transformations. The hybrid approach is based on the spherical perspective model, which is a reasonable model for human perception. Chen and Zhao (21) further developed this work, and presented an analysis of the geometric structure of moving, nonrigid point patterns and their orthographically projected images. The authors provide ways to represent and encode an image sequence of moving, nonrigid objects in terms of the initial frame and the motion parameters. They consider only one class of nonrigid motions: constant affine motions in 3D space. They utilize a "localization principle" to reduce nonrigid motion into a collection of affine motions.

Huang and Goldgof (22, 23) allow the inclusion of an isometric motion assumption in adaptive-size, physically based models. They have demonstrated the result of using the isometric constraint in an adaptive-size finite-element model of the bending surface.

3.4. Homothetic Motion

Homothetic motion involves uniform expansion or contraction of a surface; thus the stretching (amount of expansion or contraction) is equal at every point of the surface. Isometric motion is a special case of homothetic motion with the stretching parameter equal to 1 at all points on the surface. Examples of homothetic motion include a balloon being expanded or contracted, or a sphere as its radius increases or decreases (Fig. 11.3).

Goldgof *et al.* (4) consider the use of mean and Gaussian curvatures for motion classification, and deal with both articulated and homothetic motion. Stretching of the surface during motion is the additional motion parameter. They extract the stretching of the surface undergoing homothetic transformation (constant at all points), and also detect the parts of the surface where homothetic motion is violated. The same authors have also applied the above algorithm to cineangiographic left ventricular data (24) to recover stretching parameters of the heart wall. Extending this approach, Kambhamettu and Goldgof (25) proposed a curvature-based approach toward point correspondence and stretching recovery of conformal motion, with homothetic motion as a special case. The idea here is that by hypothesizing point correspondences, one can detect the correct correspondence through minimizing the deviation from the assumed homothetic motion.

3.5. Conformal Motion

Conformal motion is defined as nonrigid motion that preserves angles between curves on the surface, but not lengths. It is shown (26) that a necessary and sufficient condition for the motion to be conformal is that the ratios of the coefficients of the first fundamental form remain constant (t^2). The infinitesimal lengths are stretched by a factor of t at the given point. The parameter t can vary at different points on the surface; however, at each point the stretching is the same in all directions. Thus, recovering t will give us information on the amount of stretching at each point. *Mercator's chart* and *stereographic projection* are some of the many conformal deformations of a sphere into a plane. Stereographic projection is the most general conformal representation of the sphere upon the plane possessing the property that circles on the sphere correspond to circles in the plane. Homothetic motion is a restricted class of conformal motion where the parameter t is the same for all points on the surface.

Mishra *et al.* (27, 28) first presented an algorithm for local stretching recovery from Gaussian curvature, based on polynomial (linear and quadratic) approximations of the stretching function under conformal motion. Their expression for linear stretching in conformal motion requires at least three point correspondences. A feature of this algorithm is that it does not require a preservation of the coordinate system between any two frames of data. They have applied this algorithm to estimate the stretching of left ventricular wall in the data obtained by coronary angio-

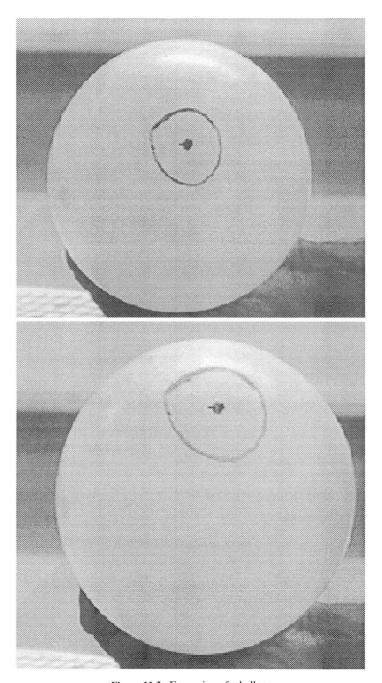

Figure 11.3. Expansion of a balloon.

graphy. An extension of this approach which incorporates knowledge of the line correspondences is described by Mishra *et al.* (29). Kambhamettu and Goldgof (30) proposed another extension and developed algorithms for point correspondence recovery in nonrigid motion under local conformal motion with constant (homothetic), linear, and polynomial stretching. They first hypothesize possible point correspondences, and form an error function for each hypothesis that represents the deviation from conformal motion. The error function is then minimized for estimating point correspondences and stretching. The advantage of this approach is that the coordinate system can be different for each frame. The authors have applied the algorithm to volumetric CT data of left ventricle to derive stretching and point correspondences between frames. Figure 11.6 shows three frames of left ventricle data (represented by the surface below the cutting plane). One can observe different elastic motion between each frame. There are 16 time frames of this data over one heart cycle. Each frame consists of $128 \times 128 \times 118$ binary voxels containing previously extracted surface information. This data was acquired by Dr. Eric Hoffman's group, now at University of Iowa.

A similar approach was used by Amini and Duncan (31). However, they use an additional bending model along with the stretching model for tracking point correspondences of the LV in motion. They consider the physical model of the LV as a thin-plate, and then track the motion involved by minimizing the bending and deviation from conformal stretching. Principal directions before and after the motion are used for setting up the coordinate system.

4. GENERAL NONRIGID MOTION

Many researchers are working on the problem of general nonrigid motion analysis. In this domain, motion has few restrictions other than topological invariance. General nonrigid motion analysis is possible in situations where we have specialized models that encode a priori knowledge about the intended application (model-based methods). More general approaches to nonrigid motion analysis, however, can make use of generic constraints such as motion smoothness.

4.1. Elastic Motion

Elastic motion is nonrigid motion whose only constraint is some degree of continuity or smoothness. Examples are the motion of elastic materials such as rubber, viscoelastic materials such as modeling clay, and plastic materials. This kind of solid-object motion is the most difficult to analyze. Elastic motion includes rigid motions plus stretching, bending, and twisting deformations.

Terzopoulos *et al.* (32) introduced a general physics-based approach to the estimation of elastic motion. Their work makes use of *deformable models*. These models are dynamic primitives made of a simulated elastic material. The material, represented mathematically in terms of generalized splines (33), provides intrinsic smoothness constraints that permit the recovery of continuous nonrigid motions. Like real-world objects, deformable models will move in response to applied forces according to the principles of Lagrangian mechanics. In this dynamic approach, external force fields serve to couple the deformable models to imaged objects. These fields are derived from potential functions that are computed from input images. As the deformable model achieves equilibrium in its external force field, it reconstructs the shape of the imaged object. When presented with image sequences of objects in nonrigid motion, deformable models are capable of estimating and tracking the motion.

The physics-based approach is also applicable to planar nonrigid motion. A simplified deformable curve model, popularly known as a "snake" (34), has been used by Terzopoulos and Waters (35) to track nonrigidly moving eyebrows, lips, and other facial features of an expressive face for the purposes of expression estimation and resynthesis.

The most common implementations of deformable models make use of finite-difference methods [as does the model in Terzopoulos *et al.* (32)] and finite-element methods. McInerney and Terzopoulos develop a "balloon" model that makes use of a quintic triangular finite element whose nodal variables include the time-varying positions and partial derivatives of the deformable surface up to second order (36). They apply their balloon model to the reconstruction and tracking of the LV in dynamic CT data.

Recursive nonrigid motion estimators have recently been developed that employ the deformable model equations of motion as system models within a nonlinear Kalman estimation framework (37–40). The system model synthesizes nonrigid motions in response to generalized forces arising from the inconsistency between the incoming observations and the estimated model state. The observation forces also account formally for instantaneous uncertainties and incomplete information. A Riccati procedure updates a covariance matrix that transforms the forces in accordance with the system dynamics and the prior observation history. The transformed forces induce changes in the translational, rotational, and deformational state variables of the system model in order to reduce inconsistency, thus deriving robust nonrigid motion estimates from time-varying visual data.

Bozma and Duncan (41) chose a deformable model-based approach, where reliable models are required for recognition of deformable objects.

They have described a segmentation system for model-based recognition of multiple deformable objects in which the modules are integrated using a game-theoretic approach. The segmentation is accomplished using an extended model-based recognition that is a combination of deformable object matching and relational matching. The deformable (flexible) model is defined as a set of independent deformable objects coupled together by loose (inequality) constraints. The matching is decomposed into individual tasks to form N-functional modules in the vision system. The authors arrive at a correspondence between the vision system and an N-player game and then use a game-theoretic approach to solve for multiple coexisting modules.

Another model-based approach is proposed by Segen and Dana (42). Authors have implemented a symbolic method for recognition of deformable shapes that is distributed in a network of general-purpose processors. Structural features were used to get a symbolic relation among local features. A graph recognition program compares the generated graph (or symbolic relation) of an object with graph models stored in a model library to select the best match. The graph model is a layered graph with a probability distribution over labels attached to each vertex. The criteria for recognition is the minimal representation complexity for a given object. Hence it tries to find the least possible graph description for an object by relating it to one of the graph models in the library.

As we observed in the earlier work on nonrigid motion, most of the approaches need point correspondences. This problem is relaxed to subset correspondences by Chaudhuri and Chatterjee (43). They have proposed the estimation of translation, rotation, and the deformation parameters for a nonrigid object using subset correspondences. Explicit point-to-point correspondence is not required in this approach. Subsets are created by grouping points lying on a single surface. Thus the correspondence problem is simplified to identifying the same surface (say, a planar patch) at two different time frames. This approach needs at least six subset correspondences to determine the motion parameters.

An algorithm for real time tracking of nonrigid objects is presented by Woodfill and Zabih (44). It requires that the object's approximate initial location is available, and the object can be distinguished from the background by motion or stereo. They use a massively parallel bottom–up approach to track and segment the object specified along the temporal sequence. The main restriction, however, is that the object's shape and position should not change too drastically. So, given a pair of images together with the position of an object in the first image, their algorithm computes the position of the object in the second image. This implies determining the 2D motion of the object.

Yamamoto *et al.* (45) presented an approach that can estimate the deformable motion parameters by solving a system of linear equations that are obtained by substituting a linear transformation of nonrigid objects expressed by the Jacobian matrix into a set of motion constraints. They use a general motion model that is composed of connected links, forming a grid. The displacement of any point can be expressed by a linear combination of the link deformations. The motion constraints include the depth constraint during motion and the intensity constraint of the image. The input data considered are from a video rate range camera that provides a registered range and intensity image sequences. The prime advantage of this approach is that point correspondences are not necessary in order to determine the nonrigid motion parameters.

Kambhamettu and Goldgof (46) proposed a method for estimating point correspondences between surfaces under small deformation using normal and curvature information. They estimate the displacement function using a first-order approximation, and then derive the motion parameters. The authors have designed three approaches for estimating point correspondences between surfaces under deformation. All three approaches can be used with and without a priori knowledge of point correspondences. The first approach involves using the changes in discriminant during small deformation. The second approach involves using changes in unit normal direction to estimate the point correspondences. The third approach uses the changes in Gaussian curvature, along with the changes in unit-normal direction to estimate point correspondences.

Huang (3) chose an application-motivated approach to general nonrigid motion analysis. As we mentioned previously, he proposed a classification

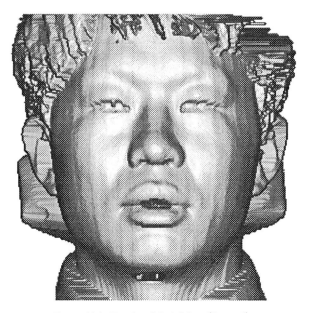

Figure 11.4. Rendered facial data (frame 1).

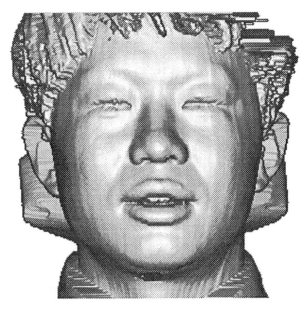

Figure 11.5. Rendered facial data (frame 2).

of nonrigid motion into articulated objects, elastic objects, and fluids. The research of his group includes modeling and analysis of heart wall motion, human face–head motion analysis and synthesis in model-based image compression, and studying the evolution of coherent structures in fluid motion. They use spherical harmonics for the modeling and analysis of heart wall motion, based on the biplane cineangiograms and CT and MRI data of the human heart. Face and head motion analysis is studied with applications toward visual communication such as teleconferencing. The surface of the face and head is approximated by triangular patches, and the facial motion is interpreted as motion at the vertices of these triangles. Figures 11.4 and 11.5 represent rendered images of two different facial expressions, which are being used for face–head motion analysis. The surface points of face were obtained in a cylindrical fashion. The data consist of 512 slices, where each slice has 512 points distributed radially around a central axis. These data were acquired using the Cyberware range scanner.

4.2. Fluid Motion

Fluid motion is the most general type of nonrigid motion. It includes the motion of liquid and gaseous objects. These motions, which need not be continuous, can exhibit highly variable topological structure as well as nonsmooth behavior such as turbulence. Compared to the other classes of motion, relatively little work has been done on fluid motion analysis.

Huang (3) and his group have been investigating the fluid motion analysis problem in order to develop automated analysis and visualization techniques for fluid flow. These techniques have applications in the acquisition of flow data, interpretation of complicated fluid motions, and the active control of flows and flow systems. The ultimate goal of this research is to study the similarities and differences among these problems and more traditional motion analysis problems, as well as to develop concepts, methodologies, and techniques applicable to various types of nonrigid motion.

5. SHAPE MODELS FOR NONRIGID OBJECTS

Shape modeling for nonrigid motion analysis is attracting increasing attention. Powerful shape models are needed to efficiently represent deformable objects and track their nonrigid motions. Globally parameterized primitives such as superquadrics and hyperquadrics have emerged as useful representations of shape. These primitives allow solids and surfaces to be constructed and easily modified using only a few parameters. Globally parameterized models are useful for object recognition using model libraries. Another useful class of shape models is the free-form mesh and spline models whose definition involves many local parameters. These models are useful for local shape control and for representing shape details as the number of parameters is increased. Recently, hybrid models have been proposed that combine the features of globally and locally parameterized representations. Dynamic, physics-based versions of certain models in all three model classes have been proposed and more are currently under development. For a survey of shape modeling methods for surface representation, see Bolle and Vemuri (47).

5.1. Local Models

Significant work in computer vision has gone into the development of reconstruction algorithms based on local shape models using generalized splines (33, 48). Dynamic generalizations of these local models were surveyed in the Section 4.1 (32, 36).

Terzopoulos and Vasilescu (49) developed adaptive meshes that can nonuniformly sample and reconstruct intensity and range data. Adaptive meshes are discrete dynamic models that are assembled by interconnecting nodal masses with adjustable nonlinear springs. The nodes are mobile and can move over the surface. The springs can automatically adjust their stiffness on the basis of the locally sampled information about depth, gradient, and/or curvature, in order to concentrate nodes near rapid shape variations. Hence the position of the nodes, and the stiffness of the springs connecting them automatically change depending on the surface (or image) properties.

Along similar lines, Huang and Goldgof (22, 50) presented a new approach to sampling and surface reconstruction that uses dynamic models. They have introduced adaptive-size meshes that will automatically update the size of the meshes (number of nodes) as the distance between the nodes changes. They have implemented algorithms for sampling of the intensity data, surface reconstruction of the range data, and surface reconstruction of 3D computed tomography LV data (Fig. 11.6). These models can also incorporate isometric and conformal constraints.

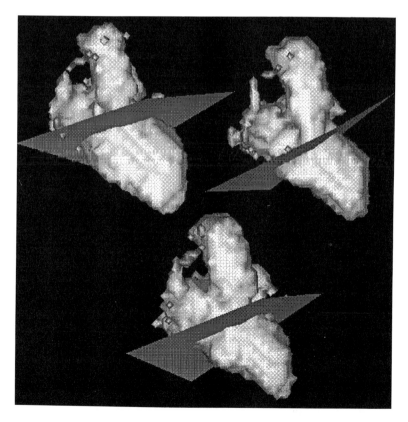

Figure 11.6. Three frames of the left ventricular data.

Recent work in this area includes that of Huang and Goldgof (51), who use a nonlinear finite-element (FEM) method to describe the object behavior. They exploit a priori information about the object's material properties and force information, and then model the object surface using nonlinear FEM. This method allows for material nonlinearity (i.e., non-Hookean materials with nonlinear stress–strain relationships) and large displacement during motion. The correct point correspondences can be obtained using image information and knowledge of material properties.

5.2. Global Models

Spherical harmonics are popular in designing global models. The spherical harmonic model (52) is a parametric representation of the closed surface that can be described by a radial function $r(\theta, \phi)$. The model, similar in concept to the Fourier descriptor, decomposes the function $r(\theta, \phi)$ into many orthogonal basis functions. The disadvantage in such a model is that its basis function is global, just like the sine and cosine functions in Fourier descriptor. Schudy and Ballard used time-varying spherical harmonics for heart volumetric representation (53). Recently, Chen and Huang (54) used superquadrics as modeling primitives for deformation analysis of 3D data. They have developed a recursive algorithm for estimating global motion and object shape, which incorporates a priori knowledge of the object information into the estimation procedure and obtains an estimate of the global motion and object shape irrespective of the biased distribution of 3D points. Matheny and Goldgof (73), extended spherical harmonics to surface harmonics that are defined on domains other than the sphere and to four-dimensional spherical harmonics. These harmonics enable the representation of shapes that cannot be represented as a global function in spherical coordinates, but can be represented in other coordinate systems. Nonrigid shapes are hence represented as functions of space and time either by including the time-dependence as a separate factor or by using four-dimensional spherical harmonics.

Quadric surfaces are the simplest models for curved shapes. They were used for position and orientation estimation, object recognition, and range data segmentation in the early 1980s (47). The disadvantage of using quadric surfaces is that the objects are described by many quadric patches. Taubin (56) and Keren *et al.* (57) have been studying higher-degree polynomials. They proposed the bounded shape polynomials for recovery and recognition. They use fourth-degree bounded polynomials as their primitives (since the third-degree polynomials are unbounded) and report very strong descriptive power. A significant advantage of shape polynomials is that they have algebraic invariants and, thus, become very useful for recognition purposes. However, higher-degree polynomials also give rise to certain disadvantages, since such polynomials involve ambiguity in representation, recovery, and recognition. Subrahmonia *et al.* used a Bayesian method to cope with such non-uniqueness problem (58).

In the past 5 years, superquadrics have become the focus of several computer vision researchers. Different from shape polynomials, superquadrics extend the quadric models by allowing the exponents to be real values. Superquadrics have small number of parameters but are flexible and powerful for describing the parts of natural objects. With the same compact equation, superquadrics can generate a continuum of forms: spheres, cuboids with rounded corners, cubes, or diamond shapes. Such shapes are difficult to model with traditional constructive solid geometry systems. Pentland's (59) *Supersketch* modeling system uses superquadrics as the basic shape primitive. The system also includes deformations to define more complex shapes.

Pentland (60) originally suggested analytically solving for all independent parameters in the superquadric parametric equations. The input might be 2D contours and shading. His second approach (61) is a combination of part model recovery and segmentation based on exhaustive search through the entire superquadric parameters pace (at 84,000 locations) to find the best initial values. Input is 3D points from range images.

Boult and Gross (62) used a gradient-descent minimization method for the superquadrics recovery, but had problems with convergence of cylindrically shaped objects. Solina and Bajcsy (63) used a modified error-of-fit function and obtained better results. Gross and Boult (64) also discussed several different error-of-fit functions and compared their effect on the shape recovery. Gupta and Bajcsy (65) presented an integrated framework for segmenting dense range data of complex 3D scenes into constituent parts using bi-quadrics and superquadrics.

Although powerful in describing shapes, superquadrics still have some drawbacks. They are intrinsically symmetric along x, y, and z axes, and their geometric bounds are just simple Cartesian cubes. In 1988, Hanson (66) extended superquadrics, proposing hyperquadrics for computer graphics applications. Hyperquadrics may be composed of any number of terms, their geometric bounds are arbitrary convex polyhedra, and the modeled shapes are not necessarily symmetric. Other properties of hyperquadric model include compactness, semilocal control, hierarchical structure, and intuitive meaning, which are all advantageous for shape representation. Han *et al.* (67) presented a fitting method that uses the hyperquadric model for the recovery of complex shapes from range data.

Pentland and Horowitz (68) presented an approach to the recovery of nonrigid motion based on a 20-node, hexahedral isoparametric, elastic finite element. The element applies a parameterized global deformation to an enclosed geometric model such as a sphere, cube, or superquadric. Their algorithm applies approximate modal analysis to decouple the degrees of freedom of the element into rigid and nonrigid vibration modes. They modeled and simulated the physics of elastic motion to estimate object shape and velocity. In Pentland *et al.* (69) they obtain both object shape and velocity estimates from contour data. Shape estimates are integrated over time by using an extended Kalman filter, resulting in a stable estimate of both 3D shape and 3D velocity.

5.3. Hybrid Models

Terzopoulos and Metaxas (70) present a physically based approach to fitting complex 3D shapes using a new class of dynamic models that can deform both locally and globally. They formulate deformable superquadrics that incorporate the global shape parameters of a conventional superellipsoid with the local degrees of freedom of a spline. In Metaxas and Terzopoulos (71), they present an approach for recursively estimating 3D object shape and general nonrigid motion, which makes use of these physically based dynamic models. The models provide global deformation parameters that represent the salient shape features of natural parts, and local deformation parameters that capture shape details. They formulate constraints that allow them to construct multibody models with deformable parts. Using these models as dynamic system models, they derive a shape and nonrigid motion estimator which takes the form of an extended Kalman filter.

Liao and Medioni (72) present representation of range data using deformable models. They have used B-spline surface patches to model the given data using an initial approximation of the surface as a simple surface such as a cylinder, or a plane. This initial surface is deformed using internal and external forces. The deformation takes place in each iteration, as the control vertices are moved around under the influence of features of the surface data. The internal and external energies are defined according to the surface derivatives, and the distance function between control vertices and the data points.

6. SUMMARY

Nonrigid motion is ubiquitous, since there is no such thing as a perfectly rigid object in the real world. In this chapter we reviewed a large body of work on nonrigid motion analysis. The reason for the recent wave of interest in nonrigid motion is twofold: (1) recent research has uncovered several promising new approaches to nonrigid motion analysis; and (2) a wealth of potential applications has become apparent, including human face–head recognition for teleconferencing, gesture recognition for virtual reality, model construction of nonrigid objects, lip reading, material deformation and soil pressure studies, tracking of cloud formations for weather prediction, crystal growth observation, and fluid flow analysis. There are also numerous biomedical applications, such as left ventrical motion analysis, lung motion studies, and tumor growth.

Nonrigid motion analysis is a burgeoning research area, and the available body of research has begun to make inroads into only a few of the many difficult problems. There are numerous open theoretical issues in motion tracking from three-dimensional data or from projections, analysis of objects undergoing large deformation, and analysis of unrestricted viscoelastic and fluid motion. For nonrigid objects, the issues of motion representation and shape representation are much more closely related than for rigid objects. Only a few researchers have considered the problems of representing nonrigid objects more complex than articulated objects. Most of this work describes "single-part" nonrigid objects. It is clear that multiple-part representations are more suitable for many nonrigid objects. Often, each part is itself a nonrigid object. Consider, for example, the human body with its numerous deformable parts, a reclining office chair with soft cushions, child swings formed by two ropes and a rubber seat, and quasiarticulated objects such as beads on a rope or a metal mesh woven out of bendable wires. Representation issues become critically important as we go beyond motion tracking and motion analysis to problems of nonrigid object recognition. New ideas for efficient representation, storage, and indexing of nonrigid shapes are needed to make automated nonrigid object recognition a practical reality.

REFERENCES

1. J. W. Roach and J. K. Aggarwal, Determining the movement of objects from a sequence of images. *IEEE Trans. Pattern Anal. Mach. Intell.* **PAMI-2**(6), 554–562 (1980).
2. T. S. Huang, Motion analysis. *Encycl. Artif. Intell.* **1**, 620–632 (1986).
3. T. S. Huang, Modeling, analysis, and visualization of nonrigid object motion. *Proc. Int. Conf. Pattern Recognition, 10th*, 1990, pp. 361–364 (1990).
4. D. B. Goldgof, H. Lee, and T. S. Huang, Motion analysis of nonrigid surfaces. *Proc. IEEE Conf. Comput. Vision Pattern Recognition, 1988*, pp. 375–380 (1988). June 5–9, 1988, Ann Arbor, MI.
5. J. A. Webb and J. K. Aggarwal, Structure from motion of rigid and jointed objects. *Artif. Intell.* **19**(1), 107–130 (1983).
6. D. D. Hoffman and B. E. Flinchbaugh, The interpretation of biological motion. *Biol. Cybernet.*, **42**, 195–204 (1982).
7. B. M. Bennett and D. D. Hoffman, The computation of structure from fixed-axis motion: Nonrigid structures. *Biol. Cybernet.*, **51**, 293–300 (1985).

8. J. O'Rourke and N. Badler, Model-based image analysis of human motion using constraint propagation. *IEEE Trans. Pattern Anal. Mach. Intell.* **PAMI-2**, 522–536 (1980).

9. M. Asada, M. Yachida, and S. Tsuji, Understanding of 3D motion in block world. *Pattern Recognition* **17**(1), 57–84 (1984).

10. M. Sallam and K. Bowyer, Generalizing the aspect graph concept to include articulated assemblies. *Pattern Recognition Lett.* **12**, 171–176 (1991).

11. B. Bruno, N. Bennett, K. Bowyer, D. Goldgof, and L. Stark, Modeling of articulated objects for machine perception. *Fla. Artif. Intell. Res. Symp.*, Ft. Lauderdale, *5th, 1992*, pp. 247–251 (1992).

12. S. Ullman, Maximizing rigidity: The incremental recovery of 3-D structure from rigid and nonrigid motion. *Perception* **13**, 255–274 (1984).

13. D. Shulman and J. Y. Aloimonos, Nonrigid motion interpretation: A regularized approach. *Proc. R. Soc. London, Ser. B* **233**, 217–234 (1988).

14. R. Jain and I. K. Sethi, Establishing correspondence of non-rigid objects using smoothness of motion. *In* "Proceedings of the Second Workshop on Computer Vision: Representation and Control," pp. 83–87, IEEE Computer Society Press, Washington, DC, 1984.

15. J. Duncan, R. Owen, L. Staib, and P. Anandan, Measurement of non-rigid motion using contour shape descriptors. *Proc. IEEE Conf. Comput. Vision Pattern Recognition*, Maui, Hawaii, pp. 318–324 (1991).

16. J. J. Koenderink, Shape from motion and bending deformation. *J. Opt. Soc. Am. A* **1**, 1265–1266 (1984).

17. J. J. Koenderink and A. J. van Doorn, Depth and shape from different perspective in the presence of bending deformations. *J. Opt. Soc. Am.* **3**(2), pp. 242–249 (1986).

18. R. Jasinschi and A. Yuille, Nonrigid motion and Regge calculus. *J. Opt. Soc. Am. A* **6**, 1088–1095 (1989).

19. S. S. Chen, Structure-from-motion without the rigidity assumption. *In* "Proceedings of the Third Workshop of Computer Vision: Representation and Control," pp. 105–112. IEEE Computer Society Press, Washington, DC, 1985.

20. S. S. Chen and M. Penna, Motion analysis of deformable objects. *In* "Advances in Computer Vision and Image Processing" (T. S. Huang, ed.), Vol. 3. pp. 179–220. JAI Press, Connecticut, 1988.

21. S. S. Chen and A. G. Zhao, Image representation of moving nonrigid objects. "Journal of Visual Communication and Image Representation." Academic Press, San Diego, CA, 1991.

22. W. C. Huang and D. B. Goldgof, Adaptive-size physically-based models for non-rigid motion analysis. *Proc. IEEE Conf. Comput. Vision Pattern Recognition*, Champaign-Urbana, IL, *1992*, pp. 833–835 (1992).

23. W. C. Huang and D. B. Goldgof, Adaptive-size meshes for rigid and nonrigid shape analysis and synthesis. *IEEE Trans. Pattern Anal. Mach. Intell.* **PAMI-15**(6), pp. 611–616 (1993).

24. D. B. Goldgof, H. Lee, and T. S. Huang, Parameter estimation of the heart motion from angiography data. *SPIE / SPSE Symp. Electron. Imaging, Conf. Biomed. Image Process.* **1245**(15), 171–181 (1990).

25. C. Kambhamettu and D. B. Goldgof, Towards finding point correspondences in non-rigid motion. *Scand. Conf. Image Anal. 7th*, pp. 1126–1133 (1991).

26. W. C. Graustein, "Differential Geometry." Macmillan, New York, 1935.

27. S. K. Mishra, D. B. Goldgof, and T. S. Huang, Non-rigid motion analysis and epicardial deformation estimation from angiography data. *Proc. IEEE Conf. Comput. Vision Pattern Recognition*, Maui, Hawaii, *1991*, pp. 331–336 (1991).

28. S. K. Mishra, D. B. Goldgof, T. S. Huang, and C. Kambhamettu, Curvature-based non-rigid motion analysis from 3D point correspondences. *Int. J. Imaging Syst. Technol.*, Vol. 4, pp. 214–225 (1992).

29. S. K. Mishra, D. B. Goldgof, and C. Kambhamettu, Estimating non-rigid motion from point and line correspondences. *Pattern Recognition Lett.*, (to be published).

30. C. Kambhamettu and D. B. Goldgof, Point correspondence recovery in nonrigid motion. *Proc. IEEE Conf. Comput. Vision Pattern Recognition*, Champaign-Urbana, IL, *1992*, pp. 222–227 (1992).

31. A. A. Amini and J. S. Duncan, Pointwise tracking of left-ventricular motion in 3D. *Proc. IEEE Workshop Visual Motion*, pp. 294–299 (1991).

32. D. Terzopoulos, A. Witkin, and M. Kass, Constraints on deformable models: Recovering 3D shape and nonrigid motion. *Artif. Intell.* **36**(1), 91–123 (1988).

33. D. Terzopoulos, Regularization of inverse visual problems involving disconti-nuities, *IEEE Trans. Pattern Anal. Mach. Intell.* **PAMI-8**(4), 413–424 (1986).

34. M. Kass, A. Witkin, and D. Terzopoulos, Snakes: Active contour models. *Int. J. Comput. Vision* **1**(4), 321–331 (1988).

35. D. Terzopoulos and K. Waters, Analysis and synthesis of facial image sequences using physical and anatomical models. *IEEE Trans. Pattern Anal. Mach. Intell.* **PAMI-15**(6), pp. 569–579. *Proc. Int. Conf. Comput. Vision, 3rd*, Osaka, Japan, *1990*, pp. 727–732 (1990).

36. T. McInerney and D. Terzopoulos, A finite element model for 3D shape reconstruction and nonrigid motion tracking. *Proc. Int. Conf. Comput. Vision, 4th*, pp. 518–523. Berlin, *1993*.

37. R. Szeliski and D. Terzopoulos, Physically-based and probabilistic modeling for computer vision. *In* "Geometric Methods in Computer Vision" (B. C. Vemuri, ed.), Proc. SPIE 1570, pp. 140–152. Soc. Photo-Opt. Instrum. Eng., San Diego, CA, 1991.

38. D. Terzopoulos and R. Szeliski, Tracking with Kalman snakes. *In* "Active Vision" (A. Blake and A. Yuille, eds.), pp. 3–20. MIT Press, Cambridge, MA, 1992.

39. D. Terzopoulos and D. Metaxas, Tracking nonrigid 3D objects. *In* "Active Vision" (A. Blake and A. Yuille, eds.), pp. 75–89. MIT Press, Cambridge, MA, 1992.

40. D. Metaxas and D. Terzopoulos, Shape and nonrigid motion estimation through physics-based synthesis. *IEEE Trans. Pattern Anal. Mach. Intell.* **PAMI-15**(6), 1993. *Proc. IEEE Comput. Vision Pattern Recognition Conf.*, Maui, Hawaii, *1991*, pp. 337–343 (1991).

41. H. I. Bozma and J. S. Duncan, Model-based recognition of multiple de-formable objects using a game-theoretic framework. *Int. Conf. Image Process. Mach. Intell.*, *12th*, Wye, UK, *1991*, pp. 358–372 (1991).

42. J. Segen and K. Dana, Parallel symbolic recognition of deformable shapes. *In* "From Pixels to Features II" (H. Burkhardt, Y. Neuvo, and J. C. Simon, eds.), pp. 387–400. Elsevier/North-Holland, Amsterdam.

43. S. Chaudhuri and S. Chatterjee, Estimation of motion parameters for a deformable object from range data. *Proc. IEEE Conf. Comput. Vision Pattern Recognition*, San Diego, CA, *1989*, pp. 291–295 (1989).

44. J. Woodfill and R. Zabih, An algorithm for real-time tracking of non-rigid objects. *Proc. Natl. Conf. Artif. Intell., Vision Sensor Interpretation, 9th, 1991*, Vol. 2, pp. 718–723 (1991).

45. M. Yamamoto, P. Boulanger, J.-A. Beraldin, and M. Rioux, Direct estimation of range flow on deformable shape from a video rate range camera. *IEEE Trans. Pattern Anal. Mach. Intell.* **PAMI-15**(1), 82–89 (1993).

46. C. Kambhamettu and D. B. Goldgof, "Estimating Point Correspondences in Small Deformations," TR. 93-01. University of South Florida, Department of Computer Science and Engineering, Tampa, 1993.

47. R. M. Bolle and B. C. Vemuri, On three-dimensional surface reconstruction methods. *IEEE Trans. Pattern Anal. Mach. Intell.* **PAMI-13**(1), pp. 1–13 (1991).

48. D. Terzopoulos, The computation of visible-surface representations. *IEEE Trans. Pattern Anal. Mach. Intell.* **PAMI-10**(4), 417–438 (1988).

49. D. Terzopoulos and M. Vasilescu, Sampling and reconstruction with adaptive meshes. *Proc. IEEE Conf. Comput. Vision Pattern Recognition*, Maui, Hawaii, *1991*, pp. 70–75 (1991).

50. W. C. Huang and D. B. Goldgof, Sampling and surface reconstruction with adaptive-size meshes. *SPIE Proc. Appl. Artif. Intell. X: Mach. Vision Robotics*, Orlando, FL, *1992*. Vol. 1708, pp. 760–770.

51. W. C. Huang and D. B. Goldgof, Nonrigid motion analysis using non-linear finite element modeling. *SPIE/SPSE Symp. Electron. Imaging, Conf. Geometric Methods Comput. Vision*, San Diego, CA, *1993*. pp. 404–414.

52. D. H. Ballard and C. M. Brown, "Computer Vision," pp. 271–274. Prentice-Hall, Englewood Cliffs, NJ, 1982.

53. R. B. Shudy and D. H. Ballard, Towards an anatomical model of heart motion as seen in 4-D cardiac ultrasound data. *Proc. Conf. Comput. Appl. Radiol. Comput. Aided Anal. Radiol. Images, 6th 1979*.

54. C. W. Chen and T. S. Huang, Nonrigid object motion and deformation estimation from three-dimensional data. *Int. J. Imaging Syst. Technol.*, pp. 385–394 (1990).

55. A. Matheny, The use of three- and four-dimensional surface harmonics for rigid and non-rigid shape recovery and representation. Master's Thesis, University of South Florida, Department of Computer Science and Engineering, Tampa, 1993.

56. G. Taubin, Estimation of planar curves, surfaces, and nonplanar curves defined by implicit equations with applications to edge and range image segmentation. *IEEE Trans. Pattern Anal. Mach. Intell.* **PAMI-13**(11) pp. 1115–1138 (1991).

57. D. Keren, D. Cooper, and J. Subrahmonia, "Describing Complicated Objects by Implicit Polynomials," TR lems-102. Brown University, Division of Engineering, Providence, RI, 1992.

58. J. Subrahmonia, D. B. Cooper, and D. Keren, "Practical Reliable Bayesian Recognition of 2D and 3D Objects Using Implicit Polynomials and Algebraic Invariants," TR lems-107. Brown University, Division of Engineering, Providence, RI, 1992.

59. A. Pentland, Towards an ideal CAD systems. *Proc. SPIE Conf. Mach. Vision Man-Mach. Interface, SPIE,* Order No. 75820 (1986).

60. A. Pentland, Perceptual organization and the representation of natural form. *Artif. Intell.* **28**(3), 3–331 (1986).

61. A. Pentland, Recognition by parts. *Proc. Int. Conf. Comput. Vision, 1st,* London, pp. 612–620. 1987.

62. T. E. Boult and A. D. Gross, Recovery of superquadrics from 3-D information. *Proc. Spat. Reasoning Multi-Sensor Fusion Workshop,* St. Charles, IL, *1987,* pp. 128–137 (1987).

63. F. Solina and R. Bajcsy, Recovery of parametric models from range images: The case for superquadrics with global deformations. *IEEE Trans. Pattern Anal. Mach. Intell.* **PAMI-12**(2), pp. 131–147 (1990).

64. A. D. Gross and T. E. Boult, Error of fit measurements for recovering parametric solids. *Proc. Int. Conf. Comput. Vision, 2nd,* Tampa, FL, *1988,* pp. 690–694 (1988).

65. A. Gupta and R. Bajcsy, An integrated approach for surface and volumetric segmentation of range images using biquadrics and superquadrics. *SPIE Proc. Appl. Artif. Intell. X: Mach. Vision Robotics,* Orlando, FL, *1992,* Vol. 1708, pp. 210–227 (1992).

66. A. J. Hanson, Hyperquadrics: Smoothly deformable shapes with convex polyhedral bounds. *Comput. Vision, Graphics, Image Process.* **44**, 191–210 (1988).

67. S. Han, D. B. Goldgof, and K. W. Bowyer, Using hyperquadrics for shape recovery from range data. *Proc. Int. Conf. Comput. Vision, 4th,* Berlin, pp. 492–496 (1993).

68. B. Horowitz and A. Pentland, Recovery of non-rigid motion and structure. *Proc. IEEE Conf. Comput.,* pp. 288–293 (1991).

69. A. Pentland, B. Horowitz, and S. Sclaroff, Non-rigid motion and structure from contour. *Proc. IEEE Workshop Visual Motion, 1991,* pp. 288–293 (1991).

70. D. Terzopoulos and D. Metaxas, Dynamic 3D models with local and global deformations: Deformable superquadrics. *IEEE Trans. Pattern Anal. Mach. Intell.* **PAMI-13**, 703–714 (1991).

71. D. Metaxas and D. Terzopoulos, Recursive estimation of shape and nonrigid motion. *Proc. IEEE Workshop Visual Motion, 1991,* pp. 306–311.

72. C. W. Liao and G. Medioni, Representation of range data with B-spline surface patches. *IAPR Proc. Int. Conf. Pattern Recognition, 11th,* The Hague, The Netherlands, *1992,* pp. 745–748 (1992).

73. A. Matheny and D. B. Goldgof, The use of three- and four-dimensional surface harmonics for rigid and nonrigid shape recovery and representation. *Tech. Report, TR 93-04,* Department of Computer Science and Engineering University of South Florida.

74. S. S. Chen and M. Penna, Shape and motion of nonrigid bodies. *Comput. Vision, Graphics, Image Process.* **36**, 175–207 (1986).

75. A. H. Barr, Superquadrics and angle preserving transformations. *IEEE Computer Graphics and Applications.* **1**, 11–23 (1981).

Chapter **12**

Analysis and Synthesis of Human Movement

THOMAS W. CALVERT and ARTHUR E. CHAPMAN

Schools of Computing Science, Kinesiology, and Engineering Science
Simon Fraser University
Burnaby, British Columbia, Canada

1. OVERVIEW

1.1. What Is Human Movement?

At a functional level, human movement is important as a means of locomotion from place to place and as a means of manipulating the objects that make our sophisticated lives possible. It provides an important means of interpersonal communication; this includes the aesthetic experiences of dance, film, and theater as well as the body language used in all human interaction. In addition, it underlies most sports activities.

In spite of the fundamental role of movement in all human activity, attempts to analyze and synthesize it have been only partially successful. If appropriate passive or active markers are placed on the body, vision systems can provide a fairly good description of the movements, but there has been almost no comprehensive work on recognizing the patterns in the data to provide a high-level description of the movement. More attention has been given to synthesis of movement from high-level commands, but animation and simulation fall well short of duplicating reality.

While there are intrinsic reasons for measuring, analyzing, and understanding human movement, there are also some very practical reasons. In clinical medicine, there is a need to assess movement abnormalities—many medical centers have "gait laboratories," which measure the way subjects walk (36). There is also a need to assess the effectiveness of prosthetic limbs and orthotic devices (braces, etc.).

In sports, there is keen interest in analyzing the effectiveness of different strokes used in games such as tennis, squash, or baseball. Similarly there is interest in assessing the best way to kick a ball, row a boat, or perform a high jump or dive.

In dance, there is a need to analyze and record how the composition of a particular choreographer is performed (25). To date, technology has been of little help—video systems can record the movement but there is no system to analyze it into its components.

1.2. Analysis and Synthesis

A view of the process involved in analyzing and synthesizing human movement is outlined in Fig. 12.1. Starting on the left with a vision system to sense movement of live humans, 2D or 3D data that describe the movement can be collected. These low-level data are a description of the movement and must be analyzed to derive a meaningful high-level description. The inverse process goes from right to left and starts with a high-level description that is interpreted to derive a detailed description. This

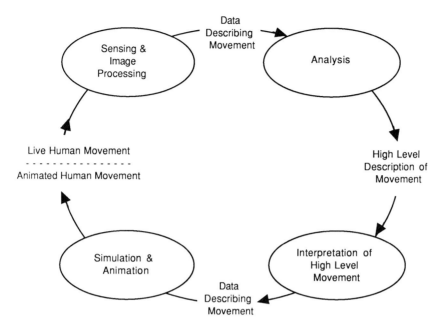

Figure 12.1. The analysis–synthesis process for human movement.

detailed description can then drive an animation or a robotic implementation of the human body that in some sense duplicates the original live
movement.

Analysis begins with a sensing system. This provides 2D or 3D data that
describe the movement over time. Typically the 3D coordinates of the
major joints are measured and recorded 10–400 times per second. The
sensing task is difficult—not only is it a challenging pattern recognition
problem to identify landmarks on the body but they must be tracked by
multiple cameras if the 3D movement is to be recovered.

The raw data describing the movement can be analyzed in a number of
ways depending on the application. For example, in clinical studies of
movement abnormalities, plots of the angle changes at the ankle, knee,
and hip joints might be studied and compared to normal patterns. To truly
understand the movement (as in biomechanics, studies of interpersonal
communication, or analysis of a dance) a high-leveled description (involving joint torques, identification of the task, etc.) must be derived.

Synthesis involves generating a 3D description of the skeleton being
animated for each time instant at which it is to be displayed. For video the
display rate is typically 30 second^{-1} and for film it is 24 second^{-1}. Thus, if
the body is defined by a minimal 23 joints, each of which has three spatial
coordinates, $3 \times 23 \times 30 = 2070$ numbers are required each second to

animate a human body on video. Unless the movement to be animated is being generated by copying live action (digitizing images from cameras, etc.), the animator requires tools to assist in the specification process.

The classical approach to 2D or 3D animation is to define a number of key frames and then interpolate between them. By building more and more knowledge into the system, the animator can dispense with detailed specification and let the system take over. For example, the detailed keyframes for a walk can be replaced by a command such as "walk 20 steps at 5 km/hour," which calls a procedure to generate the walking movement. At a higher level the command might be "Go to the next room and fetch the book which is on the table"—this depends on having a comprehensive knowledge base describing the figure and its environment, as well as having the ability to reason; in other words, an expert system is needed.

2. REPRESENTATION OF THE MOVING HUMAN BODY

Underlying the human body is a rigid skeleton (see Fig. 12.2), the segments of which are connected by joints. Soft tissue, made up of muscle, fat, connective tissue, and internal organs, forms a nonrigid body around the underlying bones. The mechanics of the whole body are difficult to measure in detail, but the rigid skeleton can be modeled fairly accurately with kinematic linkages.

2.1. Movement of a Kinematic Frame Based on the Skeleton

Although a full skeleton has over 400 bones, a useful body model can be based on 22 segments; this represents each hand and foot as one segment and approximates the 22 vertebrae in the back with 3 segments. More and more detail is achieved by adding additional segments. A 22-segment model is illustrated in Fig. 12.3.

The mathematics describing the articulated body model parallel descriptions for robotic manipulators. Each joint has 1–3 degrees of freedom, and each segment of the body is embedded in its own coordinate frame. One end of the segment, the base or the proximal end, is fixed and cannot move; the distal end is free to move. The segments can be concatenated in a chain, and the end-effector is a coordinate frame attached to the distal end of the most distal link in the chain. At each joint the rotation and displacement determine a transformation **M** between the two adjacent coordinate frames sharing the joint. The general form of the transforma-

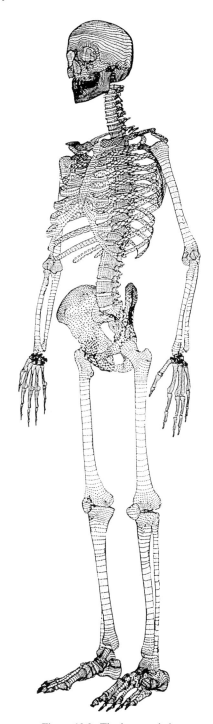

Figure 12.2. The human skeleton.

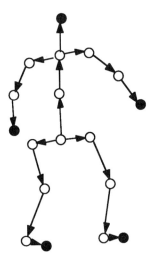

Figure 12.3. A stick figure model of the human body.

tion at joint i is $\mathbf{M}_i = \mathbf{T}$ (offset$_i$)$\mathbf{R}(\phi_i)$, where $\mathbf{T}$ (offset$_i$) is the matrix that translates joint i from its parent joint $i - 1$ (measured in the parent frame), and $\mathbf{R}(\phi_i)$ is the matrix that rotates by ϕ_i about joint i's rotation axis.

The relationship between any two coordinate systems i and j in the chain is found by concatenating the transformations at the joints encountered during a transversal from joint i to joint j:

$$\mathbf{M}_{ii} - \mathbf{M}_i \mathbf{M}_{i+1} \cdots \mathbf{M}_{j-1} \mathbf{M}_j. \qquad (1)$$

If there are 2 or more degrees of freedom at a joint, then their respective rotation matrices are concatenated with zero offset. The position and orientation of the end-effector with respect to the base frame is found by simply concatenating the transformations at each joint in the articulated body structure.

2.2. Different Approaches to a Fleshed-out Body

Because of their simplicity and because of the fact that they define the body quite well, stick figure displays based on the skeletal model have been widely used. Unfortunately, it is not completely straightforward to put flesh on the bones. The difficulty is that the tissue surrounding the underlying frame is not rigid. For any fixed stance, standard CAD modeling software can be used to approximate the shape of the body to any

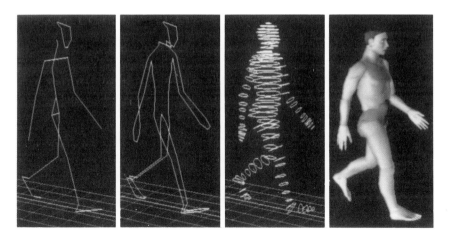

Figure 12.4. A comparison of stick, outline, contour, and smooth shaded representations for the body.

desired degree of accuracy. However, for each new stance this will generally need to be readjusted by hand since the tissue around the joints does not behave in a simple way.

Modeling the face and capturing accurate facial expressions presents a rather different problem. The movements of the surface are much smaller than around the joints, but they are more subtle and human observers are particularly attuned to the analysis of facial expression. Some animations have used interpolations between expressions digitized from live actors to create a wide range of facial expressions. This can be quite effective, but a more basic approach models changes in the facial surface that result from underlying muscle movements. In the long run this should give better results.

Figure 12.4 is a composite drawing showing stick, outline, contour, and smooth shaded representations for the body.

3. SENSING, IMAGE PROCESSING, AND PATTERN RECOGNITION

Cameras or other instrumentation are used to acquire data from which the position of a moving body in space can be deduced. When the process depends on images sensed with cameras a major problem is to identify key body landmarks in the images.

3.1. The Sensing Problem

Sensing is the process of capturing human motion as a set of numbers. This process involves some means of identifying parts of the body, recording the motion of these parts, and translating the recording into numbers. In practice, the process will combine manual and automatic control.

The major problem with sensing human motion is that the body evolved to perform a variety of movements with no apparent regard to ease of analysis. Movements are in one sense gross (motion of body segments in running) and in another sense subtle (fine control as in writing). Consequently the methods used to register human motion depend on the level of information required. Whatever the application, the investigator will have in mind an appropriate model of the system. This model should contain those aspects of the structure and motors (muscles) that are important for the problem at hand, but it will never be a complete replication of the system.

An analysis based on the assumption that the body is a set of rigid segments requires a means of registering the orientation of these segments in space. Because the general pattern recognition problem is quite difficult, this is usually done by using one or more cameras to detect markers attached to the body at specific sites. Markers can be either *passive*, in the sense that their positions will be located by manual or automated pattern recognition from a projection of an image of the subject, or *active*, in the sense that the marker actively identifies itself. A typical active marker is a light-emitting diode (LED), the position of which is captured automatically by a suitable camera. A different approach uses active devices that use an imposed electromagnetic field to provide direct measures of their position and orientation in space.

On a different level the aim might be to register joint motion. In this case markers attached to the skin are inappropriate, since the motion of the skin relative to the bones is likely to be greater than the relative motion between articular surfaces of the joint. To avoid this problem the rather drastic technique of screwing metal pins into the bones has been employed. Small light balls on the end of the pins then represent passive markers.

3.2. Sensing with Multiple Cameras

The situation where the sensing process involves one or more cameras is illustrated in Fig. 12.5. The figure being sensed is described by the 3D coordinates x_i of a series of N landmarks:

$$\mathbf{X} = [\mathbf{x}_1, \mathbf{x}_2, \mathbf{x}_3, \ldots, \mathbf{x}_N]. \qquad (2)$$

Figure 12.5. Three cameras set up to sense a moving body.

These three-space landmarks are constrained by the kinematics of the figure set out in Eq. (1), so that

$$\mathbf{x}_j = \mathbf{M}_{ji} \cdot \mathbf{x}_i. \tag{3}$$

We assume that camera C_k has location $\mathbf{p}_k$ and orientation ϕ_k where $k = 1, \ldots, M$.

Camera C_k registers an image of the scene and provide a two-dimensional projection $\mathbf{U}_k$ of the N landmarks where

$$\mathbf{U}_k = [\mathbf{u}_{k_1}, \mathbf{u}_{k_2}, \mathbf{u}_{k_3}, \ldots, \mathbf{u}_{k_N}] \tag{4}$$

and

$$\mathbf{U}_k = \mathbf{T}_k \mathbf{X} \qquad \text{for} \qquad k = 1, \ldots, M. \tag{5}$$

For each camera, the inverse transformation matrix $\mathbf{T}_k^{-1}$ can only give an estimate of the 3D coordinates of the N landmarks. However, by combining the information from all M cameras in an appropriate way a 3D estimate of $\mathbf{X}$ can be obtained:

$$\mathbf{X} = f\{\mathbf{T}_k^{-1}\mathbf{U}_k; \, k = 1, \ldots, M\}. \tag{6}$$

With more than two cameras the estimation function $f\{\ \}$ used in Eq. (6) will generally minimize the mean squared error for the overconstrained system; the estimate can be improved by using the kinematic constraints [Eq. (3)] for the articulated body structure. In practice the parameters of f{ } are obtained by using a known calibration grid after the cameras have been positioned.

3.3. Practical Aspects of Single and Multiple Views

In biomechanics much of the early work was 2D because of the relative simplicity of data reduction and the limited techniques available for recording. While a 3D analysis is clearly more realistic, there are problems with the 3D registration of movement due to points of interest becoming occluded from the sight of the recording device and the need to identify and match landmarks in different views of the body (45).

A single 2D view is adequate for actions that are primarily planar in nature, such as the major amplitude of motion in running, but is entirely inappropriate if the aim is to record the nonplanar motion of the knee joint, for example. If the aim is simply to capture kinematic information, a 2D view may be acceptable for presentation of motion to the viewer who can appreciate perspective and can mentally construct the 3D motion from the 2D view. However, at an analytical level a 2D representation of motion creates problems if any one of the body segments moves out of the plane of the view.

Three-dimensional registration of motion is clearly more complete than 2D, but data collection has a number of difficulties. The major problem in 3D is that any marker on the body must be seen by cameras that record at least two views. In some complex 3D activities it is necessary to have three or more cameras to enable body marker to be seen by two views at any one time. A further problem is to match the markers in the multiple views. In the case of cine film, a synchronizing light in the view of all cameras allows a starting frame to be identified. Even so, a timing error as great as the time between cine frames can result. Increasing the frame rate will minimize the timing error but will increase cost. However, the cost of film can be minimized by using a mirror to obtain two views on one frame of film. Even with an automatic process based on multiplexed LEDs there will be a timing error, which will be magnified as the frequency of data collection is reduced.

A further factor in 3D registration is the necessity for an accurate calibration grid. The grid needs numerous markers spread out to encompass a volume greater than that in which the activity takes place—accuracy of the 3D reconstruction of data decreases as points move away from the center of the calibration volume. While a minimal number of calibration markers are required, the accuracy of the reconstruction increases as the number of calibration markers increases. In automatic processes that use active markers, the calibration grid requires active markers, usually fixed to a metal frame. For this reason the frame must be kept to a reasonable size. Consequently it is often necessary to perform multiple calibrations by moving the calibration frame to known distances in the required volume.

3.4. Recognition of Passive Markers

When film or video is used to capture the activity it is customary to place easily identifiable markers on the body. These are usually placed on the skin at segment endpoints, either at supposed joint centers or over bony prominences such as malleoli, condyles, and epicondyles. The major source of error in such cases is movement of the skin over the bones or other subcutaneous tissues. If the subject has substantial subcutaneous tissue, the registration of motion can therefore be in serious error.

Clarity of the marker can be enhanced by using reflective material and color. Some markers are planar, but hemispheres improve clarity by standing out from the body and facilitating a visual estimate of the center of the sphere.

The major disadvantage of film or video as a recording medium is that the position of markers must be located manually from a projection of the image onto a digitizing tablet. The time spent in this process clearly increases with the number of views and the frame rate. Automatic pattern recognition avoids these problems, allowing repetition of an action in case the results are unacceptable for some reason. Unfortunately, automatic pattern recognition is not reliable enough to work without human intervention. Thus practical systems involve automatic pattern recognition proceeding under the supervision of an operator who can intervene to recognize landmarks when the system fails or to correct errors.

3.5. Active Markers

Active markers that identify themselves to the sensing system and facilitate automatic digitization of body landmarks have been used since the 1970s to avoid the tedium or manually digitizing millions of frames of film.

These can be based on LEDs or infrared-emitting diodes (IREDs). Typically the diodes are illuminated in turn by a controller that also passes synchronization pulses to the sensing system. Thus if one or more cameras sense a light impulse at a particular instant in time, it can be identified with a known marker. If, for example, the sensing time for one marker is 100 μsec, and if there are N markers, the overall sampling rate will be

$10^4/N$ samples/second. Unfortunately, both LEDs and IREDs suffer from problems of ambient light, although IREDs are better in this respect. Yet even IREDs often require a room with blackened walls to perform successfully since the infrared light from each active marker is necessarily beamed in a cone of some $60°$. This angle is required because they need to be seen as they move in 3D motion. Consequently much of the light can be reflected off the walls of the room.

The major advantage of active markers is the automatic registration of their position. The most serious problem is in ensuring that the active markers can always be seen by at least two cameras. Should a marker be lost temporarily from view, there is the possibility of interpolating the unknown positions. However, interpolation is impossible if a marker is lost either temporarily or permanently. This problem can be minimized by distributing many active markers on the segments of the body to increase their chances of being seen. The problems with this approach are that the markers may move around with motion of subcutaneous tissue, and the more markers there are, the lower will be the maximal sampling rate. Examples of commercially available IRED or LED systems include those produced by SELSPOT (Selspot Systems Ltd., 1233 Chicago Road, Troy, MI 48083) and Watsmart and OptoTrac (Northern Digital Inc., Waterloo, Ontario, Canada).

Other ways of registering movement use instrumentation on the body instead of cameras. Devices have been developed that sense an imposed electromagnetic field and provide a direct measure of the position and orientation of the sensing device relative to the imposed field. With this approach movement can be monitored directly and in real time, but the scope of the movement is limited by the extent of the field. Typical systems restrict movement to a cube of 1 m for a small system up to 8 m for a large system. The devices are attached at key landmarks on the body. Typical systems are commercially available from Polhemus (Colchester, VT) and Ascension Technologies (Burlington, VT).

Goniometers can also be used as sensors. These devices are fixed to the body across a joint and register angular displacement. The mechanism varies from simple potentiometers to strain gauge devices that can measure in two planes. For comprehensive measurements of the moving body goniometer devices have been built into a body suit. The major problem encountered in using a goniometer is that a relative angle is recorded. In order that position in space can be reconstructed from goniometric measurements, the orientation of at least one goniometer must be known. Consequently one of the techniques described previously must be used in conjunction with the goniometric method.

The electromagnetic sensors and the goniometers have the advantage that they can provide information on complex 3D motion that is unobtainable from markers sensed by cameras. Also the recognition problem is

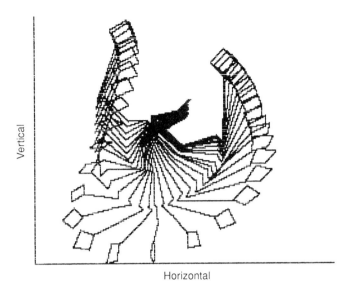

Figure 12.6. Squash forehand drives for two performers in two dimensions. Successive postures in the forehand drive of the better (top) and poorer (bottom) performers. Direction of ball projection is to the right.

avoided. The disadvantage is that the sensors and goniometers need to be connected to a controller by an umbilical cord or by telemetry, and these can limit movement.

3.6. Sequence Examples

3.6.1. Single-View Sequences

1. Squash. A 2D sequence of motion of squash forehand drives of two performers can be seen in Fig. 12.6. It was obtained from a camera whose optical axis was almost perpendicular to the line of motion of the ball. Passive markers were placed on the body as shown in Fig. 12.7. Filming was performed at 400 frames per second, digitized manually with a digitizer interfaced with an Apple computer and the 2D coordinates were plotted and joined with the same computer. A vertical 2D calibration grid was also filmed when located at the toes of the performers in the plane of ball motion. The sequence of segmental motion is seen easily as progressing in a proximal-to-distal (P/D) manner. This progression is a characteristic of expert throwing and striking skills. It involves initiation of motion of the trunk followed in sequence by the shoulder and elbow joints and ending with pronation of the forearm (13). The similarities and differences between the strikers can be appreciated from this view. However, it is little better than providing the observer with a slow motion video of the stroke.

2. Sprinting. A 2D representation of the 3D squash stroke requires interpretation by the observer. The kinematics of sprinting, which is primarily but not entirely 2D, can be captured by a single view from an

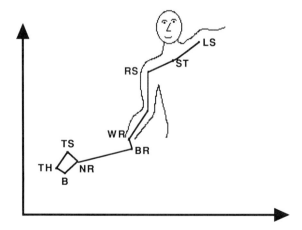

Figure 12.7. Passive markers used to monitor squash forehand drives.

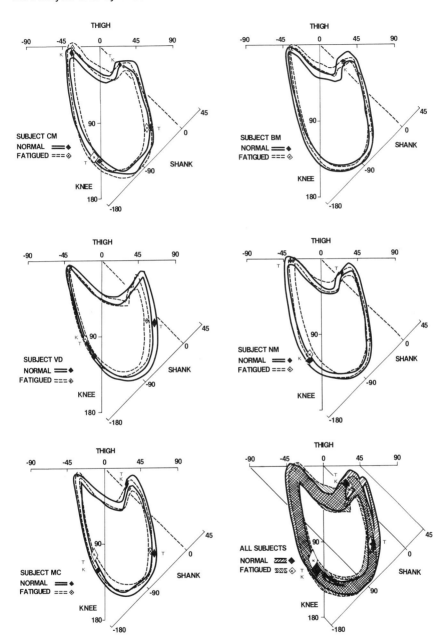

Figure 12.8. The thigh–trunk angle plotted against the knee angle.

optical camera axis that is perpendicular to the plane of motion. Again, the information obtained is little better than a hard copy of what could be seen in slow-motion video or film. However, data treatment can reveal significant information, as seen in Fig. 12.8. Here the angle of the thigh to the trunk is computed from the 2D kinematic data and plotted against the computed knee angle. Each figure is specific to one individual and has two plots that represent the pattern of motion after 100 m and 360 m of a 400-m sprint. It is clear that while fatigue induces changes in the motion patterns, it does so differentially among individuals (14).

3.6.2. Multiple-View Sequences — Squash

Filming of a squash forehand drive was performed with two cameras in order to produce accurate kinematics. The experimental setup is similar to that seen in Fig. 12.5, and Fig. 12.9 shows the calibration grid. This grid

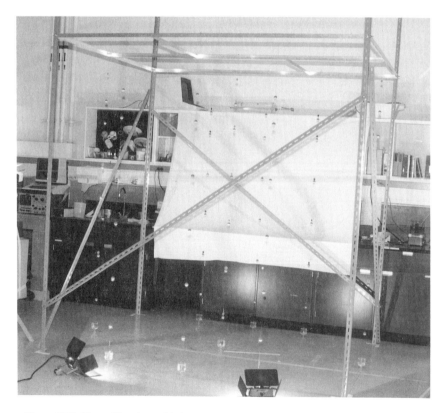

Figure 12.9. The calibration grid showing small plastic balls located on vertically hanging fishing line, and their plum bobs located in beakers of water.

Figure 12.10. The experimental subject with painted markers around joints and individual markers on the racquet.

comprised small plastic balls supported by paper clips attached to fishing line. The fishing line hung vertically as a result of the weight of a plumb bob that was immersed in a beaker of water to dampen swinging motion. Circles were painted around joints to identify joint centers rather than using markers that would disappear from the view of one or more cameras (Fig. 12.10). Markers were used on the racquet and on the forearm near the wrist in order to allow calculation of forearm pronation. Each camera view was synchronized by a camera flashlight in the view of both cine cameras, and views were digitized on an electromagnetic digitizer.

The purpose was to describe the relationship between joint angles and time with a view to determining the sequence of changes in joint angular velocity. The results showed that the motion of the forearm and wrist formed a complex combination of forearm pronation and wrist flexion-extension and abduction–adduction. This motion proved far more detailed than simple forearm pronation (13).

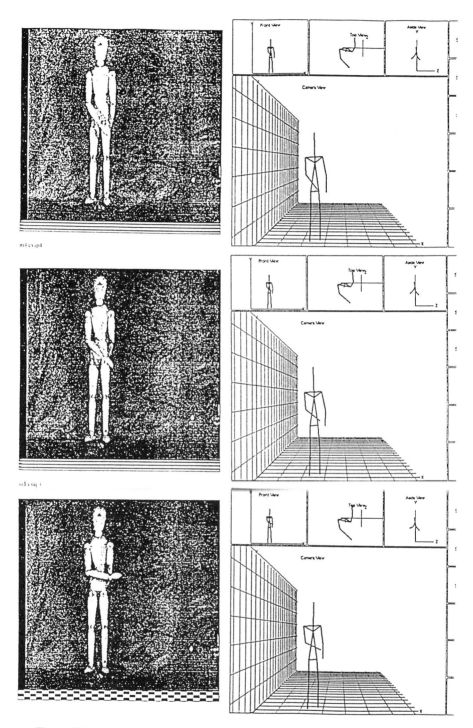

Figure 12.11. A series of single-view images of a figure are used to deduce the 3D coordinates. The estimated 3D positions are shown in the three orthogonal views on the right.

3.7. **Estimating Three-Dimensional Movement from a Sequence of Two-Dimensional Images**

While it is impossible, in principle, to calculate movement in 3D from a time sequence of 2D images, it is possible to estimate the movement (16, 21, 34). The process depends on

1. Accurately acquiring the 2D joint coordinates from the 2D images
2. Knowing the topology and segment lengths for the figure being observed
3. Having at least one frame in the sequence (preferably the first) where all landmarks are visible and the body position is known.

The basis for this approach is that the observed 2D projection constrains the 3D body to a limited number of configurations. Thus if the sequences starts from a known, standard position, the new positions in succeeding images can be calculated using knowledge of the kinematics. Normally, there will be two possible solutions for each limb segment; however, by applying additional constraints, either the impossible configurations can be eliminated or the most likely one can be selected (21). Some results are illustrated in Fig. 12.11.

4. ANALYSIS OF MOVEMENT DATA

4.1. **General**

When data have been acquired that specify the position of key points on a moving human body as a function of time, the movement has been described. Further analysis that will result in an understanding of the movement will depend on the goal of the process. For example, in biomechanics and sports the goal is to calculate the forces and other parameters that characterize the effectiveness of the movement being carried out. In dance analysis the goal is to derive a score that succinctly captures the movement of the artists in an established system of notation. In studies of human behavior the goal would be to characterize this behavior. In ergonomic evaluation of environments the goal is to characterize how economically a subject can move and carry out tasks in that environment. By far the greatest attention has been given to biomechanical analyses, and some typical approaches will be outlined here. The reader will be pointed to some references that spell out other possible applications.

4.2. Biomechanics

In biomechanics research, the goal is to develop models of the human body that explain how it functions mechanically. The structure of the biomechanical model is based on the mechanical structure of the body, and the parameters are determined by observing how the body moves in a wide variety of circumstances. In order to calculate the forces and torques between body segments the linear or angular accelerations of key landmarks must be calculated and with estimated inertial values, forces or torques can be calculated (5, 41, 43).

Activities that are analyzed range from grasping skills through locomotion of the disabled to high-level gymnastic performance. The aims and objectives of the analyses are equally varied. Much early work in this area was aimed at registering motion so that a rapid activity could simply be observed. This allowed the kinematics of the motion to be described. Subsequently the analysis involved inverse dynamic analysis (IDA), in which kinetic variables such as force and work were obtained. IDA remains a current technique in analysis of human motion, although it is based on a nonanatomic model of the body. Thus its use is being questioned, and it is being replaced by computer simulation and other methods of analysis such as solving for individual muscle forces.

4.2.1. Inverse Dynamic Analysis

This process involves the calculation of joint forces and joint moments as well as mechanical work done. The model of the body in this context is a series of rigid segments connected by either pin (in 2D) or universal (in 3D) joints (see Section 2). The process of IDA is to obtain the kinematics of segmental motion, to combine segmental translational and rotational accelerations with segmental mass and moment of inertia, respectively, and to generate a force and moment at each segmental endpoint. The process begins at a distal segment for which the externally applied force is either zero or known from a measuring device.

A simplified instance is shown in Fig. 12.12, where a single segment with moment of inertia J rotates about its lower end. Kinematic data obtained from sensing provide the orientation $\phi(t)$ as a function of time. Then the joint torque T required to produce the observed rotation will be

$$T(t) = J\ddot{\phi}(t) \tag{7}$$

This can be extended to a multisegment articulated structure. For exam-

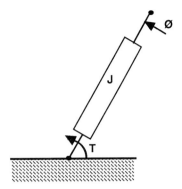

Figure 12.12. Calculation of joint torque from changes in observed orientation.

ple, in running the analysis can begin with the hand, where no external force acts, or at the foot, which lands on a force platform. Such a beginning allows forces and moments to be calculated at the proximal end of the distal segment where they become external inputs to the adjacent proximal segment.

One problem inherent in IDA is the potential accumulation of error in the serial process of calculating forces and moments in a proximal direction. Small errors in kinematic recording, estimation of segmental mass and moment of inertia, and position of the center of mass will be carried through the process and sequentially accumulated. This is why it is difficult to obtain a close match between force profiles at the feet that are calculated by IDA and measured directly by a force platform.

A further problem inherent in this approach, and one that has implications for interpretation, is its redundant nature—there are more muscles available to produce force than are necessary to drive such a simple model. The calculated moment of force about a joint is therefore the net result of the action of a number of muscles, with no available information on their relative contributions. Of greater seriousness is the fact that the calculated forces at the segment endpoints (joint forces) are not true joint reaction forces, but a vector sum of all forces acting on the segment (muscular, ligamentous and joint reaction force). Despite their artificial nature, joint forces and moments provide some insight into the mechanisms of human motion.

4.2.1.1. Example of IDA—Forces and Moments

Figure 12.13 shows calculated proximal net moments of the thigh and shank in the recovery phase of sprinting from toe-off to foot-strike. The

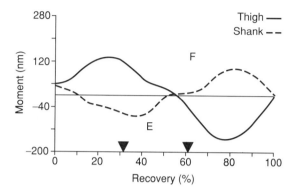

Figure 12.13. Net moments calculated for the thigh and shank during sprinting.

angular displacement resulting from the hip moment, if it was acting alone, would be 21 radians—fortunately, the moment at the knee counteracts this effect since 21 radians would lead to fracture of the hip joint! These competing moments, which are a necessary feature of the skill of sprinting, are partly automatic and result from the presence of biarticular muscles crossing both hip and knee joints. For example, the rectus femoris provides flexor and extensor moments at the hip and knee, respectively (15).

4.2.1.2. Example of IDA—Joint Force Power and Muscle Moment Power

When the scalar product of joint force and joint linear velocity is calculated, the result is power. Since the joint has only one velocity but an equal and opposite force on adjacent segments, the power represents the rate at which energy is being transferred between segments without loss. An example is the flow of energy across the hip joint during the recovery phase in sprinting. The force power due to rotation, shown in Fig. 12.14(A), is the product of the moment and angular velocity and is largely a positive energy flow from the hip to lower limb. The force power due to horizontal and linear forces, shown in Fig. 12.14(B), is initially positive as a result of pelvic axial rotation but then becomes negative as energy flows from the lower limb to the pelvis. The pelvic rotation results from contraction of muscles that are not attached to the lower limb. In this way energy can be transferred to segments whose muscles are not active. An example is the ability of the above knee amputee to produce knee flexion and subsequent extension in the recovery phase of walking without any musculature crossing the knee joint (14).

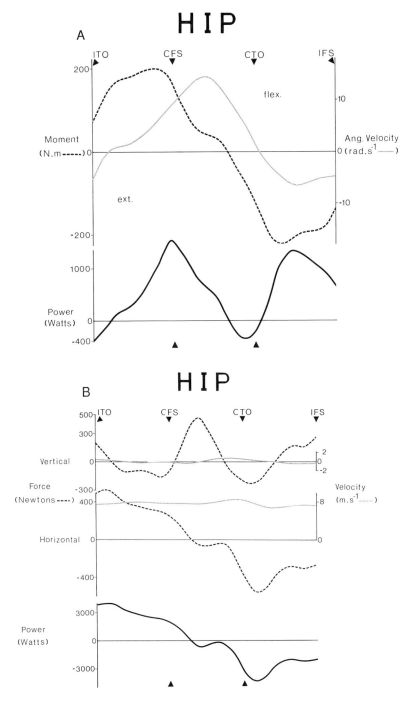

Figure 12.14. Joint force power at the hip during the recovery phase of sprinting due to (A) rotational forces and (B) linear forces; positive power represents an energy flow from the pelvis to the lower limb.

4.3. Notation Systems

A wide variety of movement notation systems have been developed to describe many aspects of human movement. For example, a notation system to describe movement in psychosocial processes has been developed by Scheflen (39), and Birdwhistell (6) has developed a complex

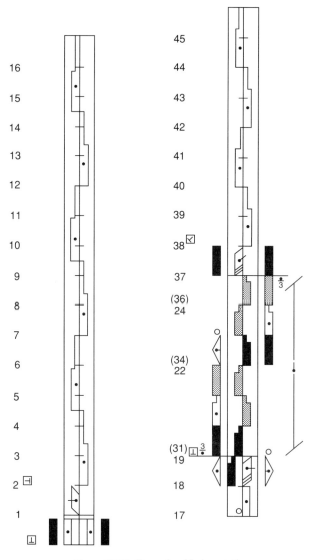

Figure 12.15. Example of Labanotation.

system to describe the movements used in interpersonal communication. However, these and other special purpose systems are unsuited for general application. Of the many general notation systems, the only three in common use are Benesh notation (4), Eshkol–Wachmann notation (19) and Labanotation (25). All three have been used to record dance; Benesh is the most popular in the United Kingdom and Labanotation (Fig. 12.15) in North America. In addition, Labanotation (after Hungarian dance theorist R. Laban) has been used in industrial time and motion study, Benesh and Labanotation have been used to record movement clinically, and Eshkol–Wachman has been used to record behavioral patterns in animals.

The strength and the weakness of all notation systems is that they rely on an intelligent human observer. Thus, they provide a way to objectively record the analysis of a movement that has been deduced by the skilled notator. Because of the difficulty in acquiring these skills there is a shortage of notators—thus there is a real need to use pattern recognition techniques to automatically develop a movement score from data describing the movement. Although a system that would recognize all the possible subtleties of human movement might be difficult to develop, it should be quite possible to automatically derive a score for most movements. This problem has received little or no attention, probably because of the difficulty and expense involved in acquiring the 3D data.

4.4. A High-Level Language for Human Movement?

No comprehensive language for human movement exists at this time (10). The wide variety of notation systems that have been developed represent movement at a very low level; the symbols of the notation represent elements that are analogous to the phonemes of speech when speech is realized from a natural language.

In designing a comprehensive language system for movement the following features are desired.

1. A natural and flexible input capability that will accept input in the form of text, graphical sketches, and possibly, analogic forms. By this we mean that it should be possible to use as input the text of a screenplay, the instructions of a play, or the notation of a dance. However, it should also be possible to indicate movement on a set with a sketch on a floorplan, where this is appropriate, and it may be desirable to allow an artist to define a specific movement pattern by example where goniometers or other advanced instrumentation is used to record the movement in a form from which it can be faithfully reproduced.

2. An efficient internal representation that captures the essence of the movement.

3. An output format that is meaningful for archival purposes and can be used as input at a later time. By making use of the consistent internal representation, it will be possible to have alternate outputs at different levels.

4. An animated output that provides an interpretation of the score in a useful way. This should provide sufficient detail to check the score for accuracy and should also be a useful tool for choreographers, film directors, and theater producers to plan a production.

5. SYNTHESIS — ANIMATION AND SIMULATION OF HUMAN MOVEMENT

The *synthesis* of human movement patterns is the inverse of the *analysis* process and follows the lower path shown in Fig. 12.1. The synthesized movement and its display as animation may be used to visualize data collected in an analysis process (as described above), it may be used for visualization of the results of a simulation, or it may be used as a way of animating human movement for the purposes of education, communication, or entertainment (12, 30). Whatever the application, synthesis requires knowledge (3). This knowledge can take one of the following forms:

1. An *explicit description* in the form of the spatial coordinates for all joints of the body at every time instant of interest. This can be from data collected from live subjects or from a series of 3D keyframes composed by an animator.
2. An *implicit description* in the form of a notation that is a shorthand for the explicit description. An example of this is the Labanotation system used in dance and ergonomic studies (25).
3. *Procedure knowledge* where a common and relatively stereotyped movement such as locomotion or grasping is captured in procedures that incorporate kinematic and dynamic knowledge about the movement (35).
4. *Declarative knowledge* where a knowledge base provides an organized way to handle the many rules and constraints needed to deduce the movement of multiple figures in a complex environment. The calculation of the resulting movement will typically involve a reasoning engine, which will in turn specify procedural movement.

These different cases will now be described and illustrated.

5.1. The Use of Explicit Knowledge

The animation of an articulated structure requires that a support position be defined in three dimensions and that three angles be specified for each body segment. Using kinematic methods, this can be obtained from live action or by interactive graphical specification of 3D keyframes.

The most basic approach is to capture the actual movement patterns of a live subject. This approach, called *rotoscoping* in the field of animation, is exactly the data collection process described in detail in Section 3. Although various forms of instrumentation assist in automating the process, some human intervention is normally required. Most of the human animation used in entertainment or advertising has been specified in this way.

The classic method of animation is still keyframing—the animator captures each important position in a keyframe and interpolation is used to generate the "in-betweens." Any computer-based animation system will incorporate 3D keyframing, and the movement specified in this way can be supplemented by movement captured from live action (20). For each figure being animated, detailed movement sequences must be choreographed and stored; the individual movement sequences become the building blocks for the animation. In describing this approach in more detail we will use the Life Forms system for animation of multiple articulated figures to illustrate the techniques (11).

In Life Forms, movement sequences are assembled in the Sequence Editor. As shown in Fig. 12.16, the main window displays a user selected projection of a 3D model of a human figure and along the side there are three small orthogonal views (front, side, and top), each of which can be selected as the main view. The different limb segments of the body can be selected directly by clicking on the part or by selection from a menu. Once selected, the orientation of the segment can be adjusted either by direct manipulation (click and drag) or by using linear or hemispherical potentiometers. Constraints have been built in to limit limb orientation to what is anatomically possible, but the constraints are complex functions and are only approximate. Using a forward kinematics approach a body stance is built up by first orienting the "root" segments, and then successively adjusting the more distal segments. For example, if support is on the right foot, this would be set first, followed in succession by the lower right leg, the upper right leg, the pelvis, and then the components of the left leg, the torso, the neck and head, and the arms.

The forward kinematic approach allows a particular body shape to be set up very accurately, but it does not lend itself very well to accurate placement of "end-effectors" such as hands. Using constrained inverse kinematics, any joint can be dragged interactively to a desired position while the joint angles in the chain are adjusted automatically (1, 2, 27, 29).

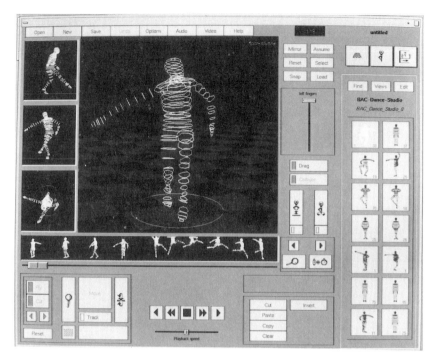

Figure 12.16. Interactive definition of keyframes and movement sequences in Life Forms.

Examples of the kinds of constraints that might be specified are "do not move torso," "do not move left leg," or "do not move foot." Thus if the hand is reaching for an object and it is close by, the torso does not need to move; however, for a more distant object the only constraint might be that the supporting foot should not move. This very powerful technique is compute-intensive but can be performed with little noticeable delay on graphics workstations.

Once a body stance has been satisfactorily defined, it is added to the movement sequence that is being assembled. The sequence consists of a string of key stances and is displayed on a strip-like window below the main display. Any stance in the sequence can be selected and brought up in the window for editing. A new stance is often developed most quickly by starting with an existing stance and modifying it. All or part of the sequence in the strip display can be played through at a speed selected by the user; the animated display is based on an interpolation between the key stances specified for the sequence. In interpolating articulated figures the use of quaternions can produce more realistic results.

The sequence can also be edited much like text in a word processor using selection, copy, cut, and paste commands, and in addition, the timing can be adjusted by moving individual stances in time, and stretching or squeezing selected sections. Playing through the animation of a sequence is helpful, but new insights can be obtained by looking at the development over time, just as a musical score shows how a piece of music develops over time. This feature has shown that it can be very helpful in capturing the dynamics of movement realistically—one of the most difficult parts of keyframe animation.

5.2. Animation of Multiple Figures

When movement sequences have been assembled for each figure being animated, they are combined together in a composition process that involves adjusting the sequences relative to each other in space and in time. Each figure has been choreographed with detailed movements of its own at the same time as moving through space relative to other figures and to the environment. If the figures are to interact closely with each other, then very careful choreography of the interaction may be necessary. Careful coordination of a soundtrack may also be necessary.

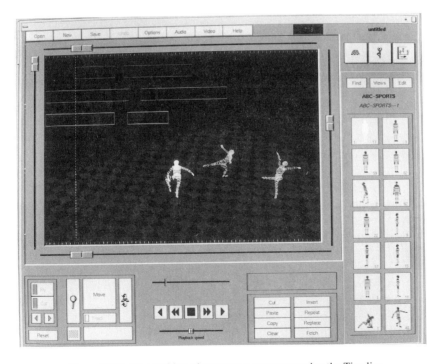

Figure 12.17. Composition of movement sequences using the Timeline.

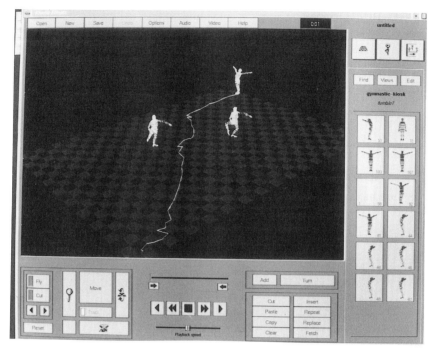

Figure 12.18. Editing movement paths.

In Life Forms composition in time is performed on the Timeline and composition in space on the Stage. In the Timeline, the sequences assigned to each figure are shown as boxes that can be edited as a unit using the select, move, copy, cut, or paste commands (Fig. 12.17). Using these word processor–like commands, the animator cannot only adjust the relative timing of sequences but also very quickly build up complex movement for each figure by building on the sequences developed in the Sequence Editor.

When a particular frame of the animation is displayed on the stage, the figures are shown in their appropriate spatial positions for that frame, but in addition, the path for the complete sequence can be displayed (Fig. 12.18). The orientation of the path can be adjusted interactively, as can its shape. The animation can then be played through in whole or in part. A soundtrack for digitized sound can also be synchronized to the movement using a separate sound window.

Because of the need to compose the animation in both space and time, users found it helpful if the Timeline was displayed on top of a Stage so that both aspects could be viewed simultaneously (Fig. 12.17).

5.3. The Use of Implicit Knowledge

Movement patterns can also be specified with notation; this approach has been used for recording dance for many decades (4, 19, 25). A number of computer-based systems have been developed to edit and/or interpret Labanotation, Benesh notation, and Eshkol–Wachmann notation scores. Our own experience with Labanotation (9) (Fig. 12.15) has shown that it is a viable method to specify animation, but that even with the addition of a macro capability, it is extremely tedious (some might compare it to programming in assembly language) and even dancers do not find it easy to learn. However, this approach has the great advantage that it relies on the animator's conceptualization of the movements required, and it certainly lends itself to the development of complicated scores. A major advantage of this approach is that the resulting score can be edited and changed.

5.4. The Use of Procedural Knowledge in Specifying Movement

The best candidates for specification with procedural knowledge are the primary movements, which are purposeful and functional. These movements include locomotion, grasping, manipulation, and such actions as throwing (24), pushing, and pulling. These movements are necessary to carry out the conscious intentions of the person involved and are distinguished from secondary movements, which are largely unconscious. We will describe our procedural approach to walking and suggest how it can be extended to grasping, manipulation, and throwing.

5.4.1. Walking

Although movements such as walking or running are conceptually well understood, a complete dynamic simulation of such actions is infeasible because generating the proper torques for a locomotion cycle is complicated by problems such as balance and coordination of the legs (44). On the other hand, kinematic approaches are inflexible and typically produce a "weightless," unrealistic animation (22, 40).

Unlike the earlier KLAW (Keyframe Less Animation of Walking) system (7, 8) which is a hybrid procedural system based on dynamics and task-level animation, the new procedural system described here is completely kinematic. Cubic spline and linear interpolation between step constraints replace the dynamic calculations with little tradeoff in realism (28). The gains from this are quite significant; the algorithm is fully

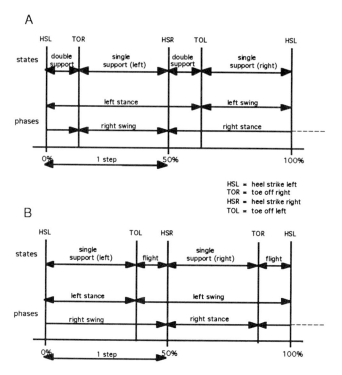

Figure 12.19. Locomotion cycles for walking (A) and running (B).

interactive and runs in real time, and thus has become a much more useful tool for animators.

Human locomotion describes an intricate activity where body translation results from rotational movements in the lower limbs (26). However, locomotion is a cyclic activity of recurring patterns with a basic unit of one locomotion stride or cycle consisting of two symmetric steps (left and right) as shown in Fig. 12.19, so we can limit our discussion to one locomotion step.

The underlying idea of our walking algorithm is twofold: it is hierarchical and step-oriented. "Hierarchical" implies that each locomotion step is determined by two independent parameters (expressed in terms of the step unit): step length and step frequency. Together with their product, which is the speed of the locomotion, they form the three *locomotion parameters* that specify a desired gait pattern as a high-level task.

A step consists of a double-support state, where both feet are on the ground, and a single-support state, where one foot is off the ground; a running step consists of a single-support state plus a flight state where both feet are off the ground. In terms of the individual legs, each state is made up from a stance and a swing phase, shifted in time. This holds for walking as well as for running. In fact, it is just the amount of "overlap" of these phases that determines whether a walking or running gait is present. In walking, the stance phases of the two legs overlap; as the step frequency increases, the duration of this overlap becomes smaller. When the duration of the double support vanishes completely, a running gait results, in which the swing phases start to overlap.

The algorithm is also "step-oriented" which means that the appearance of a walk—determined by the locomotion parameters and attributes—can be changed with the granularity of one locomotion step. For example, the step length, pelvic rotation, or amount of knee bend can be changed from one step to the next.

5.4.1.1. Algorithm

For each locomotion step, we need to calculate three *step constraints* from the high-level specification of parameters and attributes: the duration for the leg phases, the leg angles at the end of each step, and the control points that determine the movement of the hip of the stance leg during a step. Then the intermediate values from the previous step to the current step can be interpolated. The duration for the leg phases as well as the leg angles at the end of each step are calculated on the basis of the current step frequency and step length, respectively [this is explained in more detail in Brunderlin and Calvert (8)].

The computation of the control points for the hip of the stance leg is done in two parts, a vertical (y) and a horizontal (x) component. In each case, four control points per step are determined, as indicated by $t_1, \ldots, t_4$ in Fig. 12.20; the first and last points in x and y are easily derived given the current step length and the leg angles at the beginning and end of each step (at times t_1 and t_4 in Fig. 12.20). The second and third control points are computed as follows. From research on human locomotion (26) it is known that the vertical displacement is lowest around the middle of double support (t_2) and highest around the middle of the swing phase (t_3), whereas the horizontal displacement reaches a maximum (ahead of average position) around the middle of double support (t_2) and a minimum

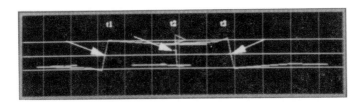

Figure 12.20. Trajectory of the stance leg hip during a walking step.

(behind average position) around the middle of the swing phase (t_3). Knowing the durations of the current step (t_{step}), the double support (t_{ds}), and the swing phase (t_{swing}) (26), we can determine the second and third control points as follows:

$$x_{mid-ds}=0.5*t_{ds}*step-length*x\_factor/t_{step}$$

$$x_{mid-swing}=(t_{ds}+0.5*t_{swing})*step-length/(t_{step}*x\_factor)$$

$$y_{mid-swing}=f(knee\_bend)$$

$$y_{mid-ds}=y_{impact}-bounce\_factor*(y_{mid-swing}-y_{Impact})/5$$

where x_factor is the change in horizontal velocity (a value of 1.1 has given good results), f is a trigonometric function of the locomotion attribute for maximum knee extension during stance, and bounce _factor is a locomotion attribute for the degree of bounciness of the locomotion; y_{impact} calculation is based on the leg angles at the end of the step.

Interpolating splines are now fitted through the two sets of four control points to generate the position of the hip for the stance leg during a step. Given the position of the toe, which is stationary during stance, the *virtual leg* principle is applied to calculate the angles for the stance leg during the current step as explained elsewhere (8).

Once the motion of the stance leg is determined, a pelvis is induced to produce three determinants of gait: pelvic rotation, pelvic list, and lateral displacement of the body. Both the default values for rotation and list of the pelvis can be changed interactively as locomotion attributes. Lateral displacement is a function of stride width and velocity (greater stride width means more and faster locomotion means less displacement).

The motion of the swing leg is divided into three subphases, in which the leg angles are obtained by linear interpolation. The upper-body motion is expressed as functions of the lower body. For example, the arm swings forward with the opposite leg, and the shoulder rotation is a function of the pelvic rotation. Both arm swing and shoulder rotation are defined as attributes and can be adjusted as desired.

The system computes a total of 56 angles for 37 joints of the default body model (24 of these joints are between vertebrae in the spine) plus a position vector in space for each time step. Different sizes and shapes of bodies can be accounted for. Since the algorithm is step-oriented, changes in the locomotion parameters and attributes over time become active with the granularity of one step. This allows for acceleration and deceleration in the locomotion, and the extreme cases, which are starting and stopping. The program is implemented as a producer–consumer, double-buffer problem synchronized with semaphores. One process calculates all the joint angles for one locomotion step based on the current parameters and attributes writing to one buffer, while the outer process handles all the graphics and interactions reading from the other buffer. As long as one process can compute a step faster than the other process is able to display the previous step, the user can adjust parameters and attributes as the figure is walking without noticeable delays. On a Silicon Graphics R3000 Indigo workstation, this real-time feedback is achieved when the contour line-drawing human figure is displayed.

5.4.1.2. Interface

One major advantage of a procedural or high-level motion control system is that it does not require the animator to meticulously specify the low-level detail; in fact, producing a movement like bipedal locomotion with traditional keyframing would require enormous skills in order to get the timing and coordination of all the body parts to look right. Of course, such a procedural approach becomes useful in practice only if it is not completely hard-coded, that is, it allows the user to flexibly choose different instances of a particular motion. The choice of the parameters to specify a desired motion is therefore crucial. It is also important to provide interactive and real-time control, so that the animator can quickly create and shape a movement idea.

In Bruderlin's system, three locomotion parameters can be set for the current step to achieve a specific stride: step length, velocity, and step frequency, as shown in Fig. 12.21. In *normal* mode, if one of the parameters is changed via a slider, the other two are automatically adjusted to maintain a "natural" gait according to the normalizing formulae. In *locked* mode, where one of the three parameters is locked at the current setting, the other two can be adjusted via sliders; for instance, to generate a slow walk at a large step length, the step length would be locked at a large value and then the velocity slider would be set to a slow speed.

In addition to the locomotion parameters, 15 locomotion attributes are also provided to individualize walks, that is, to produce walks at the same step length, step frequency, and velocity, but with different characteristics such as upper-body tilt or leg bounciness. These attributes are also illustrated in Fig. 12.21; there are 5 attributes for varying the movements of the arms: shoulder rotation, arm swing (sagittal plane), arm out (coronal plane), minimum elbow flexion, and maximum elbow flexion. There are 2 attributes for the torso—forward tilt and sway, and 2 for the pelvis—rotation (transverse plane) and list (coronal plane). Finally, there are 6 attributes for the movement of the legs—bounciness, minimum knee flexion during stance, knee flexion at impact, minimum toe clearance during swing, foot angle, and stride width.

All of these attributes as well as the parameters are initially set to default values and can be adjusted interactively via sliders while the

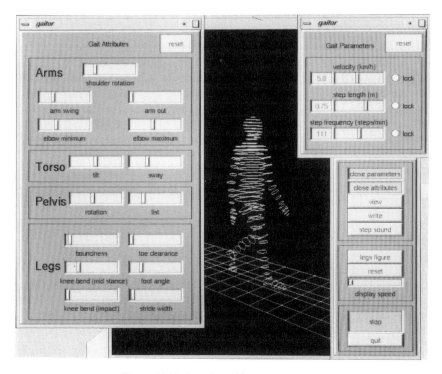

Figure 12.21. Interface of locomotion system.

motion of a human figure is displayed on the screen. Of course, many more parameters are conceivable to further personalize locomotion; however, experience has shown that too many variables lead to confusion and make it difficult to predict the outcome.

5.4.2. Grasping Movements

Grasping movements are among the most common performed by human beings; many would claim that the ability to grasp, examine, and manipulate has been crucial to our evolution. However, in contrast to locomotion, where one step is very much like another, at a detailed level two grasping movements are almost never the same. The following kinds of movements are included in this class: pick up a glass and drink, pick up a pencil and write, pick up a ball and throw it, pick up an unknown object and examine it, grasp a door knob and turn it, pick up an object and place it in a new position, and so on. Particular challenges for animation would include two figures shaking hands and a juggler with multiple balls.

A grasping movement starts with a reach, which is usually fairly rapid and covers most of the distance to the object. As the hand approaches the object to be grasped, it slows down and the thumb and fingers are held sufficiently open to encompass the object. In the final approach the closure of the fingers and thumb is coordinated with the final displacement of the hand by the arm. After the grasp has closed on the object subsequent movements for manipulation, examination, placement, etc. are carried out (42).

The choice of grasp is usually dictated more by the task than by the shape of the object to be grasped (17, 38). In a *power grasp*, the task requires considerable force and there is usually a large area of contact with the opposing surfaces—the fingers and the palm of the hand. In a *precision grasp*, in contrast, the task requires careful and accurate movements, and the opposing surfaces are the tips of the fingers and the thumb. There has been extensive study of the types of grasp used for different objects and different tasks; Cutkosky and Howe have organized these results as a *Taxonomy of Grasps* (42). Although there will be variations in the way an individual grasps a specific object to perform a specific task, this taxonomy provides useful rules for the animator. These rules have been formalized in an expert system for grasp choice (17).

5.4.2.1. Algorithm

The basic steps are as follows:

1. Look up the location of the hand and the object to be grasped. (Note that in animation, in contrast to robotics, the system normally has perfect knowledge about the shape, position, and orientation of all objects.)
2. Determine whether the object is within reach:
   a. By moving arm and without moving torso
   b. By moving arm and upper torso only
   c. By moving arm and upper and lower torso, but without moving feet
   d. By using locomotion to bring arm within reach
3. Determine the orientation of the hand needed to grasp the object. [This depends on the shape of the object—in our system all objects will carry a descriptor of the overall shape and descriptors for the different surfaces. Some objects (e.g., liquid-filled cups) will have constraints imposed on their orientation.] A model for the hand is shown in Fig. 12.22.
4. Determine a trajectory and velocity profile for the hand from its current position to the object to be grasped. (Typical trajectories are parabolic and in a plane—these are deduced from observation of

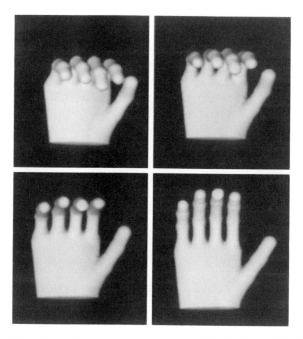

Figure 12.22. Four frames from a grasping sequence. The simple model of the hand is based on implicit surfaces.

human movement.) Constrained inverse kinematics is used to calculate the movement of other limb segments (27).

5. Determine the type of grasp to be used from the Cutkosky Grasp Taxonomy and expert system (17).
6. Calculate the movement of the fingers and thumb. (Normally the hand will approach the object with fingers extended. As the hand comes close to the object, the fingers and thumb will flex to just close on the surfaces chosen for contact.)
7. Determine the movement necessary after the hand has closed its grip on the object. Four frames from a grasping sequence are shown in Fig. 12.22.

At this time we have not considered the details of the movements that take place after the hand has grasped the object.

5.5. Declarative Knowledge

The notion of using AI and expert system approaches to capture the knowledge and skills of the animator is obvious, but the implementation is not (46, 47). At one level, it is fairly straightforward to build up a knowledge base of movement characteristics for the body. These will include basic data on the individual being animated (dimensions, moments of inertia, etc.) and such constraints as the range of movement for specific joints. The knowledge base should also include typical movement patterns for locomotion, simple voluntary movements such as grooming habits, shaking hands, and characteristics of the individual that determine how the movements are carried out (brisk, lethargic, happy, sad, etc.).

At the highest level, the system needs to be able to handle declarative knowledge where interpersonal behavior, interaction with complex environments, and the goals of the person being animated must be determined. Then a reasoning engine should be able to use this knowledge (logical statements, rules, constraints, etc.) to deduce feasible animation for goal-oriented tasks. This would include, for example, feasible movements for the three or four characters on stage in a television situation comedy, or a feasible animation for a crowd scene with a dozen people walking up and down a sidewalk. [Note that people follow quite tight rituals for their body movements when they meet strangers, those known slightly or close friends (6).]

There has been some research in this direction (47). Badler (1, 2) has used a constraint base to constrain his dynamic simulations, and Drewery and Tsotsos (18) have studied a frame-based approach to goal-directed animation. The animation produced by the Human Factory system of Magnenat–Thalmann and Thalmann (31, 32) is impressive. Another approach to this problem has been taken by Ridsdale (37), who has developed a system for human figure animation that finds feasible movement paths that take account of the feelings of the characters being animated as well as other environmental factors. Another problem that Ridsdale addressed in his Director's Apprentice system was the placement of figures in the scene. The rule base includes some of the standard rules of direction for the placement of actors on a stage and for their movement as the action proceeds. It also allows the animator to enter personal information about each character. This might take the form of "John hates Mary," "Mr. Jones is the boss of Mr. Smith," "Bill irritates Simon," or similar. Then as action proceeds, mainly through ongoing conversation between the characters, feasible movement patterns are predicted. The system is driven by a script that at this point is used only to indicate which character is speaking. Consideration of the meaning of each utterance is well beyond our current capabilities.

Not surprisingly, it has been found that the different rules of direction and the rules describing the characters are often in conflict. Thus mechanisms must be developed to provide feasible solutions that in some sense minimize these conflicts; obviously there will be no unique results, and the animator may wish to personally judge the weighting of different rules.

5.5.1. Secondary Movements

While other approaches can provide the specification of correct movement patterns to achieve high-level goals, the movement will not be realistic unless it includes those subtle secondary gestures that humans add to their primary movement. Secondary movement involves much of the body language that is so crucial to subconsious nonverbal communication (39). Morawetz (33) has developed a system that allows the animator to define the specific *personality* of the individual character (extrovert vs. introvert, cheerful vs. gloomy, assertive vs. passive, domineering vs. submissive) as well as the *moods* that affect the character from time to time (boredom, nervousness, tiredness, impatience, and fear). As implemented, the system generates secondary movement for two characters walking toward each other.

The rule base developed by Morawetz is only partially complete, and we have dubbed the system that uses it a "mock expert system," since it does not truly reason about the facts available. Considerable additional work is necessary to analyze the extensive literature on body language and to incorporate it into an expert system. Nevertheless, even this simple implementation has shown that interesting movement can be produced automatically.

6. SUMMARY

This chapter has set out the principles involved in sensing, analyzing, and synthesizing human movement. While there are impressive systems available to assist researchers, clinicians, and artists, there are still real limits on what is possible in both analysis and synthesis. Improved systems will require new application techniques from computer vision, image processing, language understanding, knowledge representation, expert systems, and image synthesis.

In spite of the availability of sophisticated and relatively inexpensive vision systems, the sensing problem is still very difficult. Accurate reconstruction of moving bodies is rarely attempted without first attaching passive or active markers to key landmarks on the body. With markers attached, there is still the problem of matching up the same markers in multiple views; this is made more difficult by the occlusion of particular markers that occurs in any complex movement. Active markers are easier to track consistently since they identify themselves unambiguously, but the tradeoff is the need to connect the active devices to a controller by an umbilical cord or a telemetry system. More consistent tracking of movement is being achieved with instrumentation that is based on sensors on the body that locate themselves relative to an imposed electromagnetic field. Since these systems are not vision-based, occlusion is not a problem, but the size of the space available is restricted to about a 3-m cube unless multiple overlapping fields are imposed with multiple transmitters. Also, as with active markers, the moving human has to be connected to the controller by umbilical or by telemetry.

While gross body movement can be assessed very well if key landmarks on the body surface can be tracked over time, surface landmarks will always be inadequate for accurate biomechanical studies since the skin moves relative to the underlying skeleton. There is no direct solution to this problem short of fixing the landmarks in the bones!

Although there are no comprehensive approaches to the analysis of movement data, sophisticated tools have been developed in the field of biomechanics to allow a quantitative analysis of the kinematics and dynamics of specific movements. These analysis tools are widely used in clinical studies of movement and in sports science to diagnose movement abnormalities and to optimize performance. At a higher level, however, there have been few attempts to deduce purposeful movement from the data describing how the body moves in space. The only techniques widely used rely on a skilled human observer to use a notation system to build up a score describing the movement. There is no reason why an automated system could not be developed to produce these scores. But even these scores are at a relatively low level, and a higher-level understanding is necessary to deduce purpose, interpersonal communication, or aesthetic content in complex movement (10). There are obvious parallels to research on natural language understanding.

If a full description is available for movement of the body skeleton, then this can be used to drive an animation. Indeed, most of the believable sequences of human animation that have been produced to date have relied on digitized (rotoscoped) live action. Obviously this approach to synthesis lacks generality, and research on human animation has concentrated on ways synthesize movement without copying live action (3). To achieve this, the system and/or the animator must provide the knowledge that describes the movement. This knowledge can have a form that is explicit, procedural, or declarative. As in classical animation, most computer-based systems are based on the explicit definition of keyframes by an animator; this approach can provide excellent results, but it requires great skill and is very time-consuming. Knowledge about some common movements such as locomotion (walking and running) and grasping is being incorporated into procedures. These procedures empower the animator by allowing a wide variety of these basic movements to be generated by specification of only a few parameters. However, the more complex and less predictable movements that occur in complex human interactions with each other and with a changing environment are not amenable to procedural definition. The complexity is best captured with a combination of logical statements, rules, and constraints that form a knowledge base. A reasoning engine (or expert system) then deduces feasible movement patterns that satisfy the rules and constraints (23). These high-level approaches are being implemented as research tools and point the way to powerful tools for complex human animation. Truly believable human animation would allow the synthesis of a scene that could not be distinguished by the viewer from one produced with live video—a sort of "Turing test" for animation. Animation tools currently under development make it possible to achieve believable movement, but the animation of realistic bodies and clothing still presents some formidable challenges (9).

REFERENCES

1. N. I. Badler, K. H. Manoocherhri, and G. Walters, Articulated figure positioning by multiple constraints. *IEEE Comput. Graphics Appl.* 7(6), 28–38 (1987).
2. N. I. Badler, J. D. Korein, J. U. Korein, G. M. Radack, and L. S. Brotman, Positioning and animating figures in a task oriented environment. *Visual Comput.* pp. 212–220 (1985).
3. B. Barsky, N. Badler, and D. Zeltzer, eds., "Making them Move: Mechanics, Control and Animation of Articulated Figures." Morgan Kaufmann, San Mateo, CA, 1990.
4. R. Benesh and J. Benesh, "An Introduction to Benesh Dance Notation." A. C. Black, London, 1956.
5. A. A. Biewener, "Biomechanics—Structures and Systems: A Practical Approach." IRL Press at Oxford University Press, New York, 1992.
6. R. L. Birdwhistell, "Kinesics and Context. Essays on Body Movement Communication." Univ. of Pennsylvania Press, Philadelphia, 1970.
7. A. Bruderlin and T. W. Calvert, Goal-directed, dynamic animation of human walking. *Comput. Graph.* **23**, 233–242 (1989).
8. A. Bruderlin and T. W. Calvert, Animation of human gait. *In* "Adaptability of Human Gait, Advances in Psychology Series." (A. E. Patla, ed.) pp. 305–330. Elsevier, North-Holland, Amsterdam, 1991.
9. T. W. Calvert, Composition of realistic animation sequences for multiple human figures. *In* "Making Them Move: Mechanics, Control and Animation of Articulated Figures" (B. Barsky, N. Badler, and D. Zeltzer, eds.) pp. 35–50. Morgan Kaufmann, San Mateo, CA, 1990.
10. T. W. Calvert, Towards a language for human movement. *Comput. Humanities* **20**(2) 35–43 (1986).
11. T. W. Calvert, C. Welman, S. Gaudet, T. Schiphorst, and C. Lee, Composition of multiple figure sequences for dance and animation. *Visual Comput.* **7**, 114–121 (1991).
12. T. W. Calvert, The challenge of human figure animation. *Graphics Interface '88, Proc.*, pp. 203–210 (1988).

13. A. E. Chapman, "Biomechanics of Squash." Canadian Squash Rackets Assoc., Toronto, Ontario, 1986.

14. A. E. Chapman and R. M. Lonergan, (1989). A biomechanical rationale for the preferred style of running. *Abstr., Int. Congr. Biomechan. 12th*, UCLA, p. 233, *1989*.

15. A. E. Chapman and C. W. Medhurst, Cyclographic evidence of fatigue in sprinting. *Hum. Movement Stud.* **7**, 225–272 (1981).

16. Z. Chen and H-J. Lee, Knowledge-guided visual perception of 3-d human gait from a single image sequence. *IEEE Trans. Syst. Man Cybernet.* **SMC-22**, 336–342 (1992).

17. M. R. Cutkosky, On grasp choice, grasp models and the design of hands for manufacturing tasks. *IEEE Trans. Robotics Autom.* **RA-5**, 269–279 (1989).

18. K. Drewery and J. Tsotsos, Goal directed animation using English motion commands. *Graphics Interface '86, Proc.* pp. 131–135 (1986).

19. N. Eshkol and A. Wachmann, "Movement Notation." Weidenfeld & Nicholson, London, 1958.

20. J. D. Foley, A. van Dam, S. K. Feiner, and J. F. Hughes, (1990). "Computer Graphics: Principles and Practice." Addison-Wesley, Reading, MA.

21. Y. Fu, Model-based recovery of human body structure from two-dimensional images. M.A.Sc. Thesis, Simon Fraser University, School of Engineering Science, Burnaby, BC, 1991.

22. M. Girard and A. Maciejweski, Computational modeling for the computer animation of legged figures. *Comput. Graphics* **19**, pp. 263–270 (1985).

23. W. S. Havens, Intelligent backtracking in the Echidna CLP reasoning system. *In* "International Journal of Expert Systems." (M. Harandi, ed.), pp. 21–45. Jai Press, London, 1991.

24. R. M. Herring and A. E. Chapman, Effects on changed segmental values and timing of both torque and torque reversal in simulated throwing. *J. Biomech.* **25**, 1173–1184 (1992).

25. A. Hutchinson, "Labanotation," 2nd ed. Theatre Arts Books, New York, 1960.

26. V. T. Inman, H. J. Ralston, and F. Todd, "Human Walking." Williams & Wilkins, Baltimore, MD, 1981.

27. P. Isaacs and M. Cohen, Controlling dynamic simulation with kinematic constraints, **21**, 215–224 (1987).

28. D. Kochanek and R. Bartels, Interpolating splines with local tension, continuity and bias control. *Comput. Graphics* **18**, 33–41 (1984).

29. P. Lee, S. Wei, J. Zhao, and N. Badler, Strength guided motion. *Comput. Graphics* **24**, 253–262 (1990).

30. N. Magnenat-Thalmann and D. Thalmann, (1985). "Computer Animation: Theory and Practice." Springer-Verlag, Tokyo.

31. N. Magnenat-Thalman and D. Thalmann, The use of high-level 3-D graphical types in the MIRA animation system. *IEEE Comput. Graphics Appl.* **3**(9), 9–16 (1983).

32. N. Magnenati-Thalmann and D. Thalmann, The direction of synthetic actors in the film Rendez-vous à Montréal. *IEEE Comput. Graphics Appl.* **7**(12), 9–19 (1987).

33. C. L. Morawetz and T. Calvert, A framework for goal-directed human animation with secondary movement. *Graphics Interface '90, Proc.* pp. 60–67 (1990).

34. J. O'Rourke and N. I. Badler, Model based image analysis of human motion using constraints propagation. *IEEE Trans. Pattern Anal. Mach. Intell.* **PAMI-2**, 522–546 (1980).

35. C. Phillips and N. Badler, Interactive behaviors for bipedal articulated figures. *Comput. Graph.* **25**, 359–362 (1991).

36. A. O. Quanbury, The clinical gait lab: Form and function. *In* "Biomechanics IX-A" (D. A. Winter, R. W. Norman, R. P. Wells, K. C. Hayes, and A. E. Patla, eds.), pp. 509–512. Human Kinetics Press, Champaign, IL, 1982.

37. G. Ridsdale and T. Calvert, Animating microworlds from scripts and relational constraints, *Proc. Comput. Animation '90*, Geneva, *1990*, pp. 107–117 (1990).

38. H. Rijpkema and M. Girard, Computer animation of knowledge-based grasping. *Comput. Graphics*, **25**(4), 339–348 (1991).

39. A. E. Scheflen, "Theory of Body Language and the Social Order." Prentice-Hall, Englewood Cliffs, NJ, 1972.

40. A. J. Van den Bogert, H. C. Schamhardt, and A. Crowe, Simulation of quadrapedal locomotion using rigid body dynamics. *J. Biomech.* **22**, 33–41 (1989).

41. C. L. Vaughan, B. L. Davis, and J. O'Connor, "Gait Analysis Laboratory." Human Kinetics Press, Champaign, IL, 1992.

42. S. T. Venkataraman and T. Iberall, eds., "Dextrous Robot Hands." Springer-Verlag, Berlin, 1990.

43. M. Whittle, "Gait Analysis: An Introduction." Butterworth-Heinemann, Oxford and Toronto, 1991.

44. J. Wilhelms, Using dynamic analysis to animate articulate bodies such as humans and robots. *Graphics Interface '86, Proc.*, pp. 97–104 (1985).

45. D. A. Winter, "The Biomechanics and Motor Control of Human Gait: Normal, Elderly and Pathological," 2nd ed. University of Waterloo Press, Waterloo, Ont., 1991.

46. D. Zeltzer, Towards an integrated view of 3-D computer character animation. *Graphics Interface '85, Proc.* pp. 105–115 (1985).

47. D. Zeltzer, Direct manipulation of virtual worlds. *In* "Making Them Move: Mechanics, Control and Animation of Articulated Figures" (B. Barsky, N. Badler, and D. Zeltzer, eds.) pp. 3–33. Morgan Kaufmann, San Mateo, CA, 1990.

Chapter **13**

Relational Matching

LINDA G. SHAPIRO

Department of Computer Science and Engineering
University of Washington
Seattle, Washington

1. INTRODUCTION

Model-based recognition of complex objects requires finding a correspondence between features of an object model and features extracted from one or more images. For instance, a two-dimensional shape may be represented by such features as points of high curvature, boundary line segments, or near-convex pieces. A three-dimensional object that appears in a single two-dimensional image may be represented by three-dimensional line segments whose two-dimensional projections can appear in the

475

**HANDBOOK OF PATTERN RECOGNITION
AND IMAGE PROCESSING: COMPUTER VISION**

image. A three-dimensional object that is acquired from range data may instead be represented by a set of its bounding surfaces.

There are a number of different methods for attempting to find the correspondence between model features and image features. The hypothesize-and-test method (7) selects a small subset of the image features, hypothesizes their correspondences to a set of object features, and constructs an estimate of the geometric transformation that would produce the image features from the model features. The transformation is then applied to the entire model to map all of its features into image space. A verification procedure decides if the projected model is close enough to a subset of the image to constitute a match. If not, a new hypothesis is generated, and the process is repeated.

Accumulator-based methods attempt to accumulate evidence for each possible transformation from model features to image features. One such method is geometric hashing (6), which represents its models in a hash-table indexed by invariant features. Each feature of the image is transformed to an index into the hash-table, a list of possible model–transformation pairs that could have produced that feature is retrieved, and accumulators representing these model–transformation pairs are incremented. After all image features have been processed, the peaks in the accumulator space indicate the best possible correspondences. A verification procedure similar to the one for hypothesize-and-test is still required, because of the likelihood of some false peaks in the accumulators. Another variation (14) votes for view classes of object models instead of transformations.

Relational matching is a powerful method for determining correspondences that can be used alone or in conjunction with either hypothesize-and-test or geometric hashing. The idea is to extract not only features, but also relationships among the features. In this manner, relational structures are used to represent both the model and the image. Relational matching finds correspondences between object features and image features that preserve the relationships as much as possible. This chapter is concerned with the definitions of relational matching, the algorithms that perform it, and the applications that use it.

2. DEFINITIONS

How can a complex object or entity be described? The object or entity has global properties such as area, height, and width. It also has a set of parts or important features. The parts each have properties of their own, and there are spatial relationships that describe their interconnections. In order to define the process of relational matching, we need a unified context in which to express these properties and relationships. We call this context a *relational description*. A relational description is a set of relations that together describe a complex object or entity. The relation is the basic unit of a relational description, so we will start with relations.

2.1. Relations

Let O_A be an object or entity, and A be the set of its parts or important features. An *N*-ary *relation* R over A is a subset of the Cartesian product $A^N = A \times \cdots \times A$ (*N* times). For example, suppose that O_A is a chair, and its part set A consists of four legs, a back, and a seat. A list of the parts is a unary relation $R_1 \subseteq A$. A list of the pairs of parts that connect together is a binary relation $R_2 \subseteq A \times A$. Other binary relations of interest include the list $R_3 \subseteq A \times A$ of pairs of parallel parts and the list $R_4 \subseteq A \times A$ of pairs of perpendicular parts. The set of triples of the form (p_1, p_2, p_3), where parts p_1 and p_3 both connect to part p_2, is a fifth relation $R_5 \subseteq A \times A \times A$. The set $D_A = \{R_1, R_2, R_3, R_4, R_5\}$ forms a relational description of the chair. This relational description describes only spatial relationships. Before we add properties to make the descriptions more robust, we discuss a method for comparing these simple relations.

2.2. Relational Homomorphisms

Let A be the part set of object O_A, and B be the part set of object O_B. Let $R \subseteq A^N$ be an *N*-ary relation over part set A. Let $f : A \to B$ be a function that maps elements of set A into set B. We define the *composition $R \circ f$* of R with f by

$$R \circ f = \{(b_1, \ldots, b_N) \in B \mid \text{ there exists}$$

$$(a_1, \ldots, a_N) \in R \quad \text{with} \quad f(a_i) = b_i, i = 1, \ldots, N)\}.$$

Figure 13.1 illustrates the composition of a binary relation with a mapping. Let $S \subseteq B^N$ be a second *N*-ary relation. A *relational homomorphism* from R to S is a mapping $f : A \to B$ that satisfies $R \circ f \subseteq S$. That is, when a relational homomorphism is applied to each component of an *N*-tuple of R, the result is an *N*-tuple of S. Figure 13.2 illustrates the concept of a relational homomorphism.

A relational homomorphism maps the primitives of A to a subset of the primitives of B having all the same interrelationships that the original

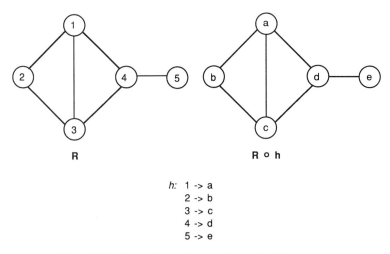

h: 1 -> a
    2 -> b
    3 -> c
    4 -> d
    5 -> e

Figure 13.1. Composition of binary relation R with mapping h.

primitives of A had. If A is a much smaller set than B, then finding a one–one relational homomorphism is equivalent to finding a copy of a small object as part of a larger object. Finding a chair in an office scene is an example of such a task. If A and B are about the same size, then finding a relational homomorphism is equivalent to determining that the two objects are similar. A *relational monomorphism* is a relational homo-

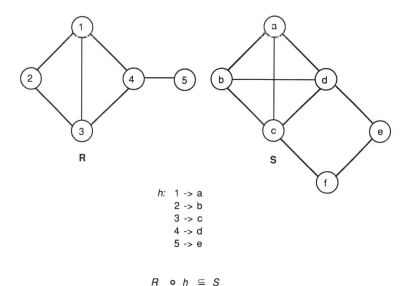

h: 1 -> a
    2 -> b
    3 -> c
    4 -> d
    5 -> e

$$R \circ h \subseteq S$$

Figure 13.2. Relational homomorphism h from binary relation R to binary relation S.

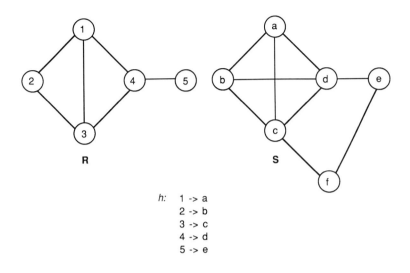

$R \circ h \subseteq S$; h is 1 - 1

Figure 13.3. Relational monomorphism h from binary relation R to binary relation S. There is a copy of R in S.

morphism that is one–one. Such a function maps each primitive in A to a unique primitive in B. A monomorphism indicates a stronger match than a homomorphism. Figure 13.3 illustrates a relational monomorphism.

Finally, a *relational isomorphism* f from an N-ary relation R to an N-ary relation S is a one–one relational homomorphism from R to S, and f^{-1} is a relational homomorphism from S to R. In this case, A and B have the same number of elements, each primitive in A maps to a unique primitive in B, and every primitive in A is mapped to by some primitive of B. Also, every tuple in R has a corresponding tuple in S, and vice versa. An isomorphism is the strongest kind of match: a symmetric match. Figure 13.4 illustrates a relational isomorphism, and Fig. 13.5 shows the difference between a relational isomorphism and a relational monomorphism.

2.3. Relational Descriptions and Relational Distance

A *relational description* D_X is a set of relations $D_X = \{R_1, \ldots, R_I\}$ where for each $i = 1, \ldots, I$, there exists a positive integer n_i with $R_i \subseteq X^{n_i}$ for some set X (X is a set of the parts of the entity being described and the relations R_i indicate various relationships among the parts). A rela-

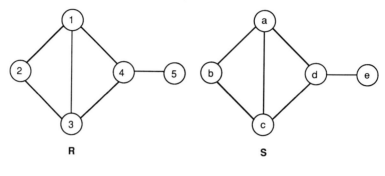

h: 1 -> a
    2 -> b
    3 -> c
    4 -> d
    5 -> e

R o h = S and h is 1 - 1

or equivalently,

R o h ⊆ S, S o h⁻¹ ⊆ R, and h is 1 - 1

Figure 13.4. Relational isomorphism h from binary relation R to binary relation S.

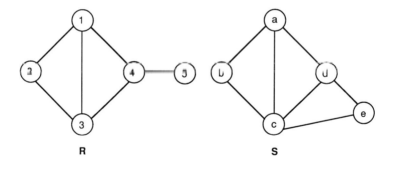

h: 1 -> a
    2 -> b
    3 -> c
    4 -> d
    5 -> e

R o h ⊆ S, h is 1 - 1, and h is onto

Figure 13.5. Relational monomorphism from binary relation R onto binary relation S. This mapping h is not a relational isomorphism, since h⁻¹ is not a relational monomorphism from S to R.

tional description may be used to describe an object model, a group of regions on an image, a two-dimensional shape, a Chinese character, or anything else having structure to it. In the spirit of the relational homomorphisms defined in the previous section, we wish to define a distance measure for pairs of relational descriptions.

Let $D_A = \{R_1, \ldots, R_I\}$ be a relational description with part set A. Let $D_B = \{S_1, \ldots, S_I\}$ be a second relational description with part set B. We will assume that $|A| = |B|$; if this is not the case, we will add enough dummy parts to the smaller set to make it the case.

Let f be any one–one, onto mapping from A to B. The *structural error* of f for the ith pair of corresponding relations (R_i and S_i) in D_A and D_B is given by

$$E_s^i(f) = |R_i \circ f - S_i| + |S_i \circ f^{-1} - R_i|.$$

The structural error indicates how many tuples in R_i are not mapped by f to tuples in S_i and how many tuples in S_i are not mapped by f^{-1} to tuples in R_i.

The *total error* of f with respect to D_A and D_B is the sum of the structural errors for each pair of corresponding relations:

$$E(f) = \sum_{i=1}^{I} E_s^i(f).$$

The total error gives a quantitative idea of the difference between the two relational descriptions D_A and D_B with respect to the mapping f.

The *relational distance* between D_A and D_B is then given by

$$GD(D_A, D_B) = \min_{\substack{f : A \stackrel{1-1}{\to} B \\ \text{onto}}} E(f).$$

That is, the relational distance is the minimal total error obtained for any one–one, onto mapping f from A to B. In Shapiro and Haralick (12) we proved that the relational distance is a metric over the space of relational descriptions. We call a mapping f that minimizes total error a *best mapping* from D_A to D_B. If there is more than one best mapping, we arbitrarily select one as the designated best mapping. More than one best mapping will occur when the relational descriptions involve certain kinds of symmetries.

2.4. Examples

Let $A = \{1, 2, 3, 4\}$ and $B = \{a, b, c, d\}$. Let $D_A = \{R_1 \subseteq A^2, R_2 \subseteq A^3\}$, and $D_B = \{S_1 \subseteq B^2, S_2 \subseteq B^3\}$. Let $R_1 = \{(1, 2), (2, 3), (3, 4), (4, 2)\}$ and $S_1 = \{(a, b), (b, c), (d, b)\}$. Let $R_2 = \{(1, 2, 3)\}$ and $S_2 = \{(a, b, c)\}$. Let f be defined by $f(1) = a$, $f(2) = b$, $f(3) = c$, $f(4) = d$. These relations are illustrated in Fig. 13.6. Then we have

$$|R_1 \circ f - S_1| = |\{(a, b), (b, c), (c, d), (d, b)\}$$

$$- \{(a, b), (b, c), (d, b)\}| = 1,$$

$$|S_1 \circ f^{-1} - R_1| = |\{(1, 2), (2, 3), (4, 2)\}$$

$$- \{(1, 2), (2, 3), (3, 4), (4, 2)\}| = 0,$$

$$E_s^1(f) = 1 + 0 = 1,$$

$$|R_2 \circ f - S_2| = |\{(a, b, c)\} - \{(a, b, c)\}| = 0,$$

$$|S_2 \circ f^{-1} - R_2| = |\{(1, 2, 3)\} - \{(1, 2, 3)\}| = 0,$$

$$E_s^2(f) = 0 + 0 = 0,$$

$$E(f) = E_s^1(f) + E_s^2(f) = 1.$$

We note that f is the best mapping and therefore $GD(D_A, D_B) = 1$.

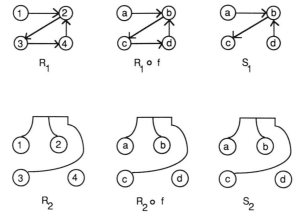

Figure 13.6. Relations R_1, $R_1 \circ f$, S_1, R_2, $R_2 \circ f$, and S_2. The notation indicates a hyperarc representing a triple.

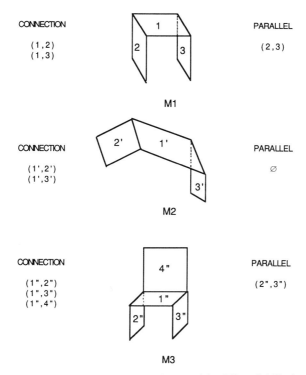

CONNECTION   PARALLEL

(1,2)   (2,3)
(1,3)

M1

CONNECTION   PARALLEL

(1',2')   ∅
(1',3')

M2

CONNECTION   PARALLEL

(1",2")   (2",3")
(1",3")
(1",4")

M3

Figure 13.7. Object model M1 and two other models, M2 and M3, that are each a relational distance of 1 from M1.

For a simple, but practical example, consider a set of object models constructed from simple parts with two binary relations: the connection relation and the parallel relation. Figure 13.7 illustrates a model (M1) and two other models (M2 and M3) that are each a relational distance of 1 from the first model. The model M4 shown in Fig. 13.8 is a variation of M3, but its relational distance from M3 is 6, due to several missing relationships induced by the additional two parts.

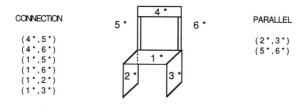

CONNECTION   PARALLEL

(4*,5*)   (2*,3*)
(4*,6*)   (5*,6*)
(1*,5*)
(1*,6*)
(1*,2*)
(1*,3*)

Figure 13.8. Model M4 that differs from M3 by a relational distance of 6.

2.5. Attributed Relational Descriptions and Relational Distance

The relational descriptions defined in the previous section describe relationships among parts, but not properties of parts, properties of the whole, or properties of these relationships. However, it is easy to extend both the concept of relational description and the definition of relational distance to include them. Intuitively, an m-tuple of attributes added to an n-tuple of parts produces an $(n + m)$-tuple that specifies a relationship plus the properties of that relationship. If $n = 1$ and $m > 0$, each tuple lists a part and its properties. If $n = 0$, $m > 0$, and the relation has only one tuple, this is a property vector describing the global properties of the object. Formally the definitions change to the following.

Let X be a set of parts of object O_X and P be a set of property values. Generally, we can assume P is the set of real numbers. An *attributed relation* over part set X with property value set P is a subset of $X^n \times P^m$ for some nonnegative integers n and m. An *attributed relational description* D_X is a sequence of attributed relations $D_X = \{R_1, \ldots, R_I\}$ where for each $i = 1, \ldots, I$, there exists a nonnegative integer n_i, a nonnegative integer m_i (where $n_i + m_i > 0$), and a property value set P_i with $R_i \subset X^{n_i} \times P_i^{m_i}$. For example, a binary parts connection relation $R \subseteq X^2$ can be extended to an attributed relation $R' \subseteq X^2 \times R$, R the set of real numbers, where an attributed pair (x_1, x_2, a) specifies that part x_1 connects to part x_2 at angle a.

Consider an attributed relation $R \subseteq A^n \times P^m$ over some part set A and property value set P. Let $r \in R$ be an $(n + m)$-tuple having n parts followed by m property values. Let $S \subseteq B^n \times P^m$ be a second attributed relation over part set B and property value set P. Let $f: A \to B$ by a one–one, onto mapping from A to B. We define the composition $r \circ f$ of attributed tuple r with f by

$$r \circ f = \{(b_1, \ldots, b_n, p_1, \ldots, p_m) \in B^n \times P^m$$

$$\mid \text{there exists} \quad (a_1, \ldots, a_n, p_1, \ldots, p_m)$$

$$\in R \quad \text{with} \quad f(a_i) = b_i, i = 1, \ldots, n\}.$$

Assume that if $(b_1, \ldots, b_n, p_1, \ldots, p_m) \in S$ and $(b_1, \ldots, b_n, q_1, \ldots, q_m) \in S$, then $p_1 = q_1, \ldots, p_m = q_m$. That is, each n-tuple of parts has only one m-tuple of properties. The error of a tuple $t = (b_1, \ldots, b_n, p_1, \ldots, p_m)$ with respect to a relation $S \subseteq B^n \times P^m$ is given by

$$e(t, s) = \text{norm\_dis}((p_1, \ldots, p_m), (q_1, \ldots, q_m))$$

$$\text{if } \exists \ (q_1, \ldots, q_m) \in P^m \quad \text{with} \quad (b_1, \ldots, b_n, q_1, \ldots, q_m) \in S$$

$$\text{else } 1.$$

where norm–dis returns the Euclidean distance (or any other desired distance) between two vectors, normalized by dividing by some maximum possible distance. Thus $e(t, s)$ is a quantity between 0 and 1. Now we can extend the definition of the structural error of f for the ith pair of corresponding relation (R_i and S_i) to

$$E_s^i(f) = \sum_{r \in R_i} e(r \circ f, S_i) + \sum_{s \in S_i} e(s \circ f^{-1}, R_i).$$

Total error and relational distance are defined as before.

3. ALGORITHMS

In Section 2 we explored several ways of defining relational matching. One can demand that two relational descriptions be isomorphic in order to say that they match, or one can be more lenient and say that there must be a relational homomorphism from the first to the second. Furthermore, it may be desirable to find the best match between an unknown relational description and a set of stored relational models. In this case, the stored model that has the least relational distance to the unknown description is the best match. Whether the object is to detect relational isomorphisms, monomorphisms, or homomorphisms or to compute relational distance, the only known algorithms that can solve arbitrary matching problems employ a tree search. In this section we describe the standard backtracking tree search and one of its variants, and we make some comments on parallel algorithms. For more details and other variants, see Haralick and Shapiro (4, 5), Rosenfeld *et al.* (8), Shapiro and Haralick (9, 10), and Shapiro (13). To simplify the discussion, the algorithms presented will be to determine all relational homomorphisms from a relation R to a relation S. The algorithms for monomorphisms, isomorphisms, and relational distance are straightforward variations of the homomorphism algorithms.

3.1. Backtracking Tree Search

Let R be an N-ary relation over part set A and S be an N-ary relation over part set B. We will refer to the elements of set A as the *units* and the elements of set B as the *labels*. We wish to find the set of all mappings $f : A \rightarrow B$ that satisfy $R \circ f \subseteq S$. Of course, the set may be empty, in which case the algorithm should fail. The backtracking tree search begins with the first unit of A. This unit can potentially match each label in set B. Each of these potential assignments is a node at level 1 of the tree. The algorithm selects one of these nodes, makes the assignment, selects the

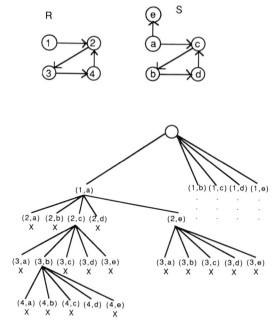

Figure 13.9. Backtracking tree search to find a homomorphism from $R = \{(1,2), (2,3),$ $(3,4), (4,2)\}$ to $S = \{(a,c), (c,b), (b,d), (d,c), (a,e)\}$ ($\times$ under a node indicates failure). The only homomorphism found is $f = \{(1,a), (2,c), (3,b), (4,d)\}$.

second unit of A, and begins to construct the children of the first node, which are nodes that map the second unit of A to each possible label of B. At this level, some of the nodes may be ruled out because they violate the constraint $R \circ f \subseteq S$. The process continues to level $|A|$ of the tree. The paths from the root node to any successful nodes at level $|A|$ are the relational homomorphisms. Figure 13.9 illustrates a portion of the back-tracking tree search for a simple digraph matching problem. The algorithm for a backtracking tree search is as follows.

procedure treesearch(A, B, f, R, S)

a := first(A);

for each $b \in B$

    {

    f' := $f \cup \{(a,b)\}$;

    OK := true;

    for each N-tuple r in R containing component a

```
      and whose other components are all in domain(f)

      if r ∘ f' is not in S

      then {OK:=false; break} endif;

   if OK then {A'=remainder(A);

      if isempty(A')

      then output(f')

      else treesearch(A',B,f',R,S)}

      }

   end treesearch;
```

3.2. Backtracking with Forward Checking

The backtracking tree search has exponential time complexity. Although there are no known polynomial algorithms in the general case, there are a number of discrete relaxation algorithms that can cut down search time by reducing the size of the tree that is searched. Forward checking is one such method. It is based on the idea that once a unit–label pair (a, b) is instantiated at a node in the tree, the constraints imposed by the relations cause instantiation of some future unit–label pairs (a', b') to become impossible. Suppose that (a, b) is instantiated high in the tree and that the subtree beneath that node contains nodes with first components $a_1, a_2, \ldots, a_n, a'$. Although (a', b') is impossible for any instantiations of $(a_1, a_2, \ldots, a_n)$, it will be tried in every path that reaches its level in the tree. The principle of forward checking is to rule out (a', b') at the time that (a, b) is instantiated and keep a record of that information.

The data structure used to store the information is called a future error table (FTAB). There is one future error table for each level of recursion in the tree search. Each table is a matrix having one row for each element of A and one column for each element of B. For any uninstantiated or *future unit* $a' \in A$ and potential label $b' \in B$, FTAB$(a', b') = 1$ if it is still possible to instantiate (a', b') given the history of instantiations already made. FTAB$(a', b') = 0$ if (a', b') has already been ruled out because of some previous assignment. When a pair (a, b) is instantiated by the backtracking tree search, an updating procedure is called to examine all pairs (a', b') of future units and their possible labels. For each pair (a', b') that is incompatible with the assignment of (a, b) and the previous instantiations, FTAB(a', b') has become 0. If for any future unit a', FTAB(a', b') becomes 0 for all labels $b' \in B$, then instantiation of (a, b)

fails immediately. The backtracking tree search with forward checking is as follows:

```
procedure forward-checking-treesearch(a,b,f,FTAB,R,S)

a := first(A);

for each b ∈ B

  if (FTAB(a,b)==1)

  then

      {

      f' := f ∪ {(a,b)};

      A' := remainder(A);

      if isempty(A')

      then output(f')

      else

          {

          NEWFTAB := copy(FTAB);

          OK := update(NEWFTAB, a, b, A', B, R, S, f');

          If (OK) forward-checking-treesearch
             (A', B, f', NEWFTAB, R, S);

          }

        endif

      endif

end forward-checking-treesearch;

procedure update(FTAB, a, b, future-units, B, R, S, f')

for each a' ∈ future-units

    {

    update := false;

    for each b' ∈ B with FTAB(a', b')==1
```

```
  if compatible(a,b,a',b',R,S,f')

  then update := true

  else FTAB(a',b') := 0

  endif;

 if (update==false) break;

 }

end update;
```

For binary relations R and S, the utility function *compatible*, which determines whether an instantiation of (a', b') is possible given instantiation (a, b), is very simple. Units a and a' constrain one another only when either (a, a') or (a', a) is in R. Thus, the algorithm for function compatible for binary relations R and S is as follows.

```
procedure b-compatible(a,b,a',b',R,S,f')

if ((a,a') ∈ R and not ((b,b') ∈ S)) or

  ((a',a) ∈ R and not ((b',b) ∈ S))

  then b-compatible := false

  else b-compatible := true endif;

end b-compatible;
```

For binary functions, the last argument f' to function b-compatible is not used, but is included here for consistency. For N-ary relations R and S, $N > 2$, those N-tuples of R where a and a' are among the components and all other components are already instantiated must be examined. The code for N-ary relations R and S is as follows:

```
procedure compatible(a,b,a',b',R,S,f')

f" := f' ∪ {(a',b')};

compatible := true;

for each r ∈ R containing a and a' whose other components

  are in domain(f")

  if r ∘ f" is not in S

  then {compatible := false; break} endif;

end compatible;
```

The binary procedure is very fast, since its time complexity is constant. The general procedure, if implemented as stated here, would have to examine each N-tuple of R. For a software implementation, it would be desirable to design the data structures for R, S, and f so that only the appropriate N-tuples of R are tested. A hardware implementation could offer even more flexibility.

4. ORGANIZATION OF RELATIONAL MODELS

In many real application areas, a robot vision system must be able to recognize a large set of objects from their stored models. While many experimental systems perform recognition by sequentially trying each model in the database, this approach is not efficient for a system that has a large database of models and uses a fairly complex recognition algorithm, like relational matching. Thus an important problem for robot vision systems is to organize the database of models in a way that allows rapid access to the most likely candidate models.

Shapiro and Haralick (10) developed a scheme for organizing relational models based on the relational distance metric. The idea is to group similar relational models into clusters and to choose a *representative* for each cluster. The representative is a relational model that is similar to each of the relational models in the cluster. An unknown object is compared to the cluster representatives to determine the most likely cluster or clusters to search further. In a single-level clustering scheme, the description of the unknown object is then matched against each model in the selected clusters to find the best match. In a multilevel scheme, which would be useful for extremely large and complex databases, each of the original clusters is also partitioned into clusters having representatives, and this process continues down to some level having manageable-size clusters. In this case, the best top-level cluster or clusters are selected, the best level 2 clusters from these are chosen, and so on down to the last level, where relational matching against the actual object models takes place. The clustering can be done by any clustering algorithm that is able to work with distances between objects as opposed to points in n-dimensional space.

Choosing the representatives is itself an interesting problem. A representative should be a relational description that is similar to all the models in a cluster. Since all the models in the cluster are already similar, this suggests an average kind of model to represent all of them. The average model may be one of the models in the cluster or something else entirely.

Suppose that a cluster C has been constructed. For any relational description D_i in C, define the total distance of D_i with respect to C by

$$T(D_i, C) = \sum_{D \in C} GD(D_i, D).$$

The relational description D_b that satisfies

$$T(D_b, C) = \min_{D \in C} T(D, C)$$

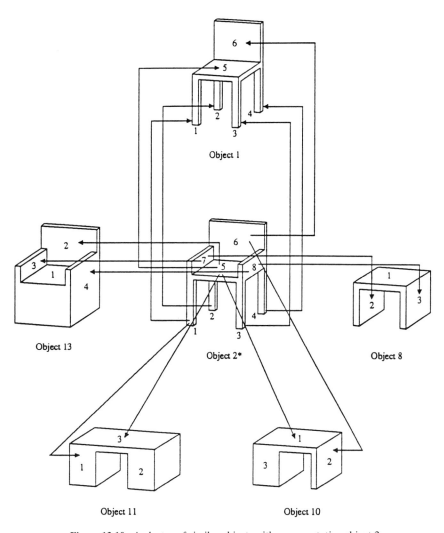

Figure 13.10. A cluster of similar objects with representative object 2.

was shown in Shapiro and Haralick (10) to be a reasonable choice for cluster representative. Figure 13.10 illustrates a cluster of similar objects with the representative defined in this manner and indicates the mappings from the parts of the representative to the parts of the other objects in the cluster that were obtained during calculation of relational distance.

5. EXAMPLES FROM VISION SYSTEMS

A number of different vision systems have used relational matching, either as the main matching paradigm or as part of a hybrid system. We will discuss three different example systems.

5.1. The Bolles – Cain System

Bolles and Cain (1) built a system for recognition of flat industrial parts. Their local-feature-focus method found one key feature, the focus feature, in an image and used it to predict a few nearby features to look for. It used graph matching to find the largest cluster of image features matching a cluster of object features near the focus feature. The clusters were typically small in size, consisting of three or four features, so the relational matching was very rapid. Once such a cluster was found, a hypothesis verification procedure added more features and also checked the boundary of the object. The features used in their example system were regions that had properties of intensity (black or white), area, and axis ratio and corners where the size of the included angle was the measured property.

The Bolles–Cain system was a knowledge-based system that knew the most important features to look for in each object and a cluster of other features that were expected to stand in certain relationships to the focus feature. The knowledge was generated automatically from training images. It was one of the earliest successful robot vision systems.

5.2. Sticks, Plates, and Blobs Models of Three-Dimensional Objects

In our earliest system (11), we used relational models to provide rough descriptions of the structure of three-dimensional, man-made objects. The primitives of the model were called *sticks*, *plates*, and *blobs*. Sticks represented long, thin parts of the object, plates represented flat parts with significant area, and blobs were three-dimensional, near-convex pieces. A chair, for example, might be modeled as two orthogonal plates (the seat and back) with four sticks that are attached to and perpendicular to the seat. If the seat of the chair has significant depth, it might then be modeled as a blob.

An object was described by an attribute-value table and five other relations: simple parts, connects–supports, triple constraint, parallel, and perpendicular. The attribute value-table contained such global attributes as number of sticks, number of plates, number of blobs, number of base supports, top part type, and so on. The simple parts relation listed each primitive and its particular attributes of type, relative length, relative area, and relative volume. The connects–supports relation gave pairs of primitives that connected in the 3D object along with several different angles of connection and the knowledge of whether one of the parts supported the other. The triple constraint relation looked at triples of connecting primitives, the topology of the connection, and related angles of connection. The parallel and perpendicular relationships merely listed pairs of primitives in these standard relationships.

The purpose of this system was to compare relational matching to simple feature matching for grouping of 3D objects. (The objects shown in Fig. 13.10 originally came from this system.) A study was run with 14 man-made objects, each represented both by the full relational model and by the attribute-value table alone. The results were as expected, showing that the relational matching was a much more powerful tool than simple feature matching in distinguishing differences and similarities between objects. Its main disadvantage was, of course, the speed of execution of a tree search matching algorithm.

5.3. The Boyer–Kak Structural Stereopsis System

Boyer and Kak (2) used the relational model for determining the mapping from the features of one image of a stereo pair to the features of the other image of the pair. The structural descriptions were derived from skeletons extracted from binary images of robotic vision scenes. The matching methods described in this chapter were expanded to include an information-theoretic interprimitive distance function, an information-theoretic relational inconsistency measure, and an entropy-based figure of merit for attribute selection and ordering during the matching process. The knowledge base required by the system was constructed from training data on real robotic images. Experiments were run on images of rodlike parts being sorted by the robot system.

5.4. PREMIO

PREMIO (3) is an object recognition–localization system that builds its objects models from CAD models of 3D objects. The PREMIO three-dimensional object model is a hierarchical, relational model with six levels: a world level, an object level, a face–edge–vertex level, a surface–boundary level, an arc–2D piece level, and a 1D piece level. The world level at the top of the hierarchy is concerned with the arrangement of the different objects in the world. The object level is concerned with the arrangement of the different faces, edges and vertices that form the objects. The face level describes a face in terms of its surfaces and its boundaries. The surface level specifies the elemental pieces that form those surfaces and the arcs that form the boundaries. Finally, the 1D piece level specifies the elemental pieces that form the arcs.

PREMIO employs line segments as the primitives for matching image structures to 3D object models. It uses the hierarchical, relational models plus knowledge of lighting and sensors to predict the detectability of features in various views of the object. From these predictions, PREMIO calculates the probabilities for each feature of being detected as a whole, being missed entirely, or breaking into pieces for each major view class of the object. It also computes the probabilities of the detection of one feature given the detection or nondetection of other features. The matching algorithm employed by PREMIO is a branch-and-bound search that

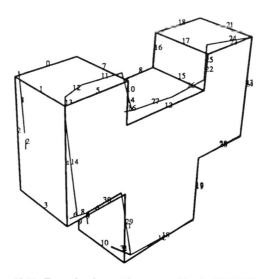

Figure 13.11. Example of a match computed by the PREMIO system.

explicitly takes advantage of the probabilities to guide the search. In terms of relational matching, PREMIO selects both the unit to match and the labels to try on the basis of these probabilities. Therefore the tree search to find the best mapping from object primitives to image primitives is very directed and, if there is a reasonable match, it will pursue it rather than performing a lot of blind backtracking. PREMIO was written in the C language and tested on 3D polyhedral objects in the robotics domain. Figure 13.11 illustrates the mapping between the image and a 3D model by calculating the pose of the object and overlaying the projection of the transformed model onto a line drawing extracted from the image.

6. MODELS FOR THE FUTURE

In this chapter we have defined relational models and relational matching for object recognition and pose determination. These models were intended for and mainly utilized for robot vision tasks involving man-made, usually polyhedral objects where the primitives are easily extractible and the relationships are clear and crisp. As computer vision progresses further, people have been working with more interesting objects including objects with curved surfaces, articulated objects, flexible objects, and natural objects. It is a challenge to computer vision researchers to develop scene analysis systems for these more difficult objects and more complex scenes. Relational matching is a powerful tool and is likely to continue to plat a role in future systems.

REFERENCES

1. R. C. Bolles and R. A. Cain, Recognizing and locating partially visible objects: The local-feature focus method. *Int. J. Robotics Res.* **1**(3), 57–82 (1982).
2. K. L. Boyer and A. C. Kak, Structural stereopsis for 3-D vision. *IEEE Trans. Pattern Anal. Mach. Intell.* **PAMI-10**(2), 144–166 (1988).
3. O. I. Camps, L. G. Shapiro, and R. M. Haralick, PREMIO: An overview. *Proc. IEEE Workshop Adv. Autom. CAD-Based Vision*, Maui, Hawaii, *1991*, 11–21 (1991).
4. R. M. Haralick and L. G. Shapiro, The consistent labeling problem. Part I. *IEEE Trans. Pattern Anal. Mach. Intell.* **PAMI-1**(2), 173–184 (1979).
5. R. M. Haralick and L. G. Shapiro, The consistent labeling problem. Part II. *IEEE Trans. Pattern Anal. Mach. Intell.* **PAMI-2**(3), 193–203 (1980).
6. Y. Lamdan and H. Wolfson, Geometric hashing: A general and efficient model-based recognition scheme. *Proc. Int. Conf. Comput. Vision, 2nd*, Tampa, FL, *1988*, pp. 238–249 (1988).

7. D. G. Lowe, Three-dimensional object recognition from single two-dimensional images. *Artif. Intell.* **31**, 355–395 (1987).
8. A. Rosenfeld, R. A. Hummel, and S. W. Zucker, Scene labeling by relaxation operations. *IEEE Trans. Syst. Man, Cybernet.* pp. 420–433 (1976).
9. L. G. Shapiro and R. M. Haralick, Structural descriptions and inexact matching. *IEEE Trans. Pattern Anal. Mach. Intell.* **PAMI-3**(5), 504–519 (1981).
10. L. G. Shapiro and R. M. Haralick, Organization of relational models for scene analysis. *IEEE Trans. Pattern Anal. Mach. Intell.*, **PAMI-4**(6), 595–602 (1982).
11. L. G. Shapiro, M. D. Moriarty, R. M. Haralick, and P. G. Mulgaonkar, Matching three-dimensional objects using a relational paradigm. *Pattern Recognition* **17**(4), 385–405 (1984).
12. L. G. Shapiro and R. M. Haralick, A metric for comparing relational descriptions. *IEEE Trans. Pattern Anal. Mach. Intell.* **PAMI-7**(1), 90–94 (1985).
13. L. G. Shapiro, The use of numeric relational distance and symbolic differences for organizing models and for matching. *In* "Techniques for 3D Machine Perception." North-Holland Publ., Amsterdam, 1985.
14. L. G. Shapiro and H. Lu, Accumulator-based inexact matching using relational summaries. *Mach. Vision Appl.* **3**, 143–158 (1990).

Chapter **14**

Three-Dimensional Object Recognition

PATRICK J. FLYNN

School of Electrical Engineering and Computer Science
Washington State University
Pullman, Washington

ANIL K. JAIN

Department of Computer Science
Michigan State University
East Lansing, Michigan

1. INTRODUCTION

The design and construction of three-dimensional object recognition systems has long occupied the attention of many computer vision researchers. The variety of systems that have been developed for this challenging and difficult task is evidence of both its strong appeal to researchers and its applicability to modern manufacturing, industrial, military, and consumer environments. The following are examples of computer vision applications with a strong 3D object recognition component:

- **Part recognition and localization**. Identification of one or more objects in an input image as instances of objects represented in a database of object models, accompanied by estimation of *pose transformation*, which (when applied to the identified database models) aligns the models with the corresponding image features. The use of previously created object models (i.e., a knowledge base) dates back almost three decades and is still the dominant theme in current research.
- **Navigation**. Continuous computation of the heading and speed required to maneuver a vehicle around known obstacles, plus the ability to learn new obstacles as they are encountered.
- **Face recognition**. Identification of a facial image as corresponding to a model face stored in a previously constructed database. The ability of the system to learn new faces is desirable.

We will emphasize the industrial–manufacturing application in this chapter (primarily because much of the research community shares this emphasis), but the reader should be aware of the widespread applicability of object recognition systems.

Three-dimensional object recognition is a problem of interest to researchers because of a desire to endow computers with robust visual capabilities and the variety of applications that would benefit from mature and robust systems. However, 3D object recognition is also a very difficult problem, and few systems have been developed for production use; most existing systems were developed for experimental use by researchers. Part of the reason for the lack of penetration into the market by 3D recognition systems is undoubtedly the high computational requirement of current recognition methods; improvements in serial processing and development of optimized parallel algorithms will make today's computationally-intensive algorithms practical in the future. Another barrier to the acceptance of 3D object recognition systems is *representational*; most current systems

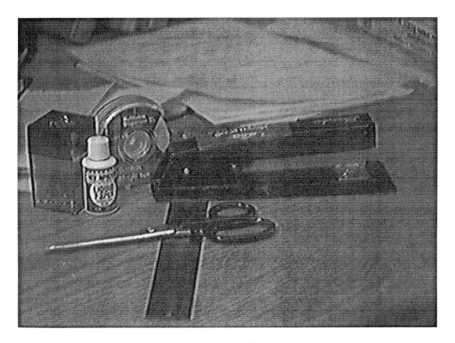

Figure 14.1. An indoor image.

cannot accommodate sculpted ("free-form") surfaces and large model databases. Many object recognition systems are designed without the ability to reject portions of the scene as unidentifiable, and are therefore limited to domains where the set of objects to be recognized is prespecified. The ability to automatically build models of such "unexpected" objects is desirable in less controlled environments. Another difficulty derives from the inadequate testing and performance characterization of research systems. It is heartening to note that all of these issues are beginning to receive attention from vision researchers.

The image in Fig. 14.1 illustrates the complexity of indoor scenes; it has relatively high contrast, and objects can be isolated strictly on the basis of edge information. Outdoor images are not as controllable as indoor images; Fig. 14.2 shows an image of a sidewalk and its surroundings. Object recognition in this environment is more difficult than recognition in indoor environments. The quality of the scene illumination affects the quality of images obtained from the scene, and therefore the features extracted from them. If the lighting is unpredictable, *active* sensing (e.g., structured light range finders) is often used. The use of other sensing modalities, either to replace or to augment the information returned from

Figure 14.2. An image of an outdoor scene.

the intensity or range sensor, is a research topic of recent interest. Certain recognition problems might best be solved using sensory data gathered from range cameras and tactile sensors, or range and color imagery, rather than a single sensor.

In this chapter, we aim to summarize the state of the art of 3D object recognition systems by describing a few such systems in detail. We also hope to give practical advice to those implementing model-based 3D object recognition systems. Our presentation is organized as follows. References to additional literature in this area are followed by a presentation of notation used in the chapter. Section 2 lays out some critical design decisions that must be addressed before a model-based object recognition system is built. Section 3 introduces a variety of image sensing modalities, feature types, and object representations that have seen significant use in the research literature. Descriptions of recognition techniques appear in Section 4, with particular emphasis on constrained-search methods, invariant feature indexing, and structural indexing. Section 5, addresses the problem of pose estimation. Section 6 is devoted to the verification (ranking) of object hypotheses. Conclusions and commentary appear in Section 7.

1.1. Surveys

This chapter is not intended as a thorough survey of this popular research area, but rather a practical guide to system building. Therefore, it is appropriate to give pointers to more complete surveys of the field. A comprehensive survey of the state of the art (ca. 1985) in 3D object representation and recognition is Besl and Jain (3). Suetens *et al.* (30) is a recent broad survey article, not limited to 3D recognition. Arman and Aggarwal (1) is a very recent survey of progress in object recognition from range data. Since several articles are available, we will limit discussion of prior work to the period since 1985.

The topic of 3D object recognition was the subject of an IEEE Computer Society Workshop on the Interpretation of 3D Scenes held in November 1989 in Austin, Texas. More recently, the October 1991 and February 1992 issues of the *IEEE Transactions on Pattern Analysis and Machine Intelligence* were devoted to 3D scene interpretation. Of related interest is the area of CAD-based vision, which was the focus of an IEEE Computer Society Workshop in June, 1991 held in Maui, Hawaii. Expanded versions of several papers presented at that workshop appear in the February, 1992 issue of *Computer Vision, Graphics, and Image Processing: Image Understanding*. Broader comments about the productivity and scope of computer vision research appear in Negahdaripour and Jain (24).

1.2. Notation

Common to almost all 3D object recognition systems is the formation of *correspondences* between *features* detected in the scene and features of similar types previously stored in *models* (or representations) of the objects of interest. The following notation for these important concepts is used throughout the chapter:

- $\mathscr{S} = (S_1, \ldots, S_{n_s})$ is the set of n_s scene features. Each feature S_i is characterized by a vector of parameters that varies with the type of feature under consideration (e.g., contours, surfaces, or volumes; see Section 3.2).
- $\mathbf{M} = \{\mathscr{M}_1, \ldots, \mathscr{M}_{n_m}\}$ is the set of n_m object models. These models are composed (in part) of features of the same or similar types as the features extracted from the scene. We typically assume that the models are already available (perhaps having been designed on a computer-aided design system, or were built by integrating information from images of a prototype object).

- $\mathscr{M}_i = \{M_{i,1}, \ldots, M_{i,n_{m_i}}\}$ is the set of n_{m_i} features associated with model i. Each feature is characterized by a type-specific parameter vector.

Given the notation above, we can now specify four subtasks typically associated with a model-based object recognition system:

- *Indexing* is the selection of a *candidate model set*

$$\mathbf{M_C} = \{\mathscr{M}_{c,1}, \ldots, \mathscr{M}_{c,n_{Mc}}\} \subseteq \mathbf{M},$$

whose members will be considered for matching. Indexing procedures are responsible for discarding models not present in the scene, as quickly as possible. In cases where multiple models are returned by the indexing procedure, the matching system would consider each candidate model in turn, and hopefully reject as many of the candidates not present in the scene as possible. We *may not* assume that all of the sets of correspondences returned by the matching procedures will be correct, or even that they involve the correct model.

- *Matching* is the selection of a *candidate model* $\mathscr{M} \in \mathbf{M_C}$ (with $n_{\mathscr{M}}$ features) and the formation of a set of n ($n < \min(n_s, n_{\mathscr{M}})$) *bindings* (or *correspondences*) between features in the scene feature set and features in the *candidate model* $\mathscr{M}$:

$$\mathscr{C} = \{(S_{i_1}, M_{j_1}), \ldots, (S_{i_n}, M_{j_n})\}.$$

An element (S_i, M_j) in the set corresponds to a decision that feature S_i is the image of M_j in the scene. The set of correspondences is sometimes called a *hypothesis*. The recognition of objects in cluttered scenes (i.e., scenes yielding features from multiple objects or yielding spurious features not corresponding to any object) requires that the matching procedure be able to select only a subset of the scene features for correspondence with model features. A common technique for incorporating unmatched features into the hypothesis is to bind them to a **NULL character** (often denoted Λ). Hence, a hypothesis involving the first three of five available scene features would be expressed as

$$\mathscr{C} = \{(S_1, M_{i_1}), (S_2, M_{i_2}), (S_3, M_{i_3}), (S_4, \Lambda), (S_5, \Lambda)\}.$$

If the scene contains multiple objects and the system is capable of generating hypotheses for multiple objects, the set of correct hypotheses

should be *disjoint*; i.e., no two hypotheses should contain a non-NULL binding for the same scene feature.
• *Localization* is the estimation of a rigid transformation **R** (incorporating both rotation and translation), which, when applied to the model features M_j in the list of correspondences, aligns them with the corresponding S_i.
• *Verification* is the evaluation of a set of correspondences for their "goodness-of-fit" to the image. Verification procedures are sometimes expected to rank the hypotheses returned by the matching module from best to worst.

The 3D object recognition systems described in the literature address these subtasks in a variety of ways. Some systems do not address localization at all; many do not address indexing explicitly. Indexing is receiving more attention in its own right as researchers begin to experiment with large model databases (hundreds or thousands of objects).

2. SYSTEM DESIGN DECISIONS

Practitioners hoping to design reliable, robust object recognition procedures should carefully think about the following issues before committing to a particular sensor, object representation, or recognition strategy. This list contains some of the most important and frequently addressed issues, but other issues (such as cost and computational requirements) may also be important to certain applications.

1. **What are the properties of the objects to be recognized?** This decision affects the choice of features used in representation (see below), but also has other implications. While almost all work in the research literature has addressed rigid objects, machine vision systems in certain domains might be required to recognize articulated or deformable objects.

2. **What is the source of object models?** There are three major sources of 3D models for object recognition systems: models built by hand (perhaps by a vision or manufacturing expert), models built from multiple views of a prototype object, and models adapted from pre-existing geometric models. If the model database used for recognition changes frequently, either of the latter two approaches may be preferable to the first. If no geometric models are available, the third method is inapplicable.

3. **What is the object representation strategy?** No design decision affects the methods used for matching, verification, and localization as drastically as the choice of object representation. If the system is intended

to operate in a computer-aided manufacturing environment, the representation used for the objects may closely parallel that used in the CAD system used to design the object.

4. **What sort of image data are available?** The two most popular types of imagery for 3D object recognition systems are intensity and range images, and are discussed below. In some situations, both intensity and range data are important to the system's operation, and the *fusion* of these different sources is beginning to receive serious attention from researchers.

5. **What are the features extracted from the input image(s)?** Once the object representation has been chosen, designers are often still left with a variety of image and model features to use in matching. For example, choice of a boundary representation for polyhedral objects implies matching could be based on either the vertices, the edges, or the planar faces of the scene and model polyhedra. A number of factors must be weighed when deciding on feature types, including *robustness* (to occlusion or sensor noise), *visibility*, *discriminability*, and *extraction cost*.

6. **What is the control strategy used to match image features to model features?** The basis of model-based object recognition is establishment of feature correspondences, but there are a variety of procedural techniques for building these correspondences. Popular techniques are based on search, graph–subgraph isomorphism, indexing using invariant features, and automatic programming. Some of these techniques are described below.

7. **What is the desired output?** Some research systems merely identify objects in the input image; they do not attempt to estimate the object's location in the sensor's coordinate system. However, many systems do estimate object pose, as it is useful if the identified objects are to be handled by a robotic manipulator, or if the recognition stage is serving as a front-end to an additional inspection procedure (e.g., metrology, in which we wish to verify that a particular object dimension is within a prespecified tolerance of a design value).

8. **What is the recognition environment?** This issue reflects the variety of locations (indoor/outdoor) and scene complexities (single-object or multiple-object scenes) for which systems have been devised. Outdoor scenes are typically less "controlled" than the indoor environment, and a competent recognition system must reliably extract features from the structures to be recognized (e.g., vehicles, road signs) from the mass of "natural" features (e.g., blades of grass, pedestrians) that occupy outdoor scenes. Many early (and some current) systems assume that any input image contains at most one object. This assumption simplifies the task of recognition significantly, and in well-controlled situations may be appropriate.

3. SENSORS, FEATURES, AND MODELS FOR THREE-DIMENSIONAL OBJECT RECOGNITION

This section provides a brief overview of image acquisition, feature extraction, and object representation techniques.

3.1. Sensors

The two most popular types of image sensors in 3D object recognition systems are *intensity* sensors, which produce images containing an intensity measurement $I(x, y)$ at each pixel location, and *range* sensors, which yield images of the location $[x, y, z(x, y)]$ of the surface point (if any) visible at the pixel location (x, y). Range sensors employing active illumination (e.g., laser lighting) produce images where no measurement of the z coordinate can be made at a particular location (x, y); such pixels are labeled *invalid*. Range sensors are often calibrated to produce images with coordinates that are directly comparable with the coordinates used in object model descriptions. The intensity measurement at an image location is a complicated function of the geometry and material properties of the object being sensed, and the number and parameters of light sources illuminating the scene. Figure 14.3 shows registered intensity and range images of a scene. These images were obtained by combining passive intensity with the shape information derived from structured light.

3.2. Features and Models

Given an input image from an intensity or range sensor, what sorts of features are commonly extracted from it for the purposes of 3D object

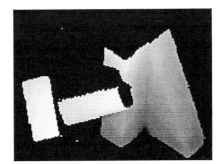

Figure 14.3. Registered intensity (A) and range (B) images of a scene.

recognition? Obviously, such features should either correspond directly to features that describe the object models to be recognized, or should form the input to procedures that compute those model features. Hence, it is most appropriate to discuss features and models together. The variety of object representations and strategies for recognition have yielded a number of feature types and extraction methods. Features that are viewpoint-invariant are frequently used in systems if they can be reliably computed, since use of view-dependent features implies that the viewpoint, along with the object, must be recognized. Image features are defined in terms of the sensor's coordinate system, while model features can be based on a model coordinate system or defined in terms of representative views of the object. Most model-based 3D object recognition systems have employed features drawn from one or more of the following four classes:

• **Point features**. Any distinguished point on the object model that can be reliably detected in the image (or inferred from it after segmentation) can serve as a feature for recognition. Examples of point features include vertices of polyhedra, point parameters of some quadric shapes (e.g., the vertex of a cone or the center of a sphere), and locations of maximal principal curvature on curved surfaces. Point features are useful for pose estimation, but if many such features are available on models or extracted from images, correspondence-based recognition procedures should be designed to employ additional constraints so that candidate correspondences are appropriate (e.g., image points corresponding to sphere centers should not be matched to model points corresponding to polyhedron vertices). Figure 14.4 shows an intensity image of several wood blocks and point features corresponding to the visible corners on one block. Two-

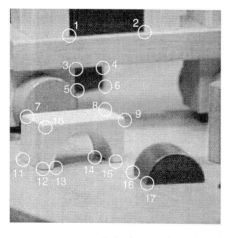

1: (31,73)
2: (26,162)
3: (70,79)

...

14: (173,102)
15: (183, 122)
16: (198,150)
17: (208,167)

Figure 14.4. Point features in an intensity image of wood blocks.

dimensional (image) coordinates for some of the point feature are listed; the origin of the image is at the upper left corner, and the point coordinates have the form (*row, column*).

• **Contour features.** Any contour (straight or curved, planar or 3D) that can be extracted from both images and models can be useful for recognition. Polyhedral objects are sometimes described as wireframes, and the edges of the model can be made to correspond to edges extracted from the input imagery. Edge detection is a well-explored area in the vision literature, and we will not discuss it further here; suffice it to say that the contour features useful for matching would typically be produced by linking edge pixels returned by one of the many edge detection strategies available. If needed, the edge thus obtained would be parametrized (e.g., by length, orientation, or curvature), and these parameters would serve as attributes of the feature. Figure 14.5 shows linear contour features (jump and crease edges) superimposed on the wood blocks image used in Fig. 14.4, along with image coordinates of a subset of the edges. Much of the previous work in 3D object recognition from 2D imagery has assumed that contour features are linear. Linearity is preserved under perspective projection, and if a correspondence between image edges and model edges is inferred, the parameters of the perspective transformation can be estimated, allowing for verification of the hypothesized correspondences.

• **Surface features.** Smooth surface patches extracted from range data have been used in many 3D object recognition systems. In such systems, models are specified as a set of surfaces accompanied by adjacency information (called a *boundary representation* in the literature). Figure 14.6 shows a range image of a polyhedron in part (A), a labeled image (i.e., a segmentation) in part (B), and equations for the planar surface fitted to each segment in part (C). Many techniques have been developed to extract surfaces from range data. Surface representations include *implicit forms* $f(x, y, z) = 0$ and *graph surfaces* $z = g(x, y)$; specific classes

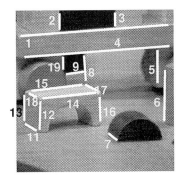

1: $(40,9) \rightarrow (23, 250)$
2: $(1,71) \rightarrow (30,71)$
3: $(1,163) \rightarrow (22,163)$
...
16: $(134,137) \rightarrow (176,137)$
17: $(118,112) \rightarrow (127,134)$
18: $(130,15) \rightarrow (137,36)$
19: $(70,78) \rightarrow (93,78)$

Figure 14.5. Contour features in an intensity image of wood blocks.

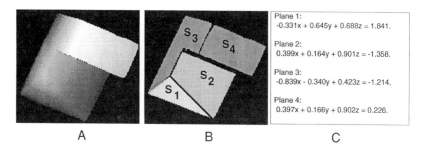

Figure 14.6. Surface features in a range image of a polyhedron.

(e.g., the natural quadric surfaces) can be described in terms of type-specific scalar and vector-valued geometric parameters. While this variety of descriptions might be seen as distinctions without a difference, the fact that we must extract these primitives from range data makes some techniques preferable to others. For example, researchers have attempted to extract natural quadrics from range data by obtaining a least-squares estimate of the 10 parameters of the general implicit quadric form using the observed range pixels. However, the parameter vector obtained from the least-squares procedure does not immediately yield the type and geometric parameters of the quadric. The primary advantage of quadric and planar surfaces in 3D object models is an ability to describe them in terms of a few parameters; however, many objects cannot be successfully characterized as piecewise-quadric or polyhedral. The difficulty in employing more complicated surface types (e.g., trimmed nonuniform rational B-spline surfaces, a popular form in computer-aided design systems) is caused by the absence of methods for extracting comparable representations for surface segments in range data. This problem has limited the usefulness and applications of 3D object recognition systems using surface descriptions.

 • **Volume features**. Since 3D objects are by definition enclosed volumes, volumetric descriptions have been employed by 3D object recognition systems for years. A popular volumetric representation is the *generalized cylinder* representation (25), in which objects are composed of a list or hierarchy of generalized cylinders, each defined as a volume swept by a planar curve translated relative to an axis. The flexibility in defining the axis shape, variations in the cross section, and the sweeping rule combine to make generalized cylinders an expressive description, but that same flexibility makes reliable extraction of their parameters from input imagery difficult. Some recent object recognition systems have viewed objects as collections of deformed "superquadric" shapes. Superquadrics are closed volumes whose boundaries are described by parametric function of two angles u and v:

$$\begin{bmatrix} x(u,v) \\ y(u,v) \\ z(u,v) \end{bmatrix} = \begin{bmatrix} \cos^{\epsilon_1} u \cos^{\epsilon_2} v \\ \cos^{\epsilon_1} u \sin^{\epsilon_2} v \\ \sin^{\epsilon_1} u \end{bmatrix}.$$

The image of the domain $(u,v) \in [-(\pi/2),(\pi/2)] \times [-\pi,\pi]$ is a closed surface within the unit cube. The parameters ϵ_1 and ϵ_2 control the surface's shape; for example, $\epsilon_1 = \epsilon_2 = 1$ yields the unit sphere, ϵ_1 close to zero and $\epsilon_2 = 1$ yields a cylinder with a circular cross section (with the convention $0^0 = 1$), and small values of ϵ_1 and ϵ_2 yield shapes approaching the unit cube. Figure 14.7 shows superquadric primitives generated from two choices of the shape parameters (ϵ_1, ϵ_2). Individual scale factors on the three components of the surface function allow shapes to be elongated, yielding ellipsoids, elliptic cylinders, and rectangular boxes. These representations are made more descriptive by adding parameterized global deformations such as tapering, twisting, or bending along a specified axis. For each global deformation, additional parameters are added to the volume description, and the problem of recovering the parameters from sampled data becomes more difficult.

Points, surfaces, and volumes by no means exhaust the sets of features that have been used in object representation and recognition. They are, however, used by the majority of researchers. Principal shortcomings of simple parameterized features such as these are their inability to represent

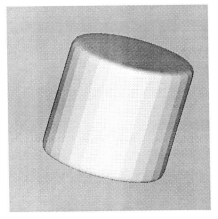 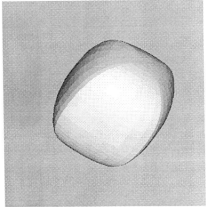

$$\varepsilon_1 = 0.1,\ \varepsilon_2 = 1.0 \qquad\qquad \varepsilon_1 = 0.8,\ \varepsilon_2 = 1.5$$

Figure 14.7. Superquadric volumetric primitives.

unstructured (or "free-form") curves, surfaces, and volumes. Later in this chapter, we will see a specialized set of features designed to accommodate complicated surfaces that do not fit into the quadratic or planar models favored by many researchers.

4. RECOGNITION TECHNIQUES

This section surveys a variety of techniques for 3D object recognition, and gives detailed descriptions of a few popular methods. As mentioned above, the survey material is not meant to be exhaustive, but merely to give the reader a flavor of the approaches that have been popular in the literature.

4.1. Constrained Search of the Interpretation Tree

A conceptually simple but often computationally demanding method for construction of candidate hypothesis is a search of the *interpretation tree* of all possible scene feature-to-model feature bindings. A separate search is involved for each object model $\mathcal{M}_i$, hence the search technique itself does not perform indexing. The root of the tree represents an empty interpretation, with no scene feature–model feature bindings. The set of tree branches immediately below the root represent bindings between one scene and one model feature (or possibly the **NULL** feature Λ, if allowed). Each branch is inconsistent with the others in that no two or more of the implied bindings can be simultaneously true. A fully enumerated tree has a set of *complete* interpretations at its terminal nodes [i.e., there are $\min(n_s, n_{m_i})$ bindings present for a search involving $\mathcal{M}_i$], which exhausts either the available scene features or the available model features. Interpretation tree search has been thoroughly explored in a recent book by Grimson (15) and has been used by many researchers as the basis for 2D abd 3D object recognition systems.

Design decisions to be considered when using a search-based recognition procedure include the following:

• **What is the ordering on the scene feature set?** One of the keys to an efficient implementation of constrained search is structuring the search tree so that pruning takes place as soon as possible (i.e., close to the root). Elements of the scene feature set that are *most discriminatory* should be considered first when fabricating the search tree, so that subtrees rooted at bindings involving them have the largest chance of being pruned. Of course, the nature of the features and the pruning constraints (see below) will sometimes dictate an ordering (or at least provide some insights regarding the most discriminatory features). In the BONSAI 3D object recognition system developed by Flynn and Jain (12), curved surface patches were considered first in a data-driven search procedure because more tree-pruning constraints were available for those surfaces than for planar patches.

• **Are NULL bindings allowed?** Earlier, we introduced the concept of a NULL binding involving a scene feature set element. Such bindings serve as place-holders for the feature involved, but attach no inference to it. No pruning decisions should be made based on a NULL binding or on a group of bindings that includes a NULL binding. These place-holders are essential to a search strategy that will cope with multiple-object scenes, models with features not visible in some views, and spurious features arising from image noise or segmentation errors. However, in some situations we may not encounter spurious features, and the expected scenes may be tightly constrained so that only a single object is present. In such cases it is advantageous to eliminate NULL bindings.

• **Are scene features reusable?** In situations where features can become fragmented by the segmentation process (e.g., linear edges being broken by occlusion), it may be helpful to allow more than one element of the scene feature to be bound to a single element of the candidate model's feature set. Reuse of scene features implies that the interpretation tree is larger (the branching factor remains constant with depth rather than decreasing), but multiple bindings involving a single candidate feature can be used to (for example) improve the quality of a pose transformation estimate.

• **How is the search effort reduced?** This decision is the most critical to efficient implementation of constrained search for 3D recognition, and utilizes domain-dependent constraints. In general, realistic search-based procedures employ one or more *constraints* (or *pruning rules*, or *predicates*), which, when given an interpretation $\mathscr{E} = \{(S_1, M_{i_1}), \ldots, (S_k, M_{i_k})\}$, returns TRUE if the bindings satisfy the constraint, and FALSE if not. If FALSE is returned by the predicate, the search tree is pruned (i.e., none of its children are explored). If TRUE is returned, the search tree node corresponding to the hypothesis is expanded and its descendants are examined. The number and nature of the predicates are dependent on the sensory data (the number and types of features), the design decisions mentioned above, and the desired output. In theory, a constraint can employ any or all of the bindings involved in the interpretation at a tree node to make a pruning decision. In practice, object recognition systems use unary and binary predicates almost exclusively. A *unary predicate* employs only the most recent binding in its decision, and a binary predicate involves the most recent and one of the previously constructed bindings in its decision. An interpretation at level k in the tree is tested using one application of the suite of unary predicates and at most $k - 1$ applications of the suite of binary predicates. Grimson (15) presented a set of constraints for recognition from linear (edge) features, including a unary edge–length constraint, a binary angle constraint, and two binary constraints on the distances between two linear edge fragments.

• **When should search be halted?** It is easy to show that the time complexity of a search-based recognition procedure is exponential in the number of scene features, when NULL bindings are allowed. A powerful technique for avoiding an exhaustive enumeration of the complete pruned search tree is known as *heuristic search termination* (15), which halts downward expansion of the search tree when an appropriate number of non-NULL bindings are present.

4.1.1. Example

Figure 14.8(A) shows a range image of a simple 3D object composed of eight faces (seven planar and one cylindrical). A region-based segmentation of the input range image is shown in part (B), and the parameters of surfaces fitted to the individual segments are shown in (C). Three planes and a cylinder were extracted from this input image.

Let us walk through an interpretation tree search using the given input image and a model of the object, as shown in Fig. 14.9. In order to keep the tree small, we will not allow NULL bindings; moreover, heuristic termination of the search will be performed. We will use the following constraints to prune the search tree.

1. **Area constraint.** A hypothesis is rejected if the scene patch in the newest binding has an observed area larger than the maximum possible area of the model patch to which it is bound.

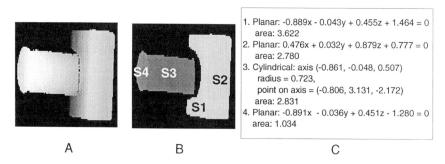

A   B   C

Figure 14.8. Input range image (A), segmentation (B), and parameters of extracted segments (C) for a scene containing one object.

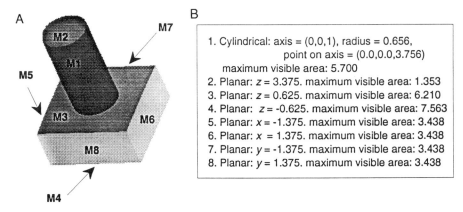

A
B

1. Cylindrical: axis = (0,0,1), radius = 0.656,
          point on axis = (0.0,0.0,3.756)
   maximum visible area: 5.700
2. Planar: z = 3.375. maximum visible area: 1.353
3. Planar: z = 0.625. maximum visible area: 6.210
4. Planar: z = -0.625. maximum visible area: 7.563
5. Planar: x = -1.375. maximum visible area: 3.438
6. Planar: x = 1.375. maximum visible area: 3.438
7. Planar: y = -1.375. maximum visible area: 3.438
8. Planar: y = 1.375. maximum visible area: 3.438

Figure 14.9. Solid model for the object shown in Fig. 14.8, (A) surfaces; (B) surface parameters.

2. **Angle constraint.** A hypothesis is rejected if the angle between the scene surfaces in any pair of bindings containing the most recent binding differs by more than 5° from the angle between the corresponding model surfaces. For this test, the axis direction is used for cylindrical surfaces, and the surface normal is used for planes.
3. **Type constraint.** A hypothesis is rejected if the most recent correspondence involves scene and model surfaces of different types.
4. **Parallel-plane constraint.** A hypothesis is rejected if the distance between any set of parallel scene planes is different from the corresponding distance between the model planes by more than 0.1 inch.

Figure 14.10 shows the interpretation tree explored by the constrained search procedure, assuming that heuristic search termination occurs when enough bindings are present to compute object pose. The subtree under the interpretation $\{(S_3, M_1), (S_1, M_4)\}$ was expanded, but all of its subtrees were subsequently pruned. Four hypotheses survived the search:

$$\mathscr{C}_1 = \{(S_3, M_1), (S_1, M_3), (S_2, M_5)\},$$

$$\mathscr{C}_2 = \{(S_3, M_1), (S_1, M_3), (S_2, M_6)\},$$

$$\mathscr{C}_3 = \{(S_3, M_1), (S_1, M_3), (S_2, M_7)\},$$

$$\mathscr{C}_4 = \{(S_3, M_1), (S_1, M_3), (S_2, M_8)\}.$$

Surviving hypotheses in this (and most other) search-based systems must be evaluated using a verification procedure, which is discussed in Section 6.

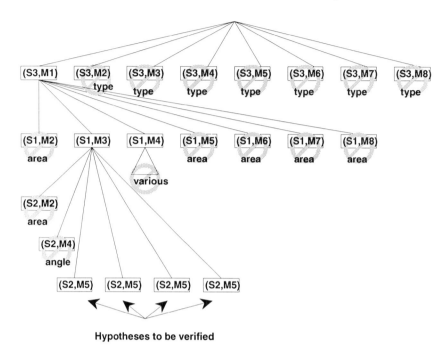

Hypotheses to be verified

Figure 14.10. Interpretation tree generated for the scene of Fig. 14.8 and the model of Fig. 14.9.

Note that the four returned hypotheses are all equivalent because of the object's fourfold rotational symmetry. Accommodation of symmetric object models has only recently been addressed in the research community.

4.1.2. Survey

Chen and Kak (8) developed a 3D object recognition system employing range data, which combined a restricted search procedure with a viewpoint-based strategy for selection of model features to use in correspondences. In essence, this system performs as little search as possible, switching to a verification procedure as soon as enough correspondences are present to estimate object pose unambiguously, and uses remaining unmatched features to support, refute, or make no contribution to the validity of that minimal hypothesis. The features used to form the minimal hypothesis are selected using relational constraints, as with the systems described above. During verification, the observed orientations of already-corresponded scene and model features, and hence the rotation transformation relating them, are used to predict the orientation of scene features from unmatched model features. To avoid searching the entire set of unmatched model features, a data structure called the *feature sphere* is created and efficiently indexed.

Camps *et al.* (7) have developed a system known as PREMIO (*Predict-ion in Matching Images to Objects*), which employs a branch-and-bound search procedure to correspond contour features extracted from intensity imagery with those present in stored object models designed on a CAD system. A prediction strategy based on knowledge of lighting and the sensor's viewpoint is used to extract features and organize them for use during recognition. The search procedure is somewhat different from the other methods described here in that there is a quality measure associated with each nonterminal node in the search tree. This cost measure has contributions from the choice of object model choice and the "quality" of correspondences in the bindings available at that node. The availability of this score allows traditional heuristic search methods (e.g., branch-and-bound methods) to be used to prune the search space.

4.2. Recognition Using Invariant Features

Some recent research has explored the use of *invariant* features (de-fined on groups of scene and model features) as indices for the construc-tion and examination of *tables* containing the information needed to form correspondences. This idea was introduced as "geometric hashing" by Lamdan *et al.* (22) and used for 3D object recognition by a number of researchers. Our description begins with an example and concludes with a short survey of systems.

4.2.1. *Interpretation Table Indexing*

Flynn and Jain (13) developed a "table-driven" object recognition system employing invariant relational features defined on pairs of surfaces. They use pairs of invariant features as indices to retrieve correspondences for three major surface patches from a precompiled two-dimensional *interpretation table*. The data in the table are called a *protohypothesis*:

$$\mathscr{PH} = \langle \text{ID}, (M_{i_1}, M_{i_2}, M_{i_3}) \rangle,$$

where ID identifies the model, and the M_i identify the model features.

The invariant relational features for pairs of planar, spherical, and cylindrical surfaces are given below. In the following, $\mathbf{n}_i$ will denote a plane's surface normal, d_i its distance from the origin, $\mathbf{a}_i$ the axis vector for a cylinder, $\mathbf{p}_i$ a point on the cylinder's axis or the center of a sphere, and r_i the radius of a sphere. The subscript i denotes the member of the pair, namely, $i \in \{1, 2\}$.

- **Plane–plane.** The relational invariant feature $\mathbf{I}_{pp}$ is the internormal angle in degrees, truncated to an integer: $\lfloor 180 \cdot \cos^{-1}(\mathbf{n}_1 \cdot \mathbf{n}_2) \rfloor$.
- **Plane–cylinder.** The relational invariant feature $\mathbf{I}_{pc}$ is the angle between the cylinder's axis and the plane's normal in degrees (between 0 and 90 because of the ambiguity in the direction of the axis), truncated to an integer: $\lfloor 90 \cdot \cos^{-1}(\|\mathbf{n}_1 \cdot \mathbf{a}_2\|) \rfloor$.
- **Plane–sphere.** The invariant relational feature $\mathbf{I}_{ps}$ is the minimum distance between the plane and the sphere's center in tenths of inches, truncated to an integer: $\lfloor 10 \cdot (d_1 + \mathbf{n}_1 \cdot \mathbf{p}_2) \rfloor$.
- **Cylinder–cylinder.** The relational invariant feature $\mathbf{I}_{cc}$ for two cylinders is the angle between their axes in degrees (between 0 and 90), truncated to an integer: $\lfloor 90 \cdot \cos^{-1}(\|\mathbf{a}_1 \cdot \mathbf{a}_2\|) \rfloor$.
- **Cylinder–sphere.** The relational invariant feature $\mathbf{I}_{cs}$ is the minimum distance between the cylinder's axis and the sphere's center in tenths of inches, quantized to an integer: $\lfloor 10 \cdot \|(\mathbf{p}_1 - \mathbf{p}_2) - \mathbf{a}_1((\mathbf{p}_1 - \mathbf{p}_2 \cdot \mathbf{a}_1)\| \rfloor$.
- **Sphere–sphere.** The relational invariant feature $\mathbf{I}_{ss}$ for two spheres is the distance between their centers in tenths of inches truncated to an integer: $\lfloor 10 \cdot \|\mathbf{p}_1 - \mathbf{p}_2\| \rfloor$.

The invariant relational features $\mathbf{I}_{xy}$ for pairs of surfaces in the segmented range image of Fig. 14.8 are given in Table 14.1. A subset of the invariant relational features computed from pairs of surfaces in the model (depicted in Fig. 14.9) appear in Table 14.2. Surface pairs involving S_3 in the first table and M_1 in the second were reordered to make the cylindrical patch appear second in the pair, to agree with our definitions of the invariant features.

The ten interpretation tables (constructed from object models and indexed by pairs of the $\mathbf{I}_{xy}$ are defined as follows:

- **Plane–plane–plane.** This 180×180 table (denoted $\mathbf{T}_{ppp}$) is indexed by two values of θ_{pp}, computed from the three different pairs of planes in the triple. The three distinct pairs of planes for the triple (M_1, M_2, M_3)

TABLE 14.1

Invariant Relational Features for Pairs of Scene Surfaces in Fig. 14.8

Surface 1	Surface 2	Invariant feature type	Value
S_1	S_2	$\mathbf{I}_{pp}$	91
S_1	S_3	$\mathbf{I}_{pc}$	3
S_1	S_4	$\mathbf{I}_{pp}$	3
S_2	S_3	$\mathbf{I}_{pc}$	88
S_2	S_4	$\mathbf{I}_{pp}$	92
S_4	S_3	$\mathbf{I}_{pc}$	4

TABLE 14.2

Invariant Relational Features for a Subset of the Pairs of Model
Surfaces in Fig. 14.9

Surface 1	Surface 2	Invariant feature type	Value
M_2	M_1	$\mathbf{I}_{pc}$	0
M_5	M_1	$\mathbf{I}_{pc}$	90
M_2	M_3	$\mathbf{I}_{pp}$	0
M_2	M_4	$\mathbf{I}_{pp}$	180
M_2	M_5	$\mathbf{I}_{pp}$	90
M_3	M_4	$\mathbf{I}_{pp}$	180
M_3	M_5	$\mathbf{I}_{pp}$	90

produce three pairs of invariant feature indices to access the table $[(\mathbf{I}_{12}, \mathbf{I}_{13}), (\mathbf{I}_{12}, \mathbf{I}_{23}), (\mathbf{I}_{13}, \mathbf{I}_{23})]$. Since we do not know in which order the scene planes will be grouped at recognition time, three entries are inserted in $\mathbf{T}_{ppp}$, one for each of the pairs above. To minimize the size of the table, we sort the two invariant feature indices so that the first is less than or equal to the second, and use only the lower triangle and the main diagonal of $\mathbf{T}_{ppp}$ to store proto-hypotheses.

• **Plane–plane–cylinder.** This 180×90 table ($\mathbf{T}_{ppc}$) is indexed by $\mathbf{I}_{12}$ and one of $(\mathbf{I}_{13}, \mathbf{I}_{23})$. As in the case above, we do not know the ordering of the planes, and must insert a protohypothesis at both $(\mathbf{I}_{12}, \mathbf{I}_{13})$ and $(\mathbf{I}_{12}, \mathbf{I}_{23})$.

• **Plane–plane–sphere.** $\mathbf{T}_{pps}$ is a 180×100 table indexed by $\mathbf{I}_{12}$ and one of $(\mathbf{I}_{13}, \mathbf{I}_{23})$. As in the case of $\mathbf{T}_{ppc}$, we insert two protohypotheses for each model triple of this type.

• **Plane–cylinder–cylinder.** $\mathbf{T}_{pcc}$ is 90×90 in size and indexed by one of $(\mathbf{I}_{12}, \mathbf{I}_{13})$ and $\mathbf{I}_{23}$. Two protohypotheses are inserted in the table for each model triple of this type.

• **Plane–cylinder–sphere.** The 90×100 table $\mathbf{T}_{pcs}$ is indexed by $\mathbf{I}_{12}$ and $\mathbf{I}_{23}$. Only one protohypothesis is inserted since the surface types are all different and only a single ordering of the surface types is possible.

• **Plane–sphere–sphere.** $\mathbf{T}_{pss}$ is 100×100 in size and indexed by one of $(\mathbf{I}_{12}, \mathbf{I}_{13})$ and $\mathbf{I}_{23}$. Two protohypotheses are inserted for each model triple of this type.

• **Cylinder–cylinder–cylinder.** $\mathbf{T}_{ccc}$ is a 90×90 table indexed by two of $(\mathbf{I}_{12}, \mathbf{I}_{13}, \mathbf{I}_{23})$. As with $\mathbf{T}_{ppp}$, multiple protohypotheses will be inserted in $\mathbf{T}_{ccc}$ if two or three of the indices are equal.

• **Cylinder–cylinder–sphere.** This table is 90×100, and is indexed by $\mathbf{I}_{12}$ and one of $(\mathbf{I}_{13}, \mathbf{I}_{23})$. Two entries are inserted in $\mathbf{T}_{ccs}$ for each model triple.

• **Sphere–sphere–sphere.** $\mathbf{T}_{sss}$ is a 100×100 table indexed by two of $(\mathbf{I}_{12}, \mathbf{I}_{13}, \mathbf{I}_{23})$. The table is symmetric, and only entries on or below the main diagonal are filled.

When a triple of patches is considered, the relational features provide the indices and the identities of the model patches form an entry to be placed in the table at that location. Since more than one triple of patches can give rise to the same index, the table entry is actually a linked list initialized to the empty list; these entries are filled as the triples are enumerated for all object models. If a triple of surfaces (M_i, M_j, M_k) produces invariant index values f_{ij}, f_{ik}, and f_{jk}, then we would create and insert the following protohypotheses at the table locations given:

Index	Protohypothesis
(f_{ij}, f_{jk})	$\langle \text{ID}, (M_i, M_j, M_k) \rangle$
(f_{ik}, f_{jk})	$\langle \text{ID}, (M_i, M_k, M_j) \rangle$
(f_{ij}, f_{ik})	$\langle \text{ID}, (M_j, M_i, M_k) \rangle$

The object model shown in Fig. 14.9 yields $(\frac{8!}{3! \cdot 5!}) = 56$ triples of surfaces. Table 14.3 shows a subset of the triples and the protohypotheses inserted in the interpretation tables. For legibility, the ID portion of the protohypothesis is omitted.

Matching scene features against model features using interpretation tables is straightforward. The invariant features are calculated for each triple of scene surfaces extracted in the segmentation process. Table entries in a small range (within five entries in either or both dimensions) about those index values are retrieved, and the model features in the retrieved protohypotheses are bound to the scene features under consideration, producing hypotheses that are then checked for validity using additional procedures.

TABLE 14.3

A Subset of the Model Surface Triples, Table Identities, Locations, and Protohypotheses Created for the Object in Fig. 14.9

Surface triple	Table	Index	Protohypothesis
$(M_1\, M_2, M_3)$	T_{ppc}	$(0, 0)$	(M_2, M_3, M_1)
		$(0, 0)$	(M_3, M_2, M_1)
(M_2, M_3, M_4)	T_{ppp}	$(0, 180)$	(M_2, M_3, M_4)
		$(0, 180)$	(M_3, M_2, M_4)
		$(180, 180)$	(M_2, M_4, M_3)
		$(180, 180)$	(M_3, M_4, M_2)
(M_3, M_5, M_7)	T_{ppp}	$(90, 90)$	(M_3, M_5, M_7)
		$(90, 90)$	(M_3, M_7, M_5)
		$(90, 90)$	(M_5, M_3, M_7)
		$(90, 90)$	(M_5, M_7, M_3)
		$(90, 90)$	(M_7, M_3, M_5)
		$(90, 90)$	(M_7, M_5, M_3)

Consider the scene surface triple (S_1, S_4, S_3) in Fig. 14.8. The type of this triple is (plane–plane–cylinder), and the invariant relational feature values are $\mathbf{I}_{pp}(S_1, S_4) = 3$ and $\mathbf{I}_{pc}(S_3, S_4) = 4$, as shown in Table 24.1 Assume that the correct correspondence set for the scene triple is $\{(S_1, M_3), (S_4, M_2), (S_3, M_1)\}$. (As noted above, the object's rotational symmetry actually gives rise to four plausible interpretations.) The corresponding protohypotheses in the table are the first two entries in Table 14.3 and retrieval of the protohypotheses in $\mathbf{T}_{ppc}$ within ± 5 index values of the pair $(3, 4)$ will yield the correct protohypothesis (along with others arising from this model and from other models).

All protohypotheses retrieved from probes of the interpretation table undergo additional testing to check their validity; most of these tests are actually geometric predicates first developed for the BONSAI system. This additional testing is necessary because the indexing procedure used to retrieve protohypotheses and bind their members to the scene features *does not verify the consistency of attributes other than those embodied in the indices.* For example, a database of polyhedra with different-sized faces, but with the same set of angles between the faces (say, 90°) will yield clustering in $\mathbf{T}_{ppp}$, because angles are not salient for that particular model database. A triple of mutually orthogonal planes extracted from the scene will yield a large number of hypotheses constructed from the corresponding entry in $\mathbf{T}_{ppp}$. The additional tests serve to filter hypotheses that obey the angle constraints, but to not obey others (such as the area orparallel-distance constraints used above).

Invariant feature indexing offers several potential advantages over constrained search as a recognition mechanism. First, the time complexity of the recognition process is cubic in the number of scene features used in matching. In constrained-search procedures, the presence of spurious features can require the use of **NULL** correspondences, which causes the search-based procedure to have exponential time complexity in the number of features. An additonal advantage of the invariant feature indexing technique is its use of pretabulated hypotheses that (if retrieved during the matching procedure) are guaranteed to obey several of the constraints that would be checked individually in a search-based system. However, the interpretation tables are typically large, and implementation of the procedure is somewhat more complicated than implementation of search.

4.2.2. Structural Indexing

Stein and Medioni (29) have developed a 3D object recognition system based on a novel object representation; the system also exploits invariance as a method for indexing and retrieving tabulated hypotheses. A distinguishing and attractive aspect of this system is its ability to build tabulated object representations from range views, rather than requiring a preexisting geometric model of the object to be present. However, if an object model is present, synthetic range images can be generated from it and would serve well as input to the system; hence this technique can still be model-based.

The invariant features in Stein and Medioni's system are estimates of the curvature and torsion at the vertices of a polygonal approximation to a 3D contour in a space of angles, which is constructed as follows. At each selected surface point $\mathbf{p}$ on the surface of interest with normal vector $\mathbf{N_p}$, a geodesic circle (called a "splash") of radius r is sampled at n equal angular increments $\Delta\theta$. Several values of r are used and their values are chosen heuristically. At each sample location $\mathbf{p}_i$, the local surface normal $\mathbf{N_{p_i}}$ is computed and compared with $\mathbf{N_p}$. The plane P_i passing through $\mathbf{p}$ and $\mathbf{p}_i$ and containing $\mathbf{N_p}$ is used to form a local coordinate system (x', y', z') with basis vectors

$$\mathbf{z}' = \mathbf{N_p},$$

$$\mathbf{x}' = (\mathbf{p}_i - \mathbf{p}) - \mathbf{N_P}[\mathbf{N_P} \cdot (\mathbf{p}_i - \mathbf{p})],$$

$$\mathbf{y}' = \mathbf{z}' \times \mathbf{x}'.$$

With the local coordinate system thus defined, two angles describe the difference between $\mathbf{N_p}$ and $\mathbf{N_{p_i}}$:

$$\phi_i = \cos^{-1}(\mathbf{N_P} \cdot \mathbf{N_{P_i}}),$$

$$\psi_i = \cos^{-1}\left\{\mathbf{x}' \cdot \left[\mathbf{N_{p_i}} - \mathbf{N_p}(\mathbf{N_p} \cdot \mathbf{N_{p_i}})\right]\right\}.$$

The set of 3D points

$$\{(\phi_1, \psi_1, \Delta\theta), (\phi_2, \psi_2, 2\Delta\theta), \ldots, (\phi_n, \psi_n, n\Delta\theta)\}$$

is interpreted as the vertices of a piecewise-linear 3D contour. Discrete estimates of the curvature and torsion of this contour at the vertices are invariant to rotation and translation and, if reliably extracted, serve as invariant feature indices, along with the radius of the geodesic circle and other information. These indices are combined to form an index in a hash-table. Hash-table entries identify the object and the splash yielding the features used to form the hash-table index. Some care is taken in selecting surface points $\mathbf{p}$ that are stable, discriminatory, and nonredundant as well. An interest operator is used to select such points from both the images used in building the hash-table and range images in which unknown objects are to be recognized.

Object recognition in this system contains aspects of both indexing and matching. Surface points selected using the interest operator are used to generate splashes, compute corresponding hash-table index, and retrieve candidate point correspondences. Incorrect hypotheses are discarded using several verification procedures that check the validity of a pose transformation estimated from the hypothesis, group hypotheses into consistent clusters using predicates similar to those described in Grimson (15), and compute a final pose transformation.

4.3. Automatic Programming

For several years, groups of researchers have been developing systems that *generate* recognition programs from object models. Such systems have great intuitive appeal; if we are currently trying to identify a particular object in the scene, a recognition program specialized to the model might well run more quickly than a more general program. The approaches taken by researchers share little in common except this central idea. Indeed, some recent work describes the automatic generation of recognition "strategies" (tree-like data structures) optimized for a particular model or model view. While these strategies are apparently not actual programs, they do guide the execution of the actual recognition system, and we feel justified in placing them in this category. All current work in this area assumes that the identity of the object model is known, but the set of correspondences between scene and model features is not.

4.3.1. Example

Let us consider the recognition of the object in Fig. 14.9, using a procedure generated automatically from a model. The procedure's goal will be to match only as many features as are required to determine the pose of the object. Before outlining the procedure, we observe that the effort involved in recognizing an object with an automatic procedure is reduced if we can create correspondences involving discriminatory features early in the execution. The tree of procedures generated by automated-programming recognition procedures is analogous to the interpretation tree searched using the techniques described earlier, and as in those systems, it is preferable to bind the most discriminatory features first and thus restrict the branching factor of the tree rather than binding less discriminatory features earlier, and perhaps undoing them later.

Our procedure generator should examine the object model and identify discriminatory features, keeping in mind that the "current" most discriminatory feature depends on what has already been matched, and what is visible. We will assume for simplicity that features are ranked as follows in terms of discriminability, with the most discriminatory appearing first:

$$\mathscr{D} = \{M_1, M_3, M_4, M_7, M_8, M_5, M_6, M_2\},$$

where M_2 is ranked last because of its size. We also assume that if a feature M_i is the first to be matched while building an interpretation, all features appearing earlier than it in $\mathscr{D}$ are not visible, were incorrectly segmented, or for some other reason cannot be identified; such features will not appear in the set of bindings returned by the procedure. The generated "tree" of procedures appears in Fig. 14.11, and can be interpreted as follows. We begin at the root of the tree with no bindings. Nonterminal and terminal nodes labeled by scene features M_i correspond to invocations of procedures designed to identify a remaining scene surface (i.e., one not already matched) as an instance of M_i. If such a surface is identified, the subtree rooted at that node is examined. The subtrees labeled **OR** indicate that there are multiple possible candidates for the next match after the parent node, and were inserted to keep the graph structures as small as possible. If during any traversal we reach a leaf node, then all the model features encountered on a path back to the root have been successfully matched against features from the scene; this tree was constructed so that reaching a leaf node produces a verifiable hypothesis.

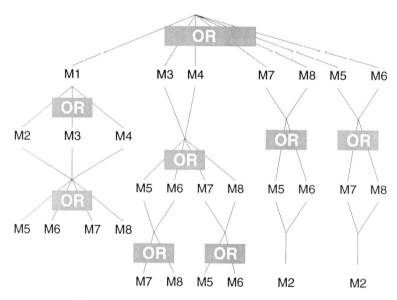

Figure 14.11. Recognition using automatic programming.

Goad (14) developed perhaps the first such automatic-programming approach to object recognition. Features in this system were linear edges, and an intensity sensor was used to obtain images of scenes to be analyzed. A hypothesis of viewer position (initially unconstrained) triggers a *prediction* operation, wherein an unmatched model edge that is guaranteed to be visible from that position is selected and its predicted position and orientation in the image calculated. This is followed by an *observation* stage, during which the list of image features is examined to see if the predicted edge is present. If the corresponding scene edge is found, its position is used in a *backprojection* step to update a pose estimate for the object, and it is added to the hypothesis. In the process of hypothesis refinement, the set of possible camera positions is typically reduced. In this way, the range of camera viewpoints that all satisfy observability constraints on the scene features is reduced, hopefully to a small range. The distinguishing feature of this system is that the possible matching decisions are embodied in a precomplied procedure, and invoked when images are obtained.

Ikeuchi and Kanade (19) have developed a *vision algorithm complier* (VAC) for 3D object localization and identification. As in Goad's system, object recognition requires a rough estimate of the object's pose with respect to the image coordinate system. However, one of the first steps in this system is to identify a specific *aspect* for the object under consideration. A discrete sampling of the two-dimensional view sphere is divided into aspects, each identified as the set of views that make the same object surfaces visible (visibility is determined by the sensor type). The attributes (surface moment, surface shape, extended Gaussian image, etc.) of surfaces visible in each aspect are extracted and their values are used for discrimination among aspects. Examination of the attributes in order of decreasing discriminability yields an efficient decision tree for identification of an object aspect. The decision tree itself is embodied in a procedure compiled from the model, and executed when features are available from input images. More recent work has been devoted to automated-programming procedures for determining precise object pose assuming that the aspect is known. Each aspect has its own pose estimation procedure associated with it; pose is estimated from alignment of corresponding edges. One remarkable feature of this system is explicit use of *sensor models* in the construction of recognition programs from object models. The type of sensor determines the detectability of image features as a function of their orientation.

Hansen and Henderson (17) described a CAD-based 3D object recognition system employing a *strategy tree*. A variety of features are extracted from the solid models used as the object database, including pointwise normals, curvatures, surface classifications, edges and arcs, and apparent symmetrics. An important contribution of this work is a systematic approach to the selection of features for recognition. *Feature filters* are employed to select the most powerful (discriminatory) features to use in recognizing a specific object, and discard the others. A strategy tree is a generalization of the tree classifier. One such tree is generated for each object in the database. Recognition of an object and computation of its pose corresponds to a descent of the strategy tree for that object. The strategy tree is constructed by placing the most discriminatory features at the first level below the root. Subtrees under the first level are known as *corroborating-evidence subtrees* (CESs), which direct a search for evidence that the first-level bindings are supported, and attempt to refine the pose estimate. If a first-level feature is detected and supported by the CES, a hypothesis is generated about the object's identity and pose. Verification of the generated hypothesis can be done either using frame correlation between the sensed image and a synthesized range image of the model, or through matching of features predicted from the model and the hypothesis with image features.

Arman and Aggarwal (1) also developed a system to generate recognition strategies from solid models designed on the CADKEY commercial solid modeler. Recognition strategies are synthesized (at run-time) from "recognition trees" (constructed off-line), which contain objects at their roots and individual features (surfaces or surface boundaries) at the leaves. Intermediate levels represent groupings of lower-level entities (e.g., similar surfaces are grouped into a type-specific node, and all surface types at that level are grouped into a generic "surface" node). Branches in the recognition tree receive numerical weights representing their discriminability. At run-time, traversal of the recognition tree causes activation of "filters" that take the scene features (surfaces) as input and produce a restricted set of candidate surfaces as output. After the issuance of multiple filters, a consistent labeling of the scene features is obtained.

4.4. Recognition of Part Models

The use of *part-based* object representations [proposed in various forms by Biederman (5) and others] has been a subject of interest to many computer vision researchers. Beyond the appeal of having systems that use representation similar to those proposed as appropriate to biological vision systems, part-based representations are typically simpler than the parameterized descriptions used by many systems. Part-based models are thus usually viewed as *qualitative* descriptions, and the extraction of parts from input imagery is a difficult problem, since most feature extractors are designed to produce quantitative features.

The *geon* (*ge*ometric i*on*) description seems to be the representation of choice for computer vision researchers employing the part model in systems. Geons are volumetric primitives with several qualitative attributes affecting their cross sections:

- *Edge*—straight or curved
- *Symmetry*—none, reflective, rotational–reflective
- *Size*—constant, expanding, expanding–contracting
- *Axis*—straight or curved

The Cartesian product space of these four qualitative descriptions yields 36 different geons. Most vision researchers employ a subset of these 36 possibilities for object representation. Complex objects are usually represented as aggregates of geon shapes. The analogy with syntactic representations is intriguing. The 36 different geons could be viewed as the alphabet of a grammar. Embodying placement, orientation, and affixment in production rules would produce a system capable of generating geon-based representations. Recognition would correspond to parsing. Figure 14.12 shows a decomposition of the object in Fig. 14.9 into two geon

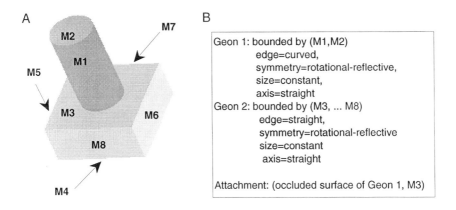

A

B

Geon 1: bounded by (M1,M2)
edge=curved,
symmetry=rotational-reflective,
size=constant,
axis=straight

Geon 2: bounded by (M3, ... M8)
edge=straight,
symmetry=rotational-reflective
size=constant
axis=straight

Attachment: (occluded surface of Geon 1, M3)

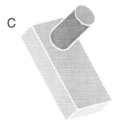

C

Figure 14.12. Geons for the object in Fig. 14.9.

shapes, accompanied by a statement of how they are attached. Part (C) of the figure depicts an object that is qualitatively similar to the object in part (A) and would be represented identically using parts.

The extraction of geons from input imagery has been attacked in several different ways. Pentland (26) was the first to propose the superquadric shape model for representation and recognition, and developed a regression technique for superquadric recovery. Solina and Bajcsy (28) and Raja and Jain (27) have also developed techniques for recovering superquadrics from dense range data. Part shapes have also been extracted from intensity data using edge-based strategies. Bergevin and Levine (2) developed a system called PARVO (*p*rimal *a*ccess *r*ecognition of *v*isual *o*bjects), which is explicitly based on geon representations and is able to extract such primitives by analyzing line drawings. Dickinson *et al.* (9) described as system that interprets intensity imagery using a geon-based volumetric object representation combined with view-dependent features.

4.5. Other Object Recognition Techniques

This section briefly addresses other strategies for 3D object recognition which have had a substantial impact on current research.

4.5.1. *Constraint Satisfaction Networks*

Bolle *et al.* (6) have developed a highly modular and parallel system for object recognition using hierarchical networks of *parameter transform* operators that either (depending on their position in the hierarchy) extract simple features from image data, organize those features into salient aggregates, provide evidence for primitive faces or volumes, or (at the highest level) provide evidence for or against the presence of a particular object in the input image. Explicit attention is paid to the indexing problem in this architecture and the homogeneity of the processing operators make this system easily extensible into new domains of features and models.

4.5.2. *Graph Matching*

It has been observed that correspondence-based object recognition can be viewed as a graph-matching problem. Object models are often expressed as relational graphs with nodes representing geometric primitives and arcs representing relational features defined on those primitives. If similar graphs can be reliably extracted from image data, then finding a graph–subgraph isomorphism essentially solves the recognition problem. Systems based on this idea typically bring additional constraints from the recognition domain to reduce the complexity of the matching algorithm.

Kim and Kak (21) combined discrete relaxation labeling and bipartite matching to recognize 3D objects in large databases. The features used are planar and quadric surfaces extracted from range data. Bipartite matching is used initially to extract a candidate correspondence between a subset of scene features and a compatible model. Predicates are developed to quickly reject models that cannot be present in the scene (this is an example of model database indexing). Remaining models undergo a bipartite matching procedure to identify candidate correspondences with the scene features. This procedure also rejects some models from consideration. Discrete relaxation labeling is used to bind surviving models to the scene features, subject to relational constraints observed in the scene and present in the object models. Multiple matches to a subset of the scene features are ranked using a pose estimation and comparison procedure.

Fan *et al.* (10) developed a 3D vision system employing multiple views as a model source. The same processing is performed on range images forming the database and the unknown views to be classified. The matching features are smooth surface patches. Heuristics are used to group patches in the image (which may come from more than one object) into classes corresponding to single objects, and patches within each class are linked with attributed relations summarizing the type of adjacency and a probability of connection. The output of the image analysis phase is a set of graphs describing scene objects. These descriptions are corresponded with graphs derived from the database images via a search procedure; estimates of object pose are produced concurrently. An analyzer module attempts to cope with segmentation or interpretation errors by modifying the graph structure.

4.5.3. Evidence-Based Recognition

Jain and Hoffman (20) developed a 3D object recognition system that accumulates evidence for object hypotheses from feature observations. The system employed global, intrinsic, and relational features defined on surface patches of three generic types. Features of the scene segments and object model descriptions are used to derive sets of scene features that are specialized to correspond as closely as possible to the object models. These modified features are then input to the recognition module, which contains codified *evidence values* for each object model. The similarity between the features in the model database and each of the modified representations is evaluated, and if one model produces a high similarity value, the unknown object in the scene is identified as that model. A distinguishing feature of this system was its ability to automatically construct evidence rules from the model database, rather than having these rules designed by a human expert.

5. POSE ESTIMATION

After forming a suitable (application- and implementation-dependent) number of correspondences between scene and model features, many object recognition systems estimate a rigid transformation that aligns the model's features with the corresponding scene features. Knowledge of the types of features being corresponded, and their ability to constrain the six degrees of freedom (three rotations and three translations) in the rigid transformation is frequently exploited in pose estimation strategies.

5.1. Three-Dimensional Pose from Two-Dimensional Features

Lowe (23) developed a system called SCERPO, which uses the principles of perceptual grouping to identify intermediate-level structures from nonaccidental relationships (proximity, collinearity, and parallelism) between line segments in 2D images. These structures are matched against candidate structures in a database of 3D models. Each matched grouping is used to generate an estimate of the 3D object's pose in the scene. The pose estimation problem attacked by SCERPO has seven parameters, namely the three rotations and translations, and the focal length of the camera used to form the perspective projection. The solution is obtained iteratively, using Newton's method on a reparametrized (linear) set of projection equations. While developed originally to derive pose from corresponding 2D and 3D points, line segments can also be accommodated in the solution, and can improve on the quality of the parameter estimates.

Huttenlocher and Ullman (18) developed a procedure for aligning corresponding feature groups obtained from the model and the scene, assuming a weak perspective projection for the image formation process. The feature types considered are triples of points (2D points in the image, and 3D points in the model) and pairs of "oriented points" such as a curved arc or a vertex adjacent to two edge fragments. Each correspondence between image and model points triples yields a pose estimate, computed using a direct (noniterative) algorithm.

5.2. Three-Dimensional Pose from Three-Dimensional Features

Computing 3D pose from corresponding 3D features has been ad-dressed in a number of different ways in the literature. Our discussion will contain a pose estimation example followed by a brief survey.

5.2.1. Example

Consider the scene features of Fig. 14.8(B), the model of Fig. 14.9(B), and the correspondences

$$\{(S_3, M_1), (S_1, M_3), (S_2, M_6), (S_4, M_2)\},$$

which is one of the correct labelings for the object. The following tech-nique for estimating the pose of the model from the correspondences was described in Flynn and Jain (12). Pose estimation is decomposed into estimation of rotation followed by estimation of translation. The method proposed by Grimson and Lozano-Pérez (16) is used to estimate the rotational component of pose. Given a pair of correspondences between two orientable scene and model surfaces $\{(S_a, M_b), (S_c, M_d)\}$, the rotation transformation is computed as follows. Let v_a, v_b, v_c, v_d represent the orientation parameters of the four surfaces involved (if the surfaces are planar, the orientation parameter is the normal vector; for rotational symmetric surfaces, the axis of symmetry can be used). We assume that v_b and v_d are nonparallel and nonantiparallel. The rotation matrix $\mathbf{R}$ that simultaneously takes v_b into v_a and v_d into v_c is constructed from an axis $\mathbf{a} = (a_x, a_y, a_z)$ (passing through the origin) about which the model is rotated, and an angle θ of rotation about that axis. In terms of the v_x, the axis and angle are given by

$$\mathbf{a} = \frac{(v_b - v_a) \times (v_d - v_c)}{\|(v_b - v_a) \times (v_d - v_c)\|},$$

$$\theta = \tan^{-1}\left[\frac{(\mathbf{a} \times v_a) \cdot v_b}{(\mathbf{a} \cdot v_a)(\mathbf{a} \cdot v_b) + (v_a \cdot v_b)}\right].$$

The rotation matrix (which postmultiplies model vectors) corresponding to these two quantities is given by

$$
\mathbf{R} = \cos\theta \begin{bmatrix} 1 & 0 & 0 \\ 0 & 1 & 0 \\ 0 & 0 & 1 \end{bmatrix} + (1 - \cos\theta) \begin{bmatrix} a_x^2 & a_x a_y & a_x a_z \\ a_x a_y & a_y^2 & a_y a_z \\ a_x a_z & a_y a_z & a_z^2 \end{bmatrix}
$$

$$
+ \sin\theta \begin{bmatrix} 0 & -a_z & a_y \\ a_z & 0 & -a_x \\ -a_y & a_x & 0 \end{bmatrix}.
$$

In cases where more than two corresponding vectors are available, all pairs of angles can be considered independently and their results averaged to get a single result.

Consider the pair of bindings $\{(S_1, M_3), (S_2, M_6)\}$ for the scene and model pictured in Figs. 14.8 and 14.9, respectively. Using the equations above, we have

$$
\mathbf{v}_a = (-0.889, -0.043, 0.455),
$$

$$
\mathbf{v}_b = (0, 0, 1),
$$

$$
\mathbf{v}_c = (0.476, 0.032, 0.879),
$$

$$
\mathbf{v}_d = (1, 0, 0),
$$

$$
\mathbf{a} = (0.029, -0.998, 0.047),
$$

$$
\theta = 5.183 \text{ radians},
$$

$$
\mathbf{R} = \begin{bmatrix} 0.454 & 0.032 & 0.890 \\ -0.053 & 0.999 & -0.009 \\ -0.889 & -0.043 & 0.455 \end{bmatrix}.
$$

Applying the estimated rotation to the M_3 orientation parameter $(0, 0, 1)$ yields the orientation parameter of S_1, as expected.

The estimated rotation applied to the model surfaces will align them but not make them coincident with the scene surfaces. To estimate the translations needed to coincide the scene and model surfaces, we observe that a pair of corresponding planes constrains translation perpendicular to themselves (but not parallel to themselves), and a cylinder constrains translation perpendicular to its axis (but not parallel to the axis). Hence, for this example, S_4 and either S_1 or S_2 will yield the translations needed.

axis). Hence, for this example, S_4 and either S_1 or S_2 will yield the translations needed.

Let us use (S_3, M_1) and (S_1, M_3) to estimate the translation vector $(\Delta x, \Delta y, \Delta z)$. The two planes S_1 and M_3 were aligned by the previous rotation, but the projection of the translation vector along the planes' surface normals should be the separation between them. The following expresses the constraint:

$$-0.889\,\Delta x - 0.043\,\Delta y + 0.455\,\Delta z = (1.464 + 0.625).$$

Now consider S_4 and M_1. We decompose the translation $(\Delta x, \Delta y, \Delta z)$ into components parallel to and perpendicular to the cylinders' axes [assumed equal to each other and to (v_x, v_y, v_z)]:

$$(\Delta x, \Delta y, \Delta z) = (\Delta x_\| + \Delta x_\perp, \Delta y_\| + \Delta y_\perp, \Delta z_\| + \Delta z_\perp).$$

Here, the subscript $\|$ denotes the parallel components, and $\perp$ denotes the perpendicular components. The translation needed to correspond to two cylinders constrains the perpendicular component but not the parallel component. If we define an auxiliary parameter t so that

$$(\Delta x_\|, \Delta y_\|, \Delta z_\|) = t(v_x, v_y, v_z),$$

then the following linear system embodies the constraint in terms of the unknown translations and the auxiliary parameter t:

$$\Delta x - tv_x = \Delta x_\perp,$$

$$\Delta y - tv_y = \Delta y_\perp,$$

$$\Delta z - tv_z = \Delta z_\perp.$$

The perpendicular translation is determined by the point $\mathbf{p}_s$ and $\mathbf{p}'_m$ on the scene and rotated model cylinder's axes, respectively, and on the axis direction $\mathbf{v}$. To extract the perpendicular component. the projection of $\mathbf{p}'_m \mathbf{p}_s$ on $\mathbf{v}$ is subtracted from $\mathbf{p}'_m \mathbf{p}_s$. In this case,

$$\mathbf{p}_s = (-1.951, 3.849, -0.952) \quad [\text{see Fig. 14.8(C)}],$$

$$\mathbf{p}_m = (0, 0, 3.756) \quad [\text{see Fig. 14.9(B)}],$$

$$\mathbf{p}'_m = \mathbf{p}_m \mathbf{R} = (-3.341, -0.161, 1.709),$$

$$\mathbf{v} = (-0.889, -0.043, 0.455),$$

$$(\Delta x_\perp, \Delta y_\perp, \Delta z_\perp) = \mathbf{p}'_m \mathbf{p}_s - (\mathbf{p}'_m \mathbf{p}_s \cdot \mathbf{v}) = (-1.167, 3.114, -1.988).$$

The system of equations produced by these values is

$$\Delta x - 0.889t = 1.167,$$

$$\Delta y - 0.043t = -3.114,$$

$$\Delta z + 0.455t = -1.988.$$

When combined with the single linear equation produced by (S_1, M_3), we have a system of four equations in four unknowns, with solutions

$$(\Delta x, \Delta y, \Delta z) = (-0.702, -3.204, 2.916)$$

Grimson and Lozano-Pérez (16) developed both the method for rotation estimation used in the preceding example and a technique for estimation of the 3D translation component using triples of planes whose normal vectors span the 3D space. In fact, the translation estimation technique described above degenerates to their method if there are only three planar surfaces involved. If there are more than three planes available for correspondence, one can (1) consider all triples and average together the resulting estimates (ignoring triples where two or all three of the planes are near-parallel), or (2) form a least-squares system to the overdetermined system defined by the planar constraints.

5.2.2. Survey

The two most popular techniques for estimation of a 3D pose transformation from 3D features are the method described above and a technique proposed originally by Faugeras and Hebert (11), which has been used in 3D-POLY (8) and other object recognition systems. Like the previous method, it estimates the rotational component of the pose transformation first, and then the translational component. The rotation is expressed as a quaternion $(\mathbf{w}, s)$, where $\mathbf{w}$ is a 3-vector in the direction of the rotation axis and s is related to the angle of rotation about that axis. The rotation operation applied to a point is expressed as a pair of quaternion multiplications, and the rotation can be obtained through an eigenanalysis of a coefficient matrix determined from orientation parameters in the scene and model. Once the rotation quaternion (and the equivalent rotation matrix) have been obtained, the translation can be estimated either by averaging the translation needed to align corresponding scene and model points (e.g., polyhedron vertices), or by alignment of planar surfaces using a technique not unlike that given above.

Besl and McKay (4) recently developed a fast iterative method for registration of a point set with a "generic" 3D shape described as a point set, a curve (parametric, or implicit), or a surface (parametric, or implicit).

The flexibility of model representation makes this an appealing technique. The rotation transformation is represented by a unit quaternion and, together with the 3D translation, forms the parameter vector modified during a procedure to minimize the registration error. The fundamental requirement of the method is a function that returns the distance between a point in the point set and the model (however represented); for certain representations, Newton's method is used to form the estimate. The overall registration procedure chooses a starting value for the parameter vector and iteratively updates it using the calculated distances and an updated point set, terminating when the change in mean-squared registration error between iterations drops below a predefined threshold.

6. VERIFICATION

Many object recognition systems generate more than one hypothesis (set of bindings) for a given input image, even if it contains only one object. This is often unavoidable since the partial information available to the sensor may admit multiple interpretations involving similar-appearing models. Additionally, the constraints used in forming the interpretation may not exploit a particular discriminatory feature that can reduce multiple interpretations. Hence, some procedure for evaluating the quality of a hypothesis is needed. This verification process typically involves a *prediction* step (in which the hypothesis and perhaps the pose estimate are used to predict the location of image features that should be visible to the sensor) and a *scoring* step (in which a search is conducted for the hypothesized features and an overall quality score for the hypothesis is updated based on these features' presence or absence). We expect the system to produce a hypothesis for each identifiable object.

We now present an example of a hypothesis verification procedure. The pose transformation obtained in Section 5 is used for verification in the BONSAI object recognition system (12) and more recent work (13) as follows:

1. Accompanying the object models are polyhedral approximations. Planar surfaces on the model are represented exactly by a single face of the polyhedron, and curved surfaces are represented as a fine mesh of planar facets. The polyhedral mesh is transformed using the estimated pose information and fed to a standard polygon renderer that produces a synthetic range image and a corresponding segmentation of the object model in the hypothesized position. The rendering is performed on an image of the same size and resolution as the input image.

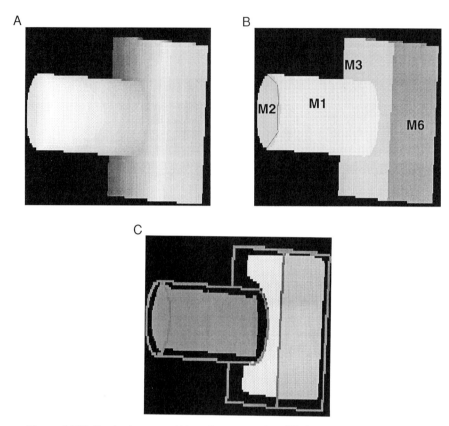

Figure 14.13. Synthetic range (A) and segmentation (B) images corresponding to a hypothesis for the scene in Fig. 14.8; (C) synthetic segmentation overlaid on input segmentation.

2. The input and synthetic range and segmentation images are compared pixel-to-pixel, and several matching scores (all between 0 and 1) are obtained, and multipled to get a final score for the hypothesis.
3. Steps 1 and 2 above yield a score for each hypothesis. The highest-scoring hypothesis is assumed to be correct.

Turning again to the example recognition experiment depicted in Figs. 14.8 and 14.9, application of the pose transformation obtained in Section 5 and rendering of the resultant polyhedron in an image grid close to that of the input image yields the synthetic range and segmentation images appearing in Figs. 14.13(A) and (B). Outlines of the segments in the synthetic image appear in part (C) of the figure, and indicate that the pose estimate is of very good quality.

TABLE 14.4

Overlapping Pixel Counts for the Synthetic Segmentation Images in Fig. 14.13[a]

	S_1	S_2	S_3	S_4
M_1	0	0	**2114**	105
M_2	0	0	0	**381**
M_3	**1299**	0	0	0
M_6	60	**2339**	0	0

[a] Boldface numbers reflect correct bindings.

For simplicity we will assume that the hypothesis has a binding for all four scene surfaces. These two synthetic images are compared with the input images, producing the following matching scores:

1. s_1 measures discrepancies in the depth at each pixel. Define N_1^+ as the number of pixels in the input range image within 0.1 inch of the predicted value, and N_1^- as the number of pixels where the predicted value is larger (i.e., closer to the sensor) than the sensed value. Intuitively, we would like N_1^+ to be larger and N_1^- to be small. s_1 is defined as $N_1^+/(N_1^+ + N_1^-)$, and lies between zero and one. In the example, $N_1^+ = 6835$ and $N_1^- = 493$, yielding $s_1 = 0.932$.

2. s_2 is a product of subscores, each calculated from observed overlaps between segments in the input and synthetic segmentation images. There are four segments in the synthetic segmentation and four in the input segmentation; Table 14.4 shows the number of pixels mapping to a particular pair of synthetic and input segmentation labels. Numbers in boldface indicate correspondences appearing in the correct hypothesis. To normalize these numbers, we need an overall count of each label in the two segmentation images. These numbers are denoted N_{M_i} or N_{S_i} and their values are given in Table 14.5. Each nonzero entry t_{ij} in Table 14.4 (which may or may not

TABLE 14.5

Populations of Segment Labels in the Input and Synthetic Images

Label	Population N_{S_i}	Label	Population N_{M_i}
S_1	1359	M_1	2989
S_2	2339	M_2	581
S_3	2114	M_3	2170
S_4	486	M_4	2883

TABLE 14.6

**Subscores for the Synthetic Segmentation Images
in Fig. 14.13**

	S_1	S_2	S_3	S_4
M_1			0.707	0.992
M_2				0.514
M_3	0.572			
M_6	0.999	0.811		

correspond to a possible bindings between S_i and M_j) yields a component of s_2.

    a. If t_{ij} came from a correct binding, the score for that entry is $t_{ij}^2/(N_{S_i}N_{M_j})$, where N_{S_i} and N_{M_j} are the total segment populations appearing in Table 14.5. Intuitively, this score will be large for segments that overlap well and low for segments that do not, or that are partially occluded.

    b. If the table yielding t_{ij} does not correspond to a binding in the hypothesis of interest, the matching score is defined as $1 - [t_{ij}^2/(N_{S_i}N_{M_j})]$. This score penalizes good overlaps since they are not present in the hypothesis, but rewards small overlaps.

The product of these subscores over all entries of the overlap matrix yields s_2. For our example, the matrix in Table 14.6 shows the individual subscores. The output value of s_2 is 0.167.

3. s_3 is a global overlap score, which is simply the sum of the "correct" overlap populations (the boldface entries in Table 14.4) divided by the sum of all overlap populations. In this example, s_3
$$= \frac{2114 + 381 + 1299 + 2339}{2114 + 105 + 381 + 1299 + 60 + 2339} = 0.974.$$

4. s_4 is the product of ratios between input and synthetic segment areas involved in the hypothesis. Table 14.7 shows the estimated surface areas of the segments in the input and synthetic images. With the information as given, $s_4 = \frac{3.022}{4.656} \cdot \frac{2.780}{3.376} \cdot \frac{2.831}{4.786} \cdot \frac{1.034}{1.217} = 0.269$.

TABLE 14.7

**Surface Areas for Segments in the Input
and Synthetic Images**

Label	Area	Label	Area
S_1	3.022	M_1	4.786
S_2	2.780	M_2	1.217
S_3	2.831	M_3	4.656
S_4	1.034	M_4	3.376

5. s_5 summarizes the closeness between the number of valid (nonzero) pixels in the input and synthetic segmentations. In Fig. 14.13, invalid pixels are black in the segmentation images. If N_i is the number of valid pixels in the input segmentation and N_s is the number of valid pixels in the synthetic segmentation, then

$$
s_5 = \begin{cases}
\dfrac{N_i}{N_s} & \text{if } N_i < N_s, \\[2ex]
\dfrac{N_s}{N_i} & \text{if } 1 < \dfrac{N_i}{N_s} < 2, \\[2ex]
0 & \text{if } \dfrac{N_i}{N_s} > 2.
\end{cases}
$$

The last clause in the conditional form for s_5 discards hypotheses where the predicted image of the hypothesized model occupies more than twice as many pixels in the synthetic segmentation as the object in the input image. In the example, $N_i = 6298$ and $N_s = 8657$, so $s_5 = 0.727$.

6. s_6 measures the number of times in the segmentation images where an invalid pixel in one corresponds to a valid pixel in the other. Let N_0 be the number of pixel locations where the synthetic segmentation has a valid pixel but the input segmentation does not, and N_1 be the number of locations where the input segmentation is valid but not the synthetic segmentation. Then

$$
s_6 = \frac{(N_i - N_0)(N_s - N_1)}{N_i N_s}.
$$

In our example, $N_0 = 2359$, $N_1 = 0$, and therefore $s_6 = 0.625$. Hence, the final score for this hypothesis is 0.019. While this number is small, the number for incorrect hypotheses is typically much closer to zero.

7. COMMENTARY, EMERGING THEMES, AND CONCLUSIONS

In this chapter, we have presented an overview of subproblems involved in 3D object recognition, surveyed existing research work, and given tutorial examples of some of the processing steps involved in object recognition. While by no means exhaustive, the survey material was intended to give the flavor of current research.

The following issues are either emerging as new areas of research in object recognition or have shown remarkable staying power and resistance to easy solution by researchers.

1. **Model database size.** Some manufacturing environments will require vision systems to identify objects belonging to a database with thousands of members. However, few existing systems have explicitly addressed the *indexing* problem associated with these databases. Recent work has begun to propose techniques for indexing and tested these techniques on a small set of real models and image data.

2. **Model-driven feature extraction.** Knowledge of recognition domain can provide useful constraints in the attributes of features to be extracted from the image data. These constraints can drive both the selection of feature extraction steps (e.g., absence of curvature estimators for scenes guaranteed to contain only polyhedra), and improve the performance of the extraction modules (e.g., using the known radii of database cylinders to reduce the dimensionality of a scene cylinder's parameter vector estimated via regression).

3. **Representation.** Existing 3D object recognition systems use object models that are limited in representational power. Current restrictions on allowable surface and volume classes (e.g., natural quadric surfaces or superquadric volumes) need to be removed, and representations used frequently in industrial environments (e.g., nonuniform rational B-spline surfaces) will need to be adopted if greater flexibility in object recognition system's behavior is to be expected.

4. **Performance characterization.** Many of the object recognition systems proposed in the literature are inadequately tested. The model database sizes are sometimes unrealistically small (a system's ability to recognize a single object is always described, but not always its ability to reject incorrect models!), and the number of test images (real or synthetic, with unknown or known noise properties) that are used to estimate the system's error rate is usually too small. Researchers have begun to create standard databases of images and models for use in system development and testing. While it is important to avoid straightjacketing the freedom of researchers to pursue creative solutions to the object recognition problem, it is equally important for the vision research community to establish a basis for comparison of systems.

5. **Parallel implementations.** The advent of parallel and distributed processing systems offers potential improvements in the performance of object recognition systems. Parallel algorithms for low-level processing (feature extraction) have been used for several years, but research on parallel techniques for higher-level processing is still in its early stages.

6. **Flexibility.** Unless they are to be operated in environments where the objects to be viewed are known in advance and not likely to change, a

competent object recognition system needs to be able to learn new objects from multiple images. A few systems have been developed for this task, but they assume that the features currently used for object recognition are appropriate to describe the new object. The tendency to use a small set of feature types is a barrier to the flexibility of 3D object recognition systems; reliable learning and recognition of new objects will require that *multiple representations* of object models be maintained, so that objects can be recognized using different feature sets. Moreover, the system should automatically determine those features that are *salient* (descriptive or discriminatory) for a given model, and give those features high priority during matching. Systems should also have the ability to reject collections of image features that do not correspond to any of the database objects.

7. **New sensing technology.** The technology of intensity sensing is fairly mature and 3D object recognition systems employing monochrome imagery are not likely to see drastic improvements in image quality. However, range sensors have steadily improved in speed and decreased in cost for several years. Improvements in stereo sensors will also make sparse range data attractive to system builders.

Drawing on the list above, we now list three specific advances in object recognition systems that would be breakthroughs (there are definitely other areas in which breakthroughs can be made; these three items are only examples): development of a system that (1) recognizes objects from a database of size 500 or larger, such recognition verified by experiments with at least 10 views of each database object; (2) recognizes "sculpted" objects (i.e., objects composed of parametric surface patches) in arbitrary position and orientation, such recognition verified by experiments with at least one hundred real images of the object(s) in the model database; or (3) is capable of learning (from real imagery) new object descriptions for recognition and successfully recognizing such objects, such ability demonstrated using objects of significantly different shapes, sizes, colors, surface textures, and other parameters.

In summary, 3D object recognition is a challenging and interesting research problem with a range of application areas. The strong interest in object recognition is evident from the many long-term research projects devoted to the topic and the variety of techniques developed to solve it. While 3D recognition systems have not yet seen as much use in industry as 2D systems, we feel that it is only a matter of time before robust, capable systems begin to make an impact in these areas.

ACKNOWLEDGMENTS

The research described in this chapter has been supported by the National Science Foundation under grants DCR-8600371 and CDA-8806599, by the GTE Graduate Fellowship program, by the Northrop Research and Technology Center, by the Department of

Computer Science and Engineering at the University of Notre Dame, by the School of Electrical Engineering and Computer Science at Washington State University, and by the Department of Computer Science and the A. H. Case Center for Computer-Aided Design at Michigan State University.

REFERENCES

1. F. Arman and J. Aggarwal, Model-based object recognition in dense range images—A review. *Comput. Surv.* **25**(1), 5–43, 1993.
2. R. Bergevin and M. D. Levine, Generic object recognition: Building coarse 3D descriptions from line drawings. *Proc. IEEE Workshop Interpretation 3D Scenes*, Austin, Tx, p. 68–74, (1989).
3. P. J. Besl and R. C. Jain, Three-dimensional object recognition. *Comput. Surv.* **17**(1), 75–145 (1985).
4. P. J. Besl and N. D. McKay, A method for registration of 3-D shapes. *IEEE Trans. Pattern Anal. Mach. Intell.* **14**(2), 239–256 (1992).
5. I. Biederman, Recognition-by-components: A theory of human image understanding. *Psychol. Rev.* **94**(2), 115–147 (1987).
6. R. M. Bolle, A. Califano, and R. Kjeldsen, A complete and extendable approach to visual recognition. *IEEE Trans. Pattern Anal. Mach. Intell.* **14**(5), 534–548 (1992).
7. O. I. Camps, L. G. Shapiro, and R. M. Haralick, PREMIO: An overview. *Proc. IEEE Workshop Directions Autom. CAD-Based Vision*, Maui, Hawaii, p. 11–21 (1991).
8. C. Chen and A. Kak, A robot vision system for recognizing 3-D objects in low-order polynomial time. *IEEE Trans. Syst., Man, Cybernet.* **SMC-19**(6), 1535–1563 (1989).
9. S. J. Dickinson, A. P. Pentland, and A. Rosenfeld, 3-D shape recovery using distributed aspect matching. *IEEE Trans. Pattern Anal. Mach. Intell.* **14**(2), 174–198 (1992).
10. T.-J. Fan, G. Medioni, and R. Nevatia, Recognizing 3-D objects using surface descriptions. *IEEE Trans. Pattern Anal. Mach. Intell.* **11**(11), 1140–1157 (1989).
11. O. Faugeras and M. Hebert, The representation, recognition, and locating of 3-D objects. *Int. J. Robotics Res.* **5**(3), 27–52 (1986).
12. P. J. Flynn and A. K. Jain. BONSAI: 3D object recognition using constrained search. *IEEE Trans. Pattern Anal. Mach. Intell.* **13**(10), 1066–1075 (1991).
13. P. J. Flynn and A. K. Jain, 3D object recognition using invariant feature indexing of interpretation tables. *Comput. Vision, Graph., Image Proc.: Image Understanding* **55**(2), 119–129 (1992).
14. C. Goad, Fast 3D model-based vision. *In* "From Pixels to Predicates" (A. P. Pentland, ed), pp. 371–391. Ablex, Norwood, Nd, 1986.
15. W. E. L. Grimson, "Object Recognition by Computer." MIT Press, Cambridge, MA, 1990.
16. W. E. L. Grimson and T. Lozano-Pérez, Model-based recognition and localization from sparse range or tactile data. *Int. J. Robotics Res.* **3**(3), 3–35 (1984).

17. C. Hansen and T. Henderson, CAGD-based computer vision. *IEEE Trans. Pattern Anal. Mach. Intell.* **11**(11), 1181–1193 (1989).
18. D. P. Huttenlocher and S. Ullman, Object recognition using alignment. *Proc. Int. Conf. Comp. Vision, 1st*, London, *1987*, pp. 102–111 (1987).
19. K. Ikeuchi and T. Kanade, Automatic generation of object recognition programs. *Proc. IEEE* **76**(8), 1016–1035 (1988).
20. A. K. Jain and R. L. Hoffman, Evidence-based recognition of 3-D objects. *IEEE Trans. Pattern Anal. Mach. Intell.* **10**(6), 783–802 (1988).
21. W.-Y. Kim and A. C. Kak, 3-D object recognition using bipartite matching embedded in discrete relaxation. *IEEE Trans. Pattern Anal. Mach. Intell.* **13**(3), 224–251 (1991).
22. Y. Lamdan, J. T. Schwartz, and H. J. Wolfson, Affine invariant model-based object recognition. *IEEE Trans. Robotics Autom.* **6**(5), 578–589 (1990).
23. D. G. Lowe, Three-dimensional object recognition from single two-dimensional images. *Artif. Intell.* **31**, 355–395 (1987).
24. S. Negahdaripour and A. K. Jain, Challenges in computer vision research: Future direction of research. *Proc. IEEE Conf. Comput. Vision Pattern Recognition*, Champaign-Urbana, IL, *1992*, pp. 189–199 (1992).
25. R. Nevatia and T. O. Binford, Description and recognition of curved objects. *Artif. Intell.* **8**(1), 77–98 (1977).
26. A. P. Pentland, Perceptual organization and the representation of natural form. *Artif. Intell.* **28**, 293–331 (1986).
27. N. S. Raja and A. K. Jain, Recognizing geons from superquadrics fitted to range data. *Image Vision Comput.* **10**(3), 179–190 (1992).
28. F. Solina and R. Bajcsy, Recovery of parametric models from range images: The case for superquadrics with global deformations. *IEEE Trans. Pattern Anal. Mach. Intell.* **12**(2), 131–147 (1990).
29. F. Stein and G. Medioni, Structural indexing: Efficient three-dimensional object recognition. *IEEE Trans. Pattern ANal. Mach. Intell.* **14**(2), 125–145 (1992).
30. P. Suetens, P. Fua, and A. J. Hanson, Computational strategies for object recognition. *Comput. Surv.* **24**(1), 5–61 (1992).

Chapter **15**

Fundamental Principles of Robot Vision

ERNEST L. HALL

Center for Robotics Research
University of Cincinnati
Cincinnati, Ohio

1. INTRODUCTION

The use of visual information to provide knowledge and guidance for a robot manipulator is desirable to facilitate the work of humans. Vision measurements also add capabilities for control since we can control only what we can measure. Visualization for recognition of targets can provide a basis for the guidance of robots and permit global navigation, collision avoidance, or other adaptation or learning techniques. Such vision-guided robots are now used in brain surgery, delivering food to patients, playing a piano, mowing the lawn, and handling hazardous materials. However, the implementations, rather than being straightforward applications of tech-

543

nology, have been extremely difficult. In general this has resulted in machines that were not robust and were limited in performance. This has also uncovered research problems on topics that are being intensively studied today. The search for a truly intelligent robot is continuing.

Robotics and machine vision are considered totally separate disciplines by many. However, the proper combination of vision sensors to a manipulator under computer control can provide an intelligent machine that can perform work useful to humans. The combination of these three components, shown in Fig. 15.1, can perform much more than the individual robot, vision system, or computer, a Gestalt accomplishment.

From the onset of the use of robots in the industrial arena, the problem of integrating these new machines with existing processes has proved difficult. Some problems have arisen because of a lack of knowledge about intelligent systems as well as difficulties in the training of end-users. Most

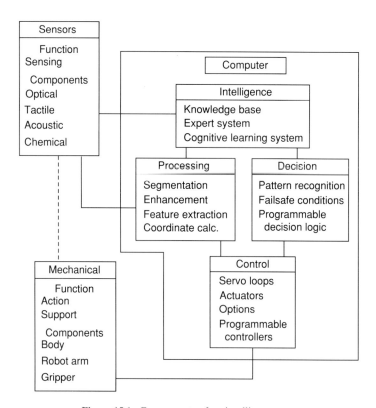

Figure 15.1. Components of an intelligent system.

robots have been used in applications where major intelligence was not a necessity and little modification was needed with existing automation. As new tasks become considered for robot utilization the development of "intelligent" devices has emerged and rekindled interest in expert system algorithms and the employment of multiple sensory systems such as vision, tactile, and ultrasonic. One area is automated materials handling and processing, which includes such problems as automated palletizing, bin picking, automated storage and retrieval, automated kitting of parts for assembly, and automated materials handling.

In Section 2, the fundamental concepts of an intelligent robot are presented in an attempt to show why robot vision is essential. Then some applications for inspection and control are presented in Sections 3 and 4, respectively. Conclusions and recommendations for further research are given in Section 5.

2. ROBOT VISION

It is easy to see intelligence or the lack of it in humans, but trying to define it in terms of machines conjures up science fiction themes. At present, robots cannot display original thought leading to complex solutions. However, with the use of expert system algorithms, a robot can appear to "think" in a logical manner and actually solve difficult problems that appear to require intelligence.

The use of intelligent robots that consist of specialized computer programs, robot manipulators, and sensors has now been demonstrated in a variety of situations. For example, various game-playing systems such as robot checkers and peg games have been developed as educational demonstrations. Game playing represents a form of intelligence that is easily understood. A game usually has a set of rules defining a competition, including the permissible set of actions. The elements of a game are defined and easily understood, and the set of actions required are also defined. The game rules specify the computer and sensor problems. The set of actions defines the robot manipulator requirements (1). If a common game is selected for a demonstration, it can rightly be called a "trivial pursuit" since the rules of the game and actions are common knowledge. However, the accomplishment of a game by an automated machine, especially for the first time, is neither commonplace nor lacking in importance, because it demonstrates the capabilities of robots for real-world applications.

2.1. Intelligent Robot Systems

2.1.1. Some Previous Intelligent Machines

Much of the early development of intelligent robots can be traced to research at the Massachusetts Institute of Technology in the early 1950s (2). Shannon in 1955 implemented a maze-following electronic mouse. In 1970, modern research in mobile robots was conducted at Stanford University with the design of Shakey by Nitzan. Mobile robotics is now a popular and growing research area. Approximately 10 years later, a robot equipped with vision was utilized by Minsky to stack blocks. Further refinements of this idea have led to the development of the expert system for palletizing random size and weight parcels at the University of Cincinnati (3).

Some recent examples of game-playing robots may be found in a book on robotics including a robot solution to Rubik's cube (4) and a checker-playing robot. Other systems that have not been as well documented include a blackjack-playing vision-guided robot developed and demonstrated by Cincinnati Milacron, several mobile robot competitions called the "seeker contest" sponsored by the Southeastern regional IEEE, the micromouse competition sponsored by the Western regional IEEE, and a recent ping-pong robot competition that originated in Great Britain but was also conducted in Europe and the United States. A vision-guided, dexterous manipulator that reads sheet music and plays an organ was developed at Waseda University and demonstrated at the World's Fair in Japan in 1984 might also be called a game-playing robot since the act of performing music has a set of rules and actions.

2.1.2. A Demonstration Manufacturing Cell

A multirobot workcell consisting of a burn stamp stand, a General Electric P50 (5-axis) robot, an A40 (4-axis) robot, a General Motors Fanuc A1 (4-axis) robot, and a General Electric Optovision II imaging system was designed and constructed to manufacture the peg solitaire game.

A typical workcell consists of the P50 robot manufacturing the game board, the A40 robot playing the game, and the A1 robot using the burn stamp to place the rules on the board. A conveyor then brings the packaged game to a predetermined destination. Implementing the vision system and artificial intelligence algorithm for peg detection, the robot plays the game to demonstrate the marriage of artificial intelligence to a robotic system to produce an "intelligence-guided" robot system (5). The technology and techniques developed to build and then find a solution to this game establish the capabilities of an intelligent robotics system to solve a real-world problem.

The game is made up of a triangular piece of wood with 15 drilled holes arranged in a bowling pin configuration. Wooden pegs are placed into all but one of the holes, and the game can commence. A move consists of the robot gripper picking up a peg, jumping an adjacent peg, placing the peg into the empty hole on the opposite side of the jumped peg, and removing the jumped peg from the board. This operation continues until only one peg is left or the player is unable to make more jumps. A robot or human player wins the game if only one peg is left standing on the board.

To communicate to the other components of the workcell, an input/output controller contains a set of switches so that any interface condition can be simulated. These switches are then linked to the interface capabilities of the robot controller and the vision system computer. Mounted on the robot wrist are three independent end-effectors or grippers. The first is simply an electric drill for boring the holes; the second can grasp the wood preforms; and the last has specialized fingers for gripping the wooden pegs during the game-playing process.

The final processing step consists of placing the preform on the burn stand stamp to have the rules and University of Cincinnati logo imprinted on the game board. After loading the board, one peg is removed and the game is placed under the vision system to determine what solution of the game to play. Since the board is symmetric, a computer simulation is executed to determine the number of possible game solutions, there are five fixed solutions for this game. The procedure of how to play them are recorded as separate robot programs and the algorithm to determine the missing peg triggers the input/output binary code to send the robot controller to solve the game. Then quickly, precisely, and with no trial-and-error learning, the robot solves the game. It is capable of achieving this goal faster than its human counterparts. A recent discovery by the authors show a new solution that leaves the peg back in the original missing peg location.

2.1.3. Mobile Robot for Material Handling

Perhaps one of the more novel intelligent robot systems designed by the Center for Robotics Research is the automated robot lawn mower. Utilization of mobility will further increase future robot capability and adaptability. For example, instead of having to modify the facility to bring the work to the robot, the mobile intelligent robot will drive to the appropriate location, carry out the assigned tasks, and then proceed to the next location.

Mobile automation is a unique area of research in which major innovation is needed not only in industry but for biomedical and military applications as well. Automatically guided vehicles are equipped with wheels, tracks, or legs; manipulator arms and special tools; sensors that permit adaptation and safe operation in a changing environment; computers for control and intelligence; and power sources. The lawn mower device may become one of the first practical domestic robots, demonstrating a new mobile robot system design and a new navigation method with a novel omnidirectional vision system.

A manual teaching operation allows the robot to generate point-to-point movement, and storage of these moves by the on-board computer is necessary to teach the robot lawn mower the moving pattern. In the manual teach programming mode, the robotic lawn mower, like most industrial robots, will learn its path from starting point to endpoint through the point-to-point motion, which is controlled by a human operator. For the point-to-point operation, a remote teach pendant and a control computer was used (6). Ultimately, the manual teach pendant phase will be replaced by one with fully automated capacities.

In order to operate in the automatic mode, some major tasks are executed that involve automatic guidance to adapt to altering work environments. These tasks include an automatic positioning procedure, automatic high-level path planning, and automatic obstacle and collision avoidance. An integral decision processing is implemented by an artificial intelligent computer. It focuses on a generic concept of automatic navigation for mobile robots (7).

2.1.4. Space-Filling Applications: Bin Packing

Space-filling techniques represent a new methodology that can be applied to industrial applications in the area of packaging a bin or container. As an example, the simple task of stacking random parcels onto a pallet seems very trivial to a human. The human implements vision to determine available locations and a high-level knowledge system to decide the most appropriate space for a given box. To accomplish this task using an automated system requires many steps to be executed. A key decision of this scheme is how to represent the pallet volume in computer memory.

The representation of three-dimensional volume may be done in several ways such as surfaces or solid representation. In the solid representation the pallet and parcel volumes are depicted by discrete volume elements or voxels. This technique permits a discrete computer representation that can be thought of as a three-dimensional array $V(x, y, z)$, where V is equal to

0 for empty regions and 1 for full regions. In order to apply region filling to the pallet, a relational database about the boxes must be established. The pallet volume could be filled with one box or with a multiple of other box volumes.

The next generation of robots must contain a computer utilizing some high-level language for the controller. These expert system robots are beginning to be developed for a variety of tasks. One such system was devised at the University of Cincinnati for the random palletizing of mixed-size and mixed-weight parcels. Most robots are able to stack cartons of the same unit load or several different unit loads without additional software. The Center for Robotics Research has developed an algorithm in OPS5 code running under list processing language (LISP) that has approximately 400 rules used to stack a good pallet of mixed size and weight parcels in a random delivery system. Because a heuristic approach is incorporated, a "good" solution may not be the optimal solution. But, with existing practice in the distribution industry, it will pass inspection as a good pallet. Some of these rules consist of interlocking and intermeshing, toxicity of contents, and crushability. The voxel elements establish the knowledge database scheme for determining stacking relationships. The expert system will also incorporate multiple sensors into its design (8).

To generalize palletizing, a robot or automated palletizer must be able to locate an object, determine how to pick up that object, and decide where to stack the object on the basis of an expert system space filling algorithm. The long-term goal of this research is to develop a useful algorithm about random palletizing for mixed size, content, and shape objects, both as a basic science problem and to perform experimental applications to illustrate its usefulness for industrial applications. Techniques devised by other researchers will augment this effort in applications such as bin picking. Improving on the earlier work is an increase in complexity as a specific solution for random palletizing is generalized for all shapes, sizes, and contents on a single pallet.

The short-term goal is to improve the logic and design of the existing space-filling expert system for palletizing. Additional shapes will be added to existing parcels to begin the generalization process of the algorithm. Another development will be the start of rewriting the existing code into a more transportable language. This will permit an increase in operational efficiency of the overall system.

2.1.5. Space-Emptying Applications: Bin Picking

Robots and robotics technology having been successfully implemented in many simple tasks. We now face the challenge of using them in more difficult applications. It is now apparent that a robot has to function in a much more adaptable manner with the environment. This may be done by expanding to move complex part geometries, novel data structures, and advanced artificial intelligence tasks, such as learning, to accomplish a difficult task. In industrial applications, a robot should be capable of picking up a workpiece from a bin, orienting it, placing it into a container or machine, and performing some operation such as welding, painting, or etching on it. Another reason for tackling a problem like bin picking is that there is a practical need for its solution. One of the remaining obstacles to the widespread introduction of industrial robots is their inability to identify and grasp parts that are not precisely positioned. The dilemma of picking randomly oriented parts from a bin could be solved if vision capability were available to analyze the mixture of parts. Intensive research in vision around the world guarantees that improved visual processing capabilities will shortly allow robots to work with overlapping objects on cluttered backgrounds with unconstrained conditions (9).

The area of investigation being studied at the University of Cincinnati involves "bin picking" using moment and instantaneous invariants. This bin-picking problem requires both object recognition and manipulation. It consists of a recognition component and a manipulation component. Three-dimensional object recognition using perspective moment invariants has been recently investigated (10–12). To acquire three-dimensional data from images, we will use surface measurements. The moment invariants approach is reasonable for three-dimensional object recognition because the moments can be global or local features of an object. Instantaneous invariants are powerful tools for the study of the inverse motion in a robot mechanism.

To manipulate an object, a robot must know where it is (position and orientation), what it is (recognition), and where to move it or what to do with it (path location). The picking problems may be considered in terms of increasing complexity or difficulty. The easiest question is picking up an isolated part from a flat two-dimensional surface, and the most difficult may be picking up an arbitrary object from an unstructured environment. Picking up an object can involve several steps. For example, consider the task of pulling a nail from a board; first, tentative objects, nail heads, must be pinpointed in terms of position and orientation; then, a force control must be used until the nail is released. This problem is quite easily accomplished by most humans, but it presents a number of difficult technical challenges for robots, because it requires coordinated vision, sensing, force control, and manipulation, none of which have been developed to a sufficient degree to make this type of task subject to economically viable automation.

A goal of such research is improved understanding of three-dimensional object recognition and manipulation under the control of a robot vision system for bin-picking problems. This requires both object recognition and manipulation. To grasp an object, it is necessary to determine the orientation and position of objects relative to a robot gripper. The movement of a robot gripper relative to objects and the relationships between objects is also important.

A principal problem of the moment invariant approach is in acquiring three- (or four-, etc.) dimensional data for object recognition. Three-dimensional object recognition may involve object manipulation because parts of the object are hidden from a simple image view. Several tentative recognition decisions may be required. In recognition using three-dimensional data, models of the object are compared to some unknown image, which may require an implementation with parallel processing. The advantage of invariant recognition is that it is possible to generate the same orientation, and ambiguity may be removed by additional region analysis derived from edge detection and line segmentation.

2.1.6. Search for Intelligent Machines

As shown by the previous examples, robot "intelligence" has been demonstrated by a variety of games and applications. In a game, perhaps a necessary ingredient is "uselessness." However, in the applications, a necessary justification of the machine is its "usefulness." What is it about these machines that makes their design such a challenge in both situations?

Perhaps the underlying mystery is that we are not cognizant of human intelligence, although we may feel confident in being able to "know it when we see it." A characteristic of all the games is that they can be described by astoundingly simple arithmetic or logical relations. The most challenging games have such an enormous state space that exhaustive enumeration of all possible solutions is not practical, say, on the order of 2^{64}. Since we have computers with 2^{32} memory locations, it seems likely that in just a few years, the games with 2^{64} states may become deterministic and, thus, lose their mystery. Examples of such games are chess, checkers, and a 64-ring tower of Hanoi. Simulated randomness can always be inserted into game decisions to retain their amusement value, but the problems they represent will be theoretically solved.

The same cannot be said about human intelligence except perhaps by psychologists or sociologists. In a demonstration of the peg solitaire robot to a group of psychology professors, the author first passed the game around to the humans with the challenge that in Psychology I, he was taught that "intelligence was what an intelligence test measured" and here was an opportunity to test their IQs. None of the audience was able to solve the game. They were then shown the robot playing the perfect game. So, if intelligence is what an intelligence test measures, machines can come out ahead. The important point is that in attempting to build intelligent robots, we may come closer to understanding human intelligence. We can, at least, present some interesting challenges to currently accepted practices.

Adaptability is another feature of intelligence in human and machine. The most intelligent robot today can be simply unplugged. One minor malfunction can incapacitate the entire machine. Redundancy of function is at least a partial solution to this. The human arm has more than 7 degrees of freedom, which may be used to move the hand to any point in three-dimensional space with any of three possible orientations, which requires only 6 degrees of freedom. Redundant degree-of-freedom machines are now being built. Self-diagnosis and self-maintenance are also being studied. To accomplish these diagnostic decisions, sensors of the state of the machine are needed for full adaptability, and sensors of the state of nature are required. The work in robot vision, tactile sensors, and other sensors is progressing; however, the problem called "multisensor fusion" has also been recognized. If more than one sensor is used to determine a state, then it is possible to have incongruence of the sensor outputs. A human in space may encounter little or no input from the balance sensors in the ear, be touching the wall as indicated by tactile and kinesthetic sensors in an arm, and see the interior of the spacecraft upside down. Vision, since humans receive over 70% of their information through their eyes, would probably be believed; however, unless at least one other sensor becomes congruent with the visual, the human might still have a difficult time moving about. For example, even an earth-bound human cannot be mobile using sight alone.

Even though we know sensors are essential to adaptability, they alone are not enough, and confusion can arise when the sensor inputs are not congruent. The expedient solution for incongruent sensors is to not move.

Learning is another feature of intelligence and a great deal of recent interest in "neural networks" can be observed. Learning has traditionally been divided into two types: supervised learning with a teacher and unsupervised learning from experience. A recent joke asks: How do you develop good judgment? Answer—experience. And, how does one develop experience? Answer—bad judgment.

The mathematical theory of statistical and structural pattern recognition is well developed, and recent advances are quite impressive. In the past, unsupervised learning or clustering has been used but the time required has often been considered impractical. With the emphasis on parallel computing, these solutions are of much more interest.

To end this discussion, we are reminded of the ancient question: How does one find the lions in the desert? Obviously, build a sieve that lets sand through but not lions. Then simply filter out the sand and what remains will be lions.

Most of our past and current research is still directed toward actions that appear intelligent. However, avoiding some actions is just as important, such as injuring humans.

2.1.7. Fundamental Theorem of Robot Vision

One may reasonably question the connection of the words *robot* and *vision*, since each noun supports a discipline of its own. Of the many answers possible, let us consider one as a rather fundamental idea.

> The manipulation of a point in space x_1 by either a robot manipulator that moves it to another point x_2 or through a camera system that images the point onto a camera sensor at x_2, is described by the same matrix transformation, which is of the form

$$x_2 = Tx_1.$$

> The transformation matrix T can describe the first-order effects of translation, rotation, scaling, and projective and perspective projections.

This theorem suggests that the sensing and manipulation of a point or collection of points on an object has some relation. Now the question is how to exploit this relation to build an intelligent robot system. We can proceed in either of the two logical approaches that have served science so well in the past: deduction or induction.

2.2. Deductive Approach

Proceeding by deduction to understand "intelligent machines" leads us into the study of human intelligence. Cognitive scientists study perception, cognition, and action. Since human behavior is what we are attempting to understand, perhaps psychologists are our best teachers. This thought led us into a year-long cross-disciplinary seminar course between our psychology and engineering colleagues. Everyone who attended this course learned a great deal. My impression at the end of the year was that human intelligence was tremendously superior to anything we have so far demonstrated in machine intelligence. The most promising technology seemed to be neural networks for learning and adaption. Nearly all the students from this course have gone on to study neural approaches but with the understanding that human behavior, although exhibiting the highest forms of intelligence, also from time to time exhibits actions that can only be described as "horrid." That is, even if we understood human intelligence, our problem of understanding intelligent machines would not be solved. We would still need work to make our robot obey Asimov's "laws of robotics." The inductive approach has led to a much greater appreciation of human intelligence and to the rise of neural networks as a major research area.

2.3. Inductive Reasoning

The other logical approach is inductive reasoning. Here we attempt to understand specific intelligent machines in the hope of discovering the fundamental laws of robot vision. This approach is currently being followed around the world because even though the fundamental laws may not be discovered, something useful may be produced with the specific machine. If we can build a machine that accomplished "action X," we may have discovered a new, useful, and nonobvious solution to an old problem. The historical developments used the inductive approach.

2.4. An Example — Flatland Robot

To provide a concrete example, let us consider a two-dimensional, or flatland robot, in sufficient mathematical detail, to illustrate the three corners, machine vision, manipulators, and controls, which box us in today's world of limited intelligent machines.

Let us start by introducing a notation that lets us move objects about. We will concentrate on rigid body motion, although the concepts can be easily extended. One of the simplest motions is a translation. Translation is a nonlinear transformation. A linear transformation, $g = T(f)$, satisfies two properties:

1. $ag = T(af)$
2. $g_1 + g_2 = T(f_1 + f_2)$ if $g_1 = T(f_1), g_2 = T(f_2)$

Let us try this with the translation: $x_2 = x_1 + h = T(x_1)$

1. $x_3 = ax_1 + h \neq ax_2$
2. $x_3 = (x_1 + x_2) + h \neq x_1 + h + x_2 + h$

Since neither of the conditions are satisfied, a dilemma is encountered at the beginning of our attempt to describe object motion mathematically. If we attempt a matrix description, we quickly see that translation cannot be represented by a 2×2 matrix operation

$$\begin{bmatrix} x_1 \\ y_1 \end{bmatrix} = \begin{bmatrix} a & b \\ c & d \end{bmatrix} \begin{bmatrix} x \\ y \end{bmatrix},$$

or

$$x_1 = ax + by,$$

$$y_1 = cx + dy,$$

but

$$x_1 = x + h,$$

$$y_1 = y + k.$$

Now, translation may be represented by a 2×3 matrix operation:

$$\begin{bmatrix} x_1 \\ y_1 \end{bmatrix} = \begin{bmatrix} 1 & 0 & h \\ 0 & 1 & k \end{bmatrix} \begin{bmatrix} x \\ y \\ 1 \end{bmatrix}.$$

However, since the matrix is not square, there is no inverse matrix. To alleviate these problems, we introduce the concept of homogeneous coordinates. The homogeneous coordinates of a two-dimensional physical point are given by the three-dimensional vector:

$$\begin{pmatrix} x \\ y \end{pmatrix} \quad \text{are} \quad \begin{pmatrix} wx \\ wy \\ w \end{pmatrix}.$$

Note that the conversion from homogeneous coordinates to physical coordinates simply requires division by w (called the *scale* term) and elimination of the third component. By using homogeneous coordinates, we homogenize the transformations (make them have the same structure). In homogeneous coordinates, translation is linear:

$$\begin{bmatrix} x_1 \\ y_1 \\ 1 \end{bmatrix} = \begin{bmatrix} 1 & 0 & h \\ 0 & 1 & k \\ 0 & 0 & 1 \end{bmatrix} \begin{bmatrix} x \\ y \\ 1 \end{bmatrix},$$

and the translation matrix has an easily computed inverse. If we move a point to the right and up with values $(-h, -k)$, we can move it to the left and down with values (h, k):

$$\begin{bmatrix} x \\ y \\ 1 \end{bmatrix} = \begin{bmatrix} 1 & 0 & -h \\ 0 & 1 & -k \\ 0 & 0 & 1 \end{bmatrix} \begin{bmatrix} x_1 \\ y_1 \\ 1 \end{bmatrix}.$$

The next common manipulation on an object is to rotate it. The rotation of a point clockwise or of the coordinate system counterclockwise may be described by

$$x_2 = x_1 \cos \theta + y_1 \sin \theta,$$

$$y_2 = -x_1 \sin \theta + y_1 \cos \theta.$$

Rotation is a linear transformation and may be represented by a 2×2 matrix operation:

$$\begin{bmatrix} x_2 \\ y_2 \end{bmatrix} = \begin{bmatrix} \cos \theta & \sin \theta \\ -\sin \theta & \cos \theta \end{bmatrix} \begin{bmatrix} x_1 \\ y_1 \end{bmatrix}.$$

The homogeneous coordinate representation is

$$\begin{bmatrix} x_2 \\ y_2 \\ 1 \end{bmatrix} = \begin{bmatrix} \cos \theta & \sin \theta & 0 \\ -\sin \theta & \cos \theta & 0 \\ 0 & 0 & 1 \end{bmatrix} \begin{bmatrix} x_1 \\ y_1 \\ 1 \end{bmatrix}.$$

The inverse is easily computed. Rotations are orthonormal transformations:

$$\begin{bmatrix} x_1 \\ y_1 \\ 1 \end{bmatrix} = \begin{bmatrix} \cos \theta & -\sin \theta & 0 \\ \sin \theta & \cos \theta & 0 \\ 0 & 0 & 1 \end{bmatrix} \begin{bmatrix} x_2 \\ y_2 \\ 1 \end{bmatrix}.$$

Scaling operations such as magnification, minification, and shearing, may also be represented by matrix operations:

$$\begin{bmatrix} x_2 \\ y_2 \end{bmatrix} = \begin{bmatrix} s_1 & 0 \\ 0 & s_2 \end{bmatrix} \begin{bmatrix} x_1 \\ y_1 \end{bmatrix}.$$

If $s_1 > 1$, magnification occurs; if $s_1 < 1$, minification occurs; if s_1 is not equal to s_2, shearing occurs.

Scaling may also be accomplished using the w term in homogeneous coordinates:

$$\begin{bmatrix} x_2 \\ y_2 \\ s \end{bmatrix} = \begin{bmatrix} 1 & 0 & 0 \\ 0 & 1 & 0 \\ 0 & 0 & s \end{bmatrix} \begin{bmatrix} x_1 \\ y_1 \\ 1 \end{bmatrix}.$$

In converting these homogeneous coordinates to physical coordinates, an inverse scaling is accomplished:

$$\begin{bmatrix} \dfrac{x_2}{s} \\[2ex] \dfrac{y_2}{s} \end{bmatrix}.$$

The nonlinear perspective transformation induced by a camera system can also be described by a linear transformation in homogeneous coordinates. The transformation from an object located at $(x_0, y_0)^T$, to an image at $(0, y_i)^T$ through a lens with center on the x axis at location $x = f$, is often presented through the use of similar triangles:

$$y_i = y_0 \left(\frac{f}{f - x_0} \right).$$

In homogeneous coordinates, the perspective transformation is

$$\begin{bmatrix} x_i \\ y_i \\ w_i \end{bmatrix} = \begin{bmatrix} 1 & 0 & 0 \\ 0 & 1 & 0 \\ -\dfrac{1}{f} & 0 & 1 \end{bmatrix} \begin{bmatrix} x_0 \\ y_0 \\ 1 \end{bmatrix}.$$

The reduction in dimensionality caused by projecting an object point onto an image plane may also be represented by a linear transformation in homogeneous coordinates. For projection onto the y axis or $x = 0$ plane, the x coordinate is essentially discarded by the following transformation:

$$\begin{bmatrix} 0 \\ y_i \\ w_i \end{bmatrix} = \begin{bmatrix} 0 & 0 & 0 \\ 0 & 1 & 0 \\ 0 & 0 & 1 \end{bmatrix} \begin{bmatrix} x_1 \\ y_1 \\ w_1 \end{bmatrix}.$$

Note that this matrix is singular and therefore has no inverse. Recovering this lost information is the goal of many three-dimensional techniques such as stereo and shape from shading.

Let us now consider a specific example that shows not only the use of the transformation matrices but also that the extension to three dimensions is relatively easy.

2.4.1. *Example 1: Perspective Transformation*

Consider a unit cube in three dimensions. It is described by the vertex coordinates:

Vertex	x	y	z
a	0	0	0
b	0	0	1
c	0	1	0
d	0	1	1
e	1	0	0
f	1	0	1
g	1	1	0
h	1	1	1

Let us determine the perspective, projective transformation on the plane defined by $z = 4$ with the camera lens centered at $(\frac{1}{2}, \frac{1}{2}, 2)^T$. To determine the transformed image, we will first translate the coordinate system to one with the lens center on the z axis. Considering the original object coordinate system as the global coordinates, we may transform to lens-centered coordinates by the following translation of the coordinate system:

$$\begin{bmatrix} x_l \\ y_l \\ z_l \\ w_l \end{bmatrix} = \begin{bmatrix} 1 & 0 & 0 & -0.5 \\ 0 & 1 & 0 & -0.5 \\ 0 & 0 & 1 & -4 \\ 0 & 0 & 0 & 1 \end{bmatrix} \begin{bmatrix} x_g \\ y_g \\ z_g \\ w_g \end{bmatrix}.$$

This transformation moves the global origin to the point $(-0.5, -0.5, -4)^T$. The perspective transformation is now simplified since the optical axis is along the z axis and the lens center is located at $z = -2$. The perspective transformation may now be written as

$$\begin{bmatrix} x_c \\ y_c \\ z_c \\ w_c \end{bmatrix} = \begin{bmatrix} 1 & 0 & 0 & 0 \\ 0 & 1 & 0 & 0 \\ 0 & 0 & 1 & 0 \\ 0 & 0 & 0.5 & 1 \end{bmatrix} \begin{bmatrix} x_1 \\ y_1 \\ z_1 \\ w_1 \end{bmatrix}.$$

This transformation produces the scaling relation:

$$w_c = \frac{z_i}{2} + w_i.$$

The projection of the transformed object points onto the image plane, $z_i = 0$, is accomplished with the following transformation:

$$\begin{bmatrix} x_z \\ y_z \\ 0 \\ w_z \end{bmatrix} = \begin{bmatrix} 1 & 0 & 0 & 0 \\ 0 & 1 & 0 & 0 \\ 0 & 0 & 0 & 0 \\ 0 & 0 & 0 & 1 \end{bmatrix} \begin{bmatrix} x_c \\ y_c \\ z_c \\ w_c \end{bmatrix}.$$

The product of these matrices may now be computed to simplify the computation. The resulting matrix is

$$\begin{bmatrix} x_z \\ y_z \\ 0 \\ w_z \end{bmatrix} = \begin{bmatrix} 1 & 0 & 0 & -0.5 \\ 0 & 1 & 0 & -0.5 \\ 0 & 0 & 0 & 0 \\ 0 & 0 & 0.5 & -1 \end{bmatrix} \begin{bmatrix} x_c \\ y_c \\ z_c \\ w_c \end{bmatrix}.$$

The original object vertex points in homogeneous coordinates are

$$\begin{bmatrix} x_g \\ y_g \\ z_g \\ w_g \end{bmatrix} = \begin{bmatrix} 0 & 0 & 0 & 0 & 1 & 1 & 1 & 1 \\ 0 & 0 & 1 & 1 & 0 & 0 & 1 & 1 \\ 0 & 1 & 0 & 1 & 0 & 1 & 0 & 1 \\ 1 & 1 & 1 & 1 & 1 & 1 & 1 & 1 \end{bmatrix}.$$

The new image coordinates are given by the following:

$$\begin{bmatrix} x_z \\ y_z \\ 0 \\ w_z \end{bmatrix} = \begin{bmatrix} -0.5 & -0.5 & -0.5 & -0.5 & -0.5 & -0.5 & -0.5 & -0.5 \\ -0.5 & -0.5 & 0.5 & 0.5 & -0.5 & -0.5 & 0.5 & 0.5 \\ 0 & 0 & 0 & 0 & 0 & 0 & 0 & 0 \\ -1 & -0.5 & -1 & -0.5 & -1 & -0.5 & -1 & -0.5 \end{bmatrix}.$$

The physical image coordinates determined with respect to the image coordinate system are as follows:

Vertex	x	y
a'	0.5	0.5
b'	1	1
c'	0.5	-0.5
d'	1	-1
e'	-0.5	0.5
f'	-1	1
g'	-0.5	-0.5
h'	-1	-1

These image points would be recorded by an image sensor. Several vision interpretation problems can now be posed. How does one recognize the object from the image data? How does one determine the centroid position of the object? How does one determine the orientation of the object? How does one recover the three-dimensional coordinates of the object vertices?

For completeness we may also compute the image vertex points with respect to the global coordinate system:

Vertex	x	y	z
a''	1	1	4
b''	1.5	1.5	4
c''	1	0	4
d''	1.5	-0.5	4
e''	0	1	4
f''	-0.5	1.5	4
g''	0	0	4
h''	-0.5	-0.5	4

If the camera position and orientation are known, then absolute object coordinates may be determined. These coordinates may be used to guide the motion of a robot.

2.4.2. Example 2: The Flatland Robot

To illustrate that the matrix transformations are also useful for robot manipulation, let us consider a two-dimensional example with a manipulator called the *flatland robot*. This example will let us see the concepts while avoiding many of the complexities of robots with more degrees of freedom. We will consider four related problems associated with this robot. The first is simply to describe where the robot is in space, the kinematics, given the parameters of the robot, and the Cartesian coordinates of the point. The kinematic descriptions involve joint angle variables for rotary joints or linear variables for prismatic joints. The flatland robot has rotational variables. The Jacobian matrix, which relates small changes between joint and Cartesian spaces is also important to relate linear and angular velocities in the two spaces. The second problem, called the *inverse kinematic solution*, involves determination of the inverse transformation from Cartesian to joint space. The next two problems deal with explaining rather than describing the motion of the robot. The dynamic equations include both static and dynamic forces and torques and relate the joint accelerations to the torques that produce the motion. The inverse dynamic equations let us determine the accelerations that will be produced by given torques. The dynamic equations also indicate the characteristics of the system that are needed for automatic control of the robot.

Again, we need a notation to permit a mathematical description of the motion. One important concept is to impose, at each joint of the robot, a coordinate system or frame. For our example, we place one at the base, another at the elbow, and another at the hand. Consider a point $\mathbf{P} = (x_1, y_1)^T$, defined with respect to the hand coordinate frame. We would like to develop the transformations to describe this same point with respect to the base coordinate frame. This may be accomplished by a series of matrix transformation that correspond to the translations and rotations required to move the coordinate system from the wrist to the base. We will again use homogeneous coordinates since they permit the same size matrices to be used for all the motions.

The point is described in homogeneous coordinates by

$$\mathbf{P} = \begin{bmatrix} x_1 \\ y_1 \\ 1 \end{bmatrix}.$$

The transformations required to describe this point in base or global coordinates are simply

$$\mathbf{x} = \mathbf{A}_4 \mathbf{A}_3 \mathbf{A}_2 \mathbf{A}_1 \mathbf{P} = \mathbf{TP},$$

where the individual matrices are

$$A_1 = \begin{bmatrix} x_2 \\ y_2 \\ 1 \end{bmatrix} = \begin{bmatrix} 1 & 0 & l_2 \\ 0 & 1 & 0 \\ 0 & 0 & 1 \end{bmatrix} \begin{bmatrix} x_1 \\ y_1 \\ 1 \end{bmatrix},$$

$$A_2 = \begin{bmatrix} x_3 \\ y_3 \\ 1 \end{bmatrix} = \begin{bmatrix} \cos\theta_2 & \sin\theta_2 & 0 \\ -\sin\theta_2 & \cos\theta_2 & 0 \\ 0 & 0 & 1 \end{bmatrix} \begin{bmatrix} x_2 \\ y_2 \\ 1 \end{bmatrix},$$

$$A_3 = \begin{bmatrix} x_4 \\ y_4 \\ 1 \end{bmatrix} = \begin{bmatrix} 1 & 0 & l_1 \\ 0 & 1 & 0 \\ 0 & 0 & 1 \end{bmatrix} \begin{bmatrix} x_3 \\ y_3 \\ 1 \end{bmatrix},$$

$$A_4 = \begin{bmatrix} x_5 \\ y_5 \\ 1 \end{bmatrix} = \begin{bmatrix} \cos\theta_1 & \sin\theta_1 & 0 \\ -\sin\theta_1 & \cos\theta_1 & 0 \\ 0 & 0 & 1 \end{bmatrix} \begin{bmatrix} x_4 \\ y_4 \\ 1 \end{bmatrix}.$$

At this point we must compute the matrix products, and the equations become rather long. For simplicity let us introduce the notation $s_i = \sin(\theta_i)$

and $c_i = \cos(\theta_i)$. The matrix products can be computed in a variety of ways. Here are some examples:

$$A_2 A_1 = \begin{bmatrix} c_2 & -s_2 & l_2 c_2 \\ s_2 & c_2 & l_2 s_2 \\ 0 & 0 & 1 \end{bmatrix},$$

$$A_4 A_3 = \begin{bmatrix} c_1 & -s_1 & l_1 c_1 \\ s_1 & c_1 & l_1 s_1 \\ 0 & 0 & 1 \end{bmatrix},$$

and

$$T = A_4 A_3 A_2 A_1 = \begin{bmatrix} c_1 c_2 - s_1 s_2 & -c_1 s_2 - s_1 c_2 & l_2 c_1 c_2 - l_2 s_1 s_2 + l_1 c_1 \\ s_1 c_2 + c_1 s_2 & -s_1 s_2 + c_1 c_2 & l_2 s_1 c_2 + l_2 c_1 s_2 + l_1 s_1 \\ 0 & 0 & 1 \end{bmatrix}.$$

Although this equation looks quite complicated, there is a special case in which it simplifies. The location of the tip of the arm is at the origin of the hand coordinate system, $(x_1, y_1)^T = (0, 0)^T$.

At this point the matrix transformation simplifies to

$$x = l_2 c_1 c_2 - l_2 s_1 s_2 + l_1 c_1,$$

$$y = l_2 s_1 c_2 + l_2 c_1 s_2 + l_1 s_1.$$

This solution may be verified from a geometric viewpoint. The generalization of this technique is called the *Denavit–Hartenberg* notation and is easily applied to any multilink manipulator (open kinematic chain). Programs are also available to perform symbolic manipulation of the matrices.

2.4.3. Inverse Kinematics

A derivation of the inverse kinematics is much more difficult than the forward kinematic equations. Examples of solutions may be found in Klaus and Horn (9) and an expert system program is described in Mu et al. (13). When one realizes that the inverse dynamic solution is essential before the construction of an industrial robot, it shows the importance of these solutions. For the flatland robot, the solution is as follows:

$$\cos \theta_2 = \frac{x^2 + y^2 - l_1^2 - l_2^2}{2 l_1 l_2}.$$

There are two solutions for Θ_2 that are of equal magnitude and opposite signs corresponding to the two arm positions that can reach the same point:

$$\tan \theta_1 = \frac{(y/x) - (l_2 \sin \theta_2)/(l_1 + l_2 \cos \theta_2)}{1 + (y/x)(l_2 \sin \theta_2/l_1 + l_2 \cos \theta_2)}.$$

The inverse kinematic equations may be used to determine the joint angles required to position the robot at a given Cartesian space point. They may also be used to determine practical facts such as the workspace of the robot or to simulate its motion.

The kinematic equations may also be written as

$$x = l_1 \cos \theta_1 + l_2 \cos(\theta_1 + \theta_2),$$

$$y = l_1 \sin \theta_1 + l_2 \sin(\theta_1 + \theta_2),$$

or

$$\mathbf{dx} = \begin{bmatrix} dx \\ dy \end{bmatrix} = \begin{bmatrix} \dfrac{\partial x}{\partial \theta_1} & \dfrac{\partial x}{\partial \theta_2} \\ \dfrac{\partial y}{\partial \theta_1} & \dfrac{\partial y}{\partial \theta_2} \end{bmatrix} \begin{bmatrix} d\theta_1 \\ d\theta_2 \end{bmatrix} = \mathbf{J}\, \mathbf{d\theta}.$$

Since we have an explicit nonlinear relation between the Cartesian and joint variables, we may easily compute the Jacobian $\mathbf{J}$, which describes the infinitesimal relationships between the two spaces:

$$\mathbf{J} = \begin{bmatrix} -l_1 \sin \theta_1 - l_2 \sin(\theta_1 + \theta_2) & -l_2 \sin(\theta_1 + \theta_2) \\ l_1 \cos \theta_1 + l_2 \cos(\theta_1 + \theta_2) & l_2 \cos(\theta_1 + \theta_2) \end{bmatrix}.$$

The Jacobian may be used to relate velocities and accelerations in the two spaces or for linear approximations about an operating point.

The robot is more than a position generator. It may also exert a force on an object. If the force $\mathbf{F}$ exerted by the tip is

$$\mathbf{F} = \begin{bmatrix} u \\ v \end{bmatrix},$$

then the joint torques $\mathbf{T}$ required to generate this force may be determined. Let us first determine this force when the robot is static. By forming force and torque balances for each link, the following relationship may be determined:

$$\begin{bmatrix} T_1 \\ T_2 \end{bmatrix} = \begin{bmatrix} l_1 \cos(\theta_1) + l_2 \cos(\theta_1 + \theta_2) & -[l_1 \sin(\theta_1) + l_2 \sin(\theta_1 + \theta_2)] \\ l_2 \cos(\theta_1 + \theta_2) & -l_2 \sin(\theta_1 + \theta_2) \end{bmatrix} \begin{bmatrix} u \\ v \end{bmatrix}.$$

The static forces and torque balance equations may be easily inverted to obtain the following relationships, which permit one to calculate the joint forces generated by given torques:

$$\begin{bmatrix} u \\ v \end{bmatrix} = \begin{bmatrix} l_2 \cos(\theta_1 + \theta_2) & -[l_1 \cos(\theta_1) + l_2 \cos(\theta_1 + \theta_2)] \\ l_2 \sin(\theta_1 + \theta_2) & -[l_1 \sin(\theta_1) + l_2 \sin(\theta_1 + \theta_2)] \end{bmatrix} \begin{bmatrix} \dfrac{T_1}{\Delta} \\ \dfrac{T_2}{\Delta} \end{bmatrix},$$

$$\Delta = l_1 l_2 \sin(\theta_2).$$

When $\sin \theta_2 = 0$, the links are parallel, and the joint torques have no control over the force component along the length of the links. When the robot moves, we must use the dynamic equations. To determine the dynamic equation we may use the Lagrangian L or the kinetic potential, which is equal to the difference between kinetic and potential energy. For each degree of freedom, the generalized momentum p_i can be expressed as

$$p_i = \frac{\partial L}{\partial q_i},$$

where q_i is a generalized coordinate. The generalized force Q_i is given by

$$\frac{d}{dt}\left[\frac{\partial L}{\partial q_i}\right] - \frac{\partial L}{\partial q_i} = Q_i.$$

For the special case of unity link lengths, the dynamic equations are

$$\begin{bmatrix} 2\left[\dfrac{5}{3} + \cos(\theta_2)\right] & \left[\dfrac{2}{3} + \cos(\theta_2)\right] \\ \left[\dfrac{2}{3} + \cos(\theta_2)\right] & \left[2\left(\dfrac{1}{3}\right)\right] \end{bmatrix} \begin{bmatrix} \ddot{\theta}_1 \\ \ddot{\theta}_2 \end{bmatrix} = \begin{bmatrix} \dfrac{T_1}{E} + \sin(\theta_2)\dot{\theta}_2\left(2\dot{\theta}_1 + \dot{\theta}_2\right) \\ \dfrac{T_2}{E} - \sin(\theta_2)\dot{\theta}_1^2 \end{bmatrix}$$

The dynamic equations permit us to determine joint torques given the arm state. The state variables are

$$\left\{\theta_1, \dot{\theta}_1, \theta_2, \dot{\theta}_2\right\}.$$

We could also use this dynamic equation for a state space description for a control system for the robot:

$$E = \tfrac{1}{2}ml^2.$$

This brief example may serve to illustrate some of the problems involved in robot design. We will now turn to a brief description of two major applications, automatic inspection and mobile robot guidance.

3. ROBOT VISION FOR AUTOMATIC INSPECTION

Robot vision systems are often used as part of the quality-control process in manufacturing. The vision system locates a defect, and the

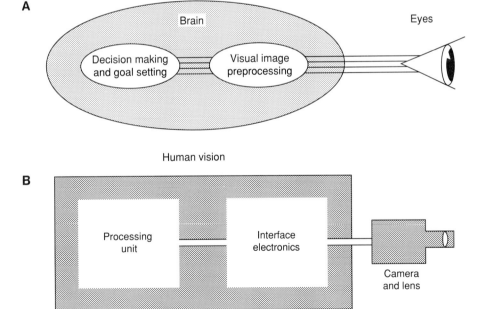

Figure 15.2. Block diagram of the human visual system (A). Block diagram of a machine vision system (B).

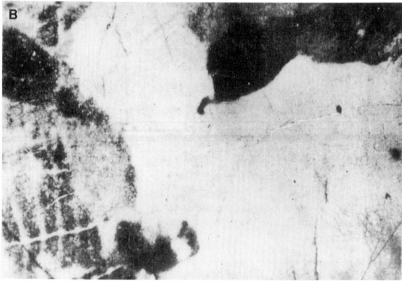

Figure 15.3. Two familiar figures illustrate the perceptual power of the human vision system.

manipulator can remove the part from the production line. A survey of automated visual inspection may be found in Chin and Harlow (14). In this section, we will present a brief introduction to machine vision techniques.

A block diagram of the early stages of the human visual system is shown in Fig. 15.2(A). Note the close relationship to a machine vision system as shown in Fig. 15.2(B). Each system has an image formation device or lens, a light-sensitive detector, and a communication path to a visual processor. However, closer examination reveals some differences. Two images of animals are shown in Fig. 15.3(A, B). The first (A) is clearly an eagle. The second (B) may require closer examination, but is simply a cow. Most

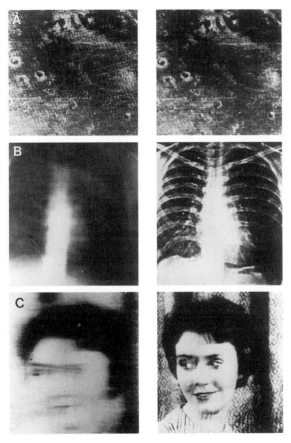

Figure 15.4. Previous research results in image enhancement and restoration: (A) removal of degradation from lunal images; (B) enhancement of chest x-ray image; (C) restoration of motion blur.

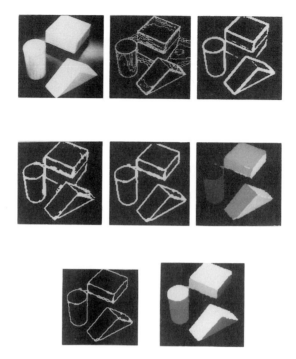

Figure 15.5. Previous research results in scene segmentation from original image through global and local processing, edge coincidence, and final segmentation into regions.

humans can recognize the cow with a few clues such as the location of the eyes and ears. No machine recognition system has yet performed such a difficult recognition.

Machine vision is now a well-established field, and only a few examples may provide the insight into the type of problems that can be solved. The composite image shown in Fig. 15.4 depicts the results of image enhancement and restoration. These two-dimensional techniques are often useful for preprocessing steps before recognition. A scene segmentation is shown in Fig. 15.5. The segmentation uses both local and global information to obtain region outlines of the objects in the image.

More recent work has expanded the measurement of three-dimensional information from images. Many of the techniques described by Klaus and Horn (9) provide three-dimensional shape from shading or other characteristics. Another approach is to use a projected pattern to solve the missing information removed by the projective transformation. Some recent results by Nurre (15) are shown in Fig. 15.6.

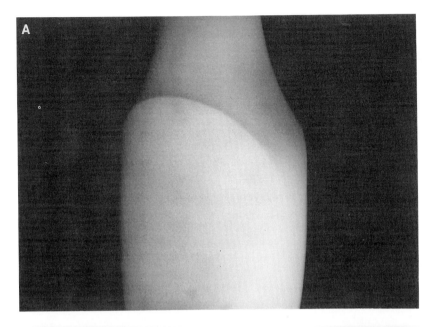

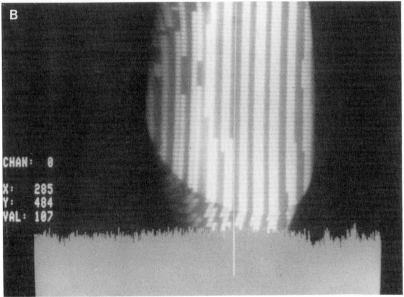

Figure 15.6. Application of computer modeling to inspection of bottles for variations in shape (*Figure continues.*)

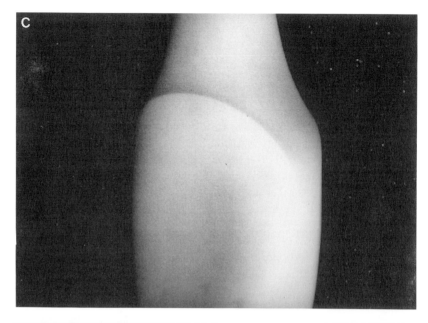

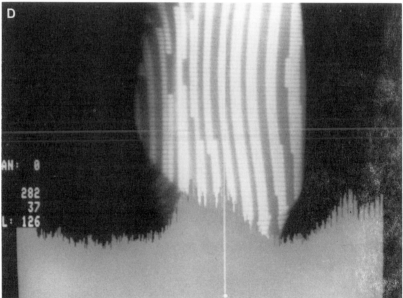

Figure 15.6. (*Continued.*)

4. VISION FOR MOBILE ROBOTS

Since humans receive a large amount of their information through the human vision system, there is reason to expect that intelligent machines that must adapt to changes in their environment will also need to collect visual information and use this information to adapt their behavior. The aspect of intelligent control addressed in this chapter involves a unique vision sensor and its integration into a mobile robot. Other aspects such as learning can be included after the fundamental analytical and architectural issues have been resolved. The visualization and recognition of an image and the guidance of robots for global navigation using omnidirectional vision systems have been studied for many years (16–18). Instantaneous viewing through an extremely wide-angle lens provides useful information on a hemispherical field of view, which, in spite of distorted geometric properties, maintains the physical relations between the object and the image field.

In our laboratory, we have been investigating the use of an omnidirectional vision system to guide a mobile robot, for use as a robot lawn mower, robot cleaning machine, and robot back hoe. A large amount of information on the basic design and the theoretical analysis has been done. The demands for the experimental analysis on the dynamic performance of the sensor, however, have increased rapidly as a result of studies on the guidance and the future development of mobile robots. To fulfill this demand, we performed experimental analyses for three relationships (19–26): on the linear relationship between the zenith angle of a target and the radial location of the image feature, the error due to relative motion, and the image processing time related to the number of blobs. These analyses have revealed some basic characteristics of the omnidirectional vision sensor (22).

The omnidirectional vision navigation system, shown in Fig. 15.7 (a global guidance system developed for a mobile robot), is used to determine accurate global position, sensing the relative location of the robot to the predefined active targets. The use of a fisheye lens that can see a 2π steradian field of view at one instant fits many robotic applications, eliminates scanning, and reduces components. The sensing system consists of four major components, a fisheye lens, an image reducing adapter, a CCD (charge-coupled-device) camera, and a vision processor. The omnidirectional vision system has two major characteristics: (1) an object and the image feature is on the same azimuth angle (azimuth angle invariability); and (2) the relation between the zenith angle—the angle between the vertical axis and a target location—and the radial distance of the image location is linear. Figure 15.7 shows the omnidirectional vision sensor and the gimbal mount installed on a test bed. The sensor consists of three

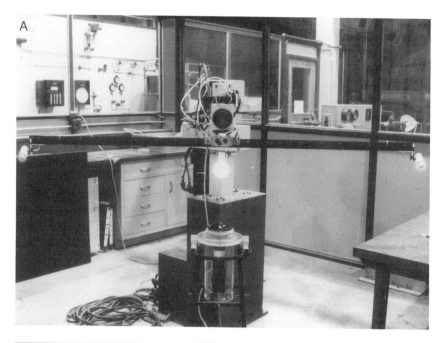

Figure 15.7. An omnidirectional vision system being tested using an industrial robot.

components: a fisheye lens, an image reducing system, and a CCD camera. The location of the image center point is the most important procedure that may affect the performance of the system. Proper calibration factors must be evaluated to minimize the error from mathematical calculations. The motion blurring effect must also be considered when the distance between the sensor and the target is close while the relative speed is high. A study of the resolution may be important in the future in deciding the size of the fisheye lens and the resolution of the camera.

Since the mobile robot may be described as a generic robot manipulator, a multiinput/multioutput system analysis may be used for the control study. For example, the θ–r manipulator is a two-input $[T(\theta), F(\theta)]$/two-output (θ, r), system. The generic mobile robot may be considered as a multiple-input/multiple-output system with a control torque input for the output steering angle, a control force input for the linear actuation of the brake, control torques and forces for a manipulator control, and so on. Although this approach seems obvious, we have not discovered any comprehensive studies that provide a theoretical foundation for omnidirectional control of mobile robots.

5. CONCLUSIONS

A major advantage of flexible manufacturing systems is their ability to accommodate a range of production rates between single products and high-rate products. Groover (23) points out two categories of mass production: (1) quantity production and (2) flow production. In both categories, material packaging and processing steps are important. In quantity production of a single item, bin picking and bin packing are often the least automated processes in the entire plant. In flow production, the "flow" is maintained only if raw materials are available in sufficient amounts and if sufficient transfer devices are available. Again many of the operations required are labor-intensive, especially in the packaging operations.

As the industrial base of the United States improves, new methods for continuing manufacturing excellence must also progress. Areas of investigation under this theme include automated packaging, palletizing, bin packing, bin picking, automated storage and retrieval, automated kitting of parts for assembly, and automated warehousing. One example of an expert system, is the space filling application for random palletizing of mixed-size and mixed-weight parcels. This system successfully utilized artificial intelligence and a robot to stack cartons for the distribution industry. Another experimental area is a new method for solving the bin-picking problem. A new technique for obtaining surface measurements has been developed so that moments and invariants can be examined to determine position and orientation of parts.

Previous examples of intelligent game-playing robots and mobile robots have served as bases for the development of expert systems. The newly developed expert system manufacturing techniques can increase production and flow. The resulting costs of manufacturing goods should be less, and quality improvement could be significant.

A cursory survey of the physical world can reveal needed improvements in all areas of technology that are better, cheaper, faster, and safer.

For further study on robot vision, consider Ayache (24). Also, a recent research study on mobile robots is given by Roning (25), and a recent text on robot manipulators and control is Lewis *et al.* (26).

The most painful thing about robot vision is how difficult it is to use after you have learned all about it. Problem solvers must be prepared to go forward, backward, and around obstacles to solutions. The prize of discovering a machine that is new, useful, and nonobvious may be worth the effort.

REFERENCES

1. G. Slutzky and E. Hall, Vision guided intelligent robot design and experiments. *Proc. SPIE — Int. Soc. Opt. Eng.* **848**, 66 (1987).
2. E. Hall and B. Hall, "Robotics: A User-Friendly Introduction." Holt, Rinehart, & Winston, New York, 1985.
3. K. Mazouz, E. Hall, and R. Shell, Expert system for flexible palletizing of mixed size and weight parcels. *Proc. SPIE — Int. Soc. Opt. Eng.* **848**, pp. 556–564 (1987).
4. E. Reich, *et al.*, Robot to solve Rubik's cube. *SAE Tech. Pap. Ser.* **830341** (1983).
5. G. Slutzky, J. Roning, F. Wu, and M. Kozak, An Intelligent Robot Work Cell. *SME Tech. Pap. MS* **MS86-773** (1986).
6. E. Hall, S. Oh, and E. Kattan, Experience with a robot lawn mower. *SME Tech. Pap. MS* **MS86-3867** (1986).
7. Y. Huang, Z. Cao, S. Oh, E. Kattan, and E. Hall, "Automatic Operation for a Robot Lawn Mower." SPIE, Cambridge, MA, 1986.
8. G. Slutzky, A. K. Mazouz, and E. Hall, "An Expert System for Palletizing Mixed Size and Weight Parcels," Final Report. Institute for Advanced Manufacturing Sciences, Cincinnati, OH, 1986.
9. B. Klaus and B. Horn, "Robot Vision." MIT Press, Cambridge, MA, 1980.
10. E. Hall and K. Park, Form recognition using moment invariants. *Proc. Int. Symp. Sci. Form, 1st*, Tsukuba, Japan, *1986*, pp. 96–108.
11. K. Park and E. Hall, Moment invariants for perspective transformations. *Proc. SPIE — Int. Soc. Opt. Eng.* **726** (1986).
12. K. Park and E. Hall, Moment invariants for perspective transformation. *Proc. SPIE, Int. Symp. 4th*, **8**, 4–34. The Hague, The Netherlands, *1987*.

13. E. Mu, J. T. Cain, and L. G. Herrera-Bendezu, Computer generation of symbolic kinematics for robot manipulators. *J. Robotic Syst.* **9**(3), 385–410 (1992).

14. R. T. Chin and C. A. Harlow, Automated visual inspection: A survey. *IEEE Trans. Pattern Anal. Mach. Intell.* **PAMI-4**(6), 557 (1982).

15. J. H. Nurre and E. L. Hall, Encoded moiré inspection based on a computer solid model. *IEEE Trans. Pattern Anal. Mach. Intell.* **PAMI-14**(12), 1214–1218 (1992).

16. R. L. Anderson, N. Alvertos, and E. L. Hall, Omnidirectional real time imaging using digital restoration. *Proc. SPIE — Int. Soc. Opt. Eng.* **348**, 807–816 (1983).

17. N. Alvertos, E. L. Hall, and R. L. Anderson, Omnidirectional viewing for robot vision. *Proc. SPIE — Int. Soc. Opt. Eng.* **449**, 230–239 (1984).

18. R. Berry, K. Loebbaka, and E. L. Hall, Sensors for mobile robots. *Proc. SPIE — Int. Soc. Opt. Eng.* **449**, 584–588 (1984).

19. M. Ehtashami, S. J. Oh, and E. L. Hall, Omnidirectional position location for mobile robots. *Proc. SPIE — Int. Soc. Opt. Eng.* **521**, 62–73 (1984).

20. Z. L. Cao, S. J. Oh, and E. L. Hall, Dynamic omnidirectional vision for mobile robots. *J. Robotic Syst.* **3**(1), 5–17 (1986).

21. Z. L. Cao, S. J. Oh, and E. L. Hall, Omnidirectional dynamic vision positioning for a mobile robot. *Opt. Eng.* **25**(12), 1278–1283 (1986).

22. S. J. Oh and E. L. Hall, A study of the characteristics of an omnidirectional vision sensor. *Proc. SPIE — Int. Soc. Opt. Eng.* **804**, 35 (1987).

23. M. Groover, "Automation, Production Systems, and Computer-Aided Manufacturing," pp. 22–23. Prentice-Hall, Englewood Cliffs, NJ, 1980.

24. N. Ayache, "Artificial Vision for Mobile Robots." MIT Press, Cambridge, MA, 1991.

25. J. Roning, Model-based visual navigation of a mobile robot. Ph.D. Dissertation, University of Oulu, Department of Electrical Engineering, Finland, 1992.

26. F. L. Lewis, C. T. Abdallah, and D. M. Dawson, "Control of Robot Manipulators." Macmillan, New York, 1993.

Index

ISBN 0-12-774561-0

90038